Sumerian Lexicon

A Dictionary Guide to the Ancient Sumerian Language

•

Edited, compiled, and arranged by

John Alan Halloran

Logogram Publishing

Los Angeles

Sumerian Lexicon: A Dictionary Guide to the Ancient Sumerian Language

Logogram Publishing
P.O. Box 75713, Los Angeles, California 90075
1-800-732-4628
http://www.sumerian.org/

FIRST EDITION.

Library of Congress Control Number: 2006927550

Softcover:
ISBN-13: 978-0-9786429-0-7
ISBN-10: 0-9786429-0-2

Hardcover:
ISBN-13: 978-0-9786429-1-4
ISBN-10: 0-9786429-1-0

0 9 8 7 6 5 4 3 2 1

"What were the steps by which men passed from barbarism to civilization?"

Voltaire, 1756

Introduction

With 6,400 entries, this is the most complete available lexicon of ancient Sumerian vocabulary. It replaces version 3 of my Sumerian Lexicon, which has served an audience of over 380,000 visitors at the web site http://www.sumerian.org/ since 1999. This published version adds over 2,600 new entries, and corrects or expands many of the previous entries. Also, following the express wish of a majority of lexicon users, I have merged together and sorted the logogram words and the compound words into purely alphabetical order. This book will be an indispensable reference for anyone trying to translate Sumerian texts. Also, due to the historical position of ancient Sumer as the world's first urban civilization, cultural and linguistic archaeologists will discover a wealth of information for research.

The Sumerian Lexicon began life in the 1980s as a collection and study of Sumerian logograms (word signs), readings of cuneiform signs that represented words in the spoken Sumerian language. The situation back in the 1980s was that no modern dictionary of Sumerian existed. To create a reliable dictionary involved relying only upon scholarly materials published since the 1950s. This dictionary brings together the lexical contributions of most of the last half-century's major Sumerologists, whose heroic achievements in recovering a dead language justly deserve praise. For the first time, the results of their separate investigations are collected together in one place. This is important because often the meaning that a scholar has found for a word in one context throws light upon its use in other contexts. In addition to continuing work on the logogram words of the original project, I have worked since 1996 to add all of the more commonly used compound words, which words are more numerous in Sumerian than are logogram-only words. Beyond the simple logogram words, three-quarters of this lexicon now consists of words that are transparent compounds of logograms.

Sumerian scribes invented the practice of writing in cuneiform on clay tablets sometime around 3400 B.C. in the large city of Uruk, which was part of the early city-state civilization of Sumer that evolved in the south of ancient Iraq. Uruk's most famous king was the legendary Gilgamesh, who spoke Sumerian. The writing on the tablets progressed from compact shorthand signs to readable texts by 2800 B.C. Archaeologists have excavated over one hundred thousand clay tablets written in Sumerian from the Old Sumerian (ca. 2800 B.C.–2350 B.C.), Old Akkadian (2350 B.C.–2150 B.C.), Neo-Sumerian (2150 B.C.–2000 B.C.), and Old Babylonian (2000 B.C.–1600 B.C.) periods. A million or more tablets written in Sumerian cuneiform may lie in the ground awaiting archaeological excavation (if these fragile clay tablets are not first destroyed by unskilled looters). The Old Babylonian period left us many Sumerian literary compositions and important bilingual cuneiform dictionaries in Sumerian and Akkadian. Akkadian is a well-understood language, belonging to the Semitic family, that was spoken by the Babylonian successors to the Sumerians. Sumerian is not genetically related to Akkadian, although the Semitic vernaculars that led to Babylonian Akkadian may have coexisted with spoken Sumerian in Greater Mesopotamia since before the invention of writing. It was probably around 1800 B.C. that Sumerian ceased to be a living language, although the Babylonian cuneiform scribes would study and write Sumerian in addition to their native Akkadian until the end of Babylonian civilization around the first century A.D.

Sumerian is a linguistic isolate, a language which is not closely connected to any other language family. Also, Sumerian writing is not alphabetic. The most important written words had their own cuneiform signs, whose origins were pictographic, as in Chinese writing. An initial Uruk IV period repertoire of about 1200 proto-cuneiform ideographic signs evolved into the standard signlist of about 900 cuneiform signs. Some of those cuneiform signs became syllabograms for writing phonetic V, VC, CV, and CVC syllables.

The Sumerian Lexicon presents Sumerian words not in cuneiform, but in readable Roman alphabet transliteration, as Sumerologists normally do when they analyze the ambiguous cuneiform symbols of an inscription and publish its text. Many cuneiform signs can be pronounced in more than one way (so that one sign can represent multiple logograms or words). The lexicon uses all upper-case or capital letters to indicate the name of a sign, usually in brackets, while lower-case or small letters indicate the word or reading of a sign. If the Sumerians wrote a word with a group of two or more cuneiform signs, a so-called `diri`-spelling, then a period will appear between each upper-case component sign, e.g., the sign group `A.PA.ĞISAL.PAD.DIRIG` for the word `addir`. If superscripted letters appear before a word, e.g., ^{iti} ^{d}dumu-zi, they represent a determinative sign that usually appeared in front of that sign in the inscriptions. Certain Sumerian words are written before a noun or name as a 'determinative', such as ^{d} for ^{dingir} being written before divine names, or ^{lu2} being written before male profession names. ^{iti} is the determinative written before month names, so that the reader will know that the sign(s) that follow refer to a month. It is thought that determinatives were not pronounced in speech, but only appear in writing.

Often two or more signs share the same pronunciation, in which case it is necessary to indicate in the transliteration which cuneiform sign is meant; Assyriologists have developed a system whereby homophones are marked by subscript numerals. The homophone numeration here follows the 'BCE-System' developed by Borger, Civil, and Ellermeier. Transcribed texts often use an acute accent (´) to mark the second homophone and a grave accent (`) to mark the third homophone, but these marks did not help in sorting all the words into the right order, so this version of the lexicon uses all subscript numerals instead. The numeration system is a convention to inform Assyriologists which, for example, of the many cuneiform signs that have the reading du actually occurs on the tablet. A particular sign can often be transcribed in a long way, such as dug_4, or in a short way, such as du_{11}, because Sumerian was like French in omitting certain amissable final consonants except before a following vowel. Due to this lexicon's etymological orientation, you will usually find a word listed under its fullest phonetic form. Transcriptions of texts often contain the short forms, however, because Sumerologists try to accurately represent the spoken language. Short forms are listed, but you are told where to confer.

The vowels may be pronounced as follows: *a* as in *father*, *u* as in *pull*, *e* as in *peg*, and *i* as in *hip*. Of the special consonants, g̃ is pronounced like *ng* in *rang*, ḫ is pronounced like *ch* in German *Buch* or Scottish *loch*, and š is pronounced like *sh* in *dash*.

Following each definition, the lexicon may indicate in a smaller font what I think is the word's etymology, usually as a compound of simpler words or less often as a loanword from Semitic Akkadian. These suggested etymologies are not the source of the word definitions, which derive from usages in context and Akkadian lexical correspondences. Etymologies are a normal part of dictionary making, but etymologies are also the most subject to speculation and debate. Sumerian studies is a very young field. There are still many learned articles yet to be written analyzing the etymologies of particular words. Etymological studies must take into account the Sumerian impulse to achieve phonetic harmony through phoneme assimilation, realizing that this tendency has disguised some original word components. But in view of the Sumerians' observed propensity for forming new words through compounding in the period after they invented cuneiform signs, it should not surprise anyone to find that this same propensity was at work in the logogram words that mostly date from before their invention of written signs.

The structure and thinking behind the Sumerian vocabulary is to me a thing of beauty. We are very fortunate to be able to look back into the minds of our prehistoric ancestors and see how they thought and lived via the words that they created. The vocabulary of proto-Sumerian and Sumerian take us back to the beginnings of human culture. There is much for the cultural archaeologist to recover in the Sumerian vocabulary. What particularly struck me as I worked on this new edition was the Sumerian knowledge of useful plants and herbs, a traditional form of knowledge that modern Western civilization has neglected. According to a 1999 United Nations report, "Amongst the 1500 or so plants used in Iraq, a large number serve medicinal and aromatic purposes." The Sumerians built their civilization in southern Mesopotamia over a continuous period of four thousand years, from the start of the Ubaid period around 6,000 BC (calibrated) to the end of the Ur III period around 2,000 BC. How much hard-won knowledge did Sumerian speakers acquire over those millennia, that can be extracted from their vocabulary?

This version of the Sumerian Lexicon includes all the variant Emesal dialect word forms in addition to the Emegir main dialect forms. We do not know the extent to which this "thin, refined tongue" or 'women's dialect' was actually spoken apart from cultic readings, but these forms do substitute for main dialect forms in literary genres that traditionally belong to women, such as laments and fertility songs. Any study of the Emesal spoken dialect question should collect the loanwords into Akkadian, such as *šabsû*, 'mid-wife, accoucheur', and *mu(t)tinnu*, 'choice wine' (cf., Sumerian $\check{s}a_3$-zu and mu-ti-in), that were transmitted in their Emesal forms.

For some verbs, the lexicon gives two sets of forms, which the Akkadians called *ḫamṭu* and *marû*, "quick, sudden" and "fat, slow". Quoting from *A Manual of Sumerian Grammar and Texts* by John L. Hayes, "The difference in function between the two has been interpreted in various ways. It has been argued that the difference was one of tense (past ~ present/future); one of aspect (perfect ~ imperfect); one of Aktionsart (punctual ~ durative, and so on). An explanation in terms of aspect seems to fit the evidence best, and they will be called aspects here." p. 46.

The shortcomings of this concise lexicon are essentially three: 1) the lexicon does not quote examples of usage; 2) aside from the notations of each sign's Archaic Frequency, taken from the electronic archaic sign list of P. Damerow and R. Englund, the lexicon rarely indicates the source period or the provenance of words or their different meanings during the language's long history (although most of our texts are from the Neo-Sumerian and Old Babylonian periods); and 3) no attempt has been made to annotate from which of the following ninety-six sources I obtained a particular meaning. The kind of large collaborative Sumerian dictionary that would offer all of these features is still many years in the future.

In the meantime, this user-friendly Sumerian Lexicon 1) provides a complete range of actually-used meanings for each word; 2) aids the reader of texts with extensive coverage of Sumerian's grammatical particles, not just its nouns, verbs, and adjuncts; 3) throws light on the origin and meaning behind words by analyzing their etymologies; and 4) assists look-ups by cross referencing short and long word forms as well as related words.

The Sumerian Lexicon has been in development for over twenty years. In date order of use, the primary sources included:

A. Deimel, *Šumerisches Lexikon*; Rome 1947.

E. Reiner, editor with R.D. Biggs, J.A. Brinkman, M. Civil, W. Farber, I.J. Gelb, A.L. Oppenheim, M.T. Roth, & M.W. Stolper, *The Assyrian Dictionary of the Oriental Institute of the University of Chicago (CAD)*; Chicago 1956ff.

W. von Soden, *Akkadisches Handwörterbuch (AHw)*; Wiesbaden 1958-1981.

R. Borger, *Assyrisch-babylonische Zeichenliste* (Band 33 in *Alter Orient und Altes Testament (AOAT), Veröffentlichungen zur Kultur und Geschichte des Alten Orients und des Alten Testaments* (Series)); Kevelaer and Neukirchen-Vluyn 1978.

R. Labat and F. Malbran-Labat, *Manuel d'Épigraphie Akkadienne, 6° édition*; Paris 1995 (this is the cuneiform sign manual used by most Sumerology students, but see Borger, MZL, for current index numbers).

M.L. Thomsen, *The Sumerian Language: An Introduction to Its History and Grammatical Structure (ThSLa)*; Copenhagen 1984 (this well-done grammar is currently the standard text - in 2001 it was reprinted in a 3rd edition with a 13-page Supplementary Bibliography).

J.L. Hayes, *A Manual of Sumerian Grammar and Texts*; Second Revised and Expanded Edition; Malibu 2000.

R. Jestin, *Notes de Graphie et de Phonétique Sumériennes*; Paris 1965.

B. Landsberger, as compiled by D.A. Foxvog and A.D. Kilmer, "Benno Landsberger's Lexicographical Contributions", *Journal of Cuneiform Studies*, vol 27 (1975).

H. Behrens and H. Steible, *Glossar zu den altsumerischen Bau- und Weihinschriften*; Wiesbaden 1983.

K. Oberhuber, *Sumerisches Lexikon zu "George Reisner, Sumerisch - babylonische Hymnen nach Thontafeln griechischer Zeit (Berlin 1896)" (SBH) und verwandten Texten*; Innsbruck 1990.

Å.W. Sjöberg, E. Leichty et al., *The Sumerian Dictionary of the University Museum of the University of Pennsylvania (PSD)*; Philadelphia 1984ff. Letters B and A through Ama have been published in book form. The complete letters A-Z now appear in brief entries on the Internet, courtesy of director Steve Tinney, at: http://psd.museum.upenn.edu/. The computerized edition of the PSD is an excellent guide to word forms.

M. Civil, unpublished Sumerian glossary for students.

S. Tinney, editor, *Index to the Secondary Literature: A collated list of indexes and glossaries to the secondary literature concerning the*

Sumerian Language, this valuable reference is unpublished, but it has been expanded and is searchable at: http://psd.museum.upenn.edu/epsd/nepsd-frame.html

E.I. Gordon, *Sumerian Proverbs: Glimpses of Everyday Life in Ancient Mesopotamia*; Philadelphia 1959 (with contributions by Th. Jacobsen).

D.C. Snell, *Ledgers and Prices: Early Mesopotamian Merchant Accounts*; New Haven and London 1982.

P. Michalowski, *The Lamentation over the Destruction of Sumer and Ur*; Winona Lake 1989.

C.E. Keiser and S.T. Kang, *Neo-Sumerian Account Texts from Drehem*; New Haven & London 1971.

S.T. Kang, *Sumerian Economic Texts from the Drehem Archive*; Urbana, Chicago & London 1972.

S.T. Kang, *Sumerian Economic Texts from the Umma Archive*; Urbana, Chicago & London 1973.

J. Bauer, *Altsumerische Wirtschaftstexte aus Lagasch*; Dissertation for Julius-Maximilians-Universität at Würzburg 1967 [appeared under same name as vol. 9 in *Studia Pohl: Series Maior*; Rome 1972].

J. Krecher, "Die *marû*-Formen des sumerischen Verbums", *Vom Alten Orient Zum Alten Testament, AOAT* 240 (1995; *Fs. vSoden* II), pp. 141-200.

K. Volk, *A Sumerian Reader*, vol. 18 in *Studia Pohl: Series Maior*; Rome 1997 (this practical, inexpensive book includes a nice, though incomplete, sign-list).

B. Alster, *The Instructions of Suruppak: A Sumerian Proverb Collection* (*Mesopotamia: Copenhagen Studies in Assyriology*, Vol. 2); Copenhagen 1974.

B. Alster, *Proverbs of Ancient Sumer: The World's Earliest Proverb Collections*, 2 vols; Bethesda, Maryland 1997.

Å. Sjöberg, *Der Mondgott Nanna-Suen in der sumerischen Überlieferung*; Stockholm 1960.

V.E. Orel and O.V. Stolbova, *Hamito-Semitic Etymological Dictionary: Materials for a Reconstruction* (Handbuch der Orientalistik, Abt. 1, Bd. 18); Leiden, New York, & Köln 1995.

M.W. Green and H.J. Nissen, *Zeichenliste der Archaischen Texte aus Uruk* [ZATU] (Ausgrabungen der Deutschen Forschungsgemeinschaft in Uruk-Warka, 11; Archaische Texte aus Uruk, 2); Berlin 1987.

P. Damerow and R. Englund, *Sign List of the Archaic Texts* (electronic FileMaker database collection of ZATU signs occurring in catalogued texts from Uruk IV to ED II); Berlin 1994.

P. Steinkeller, review of M.W. Green and H.J. Nissen, *Bibliotheca Orientalis* 52 (1995), pp. 689-713.

J. Krecher, "Das sumerische Phonem |g̃|", *Festschrift Lubor Matouš, Assyriologia* 5, vol. II, ed. B. Hruška & G. Komoróczy (Budapest, 1978), pp. 7-73.

M. Civil, *The Farmer's Instructions: A Sumerian Agricultural Manual* (Aula Orientalis-Supplementa, Vol. 5); Barcelona 1994.

M. Krebernik, *Die Beschwörungen aus Fara und Ebla: Untersuchungen zur ältesten keilschriftlichen Beschwörungsliteratur* (Texte und Studien zur Orientalistik, Bd. 2); Hildesheim, Zurich, New York 1984.

M.A. Powell, "Masse und Gewichte" [Weights and Measures: article in English], *Reallexikon der Assyriologie und Vorderasiatischen Archäologie*,.Bd. 7, ed. D.O. Edzard (Berlin & New York, 1987-90), pp. 457-517.

K.R. Nemet-Nejat, *Cuneiform Mathematical Texts as a Reflection of Everyday Life in Mesopotamia* (American Oriental Series, Vol. 75); New Haven 1993.

E.J. Wilson, *The Cylinders of Gudea: Transliteration, Translation and Index* (Band 244 in *Alter Orient und Altes Testament (AOAT), Veröffentlichungen zur Kultur und Geschichte des Alten Orients und des Alten Testaments* (Series)); Kevelaer and Neukirchen-Vluyn 1996.

D.O. Edzard, *Gudea and His Dynasty* (The Royal Inscriptions of Mesopotamia, Early Periods, Vol. 3/1); Toronto, Buffalo, London 1997.

W.W. Hallo and J.J.A. van Dijk, *The Exaltation of Inanna*; New Haven & London 1968.

D.T. Potts, *Mesopotamian Civilization: The Material Foundations*; Ithaca, New York 1997.

J. Black, A. George, and N. Postgate, *A Concise Dictionary of Akkadian* (SANTAG, Band 5); Wiesbaden 1999.

Å.W. Sjöberg, "In-nin šà-gur$_4$-ra: A Hymn to the Goddess Inanna by the en-priestess Enheduanna", *Zeitschr. f. Assyriologie, Bd.* 65 (1976; *Walter deGruyter*), pp. 161-253.

Å.W. Sjöberg, "Studies in the Emar S[a] Vocabulary", *Zeitschr. f. Assyriologie, Bd.* 88 (1998; *Walter deGruyter*), pp. 240-283.

E. Flückiger-Hawker, *Urnamma of Ur in Sumerian Literary Tradition*; Fribourg 1999 (the glossary of this book provides a window onto the Sumerisches Glossar project of P. Attinger at the Institute of Ancient Near Eastern Archaeology and Languages, University of Berne, and W. Sallaberger at the Institut für Assyriologie und Hethitologie der Universität München).

A.D. Kilmer, "Musik. A. I. In Mesopotamien." [Music in Mesopotamia: article in English], *Reallexikon der Assyriologie und Vorderasiatischen Archäologie*,.Bd. 8, ed. D.O. Edzard (Berlin & New York, 1993-1997), pp. 463-482.

M.-J. Seux, *Épithètes Royales Akkadiennes et Sumériennes*; Paris 1967.

S. Tinney, *The Nippur Lament: Royal Rhetoric and Divine Legitimation in the Reign of Išme-Dagan of Isin (1953-1935 B.C.)*; Philadelphia 1996.

M.K. Schretter, *Emesal-Studien: Sprach- und literaturgeschichtliche Untersuchungen zur sogenannten Frauensprache des Sumerischen* (Innsbrucker Beiträge zur Kulturwissenschaft, Sonderheft 69); Innsbruck 1990.

F. Karahashi, *Sumerian Compound Verbs with Body-Part Terms*; Dissertation for The University of Chicago; Chicago 2000 [UMI Microform 9978038].

R. Kutscher, *Oh Angry Sea* (a-ab-ba hu-luh-ha)*: The History of a Sumerian Congregational Lament*; New Haven and London 1975.

Jon Taylor, "A new OB Proto-Lu-Proto-Izi combination tablet", *Orientalia, Vol.* 70 N.S. (2001; *Pontificium Institutum Biblicum*), pp. 209-234.

M.A. Powell, "Sumerian Cereal Crops", *Bulletin on Sumerian Agriculture* I (Cambridge, 1984), pp. 48-72.

J.N. Postgate, "Processing of Cereals in the Cuneiform Record", *Bulletin on Sumerian Agriculture* I (Cambridge, 1984), pp. 103-113.

M. Stol, "Beans, Peas, Lentils and Vetches in Akkadian Texts", *Bulletin on Sumerian Agriculture* II (Cambridge, 1985), pp. 127-139.

J.N. Postgate, "The "Oil-Plant" in Assyria", *Bulletin on Sumerian Agriculture* II (Cambridge, 1985), pp. 145-152.

H. Waetzoldt, "Knoblauch und Zwiebeln nach den Texten des 3. JT.", *Bulletin on Sumerian Agriculture* III (Cambridge, 1987), pp. 23-56.

J.N. Postgate, "Notes on Fruit in the Cuneiform Sources", *Bulletin on Sumerian Agriculture* III (Cambridge, 1987), pp. 115-144.

M.A. Powell, "The Tree Section of ur5(=HAR)-ra=*ḫubullu*", *Bulletin on Sumerian Agriculture* III (Cambridge, 1987), pp. 145-151.

P. Steinkeller, "Notes on the Irrigation System in Third Millenium Southern Babylonia", *Bulletin on Sumerian Agriculture* IV (Cambridge, 1988), pp. 73-92.

M.A. Powell, "Evidence for Agriculture and Waterworks in Babylonian Mathematical Texts", *Bulletin on Sumerian Agriculture* IV (Cambridge, 1988), pp. 161-172.

W. Pemberton, J.N. Postgate, and R.F. Smyth, "Canals and Bunds, Ancient and Modern", *Bulletin on Sumerian Agriculture* IV (Cambridge, 1988), pp. 207-221.

K. Maekawa, "Cultivation Methods in the Ur III Period", *Bulletin on Sumerian Agriculture* V (Cambridge, 1990), pp. 115-145.

M.A. Powell, "Timber Production in Presargonic Lagaš", *Bulletin on Sumerian Agriculture* VI (Cambridge, 1992), pp. 99-122.

H. Waetzoldt, "'Rohr' und dessen Verwendungsweisen anhand der neusumerischen Texte aus Umma", *Bulletin on Sumerian Agriculture* VI (Cambridge, 1992), pp. 125-146.

M. Van De Mieroop, "Wood in the Old Babylonian Texts from Southern Babylonia", *Bulletin on Sumerian Agriculture* VI (Cambridge, 1992), pp. 155-161.

M. Stol, "Milk, Butter, and Cheese", *Bulletin on Sumerian Agriculture* VII (Cambridge, 1993), pp. 99-113.

W. Heimpel, "Zu den Bezeichnungen von Schafen und Ziegen in den Drehem- und Ummatexten", *Bulletin on Sumerian Agriculture* VII (Cambridge, 1993), pp. 115-160.

M. Van De Mieroop, "Sheep and Goat Herding According to the Old Babylonian Texts from Ur", *Bulletin on Sumerian Agriculture* VII (Cambridge, 1993), pp. 161-182.

P. Steinkeller, "Sheep and Goat Terminology in Ur III Sources from Drehem", *Bulletin on Sumerian Agriculture* VIII (Cambridge, 1995), pp. 49-70.

W. Heimpel, "Plow Animal Inspection Records from Ur III Girsu and Umma", *Bulletin on Sumerian Agriculture* VIII (Cambridge, 1995), pp. 71-171.

W. Heimpel, *Tierbilder in der sumerischen Literatur* (*Studia Pohl: Series Minor 2*); Rome 1968.

P. Mander, *An Archive of Kennelmen and Other Workers in Ur III Lagash*; Naples 1994.

D.O. Edzard, *Sumerian Grammar* (Handbook of Oriental Studies, Section One, The Near and Middle East, Vol. 71); Leiden, Boston 2003.

R. Borger, *Mesopotamisches Zeichenlexikon (MZL)* (Band 305 in *Alter Orient und Altes Testament (AOAT), Veröffentlichungen zur Kultur und Geschichte des Alten Orients und des Alten Testaments* (Series)); Ugarit-Verlag-Münster 2004 (this massive work of scholarship will be the standard guide to cuneiform sign names and indexes for a long time).

G. Visicato, *The Power and the Writing: The Early Scribes of Mesopotamia*; Bethesda, Maryland 2000.

M. Van De Mieroop, *Crafts in the Early Isin Period* (*Orientalia Lovaniensia 24*); Leuven, Belgium 1987.

J.A. Black, G. Cunningham, J. Ebeling, E. Flückiger-Hawker, E. Robson, J. Taylor and G. Zólyomi, *The Electronic Text Corpus of Sumerian Literature* (http://etcsl.orinst.ox.ac.uk/), Oxford 1998- (project glossary provides convenient access to the context of Sumerian words in translated literature).

M.L. Thomsen, as compiled by A. Taggar-Cohen, "An Index of Grammatical Terms and Particles for the Sumerian Language, by Marie-Louise Thomsen (Mesopotamia 10, Copenhagen: 1984)", *Akkadica*, vol 89-90 (1994), pp. 27-47.

C. Wilcke, "Mesopotamia, Early Dynastic and Sargonic Periods", *A History of Ancient Near Eastern Law*, vol. I, ed. R. Westbrook (Leiden, Boston, 2003), pp. 141-181.

B. Lafont and R. Westbrook, "Mesopotamia, Neo-Sumerian Period (Ur III)", *A History of Ancient Near Eastern Law*, vol. I, ed. R. Westbrook (Leiden, Boston, 2003), pp. 183-226.

J. Klein, "Some Rare Sumerian Words Gleaned from the Royal Hymns of Sulgi", *Studies in Hebrew and Semitic Languages Dedicated to the Memory of E.Y. Kutscher*, ed. G.B. Sarfatti, P. Artzi, J.C. Greenfield, M. Kaddari (Ramat-Gan, 1980), pp. IX-XXVIII.

J. Friberg, "Mathematics at Ur in the Old Babylonian Period", *Revue d'Assyriologie, vol.* 94 (2000), pp. 97-188.

T.R. Kämmerer, D. Schwiderski, *Deutsch-Akkadisches Wörterbuch* (Band 255 in *Alter Orient und Altes Testament (AOAT), Veröffentlichungen zur Kultur und Geschichte des Alten Orients und des Alten Testaments* (Series)); Ugarit-Verlag-Münster 1998.

G. Pettinato, H. Waetzoldt, J.-P. Grégoire, and D.I. Owen, *Studi per il Vocabolario Sumerico* I/3, *Glossario*, G. Reisner, *Tempelurkunden aus Telloh*; Rome, 1985.

G. Pettinato, *Untersuchungen zur Neusumerischen Landwirtschaft I: Die Felder* (1. und 2. Teil); Naples 1967.

R.C. Nelson, *PISAN-DUB-BA Texts from the Sumerian Ur III Dynasty*; Dissertation for The University of Minnesota, 1976 [UMI Microform 7627824].

K. Maekawa, "New Texts on the Collective Labor Service of the erin-People of Ur III Girsu", *Acta Sumerologica, vol.* 10 (1988), pp. 37-94.

G. Steiner, "Akkadische Lexeme im Sumerischen", *Semitic and Assyriological Studies. Presented to Pelio Fronzaroli*, ed. P. Marrassini et al. (Wiesbaden, 2003), pp. 630-647.

Th.J.H. Krispijn, "The Sumerian Lexeme *urum, a Lexico-Etymological Approach", *Veenhof Anniversary Volume*, ed. W.H. van Soldt et al. (Leiden, 2001), pp. 251-61.

J.J.A. van Dijk and M.J. Geller, *Ur III Incantations from the Frau Professor Hilprecht-Collection, Jena*; Wiesbaden 2003.

W. Sallaberger, "The Sumerian Verb na de_5(-g), "To Clear"", *"An Experienced Scribe Who Neglects Nothing": Ancient Near Eastern Studies in Honor of Jacob Klein*, ed. Y. Sefati et al. (Bethesda, MD, 2005), pp. 229-253.

W. Yuhong, "A Study of the Sumerian Words for "Animal Hole" (ḫabrud), "Hole" (burud), "Well" ($burud_2$), and "Copper" (wuruda)", *"An Experienced Scribe Who Neglects Nothing": Ancient Near Eastern Studies in Honor of Jacob Klein*, ed. Y. Sefati et al. (Bethesda, MD, 2005), pp. 374-395.

A. Falkenstein, *Die neusumerischen Gerichtsurkunden* 1-3 (Bayerische Akademie der Wissenschaften, philosophisch-historische Klasse, Abhandlungen, Neue Folge, Heft 39, 40, 44); München 1956-57.

N. Veldhuis, *Religion, Literature, and Scholarship: The Sumerian Composition Nanše and the Birds, With a Catalogue of Sumerian Bird Names*; Leiden 2004.

H. Limet, *Le travail du métal au pays de Sumer au temps de la IIIe dynastie d'Ur* (Bibliothèque de la Faculté de philosophie et lettres de l'Université de Liège, fasc. 155); Paris 1960.

H. Limet, "The Cuisine of Ancient Sumer", *Biblical Archaeologist* 50/3 (September, 1987), pp. 132-147.

M. Schretter, "Zu den Nominalkomposita des Sumerischen", *Studi sul Vicino Oriente Antico Dedicati alla memoria di Luigi Cagni*, ed. S. Graziani (Naples, 2000), vol. II, pp. 933-952.

The Sumerian lexicon has benefitted from introductory and graduate classes with Dr. Robert Englund at UCLA. Dr. Englund is in charge of an Internet project to catalog all cuneiform tablet collections and to make available in image and transliteration all the Sumerian tablets from the Ur III and earlier periods, called the *Cuneiform Digital Library Initiative (CDLI).* The Sumerian lexicon has benefitted from searches of these mostly untranslated texts using a Windows software program created by Massimo Pompeo called *The Cuneiform Texts Resources.*

I dedicate this lexicon to the memory of Dr. Robert Hetzron, with whom I had the pleasure of studying during every week of the four years that I attended the University of California at Santa Barbara. Dr. Hetzron was a professional linguist and an expert on the Semitic and Afro-Asiatic language family.

The following individuals have given financial support:

Jens Langeland-Knudsen, Carol von der Lin, Richard Kline, Murray Maynard, Colin J.E. Lupton, and Hadi Kazwini, who provided the following dedication: "For Iraq, Mesopotamia, My Homeland: May the spirit of Gudea be your uniting bond! May your coming days be as glorious as your past!"

A

a, e_4
n., water; watercourse, canal; seminal fluid; offspring; father; tears; flood. [A archaic frequency: 519]

interj., alas!; oh!; ouch!.

ã-
conjugation prefix, weakens the role of the agent, either implied or named, in a sentence, transferring focus either to the dative, comitative, ablative, terminative, or ergative - ThSLa §316; translated by Akkadian stative or passive N-stem ThSLa §318; the prefix with imperative ThSLa §321; ã- as variant of al- ThSLa §357.

-a-
variant of 2.sg. pronominal prefix -e- (in few cases also 1.sg.) ThSLa §291.

-a
imperative form, possibly indicates motion away (cf. $\tilde{g}e_{26}$-nu and g̃en-na), cf., -u_3 - ThSLa §497.

-a
suffix of adjective - ThSLa §80.

-a
locative postposition (for inanimate only), "where; in/on" ThSLa §180-183; also temporal "when" ThSLa §184.

-a
vowel harmony version of ergative or locative/terminative postposition -e - ThSLa §172.

-a
-a(k), the genitival postposition - ThSLa §161.

-a
nominalization suffix for a verbal form or clause, creating a noun - placed after pronominal suffix and before post-positions or possessive suffixes; also understood as a particularizer, at the end of a relative clause - 'the Noun that Verbs' - ThSLa §483.

-a
subordination suffix after a perfective verbal form, references previous noun qualified by the verb in a passive way - ThSLa §503, 504, 513-514.

-a
R(*ḫamṭu*)-a or Adj.-a: either of these forms makes the preceding noun definite - ThSLa §503 quotes a study by Krecher.

a-a
father (reduplicated 'offspring').

a-a-a
paternal grandfather.

a-ab-
conjugation prefix /ã-/ + inanimate pronominal element /-b-/; variant of ab- that appears only in OB texts - ThSLa §304.

a-ab-ba(-k)
the sea (cf., aba).

a-aḫ-du_{11}-ga
(cf., aḫ-du_{11}-ga).

$^{g̃iš}$A.AM
(cf., $^{g̃iš}$$ildag_2$).

A.AN
(cf., am_3).

a-ba
Emesal dialect for a-ga.

^{lu2}a-ba
scribe, scholar.

a-ba(-a)
interrogative "who" (animate) ThSLa §37; with ergative a-ba-e ThSLa §113; with possessive suffix a-ba-zu ThSLa §115 (a, 'to', + bi, 'it', + a, 'the').

a-ba-
vowel harmony transform of prospective modal prefix u_3-ba- in Old Sumerian period - ThSLa §409.

a-ba-al
'dry' asphalt (Akkadian loanword - *abālu*, 'to be dry; to mourn', may be Orel & Stolbova #2519).

a-ba-am$_3$
who is it? ThSLa §114 ('who' + enclitic copula).

a-ba-me-en
who are you? ('who' + 'to be' + '1st & 2nd person ending').

a-ba-ri-im
hunger, starvation (Akkadian *berûtu(m)*).

a-bala
drawing of water (e.g., by bucket); water drawer; broth (a, 'water', + bala, 'turn, duty').

a-bara$_2$
(cf., a-gar$_5$).

a-bi$_2$
where?, whither? (a, 'to', + phonetic ending).

a-da gub-ba
water duty ('water' + 'with' + 'to stand' + nominative).

a-da
father (cf., ada).

a-da...tuš
to live near the water ('water' + 'near' + 'to dwell (singular)').

a-da-ab
a type of song or hymn; a copper drum which accompanied such a song (also written as a-tab, 'burning tears' ?).

a-da-al
now; but now; right now - ThSLa §152.

a-da-al-ta
from now on ('now' + 'from').

a-da-ar
Emesal dialect for a-gar$_3$.

a-da-lam; i-da-al-am$_3$
now (cf., a-da-al) ('now' + 'to be').

a-da-min$_3$
contest ('when' + 'with' + 'an equal').

a-da-min$_3$...aka
to compete (with someone: -da-) ('contest' + 'to do, make').

a-da-min$_3$...dug$_4$/du$_{11}$/e
to compete; to dispute ('contest' + 'to speak, do, make').

^{uruda}a-da-pa$_3$
a type of drum (?), or a hymn accompanied by this instrument (cf., pa$_3$-pa$_3$, 'to intone'; Akk., *adapu*, *manzû*).

a-dar-tun$_2$^{ku6}
a fish ('water' + 'to slice' + 'to smash').

a-dara$_4$
(cf., a$_2$-dara$_{3/4}$).

a...de$_2$
to pour out water; to irrigate the fields; to flood, overflow (usually completed in the fifth month in Ur III Girsu) ('water' + 'to pour').

a-de$_2$
fresh ('water' + 'to pour'; cf., ku$_6$-a-de$_2$).

a-de$_2$-a
the yearly spring flood; an adjective for watered soil ('water' + 'to pour' + nominative).

a-dug$_3$
freshwater ('water' + 'sweet, fresh').

a...dug$_4$/du$_{11}$/e
to irrigate ('water' + 'to do').

a dug$_4$-ga
adj., flooded; for irrigation ('to irrigate' + adjectival -a).

a-dun-a
inshore fisherman (?) ('water' + 'lowly student' + nominative).

a-e
interj., oh! (a cry of wailing).

a-e-DU-a
inundated (said of a field, to wash away salt buildup).

a-e...gu$_7$(-a)
eroded by the water ('water' + ergative agent marker + 'to consume' (+ nominative)).

a-e$_3$-a
n., break, outlet in levee; sluice; floodgate; the work of draining water from a field ('water' + 'to emerge, exit' + nominative).

adj., overflowing.

A.EN-da-uruda
a type of copper.

$^{(dug)}$a-epig(-ga)
drinking vessel or trough for animals.

a-eštub$^{(ku6)}$
high tide, early flood (named after the fish that go into the backwaters to spawn in April) ('water' + 'river carp').

a-ga
back, rear, backside; after; back room, hall (cf., eĝir).

a-ga
whey ('water' + 'milk' + genitive; Akk. *agakkum*).

a-ga...gur
to turn back ('back' + 'to return').

a-ga-am, a-ga-am$_3$, a-ga-mu-um
artificial pond - a large, marshy, and permanent or semi-permanent lake used as a reservoir to dispose of flood waters; an occupation - female janitor (prob. loan from Akk. *agammu*).

a-ga-an-tum$_3$
a skin disease.

a-ga-aš-gi$_4$
the most awkward one ('in back' + 'the one' + 'to send, reject').

a-ga-bi-še$_3$
afterwards ('after' + adverbial force suffix + 'towards').

a-ga-de$_3$^{ki}
Agade, the capital city of Sargon's empire, somewhere on the Euphrates, but undiscovered.

a-ga-gul-la
rearmost; of lyre string: ninth and last string ('back' + 'to fall upon' + nominative).

a-ga-zu-ta
behind you ('back' + 'your' + 'from').

a-gab$_2$
(cf., ugu$_4$-bi).

a-gal
overflow of flood waters ('waters' + 'big').

a-gar$_2$-edin-na
hare (Akk. *arnabu(m)*).

a-gar$_3$
irrigated field; (communally controlled) meadow; irrigation district (cf., agar$_{(2,3)}$, ugar) ('water' + 'field'; cf., a...ĝar).

a-gar$_5$[LU$_3$]; a-bara$_2$
lead, the metal; plating of precious metal (Akk. *abāru(m) I* and *ḫumīru* from root *ḫumāru(m)*, 'to become dry'; cf., a...ĝar, 'to irrigate; to be submerged').

a-gar$_5$-ĝeštug[PI]
metal earrings, of gold or silver, weighing usually 1/3 gin$_2$, about 2.8 grams, a normal weight for a pair (e$_2$-ba-an) of modern earrings ('plated metal' + 'ears'; cf., niĝ$_2$-ĝeštug).

a...gi$_4$-a
to sluice, apply water to; to rinse off; to wash over, flood, destroy; to dye textiles ('water' + 'to restore; to surround' + nominative).

a-gig
bitter tears ('water' + 'pain').

a-še$_3$...ĝen[DU]
to go to fetch water ('water' + 'unto' + 'to go').

-a-gin$_7$
as (= when) ...; in that way; thus; how!; how? ('if, when' + 'like').

A.GU$_3$
(cf., ugu$_2$).

a-gub$_2$-ba
holy water ('water' + 'to purify' + nominative).

a-GUG$_2$
(cf., a-gar$_5$).

a-gum$_2$-ma
(cf., a-kum$_2$(-ma)).

[kuš]a-ĝa$_2$-la$_2$; a-ma-il$_2$
leather sack (for grain or flour) ('water' + 'to store' + 'to lift, carry'; Akk., *narūqum*).

a-ĝa$_2$-ri-in
a flat area (measured in sar) (cf., ĝarim).

a-ĜAR
a watery flower-based solution used to remove hair from sheepskins.

A-ĝar
(cf., e$_5$-ĝar).

a...ĝar/ĝa$_2$-ĝa$_2$
to irrigate the fields; to be submerged (usually completed in the fifth month in Ur III Girsu) ('water' + 'to store; to deposit, deliver').

a-še$_3$...ĝen[DU]
to go to fetch water ('water' + 'unto' + 'to go').

a-ĝeštin-na
vinegar ('water' + 'grape; wine' + genitive).

a-ĝi$_6$(-a)
flood ('water' + 'to be black' + nominative).

a-ḫa-an
vomit; sputum ('water' + gan, 'to bring forth'; cf., akan, 'udder').

a-ḫur-rum
(cf., ḫu-ru(-um)).

a-ia$_{10}$[A]-lum
stag, deer (loanword from Akk. *ayyalû(m)*).

a-igi
tears ('water' + 'eyes').

a...il$_2$
to carry water ('water' + 'to lift, carry').

A.KA
(cf., ugu$_2$).

A.KAL
(cf., illu).

a-ki-ta
spring, well; lower, watery end of a field; source of a river ('water' + 'from below').

a-kid
headband, sweatband; bandage ('water' + 'reed mat'; Akk. *agittû*).

a-kum$_2$(-ma), a-gum$_3$(-ma); a-gum$_2$-ma
hot water ('water' + 'to be hot' + nominative; Akk. *egumû(m)*).

a-la, a-la-la
exclamation, often of joy; exuberance; a work song (cf., la-la) ('tears' + 'happiness').

[ĝiš]a-la-la
drain, pipe (cf., alal).

(dug/gi)a-la$_2$(uruda/zabar)
a water vessel or bucket; handle ('water' + 'to lift').

a-lu
adjective for small cattle.

a-lu-lu
exclamation of woe ('tears' + 'numerous').

a-lum, ? aslum$_x$?
adjective for sheep; ram ?; long-fleeced, hairy ? (cf., as$_4$-lum) (related to Orel & Stolbova #27, Sem ***aly-** "fat tail (of sheep)" ?; cf., Akk., *ālu(m) II*, 'ram').

a-ma-il$_2$
(cf., [kuš]a-ĝa$_2$-la$_2$).

a-ma-ru
destructive flood; wave; emergency (cf., ^{kuš}e$_2$-mar-uru$_5$ and $^{(tu15)}$mar-uru$_5$/mar-ru$_{10}$) ('water' + mar-ru$_{10}$, 'flood').

a-ma-ru-kam
interj., It is urgent!; Please!; Now! ('it is of a destructive flood/emergency').

a-maḫ
flood, overflow, bursting of a dam ('water' + 'high, mighty').

a-maš
sheepfold (cf., amaš).

a-MI
(cf., a-g̃i$_6$).

a-muš-du
zig-zag furrows ('water' + 'snake' + 'going').

a-na
interrogative pronoun, "what" ThSLa §37, §116, §122; relative/independent pronoun "whatever" ThSLa §117.

-a-na
possessive suffix 3sg. + genitive -a(k) or locative -a, ThSLa §105 (-a-ni, 'his, hers', + -ak, genitive).

a-na me-a(-bi)
as many as they are; all of it; every part of - ThSLa §121 ('what there is of it').

a-na-am$_3$
thus; why; why?; what is it? ThSLa §120 ('what' + enclitic copula).

a-na-am$_3$...aka
what (will/did) X do?.

a-na-aš(-am); a-na-še
why? ThSLa §118, §201 (why is it that ...?) ('what' + terminative 'to' [+ 'to be']).

a-na-gim, a-na-gin$_7$-nam
how? ThSLa §119 ('what' + 'like'[+ abstract process]).

^{dug}a-nag̃(-nag̃)
water drinking vessel ('water' + (reduplicated) 'to drink').

a-ne
he, she - 3.sg. pronoun in OS, Gudea, & NS texts - ThSLa §37, §91, §173 (cf., e-ne).

-a-ne$_2$
transliteration to imply postposition -e after possessive suffix -a-ni - ThSLa §107.

a-ne-ne
they; these - 3.pl. pronoun in OS, Gudea, & NS texts - ThSLa §91, §173 (cf., e-ne-ne).

-a-ne-ne
possessive suffix, their - ThSLa §101; appended to a numeral forms a numeric pronoun, e.g., min$_3$-na-ne-ne, 'the two of them', ThSLa §142; sometimes analyze as -a-ni plus /-ene/, e.g., šeš-a-ne-ne, 'his brothers'.

-a-ne-ne(-k)
possessive suffix + genitive - note loss of a in -ak after plural possessive suffix, contrasts to behavior after singular possessive suffix - ThSLa §105.

-a-ni
animate 3.sg. possessive suffix, his, her - ThSLa §37, §101.

-a-ni-im
animate 3.sg. possessive suffix plus enclitic copula -am$_3$ - ThSLa §108.

-a-ni-ir
animate 3.sg. possessive suffix plus dative postposition -r(a) - ThSLa §106.

-a-ni-ra
animate 3.sg. possessive suffix plus dative postposition -ra - ThSLa §106.

a-nig̃in$_{(2)}$
standing water; pond, reservoir ('water' + 'enclosure').

a-nir
lamentation, dirge ('tears' + 'to raise high').

a-nir...g̃ar/g̃a$_2$-g̃a$_2$
to set up laments ('lament' + 'to set up').

a-nu-de$_2$-a
an adjective for unwatered soil ('water' + 'not' + 'to pour' + nominative).

a-nu-gi$_4$-a
(cf., a$_2$-nu-gi$_4$-a).

^{u2}a-numun$_2$
reeds, rushes ('water' + 'grass, rushes').

a-numun-sag̃-g̃a$_2$
water of the first seeds = watering of seeds just planted ('water' + 'seeds' + 'first' + genitive).

a-nun-na (-k)
noble stock; fear, dread ('offspring' + 'master' + genitive).

^{d}a-nun-na (-ke$_4$-ne)
the gods as a whole; the gods of the netherworld, as compared to the ^{d}nun-gal-e-ne, the great gods of heaven.

a-pap
funerary pipe (a clay pipe through which water and beer were poured into the grave) ('water' + 'elder/eldest').

a...ra
to ejaculate semen ('seminal fluid' + 'to strike, overflow').

^{dug}a-ra-ab
a clay brewing vessel with a lid (that interlocked ?) ('expel liquid' + imperative ?; Akk. *nēlepu(m)*, 'a brewing vessel', from *ēlepu(m)*, 'to sprout, grow; to interlock'; cf., ^{uruda}gag-a-ra-ab).

a-ra-li
underworld ('tears' + 'to overflow' + 'to sing').

a-ra-zu; a-ra$_2$-zu
prayer, supplication, rite (a-ra$_2$-zu is the earlier form) ('omen' + 'knowing').

a-ra-zu...e
to say a prayer [often introduces direct, quoted speech in the texts].

a-ra$_2$
way, road; solution; step(s); times (multiplication); factor (math.); the number of times that a procedure was performed; installments; discernment, understanding; omen ('where' + 'to go, carry [plural]'; cf., a-ri-a).

a-ra$_2$-bu^{mušen}
an edible water fowl ('water' + 'to go [plural]' + 'to pull, tear out'; cf., a$_{12}$-ra$_2$-bu^{mušen}).

a...ri
to engender; to ejaculate semen ('semen' + 'to pour into').

a-ri-a
one who has begotten ('to engender' + nominative).

a-ri-a; a-ru-a; e$_2$-ri-a
district; desert, waste land ('where' + remote demonstrative affix + nominative).

a-ri$_2$-na^{sar}
weed(s) ('water' + 'city'/'to guard against' + locative/nominative; cf., ^{kuš}e-ri$_2$-na).

a...ru
to dedicate; to give as a votive gift (with dative) ('water' + 'to send').

a-ru-a
ex-voto; work-people 'given' to a temple as human votive offerings; can also describe herd animals ('to give as a votive gift' + nominative).

a-ru-ub
gorge; pitfall ('water' + 'to send' + 'corner').

a-sa$_6$-ga
propitious water ('water' + sa$_6$-ga, 'to win fortune').

a-sal$_{(4)}$-bar
architrave ('water' + 'to spread' + 'to distribute, remove').

a...si
to be filled with water ('water' + 'to fill up').

^{kuš}a-si
(cf., ^{kuš}a$_2$-si).

a-si$_3$-ga, a-se$_3$-ga
placed in water, an adj., for sun$_2$ or titab$_{(2)}$, to create beer mash ('water' + 'to set in' + nominative; cf., Akk., *šūluku*, 'brought to readiness').

$^{(dug)}$a-SIG(-ga)
(cf., $^{(dug)}$a-epig(-ga)).

a sig$_9$, a si-ig(-ga)
clear water ('water' + sig$_9$, 'calm, still').

$^{(uzu)}$a-sila$_3$-g̃ar-ra
afterbirth, placental membrane ('water' + 'liter container' + 'stored' + nominative; cf., sal, 'uterus').

a-silim
potion ('water' + 'health').

^{tug2}A.SU
(cf., ^{tug2}aktum).

$^{lu2/dug}$a-su$_3$
sprinkler, moistener (as of clay); sprinkling vessel ('water' + su$_3$, 'to sprinkle').

a-su$_3$-ra$_{(2)}$
deeply laid water conduit ('waters' + 'remote, subterranean' + genitive).

a-ša-an-gar$_3$(-ra)
to lie, tell untruths; to be perverse; to deceive; to defame (cf., ešgar) (loanword from Akk. *šugguru(m)*, 'to cheat, lie', and *tašgertu(m)*, 'defamation, deception').

a-ša$_3$(-g)
(grain) field, of any size, including the holdings of a family; an area of ca. 50 hectares ('seed' + 'womb'; cf., a-gar$_3$; ašag).

a-ša$_3$-dib(-dib)-ba
the act of trimming the fields and levees of vegetation in preparation for drainage and irrigation ('fields' + 'to seize, bind, take away' + nominative).

a-ša$_3$...e$_3$
to rent a field ('to bring out a field').

a-ša$_3$(-še$_3$)...g̃en-na
who has gone to the field.

a-ša$_3$-ge kig̃$_2$...aka
to do (manual) field work ('work done in the field').

a-ša$_3$ šuku(-ra-k)
subsistence field; prebend land held by dependants of the temples or state ('field' + 'allotment'; Akk. *šukûsu(m) I*).

a-ša$_4$
(cf., a$_2$-še).

a-še-gin$_2$
probably a solution of glue in water, measured as a liquid, used in the manufacture of doors ('water' + 'glue').

a-še-ra; a-še-ru; a-še-er
Emesal form of a-nir, 'lamentation'.

a-še$_3$...g̃en[DU]
to go to fetch water ('water' + 'unto' + 'to go').

a-šed$_{12}$
cool water ('water' + 'cool').

a-$^{(IM)}$šeg̃$_3$-g̃a$_2$
rainwater ('water' + 'rain' + genitive).

a-šeš
bitter, brackish water; an adjective for soil ('water' + 'bitter, brackish').

a-ši-ir
Emesal form of a-nir, 'lamentation'.

a-šu-dab$_6$/da$_5$[URUDU]
a type of oil; an oil-producing plant ('water/liquid' + 'hands' + 'to surround').

a-šu-sa$_2$[DI]
(cf., a-šu-dab$_6$?).

-a-ta
after ... - ThSLa §208 ('when' + 'away from').

a-ta-du$_8$-a
reclaimed (by drainage), describing a field ('water' + ablative postposition + 'to crack, open' + nominative).

a-ta...e$_{11}$
to drain ('water' + 'away from' + 'to exit, drain'; cf., a-ta...g̃ar/g̃a$_2$-g̃a$_2$).

a-ta...g̃ar/g̃a$_2$-g̃a$_2$
to inundate ('water' + 'from' + 'to store; to deposit, deliver'; cf., a-ta...e$_{11}$).

a...tab
to hold or block water ('water' + 'to hold').

a-tab
irrigation ditch ('water' + 'to hold').

a-tag
a category of debit from the storehouse's account ('water' + 'to handle').

a-tar...aka
to play; to mock ('exaggerated' + 'to do, act').

a-tar...la$_2$(-la$_2$)
to deride, mock; to reveal, disclose a secret; ('surplus, excess' + lal, 'to weigh').

a-tar-di/du$_{11}$-du$_{11}$
derision, mockery ('excess, exaggerated' + 'speaking').

a-tar^{sar}
a type of grass (loanword from Akk. *(w)atāru(m)*, 'surplus, excess, exaggerated').

A.TIR
(cf., eša).

A.TU.GAB.LIŠ
(cf., $^{g̃iš}$asal$_2$).

A.TU$_5$
(cf., tu$_{17}$).

a...tu$_5$
to bathe; to wash ('water' + 'to wash').

a-tu$_5$-a, tu$_{17}$-a
lustration, ritual cleaning of statues (a ceremony performed on the day of the new moon) ('water' + 'to wash' + nominative).

a...tum$_3$
to flow with water ('water' + 'to bring, carry').

a-tur-ra; a-tur$_3$; e$_2$-tur$_3$
hollow (of the furrow) ? ('water' + 'birth-hut' for a plant seed ?; related to Orel & Stolbova #1323, ***hadar-** "darkness" ?).

a-da...tuš
to live near the water ('water' + 'near' + 'to dwell (singular)').

a-u$_3$
high water, spring flood ('water' + 'high').

a-u$_3$-a; a-u$_3$-am$_3$-ma
exclamations partly of lament, partly of a soothing nature; a type of priest.

a...u$_3$-ni-tu$_5$
'after washing', 'having washed' ('water' + 'after' + locative infix + 'to wash').

a-u$_4$-te-na
at the cool of the day ('when' + 'day' + ten, 'coolness').

a-u$_5$(-a)
ferryman; moist palate ('water' + 'to ride; to be high').

a-u$_5$-ba...g̃al$_2$
to be at its high tide ('when' + 'on top' + bi, 'its', + a, nominative, + 'to be').

a-ugu$_4$[KU]
the father who begot one ('semen' + 'to procreate').

a-URI$_3$
(cf., a-šeš).

a...uš$_2$-a
to dam up water ('water' + 'piling up an earthen dam').

a-za-lu-lu
teeming life; animal ('water' + 'voice, cry, noise' + redup. 'to multiply, to graze').

a-zal(-le)
flowing water, running water ('water' + 'to flow' (+ phonetic complement)).

^{u2}a-zal-la$_2$
a medicinal plant, probably distilled into a narcotic (described as "a plant for forgetting worries"); cannabis sativa, hashish (?) ('liquid' + 'to have time elapse' + nominative).

a-zi-ga
rising waters; water-lifting; seasonal flooding of the rivers ('water' + 'to raise, rise up' + nominative).

a-zu; a-zu$_5$; a-su
physician, healer (cf., azu).

a$_2$
arm; wing; horn; side; strength; manpower, workforce; work performance; salary, wages; moment, time. [A$_2$ archaic frequency: 3]

a$_2$ aĝ$_2$-ĝa$_2$
instructions, orders, command ('manpower' + 'to measure out', + a, nominalizer).

a$_2$...aĝa$_2$
to command; to instruct (someone: -da-); to issue an order; to pay the rental charge ('strength' + 'to measure out').

a$_2$-an
female spadix, raceme ('arm, wing' + 'sky, high').

$^{(gi)}$a$_2$-an(-la$_2$)
basket (for dates) ('reed item' + 'spadix' + 'to lift').

a$_2$-an-kara$_2$
(cf., enkara).

a$_2$-an-sur
female spadix clothed with dates ('spadix' + si, 'long and narrow', + ur, 'to surround').

a$_2$-an-zu$_2$-lum(-ma)
date spadix with its unpollinated or undeveloped clusters ('spadix' + 'date fruit' + genitive).

^{ĝiš}a$_2$-apin
wooden stilt(s) of a plow (cf., ^{ĝiš}da-pa) ('arm' + 'plow').

$^{(uruda)}$a$_2$-aš-ĝar$^{(zabar)}$
a weapon, usually of bronze, cast in a metal mold - ax (cf., a$_2$-sur/šur$^{(zabar)}$) ('arm; strength' + 'one' + 'to put'; Akk. *naptaqu*).

a$_2$-aš$_2$
what one needs; requirement ('strength' + 'to wish, desire').

a$_2$-bad-ĝal$_2$
protective ('arms' + 'spread open' + 'having').

a$_2$-bi
its hire price ('wages' + 'its').

a$_2$-bi-ĝal$_2$; a-bi$_2$-a-gal
burial priest, grave-digger ('whither' + 'to place [into]').

a$_2$...buru$_2$
to open the wings ('wings' + 'to spread out').

a$_2$-dab$_5$
hirelings ('manpower' + 'to seize, bind, hire').

a$_2$...daḫ
to assist ('strength' + 'to add').

a$_2$-daḫ
aid, help; ally; auxiliary ('strength' + 'to add').

a$_2$-dam
a human settlement; steppe-dweller; levy ('strength; wages' + 'it is from').

a$_2$...dar
to confiscate; to seize illegally; to cheat (someone) out of one's right ('wages; force' + 'to split').

a_2-dara$_{3/4}$; a dara$_4$
ibex-like, said of goats and sheep; hybrid; an ibex horn that provides musical accompaniment ('arms'/'seed' + 'ibex').

a_2-diri-ga
wages for extra work ('wages' + 'to be extra' + nominative).

a_2...dub$_2$; a_2-dub$_2$...aka
to flap one's wings (with -še$_3$ and -ši-, to fly towards) ('wings' + 'to flap' + 'to do').

a_2...e$_3$
to bring up, rear; to educate; to take care of ('strength' + 'to emerge').

a_2-e$_3$(-a)
foster child; adopted child ('to rear, care for' + nominative).

A_2-GAM
(cf., id-gurum/id-gur$_2$).

a_2-gar$_3$
embrace (?) ('arms' + 'something round and upraised').

a_2-gi$_4$-a
reimbursed wages ('wages' + 'to return, restore' + nominative).

a_2-gu$_2$-zi-ga
early morning ('arms' + 'necks' + 'rising', + a, nominalizer).

a_2-gub$_3$-bu
left; at the left side (opp. = a_2-zi(-da)) ('side, arm' + 'left' + locative).

a_2-gul-la
category of unused manpower in accounting texts - the workforce disappeared in the middle of the month/ accounting period ('workforce' + 'to disappear, run away' + nominative).

a_2...gur
to turn aside, turn away ('side' + 'circular motion').

a_2-gur(-gur)
obstinate, rebellious (redup. 'to turn aside'; cf., gur, 'to protest, contradict').

a_2-g̃a$_2$
alternate spelling for ag̃a$_2$.

a_2-g̃al$_2$
n., leader; strong one; strength; power; force; trust, reliance; circumspect judgment ('strength' + 'available').

adj., able; powerful; rich.

a_2...g̃ar
to act strongly; to win; to defeat, conquer, overcome; to resist; to oppress; to rein-force ('strength' + 'to establish').

a_2-g̃ar
strength; wall (in Gudea, Cylinder A) ('strength; side' + 'to establish'; cf., eg̃ar).

a_2-g̃e$_6$-ba-a
at night; a nighttime cultic ceremony ('side' + 'dark' + 'to divide/distribute' + locative).

a_2-g̃iš-gar$_3$-ra
work assignment ('manpower' + 'tool' + 'field' + genitive; cf., eš$_2$-kar$_3$/eš$_2$-gar$_3$/aš$_2$-gar$_3$, ešgar).

a_2-g̃iš-ur$_3$-ra
manpower required for plowing and/or harrowing, where in the Umma texts three men made up a team, but only two men needed for harrowing in Girsu texts - one or two men rested his/their weight on a harrow's beam while the remaining man drove the ox(en) ('manpower' + 'harrow' + genitive).

a_2 g̃uruš-bi
workmen's wages ('wages' + 'workers' + 'its').

a_2-ḫu-ul-g̃al$_2$
being to blame, at fault ('arm' + 'evil' + 'having').

a_2...il
to exalt, glorify ('horn' + 'to lift').

A_2-KAL
strength; plow extension ('arm' + 'strong').

(ĝiš) a_2-kar_2
armor; equipment (cf., ĝiš šu-kar_2) ('arm' + 'to encircle').

a_2 kaskal-la
migrant harvest workers ('manpower' + 'road, caravan, journey' + genitive).

iti a_2-ki-ti
calendar month 7 at Ur during Ur III; month 6 at Drehem through year 3 of Šu-Sin; calendar month 7 at Drehem after Šu-Sin 3 (loanword from Akk. *akītu(m)*, 'cultic festival frequently celebrated at the New Year; festival building'; cf., Sumerian zag-mu(-k)).

a_2-$kuš_2$-u_3
to prevail; to beat, hit; to be weary, exhausted ('strength' + 'to be tired').

ĝiš a_2-la_2
a device for moving irrigation water, involving a water bucket hanging from a swinging beam ('arm' + 'to hang').

(kuš/zabar) a_2-la_2
a type of drum or kettledrum (?), with hints that originally it may have been a stringed instrument ('side' + 'to bind').

a_2-lal, a_2-la_2; a_2-lal_2
fetters; fettered legs; paralyzed arms; handicapped, crippled person ('arms' + 'to bind').

a_2-me_3
literary term for a weapon - 'battle arm'.

a_2-mi
(cf., $ama_{(4,5)}$, ame_2).

a_2-na_2-da
bed chamber ('side, wing' + 'bed' + genitive).

a_2-ni...-ra-e_3
to escape from his/her arm ('arm' + pronominal possessive suffix + ablative infix + 'to emerge').

a_2-ni_2-za...dub_2
to be (supported) on your own ('wings' + 'self' + 'your' + 'to flap').

a_2-nu-gi_4-a
irresistable ('strength' + 'not' + 'to answer, return' + nominative).

a_2-nu-$ĝal_2$
n., slight, little one ('strength' + 'not' + 'available').

adj., powerless; poor.

a_2-nu_2-da
(cf., a_2-na_2-da).

a_2-numun-na
manpower in planting ('manpower' + 'seed' + genitive).

a_2-nun-$ĝal_2$
strongest; most powerful ('strength' + 'great' + 'available').

a_2-sag_3[PA], a_2-zag_2
slingstone; a demon (cf., a_2-sig_3 [PA]) ('arm' + sig_3/sag_3, 'to smite'; Akkadian *assukku*; *asakku(m) I*).

kuš a_2-si
whip; strap; hinge ('arm' + 'antenna-like').

uruda a_2-si
door-hinge.

a_2-sig_3[PA]; a_2-si-ga
disease (in general); sickness demon; a cause of death for which there is no blame (cf., a_2-sag_3 [PA]) ('strength' + 'to hurt'/'weak').

a_2-sikil(-la)
pure, undiluted strength ('strength' + 'pure' + nominative).

a_2...sud/su_3
to extend the arm (in accusation); to spread (around); to sail; to run (while flapping the arms); to move [intransitive] (reduplication class) ('arm' + 'to stretch; to flap').

A_2.SUḪ
(cf., aškud$_{(2)}$).

a_2-sum-ma
granted power, strength ('strength' + 'to give' + nominative).

a_2-sumur$_{(2/3)}$
canopy ('arms' + 'roof, shelter').

a_2-sur/šur$^{(zabar)}$
a type of cast bronze ax (cf., $^{(uruda)}$$a_2$-aš-g̃ar$^{(zabar)}$) ('arm; strength' + 'to divide'/'to produce a liquid').

a_2-še
attention-getting exclamation: 'hey now!', 'even now'.

a_2-šita$_4$; a_2-šu-du$_7$
parts, components (of the plow); equipment ('arm' + 'to join'/'to complete').

a_2 šu...du$_7$
to be well equipped (reduplication class) ('arm' + 'hand' + 'to be complete').

a_2-šu-g̃iri$_3$
limbs ('arm' + 'hand' + 'foot').

a_2-šu-g̃iri$_3$-ku$_5$
cripple; quadriplegic ('limbs' + 'to curse').

a_2...-ta
at the prompting of; by means of the strength of ('strength' + instrumental postposition).

a_2-taḫ
(cf., a_2-daḫ).

a_2...tal$_2$
to have broad arms; to spread wings or arms ('arms; wings' + 'to be broad; to spread').

a_2-tuku
strength; benefit; able-bodied; mighty man ('arms; strength' + 'having').

a_2-u$_4$-te-en
in the evening ('side' + 'daylight' + 'to extinguish, cool down').

a_2-u$_4$-te-na
evening ('side' + 'daylight' + 'to extinguish, cool down' + nominative).

a_2-ur$_2$
limb, limbs, extremities ('arms' + 'legs': Sumerian example of asyndetic hendiadys).

a_2-ur$_2$
secret, secrecy, hiding; armpit.

a_2-ur$_2$...dab$_5$/dib$_2$
to hide; to be in hiding ('secrecy' + 'to take'/ 'to traverse'; cf., bar...dab$_5$/dib$_2$).

a_2-zag$_2$
(cf., a_2-sag$_3$[PA]).

a_2-zi(-da)
right; at the right side (opp. = a_2-gub$_3$-bu) ('side' + 'right' + locative).

a_2-zi(-ga)
n., violence ('arm' + 'to raise' + nominative).

adj., violent.

adv., violently.

a_5
(cf., aka).

a_{12}-ra$_2$-bu^{mušen}, u$_4$-ra$_2$-bu^{mušen}
an edible waterbird ('to shine' + 'to pluck out'; cf., ara$_4$-bu^{mušen}, a-ra$_2$-bu^{mušen}; Akk. *arabû*).

ab
window; opening; niche, nook (cf., aba) [AB archaic frequency: 384; concatenates 2 sign variants (sign also used for eš$_3$ and aba - for this reading and meaning in Fara period, see Krebernik, *Beschwörungen*].

ab-
conjugation prefix /ã-/ + inanimate pronominal element /-b-/; in OB literary texts alternates with the conjugation prefix al- ThSLa §357, §304.

-ab-
(cf., -b-).

AB.AB
(cf., eš$_3$-eš$_3$).

^{iti}ab(-ba)-e_3
calendar month 10 at Nippur during Ur III.

ab-(ba)
(cf., aba).

^{ĝiš}ab-ba
(cf., ĝiš-ab-ba(-k)).

ab-ba; ab-be_2; ab[AB]; $abba_2$ [AB×ÁŠ]
father; elder; high-ranking official; ancestor (loanword from Akk. *abu(m)*).

ab-ba-ab-ba(-me)
elders, administrators.

ab-ba-uru
city elder ('elder' + 'city').

ab-ba-$ĝa_2$
of my father [such as his sheep or estate - eĝir] ('father' + 'my' + genitive).

ab-ba-$ĝu_{10}$
my father ('father' + 'my').

ab-du_3(-du_3)
to install; to drive in nails; to fix in place; a plant or vegetable ('niche, opening' + 'to build, fasten').

ab-ki-iz
clean furrow, unobstructed by weeds ('niche' + 'trimmed').

ab-lal_3
bird niche, nest (cf., ablal$_{(3)}$).

ab-sin_2; ab-si-im-ma; ab-su_3-na
furrow - seeded or irrigation ('niche' + sim/sin_2, 'to sift'; su_3, 'to extend; to immerse').

ab-sin_2-gilim-ba/ma
crossing, transversal furrow, possibly for drainage ('furrow' + 'to cross plow' (+ 'its') + nominative).

ab_2
domestic cow (a,'water, liquid', + ib_2,'middle') [AB_2 archaic frequency: 288].

ab_2-ama
mother cow ('cow' + 'mother').

ab_2-amar
mother cow ('cow' + 'calf').

ab_2-amar-ga
a collective designation of suckling she- and bull-calves ('cow' + 'bull-calf' + 'milk').

ab_2-ga
suckling she-calf ('cow' + 'milk').

ab_2-gir_{15}/gi_7[KU]
domestic cow ('cow' + 'domestic').

ab_2-gud-$ḫa_2$
herd; cattle; oxen of various ages and gender ('cow' + 'bull' + 'assorted, mixed').

ab_2-i_3-nu-de_3
a sterile cow ('cow which has not carried').

AB_2.KU
(cf., unu_3(-d); udul).

ab_2-maḫ; ab_2-$maḫ_2$[AL]
mature cow in 3rd year of life that has calved ('cow' + 'to have calved'; Akk., *ubātum*, 'fat or pregnant cow').

ab_2-$ninda_2$
breeding cow ('cow' + 'seeding tube').

ab_2-sağ
top or head strap (used by grain farmer).

ab_2-ur_2
bottom or leg strap (used by grain farmer).

ab_2-za-za
an exotic bovid, such as the zebu or water buffalo.

aba, ab
lake; sea [AB archaic frequency: 384; concatenates 2 sign variants].

^{kuš}aba
tarpaulin used to cover boats ('leather' + 'lake, sea').

abba$_{(2)}$
(cf., ab-ba).

abgal$_{(2)}$
sage, wise man, wizard (abba, 'elder', + gal, 'great') [ABGAL archaic frequency: 31].

ablal$_{(3)}$
bird niche, nest (ab, 'niche, nook', + lal, 'to be high; to hang').

abrig
a purification priest (a, 'water', + barag, 'ruler; throne') [ABRIG archaic frequency: 9].

absin$_{(3)}$
furrow, seeded or irrigation (cf., ab-sin$_2$/ab-si-im-ma/ab-su$_3$-na).

abul [KA$_2$.GAL]
gate of city or large building; outer door (loanword from Semitic for 'door', Orel & Stolbova, *Hamito-Semitic Etymological Dictionary* (1995), #287 ***bil-** 'door', Sem **ʿabul-* 'door, gate').

abzu [ZU.AB]
the 'sentient' sea - the sea personified as a god (aba/ab, 'sea' + zu, 'to know'; Akk. *apsû(m)*, '(cosmic) underground water') [ABZU archaic frequency: 28].

ad
n., shout; voice; song; sound (cf., ada) [AD archaic frequency: 36; concatenates 3 sign variants].

v., to balk.

(ĝiš)ad
raft; beam, plank (of a boat) ('water' + 'side').

ad-ad-da
paternal grandfather ('father' + 'father' + genitive).

ad-da
father (cf., ada).

ad...gi$_4$
to echo; to ponder (alone: without -da-, but with bi$_2$-); to take counsel, confer, consult (with someone: -da-) ('shout' + 'to answer').

ad-gi$_4$
advice, counsel.

ad...gi$_4$-gi$_4$
to give counsel; to converse (confidentially) (cf., ad...gi$_4$).

ad-gi$_4$-gi$_4$
advisor, counselor.

ad...ĝar
to stifle a cry ('cry' + 'to enclose, lock up').

ad-ḫal
diviner; secret ('voice, sound' + 'secret, divination expert').

ad-kid$_2$
reed mat plaiter ('raft, plank' + kid$_3$, 'to build, make', and kid$_6$, 'to weave a mat').

ad-kub$_4$, ad-gub5 [KID]
reed weaver; wicker-worker; maker of reed mats, boats, and baskets ('raft, plank' + gub, 'to install'; > Akk., *atkuppu(m)*, 'craftsman making objects of reeds', cf., *quppu(m) II*, 'box, chest, of reed or wood').

ad...mar
Emesal dialect, cf., ad...ĝar.

ad...pad$_3$/pa$_3$
to tune (a musical instrument) ('sound' + 'to seek').

ad...ša$_4$
to wail, lament, complain; to resound; to sing; to improvise vocally; to trill ('song' + 'to wail').

ad-ša$_4$
wailing (song); sound; singing; tremolo; lamentation singer.

ad-tab
harness; rein(s); collar; necklace; bead(s) ('sound' + 'to clasp; to pair off').

(ĝiš)ad-uš/us$_2$
(long)side plank, beam, board; support; wall ('plank' + 'side, edge').

ad$_2$
(cf., adda$_4$).

ad$_{3,6,7,8}$
(cf., adda).

ad$_4$ [ZA-*tenû*]
lame, cripple.

ada [AD]
n., father [AD archaic frequency: 36; concatenates 3 sign variants].

adamen$_{(2,3,4,5)}$
argument; fight (cf., a-da-min$_3$).

adda$_{(2)}$, ad$_{3,6,7,8}$
carcass, cadaver, corpse, body; skeleton [ADDA archaic frequency: 4].

$^{ĝiš/u2}$adda$_3$, ad$_5$ [U$_2$.ĜIR$_2$/ U$_2$.ĜIR$_2$*gunû*]; $^{ĝiš/u2}$adda$_4$, ad$_2$ [ĜIR$_2$]
boxthorn (*Lycium*), a tall, erect, thorny perennial shrub that often grows closely together to form impenetrable thickets from one meter to three meters high. Its smooth berries ripen to orange/red about 1 cm. in size. They can be eaten fresh or be sun-dried for winter use. Also called wolfberry, the plant and berries contain alkaloids and have medicinal uses; thorns (in general) (cf., $^{ĝiš/u2}$kišig$_{(2)}$) (Akkadian loanword from *edēdu(m)*, 'to be(come) pointed, spiky') [? KIŠIK archaic frequency: 21; concatenates 3 sign variants].

adda$_4$, ad$_2$
to dispatch, send; to drive away.

addir [A.PA.ĜISAL.PAD.DIRIG etc.]
ferry; bridge; (river) crossing; ford; fare, toll, fee, rental; wages (cf., a-u$_5$) (a, 'water', or ida$_2$/id$_2$, 'river', + dirig/dir, 'to go over').

addir$_2$ [previously addir$_x$ - PAD.BI.SI+ĜIŠ (RÉC 78)]
wages.

adkin [LAK 668/SIKI.LAM/ŠEŠ$_2$]
salted meat (cf., mu-du-lum) (ad$_3$, 'carcass', + kiĝ$_2$/kin, 'task, work').

ag
(cf., ak).

$^{(ĝiš)}$aga$_{(3)}$
a kind of ax.

^{zabar}aga
a bronze beer vessel.

^{ĝiš}aga-silig(-ga)
a double-bladed battle-ax ('ax' + 'powerful').

^{uruda}aga-silig(-ga)
a mixing tool.

aga$_{(3)}$
diadem, circlet, crown (of legitimate kingship); turban [TUN$_3$ archaic frequency: 96; concatenates 3 sign variants].

aga$_{(3)}$-kar$_2$
conqueror ('crown/axe' + 'to besiege').

aga$_{(3)}$-kar$_2$...sig$_{10}$ [SUM]
to conquer, defeat, massacre ('conqueror' + 'to apply, impose').

aga$_{(3)}$-us$_2$
policeman, constable; companion, attendant; soldier ('crown' + 'to follow').

aga$_3$ [GIN$_2$]...bar
to dress (a tree after felling it); to hew or split with an ax ('ax' + 'to pare, split').

aga$_3$-ri$_2$(-na)
(cf., agarin$_{(2,3)}$ or agarin$_{4,5}$).

aga$_3$-us$_2$ ensi$_2$
soldier of the governor ('soldier' + 'governor').

agam
swamp (a, 'water', + gam, 'to decline, incline').

agan$_2$, akan
(cf., akani).

agar$_{(2,3)}$, ugar
field; commons; communal meadow (cf., a-gar$_3$; ugur$_2$) [AGAR$_2$ archaic frequency: 16].

agar$_4$
(cf., ugur$_2$).

agargara[ku6] **[NUN-*tenû*]**
fish spawn; a fish (a, 'water', + redup. gara$_2$, 'thick milk, cream').

agarin(2,3)
father; mother; womb; mold, molding, casting.

agarin$_{4,5}$
beer-wort; crucible, vat ([zabar]aga, 'a bronze beer vessel', + rin$_2$, 'to be bright').

agrun
inner sanctuary; storage (?) chamber (Akk. *kummu(m) I*, 'cella, shrine'; *agarunnu*, 'cella'; cf., [ĝiš]li$_2$-id-ga) [ZATU-413 archaic frequency: 4].

aĝ$_2$, eĝ$_3$
(cf., aĝa$_2$; in Emesal, cf., em$_3$).

aĝ$_2$-X
Emesal dialect, cf., niĝ$_2$-X.

aĝa$_2$, aĝ$_2$, aka$_2$, am$_2$
to measure out; to mete out; to pay out; to measure (area, length, time, capacity); to check; (in Emesal, cf., em$_3$) (a$_2$,'arm', + ĝal$_2$; ĝa$_2$,'storage basket; to place, put'; cf., a$_2$-ĝa$_2$).

aĝar$_5$[IM×IM]; aĝar$_6$[IM.DUGUD]
heavy rain shower, cloudburst (a, 'water', + ĝar, 'to accumulate; to deposit').

aĝrig[IGI.DUB]
steward/stewardess, superintendent (cf., ĝiskim) (aĝa$_2$, 'to measure; to check', + rig$_7$, 'to deed, grant').

aḫ(6)
spittle (cf., uḫ$_2$, aḫ$_6$; uḫ, aḫ; uḫ$_3$).

aḫ-du$_{11}$-ga; a-aḫ-du$_{11}$-ga
spittle (of sorcery) ('spittle' + 'utterance').

aḫ...uš$_7$[KA×LI]
to spit ('saliva' + 'spittle').

aḫ$_3$; uḫ
(cf., laḫ).

aḫḫur(2,3), uḫḫur(2,3)
(cf., imḫur).

ak, ag
(cf., aka).

-ak, -ag
genitival case postposition, 'of', ThSLa §161-§168.

-/ak-eš/
because (genitival postposition + adverbial suffix).

/X ...-ak-eš/
from the X of ... - ThSLa §205 (genitival postposition + ablative-instrumental postposition).

aka, ak, ag, a$_5$
to do, act; to place; to make into (something) (with -si-); "auxiliary" verb ThSLa §532 [AK archaic frequency: 149; concatenates 2 sign variants].

aka$_3$
fleece.

akan$_2$, aka$_4$, kan$_4$[KA$_2$]
door-frame, lintel (cf., ĝiš-ka$_2$(-an)-na).

akani, akan
udder (a, 'water, liquid', + gan, kan, 'to bring forth').

akar
leather armor (cf., eg$_2$-ur$_3$).

akkil[GAD.TAK$_4$.SI]
lamentation, ritual wailing; clamor, cry (Akk. *angillu; ikillu(m)*).

[tug2]**aktum[A.SU];**
[tug2]**aktum$_2$[SU.A]**
a garment or type of heavy cloth; cape (?), rug (?).

[ĝiš]**al**
digging stick; wooden mattock, pickax; forked hoe with from 2 to 4 teeth; spade [AL archaic frequency: 95].

al-
conjugation prefix before verbal root ThSLa §303, §353, used immediately

before stative verbs ThSLa §356; indicates: 1) distance; 2) the speaker is not involved; or 3) the lack of a transitive relationship.

(ĝiš)al...aka
to work at hoeing, digging ('hoe' + 'to do').

al...di/dug$_4$/du$_{11}$/e
to desire, pray, aspire to, demand, insist (often with -ni-) ('hoe' + 'to make the motion of'; but cf., im-ma-al(-la)).

al...du$_3$
to dig; to hoe ground that is already broken ('hoe' + 'to mold, shape').

(lu2/MUNUS)al-ed$_2$/ed$_3$(-de$_3$)
n., (male or female) ecstatic; wild man (verbal prefix + *marû* form e$_3$-de$_3$(-d) of ed$_3$, e$_{11}$, 'to exit'; cf., lu$_2$-mu$_2$-da).

adj., raving, frenzied; bright, shining.

al-gazum$_x$ [ZUM+LAGAB]
an exotic spice.

al...ĝar
to use the hoe ('hoe' + 'to place').

^{ĝiš}al-ĝar
harp (?) ('hoe' + 'form, appearance').

^{ĝiš}al-ĝar-sur$_9$
plectrum, pick, drumsticks (?) ('harp ?' + 'a type of lamentation priest').

al-ḫab-ba
malodorous; very odorous, ripe (verbal prefix + participial form of ḫab, 'to stink, rot').

^{lu2}al-ḫu-nu
weak; sick; slack, relaxed; cripple (?) (verbal prefix + participial form of ḫuĝ, ḫun(-ĝ), 'to rest, repose; to abate').

al-la-ḫa-ru
a tanning agent used to produce a white color.

^{ĝiš}al-la-nu-um; ^{ĝiš}al-la-an; al-la-num$_2$[LUM]
oak tree; acorn (Akk. loanword from *allānum*, 'oak; maple (CAD A1 354b)', cf., Orel & Stolbova #31 ***'alan-/*'alun-** 'tree').

al-lul, al-lu$_5$
crab ('digger' + 'to deceive').

(ĝiš)al-lu$_5$-ḫab$_2$
a type of hunting net, said to be employed along the city wall (cf., sa-al-ḫab-ba).

al-lub/lu$_5$
a type of ax (phonetic harmony variant of al-šub ?).

(ĝiš)al...ri/ra(-ḫ)
to strike or demolish with the hoe; to punish ('hoe' + 'to break open; to strike').

al-še$_6$[NE]-ĝa$_2$
cooked (verbal prefix + 'to cook' + subordination suffix).

^{ĝiš}al-šub
ax-like hoe ('hoe' + 'to throw; to fell').

al...tag
to hoe ('hoe' + 'to handle').

(ĝiš)al-tar
construction work; demolition work; construction worker; demolishing tool (?) (some story connects this to the planet Jupiter, called both ud-al-tar and ^{d}šul-pa-e$_3$) ('hoe' + 'to cut, break').

al-ti-ri$_2$-gu$_7$^{mušen}; al-ti-ri$_2$-ga^{mušen}; al-tar(-gu$_7$)^{mušen}
a small bird; wren (?) (onomatopoeic from its cry ?; Akk., *di(q)diqqu(m)*, 'wren; small one').

al-zi-ra
destroyed (by the hoe ?); old and dry (said of reeds) (verbal prefix al or 'hoe' + zi-r 'to destroy').

^{ĝiš}al-zu$_2$
hoe ('hoe' + 'tooth').

$^{(diğir)}$alad
a life force; a male protective spirit.

alağ
(cf., alan).

$^{(dug/uruda/zabar)}$alal; alal$_x$[KI.LUGAL.DU]
pipe, conduit, gutter (of clay, copper, or bronze); pipe for making libation offerings to the deceased (a, 'water', + lal, 'lift, carry').

alal$_4$
area under cultivation (cf., ulul$_2$) (Akk., *mēreštu(m) I*).

alam
(cf., alan).

alan, alam, alağ, al$_2$
image, statue (of a god or king); figure, appearance [ALAN archaic frequency: 51; concatenates 6 sign variants].

alan-lugal
royal statue ('statue' + 'king').

alim
wild ram; bison; aurochs; powerful; weighty [ALIM=ZATU-219 [GIR$_3$] sign per P. Steinkeller, archaic frequency: 73; concatenation of 3 sign variants].

allal$_x$, alla
net, seine; crab (vowel harmony version of al-lul, al-lu$_5$).

am
(cf., am$_3$ and ama$_2$).

$^{(dug)}$am(-ma)-am
a large beer jar, that could be made of bronze or pure copper (> Akkadian *ammammu I*).

am-ra
ship timbers (Akkadian loanword, *amrû(m)*, 'beam, timber').

am-si
elephant ('wild ox' + 'horn, ray, antenna'; cf., šu-si, 'finger').

am-si-ḫar-ra-an(-na); am-si-kur-ra
camel, dromedary ('elephant' + 'road, caravan').

am$_2$
(cf., ağa$_2$).

am$_2$-u$_2$-rum
Emesal dialect for niğ$_2$-u$_2$-rum, 'favorite sister'.

am$_3$- [A.AN]
writing of conjugation prefix /ã-/ with ventive element /-m-/ in NS and OB texts - ThSLa §304, §316, §318; compared with im-ma-, ThSLa §320.

-am$_3$ [A.AN]
the Sumerian 3.sg. enclitic copula - 'to be' - in texts after OS period, ThSLa §541, occurs after nouns, adjectives, pronouns, and non-finite verbs ThSLa §526 [e.g., William king-is]; who, which, what, where; (same) as, like (in scholarly lists) - for the enclitic copula's alternation with or replacement of the equative postposition, see ThSLa §219.

am$_3$-ga
(cf., an-ga-am$_3$).

am$_3$-ma-
writing of conjugation prefixes /ã-ba-/ in OB texts - ThSLa §304.

am$_3$-mi-
writing of conjugation prefixes /ã-bi-/ in OB texts - ThSLa §304.

am$_3$-mu-
writing of conjugation prefixes /ã-mu-/ in OB texts - ThSLa §304.

am$_3$-mu-uš
Emesal dialect for eš$_5$, 'three'.

-am$_6$ [AN]
the Sumerian 3.sg. enclitic copula - 'to be' - in OS period texts, ThSLa §541.

ama
mother [AMA archaic frequency: 241; concatenates 2 sign variants].

ama$_{(4,5)}$, ame$_2$
women's quarters, chamber; living room.

ama-a-tu/tud
(cf., emedu).

ama(-ar)-gi$_4$
freedom; liberation; manumission; exemption from debts or obligations (early texts omitted the -ar) ('mother' + dative -ra + 'to restore'; cf., dumu-gir$_{15}$).

ama-gan; ama-ugu
n., natural or birth mother; child-bearing mother ('mother' + ugun$_3$, ugu$_{(4)}$, 'to beget').

adj., describes jenny asses that have foaled; pregnant.

ama-gu-la
grandmother ('mother' + 'eldest').

ama$_2$, am
wild ox or cow (aurochs, *Bos primigenius*).

amagi$_{(2,3)}$, mabi$_{(2,3)}$
ice.

amalu[AMA.AN.MUŠ$_3$]
cultic prostitute(s); goddess(es) ('mothers' + 'numerous').

amar
calf; young animal (ama$_2$, 'wild cow mother', + re$_7$, 'to accompany, plural') [AMAR archaic frequency: 297].

^{iti}amar-a-a-si
calendar month 10 at Lagaš during Ur III.

amar-ga
young calf (designation until the loss of its milk teeth ?, which starts to occur at age 1.5 years); suckling bull-calf ('calf' + 'milk').

amar-gud-am-ga
milk aurochs calf (male aurochs calf in first half year of life) ('calf' + 'wild bull' + 'milk').

amar-kud
separated, weaned young animal ('calf' + 'to cut away from').

amar-sağ^{mušen}
wild pigeon; chick, fledgling (cf., ir$_7$[KASKAL](-sağ)^{mušen}).

amar-UD
(read, amar-bir$_2$, 'foal destined for the yoke').

amaš[DAG.KISIM$_5$×LU.MAŠ$_2$]
sheepfold, cattle-pen (e$_2$, 'house', + maš, 'goat').

ambar, abbar
marsh; reeds, canebrake (imi/im, 'clay, mud', + bar, 'to obtain', but cf., ^{gi}en$_3$-bar).

amuš
(cf., am$_3$-mu-uš).

an
n., sky, heaven; the god An; grain ear/date spadix (cf., a$_2$-an) ('water' + 'high') [AN archaic frequency: 806].

v., to be high.

adj., high; tall.

prep., in front.

an-
conjugation prefix /ã-/ + animate 3.sg. pronominal element /-n-/ ThSLa §304.

-an
represents 1.sg. or 2.sg. pronominal suffix /-en/ after a verb ending in -a, ThSLa §296.

-an-
represents locative prefix /-ni-/ after ba- conjugation prefix.

an-ba
refuse; litter; dirt ('open air' + 'to give up').

an-bar(-sug4-ga)
(meteoric) iron (cf., barzil).

an-bar$_7$[NE](-gana$_2$); an-bar; an-ba-ra
noon; midday; day; the hottest, brightest part of the day; siesta-time ('sky' + 'to be bright' + 'field; surface').

an-bir$_8$[A-SUD]
noon; midday rest ('sky' + 'to be hot' ['WATER' + 'TO SIP']).

an-dul$_3$
shade; screen; protection (conjugation prefix or 'sky' + 'to cover, protect').

an-DUR
evening (?) ('heaven' + 'bond, tie' ?).

an-edin(-na)
high plain ('high' + 'steppe').

an-ga-
writing of conjugation prefixes /ã-ga-/ - ThSLa §304 (cf., in-ga-).

an-ga-am$_3$
likewise, moreover, besides, in addition, as well (cf., in-ga-na-nam).

an-gur$_4$
(cf., engur).

an-g̃a$_2$
and yet (cf., an-ga-am$_3$) (affirmative prefix ? + 'exists').

an-g̃i$_6$
eclipse (cf., an-ta-lu$_3$) ('sky' + 'black').

an-kara$_2$
(cf., enkara).

an-ki
universe ('heaven' + 'earth').

AN.MUL
starry sky (verify that AN is not the rare sign ŠU$_2$; cf., kunga[ŠU$_2$.MUL]).

an-na
in the sky; tin, pewter (metal); saltpeter (stone); yes, approval ('sky' + locative; 'sky' + 'stone'; cf., nagga; an-bar(-sug4-ga); Civil thinks an-na, 'yes', is probably an Akkadianism, but cf., affirmative na-nam, 'indeed' and in-nu, 'negation').

an-na...dug$_4$/du$_{11}$/e
to say yes ('yes' + 'to say').

^{lu2}an-ne$_2$-ba-tud[TU]
ecstatic ('heaven' + -e, loc./term. postposition, + tud, 'to give birth; to be born, reborn' ?; cf., ($^{(lu2/MI2)}$al-ed$_2$/ed$_3$(-de$_3$), 'ecstatic; wild man').

an-ne$_2$...us$_2$
to reach as high as the sky ('sky' + loc./term. postposition + 'to reach').

an-nisig(-ga)
beautiful sky, blue sky ('sky' + 'beautiful, blue').

an-nu-gi-a
(cf., a$_2$-nu-gi$_4$-a).

an-pa
zenith ('sky' + 'branch' of sun dial ?).

an-SAR
(cf., an-nisig).

an-sig$_7$-ga
the beautiful sky ('sky' + 'to be beautiful' + nominative).

an-sud
the distant heavens ('heaven' + 'distant, remote').

an-sur
(cf., a$_2$-an-sur).

an-ša$_{(4)}$-an^{ki}
Anshan - place name for powerful city in Elam - Tall-i Malyan near Persepolis in the Fars province of Iran.

an-ša$_3$(-ga)
base of the sky; center of the sky ('heaven' + 'womb, midst').

an-šar$_2$(-ra)
all of heaven, the whole sky ('heaven' + 'totality, horizon').

an-še
ear of grain ('grain ear; high/tall' + 'grain, barley').

an-še$_3$
heavenward, up ('heaven' + terminative postposition).

an-ta
from above, down; prefix (grammatical) ('heaven' + locative with remote deixis).

(lu2)an-ta
close companion, best friend.

an-ta...gi$_{(4)}$
to meet ('heaven' + 'from' + 'to return').

an-ta-ĝal$_2$
high, superior ('sky; high' + 'from' + 'being').

an-ta-lu$_3$
eclipse (cf., an-ĝi$_6$) ('heaven' + 'from' + 'to disturb, trouble').

an-ta-sur-ra, an-ta-šur-ra
a precious stone or metal; meteor, shooting star ('heaven' + 'from' + šur, sur, 'to rain; to flash, gleam' + nominative; Akk., *antasurrû, antašurrû*).

(ĝiš)an-ti-bala
banner; sign; prominent position ('high' + 'to approach' + 'to take turns').

an-ub-da
regions; "quarter" ('sky' + 'corners' + 'with').

an-ur$_2$
horizon ('sky' + 'base, floor').

an-uraš
heaven and earth; universe ('heaven' + 'earth').

an-usan; an-usan$_2$
evening; dusk; evening watch ('sky' + 'evening').

(dug)an-za-am
goblet, drinking vessel, of copper, silver, cedarwood (> Akk. *assammu*) ('high' + 'drum').

an-za-kar$_3$
tower, fort ('high' + 'stone' + 'round, high thing').

an-zag, an-za$_3$
where heaven ends; horizon ('heaven' + 'side, boundary').

an-zaḫ
heated or fused lead (an, 'tin' + 'to be calm').

an-zib$_2$(-ba)
adept; very competent (one) ('high' + 'distinguishing mark').

an-zil[NUN]
abomination; forbidden food (loanword from Akk. *anzillu(m)*, 'taboo; abomination').

anše
donkey; generic term for equid; pack animal; mare (an,'sky; high', + še$_3$, terminative postposition = 'up to' = 'to raise up, carry'; the Online Etymology Dictionary says "L. *asinus*, probably of Middle Eastern origin (cf. Sumerian ansu)") [ANŠE archaic frequency: 48; concatenates 4 sign variants;? KIŠ archaic frequency: 46].

anše-bala
pack-ass ('equid' + 'to cross over, deliver').

anše-BAR.AN
(cf., anše-kunga$_2$).

anše-bir$_3$
ass yoked in a team ('equid' + 'team').

anše-dab$_5$(-ba)/anše-dib$_2$(-ba)
ass-herdsman ('equid' + 'to take, hold, accompany').

anše-du$_{24}$-ur$_3$
(cf., dur$_9$[ŠUL]).

anše-dub
ass registered on a tablet ('equid' + 'tablet').

anše-DUN.GI
probably donkey, yoked in teams and preferred for plows and carts (occurs in ED IIIa-b period, imported from Der) ('equid' + 'yoke' ?).

anše-edin-na
wild ass, onager (occurs from ED I to Ur III) ('equid' + 'steppe' + a(k), genitival postposition).

anše-ĝir$_{2/3}$-nun(-na)
a type of mule ('equid' + 'highway').

anše-ĝiš
workass ('equid' + 'tool').

ANŠE-ka
one of the best groups of people.

anše-KU
(cf., anše-dab$_5$(-ba)).

anše-kunga$_{(2)}$ (-mi$_2$/nita$_2$)
mule (female/male); hybrid of onager + donkey (occurs from ED IIIa period) ('equid' + 'donkey'; Akk., *parû(m) I*, 'mule').

anše-kur-ra
horse (occurs frequently from Old Babylonian period on) ('foreign equid, equid of the east'; -ra phonetic complement indicates that we should not read sisi, despite OB Diri Ur 24; Akk. *sisû(m)*; cf., anše-zi-zi/anše-si$_2$-si$_2$).

ANŠE.LIBIR
(cf., dusu$_2$).

anše-mar
chariot or wagon ass ('equid' + 'wagon').

anše-ni-is-ku
fine steed; thoroughbred.

anše-nun-na
a type of mule (cf., anše-ĝiri$_{2/3}$-nun(-na)).

anše-zi-zi, anše-si$_2$-si$_2$
horse (occurs in Ur III period) ('equid that rises [off the ground]' or loanword from Akk. *sisû(m)*).

anzalub
reed pulp or pith.

anzud$_{(2)}$, anzu$_{(2)}$-(d) [^{d}IM.MI/DUGUD^{mušen}]
a mythical storm bird with the roaring head of a lion and the flying body of an eagle; vulture, eagle [ANZU$_2$ archaic frequency: 1].

^{ĝiš}apin
n., seeder plow (in the Umma texts operated by a team of four men, who could seed 2 iku of parcels per day); also a generic term for ard, sliding plow; sometimes the Sumerians merely attached a seeding-drill to a subsoil plow (a, 'seed', + bun, 'to blow') [APIN archaic frequency: 181; concatenates 3 sign variants].

adj., describes a plow animal (also apin-še$_3$).

^{iti}apin-dug-a
calendar month 8 at Nippur during Ur III.

apin-la$_2$
(cf., gana$_2$-uru$_4$-la$_2$; uru$_4$-la$_2$).

^{ĝiš}apin-numun
plow fitted with seeder attachment ('plow' + 'seed').

^{ĝiš}apin-šu
hand seeder-plow ('seeder plow' + 'hand'; Akk. *agadibbu*).

^{ĝiš}apin-tug$_2$-sig$_{18}$[KIN]; ^{ĝiš}apin-šu-sig$_{18}$[KIN]
deep-going, subsoil plow, for first plowing, usually in the fourth and fifth months of the year (cf., $^{(ĝiš)}$tug$_2$-gur$_8$/gur) ('plow' + originally LAK 483 implement + 'to cut, break, harvest').

apin-us$_2$
plowman's helper ('plow' + 'to follow; to be next to').

ar[IGI.RI]
(cf., ara$_4$).

$^{ĝiš/šim/u2}$ar-ga-nu-um; ar-ga-num$_2$
a coniferous tree or its resin; an herb with a similar resinous scent - Cedronella (loan from Akk. *argānum*).

$^{(uruda)}$ar-ma-tum
a (decorated) metal coating, such as for a door (loanword from Akk. *armatum*, from *arāmu*, 'to cover something with something').

ar-za-na, ar-sa$_3$-na
barley groats (loanword from Akk. *arzānu, arsānu*).

ar-zig
millet (Akk. *arsikku; duḫnu*).

ar$_2$
(cf., ara$_2$).

ar$_{(2)}$...de$_6$/tum$_2$
to praise ('praise' + 'to bring').

ar$_2$...e/i
to praise ('praise' + 'to speak; to send forth').

ar$_2$-mu(-r); ar$_2$-mur
ruin mounds (cf., Akk. *armūtu*, 'desolation').

$^{\tilde{g}iš}$ar$_2$-re(-eš)
(wood) stringed praise instrument - lyre ('praise' + phonetic complement + 'much').

ar$_2$-re(-eš)
praise ('praise' + phonetic complement + 'much').

adj., praiseworthy.

ar$_3$
(cf., ara$_3$).

ara$_2$, ar$_2$[UB]
n., praise, glory, fame; mound.

v., to praise, glorify.

$^{(na4)}$ara$_{3,5}$, ar$_3$, ur$_5$[ḪAR]
n., millstone, quern; miller, grinder; watercourse (cf., ḫar/ḫara, kin$_2$, kikken, ur$_5$) (ḫara - many small explosions + sliding motion) [UR$_5$ archaic frequency: 34; concatenation of 2 sign variants].

v., to coarsely grind; to destroy; to make groats or crushed flour; to chew (in redup. form, read ar$_3$-ar$_3$).

adj., ground, milled, crushed, pulverized; small; young.

ara$_4$[UD.DU]; ar; ra$_3$
v., to shine; to blaze; to appear.

adj., bright; clear; polished.

ara$_4$-bu^{mušen}
an edible waterbird ('to shine' + 'to pluck out'; cf., a$_{12}$-ra$_2$-bu^{mušen}; Akk. *arabû*).

ara$_5$[ḪAR.ḪAR]
(cf., ara$_{3,5}$; kikken$_2$).

arad$_{(2)}$, urdu$_{(2)}$, ir$_{3,11}$
(male) slave; servant; subordinate (cf., ir$_3$) (Akk. loanword from *wardum*, 'male slave, man-servant') [IR$_{11}$ archaic frequency: 10].

araḫ$_4$[E$_2$.UŠ.GID$_2$.DA]
storehouse.

arali, arala
the netherworld (ara$_3$, 'to pulverize', + la, 'youthful freshness and beauty' ?, or the name of a desert that is part of the Dumuzi myth).

arḫuš
n., womb; compassion, pity (ur$_2$, 'base; root', + ḫaš$_2$, 'lower abdomen').

v., to be sympathetic.

arib$_x$
(cf., erib).

$^{(\tilde{g}iš)}$arina, erina$_8$ [MUŠ×MUŠ.A.NA]
root(s) (cf., ^{u2}ḫirin, 'the root stalks of the spikenard') (Akk. *šuršu(m); šinbiltu*).

arkab, irkab[NIG̃$_2$.IB]^{mušen}
(cf., su-din(-dal/dara$_2$)^{mušen}).

as
(cf., aza).

as$_4$[LAGAB×A]-lum
a long-fleeced type of sheep ?; a fine quality ram/sheep for sacrifice ? (cf., a-lum) (Akk. *aslu I*, 'ram; sheep').

$^{\tilde{g}iš}$as$_4$-lum
a special cubit measure; yardstick (Akk. *aslu II*).

asa, as
(cf., aza, az).

^{ĝiš}asal$_{(2)}$, asar$_{(2)}$
Euphrates poplar tree, grown both in woods and in gardens [ASAL$_2$ archaic frequency: 16].

^{ĝiš}asal$_{(2)}$-lal$_3$
a tree, perhaps 'Strawberry tree' ('poplar' + 'honey'; Akk., *gergiššu(m)*; *tiālu(m)*).

asilal$_{(3,4,5)}$, asila, asil$_{(3,4,5)}$
(cries of) joy, gladness; celebration ('honey-filled drink ?').

aš; aš-a; aš-še$_3$
one; unique; only; alone (cf., dili).

aš
(cf., uš$_7$; aš).

-aš
writing of the terminative case post-position /eše/ after the vowel -a after the NS period - ThSLa §195 (cf., -še$_3$).

aš$_{(2)}$
emmer flour; bread (cf., eša; ĝiš-aš).

aš$_{(5)}$
spider.

AŠ-DU
accomplished; arrogant ('unique' + 'acting'; cf., dili-du(-a)).

$^{(ĝiš/gi)}$aš-ḫal-lum$^{(zabar)}$
a box-like sieve (Akk. *ašḫa(l)lum*, *mašḫalu(m)*, '(type of) sieve', from *šaḫālu(m)*, 'to sieve, filter').

aš-me
sparkle, glimmer; sundisk; star symbol; rosette - the šu-nir of Inanna ('unique' + 'function, power').

aš...tar
Emesal dialect for en$_3$...tar.

^{mu}aš-te
Emesal dialect for ^{ĝiš}gu-za.

AŠ-ur$_4$
adj., shearling; describes a lamb that is old enough (probably 16-17 months old) to have had its fleece plucked once ('one' + 'plucked').

aš$_2$
n., need; requirement; want; wish; curse; mark, sign [AŠ$_2$ archaic frequency: 5].

v., to desire; to curse.

aš$_2$ a$_2$-zi-ga...bala
to curse with violence ('curse' + 'raised arms' + 'to deliver').

aš$_2$...bala
to curse ('curse' + 'to deliver').

aš$_2$...dug$_4$/du$_{11}$/e
to curse ('curse' + 'to speak/effect').

aš$_2$-du$_{11}$-ga
cursed ('curse' + 'to speak/effect' + nominative).

$^{(SAL)}$AŠ$_2$.GAR$_3$
(cf., ešgar and eš$_2$-kar$_3$).

aš$_2$...gi$_4$
to answer with a curse ('curse' + 'to answer').

aš$_2$...mu$_2$
to curse ('curse' + 'to blow, speak').

aš$_2$...sar
to curse ('curse' + 'to write').

aš$_{3,4,8}$
six (ia$_2$, 'five', + aš, 'one').

aš$_5$
(cf., aš$_{(5)}$).

aša$_5$
(cf., ašag).

ašag, aša$_5$ [GANA$_2$]
field, plot (cf., a-ša$_3$-(g)).

ašag šuku(-ra-k)
subsistence field; prebend land periodically allotted to dignitaries and other dependants of the temples or state ('field' + 'allotment'; Akk. *šukûsu(m) I*).

ašgab
leather-dresser, currier (kuš, 'leather', + gub_2, 'to cleanse'; cf., $ḫaš_4...dab_5$, 'to hold firmly').

ašgar
(cf., ešgar).

(u2)aški
bulrush (*Typha grass*; cf, $^{u2}numun_2$) ($eš_2$, 'rope', + $kid_{(6)}$, 'to weave a reed mat').

$aškud_{(2)}$
forearm; foreleg, hooves (of animal); wedge (to block door); wedge-shape (in math.); ramp, of earth, in fields and houses; bolt, locking bar (a_2, 'arm', + $sukud_2$, 'to measure').

ašlag
(cf., $^{lu2}azlag$).

^{d}ašnan[ŠE.TIR]
the grain goddess Ashnan (cf., $^{d}ezinu_2/ezina_2/ezin_2$ [ŠE.TIR]).

ašte
need; necessity; desirable or beloved object ($aš_2$, 'to desire', + te, 'to approach'; cf., $teš_2$).

az
(cf., aza).

^{ĝiš}az-bala; ^{ĝiš}az-la_2
cage for lions, dogs, etc.; (fish-)trap ('cage' + 'hostility'/'to look after').

^{ĝiš}az-gu_2; ^{ĝiš}az-bala; ^{ĝiš}az-la_2
neck-stock (for captives); halter ('fetter' + 'neck').

aza, az, asa, as
cage; fetter; bear [AZ archaic frequency: 13].

$^{ĝiš\ (šim)}$aza, az, asa, as
myrtle (*Myrtus communis*), an evergreen shrub with scented leaves that heal wounds - its resin used to make a pleasant aromatic oil with strong anti-microbial properties (Akk., *asu(m) I*; cf., $^{(ĝiš)}$šim-$ĝir_2$).

azag[KUG.AN]
taboo.

$azag_2$
(cf., a_2-sig_3[PA]).

$^{lu2}azlag_{(2,3,4,5,6)}$, ašlag
launderer; fuller, felt-worker (a, 'water', + zalag, 'to cleanse').

azu, uzu_2, zu_5
doctor, healer (cf., a-zu; aza, 'myrtle') [AZU archaic frequency: 7].

^{u2}azugna[ḪUR.SAĜ]^{sar}, ^{u2}azukna^{sar}, ^{u2}azubir^{sar}
saffron, a spice derived from the flower of the saffron crocus - frescoes at Thera are said to prove the use of saffron in medicine during the Bronze Age - see the on-line Wikipedia article on saffron (cf., u_2-numun(-na)) (azu, 'doctor', + gin_6, 'to stabilize, strengthen, fix' + -a, nominative, or bir_2, 'to sniff'; Akkadian *azupīru(m)*).

B

-b-
inanimate (AKA nonpersonal) pronominal prefix ThSLa §37, §293.

ba-
conjugation prefix - ThSLa §337; used mostly with intransitive (non-agentive) forms - ThSLa §345, §342, §346, §349-50; case prefix for nonpersonal subjects (OB/NS) - ThSLa §344 .

ba-
conjugation prefix in year formula of NS kings - ThSLa §345; translated by Akkadian *t*-perfect in OB bilingual literary texts - ThSLa §348; with locative force - ThSLa §350.

-ba
a contraction - the possessive or demonstrative suffix -bi plus nominative -a.

ba
n., share, portion; rations, wages [BA archaic frequency: 523].

v., to give; to divide, apportion, share, distribute, split, allot; to pay; to extract (interchanges with bar).

$^{(ku6)}$ba
a shelled creature (such as a turtle or a snail); a scraping tool (cf., ba-al-gi$_{(4)}$$^{(ku6)}$).

ba-ab-si
it is more (conjugation prefix + inanimate direct object prefix + 'to be full, sufficient').

ba-al
to dig (a canal); to dredge; to channel; to unload a boat; to return (older third millenium form; cf., bal) (conjugation prefix + 'digging stick, mattock, spade').

ba-al-gi$_{(4)}$$^{(ku6)}$; bal-gi$^{(ku6)}$; ba-al-gu$_7$
tortoise; turtle (less numerous in texts than niĝ$_2$-bun$_2$-na$^{(ku6)}$) ('to dig' + 'to surround, besiege; to lock up; to eat').

ba-al-la
unloaded ('to unload a boat' + adjectival -a).

$^{ĝiš/uruda}$ba-an
a container; a five ? sila$_3$ measuring cup.

ba-an
a measure for bread and flour (cf., ban$_2$).

$^{gi/ĝiš}$ba-an-du$_8$(-du$_8$); ba-an-du$_5$
bucket for drinking; sowing basket ('container' + reduplicated 'to crack open').

ba-an-gi-in
it was examined, determined (conjugation prefix + locative prefix + 'to find true').

ba-an-gi$_4$
response; as measurement of a brick wall - taper, bevel, slant, incline (conjugation prefix + 3rd person animate affix + 'return, answer').

ba-an-za
lame, limping; crippled (conjugation prefix + 3rd person animate affix + 'to make a repetitive motion'; cf., ba-za).

ba-ba(-za)
pudding, malt-sweetened porridge (> Akk. *pappasu*).

ba-da-
comitative prefix with inanimate - ThSLa §445, §449.

$^{(ĝiri3)}$ba-da-ra
poniard; pin (from Akk. *patarru*, *pattaru*).

ba-gi-in
it was examined; it was determined (conjugation prefix + 'to find true').

ba-la$_2$
it is less (conjugation prefix + 'light, deficient').

ba-na-gi(-in)
it was awarded to him (conjugation prefix + 3.sg. animate dative prefix + 'to award').

ba-ne-gi(-in)
it was awarded to them (conjugation prefix + 3.pl. dative prefix + 'to award').

ba-ni-
locative prefix -ni- with inanimate - ThSLa §476, §480.

ba-ra-
modal prefix - with *marû* denotes vetitive (forbidding, vetoing in the future) - for use with promissory oaths; with *ḫamṭu* denotes the negative affirmative (negative assertion about the past) ThSLa §234, §366-70.

ba-ra-
writing of modal prefix ba-ra- with conjugation prefix /ĩ-/ - ThSLa §304.

ba-ra(-g)
to spread out (cf., bara$_4$).

$^{\tilde{g}i\check{s}}$ba-ri$_2$-ga
bushel; square-based measuring vessel = 6 ban$_2$ in all periods (= 36 liters in Old Sumerian period and 60 liters in Old Akkadian and Neo-Sumerian period) (cf., bariga).

ba-rV
to fly, flee (cf., bad, bar).

ba-si
OB math text term for cube root (conjugation prefix + 'to pile up; to divide').

ba-ši-
terminative prefix with inanimate - ThSLa §455.

ba-ta-tur; ba-ra-tur
it is short (conjugation prefix + earlier/later ablative case prefix + 'small, insufficient').

$^{(tug2)}$ba-tab-du$_8$-ḫu-um
a special type of woolen belt (conjugation prefix + 'to join, shut' + 'to take apart' + 'to wrestle').

$^{(\tilde{g}i\check{s})}$ba-ti-um; $^{(gi)}$pa$_4$-ti-um$^{(zabar)}$
a vessel (loan from Akkadian *baṭû(m)*).

ba-ug$_7$(-ge)
adjective for a deceased worker or ox (impersonal conjugation prefix + 'to die').

ba-ur$_4$
shorn fleece, a commodity measured in literes (impersonal conjugation prefix + 'to shear, pluck').

ba-uš$_2$[TIL]
it is dead; dead (referring to a single animal that was either slaughtered or dead of natural causes); occurs after a type of animal (cf., RI-RI-ga) (impersonal conjugation prefix + 'to die').

ba-za
n, halt or lame person (cf., ki . . . za; ba-an-za).

adj., crippled.

ba-zal
(cf., u$_4$-X ba-zal).

ba-zi
to subtract (math.); to take out; dispersed (cf., ḫa-ba-zi-zi) (impersonal conjugation prefix + 'to tear away').

$^{(\tilde{g}i\check{s})}$ba-zu$_2$
a toothed knife used by builders.

ba$_3$[EŠ]
liver; liver model; omen.

ba$_4$
Emesal dialect, cf., g̃a$_2$, 'house'.

BA$_6$-BA$_6$
(cf., ^{uruda}kuš$_3$-kuš$_3$).

ba$_7$
(cf., bar).

ba$_9$
(cf., bad).

babbar$_{(2)}$
bright; white; the rising sun (reduplicated bar$_6$, 'bright, white') [UD archaic frequency: 419].

babbar$_{(2)}$-ḫi^{sar}
purslane, an edible, nutrient-rich succulent, a summer annual - about mid-July it develops tiny, yellow flowers that open only in direct sunlight (reduplicated bar$_6$, 'to shine brightly', + 'abundance' + vegetable determinative; loan to Akk. as *parparḫû, puḫpuḫu*, 'purslane').

bad, be, ba$_9$
to open; to let out; to go away; to be at a distance (in space or time); to drive away; to separate, remove (regularly followed by ra$_2$; cf., bara$_4$ and semantics of bar; there were originally four separate signs: BAD; IDIM; TIL; UŠ$_2$) (open container with motion away from) [BAD archaic frequency: 23].

bad-bad
(cf., bad$_5$-bad$_5$).

BAD.UD
(cf., lugud).

bad_3
n., (city) wall; fortress [? EZEN archaic frequency: 114; concatenation of 3 sign variants].

v., to climb, ascend.

adj., high.

bad_3-gilim
scaling ladder ('city wall' + 'reed rope').

bad_3-niĝin
circular city wall ('city wall' + 'enclosure, circle').

bad_3-si
crenellation, parapet, battlement ('city wall' + 'long, narrow').

bad_3-si-an-na
high battlements ('parapet' + 'to be high' + nominative).

bad_3-šul-ḫi; bad_3-sil_3-ḫi
outer wall ('city wall' + 'invader'/'path' + 'numerous').

bad_4[KI.KAL]
fortress; hardship, difficulty (cf., kankal).

bad_5-bad_5[IGI.IGI]; bad-bad
to defeat; to open up; to stare (redup. bad, 'to open').

baḫar$_2$
potter [BAḪAR$_2$ archaic frequency: 50; concatenates 3 sign variants].

bal; ba.al
to dig up; to dig out (a ditch); to quarry; to tear down, demolish (cf., ba-al and bala('), bal) (ba, 'conjugation prefix' or 'turtle shell', + al, 'digging stick, hoe, spade').

bal-gi$^{(ku6)}$
(cf., ba-al-gi$_{(4)}$$^{(ku6)}$).

$^{(ĝiš)}$bala('), bal
n., spindle; bar; turn; term of office; reign; job; rotating fund; annual contribution to the state; portion; ratio; hostility; enemies; changing (of products) [BALA archaic frequency: 19; concatenates 2 sign variants].

v., to revolve; to take turns; to turn (over); to revolt; to uproot; to transgress; to change; to transfer, deliver (to someone: dative); to cross over; to pass through; to draw (water); to pour (as a libation; with -ta-); to turn around, go back (bala-e in *marû*) (the presence of a -w or -y at the end of this word is shown in that -la or -la$_2$ do not resume it, consistent with the following etymology: ba, 'share', + ila$_2$, 'to carry, deliver, bring, support', where cf. the etymology of ila$_2$).

bala-a-ri
opposite; opposing side; beyond ('to cross over' + locative + remote demonstrative affix).

bala-še$_3$...aka
to transport ('goods delivery' + 'towards' + 'to do').

bala-bala(-e)
speech, declamation; a song or hymn in the form of quoted speech, either a dialog or a monologue; pouring out (e.g., libations) (cf., inim...bala/bal-bal, 'to have a conversation'; bala('), 'to take turns').

bala-dab$_5$-ba
worker hired to work for a bala' period ('term' + 'to seize, bind, hire' + nominative).

bala eš$_2$-kar$_3$
fraction of an assignment ('term, portion' + 'work assignment').

bala-gub-ba
worker stationed to work for a bala' period ('term' + 'to stand' + nominative).

bala-ri
on the other bank ('to cross over' + remote demonstrative affix).

^{ĝiš}bala...sir$_5$
to spin with a spindle ('spindle' + 'to spin').

balağ
(spoon-shaped) round-harp, a drummable resonator, with a croaking/tweeting sound associated with frogs, crickets/locusts, and the sparrow; funeral song [? BALAG archaic frequency: 20].

balağ-di
professional mourner; dirge singer; wailer; lamentation priest ('drum harp' + 'speaking/doing').

$^{(ğiš)}$balağ-di
a drum-like musical instrument.

balağ-ila$_2$
harp carrier ('drum harp' + 'to lift').

$^{(ğiš)}$balağ-ir$_2$-ra
lamentation harp ('harp' + 'lamentation' + genitival a(k)).

BALAĞ.NAR
(cf., tigi).

ban
(cf., pana).

ban$_2$
vessel; the Biblical 'seah' - a measure of capacity or volume = 10 liters (sila$_3$) in the Ur III period; = 6 liters at Presargonic Girsu (cf., banda$_{2,4,5}$) (Akk., *sūtu(m) I*) (ba, 'portion, rations', + na, 'human being' - the Biblical 'seah', meaning 'measure', "was the ordinary measure for household purposes").

ban$_3$
(cf., banda$_3$).

ban$_3$-da
(cf., banda$_3$).

banda$_{2,4,5}$
prop, support.

banda$_3$$^{(da)}$ [TUR ^{da}]
young; junior; vigorous; impetuous; fierce; proud.

$^{dug/ğiš}$baneš [AŠ$_2$]
a 3 ban$_2$ measuring container (ban$_2$, 'a standard vessel', + eš$_{5,6}$, 'three'; Akk., *ṣimdu(m) II*, '3 *sūtu*'; with ^{ğiš}, consider *ṣimdu(m) I*, 'binding').

^{ğiš}banšur$_{(2,3)}$
table; container [? BANŠUR archaic frequency: 7; concatenates 5 sign variants].

bappir$_{(2/3)}$
beer bread (a hard bread made from raw grain barley dough mixed with sweet aromatics - this bread mixed with titab to make mash for beer); brewer [BAPPIR archaic frequency: 28; concatenates 6 sign variants].

bar
n., (out)side; exterior; outskirts; facade; fleece; soul, innards, liver, spirit [BAR archaic frequency: 306].

v., to open; to uncover, expose; to see; to remove; to dig out a canal; to be absent; to release, let go; to peel, pare, shell; to select; to divide; to split; to distribute; to keep away (with -ta-); to remain set aside (container plus to expel, remove as in ri).

adj., foreign; describes an area outside of the surveyed field plan, but included in the calculation.

prep., because of (with ...-ak-eše) ThSLa §201 (cf., bar...VERB-a-ak-eše).

bar...VERB-a-ak-eše
for the sake of, because, in a subordinate clause ThSLa §489, §491, §201.

bar...aka
to choose; to examine; to test ('to open; to see; to select' + 'to do').

BAR.AN
(cf., kunga$_2$).

$^{(ğiš)}$bar-bar
part of a weaver's loom (shuttle ?).

^{ğiš}bar-be$_2$-da
a type of rod, pole, or tool.

$^{(\tilde{g}iš)}$**bar-da**
cross-piece; cross bar ('shape of bar sign' + 'with').

bar...dab$_5$/dib$_2$
to escape ('outside' + 'to take'/'to traverse'; cf., a$_2$-ur$_2$...dab$_5$/dib$_2$).

bar...dag
to wander far away ('outside' + 'to roam about').

$^{\tilde{g}iš}$**bar-dil**
a soil-breaking plow(share) which by the Old Babylonian period had replaced the $^{(\tilde{g}iš)}$tug$_2$-gur$_8$/gur found in Ur III texts.

bar-dub$_2$-ba
a good price ('to split, distribute' + 'to knock down' + nominative).

^{tug2}**bar-dul$_{(5)}$**
a long coat; mantle ('outer body' + 'protection').

$^{\tilde{g}iš}$**bar-e$_{11}$-de$_3$**
rope braiding lever ('sides' + 'to descend' + participial ending).

^{kuš}**bar-e$_{11}$-de$_3$**
straps to attach leather wrappings to the plow ('sides' + 'to descend' + participial ending).

bar-edin-na
edge of the desert ('side' + 'steppe' + genitival a(k)).

bar-eg$_2$-ga
outer side of the levee ('outer side' + 'levee' + genitival a(k)).

bar...gub
to step outside ('outside' + 'to stand').

bar-ta...gub
to withdraw from ('side' + 'to stand aside').

bar-gun$_3$-gun$_3$-nu
chameleon ('sides' + reduplicated 'to be multicolored' + nominative with vowel harmony).

bar...g̃al$_2$
to be outside (the count); to be extra ('outside' + 'to be').

bar-g̃al$_2$(-la)
unsheared, unplucked [sheep] ('fleece' + 'to be in place' + nominative).

$^{(lu2)}$**bar-ḫu-da**
machete for harvesting reeds; a class of persons ('to open' + kud, 'to cut off' ?).

bar...ḫug̃
to appease the spirit ('spirit' + 'to rest').

bar-la$_2$
part of an irrigation system, perhaps water distributor, branching off point ('outside' + 'to lift, load, embrace, extend').

bar-LU
one of the best wool blends.

bar-rim$_4$[KAŠ$_4$](-ma)
dry land ('to uncover' + 'to travel fast'?; cf., parim).

bar...sed$_4$
to soothe the spirit ('spirit' + 'to cool, soothe').

^{tug2}**bar-sig$_9$[SI]**
head-band, turban; sash, ribbon; bandage ('sides' + 'narrow').

bar-su-ga; bar-sug$_4$-a
sheared, plucked [sheep]; calculation separate from main account but later re-entered ('fleece' + 'bare, empty' + nominative).

bar-sud
one of several rubrics or interpolated titles for part of a hymn ('outside; spirit' + 'distant; profound').

bar-šeg̃$_3$-g̃a$_2$(-e)
violence; mist ('outside' + 'to rain' + loc./term. postposition).

bar-šu-g̃al$_2$
someone who has a temper or who talks loud; inspector of slaves (?) ('soul' + 'hand' + 'to place').

$^{(mi)}$bar-šu-g̃al$_2$
midwife ('to open, expose' + 'hand' + 'to place').

bar...tab
to vanish (?) ('outside' + 'to make haste').

bar...tab$_{(2)}$
to inflame or trouble the spirit; to be feverish (opposite of bar...sed$_4$) ('spirit/outer body' + 'to burn, inflame').

bar-tam...(ak); bar...tam
to examine; to choose, select; the successful efforts of a court to establish the truth by weighing conflicting statements and evidence ('to open; to see; to select' + ablative + enclitic copula [+ 'to do']).

bar-TUG$_2$
(cf., bar-dul$_5$).

bar-ul$_3$[KIB]
dog chain ('outside' + 'leash').

bar-us$_2$^{uruda}
copper-tipped goading stick ('side' + 'to drive'; cf., gag-us$_2$).

bar$_2$
(cf., barag).

bar$_3$
(cf., barag$_2$).

bar$_{6,7}$
v., to shine, be bright; to break (of the day); to burn (cf., bar, 'to expose', which refers here to the sun; and cf., ara$_4$, 'to shine; to blaze').

adj., white.

bar$_6$-bar$_6$
(some prefer this reading, but cf., babbar$_2$).

bar$_7$-bar$_7$-ra, bir$_9$-bir$_9$-ra
flames (reduplicated 'to shine' + nominative).

bara$_2$
(cf., barag).

^{iti}bara$_2$-za$_3$-g̃ar
calendar month 1 at Nippur during Ur III.

bara$_3$
(cf., barag$_2$).

bara$_4$[BAD]
to spread out, open wide; released; separated.

bara$_{5,6}$
(cf., barag).

barag, bara$_2$, bar$_2$, para$_{10}$, par$_6$; bara$_{5,6}$
n., throne dais; seat of honor; king, ruler; cult platform, base, socle; sanctuary, chapel, shrine; stand, support; crate, box; cargo; sack; sackcloth, penitential robe; chamber, dwelling, abode (container plus ra(g), 'to pack') [? BARA$_2$ archaic frequency: 69; concatenates 2 sign variants; ? ZATU-764 archaic frequency 21].

v., to comb out; to filter; to recover dehulled sesame seed kernels from the surface of saltwater with a comb, sieve, or coarse sackcloth.

adj., combed, filtered (said of wool, goat hair, sesame, perfumes, flax).

barag-sig$_9$-ga; barag-sig$_5$-ga
house altar; small shrine ('sanctuary' + 'silence' + genitive).

barag$_2$, bara$_3$, para$_3$, bar$_3$, par$_3$[DAG]; para$_4$, par$_4$[KISAL]
n., nest [BARA$_3$ archaic frequency: 13].

v., to stretch or spread out; to pass over; to be stretched or spread out; extended (interchanges with buru$_2$) (ba, 'to apportion, divide', + ra(-g/ḫ), 'to overflow'; cf. compound word, ba-ra(-g)).

bariga [PI or UL(in Old Sumerian period)]
a dry measure of capacity - 36 sila$_3$ in the Old Sumerian period and 60 sila$_3$ in the Old Akkadian and Neo-Sumerian

periods. Equals 6 ban_2 (cf., $^{gi\check{s}}$ba-ri_2-ga). (ban_2-rig-a, 'the ban_2 from picking, gleaning').

barzil [AN.BAR]
(meteoric) iron (bar_6, 'to shine', + zil, 'to cut, peel').

be
(cf., bad).

$-be_2$, -bi
v., to diminish, lessen; to speak, say (accusative infix b 3rd pers. sing. neuter + e 'to speak'); to murmer, chirp, twitter, buzz, hum, howl, cry; mention (cf., biz; bi[z]) [KAŠ archaic frequency: 261; concatenates 4 sign variants].

be_2- [BI]
OS writing of conjugation prefix /bi-/ before verbs having the vowels [a] or [i]; normally written bi_2 [NE] ThSLa §339.

be_4, bi_6 [BA]; be_6, bi_3 [PI]; be_3, bi
to tear, cut; to tear off (with -ta-); to diminish, lessen.

be_5
(cf., bid_3).

-bi-
pron., it, them; inanimate/nonpersonal pronominal prefix; as a prefix in transitive *ḫamṭu*, /-b-/ can also refer to 3.pl. subject; often in cohortative and in transitive *marû*, /-b-/ refers to the inanimate direct object - ThSLa §293.

-bi
possessive suffix, 'its', 'their', applies to singular and plural inanimate or non-personal categories (things, animals, and collective objects) ThSLa §37, §101; used with cardinal numbers.

-bi
demonstrative suffix, this (one), that (one) - in this sense can occur with animates - ThSLa §138.

-bi
conj., and (cf., -bi-da(-ke_4)).

-bi
adverbial force suffix (ADJ.+bi; ADJ.+bi+ eš-šè) (VERB-a-bi) - ThSLa §86-89.

bi-bi-ze_2
to drip (reduplicated biz, 'to pour').

-bi-da(-ke_4)
'and'; conjunction for nouns, without the disjunctive force of /u_3/ - ThSLa §144, §193 ('with its').

BI.ĜIŠ
(cf., ĝisal).

-bi-im
inanimate 3rd person possessive suffix plus enclitic copula -am_3, ThSLa §108.

bi-iz
drop (of water); dripping, melting (cf., biz, 'to pour').

bi-ri-ig
v., to wrinkle one's nose; to sneer.

adj., obstinate (?).

bi_2
(cf., i-bi_2).

bi_2- [NE]
normal writing of inanimate directive conjugation prefix /bi-/ ThSLa §338; may represent the conjugation prefix / ba-/ for interaction with inanimates with the addition of locative-terminative /i/ or /e/ ThSLa §349-351; used to differentiate semantic meaning of certain verbs.

bi_2-i-
variant of 2.sg. pronominal prefix -e- after conjugation prefix bi_2- ThSLa §291, note 44.

bi_2-in-eš
they spoke (cf., e).

bi_2-ra
mixed, mingled (bir,'to scatter, mix' + nominative).

bi_2-za-za
frog (za,'a repeated, monotonous noise').

bi$_3$-lu$_5$-da
(cf., billuda).

bi$_6$; bi$_3$; bi
(cf., be$_4$).

bi$_7$
(cf., bid$_3$).

bibad[UZ.TUR]^{mušen}
duck, some species of which migrate down to southern Iraq in the winter (bi$_2$, conjugation prefix, + bad, 'to go away, be at a distance'; Akk. *paspasu*).

bibra[ḪUL$_2$]^{mušen}
a type of bird, equated to the dar-lugal^{mušen} (hen, chicken) (bi$_2$, conjugation prefix, + barag$_2$, bara$_3$; barag, bara$_2$, 'nest; dais, box, dwelling').

bibra[ḪUL$_2$]
a drinking vessel with the base carved in a bird-shape - rhyton.

bid$_3$, bi$_7$, be$_5$, bu$_7$[KU]; bu$_5$[BUL]
n., anus (open container with motion away from).

v., to defecate; to urinate.

bil$_{(2/3)}$
to burn; to roast; to heat (soup) (container + to lift, be high).

bil-la$_2$-a
used following iti, e$_2$-ta, or u$_4$, as in the expression 'in the new (coming) month' (cf., gibil$_{(4)}$, 'new, fresh').

bil$_{(2)}$(-la$_2$)
sour (of wine, vinegar, beer, fruit) ('to burn; sour' + adjectival -a; Akk. *emṣum I*).

bil$_{2/3}$
sprout, shoot; bud; son ('it rises'; cf., bil$_2$-lum, 'mandrake').

bil$_{2/3}$-ga
elder, ancestor (abbreviation of pa$_{(4)}$-bil$_{2/3}$-ga, 'elder suckling sprout' - a plant-breeder's terminology for human ancestor).

billuda, biluda[PA.AN]
worship; cult rite; rules, regulations, ordinances (loanword from Akk. *bēlūtu*, 'rule, government'; loaned back as *pelludû*, 'cult(ic rites)').

bir
n., destruction (cf., ellaĝ$_2$) (ba, 'to divide', + ir$_{10}$, re$_7$, 'to stir, mix') [BIR archaic frequency: 9; concatenation of 3 sign variants].

v., to scatter, mix; to wreck; to murder.

bir$_{(2,4)}$
n., mistiness (of the eyes) (ba, 'inanimate conjugation prefix', + er$_2$, ir$_2$, 'to weep' and ur$_5$, 'to smell', with possibly a hidden meaning of 'to dry' for Vr or ara$_4$ as also seen in dur$_2$).

v., to sniff, wrinkle one's nose; to dry up, shrivel up.

adj., flaccid, shriveled up (said of a penis).

bir...aka
to sow broadcast (not in furrows with a plow); to dehusk ('to scatter' + 'to do').

BIR-gun$_3$
(cf., ellaĝ$_2$-gun$_3$-gun$_3$-nu).

bir$_2$-bir$_2$
(cf., babbar).

bir$_3$[ERIM/PIR$_2$]; bir$_2$[UD]
yoke; team (of donkeys/animals) (ba, 'inanimate conjugation prefix', + ir$_{10}$, 'to accompany, lead; to bear; to go; to drive along or away', the plural *ḫamtu* for 'to go', cf., re$_7$) [?? BIR$_3$ archaic frequency: 23; concatenation of 3 sign variants; ZATU-143 ERIM archaic frequency: 175; concatenation of 3 sign variants].

bir$_3$-inim-keš$_2$-de$_6$
contractually bound worker ('yoke' + 'oath, agreement' + 'to bind').

^{ĝiš}bir$_3$-mar
wagon yoke ('yoke' + 'wagon').

bir_5[NAM]
locust, grasshopper; sparrow (cf., sim, $sin_2^{mušen}$; bir_3 for animals in plural numbers).

$bir_{6,7}$
to rip to pieces; to shred; to break (cf., bir for similar semantics).

bir_9[NE]
to blaze, flame up (cf., $bar_{6,7}$ for similar semantics).

$^{(gi)}$bisağ$_{(2/3)}$
(cf., $^{(gi)}$pisağ$_{(2/3)}$).

-biš[GIR]
3rd person inanimate possessive suffix + terminative - ThSLa §106 (bi- + šè).

biz; bi(z)
n., tears (Akk. loanword from *biṣṣu*, 'flow of tears' and *baṣāṣu*, 'to (let) drip', cf., Orel & Stolbova #256 ***baz-** 'flow, be wet').

v., to drip, trickle; to cry; to ooze; to pour; to rinse off; to impute, accuse; to push someone away; to dry (cf., bi-bi-ze_2).

$bu_{(3,7)}$
(cf., bur_{12}; $bun_{(2)}$; bul) [BU: archaic frequency: 393; concatenation of 2 sign variants].

bu(-bu)-i
n., knowledge, awareness; shoot, scion, offspring (Akk. *edûtu*; *nipru*).

v., to grasp, clench; to sprout (cf., bur_{12}/bu; $bul_{(5)}$/$bu_{(5)}$).

bu-lu-$uḫ_2$...si-il
to belch (cf., etymology of ḫal, cf., buluḫ[ḪAL]; $buru_8$[ḪAL], 'to vomit'; loan from Semitic, cf., Orel & Stolbova #1929, ***pahal**- "break through, split", Sem **pVlah-*, showing metathesis; 'break through' + 'to tear apart').

bu-luḫ
to tremble, shudder (a form of Akk. *palāḫu(m)*, 'to fear, revere'; cf., buluḫ, 'fright').

$bu_{(2/5)}$
to rush around, chase about, roam (cf., bul).

bu_3
(cf., bur_{12}; bu_3).

$bu_{5,7}$
(cf., bid_3).

bu_8
(cf., $buru_2$, bur_2)

$^{(šim)}$$bu_{13}$-lu-ḫum
(cf., šim-buluḫ)

$^{gi/ğiš}$bugiğ$_2$, $bugin_2$ [LAGAB×ĞAR/NIĞ$_2$]
(cf., buniğ).

^{ğiš}bugin
(cf., ^{ğiš}buniğ).

$bul_{(5)}$; $bu_{(5)}$
to blow; to winnow; to ignite; to sprout (onomatopoeic; cf., ul_7, 'to sprout').

bul_5^{ku6}[ZAR]
a fish (puffer ?).

bulug, buluğ
shoot, sprout; barley malt; needle; awl; drill; chisel; seal pin; latch; boundary stake, post; border, boundary (bul, 'to sprout', + aka/ag, 'to do') [BULUG archaic frequency: 4].

$bulug_2$[BUR_2]
to cut or carve up (wood) (bur_{12}, $bu_{(3,6)}$, 'to cut off, remove, chisel', + lag, 'bulk, block'; cf., $^{(ğiš)}$silig$_{(5)}$, 'ax').

buluğ$_3$
n., pupil, novice; foster-child; adopted child [$BULUG_3$ archaic frequency: 19].

v., to grow; to flourish; to grow big; to grow up; to rear, make grow.

buluğ$_4$[NAGAR]
sprout; barley malt.

buluĝ$_5$[BALAĜ]; buluĝ$_3$
v., to elevate, raise; to extoll; to praise highly.

adj., exalted; raised, elevated.

buluḫ[ḪAL]
n., fright (cf., $^{(ĝiš)}$šim-buluḫ) (a form of Akk. *palāḫu(m)*, 'to fear, revere').

v., to worry; to be nervous, anxious, frightened; to hasten, hurry.

bun$_{(2)}$; bu$_{(7)}$
n., lamp, light; blister; bag-type of bellows; rebellion (hollow container + nu$_{11}$, 'lamp' ?).

v., to be swollen; to blow; to ignite, kindle; to shine brightly (cf., bul, 'to blow; to ignite').

^{gi}bun$_2$-ĝir$_3$
feet bellows ('to blow; bellows' + 'foot').

^{gi}bun$_2$-šu
hand bellows ('to blow; bellows' + 'hand').

bunga, bungu[UŠ.GA]
suckling; young child (bun$_{(2)}$, 'to be swollen', + ga, 'milk').

$^{ĝiš/gi}$buniĝ, puniĝ, bunin, bugin[LAGAB×A]; buniĝ$_2$, bugin$_2$[LAGAB×ĜAR/NIĜ$_2$]
bitumen-coated reed container (for carrying liquids); bucket; trough; vat, tub; chest; basket (for carrying food) (bun$_2$/buĝ$_x$, 'blister; to be swollen', + niĝ$_2$, 'valuables').

^{ĝiš}buniĝ niĝ$_2$-sila$_{11}$-ĝa$_2$
dough trough ('coated reed container' + 'dough').

$^{gi/ĝiš}$buniĝ$_2$-tur
chest, box (e.g., of fisherman; for carrying bread, meat).

bur
n., meal, repast; stone bowl (cf., buru$_2$) (ba, 'portion, rations, open container', + ur$_2$, 'lap, thighs, legs') [BUR archaic frequency: 51; concatenation of 4 sign variants].

v., to pour or fill a bowl.

bur-BUN$_2$.SA$_2$
a stone vessel.

bur...gi$_4$
to offer beer ('bowl' + 'to restore'; Akk., *burgû*).

bur-gul
seal cutter, lapidary; specialist in creating cylinder seals, either from expensive stone or from inexpensive clay; a temporary cylinder seal made of clay and crudely inscribed ('stone vessel' + 'to destroy').

bur-ra
a class of priests or temple servants; one who fills bowls (?); negligence.

bur-saĝ
a kind of offering, or the people making such offerings ('stone vessel' + 'first').

$^{(na4)}$bur-šagan
a stone šagan bowl ('stone vessel' + 'oil jar').

bur-šal$_2$-la
a stone vessel ('stone vessel' + 'measuring pot' + nominative).

bur-šu-ma; bur-šu-um
elder; matriarch; old woman (Akkadian loanword, *puršumu(m)*, 'elder').

^{dug}bur-zi
(offering) bowl or cup ('stone vessel' + 'good, true') (Akk., *pursītu(m)*).

bur$_2$
(cf., buru$_2$).

BUR$_2$
a hired gang of workers.

bur$_2$-ra-bi
adv., openly.

bur$_3$
a square surface measure = 6.48 hectares = 18 iku = 3 area eše$_2$ = 1800 sar/

square `nindan` = the amount of land that supported a family (also cf., `buru`$_3$); at 1/60 `sila`$_3$ of seed per furrow and an average of 10 furrows per square nindan, this is also the area to be planted with 300 `sila`$_3$ = 1 `gur` of seed (from Akkadian *būru* IV, "hunger", but cf., *bī/ēru* IV, "space, distance").

bur_{12}, bu; bu_3; bu_7
to tear, cut off; to pull, draw; to be drawn; to tear out, uproot, weed; to pluck, pluck out; to remove, keep away (`ba`, 'to divide' + `ur`$_2$, 'base, root') [BU archaic frequency: 393; concatenation of 2 sign variants].

^{id2}buranun [UD.KIB.NUN]
Euphrates river (`bu`$_5$, 'to rush around', + `ra`, 'to flood, overflow', + `nun`, 'great, noble').

$buru_2$, $bur_{(2)}$
n., burin; thread; envelope, container; a palm product [BUR_2 archaic frequency: 45].

v., to open, loosen, free; to spread out (a garment); to dissolve; to break (a spell); to interpret (a dream); to release, put at someone's disposal; to dispose of; to pay (with `-ta`); to knap, flake off (flint); to tear out; to despoil (reduplication class; cf., `bar`, `bur`$_{12}$) (cf., `bar` and `bara`$_3$ for similar semantics).

$^{(u2)}buru_2$, bur_2
a red vegetable, perhaps beetroot; involved in making a type of beer.

$^{u2/šim}buru_{2/3}$-da
mint (?) ('to free, dissolve' + 'together with'; Akk., *urnû*).

$buru_3$(-d), bur_3
n., opening; receptacle; hole; mine; reservoir; depth (Akkadian *būru(m) I; būrtu(m) I;* 'cistern, well; pool; hole, pit', cf., Orel & Stolbova #164, ***ba'Vr-/*bu'Vr-** "well, pit").

v., to receive; to bore through, pierce, penetrate; to break into (a house); to mine; to deepen.

$buru_4^{mušen}$
a corvine bird - crow (as of Ur III period - before this referred to a bird of prey or vulture), cf., `uga`^{mušen} (cf., `buru`$_5$ for locusts/small birds, `bir` for destructive wreckers, and `bur`$_{12}$, `bu`$_{(3,6)}$ + nominative for anything that harvests or destroys plants).

$buru_4$-$dugud^{mušen}$
flock (of crows) (`dugud`, 'cloud').

$buru_5^{(mušen)}$
small birds in flocks, such as sparrows; locusts (in the post-OB period replaces `bir`$_5$).

$buru_5$-$az^{mušen}$; $buru_5$-$uz^{mušen}$
a small hole-dwelling bird; rock partridge (?) (Akk., *būṣu(m) I = iṣṣūr ḫurri*, 'bird of holes') ('small flock bird' + 'cage, fetter' - if `uz` means 'duck', then could revert to Landsberger's shelduck identification, but `uz` may just be the result of vowel harmony).

$buru_5$-ḫabrud(-da)^{mušen}
a small hole-dwelling bird; rock partridge (?) (*iṣṣūr ḫurri*, 'bird of holes') ('small flock bird' + 'pit, hole, cave, crevice' + genitive).

$buru_5$-tur
dwarf locust; very small ('small flock bird' + 'small').

$buru_7$ [GURUN]
fruit tree; fruit; berry [rare word].

$buru_8$ [ḪAL]
to vomit (Akk. *arû(m) III, parû III*, 'to vomit', cf., Orel & Stolbova #120, ***'or-** "vomit").

$buru_{14}$, bur_{14} [EN×KAR_2]
harvest; hot season, harvest time (Akk. *ebūru(m)*, 'harvest; summer', cf., Orel & Stolbova #1267, ***ḥibVr-** "harvest").

$buru_{14}$-bala
fallow land (under the alternate-year rotation system) ('harvest' + 'to rotate').

buru$_{14}$...su-su
to have the harvest be drowned (by spring floods bursting the dikes) ('harvest' + 'to drown').

buzur
(cf., puzur).

D

da
n., arm; side; nearness (to someone) [DA archaic frequency: 227; concatenation of 4 sign variants].

v., to hold; to be near; to protect; to be able, competent, powerful.

da-
Emesal dialect cohortative and optative modal prefix - ThSLa §385; or jussive prefix denoting 'be it that' - ThSLa §395, n. 87; cf., ga- and ḫa-.

-da-
comitative case prefix, 'with' - ThSLa §441; abilitative prefix, 'able to' - ThSLa §448.

-da
comitative case postposition, 'with', 'together with' - ThSLa §188-90; copula, 'and' (mainly in Sargonic date texts).

-da
phonetic variation of ablative-instrumental case postposition -ta, ThSLa §204.

da-a-ri
(cf., da-ri$_2$).

^{lu2}da-ba-ri-ri
contortionist; trickster, con man (?) (cf., da-ri).

da-ba-ri-ri
fraud (?).

^{tug2}da-ba-tum
cloth of poor quality (Akk., *tapatum*).

da-bi-a
at its side ('arm, side' + its + locative).

da-da-ga
(cf., dadag).

da-da-ra
To gird or harness oneself (as with battle gear) (redup. 'sides' + 'to branch out from').

da-ga
organization; chamber; bedroom (cf., dag; daggan).

$^{ĝiš/kuš}$da-lu(-uš$_2$)
sling; catapult ('arm' + 'many' + 'death'; Akk., *(w)aṣpu(m)*).

da-ma-al
Emesal dialect for dağal.

da-na
(cf., danna).

^{ĝiš}da-pa
wooden stilt(s) of a plow (cf., ^{ĝiš}a$_2$-apin) ('arm, side' + 'branch, wing').

-da-ra-; -da-ra-ta-; -da-ra-da-
ablative case prefix, 'from', ThSLa §467, §427, §465.

da-ra-an-šub
negligence ('to drop, let fall').

da...ri
to pay off a delivery; to adopt, sustain (an orphan) ('to lead at one's side'; cf., maš$_2$-da-ri-a; re$_7$).

da-ri
to bend (limbs) ('arm' + rig; ri, 'to pull').

da-ri
driver (of animals) (cf., da...ri, 'to lead at one's side').

da-ri-a
driven (animal) (da-ri + nominative).

da-ri$_2$[URU], da-a-ri, du-ri$_2$
long-lasting, enduring, eternal (Akkadian loanword, *darû(m)*, 'to last (for ever)'; *dāru(m) I*, 'era, eternity'; *dāru(m) II*, 'lifetime'; *dārû(m)*, 'lasting, eternal'; *dūru(m) II*, 'permanence, eternity'; Orel & Stolbova #768 ***dVwVr-** 'turn').

da-ri$_2$-še$_3$
forever ('eternal' + 'towards').

da$_5$ [URUDU]
(cf., dab$_6$).

-da$_5$-
an OS form of the comitative case prefix -da-.

-da$_5$
an OS form of the comitative suffix -da.

da$_6$
(cf., taka).

da$_{13}$
(cf., taka$_4$).

dab$_5$, dib$_2$; dab, dib; dab$_{2,4}$
n., fetter; bolt, pin (?), used in house construction.

v., to take, grasp, seize, catch; to hold; to bind, tie up; to take away; to accompany; to hire; to engage someone in work; to receive, take in charge (motion into open container).

adj., engaged in work; seized.

dab$_5$-ba
collected; used as opposed to new ('to take, accept' + nominative).

^{lu2}dab$_5$-ba
hired or conscripted man; a class of persons ('to seize, bind, hire' + nominative).

dab$_6$, da$_5$
to surround; to beset, besiege.

^{kuš}dabašin [KU$_7$]
leather fodder bag or water bag for animals.

dabin [ZI$_3$.ŠE]
coarse barley flour, barley grits; could be used as glue.

dabin-sa(-a)
toasted barley flour.

dadag [UD.UD]
v., to clean; to clear (including in the legal sense); to purify (reduplicated dag$_2$, 'brilliant, clean').

adj., bright, brilliant; pure; sacred.

dag
n., resting-place, dwelling, residence, chamber (motion as in traveling + throat-like chamber) [DAG archaic frequency: 4].

v., to add; to stretch (out); to roam about.

dag-gaz
(small) block of stone or bronze; mortar (?) ('chamber' + 'to crush').

dag-gi$_4$-a
city quarter ('dwellings' + 'to surround, lock up' + nominative).

DAG.KISIM$_5$×GA
(cf., ubur).

DAG.KISIM$_5$×GI
(cf., kiši$_7$).

DAG.KISIM$_5$×GUD
(cf., udul$_5$).

DAG.KISIM$_5$×G̃IR$_2$
(cf., kiši$_8$).

DAG.KISIM$_5$×IR
(cf., ubur$_3$).

DAG.KISIM$_5$×LU
(cf., ubur$_2$).

DAG.KISIM$_5$×LU.MAŠ$_2$
(cf., amaš; utua$_2$; udu-ua$_4$).

DAG.KISIM$_5$×U$_2$.G̃IR$_2$
(cf., kiši$_9$).

DAG.KISIM$_5$×UŠ
(cf., utua).

dag-si
saddle-hook ('resting place' + 'horn').

dag$_2$
brilliant; pure; clean ('to go out' + aga$_{(3)}$, 'diadem, circlet, crown').

daggan, dakkan
harem; living quarters; sleeping chamber (dag, 'dwelling', + gan, 'to bear').

dagrim
irrigated fields; meadow; precinct; irrigation district (same sign as g̃arim) (cf., bar-rim_4).

dag̃al
n., width, breadth (da, 'side', + gal/g̃al, 'big') [AMA archaic frequency: 241; concatenates 2 sign variants].

v., to widen, enlarge; to expand.

adj., wide, broad; vast; copious.

dag̃al-$buru_2$
spread out over a wide extent ('wide' + 'to spread out').

dag̃al...tag
to stretch out wide ('wide' + 'to handle, touch').

dag̃al-tag(-ga)
widely based ('wide' + 'to handle, touch' + nominative).

daḫ, taḫ
n., substitute; replacement; supplement, addition; second, next; partner; help, aid [DAḪ archaic frequency: 21].

v., to add; to increase; to multiply; to repeat; to replace; to say further; to help; to enhance (motion/with + numerousness).

daḫ...du_{11}-du_{11}
to overstate ('to multiply, increase' + redup. 'to speak').

daḫ-ḫu
addition; add! ('to increase' + imperative; cf., lal'u_6).

dal[RI]
n., foot-race.

v., to fly ('towards something', with -ši-; 'out of', with -ta- or -ra-); to remove; to flee, escape; to be far away; to chase (da, 'to hold, be near', + ul, 'remote, distant' and ul_4, 'to hasten').

dug dal
a large, wide-mouthed jar for oil.

(g̃iš)dal
cross beam, supporting beam; dividing line; carrying-pole for a sedan chair.

(tu15)dal(-a)
(cf., (tu15)dalḫamun(2)).

dal-ba(-an)-na
communal property; intermediate space; between ((g̃iš)dal, 'dividing line' + ba, 'portion, rations', + na, 'human being'; cf., bán, 'vessel').

dal-ḫa-mun
dust storm; decorative fancy work (dal, 'to fly'; 'ray, line', + ḫa-mun, 'contrasting, harmonizing'; cf., dalḫamun and im-ḫa-mun).

dala[RI]
(cf., dalla; dala, dal).

$dala_2$
(cf., $dalla_2$, $dala_2$).

(tu15)dalḫamun(2)
tornado; violent storm; duststorm; whirlpool; riot, revolt (dal, 'to fly', + ḫa-mun, 'mutually opposing or contrasting'; cf., dal-ḫa-mun).

$dalḫamun_4$
confusion, disorder.

dalla[IDIGNA]; dala[RI], dal[RI]
n., beam; pole; ray; crosspiece; transverse line (math.); metal ring (semantics derive from $dalla_2$, 'needle' when made with a bright metal).

v., to be or make bright; to shine.

adj., conspicuous; excellent; resplendent; magnificent.

dalla...e_3
to shine; to appear; to make clear; to make resplendent ('beam of light' + 'to become visible').

dalla$_2$, dala$_2$
thorn; needle; pin (da, 'to hold', + la$_2$, 'to pierce').

dam
spouse (husband or wife) (da, 'side; nearness; to hold, protect', + am$_3$, 'to be; who'; Akk. *aššatu(m)*, 'wife', *mutu(m)*, 'husband') [DAM archaic frequency: 10].

^{ĝiš}dam
the (curved) beam that connects the bottom of the plow to the pole.

dam-ab-ba
(professional) mourners ('spouse' + 'elder, ancestor').

^{ĝiš}dam-apin
plow sole = piece of wood on which the ard share was mounted ('spouse' + 'plow').

dam-banda$_3$[TUR] (^{da})
lesser wife ('spouse' + 'junior').

dam-dam
wife with status equal to her husband's ('spouse' + 'spouse').

dam-gar$_3$(-a)
merchant, commercial agent (Akk. loanword from *tamkārum*, 'merchant' ?, cf., *makārum* 'to do business').

dam-ĝuruš
wife of a young man ('spouse' + 'spouse').

dam-ḫa-ra
battle (Akk. loanword from *tamḫāru(m)*).

$^{\text{ukuš2/(ĝiš)ḫašḫur/šim}}$dam-šil-lum; dam-ši-lum; dam-še-lum
(cf., $^{\text{ukuš2/(ĝiš)ḫašḫur/šim}}tam_2$-šil-lum; tam$_2$-ši-lum; tam$_2$-še-lum).

dam...taka$_4$
to divorce ('spouse' + 'to leave, abandon').

(ku$_3$-/ni$_3$-)dam-tak$_4$(-a)
divorce (payment) ('silver/property' + 'spouse' + 'to leave, abandon' + nominative; Akkadian *uzubbû(m)*).

dam...tuku/du$_{12}$-du$_{12}$
to marry ('spouse' + 'to get').

dan$_3$; dan$_2$; dan$_4$; dan$_6$
to be(come) clear, pure; to launder, bleach.

dana
(cf., danna, dana).

danna, dana
road-length measure, 'march' = 30 UŠ = 1800 nindan = 21600 cubits = ca. 6.7 miles/10.8 kilometers; double hour (twelfth part of a full day) = the time it takes to march a length of 1 danna (Akkadian etymology from 'place of strength or safety') [DANNA archaic frequency: 2].

dar
v., to slice, split; to shatter (reduplication class) (da, 'sides', + ur$_4$, 'to shear, reap') [DAR archaic frequency: 36; concatenation of 4 sign variants].

n., a building at a canal.

dar^{mušen}
black francolin, a ground-nesting bird in the pheasant family (cf., Orel & Stolbova #683, ***der-** "bird").

dar-lugal^{mušen}
hen, chicken ('francolin, pheasant, partridge' + 'king').

dar-me-luḫ-ḫa^{mušen}
a black bird; chicken (?) ('francolin, pheasant, partridge' + 'Meluhha country' + genitive).

dar-ra
cured, dried (?, cf., ku$_6$-dar-ra).

$^{\text{(tug2)}}$dara$_2$, dar$_2$
n., belt, sash; sanitary towel (compare dur, 'bond, tie').

v., to bind, pack.

dara$_3$, dar$_3$
wild goat buck, mountain goat, wild bezoar ibex (not a true ibex, but the ancestor of the domestic goat); term may

have extended to the true ibex and markhor members of the goat family (Akk., *turāḫu(m)*, 'wild goat'; cf., Orel & Stolbova #2484, ***ṭuraḥ-*** "throw, fall"; cf., *darāru(m) I*, 'to roam free') [DARA$_3$ archaic frequency: 11; concatenation of 4 sign variants].

dara$_3$-maš (-da$_3$)
roe deer (?) (wild goat + gazelle).

dara$_4$, dar$_4$
n., blood (cf., dara$_2$, 'sanitary towel') [DARA$_4$ archaic frequency: 81; concatenation of 9 sign variants].

adj., red; dark, dim; high (compare dirig, 'to be darkened; to go over').

daraḫ
(cf., dara$_3$).

de [DI]
Emesal dialect for 'to go, lead, cause to march', 'to bring', 'offering', 'to throw'.

de-ḫi
(cf., $^{(ĝiš)}$teḫi$_4$).

de$_2$ [UMUN$_2$×KASKAL]
to pour (often with -ni-); to water; to libate; to fill, increase, be full; to shape, form; to instruct; to sink (for other meanings - cf., de$_{6,2}$; eg$_2$; gu$_3$... de$_2$).

de$_3$ [NE]
ashes (cf., de$_6$/de$_3$).

de$_3$-
Emesal dialect optative modal prefix - ThSLa §385, §395; or jussive prefix denoting 'be it that' - ThSLa §395, n. 87; cf., ḫa-. Emesal weak form of dug$_4$/du$_{11}$.

-de$_3$-
form of comitative case prefix, 'with', either as a contraction of -da-e- in OB lit. texts or with the vowel assimilated to a preceding -e-, ThSLa §12, §441; cf., -da-.

-de$_3$
probably a form of the comitative suffix, -da, that occurs as the final suffix after the 1. and 2. person possessive suffixes after participles to be translated by English '-ing', indicating 'with my/your (going. etc.)' in OB texts, ThSLa §521 [now read as -ne by the Oxford site].

-de$_3$
writing of *marû* verb form suffix, preceded by a vowel, denotes -ed-e; it connotes future sense, but also denotes a prospective obligation - ThSLa §255, §524. Sometimes represents subordinate *marû* verb form suffix -ed-a, ThSLa §522. Used like the terminative postposition -šè after verbal phrases to indicate intent or goal.

de$_3$-dal
ashes; embers; flame ('ashes' + 'to fly').

-de$_3$-en
(cf., -(e)n-de$_3$-en).

de$_3$-ša-na
Emesal dialect for 'mother-in-law'.

-de$_4$- [TE]
form of comitative case prefix, 'with', as a contraction of -da-e- in OB lit. texts, ThSLa §441; cf., -da-.

de$_5$(-g), di$_5$, ře [RI]
to clear; to clarify; to advise; to cleanse; to adjust; to remove (earth clods); to fall, collapse; to lie down; improper, incorrect; to void excrement (reduplication class).

de$_6$, ře$_6$; de$_2$; de$_3$
to bring, carry (-ši- or -ta- denote direction, in or from); to remove (with -ra- or -ta-); to continue on (suppletion class verb: singular object *ḫamṭu*, cf., tum$_{2,3}$, laḫ$_4$; Emesal ga$_{(14)}$).

$^{ĝiš/u2}$deḫi$_3$ [NIM]
(cf., $^{ĝiš/u2}$diḫ$_3$).

$^{(\tilde{g}iš)}$deḫi$_4$[IDIM]
(cf., $^{(\tilde{g}iš)}$teḫi$_4$).

del$_2$
(cf., dilim$_2$).

dellu[DIMGUL]
mast; mooring pole.

di(-d)
n., lawsuit, litigation, case; judgment, decision, verdict; sentence [DI archaic frequency: 99].

v., to judge, decide; to conduct oneself; to go; to escape (di[-de$_2$] used as non-finite *marû* form of dug$_4$, 'speaking, doing').

Emesal, cf., de[DI].

-di-
form of comitative case prefix, 'with' - ThSLa §441; cf., -da-.

di-bi
legal complaint, lawsuit; word, matter; agreement ('its speaking').

di-bi
manliness, virility; codpiece (Akk. *dūtu*) (dib$_{(2)}$, 'to traverse, cross; to infringe upon; to have access to').

di-bi-da
"Anshan donkey", camel [M. Civil in *JCS* 50 (1998) 11]; swollen, enlarged (Akk. *emēru II*).

di-bi di ḫé-bé
may he render a judgment in this case-the standard judicial request ('may he speak a judgment for this litigation').

di...dab$_5$
to accept a lawsuit ('lawsuit' + 'to take, accept').

di-dab$_5$-ba
case accepted for trial; decision ('decision' + 'to accept' + nominative).

di-di
to play (an instrument); in Emesal, cf., de[DI] (cf., dug$_4$).

di...dug$_4$/du$_{11}$/e
to conduct a trial; to adjudicate; to give a claim; to sue someone (with -da-) ('lawsuit' + 'to effect').

di-em$_3$[AĞA$_2$]
Emesal dialect for gim, kim, gin$_7$.

di-em$_3$[AĞA$_2$], de-em$_3$
Emesal dialect for dim$_2$[GIM].

di...gub
to judge ('judgment' + 'to set up').

di-id
Emesal dialect for diš$_{(2)}$, deš, 'one'.

di-ir-ga
cultic organization center; cultic services.

di...kud/kur$_5$/ku$_5$
to judge ('decision' + 'to cut off').

di-kud/kur$_5$/ku$_5$
judge; judgment ('decision' + 'to cut off').

di-kur$_2$
alien, hostile judgment ('decision' + 'hostile').

di-li-du-a
(cf., dili-du(-a)).

di-nu-til-la
law case for which no final verdict has been given ('verdict' + 'not' + 'to complete' + nominative).

di-ri
(cf., dirig).

di(-bi)-ta...tak$_4$
to divorce someone by means of a legal process (texts have ba-tak$_4$ and in-tak$_4$) (alternate method is by means of verbal: ka-ta) ('lawsuit' (+ adverbial force and instrumental suffixes) + 'to leave').

di-til-la
law case for which a final decision has been given ('verdict' + 'to complete' + nominative).

-di_3- [TI]
form of comitative case prefix, 'with', already in OS - ThSLa §441; cf., -da-.

di_4
(cf., tur).

di_4-di_4-ba
walking about (phonetic for dib, reduplicated + nominative).

di_4-di_4-$la_{(2)}$
children; young; small.

$dib_{(2)}$
to traverse, cross; to infringe upon; to pass (by/along); to send over; to wander; to audit; to have access to (with -ni-) [? DIB archaic frequency: 6].

dib-ba
passing, review; audit; an animal inspection during which animals could be transferred from one group to another or back to the administration ('to pass, traverse' + nominative).

$^{\tilde{g}iš}$dib-dib
clepsydra, water clock (onomatopoeic or reduplicated 'to pass, traverse').

$^{(kaš/dug)}$dida [U_2.SA]
a second-rate type of beer; beer for transport - instant beer; a dry substance used in the preparation of beer (Akk. *billatu(m)*).

didi
young, small.

didila
very small, young.

didli
separate, individual, single, each; singly working; assorted, various (reduplicated dili).

didli-bi; dil-bi
adv., one by one, one at a time ('separate, individual' + adverbial force suffix).

dig
v., to become moist, soft, workable; to be in a weakened state (redup. class) (motion + throat-like chamber, vagina).

adj., moist.

diğir, dingir
god, deity; determinative for divine beings (di, 'decision', + ğar, 'to deliver').

diğir-da...nu-me-a
without a (personal) god; unlucky ('god' + 'with' + 'not' + 'to be' + nominative).

diğir-$\tilde{g}u_{10}$ [MU]
personal god, source of luck in life ('my god').

$diḫ_{(2)}$
to sting; sting, barb, point; sickness, fever; torpidity (?) (cf., ti) (motion + cry of pain + insect).

$^{\tilde{g}iš/u2}$$diḫ_3$, $deḫi_3$, $teḫi_3$ [NIM]
a spiny plant, such as the caper shrub; thorn bushes; camelthorn (NIM is the sign for a stinging[diḫ]'flying insect') (te, 'to prick', + ḫi, 'abundant').

dili, dil [AŠ]
one.

adj., each; single; alone; unique.

adv., alone, by oneself.

dili-bad
n., the planet Venus ('alone, singular' + 'to go away, be at a distance'; cf., $bibad^{mušen}$).

adj., shining, brilliant.

dili-dili, dil-dil
one by one (cf., didli; can be variant writing of di_4-di_4-$la_{(2)}$) (reduplicated 'one').

dili-du(-a)
walking alone; individual (dili, 'alone' + 'walking; acting' + nominative).

X dili-zu(-u_3)-de_3
you alone are X (dili, 'uniqueness' + 'your' + *marû* participial suffix).

$dilib_3$
hair, locks (cf., dalla, 'beam, ray', $dalla_2$, 'needle', and dul; dal, 'to cover, clothe, hide').

$dilim_2$, $dili_2$, del_2[LIŠ]
spoon, of wood or metal; spatula; pan (of balance scale) (dal, 'to fly, remove', + eme, 'tongue').

$dilim_3$[BUN]
funnel-shaped bowl containing seeds for the drill plow.

$dilmun^{(ki)}$, $tilmun^{(ki)}$
the island of Bahrain, noted for its sweet water springs; dignitary [DILMUN archaic frequency: 35].

adj., official, important, honored, distinguished, respectful.

dim
n., bond, tie; rope; post, pillar (dam, 'spouse', modified by i, 'to sprout', that indicates long and narrow as in si) [DIM archaic frequency: 52; concatenates 3 sign variants].

v., to make fast.

(ĝiš)dim-gal
bond; a post for fastening things to, mooring post; wooden pole; mast of a boat; (dim, 'to bond, tie', + gal, 'large').

DIM×ŠE
(cf., mun).

dim_2[GIM]
to make, fashion, form, create, build (cf., dim_2-ma; šidim) (du_3, 'to build, make', + im, 'clay, mud').

ĝišdim_2
post (cf., dim).

dim_2-ma
n., mind; (fore)thought, plan(ning), intention; understanding (Akk. loanword from *ṭēmu(m)*).

adj., newly created (as opposed to dab_5-ba).

dim_2-ma...kur_2
to change one's mind or attitude ('mind' + 'to change').

dim_2-ma...$suḫ_3$
to confuse the mind, throw the mind into disorder ('mind' + 'to uproot, confuse').

dim_3
n., young child, baby; mentally ill person; fool; sickness demon, ghost; pole of a water lift.

adj., weak, helpless (di_4, 'small', + am_3, 'to be').

$dim_{(3)}$-$gi_{(4)}$$^{(sar)}$
a vegetable, compared to gu, 'flax, rope', created by the god Enki, in a fashion similar to that involving the u_2 nam-til_3-la, "the life-giving plant" (dim_3, 'weak', + gi_4, 'to restore'; dim, 'bond, rope', + gi, 'reed; to surround'; Akk. *akkullakku*, 'of the hatchet or maul', and *ṣippatu(m) II*, 'a vegetable').

dim_3-ma
figurine; statuette; doll.

dim_3-me-er
Emesal dialect for diĝir, dingir, 'god'.

dim_3-$šaḫ_2$
bear (the animal) ('sickness demon' ? + 'domestic pig').

dim_4
n., begging; tendril, clinging vine (cf., dim).

v., to approach; to cling; to bow; to beg.

adj., subservient (di_4, 'small', + am_3, 'to be').

DIM_4.SAR(-d)
maltman.

dima, dimmu
news, information; intention, decision (loan from Akk. *ṭēmu(m)*).

$^{(ĝiš)}$dimgul [MA_2.MUG]
mast; wooden post; mooring pole (dim, 'to bond, tie', + gul, 'enormous').

din
(cf., tin).

dingir
(cf., diĝir).

dinig [KI.NE]
potash; salt; crucible, kiln, brazier; air vent (de_3, 'ashes', + naĝa, 'potash').

diri, dir
(cf., dirig).

dirig, diri, dir [SI.A]
n., bridge (Akk., *titūrum*); addition; excess; slag; overdraft; trouble; amount by which credits of an account tablet exceed debits - appears in the credits section of the succeeding period's account tablet; intercalary month after either 11th month or 12th month (based as much on whether the winter crop will be ready for the harvest month as on the need to reconcile the lunar year with the solar year, which required an average of 7 intercalary months in 19 years) (cf., $^{(gi)}$ušub).

v., to go over; to exceed something; to stand out; to be extra; to be darkened, eclipsed; to be erased; to be troubled; to overwhelm; to be greater than, to surpass, to be supreme over (with dative/ locative); to set adrift; to float (with the current); to glide.

adj., superior, outstanding, surpassing; surplus; superfluous; additional; overwhelming; extravagant.

dirig-ba
additional; surplus ('to go over' + 'to give').

dirig-la(l)'u_6 [LAL.NI]
to balance ('to go over' + 'deficit').

dirig-...-še
beyond ('to go over' + 'to the').

diš$_{(2)}$, deš
one (dili, 'single', + aš, 'one'; the form resembles that of the semantically appropriate male body part, $ĝiš_{2,3}$, $ĝeš_{2,3}$; cf., mina, $min_{(5,6)}$, 'two'; cf., $teš_2$, 'together').

DIŠ; $DIŠ_2$ [AŠ]
a hired gang of workers (cf., šu).

DIŠ.DIŠ.DIŠ
(cf., $eš_5$).

du
to walk; to go; to come (suppletion class verb: sing. *marû*, cf., ĝen, re_7, sub_2; $laḫ_6$; as quality adjective cf., gin_6/ gin) [DU archaic frequency: 299].

DU(-ra)
(cf., gir_7).

-DU
(cf., gin_6/-gin; -ĝen/-$ĝe_{13}$).

du-bu-ul
to sprout, multiply; to stir (?).

du-di-da
(cf., tu-di-da).

DU.DU
(cf., $laḫ_5$).

DU&DU
(cf., $laḫ_4$; sub_2).

du-lum
burden, labor, work (Akk. loanword from *dullu(m)*, 'trouble; work, service').

DU-na
(cf., ĝen).

du-ri_2
(cf., da-ri_2).

DU-zu
(read ara_x-zu; cf., a-ra-zu).

du_2
(cf., tud and tur_5).

du_2-ru-na(-am_3)
(cf., duruna).

du_3('), $ř u_2$
n., work; totality, entirety.

v., to erect something on the ground; to raise up; to set up; to plant; to fasten, apply, hold; to build, make; to mold, cast; to fix; to do, perform (du_3-e in *marû*).

du_3-a
adj., pregnant, impregnated; well-performed, completed ('to plant' + nominative; opposite of nu/nu_2-a, 'barren').

du_3-a-bi
all of it; totality ('to erect' + nominative + 'their'; cf., ninda-bi, 'total of their bread').

du_5[GIN_2]
(cf., sug_5; tun_3; g̃iš-tun_3)

du_5-
Emesal dialect cohortative or optative modal prefix - ThSLa §385; or jussive prefix denoting 'be it that' - ThSLa §395, n. 87; cf., ga- and ḫa-.

du_5-la_2
(cf., dun_3-la_2).

du_5-mu
Emesal dialect for dumu.

du_5-mu
Emesal dialect for $tum_{12}^{mušen}$, $tu^{mušen}$.

du_6
(cf., $dul_{(6)}$).

du_6(-d)
(consider reading, ḫabrud).

du_6-du_6-da/dam/de_3
ruin mounds; the gathered together (consider reading, ḫabrud-ḫabrud-da) (redup. 'to heap up' + participial ending).

$^{iti}du_6$-ku_3
calendar month 7 at Nippur during Ur III.

du_6-ku_3
sanctuary; part of a temple ('sanctuary' + 'holy').

du_6-mar
Emesal dialect for 'dwelling place'.

du_6-mun
salt hill; an adjective for soil quality.

du_6-ul
to heap up, store, gather (cf., $dul_{(6)}$).

du_7
to be finished, complete, perfect; to be suitable, fitting; to be necessary; to push, butt, gore, toss; to rotate, dance, circle around (regularly followed by ra_2) [DU_7 archaic frequency: 7].

du_7-du_7
to rotate, dance, circle around; in math. texts, to square a number (reduplicated 'to push, rotate').

du_7-g̃ar
sum, or product, of numbers in OB math. texts ('pushed together').

du_7-na-bi
adv., in the proper way; if you please ('fitting, suitable' + ? + adverbial force suffix).

du_7-$uš_2^{mušen}$
(cf., $ḫe_{(2)}$-$uš_2^{mušen}$).

du_8
v., to crack, loosen, open; to take apart (such as a plow for storage); to untie, release; to remit (a debt); to redeem, reclaim; (in math. texts) to compute; to adorn, clothe (reduplicated); to yoke; to accumulate, amass (reduplicated); to make disgorge (reduplicated); to spread; to caulk a boat (with pitch); to gouge (eyes); to bake bread/bricks; to prepare the threshing floor (du_8 as a noun, cf., duḫ) (in *marû* singular, du_8-r or du_8-ur and in *marû* participial form, du_8-d).

adj., free.

du$_8$-du$_8$
n., weaned young; a type of vessel (reduplicated 'to untie, loosen').

adj., very plentiful.

DU$_8$-IG
(cf., gaba-ĝal$_2$).

^{na4}du$_8$-ši-a
quartz, rock crystal; stone bead; the color of this stone, either yellow or orange ('to crack, loosen' + 'concerning' + nominative).

^{kuš}du$_8$-ši-a
green (?) leather; also an adjective for linen, which rules out 'untanned leather'; consider adjective 'beaded'.

du$_9$
(cf., dun$_5$).

du$_{10}$
(cf., dug$_3$, dub$_3$).

Emesal dialect optative and affirmative verbal prefix, cf., ḫe$_2$- and du$_5$-.

du$_{10}$-ba, du$_{10}$-ub
knee(s) (cf., dub$_3$).

du$_{10}$-sa
friend, companion (cf., dub-us$_2$-sa).

du$_{10}$-us$_2$
road ('good' + 'to follow').

du$_{10}$-us$_2$-sa
bathtub (sealed with bitumen); bathroom ('gladness' + 'to follow' + nominative; Akk., *narmaku(m)*).

du$_{11}$
(cf., dug$_4$).

du$_{11}$-ga
(cf., dug$_4$-ga).

du$_{12}$
n., (manner of) speech (cf., tuku).

v., to sing or speak (a lament), to play music, play an instrument (*marû* reduplicated form with this meaning: du$_{12}$-du$_{12}$).

du$_{14}$[LU$_2$×NE or LU$_2$.NE]; du$_{17}$[NE]
quarrel, struggle, fight.

du$_{14}$...ak/ĝar; du$_{17}$...ĝar
to quarrel; start a fight (with someone: -da-) ('quarrel' + 'to do').

du$_{14}$...mu$_2$
to start a quarrel ('quarrel' + 'to ignite').

du$_{24}$
(cf., dur$_9$).

du$_{24}$-ur$_3$
(cf., dur$_9$[ŠUL]).

dub
n., (clay) tablet, document, letter; plate; proof of indebtedness (cf., kišib$_3$) (motion into open container) [DUB archaic frequency: 229; concatenates 6 sign variants].

v., to store, heap, pile up; to demarcate, divide off; to mark off a sector (for work quotas, such as in a field or along the length of a canal to be dug out); to move in a circle; to seal; to move around; to shake; to pour out; to sprinkle, strew (with -ta-); to dye (fabrics); to beat, crush, or full (cloth, wool) textiles (reduplication class ?).

adj., weak.

^{lu2}dub-alal-uruda
a temple servant ('to pour' + 'pipe' + 'copper').

^{gi}dub-ba-an
pillar made of reeds; a fence made of such pillars ('to heap up' + 'to divide' + 'to be high').

dub-bi...bala
to go over the account (with -da-) ('tablet' + 'its' + 'to pass through').

dub-gid$_2$-da
index ('tablet' + 'long' + nominative).

dub-la$_2$
platforms on either side of a portal ('to heap up' + 'to lift').

$^{ğiš (šim/mes)}$dub-ra-an
juniper; wood used to produce aromatic oil (loanword from Akk. *daprānu(m)*).

dub-sağ
leader, superior; (person) in front ('list' + 'head').

dub-sar
tablet writer; scribe (from Archaic Ur period onwards; cf., sağğa) ('tablet' + 'to write').

dub-sar-mah̬
senior scribe ('scribe' + 'foremost').

dub-sar-mar-sa
scribe responsible for shipfitting and shipyards ('scribe' + 'boat transport center').

dub-sar-tur
junior scribe ('scribe' + 'small, young').

dub-šen
copper box, treasure chest ('to store' + 'shiny').

$dub-us_2(-sa)$; $dub_3-us_2(-sa)$
younger brother; companion ('tablet; rank' + 'to follow' + nominative).

dub-dab...za
to thud, thump; to clatter (of hailstones) (see the definition for za).

dub...zi-re-dam
annulment of tablets, cancellation of records ('tablet' + 'to annul' + 'it has to be').

dub_2, tub_2
to kick, flop, flail (said of fish, newborn animals, and slaughtered animals); to flap; to fan; to strike, hammer, beat, thump; to knock down; to (make) tremble, quake; to rumble (same sign as BALAĞ, 'drummable harp') [DUB_2 archaic frequency: 2].

dub_3[H̬I]
knee(s) (cf., dug_3[H̬I]) (motion plus pair, cf., tab).

dub_3...bad(-bad)
to spread the knees; to stride, hurry ('knees' + 'to open').

dub_3...dub_2
to rest ('knees' + 'to flop').

dub_3...gam
to sit down; to kneel down ('knees' + 'to bow down, kneel').

dub_3...gur_2
to sit down; to rest ('knees' + 'to bend').

dub_3...guz
to balk, said of a donkey ('knees' + 'to clip, be lame').

dub_3-guz...la_2-la_2
to tether ('to balk' + redup. lal, 'to bind').

dub_3...$ğal_2$
to fight ('knee' + 'to put').

dub_3...ğar
to kneel down (for someone: with dative); to sit down (cf., dug_3...ğar) ('knees' + 'to place').

dub_3...nir
(cf., dug_3...nir).

dub_3(-sa)
(cf., $dub-us_2$(-sa) or du_{10}-sa).

$^{(lu2)}dub_3$-sa-dar-a
lame or handicapped person ('knees' + 'tendons' + 'to slice, shatter' + nominative; Akk. *uqquru(m)*).

dub_3 šu...bar
to run quickly ('knees' + 'to release').

dub_3-tuku
strong-legged; runner ('knees' + 'having').

dub_3($-us_2$)(-sa)
(cf., $dub-us_2$(-sa) or du_{10}-sa).

dub_3...zil
to run, flee ('knees' + 'to cut').

^{ğiš}dubšik[IL_2], dupsik
(work) basket.

dubul[ŠU.BU]
to sprout, multiply (also read ul_7; dulu; cf., du-bu-ul) (du_3, 'to plant', +

bul, 'to sprout'; Akk. *elēpu(m)*, 'to sprout, grow').

dubur$_{(2)}$
testicles; base (dub, 'to store; to pour', + ir$_{(2)}$, 'tears or any bodily secretion').

dug
standard size earthen jar, pot, jug, vessel, = 30 liters (sila$_3$), except at Presargonic Girsu = 20 liters; pictograph almost identical with pictograph for beer, kaš [DUG archaic frequency: 581; concatenates 5 sign variants].

^{ğiš}DUG
(cf., ^{ğiš}epir).

DUG-ga
(read zurzub-ga ?).

dug-tur
a standard capacity jar = 5 liters ('jar' + 'little').

dug$_3$, du$_{10}$[ḪI]
n., gladness; lap; loins; member (cf., dub$_3$[ḪI]) (motion + throat-like chamber, vagina).

v., to enjoy; to be/make enjoyable.

adj., sweet, good; beautiful; favorable; pleasing; fresh (water).

adv., nicely.

dug$_3$/du$_{10}$...aka
to repair ('gladness' + 'to make, cause').

dug$_3$-dug$_3$
very auspicious, very happy (reduplicated 'gladness').

dug$_3$-ga
good; sweet ('to enjoy' + adjectival -a).

^{kuš}dug$_3$-gan
leather bag, courier's pouch, for transporting valuable items including small tablets, with a capacity from 1 to 3 sila$_3$ ('gladness' + 'to bring forth'; Akk. *tu(k)kannu(m)*, *šutabalku(t)tu*).

dug$_3$...ğal$_2$
to be pleased, satisfied ('gladness' + 'to be available').

dug$_3$...ğar
to be/make nice, pleasant (cf., dub$_3$...ğar) ('gladness' + 'to make available').

dug$_3$...nir
to ejaculate; to have sexual intercourse ('gladness' + 'to be high; to stretch out').

dug$_3$-ud-ak
politeness (cf., dug$_3$/du$_{10}$...aka).

dug$_4$, du$_{11}$
n., speech; promise.

v., to speak, say; to order, command; to sing; to speak with, converse (with -da-); to promise; to threaten (suppletion class verb: singular *ḫamṭu* form, cf. also the sing. *marû*, plural *ḫamṭu*, and plural *marû* form, eg$_2$/e); to do (as auxiliary verb preceded by a direct obect consisting of a noun and a verb - ThSLa §532) (nonfinite form = di) (redup. form du$_{11}$-du$_{11}$ indicates conversation or repetitive activity) (to make a motion in the throat).

adj., verbal, spoken.

dug$_4$-ga, du$_{11}$-ga
utterance; command; speech; rumor; spoken; appointed ('to speak, command' + nominative).

dug$_4$-ga-na ba-ni-gi-in
he affirmed his statement ('utterance' + 'his' + locative; conjugation prefix + locative prefix + 'to agree, confirm').

dug$_4$-ga zi-da
fulfilled speech ('speech' + 'true').

dugud
n., weight; cloud [DUGUD archaic frequency: 2].

v., to be important.

adj., heavy; massive; difficult, hard (du$_7$, 'complete', + gud, 'bull').

duḫ, tuḫ, taḫ$_2$, du$_8$
residue, by-product; bran; bran mash for making beer (for duḫ as a verb or adj., cf., du$_8$) (motion + plant, grass + numerous times) [DU$_8$ archaic frequency: 29; concatenates 3 sign variants].

duḫ-gig$_2$
dark bran.

duḫ-gin
ordinary bran.

duḫ-sag$_{10}$
fine bran.

dul$_{(3,4,5,6,9)}$; dal
n., protection.

v., to cover; to clothe; to yoke; to protect; to hide (the object covered often takes the locative case) (verb can be reduplicated as in du$_6$-ul-du$_6$-ul-e) (to protect + ornament).

dul$_2$
(cf., tul$_2$).

dul$_{(6)}$, du$_6$
mound, heap; ruins, 'tell'; an adjective for a field in hilly country; cleft, cave; sanctuary; deity's throne platform in temple (redup. in plural) (cf. compound sign verb, du$_6$-ul) (du$_3$, 'to build, erect', + ul, 'ancient, enduring' or loan from Akk. *tīlu(m) I*, 'mound', *di'u(m) II*, 'throne-platform') [DU$_6$ archaic frequency: 37; concatenates 3 sign variants].

dulu[ŠU.BU]
to increase, multiply, become plentiful (also read dubul) (du$_3$, 'to plant', + lu, 'to become numerous'; Akk. *elēpu(m)*, 'to sprout, grow').

dum-dam...za
to grumble, rumble (see the definition for za; cf., gum$_2$-ga...za).

dumu
child, children; son; daughter; offspring, descendant(s); subordinate; 'citizen', 'denizen' (figuratively) (du$_2$, 'to bear, give birth', + mu$_2$, 'to sprout, grow').

dumu-arad-g̃a$_2$
the child of my slave ('child' + 'male slave' + 'of my').

dumu-aš
only son ('child' + 'one').

dumu-dab$_5$-ba; dumu-da-ba
serf; an engar's assistant/helper ('subordinate' + 'to seize, hire; hired man').

DUMU-DUMU-LA
(cf., di$_4$-di$_4$-la).

DUMU.EŠ$_2$
(cf., kun$_5$).

dumu-ga.eš$_8$
deputy (?) of a merchant ('child' + 'merchantman').

dumu-gal
eldest son or daughter ('child' + 'large').

dumu-gir$_{15}$/gi$_7$(-me)
citizen(s), including freed slaves, with all the privileges of a freeborn citizen; a kind of laborer; local inhabitants, city dwellers; Sumerians [in contrast to slaves from foreign countries] ('child' + 'native group, civilized' + plural).

dumu-gu$_4$-gur
subordinate of the engar cultivator who turns the ox(en) during plowing ('subordinate' + 'ox' + 'to return, make a circular motion').

dumu-KA
grandchild; great grandchild.

dumu-lu$_2$
freeborn man, gentleman ('son' + 'gentle-man').

dumu-lugal(-/ak/)
prince; prime ('child' + 'king' + genitive).

dumu-me-KA.UD
a cult servant ('child' + 'function' + ?).

dumu-mi_2
daughter ('child' + 'feminine').

dumu-mi_2-lu_2
freeborn woman, lady ('daughter' + 'gentleman').

dumu-mi_2-lugal(-/ak/)
princess ('child' + 'female' + 'king' + genitive).

dumu-munus
(cf., dumu-mi_2).

dumu-$nita_{(2)}$
son (cf., ibila) ('child' + 'masculine').

dumu-sag̃
first-born son ('child' + 'principal').

dumu-tab
twin sons ('child' + 'pair').

dumu-tu-da
son (born) of ('child' + 'to beget' + nominative).

dumu-uru(-k)
citizen, as opposed to a slave ('child' + 'city' + genitive).

iti ^{d}dumu-zi
calendar month 12 at Umma during Ur III.

^{d}dumu-zi(-da)
Dumuzi, the harvest bridegroom god and young husband of Inanna ('son' + 'good, lawful').

dun, du_{24}; tun, tu_{10}; tun_2, tu_{11}
n., heaping up, accumulating (cf., ku_3-dun, 'profit').

v., to heap, pile up; to scrape, dig (a field, furrow, hole); to strike, smite; to open; to dig out the sides or bottom of a canal to create extra water capacity (to move + to raise high; cf., $dul_{(6)}$).

dun
n., ward, pupil, subordinate.

$dun_{(4)}$
n., warp (threads on the frame of a weaving loom).

v., to lay a warp (onto a weaving loom); to weave (to move + to raise high).

${}^{(lu2)}$DUN-a
dependent (on), subordinate ('subordinate' + nominative).

${}^{g̃iš}$DUN.GI
a tool; a type of yoke (?) ('to scrape, dig' + 'reed' or 'firm, strong').

dun_3
(cf., sug_5; tun_3).

dun_3-la_2
depression, valley ('to bring low' + lal, 'to measure, weigh'; cf., il_2-la_2, 'elevation' and ib_2-ba-la_2, 'flat country').

$dun_{(4)}$
n., warp (threads on the frame of a weaving loom).

v., to lay a warp (onto a weaving loom); to weave (to move + to raise high).

dun_5, du_9[BUR_2]
v., to churn butter; to move around; to sway, stagger; to agitate, complain (redup. class) (see instead sun_5 if the sign is used as an adjective) (to move + to raise high).

^{IM}dungu[IM.DIRIG]
cloud, cloudbank.

${}^{(gi)}$dur
bond; rope; string, thread; strap, tie; amulet chain, necklace; umbilical cord (da, 'arm, side', + ur, 'to surround') [DUR archaic frequency: 58; concatenates 2 sign variants].

dur-an-ki
Bond of Heaven and Earth; an epithet of the city of Nippur, the Sumerian religious center (or of one of its sectors).

dur-dar^{mušen}
a speckled (gun$_3$) bird.

dur$_2$[long KU/TUŠ]
n., buttocks; anus; rectum; rear; rump, seat; dam (cf., duruna) [DUR$_2$ archaic frequency: 52].

v., to break wind; to dry out (with a dam?) (cf., duruna) (ed$_3$, 'to bring down (or up); to exit, drain' + ur$_2$, 'root, lap, thighs').

dur$_2$-dur$_2$
dam to create a reservoir (cf., duruna; durun$_x$) (reduplicated 'buttocks; to dry out').

dur$_2$...g̃ar/g̃a$_2$-g̃a$_2$
to sit, take a seat ('buttocks' + 'to set down upon').

$^{g̃iš}$dur$_2$-g̃ar
ornate chair; throne.

dur$_2$-ki...g̃ar/g̃a$_2$-g̃a$_2$
to establish one's dwelling ('to dwell (plural)' + 'place' + 'to establish').

dur$_2$-ru-un
to sit (plural); (cf., duruna; tuš).

dur$_2$-šaḫ$_2$
ham ('buttocks' + 'domestic pig').

$^{(anše)}$dur$_3$
he-ass, stallion; foal (of donkey or horse) (cf., dur$_9$) (pack animal - cf., dur, 'strap').

dur$_3$-KAS$_4$
donkey foal.

dur$_7$[BU]
(cf., mu-dur$_7$[BU](-ra)).

$^{(anše)}$dur$_9$[ŠUL]
donkey stallion (usually written du$_{24}$-ur$_3$ or dur$_9$$^{(ur3)}$) (cf., ^{anše}dur$_3$$^{(ur3)}$).

dur$_{10}$[ŠEN]
ax (compare dar, 'to slice, split').

dur$_{10}$-tab-ba
double ax, of copper or bronze ('ax' + 'to be double' + nominative; Akk., *pāštu(m)*, 'ax, adze', *ḫuppalû(m)*, 'mace, double-ax ?', *patarru(m)*, 'battle mace ?').

dur$_{11}$
(cf., tur$_5$).

dur$_x$[U$_3$]
bridge (Steinkeller in BSA IV, p. 81; cf., dirig).

duraḫ
(cf., dara$_3$).

duru$_2$, dur$_2$
(cf., duruna).

duru$_5$, dur$_5$[A]
irrigated; moist; an adjective for soil quality; full of sap; fresh; supple (de$_2$, 'to water' + ru$_5$, 'to send forth shoots'; cf., a-de$_2$, 'fresh').

durun
(cf., duruna).

duruna, durun, duru$_2$[KU/TUŠ]; durun$_x$[TUŠ.TUŠ]
n., dwelling (cf., dur$_2$).

verb plural, to sit; to be seated; to occupy, inhabit, dwell; to set down, place (objects) (suppletion class verb: plural, cf., singular tuš; also cf., dur$_2$) (dur$_2$, 'buttocks', + ug̃a$_3$/un, 'people').

$^{(im)}$duruna$_2$, tunur, tinur, dilina, dilim$_3$
clay oven for baking and roasting, the top could be closed with a cover to produce enough heat for baking cakes (Akk. *tinūru(m)*, 'oven, tannour; domestic cooking oven'; cf., im-šu-rin-na).

dusu
transportation basket, used in excavating earth from the lower levels of a canal; brick hod used by brick-layers; corvée (labor); lower levels (dub, 'to heap, pile up', + si;su, 'to fill up'; Akk. *tupšikku(m)*).

dusu e_2-ad-da
either a common family fund from which individual family members could borrow and repay with interest in annual installments (Westenholz), or a special tax that replaced an original family duty of corvée labor (Wilcke) ('corvée basket' + 'patrimony').

dusu...la_2
to carry a basket ('transportation basket' + 'to lift').

$dusu_2$[ANŠE.LIBIR]
an ass or equid yoked in teams and used as a draft animal in front of plows and wagons (occurs from Akkad to Ur III period) (du, 'to walk', + usu, 'strength'; Akk. *agālu(m) I*, 'donkey').

E

e-
(cf., eg_2-).

e
n., speaking; prayer (cf., eg_2).

v., to speak, say (suppletion class verb: e = sing. *marû*, plural *ḫamṭu*, and plural *marû*; cf. the singular *ḫamṭu* form, dug_4, also di); to do (as auxiliary verb preceded by a noun) (cf., eg_2).

interj., a vocal expression: Hey!; O!; Alas!; Eh, Ah.

e-
OS form of conjugation prefix i_3-, ThSLa §309.

-e-
2.sg. pronominal prefix (in a few cases also 1sg.) ThSLa §290-91.

-e
ergative postposition, marks the agent or transitive subject as opposed to the patient of the sentence, used with both animate and inanimate beings - ThSLa §38, §137.

-e
'locative/terminative' case postposition, in; toward; near to; forms an adverb suffixed to an abstract noun; occurs with inanimate beings only and often marks the inanimate object of a sentence - sometimes called dative case postposition for inanimate; used only with certain verbs, mostly compounds, and not generally to denote direction, for which the terminative postposition -šè is used - ThSLa §170, §174.

-e
demonstrative pron., this one; in the immediate vicinity - ThSLa §137.

-e
suffix added to regular verbs (class I or Affixation Group) to form the *marû* stem - a durative or continuative aspect marker; can also be analyzed as the pronominal suffix of the 3.sg. transitive, two-participant *marû* conjugation - ThSLa §232-33, §294, §300.

-e
(cf., /-ed/).

-e
represents 1.sg. and 2.sg. pronominal suffix -en in Gudea texts - ThSLa §296.

-e-da-
comitative prefix with 2.sg. or with 1.sg. in OB lit. texts - ThSLa §443, §442.

e-da-ku-a
(cf., $edakua_{(2)}$).

e-el[SIKIL]-lu
an interjection of unknown meaning; a (pure) sound; melody (Akkadian *ellu*, 'clear, pure').

e-ga-
writing of conjugation prefixes /ĩ-ga-/ in OS texts - ThSLa §323, §304.

e-ga-ma-
writing of conjugation prefixes /ĩ-ga-mu-/ + 1.sg. dative in OS texts - ThSLa §304.

^{ĝiš}E.KID-ma; ^{ĝiš}E.KID$_3$-ma
stick; drumstick; a type of mallet for polo (cf., ellag) (Akkadian *mekkû(m)*).

e-li-lum
cry of joy (cf., a-la/a-la-la).

e-lum
Emesal dialect for alim.

e-ma-
writing of conjugation prefixes /ĩ-ba-/ in OS texts - ThSLa §306-§308, §304, §337.

e-ne
3.sg. subject pronoun, he, she - ThSLa §91 (later form of a-ne).

-e-ne
plural suffix for animate nouns - ThSLa §67, §69.

(-e)-ne
3.pl. pronominal suffix which serves as the subject of two-part *marû* conjugations - ThSLa §294, §301, §282.

e-ne(-am$_3$)
interrogative, "what?", "how?", "where?", "why?" (cf., a-na-am$_3$).

e-ne-am$_3$
he is indeed; it is him/her; it is he indeed - ThSLa §97 (formal 3rd person pronoun + 'to be').

e-ne-da
3.sg. pronoun + comitative - ThSLa §91.

e-ne...dug$_4$/di/du$_{11}$/e
to play; to relax; to follow joyfully (3rd person pronoun + 'to do').

e-ne-di
game; play; enjoyment.

e-ne-em$_3$, e-ne-ĝ$_3$
Emesal dialect for inim, enim.

e-ne-eš$_2$
(cf., i$_3$-ne-eš$_2$).

e-ne-gim
like himself/herself - ThSLa §91 (3.sg. pronoun + equative).

e-ne...ma(-ma)
Emesal dialect for e-ne...dug$_4$/di/du$_{11}$/e.

e-ne-ne
they; them; 3.pl. pronoun.

e-ne-ne-da
3.pl. pronoun + comitative - ThSLa §91.

e-ne-ne-gim
3.pl. pronoun + equative - ThSLa §91.

e-ne-ne-ra
3.pl. pronoun + dative - ThSLa §91.

e-ne-ne-še$_3$
3.pl. pronoun + terminative - ThSLa §91.

e-ne-ra
3.sg. pronoun + dative - ThSLa §91.

e-ne-su$_3$-ud...dug$_4$/du$_{11}$/e
to rejoice; to copulate (with -da-) ('to play' + sud, 'to lengthen; to immerse').

e-ne-še$_3$
3.sg. pronoun + terminative - ThSLa §91 (cf., i$_3$-ne-eš$_2$).

e-pa-na; e$_2$-pa-na
(cf., e$_2$-ba-an).

e-pa$_5$
(cf., eg$_2$-pa$_5$(-r)).

^{ĝiš}e-ra-num$_2$
a tree and wood used for construction (cf., erin, eren).

e-re(-d), e-ri(-d)
Emesal dialect for arad$_2$.

e-re-si$_3$-ki-in
servant (?).

e-re$_7$
(cf., re$_7$).

e-ri-ib; e-rib
(cf., erib).

e-ri-iš
queen, lady (cf., ereš).

kuše-ri2-na (^{kuš}e-ri_2-na)
water resistant leather; leather treated with an extract of roots (cf., a-ri_2-na^{sar}; Akk. *erēnu II*, 'root').

e sa-dur_2-ra
(cf., eg_2 sa-dur_2-ra).

e-si-na; i_3-si-na
culm or stalk of barley.

^{kuš}e-sir_2
sandal; shoe (cf., $esir_3$).

e-sir_2
street ('levee' + 'dense').

e-sir_2-ra
in the streets ('streets' + locative).

-e-še
suffixed quotation particle in Old Babylonian texts - ThSLa §548, cf., $eše_2$[$ŠE_3$].

-e-ši-
2.sg. terminative prefix - ThSLa §453.

e-ze_2
you.

Emesal dialect for udu, 'sheep'.

e_2, e'_3, a'_3
house, household; temple; container; plot of land [E_2 archaic frequency: 649; concatenates 4 signs].

e_2-a-nir-ra
house of mourning ('house' + 'lamentation' + genitive).

e_2-a-nir-ra-gal-gal-la
euphemism for the netherworld ('house of mourning' + reduplicated 'big' + genitive).

e_2-ad-da(-/ak/)
the house of one's fathers; patrimony ('house' + 'father' + genitive).

e_2-an-na
sanctuary ('house' + 'Heaven' + genitive).

e_2-anše
donkey stable ('house' + 'equid').

e_2-ara_3(-a/ra); e_2-a-ra(-a)
mill (cf., e_2-$kikken_{(2)}$) ('house' + 'millstones' + genitive).

e_2-ba-an; e-pa-na; e_2-pa-na
a pair (e.g., shoes, wheels, chairs, castanets) (the etymology of this phonetically spelled word may relate to the pairs of oxen used to pull the ^{ĝiš}apin seeder plow).

e_2-BAPPIR
(cf., e_2-$lunga_3$).

e_2-bar-ra
a corridor or outbuilding ('house' + 'outside' + genitive; Akk. *barakku*).

e_2...bur_3
to break into a house (reduplication class) ('house' + 'to break into').

$^{(ĝiš)}e_2$-da
a small wooden box; wing (of a building), outhouse; a unit of measurement for fruit, including grapes ('house' + 'side'; cf., Akk. *edakku(m)*, 'wing (of a building)').

$^{(zid2)}e_2$-da(-di-a)
a flour offering (cf., Akk. *edadû*).

e_2-da(-ku_6)
(cf., $edakua_{(2)}$).

$^{(ĝiš)}e_2$-dim
a wooden vessel (cf., $eš_{2,3}$-dam ?) ('house' + 'bond, tie, post').

e_2-DU
(cf., e_2-tum_2).

e_2-du_3-a
house plot that has been built-on, developed; building a house; well-built house ('house' + 'to erect' + nominative; cf., Akk. *epšu(m)*).

e_2-du_6-la; e_2-dul-la
storage house or workshop ('house' + 'protection'/'sanctuary' + genitival a(k)).

e$_2$-DUB(-ba)
(cf., e$_2$-kišib$_3$(-ba)).

e$_2$-dub-ba(-a)
archive; school ('house' + 'tablet' + genitival a(k)).

e$_2$-duru$_5$
hamlet, suburb, rural settlement, hinterland, village; bridge ('houses' + 'fresh'; cf., Akk. *adurû*, 'village, outpost' and Orel & Stolbova #658, ***dar-** 'dwelling place'; also addir, 'bridge').

e$_2$-ta...e$_3$
to leave the house ('house' + 'from' + 'to exit').

e$_2$-eše$_2$
jail ('house' + 'rope').

e$_2$-gal
palace; the administrative center from which the ensi$_2$ governed the city ('house' + 'large').

e$_2$-ganba
warehouse ('house' + 'marketplace').

e$_2$-geme$_2$
a worker administrative center that reported to the Old Sumerian ensi$_2$ ('house' + 'workwomen').

e$_2$-gi$_4$-a
daughter-in-law; prospective bride ('the one who restores the house').

e$_2$-gir$_4$
bakery ('house' + 'ovens').

e$_2$-gu$_4$-gaz
slaughterhouse, abattoir ('house' + 'ox' + 'to slaughter').

e$_2$-g̃a$_2$-nun-maḫ
main storehouse, principal storeroom ('house' + 'storeroom' + noble + great; cf., g̃anun and g̃a$_2$-nun).

e$_2$...g̃al$_2$
open the house ('house' + 'to make available').

e$_2$-g̃ar; e$_2$-g̃ar$_8$
form, frame, shape; physique ('house' + 'form, appearance').

e$_2$-g̃ar$_8$[SIG$_4$]
brick wall (cf., eg̃ar).

e$_2$-g̃iš-kig̃$_2$-ti
artisan's workshop, especially devoted to the construction or reconstruction of temples ('house' + 'artisan').

e$_2$-i$_3$-gara$_2$
dairy ('house' + 'fat' + 'cream').

^{iti}e$_2$-iti-6
calendar month 8 at Umma during Ur III.

e$_2$-kaš
a public house, pub ('house' + 'beer').

e$_2$-kaš$_4$
courier's road house ('house' + 'courier').

e$_2$-KI.LAM
a storehouse ('house' + 'place' + 'abundance').

e$_2$-ki-si$_3$(-ga)
grave; tomb; pit (cf., ki-si$_3$-ga) ('house' + 'funerary offering').

e$_2$-$^{(na4)}$kikken$_{(2)}$-na
mill house, mill (cf., e$_2$-ara$_3$) ('house' + 'millstones' + genitival a(k)).

e$_2$-kišib$_{(3)}$(-ba)
storehouse; treasury ('house' + 'receipt/seal' + genitival a(k)).

e$_2$-kur
prison ('house' + 'netherworld').

e$_2$-lunga$_{(2,3)}$
beerhall; brewery ('house' + 'brewer').

e$_2$-maḫ
temple ('house' + 'great').

^{kuš}e$_2$-mar-uru$_5$[GUR$_8$]
arrow quiver ('house' + 'to immerse' + 'high, deep').

e$_2$-maš
animal stall ('house' + 'goat').

e$_2$-me-eš
summer ('houses' + 'are' + 'many').

e$_2$-mi$_2$
"woman's house"; queen's household; an administrative center for employment and production ('house' + 'woman').

e$_2$-muḫaldim[MU]
kitchen; kitchen storeroom, pantry, larder ('house' + 'cook').

e$_2$-nad$_3$
bed chamber (cf., a$_2$-na$_2$-da) ('chamber' + 'bed, couch').

e$_2$-NI
treasure-house (?).

e$_2$-nig̃$_2$(-gur$_{11}$[GA]-ra)
storehouse, treasure-house ('house' + 'things' [+ 'piled up']; cf., sag̃-nig̃$_2$-gur$_{11}$-ra(-ak)).

^{lu2}e$_2$-nig̃$_2$-ka
(cf., lu$_2$-e$_2$-nig̃$_2$-ka).

E$_2$-NUN
(cf., agrun).

e$_2$-pa-na
(cf., e-pa-na).

e$_2$-pa-paḫ
a cella or shrine in a temple or house (cf., pa-paḫ).

e$_2$-ri-a
(cf., a-ri-a).

e$_2$-sag̃
(cf., esag̃$_2$).

e$_2$ si-ga
a quiet house ('house' + 'silence').

e$_2$-SIG$_4$
(cf., e$_2$-g̃ar$_8$).

e$_2$-su-lum(-ma)
(cf., e$_2$-zu$_2$(-lum-ma)).

e$_2$-suḫur
shrine on the summit of a temple; whip holder on a chariot ('house' + 'crest'; into Akk. as *šaḫūru(m) I*; *ištuḫḫu(m)*).

e$_2$-šag$_4$/ša$_3$
house interior; (temple) cella ('house, temple' + 'midst').

e$_2$-šag$_4$-dub-ba, e$_2$-ša$_3$-dub-ba
chief accountant's office ('house' + 'contents' + 'tablet' + genitival a(k); > Akk. *šandabakku(m)*; cf., ^{lu2}ša$_{14}$[G̃A$_2$]-dub-ba).

e$_2$-šu-luḫ-ḫa^{zabar}
bronze wash basin, for cleansing, hand washing ('house; container' + 'ritual cleansing' + genitive; cf., nig̃$_2$-luḫ).

e$_2$-šu-sum-ma
warehouse ('house' + 'gift, delivery').

e$_2$-šutum; e$_2$-šu-tum
storehouse ('house' + 'portion' + 'to put, surround' + 'to bind').

e$_2$-a...ti(-l)
to live in a house ('house' + locative + 'to live').

e$_2$-$^{g̃iš}$tukul
armory ('house' + 'weapon').

e$_2$-tum$_2$[DU]
incoming goods ('house' + 'to bring, deliver').

e$_2$-tur$_3$
cattle pen; stockyard ('house' + 'stable' + genitive).

e$_2$-u$_4$-7
first crescent moon ('house' + 'day 7').

e$_2$-u$_4$-15
full moon ('house' + 'day 15').

e$_2$-u$_4$-sakar[SAR]
new moon ('house' + 'crescent moon').

e_2-u_6-nir
high temple; ziggurat ('house' + 'to be impressed' + 'to raise high').

e_2-ubur
milking pen ('house' + 'teat').

e_2-udu
sheepfold ('house' + 'sheep').

e_2-ur_3-ra
storehouse ('house' + 'bar, bolt').

e_2-ur_5-ra
debtor's prison; debt slave ('house' + 'debt' + genitive).

e_2-uru_3...gid_2
to keep watch over a house ('house' + 'watch fire' + 'to reach out, manage'; cf., $ša_3$-$še_3$...gid_2).

e_2 uš-bar
textile mill ('house' + 'weaver').

e_2-uzu_3-ga
a temple precinct (that received tithe offerings ?, where bird and fish offerings were fattened ?) ('house' + 'duck/goose' + 'milk' or uzug, 'tithe', + genitive).

(kuš/g̃iš)e_2-zu_2(-lum-ma-gigir)
arrow quiver ('house' + 'teeth, blades' + 'abundant' + 'chariot'; Akk. *laḫaruḫšum*; cf., $^{g̃iš}$ti-zu_2).

e_3, ed_2[UD.DU]; i
to go out, come out, emerge; to send forth; to issue; to lead or bring out; to consign; to rise; to sprout; to be or become visible; to appear (as a witness); to rave, become frenzied (the original final -d only appears in *marû* conjugation by the time of written Sumerian) [ED_2 archaic frequency: 12; concatenates 2 sign variants].

e_4
(cf., a).

e_5[NIN]
princely, palatial ?.

e_5-g̃ar
brick wall (cf., eg̃ar).

e_{11}
(cf., ed_3).

eb
(cf., ib).

-eb-
(cf., -b-).

eb_2
(cf., ib_2).

$ebiḫ_2$[$EŠ_2$.MAḪ]
heavy rope, strong cord; girdle (loanword from Akk. *ebēḫu*, 'to gird, belt up').

$ebir_{(2)}$
(cf., $epir_{(2)}$).

ebla
a watery type of beer - 'light beer' (ib_2, 'waist', + lal/la_2, 'to lessen').

EBUR
(cf., $buru_{14}$).

/-ed/
called 'the /-ed/ erweiterung', a verbal morpheme that usually occurs in prospective non-finite forms, but which also occurs in finite forms, never written -ed, usually just /e/ or with vowel harmony /u/, the /d/ appears when followed by a vowel - indicates something to be done in the future, ThSLa §252-259 (cf., -de_3 and example: ku_3-ta-du_8-dam, 'to be redeemed with silver').

ed_2
(cf., e_3).

ed_3, e_{11}
to exit; to rise; to descend, set; to bring down (or up); to consign; to import; to fetch; to remove; to drain (ed_3-de_3(-d) in *marû*).

$edakua_{(2)}$
fish bones (adda, 'skeleton', + ku_6/kua, 'fish'; Akk. *edakkû*).

edim
(cf., idim).

$edim_x$, edin
earthenware vat for oil and fats.

$edim_x$-a-la_2
oil cruse with a handle - could be made of gold ('oil vat' + 'handle').

edin, eden
n., steppe, plain, desert; grazing land between the two long rivers; back, spine, upperside, chest, thorax; shack; an occupation (ed_2, 'to send forth', + in, 'straw') [EDIN archaic frequency: 5].

prep., on; against.

eg_2, ek_2, ig_2, e
n., levee, embankment, bund, dike; a broad earthen bank, which sometimes accomodated a small canal running between two ridges along its top (cf., e) (a, e_4, 'water', + ig, 'door') [EG_2 archaic frequency: 12; concatenates 5 sign variants].

v., to water (cf., e).

eg_2 a-$ša_3$-ga
field bund ('bund' + 'field' + genitive).

eg_2 dal-ba-na
a dike that is shared by two watercourses or by two fields ('levee' + 'between').

eg_2-eg_2/e u_2-sag_{11}-e/a
reinforcement of the levees with cut/ bundled plants/reeds ('levees' + 'fascines').

$^{kuš}eg_2$-ib_2-ur_3 (-me_3)
siege shield (cf., eg_2-ur_3/ gur_{21}) ('dike' + 'middle, loins' + 'roof' + 'battle').

eg_2 id_2-da
canal bund ('bund' + 'main canal' + genitive).

eg_2 kal-kala-ga
work of reinforcing the levees ('levees' + 'to repair, mend' + nominative).

eg_2-pa_5(-r)
the combined structure of irrigation ditches on raised dikes; hydraulic system (of a particular farmer or of the land as a whole) ('embankments' + 'irrigation ditches'; asyndetic hendiadys).

eg_2 sa-dur_2-ra
wide levees at the low-lying end of a field which halted and contained the water for irrigating the field ('levees' + 'low-lying end of a field').

eg_2 si-ga
the work of piling up a levee ('levee' + si-ga/ge, 'to pile up').

eg_2-sur
border, boundary ('levee' + 'to delimit, bound'; Akk. *miṣru(m)*).

$^{(kuš)}eg_2$-ur_3
armor (cf., $^{kuš}eg_2$-ib_2-ur_3 and akar).

eg_2 us_2-sa-ra_2[DU]
boundary bund ('bund' + 'boundary' + genitive).

eg_2-zi-DU
a canal with floodgates, drainage canal ('levee' + 'to strengthen').

$egi_{(2)}$
(cf., $egir_{2/3}$).

$egir_{2,3}$, $egi_{(2)}$
princess ('house' + 'noble, native group'; cf., egi_2/$egir_3$[MUNUS.GI_7/GIR_{15}]).

$egir_{2,3}$-zi(d), $egi_{(2)}$-zi
a priestess ('princess' + 'faithful'; Akk. *igiṣītu*).

eg̃$_3$
(in Emesal, cf., em_3).

eg̃ar, ig̃ar
brick wall; physique (e_2, 'house', + g̃ar, 'form, appearance; to establish'; note early a_2-g̃ar in Gudea, where a_2 means 'side'; cf. also, e_2-g̃ar$_8$, e_2-sig_4, e_5-g̃ar; Akk. *igāru(m)*).

eĝir, eĝer
n., back; stern (of a ship); end; limit; future; inheritance; estate; remainder; an occupation - servant, henchman.

prep., behind.

adv., after; afterwards.

eĝir ...-a-ta
after ... - ThSLa §208, §489-90 ('from the back of').

$eḫ_3$[KU.KU]
lame; crippled.

el[SIKIL]-$lu_{(2)}$
(cf., e-el-lu).

elama, elam[NIM]
Elam; Elamite.

$elamkuš_{(2,3,4)}$
bladder ($ellaĝ_2$, 'kidneys', + kuš, 'skin').

$^{(ĝiš)}$ellag[LAGAB]
thorn; a thorny weed; wooden ball or puck for polo; a weapon that can be thrown; block of wood; a number word (cf., ^{ĝiš}E.KID-ma) (Akkadian *puquttu* and *pukku(m)*).

$^{(za/na4)}$$ellaĝ_2$[BIR = ḪI×ŠE]
kidneys; small balls, beads, pips made of carnelian, lapis, gold, silver, copper, and bronze manufactured in great numbers - used to decorate necklaces and collars (Akkadian *kalītu(m)* and *takpītu(m)* from *takāpu(m)*, 'to puncture; to stitch; dotted with colored spots').

$ellaĝ_2$[BIR]-gun_3-gun_3-nu
listed among cheeses - rennet cheese ? ('kidneys; beads' + 'to be good, beautiful' + nominative with vowel harmony; Akk. *pinnāru(m)*; note that *pinnu* is 'a bead or ornament').

em
(cf., im).

em_3, im_3[$AĜA_2$]
Emesal dialect for $niĝ_2$, 'goods, property'.

em_3[$AĜA_2$]-X
Emesal dialect, cf., $niĝ_2$-X.

em_3-da-ba
Emesal dialect for $nindaba_{(2)}$, $nidba_{(2)}$.

em_3-ze_2
Emesal dialect for ĝissu, ĝizzu.

eme
tongue; speech (cf., udu-uli[EME]-gi(-r)).

^{ĝiš}eme-apin
plowshare, blade of ard or seeder plow ('tongue' + 'plow').

eme-bala
interpreter; translator ('tongue' + 'to transfer'; Akkadian *nāpalû; targumannu(m)*; cf., inim-bala).

eme-dar
a tool, utensil ('tongue' + 'to slice, smash').

eme...e_3/e_{11}
to stick out the tongue ('tongue' + 'to send forth').

eme-gilim-ma
confused speech ('tongue' + 'to be twisted, tangled' + nominative).

eme-gir_{15}/gi_7
Sumerian language ('tongue' + 'native').

$^{(uruda)}$eme-$ĝir_2$$^{(zabar)}$
dagger blade ('tongue' + 'dagger').

eme-ĝiš-gid_2-da^{zabar}
bronze lance point ('tongue' + 'lance' + genitive).

eme-ḫa-mun
contrasting speech or languages (e.g., Sumerian and Akkadian) ('tongue' + 'mutually opposing').

eme-ḫul-$ĝal_2$
slander-demon ('tongue' + 'evil' + 'having').

^{ĝiš}eme-numun
an agricultural tool ('tongue' + 'seed').

^{ĝiš}eme-sa-du$_8$-a
a tool ('tongue/blade' + 'roasting' + 'to loosen' + nominative).

$^{(lu2)}$eme-sal
boy, or man with feminine voice ? ('tongue' + 'delicate'; Akk., *lurû(m)*).

eme-si-nu-sa$_2$
describes a person 'whose speech is not right' ('tongue' + si...sa$_2$, 'to do something in the right way' + 'not').

^{ĝiš}eme-sig
ship deck plank ('tongue' + 'small').

eme-sig
slander ('tongue' + 'small'; cf., inim-sig).

eme-sig...dug$_4$/du$_{11}$/e
to slander ('tongue' + 'small' + 'to speak').

eme-sig...gu$_7$
to slander ('tongue' + 'low; small' + 'to consume'; cf., inim-sig...gu$_7$).

eme-šub$_6$[ŠID]; eme-ušub[DIR]
lizard ('tongue' + 'to lick').

eme...šub$_6$[ŠID]
to lick with the tongue ('tongue' + 'to lick').

eme-tuku
slanderer; quarreller ('tongue' + 'to have').

^{u2}eme-ur-gi$_7$
hound's tongue, Cynoglossum, a weed with oblong leaves ('tongue' + 'dog').

eme$_2$
(cf., emeda$_{(2)}$).

eme$_{3,5,6}$
female donkey, she-ass, jenny.

eme$_4$-du$_2$(-d)
(cf., emedu).

emeda$_{(2)}$, eme$_2$
wetnurse, nursemaid, mammy (i- + ama, conjugation prefix + 'mother', + da, 'to hold, protect'; cf., umu/um, 'nurse').

emeda$_{(2)}$-ga-la$_2$
wetnurse ('mammy' + 'milk' + 'to carry').

emedu$_{(2)}$
house/estate-born slave (eme$_2$, 'mammy', + tud/du$_2$, 'to be born').

emeš$_2$
summer.

emma
(cf., enmen).

emma$_2$
(cf., enmen$_2$).

en
n., dignitary; lord; high priest or priestess; ancestor (statue); diviner [EN archaic frequency: 1232; concatenates 3 sign variants].

v., to rule.

adj., noble (cf., uru$_{16}$[EN](-n)).

-en
1.sg. or 2.sg. pronominal suffix, usually indicating the verb subject, but sometimes the direct object of a transitive verb - ThSLa §294, §281, §536.

-(e)n-de$_3$-en
1.pl. pronominal suffix - ThSLa §294, §281, §297.

en-edin-na
(cf., an-edin(-na)).

en-gal
overlord (cf., ensi$_2$-gal) ('lord' + 'large').

en-mur
a resin, possibly myrrh ('lord' + 'lungs').

en-na (...-a)
until; as long as ...; as many as ...; everywhere - ThSLa §489 ('time, enigmatic background' + nominative).

en-na ...-še$_3$
till, until - ThSLa §489 ('time' + terminative postposition, 'up to').

en-na-bi-še$_3$
until now; until the time ('this time' + 'towards').

en-na-me-še$_3$
"how long?" ('time' + 'where to?').

^{lu2}en-nam
provincial governor ('lord' + 'province').

en-nam
an OB period math. text writing for a-na, what, how much.

en-nam-šita$_4$
a priest of Enki in Eridu who could be elevated to en-priest ('governor' + 'bound/intact').

$^{(lu2)}$en-nu(-uĝ$_3$)(-ĝa$_2$)
watch, guard, guardian; watch (as a division of night time); imprisonment; prison.

en-nu(-un/uĝa$_3$)...du$_3$/ak
to watch; to safeguard; to guard against.

en-nu-da-tuš-a
one assigned to guard duty.

en-nu-gu-la
grand watch.

en-še$_3$
(cf., en$_3$-še$_3$(-am$_3$)).

en-te-en-na(-/ak/)
the cold season, wintertime ('time' + 'cold' + genitive).

-en-za-na
2.pl. pronominal suffix combined with the subordination suffix -a - ThSLa §298.

-en-ze$_2$-en
2.pl. pronominal suffix - ThSLa §294, §281, §298; imperative 2.pl. pronominal suffix when the prefix chain ends in a vowel - ThSLa §496.

en-zi
n., lead animal ('time; lord' + 'to rise up').

adj., choice, first rate.

en$_{2,3}$
n., time; enigmatic background; incantation [EN$_2$ archaic frequency: 17].

prep., until.

en$_2$-e$_2$-nu-ru
introductory formula for exorcism/incantation texts ('incantation' + 'house' + 'image, likeness' + 'to send').

-en$_3$
represents 1.sg. or 2.sg. pronominal suffix /-en/ in NS - ThSLa §296.

^{gi}en$_3$-bar
reed, reeds (cf., ambar, 'reed-bed').

en$_3$-bi-tar-re
to be subject to inquiry (cf., en$_3$... tar).

en$_3$-du
a type of song ('time' + 'walking'; note du$_{12}$, 'to sing').

en$_3$-du-an-na
high-pitched singing ('song' + 'to be high' + nominative).

en$_3$-dur
navel; umbilical cord ('enigmatic background' + 'bond, tie'; Akkadian *abunnatu(m)*).

^{u2}en$_3$-dur; en$_3$-tar; en$_3$-tur
scammony, Convolvulus Scammonia, Syrian bindweed - a twining plant having long, thick roots whose milky juice yields a black resin that is a violent purgative (Akk. *abukkatu*).

en$_3$-še$_3$(-am$_3$); en-še$_3$
until when; how long - ThSLa §127 ('time; until' + terminative postposition, 'up to' [+ enclitic copula]).

en$_3$...tar
to ask (someone: dative); to investigate; to take care of; to handle; to intercede; to pay attention to, heed ('enigmatic background' + 'to determine, inquire').

en$_3$-tukum-še$_3$
for how long; until when? ('time' + 'if' + terminative postposition). .

en$_3$-za-am$_3$
(cf., $^{(dug)}$an-za-am).

en_5[PA.TE]
(cf., $ensi_2$).

en_5[PA.TE]-si
(cf., $ensi_2$).

$-en_6$
represents 1.sg. or 2.sg. pronominal suffix /-en/ in NS - ThSLa §296.

en_7-ku_6[ZAG.ḪA]
tax collector (of tenancy dues) (cf., enkum).

en_8[ŠA]
(simplified writing of en_3[LI]).

endub, endib
cook (en, 'lord', + dub, 'to move in a circle, shake') [ENDIB archaic frequency: 6].

engar
irrigator, cultivator, farmer, peasant, estate manager, plowman (responsible for one a-$ša_3$ of ca. 50 hectares and for managing the draft animals) (en, 'lord', + gar_3, 'field'; cf., Emesal mu-un-gar_3/mu-un-ga-ar; Akk. *ikkaru* and *inkaru*, 'farmer, plow-man', allegedly from Semitic "to hoe, cultivate", cf., Orel & Stolbova #26 ***'akür-** 'till' and #70 ***'ekar-** 'farmer').

engar-gu
flax farmer ('farmer' + 'flax').

engar-gu_4(-ra)
ox-plowman ('farmer' + 'ox').

engar-gu_4-du_8-a
peasant responsible for yoked oxen ('farmer' + 'ox' + 'to yoke' + nominative).

engar-gu_4-la_2-a
peasant responsible for harnessed oxen ('farmer' + 'ox' + 'to harness, hitch' + nominative).

engar-g̃iš-i_3
sesame farmer.

engiz [ME.EN.GI]
cook; temple cook (en, 'lord', + gaz, 'to fracture, crush, slaughter') [ENGIZ archaic frequency: 22].

engur
subsoil water; subterranean sea of fresh water; deep, abyss; marshes (a, 'water', + nag̃, 'to drink', + ur_2, 'floor; root'; cf., an-gur_4).

enim
(cf., inim).

$^{g̃iš}$enkara
a weapon (cf., a_2-an-$kara_2$).

enku[ZAG.ḪA]; $enku_x$ [ZAG.ḪI.A]
fishing overseer; tax collector (of tenancy dues) (cf., en_7-ku_6; if ZAG.ḪA(-d) then cf., eššad) (en, 'lord', + ku_6/kua, 'fish').

enkum
temple treasurer; guardian deity of the foundations (cf., en_7-ku_6) [ENKUM archaic frequency: 14].

$enmen_{(2)}$, $emmen_{(2)}$, $immen_{(2)}$, $immin_{(2)}$, $emma_{(2)}$, $imma_{(2)}$
thirst (en, 'time', + mun, 'salt').

$enmen_2$, $emmen_2$, $immen_2$, $immin_2$, $emma_2$, $imma_2$
to drink beer.

$ensi_{(3)}$
dream interpreter; diviner ($en_{2,3}$, 'enigmatic background' + ?; cf., en_3...tar, 'to ask'; Akk. *šā'ilu(m)*) [ENSI archaic frequency: 8].

$ensi_2$(-k) [PA.TE.SI]
city ruler (Old Sumerian); city governor, steward (post-Sargonic) (en, 'lord, manager', + si, 'plowland', + genitive; Akkadian *iššiakkum*; cf., $nisag̃_2$, 'governor') [$ENSI_2$ archaic frequency: 1].

$ensi_2$-gal
former/ex-governor ('governor' + 'large').

enten(a)
winter (en, 'time', + ten, 'cold', + a(k), 'of').

epig, ebig[SIG]
vessel or trough for water for animals (ub_4, 'cavity', + eg_2, 'to water').

^{ĝiš}epir$_{(2)}$, ebir$_{(2)}$
wooden stand for a beer-brewing vessel (cf. etymology of ubur).

er, ere
(cf., ir).

er_2, ir_2
n., tears, weeping; lamentation; prayer; complaint.

v., to weep, lament.

er_2-du_8
lamentation singer ('tears' + 'to loosen').

er_2...gul
to stifle lament ('lamentation' + 'to destroy').

er_2...$ĝa_2$-$ĝa_2$
to set up a lament ('lamentation' + 'to make').

er_2...pad_3/pa_3
to burst into tears; to cry, weep ('tears' + 'to show').

er_2-ra
mourning, lamentation ('tears' + nominative).

er_2...sig_7
to lament ('tears' + 'to complain').

er_2-$ša_3$-ḫuĝ-$ĝa_2$
cultic songs in the Emesal dialect, mostly written down after the Old Babylonian period ('heart-soothing wail').

er_2-$ša_3$-ne-$ša_4$[DU]
lamentation prayer ('lamentation' + 'supplications').

er_2-$šem_{3,5}$-ma
Old Babylonian period hymn compositions concerning the gods sung by the gala priests in the Emesal dialect to the accompaniment of a kettledrum, i.e., timpani ('wail' + 'drum' + genitive).

er_2...$šeš_{2,4}$/$še_8$-$še_8$
to cry, weep ('tears' + 'to weep').

er_9
(cf., ir_9).

eren$_{(2)}$
(cf., erin$_{(2)}$).

ereš, eriš, erež ? [MUNUS.TUG_2]
lady; mistress, proprietress; queen; wise one (cf., e-ri-iš).

ereš-diĝir
(a possible reading for nin-diĝir).

$ereš_5$[GAL.AN.ZU]
knowing, intelligent.

erib, $arib_x$
daughter-in-law; sister-in-law (husband's sister).

$erim_2$, $erin_7$, rim$_{(3)}$ [NE.RU]
n., enemy; malefactor; wicked; destruction; oath [$ERIM_2$ archaic frequency: 20].

adj., hostile; evil; wicked.

adv., wickedly.

$erim_2$-du
wicked, evil-doer; incompetent ('evil' + 'walking'; cf., ḫul-du, 'wicked').

$erim_2$-$ĝal_2$
enemy; hostile; rebellious; wicked, evil (person) ('enemy' + 'being').

$erim_{3,4,5,6}$, $erin_{3,4,5,6}$
treasury; storehouse; treasures.

$^{(ĝiš\ šim)}$erin, eren
n., cedar tree, wood, or resin; wood highly valued and oil used as an aromatic; texts mention large deliveries of cedar-resin (Dr. Alexis Martin suggests an etymology from Hurrian ah-a-ri "cedar" plus -n, the so-called 'definite article'; but cf., the aromatic root, ḫirin and arina) [ERIN archaic frequency: 105].

v., to anoint with cedar-oil.

$^{(\tilde{g}iš)}$erin-babbar$_2$
white cedar (wood) ('cedar' + 'white'; Akkadian *tiālu(m)*).

erin$_2$, erim, eren$_2$
man, servant, soldier; conscript (for civil or military service); gang of workers; troops, army; people, folk; colonist [ERIM archaic frequency: 175; concatenation of 3 sign variants].

erin$_2$, rin$_2$
yoke; balance scale.

erin$_2$-e$_2$-sukkal
conscript of the house of the messengers ('conscripted worker' + 'house' + 'messenger').

erin$_2$-e$_2$-udu
conscript doing service at the sheepfold ('conscripted worker' + 'house' + 'sheep').

erin$_2$-eš$_3$-didli
conscript doing service at various temples ('conscript' + 'shrine' + 'separate, assorted').

erin$_2$ gi-zi
reed fodder harvesters ('conscripted workers' + 'reed fodder').

erin$_2$-ḫuš, erim-ḫuš
battle, strife ('troops' + 'furious').

erin$_2$-še$_3$-g̃en-na
become a conscript (?) ('conscript' + terminative + 'to go').

erin$_2$ še-gur$_{10}$-gur$_{10}$
harvest workers ('gang of workers' + 'grain' + reduplicated 'sickle; to reap').

$^{(\tilde{g}iš}$erina$_8$
(cf., $^{(\tilde{g}iš)}$arina).

eriš
(cf., ereš).

erum$_{2,3}$, eru$_{2,3}$
slavegirl.

es$_2$
(cf., eš).

esag̃
heir son (a/e$_4$, 'seed, offspring', + sag̃, 'first, prime').

esag̃$_2$[G̃A$_2$×ŠE]; esag̃$_x$[E$_2$×ŠE; E$_2$.ŠE; E$_2$.SAG̃]
granary, storeroom (e$_2$, 'house, temple', + sag̃, 'first, prime').

esi
(cf., esig).

esig, esi
good, fine; solid, strong (usu, 'strength', + gi, 'reed').

$^{(na4)}$esig, esi
diorite; olivine-gabbro.

$^{(\tilde{g}iš)}$esig, esi
ebony.

esir$_{(2)}$
crude bitumen, asphalt (cf., gu$_2$-gir(-esir$_2$)) (usu, 'strength' or esi, 'strong', + ir$_{(2)}$, 'liquid secretion', but cf., šur, sur, 'to flow', and esir$_2$-e$_2$-a, 'house bitumen').

esir-gibil
(liquid) bitumen, tar ('bitumen' + 'burning').

esir$_2$-e$_2$-a
'house bitumen', slime, tar, a refined liquid form for coating doors, etc. ('bitumen' + 'house' + genitive).

esir$_2$-gul-gul
'broken bitumen', used to caulk small boats ('bitumen' + reduplicated 'to break into pieces').

esir$_2$-ḫad$_2$[UD]; esir$_2$-ḫa$_2$[ḪI.A]
'dry bitumen', pitch ('bitumen' + 'dry').

^{kuš}esir$_3$
sandal; shoe (cf., e-sir$_2$).

eš[U.U.U]
n., many, much.

v., to anoint.

-eš
3.pl. pronominal suffix for the intransitive verb subject in the later periods; can indicate the direct object of a transitive verb; can denote the 3.pl. ergative subject in two-part *ḫamṭu* forms together with the prefix -n- ThSLa §294, §281, §299.

-eš
adverbial force suffix (sometimes followed by -še$_3$) ThSLa §84.

-eš
adjective suffix - ThSLa §85.

^{ĝiš}eš-ad, ^{ĝiš}es$_2$-ad
trap (phonetic spelling of ^{ĝiš}eš$_2$-sa-du$_3$ and eššad).

eš-bar
decision ('much' + 'to divide'; cf., ka-aš-bar).

eš-bar...kiĝ$_2$(-ĝa$_2$)
to arrive at a decision ('decision' + 'to seek; to order').

eš-bar-kiĝ$_2$-du$_{11}$-ga
pronounced decision ('decision' + 'message, order' + 'to speak' + nominative).

eš$_{(2,3)}$-da
ceremony; a type of vessel, goblet, jar ('shrine' + 'with; to be near'; cf., eš$_{2,3}$-dam).

eš-de$_2$(-a)
interest-free loan ('many, much' + 'to pour, increase' + nominative).

eš-še
(cf., en$_3$-še$_3$).

eš$_2$
(cf., eše$_2$).

-eš$_2$
3.pl. pronominal suffix for the intransitive verb subject in the older periods; can indicate the direct object of a transitive verb; can denote the 3.pl. ergative subject in two-part *ḫamṭu* forms together with the prefix -n- ThSLa §294, §281, §299.

eš$_2$-gana$_2$
surveyor's rope ('rope' + 'field/surface measure').

$^{\text{lu2}}$eš$_2$-gid$_2$
surveyor ('measuring rope' + 'long').

eš$_2$-kar$_3$, eš$_2$-gar$_3$; aš$_2$-gar$_3$
task; one man's daily work assignment; the oxen, plows, or work materials which perform a task; to be assigned for someone's benefit (cf. earlier form, a$_2$-ĝiš-gar$_3$-ra; cf., ešgar).

eš$_2$-kiri$_{3/4}$
nose rope (cf., eškiri) ('rope' + 'muzzle/nose').

$^{\text{(ĝiš)}}$eš$_2$-lal/la$_2$
n., halter, tether; hunting trap; bird catcher; step ladder; a siege instrument; bond, tie; cord, rope; belt, sash; fastening post; belt (for climbing palm trees); hoisting rope for a well ('rope' + 'to hang').

v., to net, catch with a net; to ensnare; to throttle, constrict, suffocate.

EŠ$_2$.MAḪ
(cf., ebiḫ$_2$).

^{ĝiš}eš$_2$-sa-du$_3$; ^{ĝiš}eš-sa-du$_3$, ^{ĝiš}es$_2$-sa-du$_3$
fishing net, trap ('rope' + 'fishing net') (compare eššad).

eš$_{(2,3)}$-da
ceremony; a type of vessel, goblet, jar ('shrine' + 'with; to be near'; cf., eš$_{2,3}$-dam).

eš$_{2,3}$-dam
epithet of a temple of the bride-goddess Inanna; brothel; tavern ('shrine' + 'spouse'; Akk. *šatû(m) II*, 'to drink').

eš$_3$
shrine; sanctuary [AB archaic frequency: 384; concatenates 2 sign variants].

eš$_3$-didli
various temples ('shrine' + 'separate, assorted').

eš$_3$-eš$_3$
a festival (All-Shrines) (reduplicated 'shrine').

eš$_3$-maḫ
major shrine ('shrine' + 'great').

eš$_3$-ta-lu$_2$
a type of singer ('man for the shrine' ?).

eš$_{5,6,16,21}$
three.

$^{(ĝiš)}$eš$_{22}$, iš$_{11}$[LAM×KUR]; iš$_{12}$, eš$_x$[(ĜIŠ.)LAM]
almond (tree, wood, nut, and oil) (cf., si-ig-dum).

eša, eše$_4$[A.TIR]; aš$_2$; aš
emmer or spelt wheat groats, coarse flour, used for offerings to the gods.

ešda
(cf., šita$_2$).

ešda$_3$
(cf., šita).

eše$_2$, eš$_2$[ŠE$_3$]
rope; leash; measuring tape/cord; length measure, rope = 10 nindan rods = 20 reeds = 120 cubits = the side of 1 square iku in area = 1,0,0 [60^2] fingers; a surface area measure, = 6 iku (can be an adverbial suffix like -eš) (eš, 'much', + eš, 'much') [ŠE$_3$ archaic frequency: 152].

-eše$_2$[ŠE$_3$]
a quotation particle which occurs as a suffix, indicates quoted speech.

eše$_2$-X
(cf., eš$_2$-X).

eše$_3$[IDIM]
a surface area measure = 2.16 hectares, 1/3 of a bur$_3$, or 6 iku.

ešemen$_{(2,3)}$
skipping rope; jump rope; game; play; celebration (eše$_2$, 'rope', + men, 'both, two').

ešgar[MUNUS.AŠ$_2$.GAR$_3$]
young she-goat, goat doe (cf., a-ša-an-gar$_3$, 'to be perverse', and aš$_2$, 'to desire'; cf., zeḫ) [? EŠGAR archaic frequency: 12].

ešgar-gaba
sexually mature female goat kid ('female goat kid' + 'breasts').

ešgiri$_2$[EN×KAR$_2$]
staff (cf., šibir$_2$; ^{ĝiš}enkara).

eškiri, ešgiri
nose rope, lead-rope, halter, bridle; jumping rope (eše$_2$, 'rope', + kiri$_3$, 'nose, muzzle').

ešsad[ZAG.ḪA]; ešsadu[AB×ḪA.ZAG.DUḪ]
fisherman; fin, flipper (of fish); wing (of bird) (^{ĝiš}eš$_2$-sa-du$_3$, 'fishing net, trap'; same signs (ZAG.ḪA) as enku).

ešša$_2$
to be satiated, full.

eššu
ear of barley or other grain.

eštub^{ku6}[GUD]
a river carp: *binnî* (Akk. *arsuppu*).

ezem
(cf., ezen).

ezen, ezem
festival, feast (uzu, 'cut of meat', + en, 'time'; > Akk., *isinnu(m)*) [EZEN archaic frequency: 114; concatenation of 3 sign variants].

^{iti}ezen-An-na
calendar month 10 at Drehem through Šu-Sin 3; calendar month 11 at Drehem after Šu-Sin 3; calendar month 11 at Ur during Ur III.

^{iti}ezen-^{d}Amar-Sin
calendar month 7 at Umma during years 6 - 8 of Amar-Sin.

^{iti}ezen-^{d}Ba-ba$_6$
calendar month 8 at Lagaš during Ur III.

^{iti}ezen-^{d}Dumu-zi
calendar month 6 at Lagaš during Ur III.

^{iti}ezen-^{d}Li$_{9}$-si$_{4}$
calendar month 3 at Lagaš during Ur III.

^{iti}ezen-^{d}Nin-a-zu
calendar month 5 at Drehem through Šu-Sin 3; calendar month 6 at Drehem after Šu-Sin 3; calendar month 6 at Ur during Ur III.

^{iti}ezen-^{d}Šu-^{d}EN.ZU(Sin)
calendar month 8 at Drehem in year Šu-Sin 3; calendar month 9 at Drehem after Šu-Sin 3.

^{iti}ezen-^{d}Šul-gi
calendar month 7 at Drehem through Šu-Sin 3; calendar month 8 at Drehem after Šu-Sin 3; calendar month 8 at Ur during Ur III; calendar month 7 at Lagaš during Ur III; calendar month 10 at Umma after year Šulgi 30.

^{iti}ezen-maḫ
calendar month 9 at Drehem through Šu-Sin 3; calendar month 10 at Drehem after Šu-Sin 3; calendar month 10 at Ur during Ur III.

ezen-maḫ
great festival ('feast' + 'great').

^{iti}ezen-me-ki-ĝal$_{2}$
calendar month 11 at Drehem through Šu-Sin 3; calendar month 12 at Drehem after Šu-Sin 3; calendar month 12 at Ur during Ur III.

^{d}ezinu$_{2}$, ezina$_{2}$, ezin$_{2}$
[ŠE.TIR]
grain, cereal, wheat; the grain goddess Ezina (cf., ^{d}ašnan[ŠE.TIR]) (uzu, 'meat, protein', + in-nu, 'straw') [EZINU archaic frequency: 24; concatenation of 4 sign variants].

G

ga
n., milk (chamber + water) [GA archaic frequency: 245; concatenation of 3 sign variants].

adj., suckling, qualifier for an infant animal.

Emesal dialect for tum$_{2}$ (cf., de$_{6}$).

ga-
modal prefix, cohortative, used for both 1.sg. and 1.pl.; in the singular with *ḫamṭu* verb forms; and in the plural with plural stem, reduplicated verb, or in some cases a *marû* verb form - ThSLa §384-§393.

ga-
modal prefix /ga-/ with conjugation prefix /ĩ-/ - ThSLa §304.

-ga-
conjugation prefix secondary to the conjugation prefix ĩ, written either e-ga, ì-ga, or in-ga, meaning 'also', often used to connect two sentences; a sequence of clauses involving nu-ga means 'neither ... nor ...'; with the modal affirmative prefix, written na-ga, na-an-ga, or nam-ga, in addition to the meaning 'indeed also', it often introduces a new section, when it is translated 'and then' or 'and now'; in a sentence with the equative -gim, it means 'as well as' - ThSLa §322-§326, §373.

ga-ab-VERB
Verbal forms like this are found as nouns, primarily from the post-Sumerian period, cf., the intransitive form ga-an-VERB.

ga-ab-kar-re
(cf., gaba-kar).

ga-ab$_{2}$-ku$_{3}$-ga
milk from pure cows ('milk' + 'cow' + 'pure' + genitive).

ga-ab$_{2}$-sig$_{7}$-ga
milk from beautiful cows ('milk' + 'cow' + 'beautiful' + genitive).

ga-am$_{3}$-
writing of cohortative modal prefix /ga-/ with conjugation prefix /ĩ-/ and ventive element /-m-/ in OB period texts - ThSLa §304.

ga-am$_3$-ku$_4$
newcomer; intruder ('I will enter').

ga-am$_3$-ma-
writing for /ga-ĩ-ba/ in OB period - ThSLa §304.

ga-am$_3$-mi-
writing for /ga-ĩ-bi/ in OB period - ThSLa §338, §304.

ga-an-VERB
Verbal forms like this are found as nouns, primarily from the post-Sumerian period, cf., the transitive form ga-ab-VERB.

ga-an-ša-ša
(cf., ka-an-ša-ša).

ga-an-tuš
(cf., gan-tuš).

ga-an-za(-za)
one that drips or bubbles ('to make a repetitive noise').

MUNUSga-an-za-za
a woman who has intercourse habitually (cf., ga-an, 'I will', ki...za(-za), 'to bow down, submit; to prostrate oneself').

ga-an-zir$_2$[ŠE$_3$-KA]; ga-an-ze$_2$-er
entrance to the netherworld; flame (cf., ganzer).

ga-ar$_3$(-ra)
powdered or finely grated sun-dried curd-cheese which can be stored and reconstituted with water or milk; instant milk; Iraqi stone-hard *kushuk* ('milk' + 'to mill, grind' + nominative; Akkadian *gubnatu* and later *eqīdu*, 'true cheese').

ga-ar$_3$-gazi
cheese seasoned with **gazi**.

ga-arḫuš-a(-ke$_4$)
the milk of mercy ('milk' + 'womb; compassion' + genitive).

ga-ba...g̃al$_2$
(cf., gaba...g̃al$_2$).

ga-ba-al
attack; fight (either related to gaba, 'rival' or Akkadian *qablu(m) II*, 'battle').

ga-ba-al...du$_3$
to challenge, contradict, quarrel ('attack; fight' + 'to make').

ga-ba-bu-um; ka-ba-bu-um
shield (Akkadian loanword, *kabābu(m) I*).

ga-ba-kar-re
(cf., gaba-kar).

ga-ba-ra(-ḫum); gaba-ra(-aḫ)
breast-beating, panic, turmoil; revolt (cf., gaba$_2$-ra) (gaba, 'breast' + ra-aḫ, 'to strike'; cf. also, gaba...ri, 'to confront'; Akkadian *gabaraḫḫu(m)*).

ga-du$_{(7)}$
lintel (above a door) (? + du$_7$, 'to finish, complete').

ga-eš$_8$[KASKAL]
traveling merchant, trading river agent (cf., ga-raš^{sar}) (> Akk. *ka'iššum*; compare ga-sa$_{10}$).

ga-ga-ra(-a)
an established account (cf., g̃a$_2$-g̃a$_2$; g̃ar-g̃ar, g̃a$_4$-g̃a$_4$(-ra)).

ga-gal
large cheese ('milk' + 'large').

ga...gu$_7$
to nurse/feed with milk ('milk' + 'to feed').

ga-gu$_7$-a
suckling foal ('milk' + 'to feed' + nominative).

GA.ḪAB
(cf., kisim$_6$).

ga-ḪAR
(cf., ga-ar$_3$).

ga-i^{mušen}
(cf., gambi$_x^{mušen}$).

ga-ila$_2$
a profession, milk carrier ('milk' + 'to lift').

ga-ki-tir-da; ga-i$_{(3)}$-ti-ir-da
curdled or fermented milk (?) ('milk' + 'forest country ?').

ga-kug
(cultically) pure milk ('milk' + 'pure').

$^{(ĝiš)}$ga-lam
(cf., galam).

ga(-a)-li$_2$(-a)-tum; ga-li$_{(2)}$
gold or bronze metal sheets ?, a quantity of which weighed one ma-na - used for weapons (loanword from Akk. *kālītu(m)*, 'part of chariot; gold ornamental item', from *kalû(m) V*, 'to hold, restrain').

ga-ma-
writing of modal prefix ga- + conjugation prefix mu- + 1.sg. dative in the Gudea period - ThSLa §304.

ga-murub$_4$; ga-mur$_x$[LAK 490]
a type of cheese, particularly in texts from Umma ('milk' + 'membrane'; strained in cheesecloth ?).

ga-na; ga-nam
interj., well; truly; indeed; come on, let's go; an affirmative or encouraging exclamation - ThSLa §153.

ga-nam-me-am$_3$
it is indeed, it was certainly - ThSLa §379, §390, §540 (cohortative + affirmative + ĩ + bi$_2$ + 'to be').

$^{(u2)}$ga-nu$_{11}$^{mušen}
the Syrian ostrich - now extinct (Akk. *lurmu(m)* [*nurmû*, 'pomegranate']; *kumû*).

ga-nunuz-TE
palm-milk ? (Akk. *uqūru(m)*).

ga-ra-an(-da)
n., bunch of grapes; heap of fruit (loanword from Akk. *karānu(m)*, 'vine; wine; grapes') (cf., kurun$_{(2,3)}$).

adj., bearing fruit.

ga-raš^{sar}
leek(s) (cf., garaš$_{3,4}$; ga-eš$_8$) (loan from Akk. *karašu(m)*; cf., *bisru*).

ga-rig$_2$
v., carding (wool); to filter with a comb.

^{ĝiš}ga-rig$_2$
n., comb.

$^{(ĝiš)}$ga-rig$_2$...aka
to card wool ('comb' + 'to apply').

ga-sa$_{10}$
tradesman ('let me buy!').

ga-se$_{12}$[SIG$_7$]-a
sour milk, from which butter and cheese are processed; yogurt ('milk + 'to dwell, complete' + nominative).

ga-sub-ba
milk sucking ('milk' + 'to suck' + nominative).

ga-ša-an
lady (Emesal dialect) (cf., gašan and nin).

ga-še-a
(variant of ga-se$_{12}$-a, particularly in texts from Umma).

ga-ti
plea, petition ('let me live!').

ga-tur
small cheese ('milk' + 'small').

ga-an...za(-za)
to drip; to bubble ('milk'(?) + 'sky, air'(?) + 'to make a repetitive noise').

ga-zi-in-bu
stake (for impalement).

ga-zil$_2$[TAG]-a; ga-zi-il-la$_3$
a type of milk, possibly colostrum, the new mother's first milk ('milk' + 'to be loving, gentle' + nominative; Akkadian *eldu*).

$^{(ĝiš)}$ga-zum
(cf., ga-rig$_2$, reading based on Diri II Ugarit 170', ka-ri-im : GIŠ.GA.ZUM).

GA$_5$.ŠU.DU$_8$
(cf., sagi).

ga$_6$
(cf., g̃a$_6$).

ga$_{14}$[KA]
Emesal dialect for tum$_2$ (cf., de$_6$).

gab$_2$(-bu)
(cf., gubu$_3$, gaba$_2$-, kab-).

gab$_3$
(cf., kab$_2$).

gaba
n., breast; bosom; chest; side, front edge (of a field or mountain); surface; coast (cf. also meanings at gaba-ri(-a)) (ga, 'milk', + ba, 'to give').

adj., semi-weaned animal, older than one month (cf., ga, 'suckling' and variant gub).

gaba-dib$_{(2)}$
breastwork, rampart, parapet; crenellation ('side, front edge' + 'to traverse'; Akk., *gabadibbu(m)*).

gaba-diri-ga
enormous strength ('rival' + 'to go over, exceed' + nominative).

gaba(-na)...dug$_4$
to speak against (someone) ('rival' + 3rd person with locative + 'to speak').

gaba-gi$_4$
opponent, adversary; opposition ('rival' + 'to besiege').

gaba...g̃al$_2$
to boast ('chest' + 'to be available').

gaba-g̃al$_2$
n., strength ('chest' + 'available').

adj., forceful; amply endowed.

$^{(g̃iš)}$gaba-g̃al$_2$(-gigir)
front part of a chariot; fairing.

gaba...g̃ar
to put out one's chest; to defy ('breast, chest' + 'to deliver').

gaba-kar(-re)
escapist ('rival' + 'to flee'; cf., gaba...zi).

gaba-ra-aḫ
(cf., ga-ba-ra(-ḫum); gaba-ra/raḫ).

gaba...ri
to confront; to meet; to sue ('breast, chest' + 'to throw out').

gaba-ri(-a)
n., rival, opponent; one who resists; match; equal; counterpart; copy, duplicate, replica; reply; "presentation" (a type of offering); opposite side; front ('breast' + 'to exchange; to beat').

adj., withstanding attack (describing a door or weapon).

gaba...ru(-gu$_2$)
to encounter ('breast, chest' + ru-gu$_2$, 'to oppose').

gaba-šu-g̃ar
resistance; rival ('breast, chest' + 'hand' + 'to place on').

gaba(-a)...tab
to hold to the breast (cf., g̃iš-gaba-tab) ('breast' (+ locative) + 'to hold, clasp').

gaba...zi(-ga)
to retreat; to depart ('breast' + 'to take away').

gaba$_2$-kar
robber (?) (Akk. *ekēmu(m)*; cf., gaba-kar(-re), 'escapist').

gaba$_2$[KAB]-ra; gaba$_2$-us$_2$; gaba$_2$-ra$_2$[DU]
shepherd's helper; sheep guardian (cf., $^{(lu2)}$kabar; Akk. loanword (?) from *kaparru(m) I*).

gaba$_2$-zu-zu
trainee, apprentice ('left hand' + 'teaching').

$^{(lu2)}$gabar
(cf., $^{(lu2)}$kabar, kapar).

gabu$_2$
(cf., gubu$_3$).

GAD(.KID$_2$).UR$_2$
(cf., umbin).

GAD.NIG̃$_2$-crossed-GAD.NIG̃$_2$
(cf., kinda).

GAD.TAK$_4$.SI
(cf., akkil).

$^{(tug2)}$gada, gad
flax; linen; linen cloth, sheet, or clothing (gu, 'flax, thread', + da, 'to protect'; Akk. *kitû(m)*) [GADA archaic frequency: 96; concatenation of 2 sign variants].

gada-bar-dul$_5$[TUG$_2$]
long linen coat ('linen' + 'long coat').

gada-dilmun-u$_3$-lal
a dress of Dilmun linen ('linen' + 'Dilmun' + pronominal prefix + 'to hang').

gada-gin[DU]
standard quality linen material ('linen' + 'ordinary').

gada gu-nu
a kind of (fine quality) linen ('linen' + gunu$_3$, 'to be good, beautiful').

gada-maḫ-g̃iš-la$_2$
spread out linen ('linen' + 'large' + 'tool' + 'to extend').

gada-nig̃$_2$-dun$_3$-du$_3$
a linen garment ('linen' + 'object' + 'to bring low' + 'to make').

$^{(g̃iš)}$gag, kak
peg; nail, spike; bone; rod; hinge, joint, knee (reduplicated to be long and neck-like; cf., gub) [KAK archaic frequency: 46; concatenates 2 sign variants].

^{uruda}gag-a-ra-ab
metal door pin ?, manufactured in great numbers ('peg' + 'brewing vessel; something that interlocks').

^{uruda}gag-ge-guru$_7$
a rare copper object ('heaping up to the peg/ knee').

^{u2}gag-gu$_5$-uš-tur
a savory herb, perhaps thyme ('small spiny undergrowth'; Akk., *sataru(m)*; cf., *ḫašû(m) III*, *zambūru*).

gag-ḫa-ḫar-ra-na
a peg or nail ('peg' + 'roads' ?).

$^{g̃iš}$GAG+LIŠ-la$_{(2)}$; $^{g̃iš}$GAG-SILA$_3$
cart; chariot (Akk., *saparru(m)*, *narkabtu(m)*).

gag-maš
a peg or nail ('peg' + 'one-half').

$^{g̃iš}$gag-si-sa$_2$
a type of arrow ('peg, nail' + 'to make straight').

$^{g̃iš}$GAG-SILA$_3$
(cf., $^{g̃iš}$GAG+LIŠ-la$_{(2)}$).

$^{(g̃iš)}$gag-ti
arrow(head) ('peg, nail' + 'arrow').

^{uzu}gag-ti
breastbone, of human or animal ('bone, joint' + 'rib').

$^{(uruda/g̃iš)}$gag-u$_4$-tag-ga
a type of arrow (cf., gu$_4$-u$_4$-tag-ga = Akk., *sâru(m)*, 'to rotate, dance').

gag-us$_2$
goad ('nail' + 'to drive'; cf., bar-us$_2$^{uruda}).

gag-zag-ga, gag-za$_3$-ga
side (?) peg ('peg' + 'side, boundary').

gag-zu$_2$[KA]$^{zabar/uruda/na4}$
nails of bronze, copper, and stone - measured in large numbers ('peg' + 'tooth').

gagar [KI]
area.

gagig
to lament; to wail (gu$_3$, 'to exclaim', + gig, 'illness; injury').

gakkul[U.DIM×ŠE]; gakkul$_3$ [U.DIM]
clay brewing-vessel, mash tun, fermenting vat; a spherical type of lettuce.

gal, g̃al
n., a large or fancy cup, in bronze, gold, silver, or copper, weighing from ½ to 1

ma-na (30 to 60 gin_2); chief; eldest son.

adj., big, large; important; mighty; great; older; adult, grown-up; fancy (milk or chamber + abundant, numerous) [GAL archaic frequency: 1004; concatenation of 2 sign variants].

adv., greatly.

gal-an-zu
(cf., gal-zu).

gal(-gal)-bi
n., its big ones; adults (redup. 'great' + 'its').

adj., great; large; voluminous.

adv., greatly; in grandiose fashion ('great' + adverbial force suffix).

gal-di
exalted, prominent; renowned ('large' + 'doing').

gal-gal-di
boaster (reduplicated 'large' + 'doing').

gal-le-eš
n., greatness ('great' + adverbial 'case marker').

adj., great; outstanding.

adv., greatly; grandly.

gal-nar
head musician ('large' + 'musician').

GAL.NI
(cf., santana).

gal-tab-bu-um
a type of fat-tailed, fat-rumped sheep with two hanging ropes of fat (that may have required a cart or contraption to support off the ground) ('large' + 'double' + 'to sprout; to pull' ? + Akkadian nominative singular ending).

gal$^{(zabar)}$-tur
a small (bronze) cup/beaker ('a fancy cup' + 'small').

gal-ug̃a$_3$
overseer ('large' + 'people'; cf., ugula).

GAL.URI
(cf., $kindagal_2$).

gal-zu; gal-an-zu
wise; omniscient; intelligent; skillful ('large' [+ 'heaven'] + 'knowing').

gal_4(-la), $gala_2$[MUNUS.LA]
vagina, vulva, female genitalia (throat-like chamber + la, 'bliss'; cf., la-ga).

gal_5, gul_3
to overwhelm.

gal_5-la_2(-gal), g̃ul$_3$-la_2(-gal)
police chief, gendarme, constable, deputy, bailiff; a demon ('to overwhelm' + 'to force into; to look after' [+ 'big']).

gala[G̃IŠ$_3$.DUR_2]
cantor, ritual singer, lamentation priest, elegist; transvestite (throat + la, 'youthful freshness and beauty').

gala-maḫ
chief lamentation priest ('cantor' + 'foremost').

$gala_{3,4,5}$
(cf., $kala_{3,4,5}$).

galam
n., stairs, rungs (of ladder) (gal, 'big, great', + lam_2, 'an awe-inspiring quality'; cf., me-lam_2).

v., to ascend, climb; to skillfully build; to artfully fashion.

adj., ingenious, clever, artistic, skillful, complicated, elaborate; tall, high.

galam-kad_5
artfully made ('artistic' + 'to bind together').

galam-ma
exalted one ('elaborate' + nominative).

galam-ma ḫu-ru
clever fool ('ingenious, elaborate' + nominative + 'idiot, hillbilly').

galla, $gulla_x$
police chief, constable; a demon (cf., gal_5-la_2).

gam
n., decline, incline; death; depth (cf., gur_2).

v., to bend, curve; to bow down, kneel (for someone: dative; direction: terminative); to shrivel; to succumb; to put to death (with comitative) (like a circle + to be).

adj., weak.

gam-gam
to submit; to subdue (reduplicated 'to bow down, kneel').

^ku6^gam-gam(-ma)
a fish (Pomadasys stridens) (cf., ^(g̃iš)^šim-gam(-gam)-ma) (reduplicated 'curved; shriveled').

^g̃iš^gam-ma
ring, handle or grip; the thwart(s) of a boat ('curved' + nominative).

gam_3 [PAP.NA_2]
n., sickle; handle; hilt (cf., zubi) (like a circle + to be).

v., to shine, glitter (like a crown, $aga_{(3)}$, + to be).

gam_3-gam_3^mušen^; gam_4-gam^mušen^
a diving water bird, probably the grebe, that feeds young at the nest (unlike ducks) (the sound of its call).

gamar
to be overwhelming (gam, 'to kneel', + mer, 'violent storm').

$gambi_x$ [SAL.UŠ.DI]^mušen^
an aquatic bird.

^u2^gamun [TIN.TIR]; ^u2^$gamun_2$ [TIR]
a spice or seed measured by weight - cumin, or caraway seed (gar_3, 'cake', + mun, 'salt'; Akk. *kamūnu(m) I*).

^(g̃iš/dug)^gan, gana, kan
n., stand, rack, support (for a vessel or food); a large container or pitcher for liquids; pestle, grinding stone (cf., g̃iš-gan(-na)) (circular + to raise high; Akk., *kannu(m) I*) [GAN archaic frequency: 125; concatenation of 4 sign variants].

v., to bring forth, bear, give birth.

adj., childbearing, pregnant.

^iti^gan-gan-e_3
calendar month 9 at Nippur during Ur III.

^(siki/tug2)^GAN-me-da
(cf., ^(siki/tug2)^ẖ$e_{(2)}$-me-da).

gan-šub-ba
mange, mites (cf., ^(lu2)^saẖar-šub-ba) ('to bear' + 'to fall, neglect' + nominative).

gan-tuš
tenant ('I shall occupy'; cf., ga-an-tuš).

gan-tuš-tur-ra
minor tenant ('tenant' + 'little' + nominative).

$gana_2$, gan_2
tract of tilled land, field parcel, plot (assigned to an individual); (flat) surface, plane; measure of surface; shape, outline; cultivated land alongside canal; cultivation (cf., ašag; iku) (cf., Orel & Stolbova #890, ***gan-** "field") [GAN_2 archaic frequency: 209].

$gana_2$-APIN
(cf., $gana_2$-uru_4).

$gana_2$-bala-a
a field being rotated ('field' + 'to revolve' + nominative).

$gana_2$-dab_5-ba
a field seized by the state ('field' + 'to seize' + nominative).

$gana_2$-ga
hill country ('land' + 'milk').

^(lu2)^$gana_2$-gid_2
field surveyor; survey team; adjective for surveying pole (gi) or rope ($eš_2$) ('field parcel' + 'to measure, survey').

$gana_2$-gu_4
plow land; demesne - a term for a unit of land administered by an institutional administrator (sag̃g̃a or šabra) and managed by a cultivator (engar) or one of his subordinates, principally to meet the internal needs of the institutional estate that owned the land; domain ('field' + 'ox').

$gana_2$-il_2
taxable land or field ('land' + 'to carry').

iti$gana_2$-maš
calendar month 1 at Lagaš during Ur III.

$gana_2$-nag̃-du_{11}-ga
a flooded field ('field' + 'drink' + 'to effect' + nominative).

$gana_2$-su_3
uncultivated or unproductive land (not necessarily unsown land; cf., $buru_{14}$-bala, 'fallow land') ('land' + sug_4/su_3(-g), 'empty').

$gana_2$-še
grain land, land for growing grain, as opposed to vegetables or trees ('land' + 'grain').

$gana_2$ šuku(-ra-k)
(cf., ašag šuku(-ra-k)).

$gana_2$-tab-ba
a field made fertile (by flooding, to wash out the salt) ('field' + 'to join; to inaugurate' + nominative).

g̃iš$gana_2$-ur_3
harrow ('field' + 'to drag across').

$gana_2$-uru_4[APIN]-a
a cultivated field ('field' + 'to cultivate' + nominative).

$gana_2$-uru_4-la_2
leasehold land for cultivating, rented to farmers for one-third or one-half of the harvest, paid in both silver and barley. The rent was less in the preSargonic period, amounting to 1/7 to 1/8 of the yield. An additional small tax ($maš_{(2)}$-a-$ša_3$-ga) to finance the cost of irrigation was paid in advance ('field' + 'to cultivate' + 'to pay').

$gana_2$-zi(-da)
cultivated field ('field' + 'to strengthen' + nominative).

$ganam_4$, $gana_4$
(cf., u_8).

$ganam_6$, $gana_6$ [$DARA_4$]
ewe.

ganba
marketplace; price equivalent, exchange rate.

$ganzer_{(2,3)}$
darkness; entrance to the netherworld; flame (cf., ga-an-zir_2) (ga-ĩ-n-ze_2-er, 'I will destroy').

gar
(cf., g̃ar).

gar_3, kar_3
knob; pommel; peak; hair lock on the back of the head (sign of a slave = Akk. *abbuttu(m)*; cf., $kiši_4$...aka); cultivated area, field; cake; filled sack (of silver ?) = purse; used for round and high objects ('circular' + 'to send forth; to protect').

gar_3(-ra)-du
warrior, soldier (Akk. loanword from *qardu* and *qarādu II*, 'valiant'; 'to be warlike').

gar_4[GUD/GUŘ]
early (the 'bull of the sun', Mercury, can only be seen right before sunrise; cf., gu_4-ud; Akk. *ḫarpu(m)*).

$gara_{2,9,10}$, $gar_{2,9,10,11,12}$
thick milk, cream; cheese (Akk. *lišdum*; ga, 'milk', + ra, 'to stir') [$GARA_2$ archaic frequency: 106; concatenation of 2 sign variants].

garadin$_{(3,4,5)}$, karadin$_{(3,4,5)}$
shock, pile of sheaves (on a harvested field) (guru$_7$, 'grain heap', + tun$_{(2)}$, 'to constrict').

garaš
straw; supply master.

garaš$_2$, karaš
military encampment; catastrophe.

garaš$_{3,4}$
decision; oracle.

garaš$_{3,4}$^{sar}
leek(s) (cf., ga-raš^{sar}).

garza
(cf., g̃arza).

gašam
n., master craftsman, artisan; skilled person; job, work; office holder; money-lender; wisdom.

adj., intelligent; clever; gifted (cf., galam, 'ingenious'; gal, 'great', + ?).

gašan
lady, mistress; queen (cf., ga-ša-an) (Emesal dialect word, in which nin becomes šan).

gaššu
(cf., gašam).

gaz$_{(2)}$
n., break, fracture; powder; war (chamber + repetitive motion; cf., [g̃iš]nag̃a$_{3,4}$, nag̃$_x$[GAZ, KUM]).

v., to break; (in math. texts) to divide; to smash, crush by pounding; to kill, slaughter (with -da-); to vanquish, defeat.

(lu2)gaz-zid$_2$-da; ka-zid$_2$-da
miller ('to crush, powder' + 'flour' + nominative).

gazi
a pungent spice - cassia or black mustard, used in meat dishes - reserved for the well-to-do (Sum. 'let it breathe'; Akk. *kasû II)* [GAZI archaic frequency: 14].

(g̃iš)gazinbu, gazimbi, gazibu[BU]
pole; stake; beam.

ge$_{(2,4,6)}$
young girl (Emesal dialect for geme$_2$).

ge-e-en$_6$
(cf., gin$_6$, gen$_6$).

ge-en-ge-en
to strengthen; to make right or stable; to perfect (cf., gin$_6$, gen$_6$).

g̃iš ge-en(-ge-na)
part of a boat or structure.

ge-eš-tu
six hundred (gež-u (?); cf., g̃eš$_2$×u).

ge$_6$
(cf., gig$_2$).

ge$_{16}$; ge, gi
judgment; verdict, sentence (cf., gi$_{16}$-sa; gilim-(b); gib) (Akkadian *šipṭu(m) I*).

gel-le-em$_3$
Emesal dialect for ḫa-lam or gilim.

geme$_2$, g̃eme$_2$(?)
full-grown woman; workwoman (equivalent in rank and stature to male g̃uruš worker, though usually paid half the wages); female slave; servant; maid; domestic staff; second wife, concubine (gi$_{(4)}$, 'to lock up', cf., gi$_4$-in, 'slave-girl' and gi$_7$-nun, 'slave-girl', or g̃eš, 'tool', + mi$_2$, 'woman').

geme$_2$(-e$_2$)-kikken$_{(2)}$-na
female mill worker ('work-woman' + 'mill house' + genitival a(k); Akk. *ararratu*).

geme$_2$-i$_3$-šur-šur
female oil presser ('work-woman' + 'preparer of sesame oil').

geme$_2$-kar-kid$_{(3)}$
prostitute ('work-woman' + 'prostitute').

$geme_2$-maš
female tender of goats ('work-woman' + 'goats').

$geme_2$-nam-ra(-aka)
female captive ('female slave' + 'taken as prisoner').

$geme_2$-šu-gi_4
old female worker ('work-woman' + 'old').

$geme_2$-uš-bar
female weaver ('work-woman' + 'weaver').

gen_6
(cf., gin_6).

gena, gina[TUR+DIŠ]
(cf., genna, gena, ginna, gina).

genna, gena, ginna, gina[TUR+DIŠ]
n., the planet Saturn; child, baby; son; daughter (possible loan from Akk. *kayyamānu*, *kayyānu*, and *kānu* 'constant'; loan back into Akkadian as *ginû II*, 'child'; cf., gin_6, gen_6 and g̃in, g̃en).

adj., constant; regular; small.

geš
(cf., g̃iš).

gešta, $geš_{2,3,4}$, $giš_{2,3}$
(cf., g̃ešta, g̃e$š_{2,3,4}$, g̃i$š_{2,3}$).

gi, ge
reed; length measure, reed = 6 cubits = 3 meters (circular + to sprout) [GI archaic frequency: 484].

gi, ge
(cf., gin_6, gen_6; ge_{16}).

$gi_{(4)}$
to surround, besiege; to lock up (circle + to descend into).

$gi_{(17)}$
n., young man, lad (cf., gi-ru).

adj., small (cf., sig_{17}).

Emesal dialect for tur.

gi-a-dag
raft ('reed' + 'water' + 'resting place').

gi-di(-da)
reed pipe, flute; (drinking) straw ('reed' + 'doing').

gi-dili(-du_3)
a solitary reed (idiomatic expression) ('reed' + 'single' + 'to plant').

$^{g̃iš}$GI.DIM_3.$MA^{meš}$
olive tree; olive(s) (Akkadian *serdu(m)*).

gi(-a)-dirig(-ga)
raft (cf., $^{(gi)}$ušub) ('reed' + 'water' + 'to float' + nominative).

gi-diš-nindan
(cf., gi-nindan).

gi-du_3-a
reed hut; reed fences; high-quality writing stylus ('reed; to surround' + 'to erect' + nominative).

gi-dub-ba
stylus ('reed' + 'tablet' + genitive).

gi-dug_3-ga
sweet reed - perhaps sweet-smelling Cymbopogon ('reed' + 'sweet' + nomin.).

gi-dur
umbilical cord ('reed' + 'bond, tie').

^{šim}gi-dur-ra
aromatic gum resin from the bdellium tree/shrub, similar to myrrh, used in medicines and perfumes ('the binder'; Akk. *budulḫu*).

gi-$duru_5$[GI.A]
supple, swaying reed ('reed' + 'fresh').

gi-er_2-ra
reed pipe for laments; shepherd's pipe ('reed' + 'to lament' + nominative).

gi-ga; gi-gi
(cf., gig-ga).

gi-gi
(variant writing for gilim).

gi-gi-ir; gi_4-gi_4-ra
constantly self-renewing (Akkadian *eddēšû(m)*) (Emesal dialect for $gibil_{(4)}$).

gi-gid_2
musical reed pipe, flute, which could be made of bronze, gold, or silver; a composition or song for such an instrument; a type of garden tree ('reed' + 'to be long'; cf., gi-zi-gid_2-gid_2; Akk., *ebbūbu(m)*).

gi-gu_4-ud
catapult ('reeds' + 'to leap').

gi-gun_4(-na), gi-gu_3-na
sacred building, raised temple, perhaps with 'planted trees', tir; in apposition to u_6-nir, 'ziggurat' (also read as giguna) ('reeds' + 'decorated temple').

gi-gur
reed basket (cf., $^{(gi)}$gur, kur_3) ('reeds' + 'basket').

gi-gur-a-bala
bitumen-sealed basket for carrying water ('basket' + 'water' + 'to transport').

gi-gur-da
a large carrying basket ('basket' + 'to hold').

gi-gur-še-bala
basket for carrying grain ('basket' + 'grain' + 'to transport').

gi-ḫal
a small basket.

gi-il-gi-il-la
harnessed (?) (redup., gil, 'to cross, lie athwart').

gi-ila_2
reed carrier ('reeds' + 'to lift').

gi-in
(cf., gi_4-in, gin_6 and gim/gin_7).

gi-izi-la_2
torch ('reeds' + 'fire' + 'to hold up').

GI.KID.MAḪ
(cf., $muru_{12}$).

GI.KID.$ŠU_2$.MA_2
(cf., $muru_{12}$).

gi...ku_5
to cut reeds ('reeds' + 'to cut').

gi-kud(-a)
cut reed, used to make measurements ('reed' + 'to cut' + nominative).

gi-ma_2-gan^{ki}
reed of Magan = bamboo ('reed' + 'Magan').

^{ĝiš}gi-muš
punting pole for boatman; also, steering oar ('reed' + 'snake').

gi-na
consent; regular contribution (to temple) (cf., gin_6 and ^{gi}na) ('just, firm' + nominative a).

GI.NA.AB.UL; GI.NA.AB.TUM
(cf., šutum; $šutum_2$).

^{lu2}gi-na-ab-$tum_{(2)}$; ^{lu2}ki-na-ab-dam
guarantor of a sale, functioning as a co-seller, against whom the buyer could proceed if the seller did not meet his obligations.

gi-na-tum
security deposit; surety guarantee (Akk. loanword, *kinātum*, plural of *kittu(m) I*, 'reliability').

gi-NE
unsorted, mixed reeds; a class of reeds which workers were able to make in greater numbers than split reeds (gi-šid); could be fed to sheep as fodder ('reeds' + ?).

gi-ne_2-dam
they will prove it (cf., gin_6 and /-ed/).

gi-NI
a scented substance ('reed' + 'oil').

gi-niĝ$_2$(-kaš)-šur-ra
drinking tube or straw ('reed' + 'thing' + 'beer' + 'to flow' + nominative).

gi(-diš)-nindan
measuring rod of one nindan; a symbol of authority ('reed' + 'one' + six meter length measure).

GI.PAD
(cf., ^{gi}šutug).

gi-rim
(cf., gurun).

gi-rin[LAGAB]; gi-rin$_2$; gi-ri$_{(2)}$-in
n., blossom, flower; red carnelian; also a syllabic writing for gurun, 'fruit' (cf., kur-gi-rin$_{(2)}$(-na)^{sar}) ('reed' + 'bright'; cf., u$_2$-ri-in).

adj., pure, spotless; bright, shining; blooming, fruitful; flowered.

gi-ru
young man, lad (in Emesal).

Emesal dialect for tur.

gi-RU.UŠ
uneaten waste from fodder reeds (cf., gur$_5$-RU.UŠ).

gi-sa, ki$_2$-sa; gi(-niĝ$_2$)-sa-ḫa$_2$
bundle (of reeds); math. shape, truncated cone; abutment or platform; used to make lower two-thirds of triangular 'causeway, bund' in river called *appu(m)* (cf., gi$_{16}$-sa) ('reeds' + 'mat, bundle').

gi-saĝ
(reed) fence, enclosure; delicate reed ('reed' + 'first class, prime' ?).

gi-saĝ-ḫul
a type of reed ('reed' + 'head' + 'bad').

gi-sal
reed screen on the roof; eaves ('reeds' + 'to be thin and wide').

gi-SI.A
(cf., $^{(gi)}$ušub; gi(-a)-dirig(-ga)).

gi-sig$_{(3)}$
reed wall, hut ('flattened reed'; Akk. *kupû*).

gi-sun
mature reed used for kindling ('reed' + 'old').

gi-ša$_3$-sur, gi-ša$_3$-šur
sieve ('reeds' + 'intestines' + 'to flow, drip').

gi-šid
split reed for mats, baskets, etc. ('reed' + 'to join, link'; cf., gi-NE).

gi-šul-ḫi
a reed or plant that was used as a medicine (Akk. loanword, *šalāḫu(m)*, 'to pull out, uproot').

gi-til(-le)
to make a verdict final; to enforce a judgment (gi$_{(4)}$, 'to lock up' + 'to finish, complete').

gi-u$_2$(-la$_2$); gi-u$_2$-du$_3$(-du$_3$)
(cf., ^{gi}u$_2$(-la$_2$); ^{gi}u$_2$-du$_3$(-du$_3$)).

gi-UNUG
(cf., giguna, gi-gunu$_4$).

gi-uri$_3$
standard, emblem, post, banner ('reed' + 'standard').

gi...ze$_2$
to cut reeds ('reeds' + 'to cut').

gi-zi, gi-ze
fodder reed; green or cut reed ('reed' + 'life/cut').

gi-zi-gid$_2$-gid$_2$
musical reed pipes ('reed' + 'to breathe' + redup. 'to be long').

$^{(u2/\tilde{g}iš)}$gi-zu$_2$-lum-ma
mullein (*Verbascum*); lampwick (made of mullein leaf); butterfly plant used as drug (cf., ĝiš-lam$_7$) ('reed' + 'date fruit';

Akk. *buṣinnu*, 'mullein', and ^{u2}*kurṣiptu*, 'butterfly plant').

gi_2, ge_2[KID]
reed mat.

$^{(uruda)}gi_2$-dim
spade; water scoop (?) ('reed mat' + 'bond, tie, post'; Akk. *gidimmu*, 'perhaps, water scoop').

gi_3, ge_3[DIŠ]
(cuneiform) wedge; sign.

gi_4, ge_4; gi
to return, come back; to send (back) (with -ši-); to reject, dislike; to overturn; to restore; to put back; to answer (person to whom answer is given resumed by dative verbal prefix, and with -ni-) (*marû* aspect form : gi_4-gi_4) (circular motion + to go out, send) [GI_4 archaic frequency: 37; concatenation of 3 sign variants].

gi_4-an
cultically unfit ? ('to reject' + 'heaven').

gi_4-du_3[GAG]
a rare occupation (cf., zi-gi_4-du_3).

gi_4-gi_4-ra
(cf., gi-gi-ir).

gi_4-in
slave (girl) (occurs in Emesal for $geme_2$) ('to lock up' + 'he, she').

gi_4-me-a-aš
colleague, fellow (cf., nam-gi_4-me-a-aš) ('to return, come back' + 'office, function' + locative + plural suffix).

gi_6
(cf., gig_2).

gi_7
(cf., gir_{15}).

gi_7-nun
slave (girl) ('to lock up' + 'master').

gi_9, ge_9
(cf., gir_{10}).

gi_{16}
(cf., ge_{16}, gib, and gilim-(b)).

gi_{16}[GIL]-da
basket.

gi_{16}-il-gi_{16}-il
Emesal dialect for gilim, 'to destroy'.

gi_{16}-sa(-a); gi-sa; gi_{16}
parched wheat, Arabic *frikeh*, in which usually durum wheat but sometimes bread wheat is harvested while still green and then parched or roasted; (lasting) treasures; jewelry ('wheat' + 'to parch').

adj., lasting; of lasting value.

gi_{16}[GIL]-sa...aka
to treasure highly; to make permanent.

gi_{17}
(cf., gig and $gi_{(17)}$).

gib[GIL],gi_{16}; gib_3[GIG](-ba)
wheat, probably the hard, long-lasting durum wheat which is high in protein and gluten but low in moisture (cf., gilim[-b]).

$gibil_{(4)}$
n., renewal (gub_2, 'to purify, cleanse', + ul, 'to shine') [GIBIL archaic frequency: 77].

v., to renovate; to be(come) new.

adj., new; fresh.

gibil-bi
adv., the first time; anew; in a new way ('new' + adverbial force suffix).

gibil-bi-$še_3$
adv., in a new way ('new' + adverbial force suffixes).

$^{(gi/ĝiš)}$gibil; $gibil_2$[$ŠU_2$.$AŠ_2$]
n., burning tinder, stick; fire-brand, taper; burning (gi, 'reed', + bil, 'to burn') [GIBIL archaic frequency: 77].

v., to burn, incinerate.

adj., glowing; parched.

^{d}gibil$_6$[NE.GI]
the fire god.

gid$_2$[BU]
n., length [BU: archaic frequency: 393; concatenation of 2 sign variants].

v., to stretch out; to lengthen; to flay (hide or skin); to draw, pull, tow; to haul upstream; to measure out; to survey a field; to tax; to manage; to reach out (to take); to receive (to be long and throat-like with motion away from).

adj., long; distant.

^{gi}gid$_2$
flute, pipe.

gid$_2$-bi
its length.

gid$_2$-i
to pull out, to tighten, to increase (such as a musical string) ('to draw, pull, stretch out' + e$_3$; i, 'to go out, emerge; to lead or bring out; to rise; to sprout; to be or become visible ').

gidim$_{(2,4,7)}$
spirit of illness or death; ghost, shade (gig, 'to be sick', + dim$_3$, 'sickness demon', or gi$_6$, 'black', + dim$_4$, 'to approach').

gidim$_6$, gidi$_6$
eclipsed, darkened (gig$_2$/gi$_6$, 'black', + dim$_2$, 'to make').

gig, gi$_{17}$[GIG$_2$.NUNUZ]
n., illness; injury (cf., gib$_3$(-ba)) (throat + i, 'cry of pain', + throat) [GIG archaic frequency: 16].

v., to be/make sick; to be painful to (with dative); to reject.

adj., sick; painful; bitter.

adv., painfully; bitterly.

gig-ga; gig-a; gi-ga; gi-gi
n., wound, lesion; suffering ('injury; bitter' + nominalization suffix -a).

adj., very painful; bitter.

adv., painfully; bitterly.

gig(-še$_3$)...g̃ar
to cause trouble; to be angry at ('injury' + terminative + 'to set').

GIG-ma
(cf., sim$_x$[GIG]-ma).

gig$_2$, gi$_6$(g), ku$_{10}$[MI]
v., to be black or dark (ku$_{10}$: reduplication class; cf., g̃i$_6$, 'night/ shade') [GI$_6$ archaic frequency: 105].

adj., black; dark; shady (cf., kukku$_2$).

gig$_3$
(cf., gib).

gigam[LU$_2$.LU$_2$@180; LU$_2$&LU$_2$]
quarrel, conflict, war (cf., gug$_5$, 'hostility, war'; inbir, 'conflict, war'; gig, 'injury', + am$_3$, 'to be').

$^{g̃iš}$gigir$_{(2)}$
wheel(s); chariot; wagon; coach (reduplicated gur$_4$/gir$_8$, 'to turn, roll') [PU$_2$ archaic frequency: 37].

gigri$_2$[KAŠ4.KAŠ4/GIR5.GIR5]; gigri[SUḪUŠ.SUḪUŠ/GIR6.GIR6]
to go into hiding; to creep, slink, wiggle; to slip into; to dive; to sink, founder (reduplicated giri$_5$, 'to seek refuge'; Akk., *šerû I*, 'to take refuge').

giguna[GI.UNUG(.GI)]
(cf., gi-gunu$_4$).

gig̃$_4$
(cf., gin$_2$).

gil
(cf., gilim).

gil-le-em$_3$
Emesal dialect for ḫa-lam or gilim.

$^{(gi)}$gilim(-b), gilib$_x$, gili, gil, gi$_{16}$, ge$_{16}$
n., reed bundle; reed rope; reed post; dancer; bride crown (cf., gi$_{16}$-sa) (gi, 'reeds', + lam, 'abundance'; Akk. *kilimbu*, 'reed bundle') [GIL archaic frequency: 1].

v., to twist, twine together; to twine reeds into a bundle or rope; to bend, bow; to cross, bar, block; to fence off; to lie athwart; to go across; to cross plow; to mess up; to destroy.

adj., to be twisted, tangled; opaque; to be corrupted, confused; destroyed (cf., gil-le-em_3 and ḫa-lam).

gim
(cf., dim_2).

-gim, kim, gin_7
equative postposition; as, like; instead of; equals; just as, during - ThSLa §214 - §220 (syllabic spellings indicate both gim and gin_7; cf., Akk. *kīma* with same meanings).

GIM-ma
(cf., dim_2-ma).

gim_4, im_2
n., runner (cf., $kaš_4$).

v., to trot, run (mainly said of animals). (gi_4, 'to come back' + im, 'wind').

gim_7
(cf., kim_3).

-gin[DU]
(cf., gin_6/-gin; g̃en, g̃in).

gin_2, $gig̃_4$[DUN_3*gunû*]
small ax; adze; axehead used as money; shekel (of silver) = ca. 8.333 grams; a surface area measure, 1/60 square nindan (sar) = 180 surface še = 2160 (=36,0) square fingers; a volume measure, = 0.3 cubic meters (Akk. *pāšu(m)*, 'axe, adze'; *šiqlu*, 'shekel') (Akk. *kīnu* 'true measure', cf., Orel & Stolbova #1459, ***kin-** "count") [TUN_3 archaic frequency: 96; concatenates 3 sign variants].

$^{uruda}gin_2$-sal
a light metal hoe.

gin_2-tur
a surface area measure, little shekel = 1/60 shekel = 1/3600 square nindan (sar) = 3 surface še = 36 square fingers = surface of the side of a cube of 1 $sila_3$ capacity.

gin_3[KUR]
lapis lazuli (igi, 'eye', + na_4, 'pebble, stone', but cf., $gunu_3$, 'decorated with colors, lines, spots').

gin_4
a kind of grass (Akk. *kuštu*).

gin_6, gen_6, gi, ge[GI]; gi-in; gi-na; -gin[DU]
n., verdict; steadiness, reliability, constancy.

v., to act justly; to stabilize, strengthen, support; to fix; to examine, confirm, prove, determine; to consent, agree; to establish something as the property of someone (dative); to award, transfer; to standardize (loanword from Semitic, Orel & Stolbova #1403, ***ka'Vn-** 'be true', Akkadian *kânu*; cf., g̃in, g̃en).

adj., ordinary; firm, solid, steadfast; fixed; just; reliable, trustworthy; correct.

adv., usually.

-gin_7
(this is sometimes the preferred form, but cf., gim).

-gin_7-nam
just as - occurs after finite verb in temporal sense; equals (in OB math. texts) - ThSLa §218 ('to be as').

gir, kir
cow or mare of intermediate age; sow; a fish, possibly a carangid (cf., $^{(dug)}kir_2$, gir_9; $^{(dug)}kir$, gir) (ki, 'place', + $ir_{(2)}$, 'fluid secretion') [GIR archaic frequency: 28; concatenation of 4 sign variants].

$^{(ku6)}$GIR-ab-ba
fish from the sea marsh - could be read peš-ab-ba ('cow' + 'sea'; cf., IE **peisk(o)**).

gir-gi4-$lu_2^{mušen}$
(cf., $g̃ir_3$-gi-lum/$lu^{mušen}$).

$^{(ku6)}$GIR-gid_2
a variety of fish ('cow' + 'long').

gir_4, kir_{13}[U.AD]
kiln (for lime or bitumen); oven (cf., $udun_x$) (ki,'place', + ara_4, 'to shine, blaze'; Akk. *kīru(m) I*, 'oven, kiln') [GIR_4 archaic frequency: 1].

gir_4-bil
furnaceman, stoker ('kiln' + 'to burn').

gir_5[$KAŠ_4$], $giri_5$
n., refugee, stranger (seems cognate to $\tilde{g}iri_{2,3}$ and $\tilde{g}iri_{16}$, but no lexical evidence for $\tilde{g}iri_5$ reading).

v., to run, trot; to seek refuge, hide; to dive; to drown.

gir_5-gir_5^{ku6}
a fish (reduplicated 'to seek refuge, hide'; cf., $gigri_2$).

gir_5-ra
courier ('to run, trot' + nominative).

gir_7[DU]
to carry.

gir_9
(cf., kir_2).

gir_{10}, gi_9, ge_9[NE]
anger, fury (compare bir_9).

$giri_{11}$, gir_{11}[KEŠDA]
to be tidy, neat; to bind up (cf., ḫir, kirid) (gi_4,'to restore', + ri, 'to sweep away').

gir_{15}, gi_7 [KU]
domestic, civilized; belonging to the native in-group; noble (circle + city) [$ŠE_3$ archaic frequency: 152].

gir_{15}/gi_7-nun
lofty noble (an adjective applied to Enlil) ('noble' + 'royal').

$^d gira_3$, $^d gir_{18}$[NE.GI]
the fire god (compare $^d gibil_6$).

$giri_{16}$
(cf., $\tilde{g}iri_{16}$).

$giri_{17}$, gir_{17}
(cf., $kiri_3$).

$giri_{17}$-zal
(cf., $kiri_3$-zal).

$^d gir_{18}$
(cf., $^d gira_3$).

girim, girin, gir_8
piece of clay; to detach a piece of clay; to creep or glide on the ground (gur_5, 'to separate, divide', + imi/im, 'clay'; cf., gurun).

$girim_3$, $girin_2$
(cf., gurun).

giriš
butterfly; moth.

gissu
(cf., g̃issu, g̃izzu).

giš
(cf., g̃iš).

gu
string, thread; wool yarn; flax (used for linen); hemp; rope; snare; net; orig. word for needle (circular + grass-like) [GU archaic frequency: 53].

Emesal dialect for gu_2, 'legumes'.

gu-dili(-a)...e_3
'stringing [their heads] on one string'; enumerate their number, from a counting device to keep track of people (per M. Civil in *Wisdom, Gods, and Literature* - W.G. Lambert festschrift) ('string' + 'single' + locative + 'to bring out').

gu-du; gu-di
anus; rump; spider's spinneret; a musical instrument ('thread' + 'it comes').

gu-du gun_3-a
multi-colored thread.

gu...dub_2; gu...tag
to align; to adjust (with a string) ('string' + 'to strike/to touch').

gu-gu-tum
a fodder plant.

gu-kilib(-ba)
bale - preferred reading now is gu-niĝin$_2$-ba ('net' + Umma reading for LAGAB, 'package, bundle' + inanimate pronoun + locative).

gu-la
large, great; eldest (cf., gal; gu-ul).

gu...lal/la$_2$
to set out a snare; to bind ('string' + 'to place, set, stretch, extend').

gu-lal/la$_2$
a measure of unknown size from Nippur; snare; trapper ('string' + 'to place, set, stretch, extend').

gu-mur$_7$
backbone ('needle; string' + 'neck, back, ridge').

gu-niĝin$_2$[LAGAB](-na)
bale ('net' + 'circle, whole').

gu-nu
(cf., gunu$_3$).

gu-ru-um
(cf., gurum).

gu-su$_9$
shaggy (phonetic for guz, guzu).

gu$_{(3)}$-sum
impression or line on a tablet; wedge; sign ('sound' + 'to give'; cf., gi$_3$).

gu ša$_3$-gu
a fine quality linen thread ('thread' + 'heart' + 'flax').

gu-ud^{ku6}
carp (cf., eštub^{ku6}[GUD]) ('dancing, leaping fish').

gu-ul
to enlarge; to mature; to increase; to make numerous; to be great, exalted; sometimes = gul, 'to destroy' (cf., gal; gu-la).

gu-ur$_2$^{mušen}
syllabic writing for buru$_4$^{mušen}.

$^{(ĝiš)}$gu-za
throne; armchair (Akk., *kussû(m)*, 'chair, stool, throne', direction of loan unclear - metathesis of Orel & Stolbova #153 ***'Vsuk-** 'dwell, sit' ?; cf., guzza).

gu-za-la$_2$
throne-bearer; chair-bearer; a functionary or bureaucrat (who followed the ruler with his chair in readiness ?) ('throne; chair' + 'to hold up').

^{ĝiš}gu-za-sir$_3$-da
litter, sedan chair ('throne, chair' + 'carrying-pole').

gu$_2$
neck; nape; river bank; side; other side; edge; front; vegetable, legume, pulse, chick pea (for 'land, district' cf., gun$_2$; for 'load, burden; talent' cf., gun; gun$_2$, gu$_2$) (circular + u$_5$, 'on top of'; cf., Orel & Stolbova #982, ***gun-** "occiput, neck, nape") [GU$_2$ archaic frequency: 34].

gu$_2$
entirety, assemblage, all (cf., gukin$_{(2)}$; gu$_2$...dirig / gu$_2$...si(-a); gu$_2$-en(-na)).

gu$_{2,4}$
(cf., gud$_{(2)}$).

gu$_2$...aka
to submit; to bow, to someone: dative ('neck' + 'to do'; cf., gu$_2$...ĝar).

gu$_2$-an-še$_3$
sum, of goods received; all things considered ('loads' + 'up').

gu$_2$-bala
the turning edge ('edge' + 'to revolve').

gu$_2$-bar
mane; nape of the neck; lock of hair at the back; hair-style; halter, tether; enemy ('neck' + 'outside; fleece').

gu$_2$...dirig
to sum accounts ('loads' + 'to add'; cf., gu$_2$...si(-a)).

gu$_2$...du$_3$
to despise; to neglect ('neck' + 'to fasten, plant').

gu$_2$-du$_3$-a
enemy; disliked, hated ('neck' + 'to fasten, plant' + nominative).

gu$_2$...du$_8$
to remove the burden ('neck/load' + 'to loosen, release').

gu$_2$...e$_3$
to cover; to clothe; to insulate ('neck; edge' + 'to extend').

$^{(tug2)}$gu$_2$-e$_3$
wrap, stole, shawl; insulation; armor; fat, tallow ? (on a goat).

gu$_2$-en(-na)
assembly; entire assemblage; assembly chamber; throne room (cf., im-gu$_2$(-en-na)) (cf., gu$_2$...si(-a), 'to assemble').

gu$_2$-en-bar-ra
outer throne room.

gu$_2$-erim$_2$
enemy ('neck' + 'evil, hostile').

gu$_2$-erim$_2$-ĝal$_2$
wicked, hostile ('neck' + 'evil, hostile' + 'having').

^{ĝiš}gu$_2$-eš; ^{ĝiš}gu$_2$-uš
wooden neck(-part) (of the lyre) ('neck' + 'many').

$^{(u2)}$gu$_2$-gal(-la)
big pulse, which evidence shows to be a winter crop, probably the broad bean (fava bean) or the chick pea; red berry of box-thorn (*abulīlu*) ('the bean that is large').

gu$_2$-gal
foremost; leader, king ('neck' + 'large').

gu$_2$-gal-ḪAR-ra
ground beans ('large bean' + ar$_3$/ur$_5$, 'to grind', + nominative).

$^{(lu2)}$gu$_2$-gal; ku$_3$-ĝal$_2$
irrigation controller; village-based canal inspector ('river bank' + 'large').

gu$_2$...gid$_2$
'to stretch the neck' as something that mourners do; to bend downwards; to lodge; to spy; to rob ('neck' + 'to stretch out').

^{ĝiš}gu$_2$-gid$_2$-gid$_2$
an agricultural tool ('neck' + reduplicated 'long').

gu$_2$...gil
to strike a person down ('neck' + 'to cross; to lie athwart').

gu$_2$-gil
criminal, wrongdoer; inciter, agitater (?).

gu$_2$-gir(-esir$_2$)
collection/processing of bitumen, asphalt - found in pools or on the surface of water, having seeped up from the formations below; an occupation ('edge of pool' + 'place of liquid secretion' + 'bitumen, asphalt').

gu$_2$-gu$_2$
various pulses/legumes (reduplicated 'pulse/legume').

gu$_2$-gu$_2$-GUD
a type of pea (reduplicated 'chick pea/bean' + 'ox, bull').

gu$_2$-gu$_2$-UḪ
a type of pea (reduplicated 'chick pea/bean' + 'insect, vermin').

gu$_2$...gur
to gather, collect, amass, pile up (often with -da-; often reduplicated) ('chick pea/bean' + 'basket').

gu$_2$-gur$_5$(-uš)...dug$_4$/du$_{11}$/e
to cut down; to strip; to be stripped ('neck' + 'to separate' + 'to lift, support' + 'to effect').

gu_2 (ĝiš)...$ĝal_2$
to submit (to someone: dative); to obey ('neck' + 'yoke' + 'to place').

gu_2...ĝar/$ĝa_2$-$ĝa_2$
to collect, gather, assemble; to stack up, pile ('neck; load' + 'to deliver').

gu_2...ĝar/$ĝa_2$-$ĝa_2$
to submit (intransitive use); to subdue, subjugate (transitive use) ('neck' + 'to set down'; cf., gu_2...aka).

gu_2-a...ĝar/$ĝa_2$-$ĝa_2$
(cf., ugu_2...ba-a-ĝar which is the later Neo-Sumerian form of this Old Sumerian original) ('neck' + 'upon' + 'to place [a load of debt]').

gu_2-$ĝiri_{3/16}$
breach (cf., gu_2 $ĝiri_{16}$...ĝar).

gu_2 $ĝiri_{16}$...ĝar/$ĝa_2$-$ĝa_2$
to breach walls ('to subjugate' + 'fortress').

gu_2-ĝiš
(cf., gun_2-ĝiš).

gu_2 i_7(-da)
bank; quay ('bank' + 'river').

gu_2-ki-$ĝal_2$
submissive ('neck' + 'ground' + 'placing').

gu_2-$kiĝ_2$
(cf., $gukin_{(2)}$).

gu_2...kud
to cut (off) the neck ('neck' + 'to cut').

gu_2...lal/la_2
to bow down; to kneel; to lean over (a wall, bad_3); to yoke, hitch up, harness; to embrace; to wrap; to tie up, knot; to throttle, constrict ('neck' + 'to hang; to stretch, reach').

gu_2-la_2
neck collar, harness, yoke; plow-team; (cloth) cover, wrap.

gu_2-da...lal/la_2
to embrace, join ('neck' + comitative suffix 'with' + 'to stretch').

gu_2-ki-$še_3$...lal/la_2
to fall prostrate ('neck' + 'ground' + terminative postposition + 'to hang, stretch').

gu_2-tar...lal/la_2
to style or dress hair; to bind an animal's mane ('neck' + 'to cut, determine' + 'to lift').

gu_2-zag(-ga)...lal/la_2
to lie (transversely) across; to loll (lifelessly) ('neck' + 'barrier' + 'to stretch').

gu_2...mar
Emesal dialect for gu_2...ĝar, 'to pile up'.

$^{(kaš)}gu_2$-me-ze_2
a type of beer, ale; an expensive and noisy (?) beer suitable for libations.

gu_2-mun
caraway ('pea' + 'salt').

gu_2-na; gu_2-un
burden; tax; (annual) tribute; fee; rent (cf., gun[GU_2-UN]; gun_2/gu_2; 'neck' + locative).

$^{ĝiš}gu_2$-ne-saĝ(-$ĝa_2$)
a cabinet in the place of first fruit libation offerings.

$^{(kaš)}gu_2$-ne-saĝ(-$ĝa_2$)
(cf., $^{(kaš)}gu_2$-nisaĝ).

$^{(GIG)}gu_2$-nida[NUNUZ]
a type of gluten enriched grain used for breads and pastries; naked barley (Akk., *gulbūtu*; cf., ziz_2-gu_2-nida).

gu_2-$niĝ_2$-ar_3-ra
common vetch or bitter vetch (Akkadian *kiššanu*) - similar to lentils, but bitter vetch requires cooking to remove a neurotoxin; lentils (Akkadian *kakkû(m)*) (only during the Old Babylonian period); a leguminous vegetable grown mainly as animal

fodder ('pea for grinding - lentil seeds are indigestible if the outer skin of the seeds is not removed through roasting or grinding'; cf., $ni\tilde{g}_2$-ar_3-ra, 'milled grain; barley groats', gu_2-tur, 'field pea or lentil', and gu_2-šeš, 'bitter vetch' in Hittite texts).

(kaš)gu_2-nisağ; (kaš)gu_2-ne-sağ (-$\tilde{g}a_2$)
first fruits libation offering beer (cf., nisağ).

gu_2...peš
to stiffen the neck ('neck' + 'to expand'; cf., šu...peš).

gu_2-PU_2
an occupation ('side, bank' + 'reservoir'; cf., (lu2)gu_2-gal; ku_3-$\tilde{g}al_2$).

gu_2-ri(-ta)
on the opposite bank; from the other side ('side, bank' + 'that' + 'from').

gu_2-sa(-a-gig)
neck tendon ('neck' + 'sinew, tendon' + 'bitter tears' ?; Akk., *dâdānū*, 'tendon of the neck').

gu_2...si(-a)
to assemble, organize, gather around (with loc.term. suffix -e on inanimate indirect objects) ('necks' + 'to be upright, in order, and still'; cf., gu_2...dirig).

gu_2-si-a; gu_2-sa
entirety.

gu_2-su_4
shaggy (phonetic for guz, guzu).

gu_2-$še_3$
up to the edge; to the other side ('side, bank' + terminative postposition).

gu_2-šeš
Sumerogram in Hittite texts, bitter vetch, used for human consumption after proper cooking to remove a neurotoxin ('pea' + 'bitter'; cf., gu_2-$ni\tilde{g}_2$-ar_3-ra).

gu_2...šub
to be lax with respect; to scorn; to neglect (with -ši-) ('neck' + 'to make fall').

gu_2-šub-ba
arm; anger ('neck' + 'to fall').

gu_2-tar; gu_2-tal_2
back; back of the head; shoulders ('neck' + 'to cut (hair)'/'to spread, unfold'; Akk., *kutallu(m)*).

gu_2-tar...lal/la_2
to style or dress hair; to bind an animal's mane ('neck' + 'to cut, determine' + 'to lift').

gu_2-tuku
proud; splendid; ideal; mighty; foremost; perfect; most elegant ('neck' + 'having'; cf., sağ-tuku).

gu_2-tur(-tur)
small pulse, either the field pea or lentil ('chick pea/bean' + 'small'; Akk., *kakkû(m)*).

GU_2.UN
tribute, tax; load (cf., gun).

gu_2-ur_5^{mušen}
syllabic writing for $buru_4$^{mušen}.

gu_2...us_2
to raise the neck ('neck' + 'to join').

$^{\tilde{g}iš}gu_2$-uš
(cf., $^{\tilde{g}iš}gu_2$-eš).

gu_2-za
a piece of jewelry ('neck' + 'precious stone').

gu_2-zag(-ga)...lal/la_2
to lie (transversely) across; to loll (lifelessly) ('neck' + 'barrier' + 'to stretch').

gu_2-zal
rogue, scoundrel, criminal ('neck; load' + 'to tarry, wait').

gu_2...zi(-g)
to have success ('neck' + 'to raise').

gu_2-zi-ga
(cf., a_2-gu_2-zi-ga).

gu_2-zi-iz
(cf., ziz_2-gu_2-nida).

gu_3 [KA]
n., noise, sound; voice.

v., to exclaim; to utter a cry (said of an animal) (throat + $u_{(3,4,8)}$, 'cries, screams').

gu_3-an-ne_2-si (-a)
thunder (cf., gu_3...si-il + 'in heaven').

gu_3...balağ
(cf., gu_3...dub_2).

gu_3...de_2
to say; to talk; to speak (to someone); to call (someone); to cry; to exult, sing; to read (aloud) ('sound' + 'to pour out, shape').

gu_3...dub_2
to shout, make a loud noise ('voice' + 'to make tremble').

gu_3...dug_4/du_{11}/di/e
to make a noise or sound ('noise' + 'to effect').

gu_3...e_3
to roar, shriek, cry ('voice' + 'to go out; to send forth').

gu_3...ğar
describes the twanging of bows; to shout; to make a legal claim to something (against someone) (Wilcke prefers this reading to the traditional inim...ğar) ('sound' + 'to deliver').

gu_3-$ğiri_3$
path ('noise' + 'feet').

gu_3-ḫa-mun
harmony ('voice' + 'contrasting, harmonizing').

gu_3-$kiri_6$ [SAR]
battle cry ('sound' + 'orchard' ?; cf., gu_3-ri-a and akkil; Akk. *tanūqātu(m)*).

gu_3...mur
to roar, bray, bellow, shout; to rumble (of storm) ('sound' + 'lungs').

gu_3-mur-aka
hero; professional mourner ('to roar, bray' + 'to do').

gu_3-nun...di/e
to make a pleasant/loud sound; to low loudly ('sound' + 'fine, great, deep' + 'to say, do').

${}^{gi}gu_3$-nun-di
flute.

gu_3...ra (-ra)
to shout, roar; to make a complaint, lay a claim ('sound' + 'to strike'; Akk. *šasû(m)*).

gu_3...ra-aḫ
to chatter ('sound' + 'to strike repetitively, shake').

gu_3-ra-aḫ
chattering, noise-making ('sound' + 'to strike repetitively, shake').

gu_3-ri-a
clamor, uproar, protest; cry for aid, help; cry of animals, birds; shouting ('sound' + 'driven').

gu_3...si-il
to scream with an ear-splitting voice ('voice' + 'to split').

gu_3...si-si-ig
to read silently ('voice' + 'to silence').

gu_3...si_3 [SUM]
to bellow (said of cattle) ('sound' + 'to smite; make quake').

gu_3-$teš_2$-a...sig_{10} [SUM]
to be united; to make obedient; to instill harmony ('voice' + 'to come together' + locative + 'to impose, apply').

gu_3...sum
to repeat; to echo; to speak; to talk to (with dative); used especially when speaking to superiors (cf., ka...ba) ('sound' + 'to give, lend').

gu_3-sum
cuneiform wedge; sign (also, gu-sum).

gu_3...ta/ra-de_2
to read out, read aloud, recite ('voice' + ablative infix 'from' + 'to pour out').

gu_3-teš$_2$-a...sig$_{10}$[SUM]
to be united; to make obedient; to instill harmony ('voice' + 'to come together' + locative + 'to impose, apply').

gu_3...tum$_{2/4}$
to call ('noise' + 'to carry').

gu_3-zal
(cf., gu_2-zal).

gu_4-
(cf., gud-).

gu_4-ud
n., the planet Mercury ('bull' + 'sun').

v., to jump; to flutter; to twitch; to dance (reduplication class: gu_4-gu_4-ud).

gu_5-li
(cf., ku-li).

gu_5-ul
great (cf., gal; gu-ul).

gu_7, ku_2
n., food, sustenance; fodder; angle [GU_7 archaic frequency: 236].

v., to eat, swallow, consume, use; to eat up, finish off; to graze; to feed, nurse, fatten, benefit (with -ni-) (throat + u_2, 'food').

gu_7-kur-kur-ra
bread-basket of all the lands ('food, sustenance' + 'lands' + genitive).

gub[DU] (-ba)
v., to stand; to be present; to appear (in court); to be stored; to stand on (with -ni-); to set, erect, install, appoint (singular); to set down in writing; to stand by, to serve (with -da-); to serve somebody (with dative verbal prefix); to do service (with -ši-); to stand aside (with -ta-) (suppletion class verb: singular stem; cf. sug_2) (to be long and throat-like in open container).

adj., describes a young but sexually mature lamb (applied from five months to two years old); weaned or semi-weaned (cf., gaba).

gub-ba-am$_3$
plow animal group assets ('to be standing' or imperative 'station them').

gub_2
to purify, cleanse.

$gubu_3$, gub_3, $gaba_2$, $gabu_2$, gab_2(-bu)
left (hand/side) (cf., ḫab and ḫub$_2$; the left was the hand that stank from wiping excrement) [GUB_3 archaic frequency: 15; concatenation of 4 sign variants].

gub_3-bu
left arm ('left-hand' + nominative with vowel harmony).

gub_3-kaš$_4$
stud farm manager (?) ('left-hand' + 'speed, fluency').

gud, gur̆$_x$, gu_4
n., domestic bull (intact male); steer, bullock (castrated male); ox (steer dedicated to draft work) (regularly followed by ra_2; cf., $gur_{(4)}$) (voice/sound with repetitive processing - refers to the bellow of a bull) [GU_4 archaic frequency: 182].

v., to dance, leap; to skip (a line in a text) (cf., gu_4-ud).

gud^{ku6}; gu-ud^{ku6}
carp (cf., eštub^{ku6}[GUD]) ('dancing, leaping fish').

$gud_{(2)}$, $gu_{2,4}$
warrior.

gud-ab$_2$(-ba)
breeding bull ('bull' + 'cow' + genitive).

gud-ab$_2$(-ḫa$_2$)
herd(s); oxen of various ages and gender; cattle, bovines (collective) ('bull' + 'cow' + 'mixed').

gud-alim
bison ('bull' + 'bison').

gud-am; gu_4-dam
wild bull; a mythological entity ('bull' + 'wild ox'; cf., gud - sun_2).

gud-anše (-ḫa_2)
large animals; livestock ('ox' + 'horse' + 'mixed').

gud-apin
plow ox; generic term for draft oxen ('bull, ox' + 'plow').

gud-apin-ni$\tilde{g}_2$-tug_2
blanket for a plow ox ('bull, ox' + 'plow' + 'thing' + 'cloth garment').

gud-du_7 (-du_7)
perfect, unblemished bull; fierce, spirited, goring ox ('bull, ox' + 'complete, suitable; to butt, gore, toss').

gud-dub
ox (recorded) on a tablet ('bull, ox' + 'tablet').

gud (al/šu_4)-dul_4
an ox that has been yoked ('ox' + al -, 'conjugation prefix', or šuš/šu_4, 'to cover', + 'to yoke').

gud-dun-a
subordinate ox ('bull, ox' + 'subordinate' + nominative).

gud-e-us_2-sa
following the oxen ('cattle' + 'near to' + 'to follow' + nominative; cf., niga gud - e - us_2 - sa).

gud e_3
oxen taken out (of work) ('bull, ox' + 'to exit').

gud e$š_2$-gar_3
working oxen ('bull, ox' + 'assigned task').

gud-gal-gal
full-grown ox ('bull, ox' + reduplicated 'great').

gud-$gana_2$ (-SI)
a festival ('oxen' + 'field parcel'; cf., gud - numun - $gana_2$ and gud - numun - diri, where SI.A = diri, 'excess').

gud-g̃iš
work ox, yoked ox (anywhere from two to seven oxen could be on a plow-team, with four and six being standard); full-grown ox ('bull, ox' + 'tool, yoke, plow').

gud g̃iš (-ur_3)
draft oxen for the harrow, worked immediately after the subsoil plowing ('bull, ox' + 'beam, harrow').

gud g̃iš-du_3-a
breeding bull, seed bull ('full-grown bull, ox' + 'to fasten, plant' + nominative).

gud-la_2-a
harnessed ox ('ox' + 'to harness, hitch' + nominative).

gud-la$ḫ_5$ [DU-DU]
ox driver ('bull, ox' + 'to drive').

gud-mu-x
x years-old ox ('bull, ox' + 'name, year' + number).

gud-murub
(second) front oxen/middle oxen ('bull, ox' + 'middle').

gud-niga
fattened, grain-fed ox ('bull, ox' + 'fattened').

gud-$ninda_2$
breed bull; bull-calf ('bull' + 'seeding apparatus').

gud-numun
draft oxen set to sowing/planting with a seeder-plow, usually mentioned in texts from the sixth, seventh, and eighth months of the year ('ox' + 'seed').

gud-numun-diri
reserve oxen for sowing; or oxen for sowing irregular parcels ('oxen for sowing' + 'excess').

gud-numun-$gana_2$
oxen for sowing on the field ('oxen for sowing' + 'field parcel').

gud-ra
ox driver ('bull, ox' + ra_2, 'to drive along').

gud-saĝ
(first) front oxen ('bull, ox' + 'foremost').

ĝišgud-si-dili [AŠ]
battering ram; siege engine ('single-horned bull'; Akk. *yašibum*).

itigud-si-su
calendar month 2 at Nippur during Ur III.

gud-su_7-ra
threshing ox ('bull, ox' + 'threshing floor').

gud-suḫub_2 [MUL]
grazing or trampling oxen, placed in newly converted wasteland prior to manual cultivation with the ĝiš-gaba-tab, at least partly to kill reeds and unwanted plants; also placed in reservoirs ('bull, ox' + 'to step; to graze').

gud-sun_2
wild-cow; Wild Bull (an attribute of the god Enlil) ('bull, ox' + 'aurochs cow').

gud-šar_2(-a)
perfect bull ('bull' + 'to be many; to slaughter' + nominative).

gud-šu-gi_4
old ox ('bull, ox' + 'old').

gud-šuḫub_2
(cf., gud-suḫub_2).

gud(-apin)-tug_2-sig_{18} [KIN]
ox (yoked) for deep plowing ('ox' + 'plow' + 'to deep plow').

gud-ud-diri(-ga)
(second) rear oxen/additional oxen ('bull, ox' + 'extra').

gud-ud-ri
spare oxen ('bull, ox' + 'to exchange').

gud-ur_3-ra
(first) rear oxen (?) (cf., gud ĝiš(-ur_3)) ('bull, ox' + 'beams').

$gud_{(2)}$, $gu_{2,4}$
warrior.

gud_3 [U_2.KI.SI_3.GA]
nest; shelter.

gud_3...us_2
to build a nest ('nest' + 'to moor, join').

gud_8
short (related to but opposite in meaning to gid_2; cf., lu_2-gud_4, 'short person, dwarf').

$gudibir_2$
war ($gud_{(2)}$, 'warrior', + bir, 'to wreck, murder').

$gudu_4$(-g), $guda_2$ (?)
a ritually pure, linen-clothed priest who cares for and feeds the gods; a low-ranking priest; divinely anointed (gu, 'flax, thread', + dug_3, 'loins'; cf. etymology of gada, 'linen').

gug [ZA.GUL]
monthly offering; brand, birthmark, mole; carnelian stone, sharp blade stone (with na_4).

gug; gug_6
blade; bite; beak; tooth.

gug-kal
shortage, famine (gug, 'monthly offering', + kal-la-kal-la, 'barren, empty').

nindagug_2
cake; pressed-date bread - eaten by royalty, not common folk (gu_7, 'to eat, swallow, consume' + round and neck-like) [GUG_2 archaic frequency: 70; concatenation of 2 sign variants].

u2gug_4; u2gug
a tough clumpy grass such as bulrush, sedge, or cat's tail (cf., (u2)šub_5; (u2)n$umun_2$; ZI&ZI.LAGAB; u_2-gug).

gug_5
hostility, war (might be reduplicated $ug_{5,7,8}$, 'to kill; to die'; cf., gigam).

guḫšu[SIG_4&SIG_4.$ŠU_2$]
altar or table, for holding various food items - a large bowl or stacks of bread.

gukin$_{(2)}$
entire inhabited world (gun$_2$, gu$_2$, 'land, district', + kiĝ$_2$, 'to send orders'; cf., gu$_2$-kiĝ$_2$; Akk. *kiššatu(m) I*, 'totality, world').

gukkal[LU.ḪUL$_2$], kungal
fat-tailed sheep, producing first class wool, usually distinguished from 'native' sheep (udu-gir$_{15}$) (kun, 'tail, rump', + gal, 'big') [GUKKAL archaic frequency: 36; concatenation of 4 sign variants].

gukkal-IB$_2$-la$_2$
a type of fat-tailed sheep ('fat-tailed sheep' + 'waist' + 'to bind, carry').

gul
v., to destroy, demolish (as preparation for rebuilding); to pound, break to pieces (e.g., bitumen); to be destroyed; to obstruct; to hold back, restrain; to extinguish; to cease; to disappear, run away; to fall upon (with -ši-); to wreck, to destroy utterly (with -ta-) (reduplication class) (can be a writing for gu-ul, 'to increase, make numerous') (gu$_7$, 'to consume' + ul, 'ancient, enduring') [GUL archaic frequency: 24].

adj., evil; enormous; (redup.) broken, chipped, as in teeth.

^{ĝiš}GUL-BU, dulbu$_x$
a kind of tree and wood referenced in pre-Sargonic texts, a versatile wood used by carpenters and for firewood (cf., ^{ĝiš}tu-lu-bu-um).

gul-lum
cat (occurs as 'cat of Meluhha' in a proverb [Akk. *šurānu(m) I*]; the usual word is sa-a) ('to fall upon, destroy, extinguish' + 'fertile'; cf., ki-gul-la and Akk. *qallu(m)*, 'small' of person, animal, building).

gul$_3$
(cf., gal$_5$).

gum
(cf., kum).

gum$_2$, gun$_5$
to influence; to neglect, ignore (ga, 'milk' + um, 'old woman').

gum$_2$-ga...za
a sound made by blowing into a bull's horn (cf., dum-dam...za).

gun[GU$_2$.UN]; gun$_2$, gu$_2$
back of a man's neck = load, burden = a talent in weight = 30 +/- 2 kg. = 60 *mina* (ma-na); tribute, tax, dues, rent (gu$_2$, 'neck; nape' + uĝa$_3$, un, 'people'; cf., gu$_2$).

gun$_2$, gu$_2$
land, region, district (gu$_2$, 'edge' + uĝa$_3$, un, 'people, population').

gun$_2$-ĝiš
wood load ('load' + 'wood').

gunu$_3$, gun$_3$
n., colored dot, spot (circle + discrete point; cf., ugun) [GUN$_3$ archaic frequency: 23; concatenation of 2 sign variants].

v., to decorate with spots, lines, colors; to sparkle; to be good; to be beautiful; to put on kohl, antimony paste makeup.

adj., dappled; speckled, spotted; mottled; striped; spangled; variegated, multi-colored; iridescent; embellished, decorated; brilliant.

gun$_3$-a
adj., multi-colored, describing a domestic animal ('colored spot' + adjectival -a).

gunu$_4$, gun$_4$[UNUG]
(cf., gi-gun$_4$(-na), gi-gu$_3$-na).

gun$_5$
(cf., gum$_2$).

gunni[KI.NE]
kiln; stove (gunni not a standard reading of KI.NE; cf., dinig and nimur).

$^{(gi)}$gur, kur$_3$

n., reed basket; measure of dry capacity - Biblical **kor** (= 300 sila$_3$ in Old Akkadian and Neo-Sumerian periods; = 144 sila$_3$ in Old Sumerian Girsu/ Lagash; in admin. texts = 2 bariga); these units expressed by horizontal number signs; carrier (cf., ^{tug2}šu-gur-ra; gur-ra; gi-gur) (Akk. *kurru(m) I*) [? GUR archaic frequency: 14] (circle + to reap; to send).

v., to make a circular motion; to go around; to come back; to return (to); to give back; to protest, contradict, contest, deny; to reject evidence or witnesses (in a legal case); to turn away from, refuse (object has ablative -ta); to wipe off.

$^{(tug2)}$gur

(cf., ^{tug2}šu-gur-ra; gur).

gur-2-ul

a capacity measure of 72 sila$_3$ in Presargonic Girsu.

gur-da

a type of worker in the fields.

^{gi}gur-dub

a reed basket with a capacity from 30 to 90 liters; used to transport grain or flour; to make such a basket required 2/3 to 1 ½ reed bundles (cf., gi-gur).

gur-lugal

a capacity measure - the royal gur (of 300 sila$_3$ promulgated by King Shulgi).

gur-ra

adv., in return ('to return' + subordination suffix -a).

gur-sa$_2$-dug$_4$

a capacity measure, = 160 sila$_3$ ('reed basket' + 'offering; measuring container of either 24 or 40 sila$_3$').

gur-sağ-ğal$_2$

a capacity measure, = 240 sila$_3$, where Civil says the difference is that this gur has been filled from measuring containers topped off with a 'head' of grain instead of being leveled off at the top ('reed basket' + 'head' + 'having'; cf., sağ-du$_3$, 'triangle').

gur-^{d}šul-gi

a capacity measure - the gur of (king) Shulgi.

X-gur-ta

grain yield formula for a particular area found on Ur III round tablets, "at X gur (per iku)".

gur$_2$

n., sphere; circle, ring; loop; hoop (circle + ur, 'to surround').

v., to bow down, submit; to curb, subdue; to die (cf., gam).

guru$_3$, gur$_3$

to bear, carry; to be imbued with; to be full, loaded, laden (Umma reading for ila$_2$ sign) (circular container + er, 'to bring'; cf., gur, kur$_3$, 'basket').

gur$_{(4)}$, kur$_4$, gir$_8$

v., to be, feel, or make big/fat; to be endowed with; to turn, roll over; to run; to gallop; to grind (reduplication class) (circle + flowing motion).

adj., thick, coarse; fattened, plump; bright, preeminent; very strong; great (cf., gud, guř$_x$, 'bull').

GUR$_4$-da

read lugud$_2$-da, 'short'.

gur$_4$-gur$_4$ [LAGAB+LAGAB]

a standard size container for wine, beer, and oil, = 10 liters (reduplicated 'thick, round, plump').

guru$_5$, gur$_5$, kur$_{12}$

n., fangs; a short reed mat, sometimes used to make a door; a piece sliced from a plant stem or reed, for use in making a drug.

v., to separate, divide; to chop; to cut, pull (weeds) (gu$_2$, 'neck; nape' + ra, 'to strike'; cf., kud, kur$_5$; and gu$_2$-gur$_5$...dug$_4$/du$_{11}$/e).

adj., chopped.

gur$_5$[KA×GU]-RU.UŠ
to pluck, pick off; to grind or cut away or off (cf., gi-RU.UŠ).

gur$_5$[KA×GU] (-RU.UŠ$_{(11)}$)...bur$_2$
to bare the fangs, snarl (sign for 'mouth-needles' (+ 'to send' + 'poison') + 'to release').

guru$_6$
(cf., kara$_2$).

guru$_7$, gur$_7$, kara$_6$
grain heap; (stacked) pile; granary, silo; a standard capacity measure for dry and liquid substances, ca. 909 liters (cf., gur, 'basket'; gurum, 'heap'; Akk., *karû(m) I*).

guru$_7$-a im ur$_3$(-ra)
describes the labor-intensive work of sealing up the grain in a storage structure; the older interpretation was that im- was a verbal prefix and that this described hauling the grain to the granary ('granary' + locative + 'clay' + 'to bolt, shut; to smear').

guru$_7$-du$_6$
grain stack ('granary' + 'heap').

guru$_7$-maš
grain depot ('granary' + 'interest, profit').

guru$_8$, gur$_8$ [TU]
n., load (cf., gurum; $^{(\tilde{g}iš)}$ma$_2$-gur$_8$).

adj., high; deep.

gur$_8$-gal^{mušen}
(cf., g̃ir$_3$-gi-lum/lu^{mušen}).

gur$_8$-gur$_8$
adjective for sheep and cattle, pot-bellied (?) (reduplicated 'deep').

$^{(uruda)}$gur$_{10}$[KIN]; gur$_{15}$[UR$_4$]; gur$_x$[ŠE.KIN]
n., copper sickle (I disagree that Hh XI 414 indicates a reading of kin for sickle - gin$_2$ is an adjective for a type of sickle, since equated to *pāšu*; cf., gin$_2$) (semi-circle + flowing motion).

v., to reap, harvest; to pluck; to shear (sheep); to gather in; to catch (in a net); to gather together; to join in assent (probably reduplication class) (cf., saga$_{11}$[KIN]).

^{uruda}gur$_{10}$-sumun
a used copper sickle (cf., kig̃$_2$...til) ('sickle' + 'old, used').

$^{(kuš)}$gur$_{21}$, guru$_{21}$[E.IB$_2$]
shield; decorative inlay; (metal) band; belt; an encircling snake (cf., eg$_2$-ur$_3$).

$^{(kuš)}$gur$_{21}$-ša$_3$-ba-tuku
shield ('shield' + 'padded, thick').

$^{(gi)}$gurdub$_{(2)}$
reed basket (cf., ^{gi}gur-dub and gi-gur).

gurud$_{(2)}$
to plop down; to throw down; to throw away, discard (gur$_3$, 'to carry, be loaded' + ed$_3$, 'to descend, bring down, remove').

gurum[GAM]; guru$_8$
n., heap, pile; arched beam; bending.

v., to be bent; to subdue.

gurum$_2$
(cf., kurum$_7$).

gurun, gurin, guru$_{20}$; girin, girim; girim$_3$, girin$_2$
fruit; berry; flower (cf., gi-rin) (gur$_2$, 'sphere', + an, 'high'; cf., kurun).

gurun$_6$
(cf., kurun$_2$).

guruš
(cf., g̃uruš).

guruš$_{3,4}$, guru$_5$, gur$_5$; kur$_5$
to trim away, strip; to cut, clip (a part of the body); to notch, incise; to fell trees; to be parted, relieved of; to circumcise (?) (cf., gur$_5$-RU.UŠ; gur$_{10}$, 'sickle', + ĝiš$_3$/uš, 'penis' ?).

gurušda
(cf., kurušda).

guz, ḫuz[LUM]
v., to gnash the teeth; to bare the teeth; to rage at; to cut, trim, clip; to castrate (reduplication class: ḫu-ḫu-uz) (gu$_3$, 'noise', + zu$_2$, 'teeth').

adj., long, shaggy, tufted (hair); lame (Akk., *ḫuzzû*).

^{tug2}guz-za
a type of cloth.

^{tug2}guz-za-su$_3$-a-šar$_3$
plush or long, regal (quality) guz-za cloth ('a type of cloth' + 'to sink; to stretch' + nominative + 'royal (quality)').

^{tug2}guz-za-us$_2$
second quality guz-za cloth ('a type of cloth' + 'to follow').

^{tug2}guz-za-us$_2$-šar$_3$
second quality regal guz-za cloth ('a type of cloth' + 'to follow' + 'royal (quality)').

guzza[KU.NIĜ$_2$]
throne; armchair (cf., $^{(ĝiš)}$gu-za).

G̃

ĝa$_2$
(cf., ĝal$_2$, ĝar, ĝe$_{26}$ and ma$_{(3)}$).

ĝa$_2$
box; basket; house; stable; shrine (cf., ĝar) [GA$_2$ archaic frequency: 125; concatenation of 5 sign variants].

Emesal dialect for ma, 'for me' and for e$_2$, 'house'.

-ĝa$_2$(-k)
/-ĝu$_{10}$-ak/, 1.sg. possessive suffix + genitive = 'mine' or locative -a, ThSLa §105.

ĝa$_2$-a-ra; ĝa$_2$-a-ar
to me - ThSLa §91, §93, §96.

ĝa$_2$-a-še$_3$
towards me - ThSLa §91, §96.

^{lu2}ĜA$_2$-dub-ba
(cf., ^{lu2}ša$_{14}$-dub-ba).

ĝa$_2$-e
I; myself - ThSLa §91, §173 ('I' + subject ending).

ĝa$_2$-e-me-en
it is me; I am one who... - ThSLa §97 ('I' + enclitic copula + 1st or 2nd person ending).

ĝa$_2$-gi$_{(4)}$(-a)
(cf., ĝagia).

ĝa$_2$-ĝa$_2$
adding, addition (reduplicated form of ĝar, 'to accumulate'; cf., ĝar-ĝar-ĝar).

ĝa$_2$-ĝa$_2$-de$_3$
in order to place, for depositing - non-finite prospective *marû* (cf., ĝar).

-ĝa$_2$(-k)
/-ĝu$_{10}$-ak/, 1.sg. possessive suffix + genitive = 'mine' or locative -a, ThSLa §105.

ĝa$_2$(-a)-kam
it is mine - ThSLa §98 ('I' + /ak/ + enclitic copula).

ĝa$_2$-la...dag; ĝal$_2$-la...dag
to cease (doing something) (often with -ta-); to lie idle ('to be somewhere' + 'resting place'; Akk., *egû(m) III*, 'to be(come) lazy; be negligent').

ĝa$_2$-la...nu-dag
to be incessant, tireless; to never neglect ('to cease' + 'not').

^{kuš}ĝa$_2$-la$_2$
(cf., ^{kuš}a-ĝa$_2$-la$_2$).

ĜA$_2$-nam-ma-da
(cf., ĝe$_{26}$-nam-ma-da).

ĜA$_2$-nu
(cf., ĝe$_{26}$-nu).

ĝa$_2$-nun
storeroom; private chamber; storehouse; barn; granary (ĝar, 'storeroom' + 'noble').

ĝa$_2$-nun-da tuš-a-me
engaged in service at the storehouse ('storeroom' + 'with' + 'to sit' + 'to be').

ĝa$_2$-nun-ĝiš-ka gub-ba
engaged in service at the storehouse of the wood ('storeroom' + 'wood' + genitive + locative + 'to stand' + nominative).

ĝa$_2$-nun-maḫ
main storehouse, principal storeroom ('storeroom' + 'great, high').

ĝa$_2$-ra
loaded (cf., ma$_2$-a-ĝar-ra).

ĝa$_4$-ĝa$_4$
(cf., ĝar-ĝar).

ĝa$_6$(-ĝ)
to bear, carry (Umma reading for íla sign; cf., šu...ĝar/ĝá-ĝá).

ĝadub
tablet container (ĝar;ĝa$_2$, 'to store', + dub, 'clay tablets'; cf, ^{lu2}ša$_{14}$[ĜA$_2$]-dub-ba).

ĝagia
cloister, for priestesses; reed basket; a measure of fish, dates, apples, figs, and pomegranates (cf., ĝa$_2$-gi$_{(4)}$(-a), 'the house/basket that is locked up').

ĝal$_2$, ĝala$_7$[IG]; ĝa$_2$
to be available; to exist, be (somewhere); to be on hand; to remain; to place, put (with -ni- or bi$_2$-); to reach or place into (with -ši-); to be with someone (with -da-); to have on one's person (with -da-); to be possible (with -da-); to take an oath; to hold; to guard, protect; to unblock a river; to dwell (ĝa$_2$, 'storage basket' + la, 'abundance').

ĝal$_2$...taka$_4$
to open (with loc.term. suffix -e on inanimate indirect objects) ('to be somewhere' + 'to open').

ĝalga, malga
advice, counsel; wise one; reflection, consideration, judgment (loan from Akkadian *milkum*; cf., Orel & Stolbova #1791 ***mulak-/*mulik-** 'stranger, chief') [GALGA archaic frequency: 16; concatenation of 2 sign variants].

ĝalga-suḫ$_3$
nitwit; confusing advice ('consideration' + 'to be confused').

ĝansis, ĝasis$_x$
darkness; the netherworld; eclipse.

ĝanun[ĜA$_2$×NUN]
barn, storehouse, granary (ĝar;ĝa$_2$, 'storeroom', + nun, 'great') [GANUN archaic frequency: 3].

ĝar[NIĜ$_2$] (-ra)
n., storeroom; form, appearance; setting (to be + to send) [GAR archaic frequency: 409].

v., to store, accumulate; to deliver, deposit; to put, place, lay, set down upon; to settle down; to prepare; to make, establish, organize, restore (with -ši-); to change; to set the mode of a song; to remove and set elsewhere, set aside (with -ta-); to expel, put aside (with -da-) (ĝa$_2$-ĝa$_2$ in *marû*).

ĝar-ĝar, ĝa$_4$-ĝa$_4$(-ra)
n., an account summary.

v., to add together (math.) (redup. ĝar, 'to store'; cf., ĝa$_2$-ĝa$_2$).

ĝar-ĝar-ĝar
careful preparation; hospitality (redup. ĝar, 'storeroom; to establish, restore'; cf., ĝa$_2$-ĝa$_2$).

ĝar-ra
posited or set conditions (OB period math. exercises); covered or encrusted with (e.g., gold) ('to set down' + nominative).

ĝar$_7$-du$_2$
(cf., ^{lu2}MAR-TU[-KI]).

ĝarim
meadow; irrigated fields; pool, pond; irrigation district (same sign as dagrim) (ĝar, 'storeroom', + imi/im, 'clay, mud'; cf., ugur$_2$; agar$_{(2,3)}$, ugar).

$^{(lu2)}$ĝarza, ĝarzu[PA.DIĜIR]; $^{(lu2)}$mar-za
custom(s); rite(s); religious obligation; divine or royal orders; can describe an institutional witness of a court decision; administrative representative (ĝar, 'form, appearance' or ĝar, 'to deliver', + zu, 'to know').

ĝarza$_2$, ĝarzu$_2$, ĝirza[PA.LUGAL]
office, duties; rules.

ĝe
(Emesal reading of the verb me, to be).

ĝe$_6$
(cf., gig$_2$).

ĝe$_{26}$, ĝa$_2$
I; me; myself; my.

ĝe$_{26}$[ĜA$_2$]-e
I; me; myself, cf., ĝa$_2$-e.

ĝe$_{26}$-nam-ma-da
come with me! (ĝe$_{26}$-na, imperative form of ĝen, 'to go, come' + conjugational prefixes ĩ-ba with locative force + 'with').

ĝe$_{26}$-nu
imperative, come!.

ĝele$_3$
(cf., meli$_2$).

ĝeme$_2$
(cf., geme$_2$).

ĝen, ĝin[DU] (-na)
(as noun or adj. cf., gin$_6$/gin).

v., to go; to arrive; to send; to come (with dative or -ši-) (suppletion class verb: sing. *ḫamṭu*, cf., du, re$_7$, sub$_2$) (Akk. *gana* 'come!', cf., Orel & Stolbova #892, ***gan-/*gin-** "go").

ĝen-na
imperative, go! (Emesal dialect for kim$_3$, 'willow tree').

-ĝen, -ĝe$_{13}$
Emesal dialect for -me-en (ĝen[DU] = men$_3$[DU]), 1sg. and 2sg enclitic copula, ThSLa §541.

ĝeš-
(cf., ĝiš-).

ĝeš$_{2,3,4}$, ĝiš$_{2,3}$, geš$_{2,3,4}$, giš$_{2,3}$
sixty (cf., ĝešta).

ĝeš$_2$×u, ĝeš'u
six hundred ('sixty' + 'ten'; cf., ge-eš-tu).

ĝešbu, ĝešpu, ĝešba, ĝešpa[ĜIŠ.ŠUB]
bow; boomerang; throw-stick (ĝiš, 'tool', + šub, 'to cast, throw', + nominative a; ending reflects vowel harmony prior to vowel contraction).

ĝešbu$_2$, ĝešpu$_2$[ŠU.DIM$_4$]
fist(s); hook; handle; grappling hook for a wrestler; wrestling (often linked with lirum$_3$, 'athletics') (ĝiš, 'wooden tool', + bu$_{(6)}$, 'to pull, draw').

ĝešta, ĝeš$_2$, ĝiš$_2$[DIŠ]; ĝeš$_{3,4}$, ĝiš$_3$
sixty (cf., ge-eš-tu, 'six hundred', and ni-gi-da, 'thing of sixty'; read instead (?) gešta, geš$_2$, giš$_2$; cf., igi-še$_3$...du, 'to walk in front of', Akk., *igištû*, *gešṭû*, 'very first, leading'; *gišṭû*, '(writing) board'; Sum., igištu, geštu$_4$ [IGI.DU]; cf., ugula-ĝeš$_2$-da, 'officer in charge of sixty men'; Akk., *šūši*, 'sixty').

g̃eštin
grapevine; bunch of grapes [measured with dry capacity measures in most earlier Pre-Sargonic and Ur III texts]; wine; grape juice (g̃iš, 'tree', + tin, 'life; wine'; cf., Emesal mu-ti-in/mu-tin) [GEŠTIN archaic frequency: 42; concatenation of 2 sign variants].

g̃eštin-bil$_{(2)}$-la$_2$
sour grapes; vinegar ('grapes' + 'sour').

g̃eštin-duru$_5$
fresh grapes ('bunch of grapes' + 'moist').

g̃eštin-gurum-ma
stock or trunk of the grape vine ('grape vine' + 'heap, pile, arched beam').

^{giš}g̃eštin-g̃ir$_2$(-ra)
bramble (?); wild rose (?); blackberry (?) ('grape vine' + 'thorns').

g̃eštin-ḫad$_2$
dried grapes, raisins ('bunch of grapes' + 'dried').

g̃eštin-KA
vinegar.

g̃eštin-ka$_5$-a
fox-grape, cf., Vitis vulpina (literally the vixen-grape) - 'foxes are supposed to be attracted to the fruit of this species'; used in medicine ('grapes' + 'fox').

g̃eštug$_{(2,3)}$, g̃eštu$_{(2,3)}$ [PI]
n., ear(s); hearing; understanding, intelligence (g̃iš, 'tool', + tuku/tug, 'to receive') [GEŠTUG archaic frequency: 108; concatenation of 5 sign variants].

v., to hear; to understand.

g̃eštug$_{(2,3)}$...gub
to plan; to pay attention to, heed (with -ši-); to be attentive ('understanding' + 'to set').

g̃eštug$_{(2,3)}$...g̃ar/g̃a$_2$-ar
to listen, pay attention (to: with -ši-); to think ('ears, understanding' + 'to make available [to]').

g̃eštug$_{(2)}$-lal/la$_2$
deaf; mentally handicapped ('ears, understanding' + 'deficit').

g̃eštug$_{(2,3)}$-ga...ri/de$_5$
to listen; to comprehend ('ears' + locative case postposition + 'to put into').

g̃eštug$_{(2,3)}$-ga-ri(-a/-im)
understanding ('to listen' + participial ending).

g̃eštug$_{(2,3)}$...sum
to listen to (with dative); to give wisdom ('ears' + 'to give').

g̃eštug$_{(2,3)}$...šu$_2$
to stop one's ears ('ears' + 'to cover').

g̃eštu$_{(2,3)}$-tuku
possessing intelligence ('ears, understanding' + 'having').

g̃eštug$_{(2,3)}$-ga...u$_{18}$-lu
to forget ('ears, understanding' + locative case postposition + 'great storm').

g̃eš'u
(cf., g̃eš$_2$xu).

g̃i$_6$, g̃e$_6$ [MI]
night; shade (cf., gig$_2$, 'black/dark') [GI$_6$ archaic frequency: 105].

g̃i$_6$-an-na
at night ('night' + 'heaven' + locative).

g̃i$_6$...di
to pass the night ('night' + 'to go'; cf., u$_3$-di).

g̃i$_6$-eden
(cf., izi-g̃i$_6$-eden-na).

g̃i$_6$-da...gub
serving at night ('night' + 'with' + 'to serve').

g̃i$_6$-par$_{3/4}$
residence of the en priest or priestess; cloister ('night; shade' + 'to spread, stretch out').

^{ĝiš}ĝi$_6$-par$_{3/4}$
a shady fruit tree, whose fruit could be dried (ḫada$_2$); suggestions include mulberry (*Morus nigra*), pear, and quince ('shade' + 'to stretch, spread out'; Akk. *libāru(m)*).

ĝi$_6$...sa$_2$
stay to midnight ('night' + 'to make equal').

ĝi$_6$-sa$_2$
midnight, early morning ('night' + 'to make equal').

ĝi$_6$...sa$_9$
stay to midnight ('night' + 'half').

ĝi$_6$-u$_3$-na(-k)
'dead of night', middle of the night (cf., ĝi$_6$-sa$_2$, 'midnight'; u$_3$-sa$_2$, 'sleep'; ĝi$_6$-an-na, 'at night').

ĝi$_{25}$[DUGUD]
cloud (Borger questions this logogram).

^{ĝiš}ĝidru, ĝidri[PA]
stick; staff; scepter; stick used to measure the height of a pile of grain (ĝiš, 'wood', + duru$_2$, 'low end, base' where stick was thrust to the base of a grain pile; cf., duru$_6$ reading of PA, Emesal variant mu-u$_2$-a, and še ĝiš-e$_3$-a).

ĝidru-še$_3$...nu$_2$
to lay (heaped-up grain) under the (measuring) stick ('stick' + terminative + 'to lie down').

ĝidru(-mu)-u$_4$-su$_3$-ra$_2$
a scepter of long (years and) days ('scepter' (+ years) + 'days' + 'lasting, far away' + genitive).

ĝig$_2$
(cf., gig$_2$).

ĝili$_3$
(cf., meli$_2$).

ĝin
(cf., ĝen, ĝin).

ĝin-na
ordinary ('ordinary' + nominative).

^{ĝiš}ĝipar
(cf., ^{ĝiš}ĝi$_6$-par$_4$).

ĝir$_2$, ĝiri$_2$
n., knife, dagger, sword; razor, shaving blade, surgeon's knife; thorn; scorpion; lightning flash; road; expedition, trip (ĝiš, 'tool', + ra, 'to strike, stab, slay' with vowel harmony) [GIR$_2$ archaic frequency: 114].

v., to stab; to fulgurate, lighten, flash.

$^{\text{ĝiš/u2}}$ĜIR$_2$/ĜIR$_2$*gunû*
(cf., $^{\text{ĝiš/u2}}$adda$_4$; $^{\text{ĝiš/u2}}$kišig$_2$).

ĝiri$_{2,3}$, ĝir$_{2,3}$
n., booty; captive (additional associations of 'road' and 'sword').

v., to pillage; to capture; to drive away; to take away; to be taken.

ĝir$_2$-ad-dag^{zabar}
crooked blade dagger ('knife' + Akk. *atāku*, 'to be bent, crooked').

$^{\text{(uruda)}}$ĝir$_2$-ašgab$^{\text{(zabar)}}$
currier's knife, for working with hides and leather ('knife' + 'currier').

ĝir$_2$...DU$_3$
to cut off (?) ('knife' + 'to erect').

ĝir$_2$-gal
sword ('knife, dagger' + 'large').

ĝir$_2$-gu-la; ĝir$_2$-gul
knife used in plucking/shearing dead sheep ('knife' + 'great; to destroy').

$^{\text{(uruda)}}$ĝir$_2$-gur$_{10}$[KIN]
knife for harvesting ('knife' + 'to reap, pluck, shear').

ĝiri$_2$...ĝar
to clear the way ('road' + 'to place, establish').

$^{\text{(lu2)}}$ĝir$_2$-la$_2$
sword; butcher ('knife' + 'to raise').

ĝiri$_{2/3}$-nun
highway (cf., anše-ĝiri$_{2/3}$-nun(-na)) ('road' + 'high, fine').

ĝir$_2$-pa
butcher knife; a marsh-bird ('knife' + 'branch').

ĝir$_2$-su
burning; purification ('lightning flash' + 'body').

ĝir$_2$-šu-i(-ne)^{zabar}
bronze barber's razor(s)·('knife' + 'barber' + 'bronze').

ĝir$_2$-tab
scorpion ('knife' + 'sting').

ĝir$_2$-tur
an offering knife ('knife, dagger' + 'small').

ĝir$_2$-udu-uš$_2$$^{(zabar)}$; $^{(uruda)}$ĝir$_2$-udu-šum$^{(zabar)}$
a knife to slaughter sheep ('knife' + 'sheep' + 'to kill, slaughter').

ĝir$_2$-ur$_3$-ra$^{(zabar)}$; ĝir$_2$-ur$_2$-ra$^{(zabar/an)}$
sharpened knife, of bronze or tin (cf., $^{(ĝiš)}$mi$_2$-us$_2$) ('knife, dagger' + 'ground smooth'; cf., lu$_2$-ur$_3$-ra and šu-ur$_3$-ra).

^{ku6}ĝir$_2$-us$_2$
an inexpensive fish ('knife' + 'length; second-class').

ĝir$_2$-zal
scalpel ('knife' + 'to shine').

$^{(na4)}$ĝir$_2$-zu$_2$-gal
a flint or obsidian dagger ('knife' + 'flint; obsidian').

ĝir$_2$-zu$_2$-zabar
a dagger ('dagger' + 'bronze').

ĝiri$_{2,3}$, ĝir$_{2,3}$
n., booty; captive (additional associations of 'road' and 'sword').

v., to pillage; to capture; to drive away; to take away; to be taken.

ĜIR$_3$
(cf., ĝir$_3$, ir$_9$, piriĝ, šakan$_2$, ĝiri$_3$).

ĝir$_3$, kir$_{10}$
proud, splendid (Akk. *šarāḫu(m) I*).

ĝiri$_3$, ĝir$_3$
n., foot, feet; step; way, path, road; intermediary (ĝiš, 'tool', + uru$_9$, 'support'; ur$_2$, 'leg(s)'; cf., ĝidri and ĝušur for similar and different phonetic developments).

prep., via; under the responsibility of (person's name).

ĝiri$_3$-bala
destructive weather, flood; battering; destruction ('path' + 'to change, uproot').

ĝiri$_3$...dib$_{(2)}$
to take a path, be on one's way; to follow the instruction ('path' + 'to traverse, pass along').

ĝiri$_3$-kur$_2$...dib$_2$
to take the wrong path; to go astray; to bypass, avoid ('path' + 'strange' + 'to traverse').

ĝiri$_3$-dili
(cf., ĝiri$_3$...gub).

ĝir$_3$-gi-lum/lu^{mušen}; gir-gi4-lu$_2$^{mušen}; gur$_8$-gal^{mušen}
an edible water-fowl - a kind of gull (?); Akkadian equivalent *ṣayyāḫu* means 'laughing' bird ('foot' + 'reeds + 'abundant; numerous'; Akk. *gergīlu(m)*, 'a bird').

ĝiri$_3$...gub
to wait for; to step on/in/out (ĝiri$_3$ modified by dili can either mean 'alone' or mean 'with one foot; one step') ('foot' + 'to stand').

$^{(ĝiš)}$ĝiri$_3$-gub(-ba)
step; footstool; pedestal ('foot' + 'to stand').

g̃iri$_3$...gur
to go around ('foot' + 'to make a circular motion').

g̃iri$_3$ KU-bi-še$_3$...g̃al$_2$
to be subjected ('foot' + 'at their place' + 'to be located').

g̃iri$_3$...g̃ar
to step forward; to trample (with -ni-); to travel; to prepare or lay down the road ('foot; road' + 'to place, set down').

g̃iri$_3$-še$_3$...g̃ar
to place something under the authority of someone ('foot' + terminative + 'to place, set down').

g̃iri$_3$-g̃en[DU]-na
walkway; path, way; procedure, method ('foot; road' + 'to go' + nominative).

g̃iri$_3$-ḫum
deformed or missing feet, such as from diabetes (cf., ḫum-ḫum, 'swollen up, as with edema'; Akk. *galāšu*, 'to flatten off ?'; *ḫamāšu(m) I*, 'to snap off'; *ḫamšu(m) II*, 'snapped off').

g̃iri$_3$...kur$_2$
to change ('foot; path' + 'to change').

g̃iri$_3$-kur$_2$...dib$_2$
to take the wrong path; to go astray; to bypass, avoid ('path' + 'strange' + 'to traverse').

g̃ir$_3$-lam
a small basket for eggs, fish, and fruit such as dates, figs, pomegranates, and apples ('way, path' + 'abundance'; Akk. *kirlammu*, 'a container').

^{giš}g̃ir$_3$-ma$_2$-du$_3$
floorboards of a ship ('way, path' + 'ship's plank'; Akk. *germadû*).

G̃IR$_3$.NITA$_2$+G̃IR$_3$.NITA$_2$
military governor; general (cf., šaggina).

g̃iri$_3$-pad-ra$_2$[DU]
bone(s); skeleton ('foot' + 'to break off a piece' + nominative).

g̃iri$_3$...ra(-ra)
to beat, batter; to break; to kill; to stumble ('foot' + 'to strike, stir').

g̃iri$_3$-saga$_{11}$/ sig$_{18}$[KIN]...dug$_4$/du$_{11}$/e
to trample; to stamp out; to crush, destroy ('foot' + 'to harvest'(?) + 'to effect').

g̃iri$_3$-si
toes; sandals ('foot' + 'narrow thing').

g̃iri$_3$...si
to strap on sandals ('foot' + 'narrow thing; strap').

g̃iri$_3$ si..sa$_2$
to make the roads passable ('road' + 'to put in order').

g̃iri$_3$...sig$_{10}$-ga, g̃iri$_3$... se$_3$-ga, g̃iri$_3$...si$_3$-ga
to serve ('foot' + 'to serve, provide').

g̃iri$_3$-se$_3$-ga, g̃iri$_3$-sig$_{10}$-ga
menial(s), domestic(s); palace or temple attendant(s); personnel ('foot' + 'to serve, provide'; Akk. *gerseqqû*, 'palace, temple attendant').

g̃iri$_3$-se$_3$-ga-uru
state personnel ('personnel' + 'city').

g̃iri$_3$...sig$_{18}$[KIN]
(cf., g̃iri$_3$-saga$_{11}$...dug$_4$).

g̃iri$_3$ su-ul-su-ul
crippled (Akk. *pussulu(m)*).

g̃iri$_3$-suḫub$_2$[MUL]
hoof ('foot' + 'boot').

g̃iri$_3$-tag
deformed foot ('foot' + 'afflicted').

g̃iri$_3$...us$_2$
v., to follow on foot; to set one's foot on; to firmly plant one's foot; to make one's way ('foot' + 'to follow; to join').

ĝiri$_3$-us$_2$
n., road; footprint, track; step; companion.

ĝiri$_3$...ze$_2$-er
to lose one's footing, slip, slide ('feet' + 'to remove'; cf., ki-ma-an-ze$_2$-er).

ĝiri$_5$
(cf., gir$_5$).

ĝiri$_{16}$, ĝir$_{16}$ [ĜIR$_3$×KAR$_2$]
fortress, refuge (cf., giri$_5$ and gu$_2$ ĝiri$_{16}$... ĝar/ĝa$_2$-ĝa$_2$).

^{giš}ĝisal[BI.ĜIŠ]
steering oar; rudder (ĝiš, 'wooden tool', + sal, 'thin, wide') [GISAL archaic frequency: 3; concatenation of 2 sign variants].

ĝiskim, ĝiškim, iskim, izkim, ĝizkim[AĜRIG]
sign, signal; password; answer; instruction, order; omen (ĝiš, 'tool', + kiĝ$_2$, 'message').

ĝiskim-ti, ĝiskim-til$_3$
n., object of trust, support ('signal' + 'to stay alive').

adj., recognized, familiar, trustworthy.

ĝiskim...tuku
to get recognition ('signal' + 'to get').

ĝiskim-zi an-na
good omen from heaven ('signal' + 'good, firm' + 'heaven' + genitive).

ĝissu, ĝizzu[ĜIŠ.MI]
shadow; shade (ĝiš, 'tool, agent', + su, 'substitute'[Akk. *tarīb(t)u(m)*]).

ĝissu...lal/la$_2$
to cover with a shadow; to stretch out a shade; to shelter ('shadow' + 'to extend, reach').

ĝissu-gi$_4$-a
roof; shelter ('shadow' + 'to restore, return' + nominative).

ĝissu-la$_2$
shade; shelter; evening ('shadow' + 'to extend, reach').

ĝiš, ĝeš
n., tree; wood; wooden implement; scepter; tool; weapon; organ; plow; yoke; natural phenomenon (describes a trunk that goes out into many branches and leaves) [GIŠ archaic frequency: 381].

adj., describes an animal assigned to the plow (sometimes ĝiš-še$_3$); mature, for breeding.

^{giš}ĝiš
plow ('the' tool, par excellence).

ĝiš-ab-ba(-k)
a type of thorn tree; bramble; a wood used for fuel and to make boats, sickle hafts, handles, hoes, stools, etc. ('wood' + 'sea' + genitive; imported from the Gulf area, but also grown locally; loan into Akkadian as *kušabku(m)*).

ĝiš-aš
adj. for type of bread, probably a brick-shaped loaf or baguette ('implement, scepter, weapon' + 'emmer flour, bread'; cf., Akk., *patāqu(m) I*).

ĜIŠ-BAD
in the Akkad period, a length measure equal to 1 cubit, 1 kuš$_3$.

ĝiš-bad(-ra$_2$)
a basket with a wooden handle; threshing sledge.

ĝiš-bala
dried wood; roof-room, second story; change, spare (cf., $^{(ĝiš)}$bala) ('tool' + 'change').

ĝiš-bar-ra
fire; fire-god (cf., ĝiš-par$_2$) ('wood' + 'to remove' + 'that which').

ĝiš-bar-ra...lal/la$_2$
to catch fire, be set aflame ('fire' + 'to reach; to diminish; to become reduced').

ĝiš-bil$_2$
father ('tool' + 'sprout, shoot').

g̃iš-BU
(cf., $^{(g̃iš)}$gazinbu, gazimbi, gazibu[BU]).

g̃iš-buru$_2$
trap; net; snare; fetters; throwing stick; magic staff; a door-ornament ('tool' + 'to spread out, release' + nominative with vowel harmony; cf., g̃iš-par$_3$; su-buru$_2$).

g̃iš-da
(writing) board, infilled with wax (cf., g̃ešta); part of a boat ('tool' + 'arm; to hold'; Akk. *gišṭû; lē'u(m)*).

g̃iš-dala
cross-bar (on door) (cf., $^{(g̃iš)}$dal) ('tool' + 'beam; transverse line').

g̃iš-de$_5$, g̃iš-di$_5$[RI]
cross-bar, on toilet, throne, or table (Akk. *gištûm*; cf., de$_5$, 'to void excrement').

g̃iš-DIM$_4$
(cf., g̃ešbu$_2$, g̃ešpu$_2$[ŠU.DIM$_4$]).

g̃iš-du$_3$(-a)
n., timber; stick ('wood; penis' + 'to plant' + nominative).

adj., pregnant; breeder (describing an animal).

$^{(na4)}$g̃iš-dub
an ornamental plaque of precious stone or metal on the front of a chariot (Akk. *gištuppu(m)*).

g̃iš-e$_3$; g̃iš-e$_{11}$
key; door pin ('tool' + 'to go out; to exit').

g̃iš-eme
a utensil; tongue to hold socketed 'tooth' of ard plow ('tool' + 'tongue').

-g̃iš-en
irrealis suffix, 'unreality' form suffix, 'were it that' - ThSLa §551 ('tool' + 'enigmatic background').

g̃iš-ERIN$_2$
(cf., g̃iš-rin$_2$).

g̃iš-eš$_2$-la$_2$
(cf., $^{(g̃iš)}$eš$_2$-lal/la$_2$).

g̃iš-gaba-tab
a one-nindan-long pole held to the breast of ten or twelve laborers advancing in parallel and manually dropping cereal seeds by hand into each furrow (per Maekawa); a pole suspending left and right bags of seeds for broadcast sowing by an individual laborer (per Englund) ('stick' + 'to hold to the breast').

g̃iš-gal
(cf., g̃išgal).

g̃iš-gan(-na)
(wooden) pestle; clapper (Akkadian *bukānu(m)*) ('wood' + 'pestle' + phonetic complement).

g̃iš-gan(-na)
door bolt (Akkadian *sikkūru(m)*) ('wood' + 'pestle' + phonetic complement).

g̃iš-gan...bala
to conclude a sale, transferring possession of a slave or animal ('pestle/stick' + 'to cross over').

g̃iš-gana$_2$-ur$_3$-ra
harrow, drag ('tool' + 'field' + 'to drag over the ground').

g̃iš-GAZ
(cf., $^{[g̃iš]}$nag̃a$_3$).

g̃iš-gaz
cudgel ('tool' + 'to crush, vanquish'; Akk. *mašgašu(m)*; cf., g̃iš-ḫaš/ḫaz, 'wooden battle mace').

g̃iš-gaz-me$_3$
battle cudgel ('cudgel' + 'battle').

g̃iš-ge-en(-ge-en)-na; g̃iš-gi-na
limb; limbs ('tool' + gen$_6$, 'to stabilize, strengthen, support' + nominative).

g̃iš-gi
reed bank, thicket, canebrake ('tree' + 'reed').

^{lu2}g̃iš-gi
a ritual officiant.

g̃iš-gi$_{(4/5)}$-g̃al$_2$
antiphon, answering chorus, refrain (Akk. *meḫru(m)*) ('tool/ear' + 'to answer' + 'being').

g̃iš-gid$_2$-da
long wood; punting pole; javelin, spear, lance ('wood' + 'long' + nominative; Akk., *ariktu*).

g̃iš-gig$_2$
a date palm ('tree' + 'black, dark').

g̃iš-gu$_2$
shackle, neck-stock; ladder ('tool' + 'neck').

g̃iš-gu$_2$-ba
a piece of tableware ('tool' + 'chick pea, bean' + 'to give').

g̃iš-gu$_3$-de$_2$; g̃iš-gu$_3$-di
a loud stringed musical instrument ('tool' + 'to make a noise or sound').

g̃iš...g̃ar
to assign ('tool' + 'to deliver').

g̃iš-g̃iri$_3$
fetters, for feet ('tool' + 'feet'; Akk. *kurṣû(m)*).

g̃iš-g̃iš-la$_2$
battle ('tools' + 'to raise'; cf., ki-g̃iš-g̃iš-la$_2$).

g̃iš-ḪAR
dredging (?) work in the canal (cf., g̃iš-kin$_2$) ('tool' + 'obligation' ?).

g̃iš-ḫaš
wooden battle mace ('tool/wood' + 'to break up; to pulverize'; cf., g̃iš-gaz, 'cudgel').

g̃iš-ḫaš...aka
to slaughter ('tool' + 'to thresh' + 'to do'; cf., gaz, 'to slaughter').

g̃iš-ḫe$_2$
firmament, sky; heap, accumulation (of stars ?) (cf., UL-ḫe$_2$) ('tool' + 'numerous').

g̃iš-ḫum
bench on a wagon; cabin on a boat or barge; structure for shade ('wood' + 'in motion').

g̃iš...ḫur
to draw; to design; to make plans; to give orders ('tool' + 'to draw').

g̃iš-ḫur
plan; design; drawing; scheme; statute, rules ('tool' + 'to draw, sketch'; cf., lal$_3$-ḫur).

g̃iš-i$_3$
husks, bran; sesame plant (cf., še-g̃iš-i$_3$).

g̃iš-KA$_2$
(cf., akan$_2$).

g̃iš-ka$_2$(-an)-na
door-lintel, door frame ('piece of wood' + 'gate' + 'high' + genitival postposition).

g̃iš-kad$_5$
stepladder ('tool' + 'to tie, bind together').

g̃iš-kar$_{2/3}$
task (cf., eš$_2$-kar$_3$).

g̃iš-ki-g̃al$_2$
(cf., g̃iš-gi$_5$-g̃al$_2$).

g̃iš-kig̃$_2$-ti
(industrial) kiln; craftsmen, artisans; workshop (cf., e$_2$-g̃iš-kig̃$_2$-ti) ('tool' + kig̃$_2$...ti, 'to assign work'; cf., kin and KI.NE, 'kiln').

g̃iš-kim$_3$[BU]
wooden clapper or pestle; willow (Akk. *bukānu(m); ḫilēpu(m)*).

g̃iš-kin$_2$[ḪAR]
a type of tree, used for drug, as wood for chairs, whose bark was used for the outer covering [g̃iš-bar-kin$_2$] of composite bows, which furnished a basket of seeds, and which is described as black, white, red, green, and speckled (Akk. *kiškanû*).

ĝiš-KU
(cf., ^{ĝiš}tukul).

ĝiš-KUM
(cf., $^{[ĝiš]}$naĝa$_4$).

ĝiš-kun
hind legs; rump ('tool' + 'tail'; Akk. *rapaštu(m)*).

ĝiš-la$_2$
(cf., ĝiš-ĝiš-la$_2$).

ĝiš...lal/la$_2$
to be silent; to pay heed (cf., ĝeštug$_{(2)}$-lal; 'deaf').

ĝiš-la$_2$-bi
n., silence.

adv., silently ('to be silent' + adverbial force suffix).

ĝiš-lam$_7$[LAM×KUR]
mullein (*Verbascum*), a plant with 2 foot-long velvety leaves, used for lampwicks, toilet paper, and in medicine as an antibiotic and cough remedy (cf., $^{(u2/ĝiš)}$gi-zu$_2$-lum-ma) ('tree' + 'abundance, luxuriance'; Akk. *gišlammu*).

ĝiš-LUGAL
(cf., ^{ĝiš}rab$_3$).

ĝiš-MA
(cf., ^{ĝiš}peš$_3$).

ĝiš-maḫ
a stepladder (cf., ĝiš-kad$_5$) (Akk. *merdītu*).

ĝiš-mud
socket for door bolt or pick handle; metal tube, pipette (for liquids); (tree) stump.

ĝiš-na$_2$
bed; resting place; bedspread ('tool' + 'to sleep' + nominative).

ĝiš-na$_2$-aš-na$_2$
couch ('bed' + 'one, alone' + 'to sleep' + nominative).

ĝiš-naĝ
wooden water pail ('wood' + 'to drink').

ĝiš-nam-tar; ĝiš-nam-ri$_2$-za
magical figurine from mandrake root ('wood' + 'fate' + 'cut'/'small board').

ĜIŠ-NI
a type of wool (cf., ĝiš-i$_3$).

ĝiš-nim
in the east; sunrise (cf., ĝiš-šu$_2$) ('tool' ? + 'east, early, upper'; Akk. *ṣītān/š*).

ĝiš-NIM
(cf., $^{ĝiš/u2}$diḫ$_3$[NIM]).

ĝiš-nu$_2$
(cf., ĝiš-na$_2$).

ĝiš-nu$_{11}$[ŠIR]
lamp, light; white sandalwood from India (?) ('tool; tree' + 'light, fire, lamp'; Akk. *samullu(m)*).

^{na4}ĝiš-nu$_{11}$-gal
alabaster; marble.

ĝiš-PA
(cf., ^{ĝiš}ĝidru).

ĝiš-pa-ku$_5$-da
cut branch, stick, palm frond ('wood' + 'branch' + 'to cut off' + nominative).

ĝiš-par$_3$; ĝiš-par$_2$
trap, snare (Akk., *gišparru*; cf., ĝiš-buru$_2$).

ĝiš...ra
to thresh; to beat ('stick' + 'to beat').

ĝiš-RI
(cf., $^{(ĝiš)}$dal; ĝiš-de$_5$; ĝiš-dala).

ĝiš-rin$_2$
weighing scale; yoke (of cart) (cf., erin$_2$, rin$_2$).

ĜIŠ-RU
(cf., ^{ĝiš}illuru; ĝešbu; ^{ĝiš}LAGAB.RU).

ĞIŠ-SAR
(cf., $^{\tilde{g}iš}$kiri$_6$).

g̃iš-si$_4$
a date palm ('tree' + 'red-brown').

g̃iš-sig$_3$[PA] (-sig$_3$)
a wooden percussion musical instrument ('wood' + 'to beat rhythmically').

-g̃iš-še-en
(cf., -g̃iš-en).

g̃iš-še$_3$
fit for the yoke ('tool, yoke' + terminative postposition, 'unto').

g̃iš-ŠIR
(cf., g̃iš-nu$_{11}$).

g̃iš-šu
shackle; haft; tool ('tool' + 'hand').

g̃iš-šu-kin
(cf., $^{\tilde{g}iš}$šu-KIN).

g̃iš-šu$_2$
in the sunset; in the west (cf., g̃iš-nim) ('tool' ? + 'to set, become dark'; Akk. *šīlān*).

g̃iš-šub(-ba)
lot, share; spell; a musical interval sounded by lyre strings 1+3 ('tool' + 'to cast, throw, drop' + nominative).

ĞIŠ-ŠUB
(cf., g̃ešbu).

g̃iš-šudum-ma
herder's tally sticks, placed in the ground at night, to record the count for each type of animal (cf., The debate between Sheep and Grain); records (here is the origin of the Sumerian terminology for counting with numbers; cf., šita$_5$).

g̃iš...tag
to make a religious offering, sacrifice (often with dative) ('tree' + 'to adorn').

g̃iš...tuku
to hear, listen to (with loc.term. suffix -e on inanimate indirect objects) ('tool' + 'to receive'; cf., g̃eštug$_{(2,3)}$, 'ears').

g̃iš-tuku
attentive ('tools' + 'having').

g̃iš-tun$_3$[GIN$_2$]
a small wooden container; a type of ax.

g̃iš-u$_2$-gibil-la
firewood ('tree' + 'vegetation' + 'tinder, firewood' + genitive).

g̃iš-ur$_2$
tree trunk ('wood' + 'base, trunk').

g̃iš...ur$_3$
to harrow, level, grade (often with -ni-), done several times, usually but not necessarily after a first plowing in months four and five, and completed before sowing ('tool' + 'drag').

g̃iš-ur$_3$(-ra)
tree trunk, felled log; beam, rafter (e.g., of a roof); timber; harrow, strickle, leveler, grader ('wood' + 'roof').

g̃iš-zi
wall ('wood' + 'to rise up').

g̃iš-zu$_2$
flat, triangular spearhead of ard plow share ('tool' + 'tooth').

g̃iš$_{2,3}$, g̃eš$_{2,3}$, uš
penis; man (self + to go out + many; cf., nitaḫ$_{(2)}$ and šir) [GIŠ$_3$ archaic frequency: 16; concatenation of 2 sign variants; UŠ archaic frequency: 101; concatenates 2 sign variants].

g̃iš$_3$ a$_2$-zi...e
to commit rape (g̃iš$_3$, 'penis', + 'violence' + 'to do').

g̃iš$_3$...du$_3$
to have sexual intercourse (g̃iš$_3$, 'penis', + 'to plant').

g̃iš$_3$...dug$_4$/du$_{11}$/e
to copulate with; to have sex with; to make love to; to inseminate (g̃iš$_3$, 'penis', + 'to do').

g̃iš$_3$-nu-zu
virgin (said of animals) (g̃iš$_3$, 'penis', + 'not' + zu, 'knowing').

g̃iš$_3$...zig$_3$/zi-zi
to have an erection (g̃iš$_3$, 'penis', + , 'to stand up, rise').

g̃iš$_3$-zu
having born young; open (g̃iš$_3$, 'penis', + zu, 'knowing').

g̃išbun [KI.BI.NINDA]
(cultic) feast, banquet.

g̃išbun gal-gal
huge banquet tables ('feast' + reduplicated 'large').

g̃išgal
pedestal; seat; throne-base; station (g̃iš, 'wooden thing', + gal, 'big, great') [GIŠGAL archaic frequency: 9].

G̃IŠGAL-di
(cf., ulu$_3$-di).

^{giš}g̃išimmar, ^{giš}g̃išnimbar
date palm; trunk of a date palm tree ('tree' + nim, 'to be high', + bar, 'to release') [GIŠIMMAR archaic frequency: 55; concatenation of 5 sign variants].

^{giš}g̃išimmar-kur-ra
a kind of tree, with cones, and used for drug ('foreign date palm').

g̃iškim
(cf., g̃iskim).

g̃itlam$_{(2,3,4)}$, nit(a)lam$_{(2,3,4)}$
lover; honeymooner; first husband; spouse (cf., murub$_5$) (g̃iš$_3$, 'man; penis', or nitaḫ, 'male, man', + lam, 'luxuriance', or Semitic kinship root *tlm* in Akk., *talīmu(m)* and *talīmtu(m)*, 'favorite brother or sister').

g̃izzal [G̃IŠ-TUG$_2$-PI-ŠIRtenu/ ŠIR-SILA$_3$]
attention; intelligence (g̃iš, 'tool', + zal, 'to pass time'; cf., mu-uš-zal) [? GIZZAL archaic frequency: 1].

g̃izzal...aka
to pay attention ('attention' + 'to do', cf., sağ-keš$_2$...aka).

g̃izzal-kalam-ma(k)
the most intelligent person in Sumer ('intelligence' + 'land (of Sumer)' + genitive).

g̃izzu
(cf., g̃issu).

-g̃u$_{10}$ [MU]
1.sg. possessive suffix, my - ThSLa §101.

-g̃u$_{10}$-um
1.sg. possessive suffix plus enclitic copula -am$_3$ (example: mašda$_2$-g̃u$_{10}$-um, 'he is my dependant') - ThSLa §108.

-g̃u$_{10}$-ur$_2$
1.sg. possessive suffix plus dative postposition -ra - ThSLa §106.

-g̃u$_{10}$-uš
1.sg. possessive suffix plus terminative postposition -še$_3$ - ThSLa §106.

g̃uruš, guruš
adult workman, laborer; young man (g̃ir$_3$/ir$_9$, 'splendid, very strong', + uš, 'to support, lift'; a scribal etymology is seen in this logogram's pictographic sledge sign, representing g̃iri$_3$, 'feet; road', or gur$_2$, 'wheels' [cf., gigir], + uš, 'to stand upon'; the g̃ pronunciation indicated by Ebla sign name *nu-rí-šúm*) [? GURUŠ archaic frequency: 68; concatenation of 2 sign variants].

g̃uruš-nig̃$_2$-gul
a worker who prepared a field's seed bed with a maul, a hammer-like implement used to break the clods left after harrowing ('worker' + 'maul').

g̃uruš-nu-dab$_5$(-ba)
a worker who is not conscripted ('laborer' + 'not' + 'to seize' + nominative).

g̃uruš ša$_3$-amar-du$_8$
a worker who yokes the steers ('laborer' + 'essence' + 'calf' + 'to yoke').

g̃uruš ša$_3$-gud-:n:-al-sar-ta
ox driver who tills n sar (of field per day) ('laborer' + 'essence' + 'ox' + amount +

'hoe' + 'surface area measure = 1/100 iku' + 'each').

g̃uruš ša$_3$-saḫar
earth moving workers ('laborer' + 'interior' + 'earth').

g̃uruš ša$_3$-ur$_3$-ra
a worker who harrows the field ('laborer' + 'essence' + 'to drag across' + nominative).

g̃uruš-u$_2$(-kud)-a
a worker who cuts grass ('laborer' + 'grass' + 'to cut off' + nominative).

g̃uruš-u$_2$-ze$_2$
a worker who pulls weeds ('laborer' + 'plants' + 'to pluck').

g̃uruš-zaḫ$_3$
an escaped worker ('laborer' + 'to flee').

g̃uškin
(now read as ku$_3$-sig$_{17}$).

g̃ušur
rafter beam (g̃iš, 'wood, tool', + ur$_3$, 'roof; beam'; cf., g̃iš-ur$_3$(-ra)).

Ḫ

***ḫa**
fish (not the usual word for fish, but the fish sign may get its syllabic reading of ḪA from *ḫ 'many' + a 'water' = 'fish', an alternative to the usual ku$_6$, kua) [KU$_6$ archaic frequency: 282; concatenates 3 sign variants].

ḫa^{sar}
fennel; anise (Akk., *šimru*).

ḫa-
optative/precative (*marû*) or affirmative (*ḫamṭu*) modal prefix; optative/precative meaning, 'may, let it be', with *marû* verb form or sometimes with an intransitive *ḫamṭu* form; affirmative meaning, 'indeed', with *ḫamṭu* verb form - ThSLa §394-§403.

ḫa-
sometimes used for cohortative modal prefix ga- ThSLa §386; cf, identical Emesal dialect cohortative and optative modal prefix da- ThSLa §385.

ḪA.A
(cf., zaḫ$_2$).

ḫa-ad
(cf., ḫad; ḫada$_2$).

ḫa-al-ma
vandals (ḫa-lam + nominative).

ḫa-am$_3$-
writing of precative and affirmative modal prefix /ḫa-/ with conjugation prefix /ĩ-/ and ventive element /-m-/ in NS period - ThSLa §304.

ḫa-az
(cf., ḫa-za).

ḫa-ba-zi-zi
agricultural worker; agricultural yield ('let it be taken out'; cf., ba-zi; Akk., *ḫabazûm*).

ḫa-bi$_2$-
writing of modal prefix ḫa- + conjugation prefix /bi-/ in NS period - ThSLa §304.

$^{(uruda)}$ḫa-bu$_{(2,3,6)}$-da
a heavy copper hoe, used for cutting reeds (Akkadian loanword, *ḫap/būtum*).

^{d}ḫa-ia$_3$^{mušen}
peacock (onomatopoeic from the bird's cry).

ḫa-la(-a)
n., (inheritance) share, division, lot (cf., ḫal).

v., to apportion, divide.

ḫa-lam
n., destruction (cf., *ḫilammu*, 'locusts', ḫul$_{(3)}$ and gilim).

v., to ruin; to destroy (often with -ta-); to forsake, to forget.

$^{g̃iš}$ḫa-lu-ub$_2$, $^{g̃iš}$ḫu-lu-ub$_2$
oak; wood used for vessels and furniture, especially chairs; its seeds, twigs, and bark used in magic and medicine (cf.,

še-^{ĝiš}ḫa-lu-ub$_2$) (Akk. loanword, *ḫaluppu(m)*).

ḫa-luḫ
(cf., ḫu-luḫ).

ḫa-ma-
writing of modal prefix ḫa- + conjugation prefix mu- + 1.sg. dative - ThSLa §336, §304.

ḫa-mun
mutually opposing; contrasting, harmonizing; clashing ('mixed spices' ?, like salt and pepper, cf., gamun and gu$_2$-mun).

ḫa-ra-an
(cf., ḫar-ra-an).

$^{(ĝiš)}$ḫa-šu-ur$_2$; ḫa-šur
a type of cypress tree or its scented resin (cf., $^{(ĝiš)}$šu-ur$_2$-min$_3$) (Akk. loanword ?, *ḫašūrum*).

ḫa-za
v., to hold, grasp; to retain; to maintain (Akk. *aḫāzum*, Orel & Stolbova 25).

ḫa-za
n., lettuce; salad (loan from Akkadian *ḫassû*; possible Emesal dialect form, cf., ḫi-iz^{sar}).

ḫa-za-num$_2$; ḫa-za-nu
local mayor; village headman (Akk. *ḫazannu(m) II*).

$^{(uruda)}$ḫa-zi(-in)
ax; ax handle (loanword from Akk. *ḫaṣṣinnu(m)*, Orel & Stolbova 1318, cf., 1305).

ḫa$_2$
numerous; diverse; assorted; mixed (cf., ḫi-a).

ḫa$_3$, ḫu$_3$, a$_6$, u
ten (usually written: u) (Ebla indicates ḫaw > o, u).

ḫab$_{(2)}$
n., foul smell; Opopanax or madder (?) (cf., $^{(ĝiš)}$šim-ḫab$_{(2)}$; ta-ḫab$_{(2)}$; u$_2$-ḫab$_2$) (attracting many vermin in open container; Akk., *bīšu I*, 'bad; malodorous', *ekēlu(m)*, 'to become dark', *ḫappu*, 'stinking, fetid').

v., to stink; to rot; to become dark.

adj., malodorous; fetid; stained.

ḫabrud
animal burrow; pit, hole; cave, cavern; crevice (ḫab, 'to stink', + buru$_3$(-d), 'hole'; cf., ub$_4$).

ḫad[PA]; ḫa-ad
scepter, which could be of silver (Akkadian loanword from *ḫaṭṭu(m)*, 'stick, scepter').

ḫada$_2$[UD], ḫad$_{(2)}$, ḫa-ad
v., to dry; to shine brightly (ḫe$_2$, 'let it become', + dag$_2$, 'brilliant').

adj., dry; arid; dried (e.g., fish); white.

ḫal
n., crotch, upper thigh; secret; divination expert; portion, share (cf., gi-ḫal, ḫa-la and pap-ḫal(-la)) (loans from Akkadian *ḫallu* I and *paḫallu*; cf., Orel & Stolbova #1928, ***pahal-** "leg, thigh" and #1929, ***pahal-** "break through, split") [ḪAL archaic frequency: 53].

v., to stream, run; to drain a reservoir (in order to irrigate land); to divide, separate; to deal out, distribute, allot, assign, allocate (ḫal-ḫa in *marû*).

$^{(ĝiš)}$ ^{šim}ḪAL
(cf., $^{(ĝiš)šim}$buluḫ).

ḫal-ḫal
to roll along; designation of the Tigris as the 'rolling river' (although one text from Ras Shamra equates it to the Euphrates); description of a plant (Akkadian *ammu II*, 'a name of the Tigris', *qarāru(m)*, 'to writhe, grovel, roll around').

$^{(ĝiš/uruda)}$ḫal-ḫal
basket; drum (Akkadian, *ḫalḫallu(m) II*, 'a basket'; *ḫalḫallatu(m)*, 'a kind of drum').

$^{(lu2)}$ḫal-ḫal-la
n., slanderer.

adj., dissolved; completely destroyed.

ḫal(-la)-tuš-a
apprentice ('one who sits on the thigh').

ḫalba$_{(2,3)}$, ḫalbi$_{(2,3)}$
frost, freezing.

ḫar, ḫara
ring; link (in a chain); coil or spiral of silver or other precious metal that can be worn as a ring or bracelet and was used as money (cf., ara$_{3,5}$, kin$_2$, kikken, ur$_5$) (Akk. *šawirum*, 'ring; torc for hand, foot, of precious metal') (originally ḫara, ara$_3$, 'circular millstone', cf., ara$_3$) [UR$_5$ archaic frequency: 34; concatenation of 2 sign variants].

^{ĝiš}ḪAR
(cf., ĝiš-kin$_2$).

$^{(u2)}$ḫar-an
a plant used for maintaining canal systems - perhaps a grass planted to halt erosion ('ring' + 'high').

^{na4}ḫar-gu$_2$-gil
neck ring, torc ('ring' + 'neck' + 'to cross; to lie athwart').

ḪAR-gud
(cf., mur-gu$_4$).

ḫar-ĝiri$_3$
ankle bracelet, of silver, gold, bronze, or precious stone; fetter ring ('ring' + 'foot'; Akk., *semeru*).

ḪAR-ḫa-da
a threshing sledge, *tribulum*, a raft-like lattice of staves bound in place with leather and with bitumen holding in place the thick flint blades inserted between the staves that cut the crop when dragged over the field by mules (millstone + many + with; cf., $^{(ĝiš)}$za-ḫa-da, mur, and mur-gu$_4$; cf., Akkadian *mur(u)dû(m)*, 'lattice, grating', and *ḫarādu(m) III*, 'to fit together, fabricate, mat, battering ram').

ḪAR-ḪAR
(cf., ara$_5$; kikken$_2$).

^{ĝiš}ḫar-ḫar
a musical instrument; chain (reduplicated 'ring, bracelet').

ḫar-ka-gu$_4$$^{(ku3-babbar)}$
ring (of silver) to muzzle (?) an ox ('ring' + 'mouth' + 'ox').

^{ĝiš}ḫar-mušen-na
bird snare ('ring' + 'bird' + genitive).

ḪAR-ra
(cf., ur$_5$(-ra)).

ḫar-ra-an; ḫa-ra-an
road, path, way; route, passage; journey, caravan; military campaign (Akkadian loanword, *ḫarrānu(m)*, from a 5,000 year-old city inhabited principally by Hurrians at the intersection of trade routes to Anatolia and the Mediterranean, mentioned in mid-3rd millenium Ebla tablets as *ḫar-ra-nu*^{ki}).

ḫar-šu
ring or bracelet, of silver, gold, bronze, or precious stone (cf., na$_4$-ara$_3$/ur$_5$-šu-se$_3$-ga) ('ring' + 'hand'; Akk., *semeru*).

ḫara$_3$
rogue, ruffian.

ḫara$_5$
spout; vessel with a large spout (ḫa-, optative prefix, + ra, 'to branch out from the side of').

ḫarub[DAG.KISIM$_5$×U$_2$.ĜIR$_2$]
carob.

ḫaš, ḫaz
n., wood shavings; pieces of cut wood (ḫa$_2$, 'numerous', + ša$_5$, 'to cut, break' or ze$_2$, 'to cut, pluck').

v., to break or cut off (twigs, branches); to snap a reed; to clear away, strip off plants from land; to break up; to pulverize; to thresh grain.

ḫaš$_2$ [ZIG] ; ḫaš$_4$ [ZUM]
lower abdomen; loins; back; upper thighs, buttocks; haunches (ḫa$_2$, 'mixture', + a, 'water/urine', + še$_{10}$, 'excrement'; cf., etymology of šag$_4$).

ḫaš$_{2/4}$-gal
upper thighs; buttocks; groin region ('loins' + 'large').

ḫaš$_4$...dab$_5$
to hold firmly ('thighs' + 'to hold, seize').

ḫaš$_4$...dug$_4$/du$_{11}$/e
to have sexual relations ('loins' + 'to do').

ḫaš$_4$...g̃a$_2$-g̃a$_2$
to rejoice ('loins' + 'to place').

ḫaš$_4$...tal$_2$ [PI]
to rejoice ('upper thighs' + 'to spread, unfold').

$^{(g̃iš)}$ḫašḫur [MA*gunû*]
apple (tree); apples found dried and kept on strings in the Royal Cemetary of Ur (ḫaš, 'to break off (twigs or branches)', + gurun; gur$_2$, 'fruit; sphere') [ḪAŠḪUR archaic frequency: 101].

$^{(g̃iš)}$ḫašḫur-duru$_5$
fresh apple ('apple' + 'moist').

$^{(g̃iš)}$ḫašḫur-ḫad$_2$
dried apple (slice) ('apple' + 'dried').

$^{(g̃iš)}$ḫašḫur-kur-ra
pear (tree) (Akk. *kamiššaru(m)*); quince (tree) (Akk. *supurgillu(m)*); apricot (?) (tree) (Akk. *armannu(m)*) ('foreign apple', 'apple from the east').

$^{(g̃iš)}$ḫašḫur-ma-da
pear (tree) (Akk. *kamiššaru(m)*) ('apple of the district').

ḫaz
(cf., ḫaš).

$^{g̃iš}$ḫaz...aka
(cf., g̃iš-ḫaš...aka).

ḫe
(cf., ḫi, ḫe).

ḫe$_{(2)}$
abundance; abundant.

ḫe-BAD^{mušen}
(cf., ḫe$_{(2)}$-uš$_2$^{mušen}).

$^{(siki/tug2)}$ḫe-me-da
(cf., $^{(siki/tug2)}$ḫe$_2$-me-da).

ḫe-eš$_{19}$-ši
captive; detained (cf., ḫeš$_5$).

ḫe$_2$-
optative/precative or affirmative verbal prefix before conjugation prefix /bi-/ and /ĩ-/, which it incorporates, cf., ḫa-; this form by itself can be an abbreviation of ḫé-àm, 'so be it' - ThSLa §394, §400-§402.

ḫe$_2$-...nam-...
let it be.

ḫe$_2$-am$_3$; ḫe$_2$-a
'so be it', 'let it be (so)'; 'whether it be, though it be'; 'yes'; consent, approval; wish - ThSLa §400, §540 (optative prefix + ĩ + 'to be').

ḫe$_2$-am$_3$...dug$_4$
to accede, approve; to say yes ('consent' + 'to speak').

ḫe$_2$-am$_3$-me-am$_3$
[that] is our wish ('wish' + ĩ + 'to be').

ḫe$_2$-ba-
writing of modal prefix ḫa- + conjugation prefix /ba-/ in NS period - ThSLa §304.

ḫe$_2$-be$_2$-
writing of modal prefix ḫa- + conjugation prefix /bi-/ in OS period - ThSLa §304.

ḫe$_2$-bi$_2$-
writing of modal prefix ḫa- + conjugation prefix /bi-/ in NS, IL, and OB periods - ThSLa §304.

ḫe$_2$-dab$_5$ (-ba)
a class of workers and persons (optative prefix + 'to seize, bind, hire').

ḫe$_2$-du$_7$
decoration; adornment; that which is suitable or fitting; that which is destined ('let it be suitable, fitting').

ḫe$_2$-em-
writing of precative and affirmative modal prefix /ḫa-/ with conjugation prefix /ĩ-/ and ventive element /-m-/ - ThSLa §304.

ḫe$_2$-em-ma-
writing of modal prefix ḫa- + conjugation prefixes /ĩ-ba-/ ThSLa §336, §304.

ḫe$_2$-em-mi-
writing of modal prefix ḫa- + conjugation prefixes /ĩ-bi-/ ThSLa §394, §304.

ḫe$_{(2)}$-en-du(-du)
way, path (optative prefix + 3rd person animate pronominal element + 'to walk, go'; cf., in-di; ki-in-du).

ḫe$_2$-en-ga-
writing of modal prefix ḫa- + conjugation prefixes /ĩ-ga-/ in OB period - ThSLa §304.

ḫe$_2$-en-na-nam-ma-am$_3$
may it indeed be so - ThSLa §379 (optative prefix + ĩ + na-nam, 'indeed' + enclitic copula, 'to be').

ḫe$_2$-en-ze$_2$-er
very small, tiny (ḫe$_2$-ĩ-n-ze$_2$-er, 'may it be torn up'; cf., ḫenzer, 'weakling; cripple').

ḫe$_2$-g̃al$_2$
overflow; abundance ('let there be available' or 'having abundance').

ḫe$_2$-ma-
writing of modal prefix ḫa- + conjugation prefixes /ĩ-ba-/ in Gudea period; also writing of modal prefix ḫa- + conjugation prefix mu- + 1.sg. dative in the NS period - ThSLa §304.

ḫe$_2$-me-
writing of modal prefix ḫa- + conjugation prefixes /ĩ-bi-/ in OB period - ThSLa §304 (cf. also, -me-en; -me-e).

$^{(siki/tug2)}$ḫe$_{(2)}$-me-da
red-dyed (wool/cloth) (Akkadian *tabarru* and *nabāsu(m)*).

ḫe$_2$-mi-
writing of modal prefix ḫa- + conjugation prefixes /ĩ-bi-/ ThSLa §394, §304.

ḫe$_2$-...nam-...
let it be.

ḫe$_{(2)}$-nun
abundance, fruitfulness, plenty ('may it be; numerous' + 'great, fine, deep').

ḫe$_2$-ši; ḫe-ši; ḫe-še
gloom; darkness; to turn pitch dark (loan from Akk. *ḫašû I*, 'dark', *ḫašû V*, 'to become dark'; Orel & Stolbova #1320 ***ḫaš-** 'become dark').

ḫe$_{(2)}$-uš$_2$^{mušen}
a small diving water-fowl ('numerous' + 'to kill').

ḫe$_2$-zu-ḫe$_2$-zu; ḫe$_2$-zu-ḫe$_2$-za
knowledge (reduplicated 'let it be known' + nominative).

$^{(gi)}$ḫenbur$_{(2)}$
(green) reed shoots, stalks; the succulent part of a reed or rush, used in making beer ('let it be harvested, opened, loosened, released' ?; Akkadian *ḫabbūru(m)*).

ḫenzer
weakling; cripple; infant (cf., ḫe$_2$-en-ze$_2$-er).

ḫeš$_5$
(cf., šag̃a).

ḫi, ḫe
v., to mix (cf., šar$_2$/sar$_2$) [ḪI archaic frequency: 291].

adj., mixed, averaged - such as the lengths of the parallel sides of a roughly rectangular field (cf., kur; mer).

ḫi-a; ḫi-da
mixed; alloyed; various; unspecified; numerous - ThSLa §75 (cf., ḫa$_2$) ('to mix' + subordination/comitative suffix).

ḪI-GUZ
(cf., dub$_3$...guz).

ḫi-in-tum
a type of bead for a necklace, usually of carnelian stone (cf., tu-dur) (loan from Akkadian *ḫiddu(m), ḫindu(m)*).

ḫi-iz^{sar}, ḫi-is^{sar}
lettuce (loan from Akkadian *ḫassû*).

ḫi-iz-tur^{sar}
a bitter leaf vegetable, e.g., chicory (Akk., *murāru(m)*).

ḫi-li
beauty; (sexual) charm, appeal; luxuriance; wig ('numerous' + 'to be happy; to sing').

ḫi-li...aka
to behave gracefully ('beauty' + 'to do').

ḫi-li-ba
the underworld ('beauty' + 'to give'; cf., ḫilib).

ḫi-li...du$_8$(-du$_8$)
to apply adornments ('beauty' + 'to adorn; to spread').

ḫi-li-em$_3$
Emesal dialect for ḫa-lam.

ḫi-li...gur$_3$-ru
to be full of opulence ('beauty' + 'to bear, carry').

ḫi-li-ḫi-li
v., to experience great pleasure; to rejoice (redup. 'beauty, charm').

adj., alluring.

ḫi-li...su$_3$(-su$_3$)
full of appeal ('beauty' + 'to furnish; to rejoice'; cf., me-lam$_2$...su$_3$-su$_3$).

ḫi-nun
(cf., ḫe$_2$-nun).

ḫi-ri(-a)-tum
an ornament, of gold or lapis, weighing 2 or 3 gin$_2$ (Akkadian loanword from *ḫirītum II*).

ḫi-ri-tum$_2$
trench, channel; canal; moat (Akkadian loanword from *ḫirītu(m) I*).

ḫi-ši; ḫi-še
(cf., ḫe$_2$-ši).

ḫilib, ḫalib[IGI.KUR]
entrance to the netherworld (cf., ganzer$_3$) (loanword from Akk. *ḫālipu*, 'accuser, prosecutor' ?; cf., ḫi-li-ba).

ḫir[KEŠDA]
n., produce, yield (abundance + to go out + to flow).

v., to squeeze, tighten (cf., giri$_{11}$, kirid).

^{u2}ḫirin, ḫirim[KI.KAL]
the root stalks of the spikenard, an aromatic rhizome in the valerian family, imported from India, and used in perfumes; a weed grass or the wasteland in which it grows (cf., ^{u2}KI.KAL; $^{(ĝiš)}$arina/erina$_8$) (ḫe, 'abundant', + ir, 'perfume', + in, 'straw'; Akk. *arantu* and *lardu*).

ḫu, u$_{11}$
bird (earlier word than mušen).

ḫu-
modal prefix ḫa- before conjugation prefix mu- in OB lit. texts and Isin/Larsa texts - ThSLa §394, §304.

$^{(ĝiš/uruda)}$ḫu-bu-um, ḫu-pu-um; ḫu-bu$_3$-um
axle; wheel assembly (Akkadian loanword, *ḫūpu(m) I*, '(wheel) rim; ring').

$^{(lu2)}$ḫu-dab$_5$-bu
a category of worker.

ḪU-GAG
(cf., mušen-du$_3$).

ḪU.ḪI
(cf., mud).

ḫu-ḫu-uz
(cf., guz, ḫuz).

^{ĝiš}ḫu-lu-ub$_2$
(cf., ^{ĝiš}ḫa-lu-ub$_2$).

ḫu-luḫ, ḫa-luḫ
to scare; to become scared, frightened ('birds/fish' + 'to sweep away').

ḫu-luḫ-ḫa
adj., angry, terrifying (cf., uruda(-ḫu)-luḫ-ḫa) ('to scare' + adjectival -a).

ḫu-LUM
(cf., ḫu-nu-um/ḫu-num$_2$).

ḫu-mu
(cf., ḫuĝ-u$_3$ and ḫu-nu/ḫu-ḫu-nu).

ḫu-mu-
writing of modal prefix ḫa- + conjugation prefix /mu-/ in Isin-Larsa and OB period - ThSLa §304.

ḪU.NA$_2$
(cf., sa$_4$, še$_{21}$).

ḫu-nu, ḫu-ḫu-nu
helpless (participial form of ḫuĝ, ḫun(-ĝ), 'to rest, repose; to abate'; cf., ^{lu2}al-ḫu-nu).

ḫu-nu-um; ḫu-num$_2$
a kind of table (Akkadian loanword, *ḫunnum*).

ḫu-pu-um
(cf., ḫu-bu-um).

ḫu-ri$_2$-in^{mušen}, u$_{11}$-ri$_2$-in^{mušen}
eagle, lammergeier vulture (?) (Akkadian loanword, *urinnu I*; Orel & Stolbova #52 ***'ar-/*war-** 'eagle'; note that AHw says that *urinnu II*, 'standard, totem', is a Sumerian loanword).

$^{(u2)}$ḫu-ri$_2$-um; $^{(u2)}$ḫu-ri$_2$-a-num$_2$
a spice (Akkadian *ḫurium* or *uriyānu(m)*, 'fennel' ?).

ḫu-ru(-um)
n., idiot, fool, hillbilly, boor; social inferior (Akkadian loanword, *aḫurrû*, 'younger child').

adj., compliant, submissive.

ḪU.SI
(cf., u$_5$).

ḫu-su
(cf., ḫaš$_2$).

ḫu-ur$_2$-sa$_2$-ĝa$_2$/ne
(cf., ḫur-saĝ).

ḫub
hole, recess, pit (cf., tun; ub$_4$) (Akk. *ḫuppu(m) II*) [ḪUB archaic frequency: 1].

ḫub$_2$, ḫup$_2$
acrobat, athlete, a cultic dancer; foot; a type of weaver; a left-handed or ambidextrous person (?) (Akk. *ḫuppû(m) II*) [ḪUB$_2$ archaic frequency: 2].

ḫub$_2$-dar...aka
to run; to race; to rush around; to send running ('foot' + 'to slice' + 'to make'; cf., kaš$_4$...dar).

ḫub$_2$-gaz
slaughter ('athlete' + 'to slaughter').

ḫub$_2$...sar; ḫub$_2$...du$_{10}$
to run (fast); to speed; to end in a point, like an arrow ('foot' + 'to run').

ḫub$_2$...šu$_2$
to gallop; to trample (?) ('foot' + 'to cover').

ḫub$_2$...ze$_2$
Emesal dialect form for ḫub$_2$...sar; ḫub$_2$...du$_{10}$.

ḫubur
netherworld (ḫab, 'to rot, stink', + ur$_2$, 'root; base').

$ḫud_2$
morning [UD archaic frequency: 419].

ḫug̃, ḫun(-g̃)
to hire or rent (someone or something); to introduce (to a job); to enthrone (a ruler); to rest; to repose; to abate; to placate (cf., al-ḫu-nu, ḫu-nu, and ḫu-ḫu-nu) (many + to mete out to).

ḫug̃-u_3
to rest (*marû* form) ('to hire; to rest', + 'to sleep'; cf., $kuš_2$-u_3 and ḫu-nu/ḫu-ḫu-nu).

ḫul, ḫula, ḫulu[IGI.UR]; $ḫul_3$
n., evil (vermin + abundant, numerous; cf., *ḫilammu*, 'locusts', ḫa-lam, 'destruction') [ḪUL archaic frequency: 1].

v., to destroy; to ruin; to damage, harm.

adj., bad, evil; hated; damaged; ugly; hostile, malicious.

adv., painfully; violently; maliciously; in an evil mood.

ḫul-bi
adv., in an evil way ('evil' + adverbial force suffix)

ḫul...dim_2
to hurt, cause pain ('evil' + 'to create, make')

ḫul-dim_2-ma
evil; wickedness ('evil' + 'to create, make' + nominative).

ḫul-du
wicked ('evil' + 'walking'; cf., $erim_2$-du, 'wicked').

ḫul...gig
to hate ('evil' + 'to be sick').

ḫul-gig(-ga)
n., hate; poor quality beer.

adj., hated, loathsome; difficult.

ḫul-g̃al_2
evil, wicked (ones) (cf., a_2-ḫu-ul-g̃al_2) ('evil' + 'being').

ḫul-ḫul
to devastate (redup. 'to destroy, ruin').

ḫul-mu_2-a
bad weed(s) ('evil' + 'growth(s)').

ḫul-tag(-tag)
devastated; an adjective for soil quality ('evil' + 'to afflict').

$ḫul_2$
n., joy (many + abundance, from the joy of many children, cf., tuḫul; bibra).

v., to be happy; to rejoice over (usually with -da-, but also -ši-).

adj., joyous.

adv., joyously.

$ḫul_2$-la
very happy; joyful ('joy' + subordination suffix -a).

$ḫul_3$
neck ring, torc, collar (Akk. *ḫullu(m)*).

ḫuluḫ
to tremble; to be terrified; to terrify.

ḫum
to wrestle; to be passionate; to bruise; coagulated blood; to smash, break, snap off; to thresh grain; to paralyze or be paralyzed; to make low; to be in motion; to send (many + $u_{(3,4,8)}$, 'fight, dispute' + $me_{3,7,9,11}$, 'battle').

(lu2) ḫum-ḫum
swollen up, as with edema (swelling) from diabetes; impoverished, destitute (Akk. *ḫubbušu(m)*; *luppunum*; cf., g̃iri_3-ḫum, 'deformed or missing feet').

ḫun
(cf., ḫug̃).

ḫur, ur_5[ḪAR]
n., hole; limb, stem, handle (Akk. *ḫurru(m)*, "hole"; Orel & Stolbova #1376 ***ḫur**- 'hole, pit' derived from #1375 ***ḫur**- 'dig', Akk. *ḫerû(m) II*, "to dig; excavate").

v., to scratch, mark, draw, sketch, inscribe, incise, outline; to grind; to dig (many small explosive sounds + ur_3, 'to drag').

adv., ever (after or again) (Akkadian loanword *ḫurri*).

ḫur-sag̃
hill-country; mountainous region ('holes, valleys' + 'points, peaks').

ḫur-sag̃-galam(-ma)
literary term for a stepped pyramid, ziggurat, particularly at Nippur and Ur ('mountain' + galam, 'to ascend; to skillfully build' + nominative).

^{u2}ḪUR.SAG̃^{sar}
(cf., ^{u2}azugna^{sar}, ^{u2}azukna^{sar}, ^{u2}azubir^{sar}).

ḫuš
v., to be angry (compare guz, ḫuz).

adj., furious, terrible, terrifying, awesome, fierce; wild (said of animals); fiery red (Akk. *ruššû*).

adv., fiercely; furiously.

ḫuš-a
something red ('angry' + nominative).

ḫuz
(cf., guz, ḫuz).

I

i
n., cry of pain (Akk. *nâqu(m) I*, 'to cry (out), wail'; derived from er_2, ir_2, 'tears; complaint' ?; cf., i-^{d}utu; i-lu) [I archaic frequency: 17].

v., to capture, defeat, overcome (cf., e_3; i) (Akk. *kamû(m) II*, 'to bind').

i(-r)
(cf., ir).

i-bi_2[BIL]; i_3-bi_2
smoke ('to go out, rise' + 'to burn').

Emesal dialect for igi, 'eye; face; to see; before, in front of'.

i-bi_2-eš-du; i-de_3-eš-du
Emesal dialect for igi-du and igi-$še_3$...du.

i-bi_2-za
(financial) loss; legal quarrel ('smoke' + 'cry, noise').

i-da-al(-am_3)
(cf., a-da-lam).

i-dib
threshold; flagstone, slab; device, contrivance ('to go out' + 'to traverse, cross').

i-gi_4-in-zu
indeed!; moreover; as if, like (used in hypothetical comparisons) - ThSLa §149.

i-i
to rise, sprout; to praise, extol (reduplicated e_3).

i-im-ma
Emesal dialect for min, 'two'.

i-lim
awesome radiance (e_3, ed_2; i, 'to be or become visible' + 'thousand; awesome'; cf., pa...e_3, 'to shine'; su-lim, 'terrifying appearance'; Akk. *rašubbatu(m)*; *šalummatu(m)*).

i-lu
sad song, lament, dirge, wailing (cf., a-la/a-la-la) ('cry' + 'to multiply'; Akk. *nubû*).

i-lu-di; ulu_3-di
a priest devoted to ritual lamentations; frequently used as a personal name ('sad song, lament' + 'speaking/doing'; cf., i-lu...du_{11}/e, 'to sing a dirge'; Akk., *munabbûm*).

i-lu...du_{11}/e
to sing a dirge ('dirge' + 'to speak, sing').

i-lu-lam-ma
a 'productive' lament or prayer; the noise of wailing.

i-mi-tum
(cf., $middu_{(2)}$, $mitum_{(2)}$).

i-ne-eš$_2$
(cf., i$_3$-ne-eš$_2$).

i-ni-im
(cf., inim).

i-ra
(cf., er$_2$).

i-ri-; i-ri$_2$-
writings of conjugation prefix /ĩ-/ + 2.sg. dative -ri- ThSLa §478.

i-ri(-im-ma)
(cf., erim$_2$).

(ğiš)i-ri$_9$-na, i-ri$_8$-na
root(s) (cf., (ğiš)arina/erina$_8$).

i-si-iš
complaint; lament; wail; sorrow (cf., isiš$_{2,3}$).

i-si-iš...ğar
to wail (to someone: dative) (cf., si$_{12}$-si$_{12}$...ğar) (isiš$_{2,3}$, 'moaning' + 'to set').

i-si-iš...lal/la$_2$
to sit in anguish (isiš$_{2,3}$, 'sorrow' + 'to carry').

i-ti
(cf., itud).

i-^{d}utu
outcry; complaint; cry for justice; 'Oh, Shamash!' ('cry' + divine determinative + 'god of justice').

i-ze-em$_3$, i-zi-iğ$_3$
Emesal dialect for ezen/ezem.

i-zi
wave(s) (cf., iz-zi) ('to go out, rise' + 'to rise, go out').

ĩ-
(cf., i$_3$-).

i$_2$
(cf., ia$_{2,7,9}$, i$_2$).

i$_2$-ku$_2$
inclined angle, inclination (e.g., 45 degrees - the angle formed by animals eating fodder).

i$_3$[NI]
oil; dairy fat; cream; a thickened spread, butter.

i$_3$-
impersonal verbal conjugation prefix, opposite of mu-, indicates distance from speaker, or social distance between actor and a person of lower social standing, a nasalized vowel ĩ (example: i$_3$-sa$_{10}$, 'I bought') - ThSLa §306-314.

i$_3$-ab$_2$
fat of cows, cream (?) ('fat' + 'cow').

i$_3$-ab$_2$-si$_3$-ga
clarified butter, ghee (Old Sumerian) (cf., i$_3$-nun) ('cow fat' + 'to make flat [by boiling away the water]').

i$_3$-ba
monthly oil rations; ointment ('oil' + 'portion, rations').

i$_3$-bara$_2$-ga
purified sesame oil; a high quality edible oil pressed from hulled sesame seed kernels (as opposed to oil pressed from unhulled sesame seeds) ('oil' + 'to comb, filter' + nominative).

i$_3$-bi$_2$
(cf., i-bi$_2$).

i$_3$-bi$_2$-
writing of prospective modal prefix u$_3$- + /bi-/ in Gudea texts - ThSLa §409, §304.

i$_3$-bi$_2$-la
(cf., ibila).

i$_3$-bi$_2$-za
loss; reimbursement, compensation, remuneration ('when it bleats').

i$_3$-dab$_5$
in charge of - the third level in the herding hierarchy (impersonal verbal conjugation prefix + 'to hold, hire, receive').

i$_3$...de$_2$
to make oil/fat ('oil' + 'to pour').

$^{(lu2)}$i$_3$-du$_8$
doorkeeper; gatekeeper; porter; janitor (impersonal verbal conjugation prefix + 'to crack, open').

$^{(lu2)}$i$_3$-du$_8$-guru$_7$
granary guard ('doorkeeper' + 'granary').

i$_3$-dub
depot, granary, silo, storehouse; storage jugs (impersonal verbal conjugation prefix + 'to store, heap up'; Akkadian *išpiku(m)*, 'stores (of crops); grain-bin').

i$_3$-dug$_3$(-ga), i$_3$-du$_{10}$-ga
perfume; good oil ('oil' + 'sweet').

i$_3$-ga
dairy products ('butter' + 'milk').

i$_3$-ga-
writing of conjugation prefixes /ĩ-ga-/ in OAkk and Gudea texts - ThSLa §323, §304.

i$_3$-ge$_{(4)}$-en
really, actually; an expression, 'but no' - ThSLa §150.

i$_3$-gu-la
perfumed oil ('oil' + 'flax' + 'beauty, desire').

i$_3$-gu$_7$
a rare OB math. expression for multiplication ('he eats').

i$_3$-g̃iš
sesame oil; not just eaten, also used in textile/leather manufacturing ('oil' + 'tree').

i$_3$-ḫe-nun(-na)
precious oil ('oil of plenty'; Akk. *iḫenunnakku*; cf., ḫe$_2$-nun; ḫi-nun).

i$_3$-ib$_2$-
verbal chain prefix possibly with locative-terminative morpheme /-i-/ and element /-b-/, either the inanimate pronoun or an 'ientive' element, denoting 'spatial and emotional movement away from the speaker' - ThSLa §331, §333-§334.

i$_3$-im-
verbal chain prefix possibly with locative-terminative morpheme /-i-/ and ventive element /-m-/ - ThSLa §329-§335.

i$_3$-in-
verbal chain prefix possibly with locative-terminative morpheme /-i-/ and animate 3.sg. pronominal element /-n-/ in NS texts - ThSLa §333-§334.

i$_3$-ir-a
fragrant ointment, salve ('oil' + 'perfume' + nominative).

i$_3$-ku$_6$
fish oil ('oil' + 'fish').

i$_3$-la$_2$
(cf., in-la$_2$).

i$_3$-laḫ$_4$
a profession (impersonal verbal prefix + 'to fling away').

i$_3$-li$_2$; i$_3$-li
fine oil (jar); balm (cf., a-zal-le) ('oil' + 'true measure; fine oil').

i$_3$-lu
(cf., i-lu).

i$_3$-ma-
writing of conjugation prefixes /ĩ-ba-/ in OS texts - ThSLa §306-§308, §304, §337.

i$_3$-mi-
writing of conjugation prefixes /ĩ-bi-/ in OS and Gudea texts - ThSLa §338, §304.

i$_3$-ne-eš$_2$; i$_3$-ne-še$_3$; i-ne-eš$_2$; e-ne-eš$_2$
now - ThSLa §151 (cf., en-na-bi-še$_3$).

i$_3$-nun
butter; clarified butter, ghee (Neo-Sumerian) (cf., i$_3$-ab$_2$-si$_3$-ga) ('fat, oil' + 'noble').

i_3-ra_2-ra_2
ointment mixer, perfume-maker ('fat' + reduplicated 'to stir, mix').

i_3-sag̃
best, fine oil ('oil' + 'prime').

i_3-si-na
(cf., e-si-na).

i_3-šaḫ
pig lard ('fat' + 'pig').

i_3-šur
preparer of sesame oil ('oil' + 'to press out a liquid').

i_3-ti
moonlight (cf., itud).

i_3-udu
fat, tallow ('fat' + 'sheep').

i_3-zi
(cf., i-zi).

i_3-zu_2-lum
date oil ('oil' + 'dried date-fruit').

i_5-g̃ar[KA.G̃AR]
to promise, predict; ominous remark (inim, 'word' + 'to make, establish').

i_7
(cf., ida_2).

$ia_{2,7,9}$, i_2
five.

ia_3
(cf., i_3).

ia_4, i_4
pebble, counter.

ib, eb
corner, angle, nook [IB archaic frequency: 252; concatenates 2 sign variants].

ib-gal
oval terrace/temple ('angles' + 'large').

ib-$si_{(2/8)}$
square ('angles' + 'equal'; cf., ib_2-si_8, 'equal side').

ib_2, eb_2
n., middle; waist; hip; loins; thighs.

v., to be angry; to flare up in anger; to curse, insult.

ib_2-
conjugation prefix /ĩ-/ + inanimate pronominal element /-b-/, 'it', ThSLa §307, §304.

ib_2-ba
at the hip; at waist-level ('waist, hip' + locative).

ib_2-ba
n., anger (cf., $ša_3$-ib_2-ba(-/ak/)).

v., to be full of rage.

adv., in anger ('to be angry' + adverbial -bi + locative).

ib_2-ba-la_2
plains, flat country ('at waist-level' + lal, 'to measure, weigh'; cf., il_2-la_2, 'elevation' and dun_3-la_2, 'depression').

ib_2-dam-za
anger ('to be angry' + dum-dam...za, 'to grumble').

ib_2-gig
a disease of the loins/hip area that afflicts female animals ('middle' + 'disease').

ib_2-ku_5
crippled hip, leg ('waist, hip, thigh' + 'to curse'; cf., tugul-ku_5, 'crippled hip').

(tug2) ib_2-lal
belt, sash, tie, band, headband ('hips' + 'to hang, stretch, extend').

ib_2-si
enough! ('it is full, sufficient').

ib_2-si_8[DI]
(in math. texts) equal-side; N-e M ib_2-si_8: M is the square root of N, i.e., M squared equals N ('N is M equal-sided'; cf., ib-si_8, 'square').

ib_2-$taka_4$
leftover, remainder ('it is disregarded').

$^{kuš}ib_2$-ur_3
(cf., $^{kuš}eg_2$-ib_2-ur_3).

ibila
son(s); heir(s), successor(s) to the father's whole estate, both assets and liabilities; inheritance (ib_2 (subj. prefix) + ila_2, 'he carries it'; cf. rare i_3-bi_2-la; Akk., *aplu(m) II*, 'heir, son').

ibira
(cf., $tibira_2$).

$^{(uruda)}$id-gurum, id-gur_2
a large standard vessel containing 4 shekels (gin_2) of oil (Akkadian loanword, *itqūru(m)*, 'spoon').

ida_2, id_2, i_7
river; main canal; watercourse; an adjective for soil at the canal (ed_2, 'to issue', + a, 'water').

id_2-a-dug
irrigation project ('canal' + 'water' + 'vessel').

id_2 ki sur-ra
boundary canal ('canal' + 'to set the boundary').

$id_{4,8}$, it_4
(cf., itud).

idigna
the Tigris river; sluice (ida_2/id_2, 'river', + i_3, 'impersonal verbal conjugation prefix', + ĝen, 'to go', + nominative a, "the river that goes", the Tigris was a faster-moving river than the Euphrates; it was less likely to overflow because, not depositing as much silt, it did not built up its bed as high) [? IDIGNA archaic frequency: 25].

idim, edim
n., spring, underground water; weight, mass (ida_2, 'river', + mu_2, 'to sprout, appear').

v., to shut or close up.

adj., wild, raging, rabid, mad; considerable, distinguished, honored.

IDIM/BAD
heaven (cf., Sjöberg, "Emar S[a] Voc", #683').

IDIM/IDIM.BUR
(cf., $banšur_2$).

$^{(ĝiš/gi)}$ig
door, entrance [IG archaic frequency: 43; concatenates 2 sign variants].

$^{(ĝiš)}$ig-šu-ur_2
bolt; bar ('door' + 'hand' + 'trunk').

^{ĝiš}ig-šu-ur_2...DU
to bolt the door ('bolt' + 'to go').

igi
n., eye(s); glance; face; aspect, looks; front (reduplicated ig, 'door') [IGI archaic frequency: 21].

v., to see.

adj., the main component of many stone names.

prep., before, in front of; in the presence of (with ...-a(k)-šè) - ThSLa §159, §201.

igi
reciprocal of a number (= the multiplier that will give 60; the igi of 5 is 0;12) (abbreviation of igi-$ĝal_2$, 'that which is opposite').

igi-a-a-na-$še_3$
before his father ('front' + 'father' + ni-a(k), 'his' + genitive + terminative postposition, 'unto').

igi...bad
to open one's eyes ('eye' + 'to open').

igi-bala
traitor, turncoat; shiftiness ('eyes' + 'to turn, change, revolt').

igi...bar
to look, to see (often with -ni-); to look at or upon (with -ši-); to look

closely; to look after, care for ('eye' + 'to open').

igi-zi...bar
to choose; to legitimate ('to look at' + 'legitimate; to strengthen').

igi-bar
sight.

$^{(lu2)}$igi-bar-ra
inspector, exposer; keen-sighted ('eye' + 'to open' + nominative).

igi-daĝal
wide seeing eyes ('eyes' + 'wide').

igi(-še$_3$)...dib$_{(2)}$
to pass in front of/before ('face' + terminative postposition + 'to pass by').

IGI.DIB
(cf., u$_3$).

igi-du
adj. for a lead animal; leader (also read as palil and igištu) ('front' + 'walking').

igi-še$_3$...du
to walk in front of ('to the front' + 'to walk').

igi...du$_3$
to be on the lookout for (with -ši-) ('eye' + 'to raise erect').

IGI.DU$_3$
(cf., šukur).

igi...du$_8$
to see (often with -ni- or bi$_2$-); to witness; to experience; to discover; to inspect; to spy; to read (with -r auslaut in *marû* singular) ('eye' + 'to crack open').

igi-du$_8$(-a)
onlooker; observer; overseer; controller; attendant.

igi-du$_8$-a
visibility (of the moon) ('to see' + nominative; Akk. *tāmartu(m)*, 'view(ing); audience-gift').

IGI.DUB
(cf., aĝrig; ĝiskim).

IGI.E$_2$
(cf., ug$_6$, u$_6$).

IGI.ERIM
(cf., sag$_{10}$, sig$_5$; kurum$_7$).

IGI.ESIR$_2$
a type of bitumen.

IGI.EŠ$_2$
(cf., libir).

IGI.GAG
(cf., šukur).

igi...gi$_4$
to change the appearance ('face, appearance' + 'to reject, overturn').

igi(-tur)...gid$_2$
to despise, look upon with disfavor or anger ('eye, face' + 'little' + 'to lengthen'; cf., saĝ-ki...gid$_2$).

igi-gu$_4$
a stylized biconvex geometric figure constructed from 120 degree arcs ('eye' + 'ox').

igi...gub
to look at; to stand before ('eye; face, front' + 'to set; to stand').

igi-gub(-ba)
coefficient ('inverse' + 'fixed').

igi-gun$_3$-gun$_3$
flashing eyes ('eyes; face' + 'to sparkle; to have on makeup').

igi...ĝal$_2$
to (be able to) see; to understand; to look upon, behold (often with -ši-) ('eye' + 'to place [into]').

igi-ĝal$_2$(-la)
n., insight, wisdom; wise one; in math, that which is opposite = reciprocal ('eyes' + 'available' + nominative).

adj., clever, intelligent.

participle, seeing as, taking into account that.

igi-4-g̃al$_2$
1/4.

igi-6-g̃al$_2$
1/6 (cf., šušana = 2/6).

igi-g̃al$_2$-tuku
wise ('wisdom' + 'having').

igi...g̃ar
to face, look at (with -ši- adds intensity to the gaze); to consider, contemplate; to appear before someone; to appear in court; to prepare to (...) ('eye; face' + 'to set').

IGI-G̃AR(-m)
(cf., kurum$_7$).

igi-ḫul...dim$_2$
to put the evil eye (on someone) ('eyes/face' + 'evil' + 'to fashion').

igi...ḫuš
to frown at; to frighten ('eyes/face' + 'fierce').

IGI.IGI
(cf., bad$_5$-bad$_5$; šeš$_{2,3,4}$).

igi...il$_2$
to direct the eyes to (with -ši-, at a specific object); to view; to look over ('eyes' + 'to lift').

igi-il$_2$-la
choice ('eyes' + 'to lift' + nominative).

igi-kal
wild-eyed; brazen; dangerous ('eyes' + 'strong').

igi...KAR$_2$(guru$_6$?)
to look upon; to examine, inspect; to select (often with -ši-) ('eyes' + 'to illuminate').

igi-KAR$_2$(guru$_6$?)
observation; check, inspection; provisions.

igi...lal/la$_2$
to close one's eyes; to look at; to read ('eyes' + 'to diminish, retreat'/'to lift high').

igi-la$_2$
(cf., igi-tum$_3$-la$_2$).

igi...lib$_{(4)}$
to be sleepless, awake ('eyes' + 'to be sleepless').

igi-lugala
before the king ('front' + 'king' + a(k), genitive).

igi-me$_3$(-/ak/)
before the battle; vanguard ('before; front' + 'battle' + genitive).

IGI.NIG̃$_2$
(cf., kurum$_7$).

igi-nig̃in$_2$
treachery ('eye' + 'to wander, turn away').

igi-nim(-ma)
above; upper country - from Sumer either the east or the northwest ('to face' + 'east').

igi-nu-du$_8$(-a)
blind person - a foreigner slave; unskilled worker ('eyes' + 'not' + 'cracked open').

igi-nu-g̃al$_2$
blind ('eyes' + 'not' + 'available').

IGI.RI
(cf., ar).

IGI.RU
(cf., pad$_3$).

igi-sag$_{10}$
sorted (e.g., onions) ('eye' + 'mild, sweet, good; of fine quality ').

igi-sag̃-g̃a$_2$
sorted; selected ('eye' + 'prime, first-class' + adjectival -a; cf., igi-zag̃$_3$-g̃a$_2$; igi-zag$_3$-ga).

igi...si(-g)
to see ('eyes' + 'to fill').

igi-sig$_3$-sig$_3$[PA-PA]
an insulting face ('face' + reduplicated 'to strike, knock down'; cf., ka-sig$_3$).

igi-sig$_7$-sig$_7$
jaundice ('eyes' + 'to be yellow').

igi-su
(cf., i-gi$_4$-in-zu).

igi...suḫ
to stare angrily; to frown at, regard malevolently; to fight, stop; to stare with wide-open eyes; to choose, select (variant of igi...zag$_3$) ('eyes' + 'to pop out').

^{lu2}igi-suḫ
foreigner (?).

igi...sum
to see ('eyes' + 'to give').

igi-še$_3$(-du)
first; initial; first-fruits (?) (cf., igi-še$_3$...du) (Akk., *igištûm*, 'the very first').

igi-X-še$_3$
in the presence of X ('face, front' + X + terminative postposition).

igi...te-en
to unite ('eyes' + 'to soften, allay').

igi-te-en
n., fraction; quotient; proportions; symmetry; mesh, interstice.

adj., fine-meshed (net).

igi-tum$_3$-la$_2$
coveting, longing, greedy eyes; spying eyes; a starving person ('eyes' + 'to obtain, carry away' + 'to weigh').

igi...tur
to look down upon; to despise ('eyes' + 'to make small').

^{ĝiš}IGI.TUR.TUR
(cf., ^{ĝiš}ŠI.TUR.TUR).

igi-u$_4$-e$_3$-a
facing the sunrise, facing east ('face; before' + ^{d}utu-e$_3$, 'sunrise' + locative).

IGI.UR
(cf., ḫul).

igi...uru$_3$
to be on guard, vigilant ('eyes' + 'to watch, guard').

igi...zag$_3$
to choose, select ('eyes' + 'to choose').

igi-zaĝ$_3$-ĝa$_2$; igi-zag$_3$-ga
select, precious ('eyes' + 'to choose' + nominative).

igi-ze$_2$-ze$_2$
dry-eyed (?); partially-sighted (?) (Akk. *ṣuḫḫutu(m)*, 'squeezed, pressed' = glaucoma ?; in the Emesal vocabulary, i-bi$_2$-ze$_2$-ze$_2$ = igi-du$_8$-du$_8$).

igi-zi...bar
to choose; to legitimate ('to look at' + 'legitimate; to strengthen').

igi-zu
(cf., i-gi$_4$-in-zu).

igi-zu(-še$_3$)
in front of you ('before; in front of' + 'you' + terminative).

igi$_3$[KI.SAĜ]
front; face (Akk. *pānu(m)*).

igira$_2$, igiru [KI.SAĜ.MUNUS]^{mušen}
heron (igi, 'the eye', + ra, 'to strike' or loan from Akk. *igirû(m)*; KI.SAĜ = igi$_3$).

igištu[IGI.DU]
the very first (igi-še$_3$...du, 'to walk in front'; Akk. *igištûm*).

iku
a surface area measure of 3600 meters^2 = 100 sar = 1 square 'rope' = 1/18 bur$_3$ (plural Akk. form of eg$_2$, ek$_2$, 'levee').

$^{(\tilde{g}i\check{s})}$il-lu-ur
a syllabic writing for $^{\tilde{g}i\check{s}}$illuru; a tree, perhaps Melia azedarach, 'Chinaberry' (Akk., *zanzaliqqu*).

il_2
(cf., ila_2).

il_2-la_2
elevation; heights ('to raise, lift up' + lal, 'to measure, weigh'; cf., dun_3-la_2, 'depression' and ib_2-ba-la_2, 'flat country').

il_5
(cf., ili_5).

ila_2, ili_2, il_2
n., carrier; basket; head load (loan from Akkadian *elû(m) III*, 'to raise/be high'; cf., Orel & Stolbova #1102, ***ʻilay-** "rise").

v., to lift, carry, bear; to gather, deliver, bring; to endure; to support; to promote; to carry forward (in accounting); to be high; a rare OB math. term, to multiply; to shine (il_2-i in *marû*).

adj., raised, honored, elevated.

$^{\tilde{g}i\check{s}}$ilar
(cf., $^{\tilde{g}i\check{s}}$illuru).

$^{\tilde{g}i\check{s}}$ildag$_{(2,3)}$
a species of poplar tree (il_2, 'to be high; to shine', + dag_2, 'brilliant').

$ildag_2$[A-AM]-zi-da
pleasant poplar tree ('poplar tree' + 'good').

ilduma$_{(2,3)}$, ildum$_{(2/3)}$, ildu$_{(2/3)}$
family group, clan, lineage; band, group, pack, crowd, team (loan from Akkadian *illatum*; cf., Orel & Stolbova #2540 ***wiled-** 'give birth'; cf., ki-ulutim) [ILDUM archaic frequency: 5; concatenation of 2 sign variants].

ili_5
to rise, get up.

ilimmu
nine (ia_2/i_2, 'five', + limmu, 'four').

illat[KASKAL.KUR]
help; reinforcement (Akkadian *tillatu(m) I*, '(military) support, reinforcements'; cf.,ilduma).

illu[A.KAL]
high water, flood; (amniotic) fluid; exudation, resin; reservoir, water basin (designation of soil in land survey texts).

$^{\tilde{g}i\check{s}}$illuru, illulu, illar, ilar
throw-stick; bow; arc (made from poplar, apple, and oak tree wood) (ila_2, 'to lift', + ru, 'to send').

IM
see tu_{15} for meaning 'wind' or 'cardinal direction'.

im, imi, em
clay, loam, mud; paste; clay tablet, account tablet [IM archaic frequency: 67; concatenation of 2 sign variants].

im, imi, em
storm; cloud; rain; weather (cf., tumu).

im-
writing of conjugation prefix /ĩ-/ with ventive element /-m-/ in Gudea, NS, Isin-Larsa, and OB texts - ThSLa §304.

IM.A.AN
(cf., $\check{s}e\tilde{g}_{14}$).

im-ba
loss ('the paid out').

im-ba-šur
an illness with shivering and cramps; diarrhea ('mud' + conguation prefix + 'to flow, drip, spray out'; cf., šurun, šurim).

im-babbar$_{(2)}$; $ni\tilde{g}_2$-$babbar_2$-ra
chalk, lime; gypsum; lime whitewash; an alkali cleansing agent like fuller's earth, an oil-absorbing clay used to remove hair and fat from hides ('clay' + 'white').

IM...dirig
(cf., ni_2...dirig; dungu).

im-du_3-a; im-du_8-a
wall either of rammed earth or stacked clay bricks; adobe wall; a type of

construction used in clay walls or clay foundations like the clay core of a *ziqqurrat* ('mud' + 'to erect, stack' + nominative).

im-du$_8$
clay/mud making - an activity to which workers can be assigned (cf., im-duḫ) ('clay' + 'to accumulate, spread').

im-dugud; im-dug
lump of earth or metal; slingstone (cf., ağar$_6$; anzud; muru$_9$) ('clay, earth' + 'weight').

im-duḫ
moisture, dew (rain + residue, by-product).

im-e-taka$_4$(-a)
registered, recorded ('clay tablet' + locative/terminative postposition + 'to entrust' + subordination suffix).

IM.EN×EN
(cf., mermer$_3$).

im gaba-ri$_2$[ZUM]
copy or replica tablet (cf., gaba-ri(-a), 'copy'; Akk., *gabarû*, 'copy, duplicate').

IM-gal
(cf., ni$_2$-gal).

im-gid$_2$-da
small, one column tablet ('clay tablet' + 'long' + nominative).

im-gu-ra
(cf., engur).

im-gu$_2$(-en-na)
river mud, silt; a dark earth for dyeing ('clay, earth' + 'river bank').

im-gu$_2$-la$_2$(-ğiš-tuku)
library for tablets ('tablet' + 'to tie up' + 'attentive').

im-ğir$_2$
lightning storm ('storm' + 'lightning flash').

im-ḫa-mun
a dark-colored earth used for a high-contrast dye ('clay, earth' + 'contrasting'; cf. also, im-ri-ḫa-mun).

im-ḫul
destructive wind; storm (Akkadian *imḫullu*) ('weather' + 'evil').

im-il$_2$
clay/mud carrier or delivery ('clay' + 'to carry').

IM-KA
(cf., lu$_2$-ni$_2$-zuḫ).

im-la$_2$
container; width ('tablet' + 'to hold'; cf., im-gu$_2$-la$_2$(-ğiš-tuku)).

im-lag[ŠID]
lump of clay; pellet (cf., im-te$_6$, im-zadru) ('clay' + 'piece').

im...lu
to mix clay or building mud ('clay' + 'to mix').

im-ma
last, previous (year); the elapsed year ('the named').

im-ma-
writing of conjugation prefixes /ĩ-ba-/ in Gudea and later texts - ThSLa §306-§308, §304, §337.

im-ma-al(-la)
milk cow (cf., immal$_{(2)}$) ('previous year' + 'opened, penetrated').

(na4)im-ma(an)-na
glass ('clay tablet' + 'sky' + genitive; Akk. *immanakku*).

im-ma...gub
to register on a clay tablet ('clay tablet' + locative + 'to write down'; cf., im-šu-gub).

im-ma-si-im-ma-diri-ga
'it is too much' - the scream of suffering men or of women in travail (a deverbalized fixed form).

IM-MAR-TU
(cf., tu$_{15}$-ğar$_7$-du$_2$).

im-me
to be the one for (i$_3$ + me + a).

im-me-
either a writing of im-mi- or a contraction of im-mu-e- - ThSLa §304, n. 48.

im-mi-
writing of conjugation prefixes /ĩ-bi-/ in Gudea and later texts - ThSLa §338, §304.

im-mu-
writing of conjugation prefixes /ĩ-mu-/ in OB texts - ThSLa §306-§307, §304.

im-nu-g̃al$_2$(-la)
void, invalidated tablet(s) ('clay tablet' + 'not' + 'available'; Akk., *seḫšu(m)*).

im-nu-ila$_2$
adjective for a kind of laborer.

im-nun
edge of the civilized world ('writing tablets' + 'noble').

im-ri(-a), im-ru(-a)
relatives, family, clan ('the sent out; the engendered'; cf., ri-a, 'engendered').

IM-RI-ḫa-mun; IM-RI-a
(cf., (tu15)dalḫamun$_{(2)}$; (tu15)dal(-a)).

im-rig$_{11}$[ŠID.RU]
clay bulla; clay sealing.

im-sar(-ra)
inscribed clay tablet; document ('clay' + 'to write' + nominative).

im-sig$_7$-sig$_7$
a dark yellow paste; antimony (paste), kohl ('clay, mud' + redup. 'green, yellow; beautiful').

im...šeg̃$_3$
to rain; to form dew ('storm' + 'to rain').

im-ši-
writing of conjugation prefix /ĩ-/ + inanimate /-m-/ + terminative prefix - ThSLa §455.

im-šu
hand tablet, a small lenticular (round) or rectangular tablet used for exercises and rapid notations in OB period schools; paragraph, section, extract (on a tablet) ('clay tablet' + 'hand; portion').

im-šu-gub-ba
list tablet ('sections' + 'to write down' + nominative; cf., im-ma...gub).

im-šu-rin-na
oven ('hand tablets' + 'to make bright' + nominative).

im-ta-ḫab
wet mud, silt ('mud + 'soaked'; Akk., *rušumtu*).

IM×TAK$_4$; IM.TAK$_4$; TAK$_4$; TAK$_4$.IM
to cut; to be cut out.

im-te$_6$[ŠID], im-zadru[ŠID]
box to hold matching clay tally halves as proof of credit or debt, the Sumerian version of the split tally system known from other historical cultures (cf., im-lag) ('clay' + te, 'to approach, reach, meet'/ zandara, 'one-half (share)'; Akk., *pišannu(m)*, 'box, chest').

IM.UD
(cf., im-babbar).

im...ur$_3$
to seal ('clay' + 'to surround').

IM-zuḫ
(cf., lu$_2$-ni$_2$-zuḫ).

im$_2$
to run (cf., gim$_4$).

im$_3$[AG̃A$_2$]-X
Emesal dialect, cf., nig̃$_2$-X.

img̃ag̃a$_{(2,3)}$
husked, processed (?) emmer wheat; spelt wheat (?).

imḫur[IGI.A]
foam.

imi
(cf., im).

imin$_{(2,3)}$
seven; totality; innumerable; all (ia$_2$/i$_2$, 'five', + min, 'two').

imma
(cf., enmen).

immal [NUN.LAGAR×BAR]; $immal_2$ [NUN.LAGAR×MUNUS]
milk cow (cf., im-ma-al(-la)).

immen, immin, imma
(cf., enmen).

$immen_2$, $immin_2$, $imma_2$
(cf., $enmen_2$).

immindu
roasting, baking oven (imi/im, 'clay', + ninda, 'bread').

in
he, she; straw, hay; border line marker; insult, offense, invective [IN archaic frequency: 21].

in-
writing of conjugation prefix /ĩ-/ and animate 3.sg. pronominal element /-n-/ in all period texts - ThSLa §307, §304.

in...bu_5-bu_5; in...bul_5-bul_5
to blow away the chaff; to winnow ('straw, hay' + redup. 'to blow'; cf., bul).

/ in all period texts - ThSLa §307, §304.

in-bu_5-bu_5
(worthless) chaff; waste product.

in-dal
chaff ('straw' + 'to fly').

in...de_2-a
cleaning straw after winnowing ('straw' + 'to pour' + nominative).

in-di
path; way of life; shade (i_3, 'impersonal verbal conjugation prefix', + 3rd person animate pronominal element + 'to conduct oneself; to go'; cf., ḫe$_{(2)}$-en-du(-du); ki-in-du).

in...dub
to mark out a border line; to demarcate boundaries ('straw, border line marker' + 'to heap up').

in-dub
marked out border, demarcation.

in(-nu)(-$še_3$)...dub_2
to insult; to taunt (with -ni-) ('insult' (+ terminative postposition) + 'to thump').

in-ga-
again; also; equally (frequently follows -gim); writing of conjugation prefixes /ĩ-ga-/ in OB texts - ThSLa §322-§328, §304.

in-ga-na-nam
it is also - ThSLa §379 ('equally' + emphatic + 'to be').

in-gi-in
he has proved it (i_3, 'impersonal verbal conjugation prefix', + 3rd person animate pronominal element + gin_6, 'to determine').

in-g̃ar
(a rare math. text expression) the result is ('he sets down').

in-la_2
weighed out; to be reduced (i_3, 'impersonal verbal conjugation prefix', + 3rd person animate pronominal element + 'to weigh' = 'he weighs').

in-na
insult (cf., en-na, 'as long as').

in-nam-gid_2-da
storehouse (rare variant of uš-gid_2-da).

in-nin$_{(9)}$
lady, mistress (redup. 'mistress').

in-nu
'no'; 'it was not'; negation (i_3, 'impersonal verbal conjugation prefix', + negative indicator; cf., an-na, 'yes').

in-nu(-da)
straw ('straw' + nud, 'bed' + genitive).

in-nu-ḫa
(cf., še-in-nu-ḫa).

in-nu-UŠ
a soap plant (?) ('second-class (?) straw'; Akk. *maštakal*).

in-TI, in-di_3
(cf., ki-in-du).

in-ZAR
pile of straw/hay, haystack.

in...ZAR-ZAR
to stack hay ? (cf., in...bul_5-bul_5).

inbir[LU_2.LU_2]
conflict, war (cf., gigam, 'quarrel, conflict, war'; Akk. *ippīru*).

inim, enim[KA]
word(s); statement; command, order, decree; oath, agreement; matter, affair, concern, subject (in, 'one discrete individual', + eme, 'speech').

inim...bala/bal-bal
to have a conversation; to interpret; to translate ('words' + 'to revolve').

inim-bala
interpreter; translator (Akkadian *nāpalû; targumannu(m)*; cf., eme-bala).

inim-bur_2-ra
breach of treaty ('words' + 'to dissolve, loosen' + nominative).

inim...de_6[DU]
to bring (good) news (cf., ka...de_6) ('word' + 'to bring').

inim-dirig
exaggeration; lie; arrogance, hubris ('words' + 'to exceed').

^{lu2}inim-dirig-du_{11}-du_{11}
exaggerator; liar ('exaggeration; lie' + redup. 'to speak'; cf., daḫ...du_{11}-du_{11}).

inim-du_3-a
message, report (cf., ka-du_3-a and inim-sikil-du_3-a) ('word' + 'to erect' + nominative).

inim-dug_3
good word ('word' + 'sweet, good').

inim...dug_4/du_{11}/e
to say; to arrive at a decision; to give a decision ('words' + 'to speak').

inim-e_2-gal
abuse, insult, iniquity, slander ('words' + 'palace').

inim...gi_4
to answer (takes dative infix followed by locative infix -ni-); to call back one's word (with bi_2-); to reject (with loc./term. postposition) ('word' + 'to return').

inim...$\tilde{g}al_2$
to let orders be; to file a complaint; to put orders into something (with locative -ni-) ('word' + 'to be; to place').

inim-$\tilde{g}al_2$(-la)
n., legal claim ('words' + 'to be; to place' + nominative).

adj., eloquent.

inim...g̃ar
to bring an action against someone (before the court); to claim; to sue (cf., gu_3...g̃ar; 'word' + 'to set, fix').

inim-g̃ar
(ominous) utterance; omen; spoken opinion; reputation (Akkadian *egerrû*).

inim...$ki\tilde{g}_2$
to seek or find the right word ('word' + 'to seek, fetch').

inim...ku_5(-r)
to swear ('word' + 'to cut, curse').

inim...kur_2
to change the word ('word' + 'to change').

inim-mud-$\tilde{g}al_2$
eloquent ('words' + 'begetter').

inim...sag_9-sag_9(-g)
to pray ('word' + redup. 'to please').

inim-ma...se_3(-g) [SUM]
to imagine, conceive an idea ('in a word' + 'to place').

inim-sig...gu_7(-gu_7)
to (produce) slander ('word' + 'low; small' + 'to consume'; cf., eme-sig...gu_7).

inim-sig-ga
slander ('word' + 'low; small' + nominative; cf., eme-sig).

inim-sikil-du_3-a
insult; blasphemy ('word' + 'purity' + 'to plant (the penis)' + nominative; cf., $\tilde{g}iš_3$...du_3, 'to have sexual intercourse', ka...du_3, 'to accuse', ki-sikil, 'young woman; virgin', and gud $\tilde{g}iš$-du_3-a, 'breed bull').

inim-su_3-ga
deceit; boasting ('word' + 'empty, deceitful').

inim...$šar_2$
to search for clarification ('word' + 'to request, implore').

inim...šub
to hand down an order, issue a decree (by the king/palace) ('word' + 'to drop').

inim-$šud_3$(-da)
a word of prayer ('word' + 'to pray' + nominative).

inim-PN-ta
by order of PN ('words' + ablative-instrumental case postposition).

inim...TAR
(cf., inim...ku_5(-r)).

inim-ma...tuš
to obey ('to sit to the word').

inim-zu
one who knows the (proper) words; learned ('words' + 'knowing').

$ir_{(10)}$, er(-ra)
v., to bring; to lead away; to capture; to carry off; to go (Emesal dialect for tum_2, cf., re_7).

ir, er; ir_7
n., sweat; smell, odor, scent; perfume, fragrance [IR archaic frequency: 53; concatenation of 4 sign variants].

adj., scented, perfumed, fragrant.

ir...ši-še
(cf., er_2...$šeš_{2,4}$/$še_8$-$še_8$).

ir-pag
plan, scheme.

ir-pag...aka
to entrust; to assign; to scheme with ('to lead, bring' + 'to cage, shelter' + 'to do').

ir-si-im; ir-sim
fragrant aroma, scent ('perfume' + sim, 'fragrant').

ir_2
(cf., er_2).

$ir_{3,9}$
strong, powerful, manly (Akk. *īru* and *gašru* with same meanings; cf., $\tilde{g}ir_3$; ni_2-ir_9; nir).

$ir_{3,11}$
(cf., $arad_{(2)}$).

ir_7[KASKAL](-sa$\tilde{g}$)^{mušen}
wild pigeon - a larger bird, such as the wood pigeon, as it consumed 6 gin_2 of grain, while the dove tum_{12}-$gur_4^{mušen}$ only got 4 gin_2 ('journey' + 'head, leader, point', cf., sa$\tilde{g}$-du_3, 'triangle'; Akkadian *amursānu, uršānu(m)*).

ir_{10}
(cf., re_7).

iri
the third millenium lexical reading of uru, 'city'.

iri-
either a rare modal prefix found with the combination verb mi_2(-zi)...dug_4/du_{11}/e or a writing of the conjugation prefix /ĩ-/ + 2.sg. dative -ri- ThSLa §478.

iri_{11}
(cf., $uru^{(ki)}$, eri, iri, ri_2; uru_2; iri_{11}).

irigal
(cf., urugal).

is-ḫab$_2$
fool; villain, rogue ('organ' + 'foul-smelling'; Akk. *isḫappu*).

isi
pit; clay pit.

isimu$_{2,3}$, isim$_{2,3}$
shoot, sprout; offspring, descendant (i, 'sprout', + si, 'straight, long, narrow', + mu$_2$, 'to grow').

isiš$_{2,3}$
n., moaning; laughter (cf., redup. šeš$_{2,3,4}$, 'to weep').

v., to weep; to laugh.

iskim
(cf., g̃iskim).

iš
(cf., iši).

iš-gana$_2$
supplementary payment; extra payment in kind in a fixed ratio to the price; concluding payment settling the transaction (Akkadian loanword, *iškinū*, from *šakānu*, 'to deposit'; cf., NÍG̃-KI-G̃AR).

g̃išIŠ-gi$_4$
a tool.

iš$_{11}$; iš$_{12}$
(cf., eš$_{22}$, iš$_{11}$; iš$_{12}$, eš$_x$).

iši
mountain [IŠ archaic frequency: 88; concatenates 3 sign variants].

išib
n., priest who performs exorcisms, incantations, lustrations and purification (Akkadian *(w)āšipu(m)*).

adj., clean; anointed.

išin [PA.ŠE]
stalk (g̃iš, 'stick', + in, 'straw').

iti$_6$[UD.dNANNA]
moonlight.

itima, itim, idi; itima$_2$
cella, chapel; the dark room holding the temple deity's cult statue; Holy of Holies.

itu, iti
(cf., itud).

itu-da
monthly (itud, 'month', + a(k), in genitive compounds).

itu-ta-zal-la
rare category of unused manpower in accounting texts - those who have not worked from the first of the month ('month' + 'from' + 'to be idle, waste time' + nominative).

itud, itid, itu, iti, id$_8$; it$_4$,id$_4$
moon; month; moonlight (i$_3$-, 'impersonal verbal conjugation prefix', + tud, 'to give birth; to be born, reborn').

iz-zi[G̃IŠ-ZI]; iz-zi$_8$[G̃IŠ-KAL]
house wall; fire; current, flood ('wood/tool' + 'to rise up').

izi[NE]
fire; fever (cf., iz-zi) [NE archaic frequency: 303; concatenation of 4 sign variants].

(g̃iš/gi)izi-g̃ar
torch; light; sunlight; brilliance; ray; oven; quarrel ('fire' + 'to store, place, deliver').

izi-g̃i$_6$-eden-na
shadow, deep shade ('fire' + 'night' + 'open country').

izi-ku$_3$
lost (in the making of metal objects or wool material) ('fire' + 'silver').

izi...la$_2$
to purify with fire ('fire' + 'to raise up').

izi-la$_2$
n., torch ('fire' + 'to raise up').

adj., burned.

izi...ne-ne(-r)
to fan the fire ('fire' + reduplicated nir, 'to winnow').

izi...ri(-ri)
to kindle a fire ('fire' + 'to touch; to beget').

izi...sig$_3$[PA]
to set on fire ('fire' + 'to knock down, demolish').

izi-su$_3$(-ud)
bright torch (cf., su$_3$(-ud/ra$_2$)-aĝa$_2$, 'brilliant'; Akk., *dipāru(m)*, 'torch').

izi...šub
to hurl fire ('fire' + 'to throw').

izi-ta nu$_2$-a ku$_6$
a type of baked fish ('to kill by fire' + 'fish'; Akk., *temrum*, from *temēru(m)*, 'to cover (in earth), bury').

izi...te
fire approaches ('fire' + 'to approach').

izi...te-en
to extinguish or calm a fire ('fire' + 'to calm, extinguish').

izi$_2$[KI-IZI]-ur$_5$
coal ('fire-place' + 'liver, soul').

izkim
(cf., ĝiskim).

K

ka(-g)
mouth; opening, branching (of a canal) [KA archaic frequency: 108; concatenates 2 sign variants].

ka
in late usage, the difference between a rough measuring and a final measuring of a quantity of grain.

KA-a-ab-ba; KA×ĜIR$_2$-a-ab-ba
(cf., zu$_2$-a-ab-ba).

KA.AḪ
an unknown type of wool.

ka-al
clay pit (cf., ki-lal, 'trench').

ka(-al)-lu$_5$
a vessel, bowl (Akkadian loanword, *kalû*; Orel & Stolbova #1423, ***kalVy-**, 'vessel').

KA-AN-NI-SI
(cf., kurku$_2$; gu$_3$-an-ne$_2$-si).

ka-an-ša-ša
overpowering (cf., ka...ša-an-ša-ša).

ka-aš...bar
to render a decision.

ka-aš-bar
decision ('mouth' + 'decision'; cf., eš-bar).

ka...ba
to open the mouth; to speak, talk; to converse; used when speaking to social inferiors - to belittle (cf., gu$_3$...sum) ('mouth' + 'to give').

ka-ba-bu-um
(cf., ga-ba-bu-um).

KA×BAD
(cf., KA×UŠ$_2$).

$^{(lu2)}$ka-bar
(cf., $^{(lu2)}$kabar, kapar).

KA...de$_2$
(cf., gu$_3$...de$_2$).

ka...de$_6$
to bring news (cf., inim...de$_6$) ('mouth' + 'to bring').

ka...du$_3$
to accuse (reduplication class) (cf., inim-sikil-du$_3$-a) ('mouth' + 'to build, make').

$^{(kuš)}$ka-du$_3$
a leather wrapping for part of the plow; cover; sleeve.

ka-du$_3$-a, ka-du$_3$-du$_3$
fierce, accusing, or mocking mouth (cf., inim-du$_3$-a).

^{ĝiš}KA-dub$_2$-ba
a field tool (?).

ka...du$_8$[duḫ]
to open the mouth ('mouth' + 'to crack open').

ka-dug
nozzle of a jug ('mouth' + 'jar').

ka-duḫ(-a)
n., opening ('mouth' + 'to crack open' + nominative).

adj., with open mouth.

^{dug}ka-gag
beer-jar ('vessel' + 'mouth' + 'peg'; Akk. *pīḫu(m)*, from *peḫû(m) II*, 'to close up, seal').

ka-garaš$_2$-a
catastrophe ('mouth' + 'military encampment' + nominative).

^{na4}KA-gi-na
hematite; iron ore ('mouth; tooth' + gin$_6$, 'steady, reliable').

^{na4}KA-gi-na-dab-ba
magnetite, lodestone ('hematite' + 'holding').

KA×GUR$_7$
(cf., kugur; ka-guru$_7$).

ka-guru$_7$
granary supervisor; storekeeper ('mouth' + 'silo').

KA-ĝiri$_3$
path, road ('mouth' + 'feet; way, path'; cf., ki-ĝiri$_3$; gu$_3$-ĝiri$_3$).

KA...ḪAR
(cf., zu$_2$...ur$_5$; gu$_3$...mur; kiri$_{3/4}$...ur$_5$; kir$_4$...ḫur).

ka-id$_2$-da
canal intake ('mouth' + 'river' + genitive).

KA-inim-ma(-k)
composition; incantation; wish; plan; wisdom, eloquence ('mouth' + 'word' + genitive; cf., lu$_2$-inim-ma).

ka-izi
roasted, seared; burned up ('mouth' + 'fire').

KA.KA.SI.GA
pronunciation, syllabic value; in lexical texts, denotes a sign which has only a phonetic value.

ka-ta...kar
to take away ('mouth' + 'from' + 'to take away').

KA×KARA$_2$
(cf., bu$_3$; buzur$_5$; kana$_6$).

$^{(ĝiš)}$ka-kara$_4$[KAD$_4$/KAD$_5$; ŠU-KAD$_3$]
an elaborate table ('mouth' + 'tool' + 'to bind' + genitive; Akk. *kannaškarakkum*).

KA...keš$_2$(-ra$_2$)
to organize; to have/close an agreement; to enroll; to put or gather together; to tie (up); to become entangled; to become undone, disorganized (with -ta-) ('mouth/tongue' + 'to bind (under oath)').

KA-keš$_2$(-ra$_2$)
knot; conglomeration; corral; regiment; contingent; rental (payment) ('to organize' + nominative).

ka-ki(k)
recorder, a city official who recorded sales ('mouth' + 'place' + genitive; Akk., *kakikkum ?*).

ka ki...zu-zu
to kiss the ground ('mouth' + 'ground' + reduplicated 'to know').

ka-ku$_3$-ĝal$_2$
incantation priest; exorcist ('mouth' + 'pure, holy' + 'having').

ka-lal$_3$
a sweet person ('mouth' + 'honey').

KA×LI
(cf., tu$_6$, mu$_7$, zug$_4$, zuḫ$_x$, uš$_7$, and meli$_2$).

KA×LI...di/e
(cf., gu$_3$-nun...di/e).

KA×LI...gi$_4$(-gi$_4$)
(cf., šeg$_x$..gi$_4$).

ka-lu$_5$
(cf., ka-al-lu$_5$).

KA-mud-ĝal$_2$
(cf., inim-mud-ĝal$_2$).

ka-na-aĝ$_2$(-ĝa$_2$); ka-naĝ(-ĝa$_2$)
Emesal dialect for kalam, 'land'.

ka-na-da
(cf., ka-naĝ-ĝa$_2$-da).

KA-NE
(cf., zu$_2$...bir$_9$-bir$_9$).

KA×NE
(cf., murgu$_3$).

KA-nun...di/e
(cf., gu$_3$-nun...di/e).

[MUNUS]ka-piriĝ[ĜIR$_3$]
incantation priest or priestess; exorcist ('mouth' + 'lion').

KA×SA
(cf., sun$_4$, sum$_4$, sul$_3$, su$_6$).

ka...sag$_9$-sag$_9$
to make the mouth pleasant ('mouth' + reduplicated 'good, pleasing').

KA.SI.KA
(usually preceded by ĝiri$_3$, 'under the responsibility of the shearer'; cf., zu$_2$-si(-ga)).

ka-sig$_3$[PA]
an insulting mouth ('mouth' + 'to strike, knock down'; cf., igi-sig$_3$-sig$_3$).

ka-su$_3$-ga
an empty mouth (cf., inim-su$_3$-ga) ('mouth' + 'to be empty' + nominative).

ka...ša-an-ša-ša
to overpower (Akk. *kašāšu(m) I*, 'to gain control of').

ka-šakan
supervisor of the fat stores ('mouth' + 'large oil jar').

KA-ŠER$_3$
(cf., KA-keš$_2$(-ra$_2$)).

KA šu...ĝal$_2$
(cf., kiri$_4$ šu...ĝal$_2$).

ka-ta...kar
to take away ('mouth' + 'from' + 'to take away').

ka-ta-du$_{11}$-ga; ka-ta-e$_3$-a
saying, utterance ('mouth' + 'from' + "to speak/go out' + nominative).

ka-tab
n., helper; jar lid or cover, of sheepskin ('mouth' + 'to clasp'; cf., ša$_3$ ka-tab; saĝ-tab).

v., to be clogged; to block.

ka-tar
n., praise; challenger; a type of fungus, mold, or rot ('mouth' + 'to decide; to destroy').

adj., princely, noble.

ka-tar...si-il
to praise ('praise' + sil, 'to praise').

ka-teš$_2$
peace, amity; unison; mutual understanding ('mouth' + 'together').

ka-tu$_6$-ĝal$_2$
an incantation formula; exorcist, incantation priest ('mouth' + 'incantation formula' + 'having').

KA-us$_2$-sa
an individual type of worker, to whom grain could be distributed (read du$_{11}$-us$_2$-sa ?).

KA×UŠ$_2$
(cf., uš$_{11}$).

KA-zal
(cf., kiri$_{3,4}$-zal).

$^{(lu2)}$ka-zid$_2$-da
(cf., $^{(lu2)}$gaz-zid$_2$-da).

ka$_2$
gate (cf., akan$_2$) [? KA$_2$ archaic frequency: 11; concatenates 4 sign variants].

ka$_2$-bar-ra
outer door ('gate' + 'outside' + nominative).

KA$_2$.GAL
(cf., abul).

ka$_2$-me$_3$
wings of a temple door ('gate' + 'battle').

ka$_5$-(a)
fox.

ka$_6$
mongoose.

ka$_9$
(cf., kas$_7$ and niĝ$_2$-kas$_7$/ka$_9$).

$^{(ĝiš)}$kab
a wooden or metal cross piece on a harness or bridle - bit; the lead rope or bridle itself; fetter, shackle; cage; trap; chamber, cell (cf., gubu$_3$[KAB]).

$^{(ĝiš)}$kab-il$_2$(-gigir)
weight-bearing beams on a chariot; axle ('cross-piece' + 'to raise, support').

KAB-ra; KAB-us$_2$; KAB-ra$_2$
(cf., gaba$_2$-ra; gaba$_2$-us$_2$; gaba$_2$-ra$_2$).

$^{(lu2)}$kab-sar
stone carver ('cross-piece' + 'to inscribe').

kab$_2$
flaxen measuring string ?.

kab$_2$...dug$_4$
to measure or count commodities for accounting or taxation ('string' ? + 'to do').

$^{(dug)}$kab$_2$-dug$_4$-ga; kab-dug$_4$-ga
a measuring jar with a capacity of 20 sila$_3$ - the Flood narrative connects these to the institution of kingship and thus to taxation.

kab$_2$-ku$_{(5)}$
container, vessel (for apples or onions).

$^{(lu2)}$kabar, kapar
[PA.DAG.KISIM$_5$×GAG]
shepherd boy, shepherd's assistant; milk churner (cf., cf., gaba$_2$-ra; gaba$_2$-us$_2$; gaba$_2$-ra$_2$; Akkadian loanword (?) from *kaparru(m) I*).

kad$_{3,4,5}$
to tie, bind together [KAD$_4$ archaic frequency: 13; concatenates 4 sign variants].

kadra$_{(2)}$
gift, offering, bribe (kad$_4$, 'to tie together', + ru, 'present, gift'; Akk., *kadrû*, 'present, greeting gift').

kak
(cf., gag).

kal-(l)
v., to esteem, value; to be rare; to make dear, endear; to be appreciated (cf., kalag) (ka, 'mouth' + la, 'youthful beauty, abundance') [KAL archaic frequency: 60; concatenates 3 sign variants].

adj., excellent; precious, valuable (cf., kalag).

^{d}KAL
(cf., ^{d}lamma, lama$_3$).

kal-kal(-la); ka-al-ka-al
highly esteemed or valued; precious; unaffordable (reduplicated 'to esteem, value').

kal-la-kal-la
barren, empty ('to be rare').

KAL-na
(cf., sun$_7$).

kala
(cf., kalag).

kala$_{3,4,5}$, gala$_{3,4,5}$
store-pit; cellar (cf., ki-lal/la$_2$, 'cellar granary, silo' with vowel harmony).

kalag, kala(-ga)
v., to repair, mend, fasten, strengthen (kal, 'excellent', + aka/ag, 'to make').

adj., strong, mighty; swift [GURUŠ+2-N14 (wagon pictogram) archaic frequency: 7; concatenation of 3 sign variants].

kalama, kalam[UN]
the land (of Sumer); nation (of Sumerians) (kal, 'excellent', + eme, 'speech, speaking' ?) [KALAM archaic frequency: 91; concatenates 6 sign variants].

kalam...til
to decimate the land ('land' + 'to finish, put an end to').

-kam
(cf., $\tilde{g}a_2$(-a)-kam).

-kam-ma
Used with ordinal numbers.

$kam_{(2)}$
n., grasp, grip; tuning (?).

v., to desire (cf., ki...$a\tilde{g}_2$, 'to love').

$kam_{(2)}$-$kam_{(2)}$-ma(-tum)
earring(s); ring; modified by determinatives for copper, bronze, silver, stone, and lapis lazuli; a percussion musical instrument, ring-jangles (?) (redup. Sumerian root means 'to desire', but word ending is typical of Akkadian loanwords).

kam_3
n., tablet; round disk (of metal or wood) (ka, 'mouth' + im, 'clay').

v., to alter, change; to overturn; to banish, drive out (these verbal meanings make me wonder if this became the Sumerian word for a changeable wax-coated writing tablet).

kan
(cf., gan).

$kana_{3,5,6}$, $kan_{3,5,6}$
n., apprehension, worry; affliction, trouble, misfortune; sorrow (ka, 'mouth' + ni_2; ne_4, 'fear'; Akk. *adāru(m) II*, 'to be afraid; fear').

v., to be troubled.

kan_4
(cf., ka_2, $akan_2$).

kankal[KI.KAL]
uncultivated, inarable land, barren soil (cf., ki-$\tilde{g}al_2$; bad_4).

kapar
(cf., kabar).

kar[TE.A]
n., embankment; quay-wall; mooring-place; wharf; harbor; marketplace; port authority; rescued (people) (place + water + to flow, send, take, drive away; cf., kur_9, 'entrance') [KAR archaic frequency: 7].

v., to take away from, remove (with ablative -ta-); to steal (with locative infix -ni-); to raid, capture, pillage; to escape, run away, flee (with comitative infix -da-); to run swiftly; to avoid (kar-re in *marû*).

(MUNUS)kar(-e)-kid
prostitute (B. Alster reads munus-kar-ke_4) ('marketplace' + 'reed mat'; Akk., *karkittu*, 'prostitute', *ḫarimtu(m)*, '(temple) prostitute').

kar(-ra)...us_2
to reach the quay (in a boat) ('quay' + locative + 'to reach, moor to').

$kara_2$, kar_2, $guru_6$[GAN_2-*tenû*]
to encircle, besiege; to impute, accuse; to (make) shine, illuminate; to be bright (of light, day) (reduplication class) (sometimes written for kur_2) (place + ur, 'to surround', + a, nominative ending, and ara_4, 'to shine') [? KAR_2 archaic frequency: 68; concatenates 2 sign variants].

kar_3
(cf., gar_3).

$karadin_{(3,4,5)}$
(cf., $garadin_{(3,4,5)}$).

kas_2
(cf., kaš).

kas_7, ka_9
deduction, calculation; settlement of accounts; possession (back-formation from $ni\tilde{g}_2$-kas_7/ka_9, which see).

kaskal
expedition, caravan; road, course; journey ($ka\check{s}_4$/kas_4, 'to travel fast', + kalag/kal, 'swift') [KASKAL archaic frequency: 35].

KASKAL(-SAĜ)^{mušen}
(cf., ir_7-$sa\tilde{g}^{mušen}$).

KASKAL.KUR
(cf., illat).

kaskal...sig_{10}/si_3(-g)
to clear a road ('road' + 'to place, put in; to engrave; to make flat, even').

kaš, kas_2; $ka\check{s}_2$
barley-beer (not flavored with hops); alcoholic beverage (ka, 'mouth', + $a\check{s}_2$, 'to desire') [KAŠ archaic frequency: 261; concatenates 4 sign variants].

kaš-a gub-ba
one who works in beer production ('beer' + locative + 'to stand' + nominative).

kaš-de_2...aka
to put on a banquet ('banquet' + 'to do').

kaš-de_2-a
banquet, libation, wedding offering, party ('beer' + 'to pour' + nominative).

kaš-dug_3/du_{10}
sweet drink ('beer' + 'sweet, fresh').

kaš-gig_2
dark beer ('beer' + 'black, dark').

kaš-gig_2-dug_3-ga
good dark beer ('beer' + 'black, dark' + 'sweet, fresh' + nominative).

kaš-kal
strong (?) beer ('beer' + 'strong; excellent').

kaš-sag_{10}, kaš-sig_5
fine beer ('beer' + 'good, fine quality').

kaš-saĝ
prime beer, first-class beer ('beer' + 'prime').

kaš-si_4
reddish-brown beer ('beer' + 'red-brown').

kaš-sig_{15}
light beer ('beer' + 'pleasing; valuable'; cf., zid_2-sig_{15}).

kaš-šur-ra
pressed out beer ('beer' + 'to press; to brew' + nominative).

$ka\check{s}_3$
urine (an etymology involving $\check{s}e_{10}$, 'excrement', would have to be forced so much, that the homophone kaš, 'beer', with its similar appearance, probably replaced the use of a, 'water', to mean 'urine' at some point).

$ka\check{s}_3$...šur
to urinate ('urine' + 'to expel a liquid').

$ka\check{s}_4$, kas_4
n., speed; runner, courier, messenger; nonresident, noncitizen, tourist (place(s) + locative + many) [KAS_4 archaic frequency: 1].

v., to run fast; to gallop; to travel fast.

adj., quick; fluent.

$ka\check{s}_4$...dar
to run (joyfully); to bound along ('speed' + 'to slice, split'; cf., $\text{ḫ}ub_2$-dar...aka).

$ka\check{s}_4$-di
adj. or adv., running ('speed' + 'doing').

$ka\check{s}_4$...du
to run ('speed' + 'to go; to come').

$ka\check{s}_4$...dug_4/du_{11}/e
to run ('speed' + 'to effect').

$ka\check{s}_4$...kar
to run fast ('speed' + 'to escape, run away').

$ka\check{s}_4$...sar
to run quickly ('speed' + 'to make hurry, run'; cf., $\text{ḫ}ub_2$...sar).

kašbir
small beer; sweetened beer (kaš, 'beer', + bir$_2$, 'to sniff').

ke-en-gi; ke-en-ge-ra
(cf., ki-en-gi(-r)).

-ke$_4$
often occurs at the end of a genitival compound which functions as the actor or agent of the sentence - ThSLa §161ff., §170 (ak, genitival postposition 'of', + e, ergative agent marker).

keš$_2$[KEŠDA]
(cf., kešda).

keš$_2$-de$_6$[DU]
a fish measure ('to join, tie' + 'to carry').

$^{g̃iš}$keš$_2$-ra$_2$[DU]; $^{g̃iš}$keš$_2$-da
regulator for adjusting the level of water in a canal; dam, weir; sluice; floodgate.

kešda, kešedr?, keše$_2$(-d), keš$_2$
n., knot; tether; contract; lease; hiring; team; taboo; inhibition (usually followed by -da, but also by -ra$_2$[DU]; for keš$_2$-r, cf. also, $^{g̃iš}$keš$_2$-ra$_2$, ḫir and giri$_{11}$, gir$_{11}$) (ki, 'place', + šita$_4$, 'to bind'; cf., kurušda) [KEŠ$_2$ archaic frequency: 6].

v., to bind, wrap, tie; to join; to fasten, attach; to tether; to harness; to snatch; to close up, to dam up.

$^{g̃iš}$kešda[KEŠDA]
regulator for adjusting the level of water in a canal; dam, weir; sluice (cf., $^{g̃iš}$keš$_2$-ra$_2$).

ki
n., earth; place; area; location; ground; grain ('base' + 'to rise, sprout') [KI archaic frequency: 386; concatenates 2 sign variants].

prep., where; wherever, whenever; behind.

ki-PN
(disbursed) for PN, where PN is a personal name ('to the place of PN').

Emesal dialect variant for gi$_4$.

ki-A
(cf., ki-duru$_5$).

ki-a-nag̃
libation place; death offering; place of liquid offerings to the dead ('place' + 'water' + 'to water').

ki-a$_2$-ag̃$_2$-(g̃a$_2$)
the place of issuing orders (cf., a$_2$-ag̃$_2$-g̃a$_2$, 'instructions, orders').

ki...ag̃$_2$-(g̃)
to love (animate someone: with dative infix; inanimate something: with locative/loc.-terminative infix); to show affection ('ground' + 'to measure' = the first recorded euphemism ?, or the result of popular etymology from kam$_{(2)}$, 'to desire'; cf., ki-na$_2$...aka; also kig̃$_2$, 'to seek').

ki-ag̃$_2$
beloved.

ki-(PN)-ak-a
with Personal Name - ThSLa §159 ('at PN's place' - locative).

ki-(PN)-ak-ta
from Personal Name; 'from' an animate being - ThSLa §159, §205 ('from PN's place' - ablative).

ki-bad-ra$_2$
distant places ('places' + 'to be at a distance' + nominative).

ki-bala
rebellious country, rebel land ('place' + 'to revolt').

KI.BI.G̃AR
(cf., g̃išbun; ki-bi-še$_3$...g̃ar).

ki-bi-še$_3$...g̃ar; ki-be$_2$...g̃ar; ki-ba...g̃ar
to put (back) in its place; to exchange, substitute ('place' + 'its' + 'towards/the' + 'to place'; Akk. *pūḫu(m)*).

ki-bi-še$_3$
adv., to that place, there ('place' + 'its' + 'to').

prep.,to, towards.

ki-bi-ta
adv., from that very place, from there ('place' + 'its' + 'from').

ki-bur$_2$
solution, answer; place of relaxation ('place' + 'exposed').

ki-buru$_{14}$
harvest area ('place' + 'harvest').

ki...dar
to break the ground; to sprout; to make a funerary offering ('ground' + 'to split'; cf., ki(-in)-dar).

ki...de$_6$
to bury ('ground' + 'to bring; to continue').

ki-di-ku$_5$-da/ru
place of judicial decisions ('place' + 'decisions' + 'to cut, decide' + nominative without/with vowel harmony).

KI.DU.GAG
(cf., šiten).

ki-dul
secret; obscure point ('place' + 'to cover, hide').

ki-dur$_2$
nest or den for animals (plural, cf., ki-tuš); a kind of chair or stool ('place' + 'to dwell (plural)'; Akk., *ki(t)tu(r)ru II*).

ki-duru$_5$
parts of a field where the ground remains wet after flooding, where it is moist and productive, sometimes used for small garden plots; riverbank; generosity (cf., piš$_{10}$, peš$_{10}$[KI.A]) ('ground' + 'moist').

ki-e-ne-di
play area; (place of) dancing (also read as ešemen) ('place' + 'to play').

ki-e$_3$
exit ('place' + 'to go out').

ki-en-du
(cf., ki-in-du).

ki-en-gi(-ra$_2$); ki-en-gir$_{15}$/gi$_7$(-r)
Sumer ('place' + 'lords' + 'civilized' + genitive).

adj., domestic.

ki-gal
(building) platform, foundation platform; foundation pit (?); statue pedestal, socle, circular base (for a statue of the king); great Earth, underworld (as opposed to an-gal, 'great Heavens') ('place' + 'big').

ki-(bi-še$_3$)...gi$_4$
to restore (usually with bi$_2$-, or with dative prefix) (lit., return [to its] place) ('place' [+ 'its' + 'to'] + 'to return, restore').

ki-gibil-gibil-la$_2$
constant renewal ('place' + reduplicated 'renewal' + nominative).

ki-a...gub
to assist ('ground' + locative + 'to serve').

ki-gub(-ba)
assigned place to stand, station; socle; walkway (cf., ki-tum$_2$) ('place' + 'to stand' + nominative).

(lu2)ki-gul-la
destitute person; waif ('ground' + 'to fall upon' + nominative; cf., gul-lum).

ki-g̃al$_2$
waste land; threshing floor ? ('place, ground' + 'available')

ki-g̃ar
grounds; settled place; place where something is built ('ground' + 'to place').

ki...g̃ar
to found, establish, erect, install (usually a building, town, or house, but sometimes abstract things such as

prayers or a song) (often with -ni- or bi$_2$-); with redup. g̃ar - to soothe, allay ('ground' + 'to place').

ki-bi-še$_3$...g̃ar; ki-be$_2$...g̃ar; ki-ba...g̃ar
to put (back) in its place; to exchange, substitute ('place' + 'its' + 'towards/the' + 'to place'; Akk. *pūḫu(m)*).

ki-še$_3$...g̃ar
to fall/throw upon the ground ('ground' [+ 'onto'] + 'to set').

ki-g̃iri$_3$
path ('place' + 'feet; way, path').

ki-g̃iš-g̃iš-la$_2$
battlefield ('place' + 'tools' + 'to raise'; cf., g̃iš-g̃iš-la$_2$).

ki-ḫul
mourning rites ('ground' + 'to destroy; evil').

ki...ḫur
to scratch the earth; to paw the ground ('ground' + 'to scratch').

ki-ib-mušen
(cf., kib-mušen).

ki-ig-ga-ag̃$_2$; ki-ig-ag̃$_2$; ki-ga-ag̃$_2$; ki-en-ga-ag̃$_2$
Emesal dialect for ki...ag̃$_2$-(g̃).

ki(-in)-dar
hole, crack, crevice, cleft ('ground' + i$_3$, 'impersonal verbal conjugation prefix', + 3rd person animate pronominal element + 'to split' = "the ground/place that one splits"; cf., ki...dar).

ki-in-du; in-di$_3$; ki-en-du
stretch of road; way, course, route; river bed; typical behavior ('ground' + i$_3$, 'impersonal verbal conjugation prefix', + 3rd person animate pronominal element + 'to walk' = "the ground that one walks'; Akk., *mālaku(m) I*).

ki-in-gi$_4$-a
(cf., kin-gi$_4$-a).

ki-inim-ma
place of testimony (cf., lu$_2$-ki-inim-ma) ('place' + 'oath' + genitive).

ki-ir-ga
(cf., di-ir-ga).

ki-iz
to trim, to clean (of hair, leaves, or vegetation) (cf., guz).

KI.KAL
base, floor; sole (of shoes); bottom of container (cf., bad$_4$; kankal; ulutim in ki-ulutim(-ma); sas; consonantal harmony version of ki-g̃al$_2$; Akk. *sassu(m)*).

^{u2}KI.KAL
grass, turf (cf., ^{u2}ḫirin, ḫirim; ^{u2}sas; Akk. *sassatu*).

ki-kal-kal-la
the very precious place ('place' + reduplicated 'to value, esteem' + nominative).

ki-kal-la-kal-la
the barren place = the netherworld ('place' + 'barren, empty').

ki-kalag
hard ground; inarable land ('ground' + 'strong'; cf., kankal).

ki-kid
a place of reed mats ('place' + 'reed mat').

ki...kig̃$_2$, kin
to seek (with -ši- denoting the object of the search) ('place, ground' + 'to seek, scour').

ki-kur$_2$(-ra)
foreign country ('place' + 'mountains, foreign country' + genitive; cf., lu$_2$-kur$_2$-ra).

ki-kukku$_2$
dark place ('place' + 'dark').

ki...la$_2$
to heed, pay attention to; to prostrate oneself, grovel; to dig, excavate ('ground' + 'to stretch, extend').

^{ĝiš}ki-la$_2$
water meter.

ki...la$_2$-la$_2$
to weigh out, pay ('area' + redup. 'to weigh, lift').

ki-lal/la$_2$(-bi)
(its) weight, where weight refers to area or volume; excavation, trench, grave; underground cellar granary or silo; shape, arrangement (Akk., *šuqultu(m)*; *kalakku(m)*) ('area' + 'to weigh, lift').

ki-la$_2$ tag(-ga)
woven on a warp-weighted loom ('weights' + 'to weave' + subordination suffix).

KI.LAM
(cf., ganba).

ki-li$_2$-lum (u$_4$-sakar)
crescent-shaped wreath (of gold and crystal) (Akk. loanword, *kilīlu(m)*, 'wreath; head ornament for humans, gods').

KI.LUGAL.GUB
royal offering place (could be read ki-lugal-gub(-ba), alal$_x$ or šiten$_x$) ('place' + 'king' + 'to stand').

ki-lugal-še$_3$
for the king ('place' + 'king' + terminative).

ki-lul-la
place of murder or violence ('place' + 'malicious act' + genitive).

ki-ma-an-ze$_2$-er
a slippery place ('a place where it slips for me'; cf., ĝiri$_3$...ze$_2$-er).

ki-maḫ
high place; place of honor; tomb, funeral place, cemetery ('place' + 'exalted').

ki-mar(-mar)-ra
n., pacification, mollification (Emesal dialect for ki-še$_3$...ĝar ?).

adj., submissive.

KI.MIN
in lexical texts, the same as the previous entry, idem ('place' + 'two').

ki-min-a
in two places ('place' + 'two' + locative).

ki-mun
heavily salinated land ('land' + 'salt').

ki na-me-šè
to any other place - ThSLa §128 ex. 91.

ki-na$_2$(-a), ki-nu$_2$(-a)
sleeping quarters; bed, bedding ('place' + nud/nu$_2$, 'to lie down', + nominative).

ki-na$_2$...aka; ki-na$_2$...dug$_3$/du$_{10}$
to make love; to lie at ease ('bed' + 'to do').

ki-nam-erim$_2$(-kud-a-ka)
the place of solemn oath swearing ('place' + 'terrible oath' + 'to cut' + nominative + genitive + nominative).

ki-nam-nitaḫ
battlefield ('place' + 'manliness').

KI.NE
(cf., dinig, nimur, and gunni; also, KI.NE.NE and Akkadian *kinūnu(m)*, 'brazier; oven').

ki-ni$_2$-te
resting place ('place' + ni$_2$...te-en, 'to calm down').

ki-nin-še$_3$
for the queen ('place' + 'queen' + terminative).

ki-ninda-gu$_7$
place to eat bread ('place' + 'bread' + 'to eat').

ki-nu-gi$_4$
netherworld ('land' + 'not' + 'to return').

ki-nu$_2$(-a)
(cf., ki-na$_2$(-a)).

ki...ri(-ri)
to scratch the ground; to run around (redup.) ('ground' + 'to touch; to gather').

ki-ru-gu$_2$
song, chant; a musical interval; one of several stages in the processional

performance of a text (?) ('place' + 'to oppose; to face').

ki-sa$_2$(-a)
footing, plinth, socle, platform; support for a wall, abutment; an office that dispensed goods ('place' + 'to compare with' + nominative).

ki-sa$_2$-al-ma-ḫe
syllabic writing for kisal-maḫ-e, 'in the great courtyard'.

ki-sağ-ğal$_2$-la
tower, stronghold ('place' + 'to confront' + nominative).

KI.SAĞ.MUNUS^{mušen}
(cf., igira$_2$^{mušen}).

ki-saḫar
place of silt deposits ('place' + 'silt').

ki-si$_3$-ga; ki-si-ga
funerary offering; (quarantine) hut ('place at which one is struck flat'; Akk., *kisiggû*).

ki-siki
wool workshop (cf., nu-siki) ('place' + 'wool').

^{iti}ki-siki-^{d}Nin-a-zu
calendar month 4 at Drehem through Šu-Sin 3; calendar month 5 at Drehem after Šu-Sin 3; calendar month 5 at Ur during Ur III.

ki sikil
untouched ground ('place' + 'pure').

$^{(lu2)}$ki-sikil
young woman; maiden; virgin ('place' + 'pure').

ki-sikil-tur
adolescent girl ('young woman' + 'child').

ki-a...su-ub
to kiss the ground; to prostrate oneself ('ground' + locative + 'to suck').

ki-su-ub...aka
to kiss the ground; to make obeisance ('to kiss the ground' + 'to do').

ki-sum-ma
onion-growing land; garden plot; land for growing garden crops such as onions, garlic, pulses, coriander, cumin, and flax ('land' + 'onions' + genitive).

ki...sur
to fix the boundary; to demarcate territory ('place' + 'ditch; to delimit').

ki-sur-ra
border; boundary ditch, sometimes filled with water ('place' + 'to delimit' + nominative).

ki-sura$_{12}$, ki-su$_7$(-ra)
threshing floor, select fallow land whose surface was conditioned to act as a threshing floor ('place' + 'threshing floor' + locative; cf., kislaḫ; sur$_{12}$).

ki-šar$_2$
horizon; everywhere ('place' + 'totality').

ki-še-er
fence; enclosure; limit ('place' + šar$_2$, 'to be many'; cf., še-er-tab-ba').

ki-še-er
profit, success (Akk. *kušīru(m)*, 'success, profit').

ki-še-er...ğar
to bring success ('success' + 'to establish').

ki-še$_3$
below; down ('earth' + 'into').

ki-PN-še$_3$
for PN ('place' + terminative).

ki-še$_3$...ğar
to fall/throw upon the ground ('ground' [+ 'onto'] + 'to set').

KI.ŠEŠ.GAG
(cf., kissa).

ki-šu(-k)
cult center ('place' + 'hand' + genitive; Akkadian *māhāzu(m)*, 'place of taking').

ki-šu-peš (5/6/11)
cult center; (market) town; place for spreading out the harvest ('place' + 'to

spread out'; cf., šu-peš$_5$-ri-a, 'division of the harvest').

ki-šu-tag
cult center; (market) town ('place' + 'to decorate; to seize').

ki-šu$_2$
enclosure; confinement, for prisoner; finale of song, concluding cadence ('place' + 'to cover; to set, go down, become dark').

ki-šub-ba
waste ground or plot ('place' + 'to drop, neglect').

ki-šur$_2$
n., snake hole; grave; cavity in the ground ('place' + 'fierce').

adj., frightening; fearful.

ki-ta
from below, up; lower; suffix (grammatical) ('ground' + locative with remote deixis).

ki-PN-ta
disbursed by PN, from PN, on the part of PN ('from the place of PN').

ki...tag
to lay something (on the ground); to lay the foundation (of a building); to plant; to sow; to lay one or more eggs; to drop excrement (said of cattle); to miscarry (said of animals) ('ground' + 'to adorn').

ki...tum$_{2/3}$
to bury (a dead person) ('ground' + 'to prepare; to bring').

ki-tum$_{2/3}$
burial; grave.

ki-tuš
seat; dwelling place, apartment (singular, cf., ki-dur$_2$) ('place' + 'to sit, dwell (singular)').

ki-u$_2$-du$_{11}$-ka
fallow land/pasture ('ground' + 'vegetation; pasture' + 'to order, do' + genitive + nominative).

ki-u$_2$-du$_{11}$-ka
fallow land/pasture ('ground' + 'vegetation; pasture' + 'to order, do' + genitive + nominative).

ki-u$_4$(-ba)
(at that) time ('place, point' + 'time' + inanimate pronoun + locative).

KI-UD(-k)
desert land ('place' + 'sun; dry').

ki-ulutim[KI.KAL](-ma), ki-uludim(-ma)
birthplace (Akk. loanword - cf., ilduma).

ki-ur$_3$
territory; living grounds, home; foundation ('place' + 'roofs').

ki-uri
the land of Akkade ('place' + 'protectors ?').

ki-uru
city territory (designation in land survey texts).

ki...us$_2$
to set firmly on the ground; to throw to the ground; to establish, institute (often with -ni-) (with loc.term. suffix -e on inanimate indirect objects) ('ground' + 'to moor, join').

ki-us$_2$
foundation; cult dais (?).

ki-uš$_2$
lifeless land, steppe (designation in land survey texts).

ki-^{d}utu-e$_3$(-a)
sunrise; east ('place' + ^{d}utu-e$_3$, 'sunrise' + nominative).

ki...za(-za)
to bow down, submit; to prostrate oneself (reduplication class) ('ground' + 'to make a repetitive motion').

ki-za...bad; ki-za...su$_3$
to make homage far from ('homage' + 'to be at a distance, remote').

ki-za...tum$_2$
to obtain homage; to refuse obeisance ('homage' + 'to obtain').

ki-zaḫ$_3$
a sacred locality ('place' + 'to hide').

ki-zu$_2$-ur$_5$-ra
sharp edge ('place' + 'teeth' + 'mill stone; to chew' + nominative).

ki$_2$-sa
(cf., gi-sa).

ki$_3$
(cf., kid$_3$).

ki$_3$-ki$_3$-da
ritual (redupl. kid$_3$, 'to act'; Akkadian *kikiṭṭû*, 'ritual procedure').

kib[ĜIŠ×ĜIŠ]
an object, that could be made of gold.

kib-mušen; ki-ib-mušen
a type of freshwater-bird; loop trap for birds ('place' + 'nook' + 'bird'; cf., Akkadian *kippu(m)*, 'loop', and *kippatu(m)*, 'circle, hoop, ring').

^{ĝiš}KIB.UD
(cf., ^{ĝiš}šennur-babbar).

kibir$_2$
firewood, kindling.

^{ĝiš}kibir$_2$
pitchfork.

^{gi}kid
reed mat; something plaited or interwoven [KID archaic frequency: 76; concate-nates 5 sign variants].

$^{(uruda)}$KID-dim
(cf., $^{(uruda)}$gi$_2$-dim).

^{gi}KID.MAḪ
(cf., muru$_{12}$).

^{gi}KID.ŠU$_2$.MA$_2$
(cf., muru$_{12}$).

kid$_{2,6,7}$
to pinch off (clay); to break off; to pluck out; to remove; to divorce; to dispossess; to open (ground with motion away from; etymologically related to kud/kur$_5$, cf., kir$_3$, 'to nip off clay').

KID$_2$-alam
sculptor ('to pinch off clay' + 'statue').

kid$_3$, ki$_3$
to build; to make; to act (cf., ki$_3$-ki$_3$-da) (ground/floor plus motion).

kid$_6$, kad$_{6,8}$
to weave a mat; to fit together, fabricate (ground/floor plus motion).

kiĝ$_2$, kin
n., message, order; task, work; clay/brick work on a dam (ki, 'places', + a$_2$...aĝa$_2$, 'to command') [KIN archaic frequency: 9].

v., to send orders; to seek, fetch (with locative-terminative -ni-); to prowl; to send; to order (reduplication class).

kiĝ$_2$/kin^{ku6}
a fish.

kiĝ$_2$...aka
to work; to manufacture ('orders' + 'to do').

kiĝ$_2$-še$_3$...aka
to put to work ('orders' + terminative + 'to do').

kiĝ$_2$-du$_3$-a
construction work; completed work ('tasks' + 'to build, erect; to do, perform' + nominative).

kiĝ$_2$-dub$_2$-ba
hammering work ('tasks' + 'to strike, hammer' + nominative).

^{iti}kiĝ$_2$-ga-ša-an-an-na
Emesal dialect for ^{iti}kiĝ$_2$-^{d}Inanna.

$^{(lu2)}$kiĝ$_2$-gi$_4$-a
messenger, envoy; message ('messages' + 'to return' + 'the one who').

adj., describes a goat buck, goat kid, sheep or lamb whose entrails were examined for omina.

kig̃$_2$...g̃a$_2$
to work ('orders' + 'to make, deliver').

$^{(g̃iš)}$kig̃$_2$-g̃eštin
cluster of grapes ('task' + 'grape vine').

^{iti}kig̃$_2$-^{d}Inanna
calendar month 6 at Nippur during Ur III.

kig̃$_2$-nim
morning meal; time of the morning meal ('tasks' + 'early').

kig̃$_2$-saḫar
earth-moving work ('tasks' + 'earth, silt').

kig̃$_2$-sig$_{(7/17)}$(-g), kig̃$_2$-se$_{11/12}$(-g)
evening meal; time of the evening meal; evening, late afternoon; cool of the evening; substitute, equal (?) ('tasks' + 'late').

kig̃$_2$-sig-gin$_7$
during the evening ('evening' + 'during').

kig̃$_2$...ti
to assign work ('orders' + 'to keep alive').

kig̃$_2$[-kig̃$_2$]...til/til$_3$
to finish one's work ('work' + 'to make complete').

kig̃$_2$-tur$^{(ku6)}$
toad, frog ('sender (?)' + 'little'; loan into Akkadian, *kitturu I*).

kig̃$_2$-u$_2$-saḫar
canal cleaning ('work' + 'vegetation and earth').

^{na4}kikken, kikkin[ḪAR]
grinding slab; mortar.

kikken$_2$, kikkin$_2$[ḪAR.ḪAR]
milling; mill house; adj. for milling women (reduplicated kin$_2$, 'hand mill').

kilib[LAGAB]
package, bundle, bale.

kilib$_3$, kili$_3$
totality; all; star(s); assembly.

kilib$_{(3)}$-ba
in all; all together ('totality' + locative).

kilim, gilim$_2$, gilili[PEŠ$_2$]
group of (wild) animals; rodents or other very small mammals.

kilim-gal
mongoose (cf., ^{d}nin-kilim; ka$_6$).

kim$_3$[BU], gim$_7$
willow tree.

kin
(cf., kig̃$_2$).

^{uruda}KIN
(cf., gur$_{10}$).

^{na4}kin$_2$[ḪAR]
hand mill (saddle quern for grinding); millstone (base/ground + stone) [KIN$_2$ archaic frequency: 11; concatenates 4 sign variants].

^{na4}kin$_2$-an-na
upper millstone ('millstone' + 'to be high' + nominative).

kinbur
bird's nest or perch (ki, 'place', + an, 'high', + buru$_3$/bur$_3$, 'receptacle').

kinda[GAD.NIG̃$_2$-crossed-GAD.NIG̃$_2$]
barber, hairdresser; surgeon.

$^{(uruda)}$kinda$_2$[URI]; kinda$_x$[LAK-419]
a large vessel for measuring barley or holding water (cf., gin$_2$, 'a volume measure'; nindan, ninda, 'a length measure').

kindagal, kindag̃al
overseer of a group of (five) slaves.

kindagal$_{(2)}$
chief barber (Akk. *(w)aklu(m)* and *gallābu(m)*).

kingal
commander, director (kiĝ$_2$, 'to order', + gal, 'big, great') [KINGAL archaic frequency: 39].

kingusili
greater part; five-sixths (5/6) (kiĝ$_2$, 'task', + silig$_2$, 'hand [of five fingers]').

kinkin
(cf., kikken).

kir
(cf., gir).

$^{(dug)}$kir$_2$, gir$_9$; $^{(dug)}$kir, gir
a large vessel; beer keg (ki, 'place', + ir$_{(2)}$, 'fluid secretion'; cf., gir, kir, 'cow or mare'; Akk., *kirru(m)*).

kir$_3$[LAGAB]
to nip off (clay); to fashion (a clay pot) (ki, 'earth', + ur$_4$, 'to shear, reap'; cf., kud, kur$_5$; and kid$_{2,7}$, 'to pinch off').

kir$_4$
(cf., kiri$_3$).

kir$_{6,4}$
stream dam, weir (cf. also, kiri$_{3,4}$) (ki, 'place', + ir$_{(2)}$, 'fluid secretion'/ra, 'to flood').

kir$_{11}$[MI$_2$.SILA$_4$]
female lamb, ewe-lamb [KIR$_{11}$ archaic frequency: 3].

kir$_{11}$-nu-ur$_4$
unshorn female lamb ('female lamb' + 'not' + 'to shear, pluck').

kir$_{13}$
(cf., gir$_4$).

kiraši
emmer wheat for making beer.

kiri$_3$[KA], kiri$_4$[BIR$_6$], kir$_4$[KA], giri$_{17}$[KA], gir$_{17}$
nose; muzzle (of an animal); hyena, the animal that eats bad-smelling food (cf., kir$_{6,4}$) (ki, 'place', + ir, 'smell').

kiri$_3$-dib/dab
groom (for leading donkeys and horses and as a title of a court official) ('nose' + 'to catch, hold').

kiri$_3$-ḫab$_{(2)}$
scurvy ('nose' + 'putrid smell').

kiri$_3$...ḫur
to cleave, pierce, prick with a spindle ('nose' + 'to scratch').

kiri$_{3/4}$-šu-du$_3$
supplication(s) ('nose' + 'hand' + 'to fasten, apply').

kiri$_{3/4}$ šu...ĝal$_2$/tag
to pay homage to; to greet (dative); to offer salutations ('nose' + 'hand' + 'to place on').

kiri$_{3/4}$...te-en
to sneeze ('nose' + 'cold').

kiri$_{3/4}$...ur$_5$
to sniff at; to sneer at; to snort; to flare the nostrils; to rub noses ('nose' + 'to smell').

kiri$_{3/4}$-zal
prosperity, splendor; (ceremony of) celebration; proud one ('dam in a stream; nose' + 'to be full, abundant; to shine').

adj., splendid, wonderful, princely, noble.

adv., proudly.

^{ĝiš}kiri$_6$[SAR]
orchard, garden, palm grove, plantation (ki, 'place', + ru$_5$, 'to send forth shoots, buds, or blossoms').

kiri$_6$...du$_3$
to lay out a garden ('garden' + 'to set up; to plant').

kiri$_6$...gub
to plant an orchard ('garden' + 'to erect').

^{ĝiš}kirid, kiri$_7$[KEŠDA]
hairpin, clasp (?) (cf., ḫir, giri$_{11}$).

kisal
temple or palace courtyard; weight measure (ki, 'place', + sal, 'spacious') [KISAL archaic frequency: 145 ?; concatenates 5 ? sign variants].

$^{\tilde{g}i\check{s}}$KISAL(-ḫada$_2$)
(cf., $^{\tilde{g}i\check{s}}$g̃i$_6$-par$_{3/4}$).

kisal-luḫ
courtyard sweeper ('courtyard' + 'to clean').

kisal-maḫ
main courtyard; athletic court ('courtyard' + 'foremost').

kisi
chamber pot (kaš$_3$, 'urine', + si$_{14}$, 'a small pot').

kisim$_{(3,5,6,7)}$
butter fat from sheep or goat milk; milk-processing wasters; spoiled milk; sharp cheese, stinky cheese (ki, 'place', + sim, 'to sniff') [KISIM archaic frequency: 67; concatenates 3 sign variants].

kisim$_{(4)}$
cheese maggot.

kisim$_{2,3,5}$
stable, pen (ki, 'place', + sim, 'to sniff').

kislaḫ, kizlaḫ[KI.UD = KI.ZALAG]
empty lot, with wild growth; threshing floor; dry land (ki, 'place' + zalag/ zalaḫ, 'to cleanse'; cf., ki-su$_7$; sur$_{12}$).

kissa
supporting wall.

kiši, kiš, keš
totality, entire political world (name of the powerful city in the north of Sumer that first bound together and defended the cities of Sumer) (places + many) [? KIŠ archaic frequency: 46].

KIŠ.NITA$_2$
(cf., šaggina).

kiš-nu-g̃al$_2$
brightly lit (??) (cf., igi-nu-g̃al$_2$, nir-nu-g̃al$_2$, g̃iš-nu$_{11}$).

$^{\tilde{g}i\check{s}}$kiša$_{(2)}$
(cf., kišig$_{(2)}$).

kiši$_4$
half; forelock (sign of a freeman; contrast gar$_3$, kar$_3$) (ki, 'place', + še$_3$, 'portion').

kiši$_4$...aka
to shave half the head as punishment or sign of slavery; to excise tattoo ? ('forelock; half' + 'to do'; Akk., *muttata gullubu(m) II*).

kiši$_{5,10}$
mouse (cf., kišib$_2$, kiši$_5$[PEŠ$_2$]; kiši$_{10}$[KUŠU]).

kiši$_{6,7,8,9}$
ant (ground + many).

kiši$_6$-bar^{mušen}[ŠEG$_9$-BAR]
egret (?) - a water-side bird whose plumage shines as if dressed in linen ('ants' + 'to uncover').

$^{\tilde{g}i\check{s}}$kiši$_{16/17}$
(cf., kišig$_{(2)}$).

kišib$_{(3)}$
n., hand; fist; paw; cylinder seal; sealed bulla, document; receipt (followed by the PN or office doing the receipting) (lexicalized imperative of keš$_2$, 'to snatch; to bind' - 'bind it!').

v., to seal.

kišib-ensi$_2$-ka
the governor's seal ('seal' + 'city governor' + genitive + genitive).

kišib-g̃al$_2$
seal-keeper ('seal' + 'having').

kišib-la$_2$
wrist; archivist ('hand; seal' + 'to hang; to carry').

kišib nam-ša$_3$-tam
sealed under the treasurership of [Personal Name] ('seal' + 'treasurership').

kišib...ra(-ra)
to seal (a tablet); to subpoena ('seal' + 'to roll, impress').

kišib$_2$, kiši$_5$[PEŠ$_2$]; kiši$_{10}$[KUŠU]
small rodent; mouse ('grab it!'; cf., kišib$_{(3)}$).

$^{ĝiš/u2}$kišig$_{(2)}$, kišik$_{(2)}$, kiša$_{(2)}$, kiši$_{16/17}$(-g) [U$_2$.G̃IR$_2$/U$_2$.G̃IR$_2$*gunû*]
a thorny plant/bush that required many days of cutting work - Syrian mesquite (*Prosopis farcta*) or camelthorn; *Prosopis* tends to invade land that has been overgrazed by sheep, but its seed pods can be ground into animal fodder (cf., $^{ĝiš/u2}$adda$_3$) [? KIŠIK archaic frequency: 21; concatenates 3 sign variants].

ku
to base, found, build; to produce; to spread out, open wide, remove clothing; to (cause to) lie down; to lie still; to sleep (reduplication class) (cf., u$_3$...ku$_{(4)}$, probably pronounced *o ko*) [KU archaic frequency: 64; concatenates 3 sign variants].

KU
an occupation - from context, herder - reading uncertain, perhaps nu$_{10}$ (cf., unu$_3$(-d)[AB$_2$.KU]).

^{uruda}KU ^{ĝiš}ig
part of a door weighing as much as 9 ma-na - handle (?) (read KU as tukul or as dur$_2$?).

$^{(ĝiš)}$KU.AN; KU.BAD
(cf., $^{(ĝiš)}$mitum$_{(2)}$).

ku-bu-ul-lum
a delectable food that could be mixed with clarified butter (cf., Orel & Stolbova #1529 ***k,abul-** 'heart, stomach').

ku-du$_3$^{zabar}
a rare bronze object ('solid base' + 'to mold, make').

ku-dun...dug$_4$
to profit ('solid base' + 'to heap, pile up' + 'to speak, do').

KU.ḪA
(cf., suḫ$_5$-ḫa).

KU-KU
n., ancestors (?); grain, barley (cf., durun$_x$[TUŠ.TUŠ] and ninda-durun$_x$) ('to found; to lie down').

v., to rest, lie down.

KU.KU
(cf., eḫ$_3$).

^{dug}ku-kur-du$_3$
(cf., ^{dug}kur-ku-řu$_2$).

ku-li(-li), gu$_5$-li
friend; a standard size clay beer pot in range 0.5 - 1.2 liters ('solid base' + 'true measure').

ku-li(-li)-an-na
friend of heaven; dragonfly ('friend' + 'sky' + genitive; Akk., *kulīlu I*, 'dragonfly').

ku-mul
cumin (Elamite ? loanword; 'to spread out' + 'stars'; cf., gamun).

ku-nu
to approach; to be near.

ku-ša-nu-um
cushion (Akk., *gusānu(m)*, "a leather sack, often containing wool", possibly from Hittite).

ku$_2$
(cf., gu$_7$).

ku$_3$
(cf., kug).

ku$_3$-a$_2$-tuku
success with wealth; profit from silver ('silver' + 'mighty').

ku$_3$-babbar
silver ('noble metal' + 'white').

ku_3-bala
to exchange money ('silver' + 'to change, transfer').

ku_3-bu; ku-bu
fetus, foetus (Akk. loanword, *kūbu(m) I*, "foetus").

ku_3-dam-tak_4-a
divorce settlement, property division (cf., $ni\tilde{g}_2$-dam-tak_4-a) ('silver' + 'to divorce' + nominative).

ku_3-dam-tuku
bride payment ('silver' + 'spouse' + 'having').

ku_3-diĝir
(cf., kug-an).

ku_3-dim_2
goldsmith, silversmith, precious metal worker ('noble metal' + 'to fashion').

ku_3-diri(-ga)
to accumulate, increase wealth ('silver' + 'addition').

ku_3-du_8
ransom money (for a slave) ('silver' + 'to untie').

ku_3-dun
profit, business ('silver' + 'to heap up').

ku_3-GI
(cf., ku_3-sig_{17}).

ku_3-$\tilde{g}al_2$
holy (cf., ${}^{(lu2)}gu_2$-gal).

ku_3-im-ba(-aš...ku_4)
reduced wealth; to lose money ('silver' + 'loss' (+ plural marker + 'to enter, turn into').

ku_3...la_2
to settle an account; to pay ('silver' + 'to weigh').

ku_3-luḫ-ḫa
refined silver ('noble metal, silver' + 'to clean' + nominative).

ku_3-ma-al
Emesal dialect for ${}^{(lu2)}gu_2$-gal.

ku_3-me-a
pure silver ('silver' + 'purified, refined'; cf., me-a).

ku_3-ne(-a)
refined silver (variant of ku_3-me-a).

ku_3-pad-ra_2; ku_3-pad-da
block or lump of silver ('noble metal' + 'to break off a piece' + nominative; Akk., *šibirtu(m)*).

ku_3-sig_{17}
gold; golden ('noble metal' + 'yellow').

ku_3-sig_{17} ḫuš-a
reddish gold - a valued native gold that contained little silver ('gold' + 'to be fiery red').

ku_3-šu-na(-ta)
with his own money ('by means of silver of his hand/control').

ku_3-ta-du_8-dam
to be redeemed/ransomed with silver ('silver' + instrumental case postposition, 'by means of' + 'to untie, release, redeem' + /-ed/ erweiterung + -am_3, enclitic copula).

ku_3-ta-gub-ba
pledge, security (in silver) ('silver' + instrumental case postposition, 'by means of' + 'to stand' + subordination suffix).

ku_3-ta sa_{10}-a
purchased with silver ('silver' + instrumental case postposition, 'by means of' + 'to buy').

ku_3-tuku
one who has silver, wealthy one ('silver' + 'having').

ku_3-zi(-ga), ku_3-si_2(-ga)
(variant of ku_3-sig_{17}).

ku_3-zu
expert, erudite, clever, wise; wisdom ('bright' + 'knowing').

ku_3-zu-ni_3-nam-ma
the all wise ('expert' + $ni\tilde{g}_2$-na-me, 'anything' + genitive).

ku_4
(cf., kur_9).

ku_5
(cf., kud).

ku_5-ku_5-ra_2
a lame person, cripple (reduplicated 'to curse' + nominative; cf., a_2-šu-$\tilde{g}iri_3$-ku_5, 'cripple', and tuḫul-ku_5, 'crippled hip').

ku_5-ra_2[DU]
a type of offering.

ku_5-ra_2 us_2-sa
rent due on leased fields; interest due when an installment purchaser of a field defaults; 20% was the normal interest rate for silver and 33% was the normal interest rate for barley; encumbered with duties, refer-ring to a temple field ('offerings' + 'to follow' + nominative).

ku_6, kua[ḪA]
fish (ku_2, 'food', + a, 'water') [KU_6 archaic frequency: 282; concatenates 3 sign variants].

ku_6-a-de_2
fresh fish ('fish' + 'fresh').

ku_6-ab-ba[ku6]
salt-water fish ('fish' + 'sea' + genitive).

ku_6-banšur-ra
fish for the (offering) table ('fish' + 'table' + genitive).

ku_6-da
a type of carp fish that lives in the marshes.

ku_6-dar-ra
dried fish ('fish' + 'to slice' + nominative).

ku_6-engur(-ra-k)
fish of the marshes ('fish' + 'fresh waters' + genitive).

ku_6-gi-ḫal
fish basket ('fish' + 'a small basket').

ku_6-gibil
fresh fish; smoked (?) fish ('fish' + 'new, fresh').

ku_6-il_2
fish carrier or delivery ('fish' + 'to carry').

ku_6-ma-al
Emesal dialect for $^{(lu2)}gu_2$-gal.

ku_6-$ša_3$-bar
cleaned fish ('fish' + 'intestines' + 'to cut open, remove').

ku_6-$še_6$[NE] (-$\tilde{g}a_2$)
cooked fish ('fish' + 'to cook' + nominative).

ku_7
n., honey (cf., kuruš; ku_7-ku_7(-da)) [GURUŠDA archaic frequency: 61].

adj., sweet; good.

ku_7-ku_7(-da)
sweetened (with honey); very sweet (reduplicated ku_7, 'sweet').

ku_{10}
(cf., gig_2).

kud, kur_5, ku_5[TAR]
to cut off (with -ta-); to breach (a dike); to cross plow a field after a harvest; to separate; to wean; to divide, divert; to levy tax or tribute; to curse (regularly followed by ra_2; cf., gur_5, kir_2, ku_5-ku_5-ra_2, gur_{10}, and lu_2-gud_4) (base with motion away from).

kug-
(cf., ku_3-).

kug, ku_3
n., silver; precious metal; money; noble (ku, 'to base, build' + $aga_{(3)}$, 'diadem, circlet, crown') [KU_3 archaic frequency: 181; concatenates 3 sign variants].

v., to cleanse, purify; to make cultically pure.

kug-an

adj., 1) shining, bright, dazzling; white; clean, pure; precious; 2) sacred, holy - unusual among adjectives in that it can come before the divine name that it modifies - ThSLa §79; 3) free (of claims); noble.

kug-an
a precious metal (cf., azag; barzil; an-bar).

kugur [KA×GUR$_7$]
(cf., ka-guru$_7$).

kukku$_2$ [MI.MI], ku$_{10}$-ku$_{10}$, gi$_6$-gi$_6$
dark, darkened (the reading kukku$_2$ appears to be a Semiticism; cf., Orel & Stolbova #1509 *kuw- 'be dark', Egyptian *kkw*, 'dark'; Akk., *kukkūm*, 'darkness').

kukkuš, kukkuž ? [IŠ]
a type of flour.

kul
n., handle (base + ul, 'pleasure; ornament').

v., to bring together, unite; to collect, glean; to roam, run.

adj., heavy; thick; sexually mature.

^{uruda}kul-du$_7$ [UL]
rotating copper door handle ('handle' + 'to push; to rotate').

kum, gum
n., mortar (for grinding) [GUM archaic frequency: 47; concatenation of 2 sign variants].

v., to crush, bruise by pounding (cf., ḫum; alternation between ḫ and k/g like the alternation between ḫab, ḫub$_2$ and gub$_3$).

kum$_2$
n., heat; summer; fever (ku$_3$, 'bright' + to be).

v., to heat.

adj., hot.

kum$_4$ [UD]
an adjective describing flour [that would be ground in a mortar, kum] and bread.

kum$_x$-kum$_x$ [PA.PA]
roasted, parched.

kun, kug̃$_x$
tail; reservoir, storage basin, outlet (of a canal); grasp (base/seat + high/to mete out) [KUN archaic frequency: 2].

kun-GAG
(cf., kun-řu$_2$).

kun-gid$_2$
a type of sheep with a long fat-tail ('tail' + 'long').

kun-g̃ar
a type of musical composition (cf., kur-g̃ar-ra).

kun-ka$_3$-an...za
to bubble (see the definition for za).

kun...la$_2$
to make an outlet reach ('canal reservoir' + 'to stretch, reach').

kun-LAGAB
(cf., kun-řu$_2$; kun-rim[LAGAB]).

kun-řu$_2$ [GAG] $^{(zabar/ku3-babbar/ku3-sig17)}$**; kun-rim[LAGAB]**
a metal libation vessel (cf., šen-dili$_{(2)}$) ('canal reservoir' + 'to erect, dedicate'; Akk., *maslaḫtu(m)*).

kun-sag̃
staircase of the sanctuary ('tail; staircase' + 'head, chief').

kun-sig$_3$
mane, tuft of hair ('tail' + 'to shake rhythmically').

kun-su$_{3/13}$ (-su$_{3/13}$)
long-tailed ('tail' + 'to stretch; to wag a tail; to be long').

kun-zi(-da)
weir; dam ('canal reservoir' + 'to strengthen').

^{ku6}kun-zi(-da)
fish-pond fish.

kun_2 [PA] (-na)
to shine (the sun illuminated the $^{(\tilde{g}i\check{s})}$kun$_4$, 'ladder', through the roof entrances of homes; for the chosen orthography, cf., pa, 'sprout, branch'; pa...e$_3$, 'to let shine'; mul, 'to sparkle, shine; to branch out').

$^{(\tilde{g}i\check{s})}$kun$_{4,5}$
ladder; stairs, staircase; threshold, slab, doorsill (base/ground + high - dates back to Neolithic dwellings sharing common walls and roof-level entrances).

kunga [ŠU$_2$.MUL]; kunga$_2$ [BAR.AN, ŠU$_2$.AN]
donkey (cf., anše-kunga$_{(2)}$).

kungal
(cf., gukkal).

kuniĝ$_x$, kunin$_2$
refined asphalt, bitumen (ku, 'to build', + niĝ$_2$, 'assets').

kur
n., mountain; highland; (foreign) land or country; the netherworld; the east; short side, of rectangular field inscribed on round tablet (ki, 'place', + ur$_3$, 'roof, mountain pass'/ur$_2$, 'root, base'; cf., Orel & Stolbova #1504, ***kur-** "mountain", #1552, ***kar-** "mountain") [KUR archaic frequency: 145; concatenates 3 sign variants].

v., to reach, attain; to kindle; to rise (sun).

adj., eastern.

kur-bad$_3$
high mountains, peaks - home of wild mountain goats and deer ('mountains' + 'high').

^{ukuš2}kur-dil-lum
a type of squash or cucumber (kur, 'foreign', + dil, 'alone, individual', + lum, 'to grow luxuriantly').

kur-$^{\tilde{g}i\check{s}}$erin-na
mountain of cedar trees ('mountain' + 'cedar' + genitive).

kur-gal
Great Mountain - a metaphor for temples, for Sumer as a place where earth and sky meet, and for Enlil, the god of Nippur ('mountain' + 'big').

$^{(\check{s}im)}$kur-gi-rin$_{(2)}$ (-na)^{sar}
turmeric, curcumin - a member of the ginger family, the root of which is very deep orange, almost red, from which an anti-inflammatory spice is made, and from which is extracted a yellow-orange oil or dye, "just the tiniest drop of which will color things very brilliantly." ('foreign' + 'reed' + 'bright'; Akk. *kurkanû*).

kur-gi$_{(4/16)}$^{mušen}
goose, geese ('foreign lands' + 'to return'; Akk. *kurkû(m)*).

kur-ĝar-ra
a cultic devotee, armed with sword and mace, who performed a variety of ritual dances, songs, and music - a prebend office; entertainer, clown ('mountain' + 'to set' + nominative; cf., kun-ĝar).

kur-ḫe$_2$-ĝal$_2$-la
mountain of abundance ('mountain' + 'overflow; abundance' + genitive).

^{dug}kur-ku-řu$_2$ [GAG]; ^{dug}ku-kur-řu$_2$; ^{dug}kur-ku-du
an Ur III storage jar for holding between 30 and 600 sila$_3$ of oil or fat - pythos ('mountain' + 'solid base' + 'to erect'; Akk., *gugguru(m), gukkurum*, 'a sealed clay vessel holding lard').

kur-kur
foreign countries, foreign lands (redup. 'foreign land/country').

$^{(u2)}$kur-ra$^{(sar)}$
a medicinal plant in the lexical lists, perhaps *"Ammi"* (cf., u$_2$-kur; Akk. *ninû(m)*).

kur-ra diri-ga
supreme over the lands ('lands' + locative + 'to be supreme' + nominative).

kur-sig
deep mountain ('mountain' + 'low').

kur-ša$_3$(-ga)
center of the mountains ('mountains' + 'womb, midst'; cf., an-ša$_3$(-ga)).

kur-ur$_2$(-ra)
foot of the mountains ('mountains' + 'base, floor' + genitive).

kur$_2$[PAP]
n., stranger; enemy; hostility (base + flowing motion; semantics reflect symbiosis with kur,'foreign land' and Akkadian *nakāru(m)*, 'to be(come) different, strange, hostile', and *nakru(m)*; 'strange, foreign', Orel & Stolbova #1840 ***nakar-/*nakir-** 'refuse, deny', Semitic **nVkar-* 'ignore, disapprove').

v., to be different; to change; to alter; to break a seal (often with -da-); to deny (kur$_2$-re in *marû*).

adj., altered; strange, alien; foreign; hostile; in the future.

kur$_2$...di
to speak hostile words ('hostile' + 'to speak').

kur$_3$
(cf., gur).

kuru$_4$, kur$_4$
(cf., gur$_4$).

kuru$_5$, kur$_5$
(cf., kud).

kur$_6$
(cf., kurum$_6$).

kuru$_7$, kur$_7$
(cf., kurum$_7$).

kur$_9$, ku$_4$
n., entrance (ki,'place', + ur$_3$, 'entrance').

v., to enter; to bring; to pronounce a slave free; to deliver (-ni- specifies delivery location); to enter before someone (with dative verbal prefix); to let enter (with -ni-); enter into the presence of (with -ši-); to turn round; to turn into, transform (with -da-) (ku$_4$-ku$_4$(-de$_3$) in *marû*) (suppletion class verb ?: singular [?] reduplication class stem; cf., sun$_5$).

kur$_{12}$
(cf., guru$_5$).

kurku$_{(2)}$
bounty, abundance; triumph (reduplicated kur$_9$, 'to deliver').

kurum$_2$
(Deimel's index for kurum$_7$).

kurum$_6$, kur$_6$
a basket of food-rations; share(s) (Akkadian loan from *kurummatu(m)*; especially if followed by -ra$_{(2)}$, read as šuku).

kurum$_7$, gurum$_2$, kuru$_7$, kur$_7$ [IGI.ERIM or older IGI.NIĜ$_2$/ĜAR]
n., lookout, spy; review, inspection, examination, supervision; delivery (ki, 'place', + uru$_3$(-m), 'to watch, guard').

v., to watch; to check, take stock; to review; to allocate, entrust; to place in crucible or dyeing vat.

kurum$_7$...aka
to inspect, review, check, control; fire, bake (clay); dye (red) ('review' + 'to do').

kurum$_7$-aka
inspection record.

kurun$_{(2,3)}$
sweet red wine; wine grape, grapevine, or grape cluster (cf., gurun and ga-ra-an).

kurušda[KU$_7$], gurušda, kuruš, guruš$_2$, kuš$_6$
n., sweet fodder (for fattening cattle); fattener (of cattle); stock-breeder, cattleman, stockyard chief (cf., ku$_7$) (kurun, 'sweet grape'/gurun, 'fruit, berry, flower', + šita$_4$; ešda$_3$, 'to bind'; cf., kešda and gur$_{(4)}$/kur$_4$, 'to make big/fat';

from W. Yuhong, kuru$_4$ še-da, 'to fatten with barley') [GURUŠDA archaic frequency: 61].

adj., plump, fat.

kuš, kus[SU]
skin, animal hide, leather (ku$_5$, 'to cut', + us$_2$, 'to be joined, next to'/še$_3$, terminative postposition/šu$_2$, 'to cover').

kuš-a-ĝa$_2$-la$_2$
(cf., ^{kuš}a-ĝa$_2$-la$_2$).

kuš-a-ĜAR-naĝ-a; kuš-a-ĜAR-gu$_7$-a
dehaired skins; animal hides that have gone through the pretanning process ('leather hides' + 'a watery solution' + 'to drink'/'to eat' + locative/nominative; cf., kuš-siki-mu$_2$; a-ĜAR).

kuš-AB
(cf., ^{kuš}aba).

kuš-ab$_2$
cowhide ('leather, hide' + 'cow').

kuš-amar
calfskin ('leather, hide' + 'calf').

kuš-anše
donkey hide ('leather, hide' + 'donkey').

kuš...du$_3$
to treat or dress skin ('leather' + 'to raise up, make').

kuš-du$_3$
treated or flayed skin.

kuš-du$_3$-du$_3$
leather-dresser.

kuš-gid$_2$-da
flayed skin ('hide' + 'to stretch out, flay' + nominative).

kuš-gu$_4$
oxhide ('hide' + 'ox').

kuš(-gu$_4$)-ḫul
damaged (ox-)hide ('hide' + 'ox' + 'damaged, ugly').

kuš-gu$_7$, kuš-ku$_2$
rash, inflammation, redness; a skin complaint (cf., su-gu$_7$/ku$_2$) ('skin' + 'to eat').

kuš-gug
(cf., su-gug).

kuš-KU$_7$
(cf., ^{kuš}dabašin).

kuš-la$_2$
leather cord ('leather' + 'to hang; strap').

kuš-maš$_2$
goatskin ('hide' + 'goat').

kuš-naĝ
leather water pail or hose ('leather' + 'to drink').

kuš-siki-mu$_2$
hairy skins; animal hides from which the hair has not been removed ('leather hides' + 'hair' + 'to grow tall'; cf., kuš-a-ĜAR-naĝ-a).

kuš-udu
sheepskin ('hide' + 'sheep').

kuš$_2$
to be or become tired, exhausted; to be out of breath; to worry; to calm (kuš$_2$-u$_3$ in *marû*) (aka, 'to do, act', + uš$_2$, 'dead').

kuš$_2$-a
hardship ('to be tired; to worry' + nominative).

KUŠ$_2$.DU
(cf., šur$_2$-ra$_2$).

kuš$_2$-u$_3$
to be tired (*marû* form); to be troubled about (with loc.term. suffix -e on inanimate indirect objects) ('to be tired', + 'to sleep'; cf., ḫuĝ-u$_3$).

kuš$_3$[U$_2$]
ell/cubit = ½ meter = 30 fingers [šu-si] = distance from elbow to fingertips; forearm; channel; mold (cf., šu-da) (ku, 'to base, found, build', + many).

$^{(uruda)}$**kuš$_3$-kuš$_3$**
(copper) gutter (Akkadian *rāṭu(m)*).

kuš$_3$-numun
in the Akkad period, a length measure equal to 2 cubits, 2 G̃IŠ-BAD, = 1 meter.

kuš$_6$
(cf., kuruš).

kuš$_7$[IŠ]
devastation, destruction (also read šuš$_3$; cf., šuš, 'to overthrow'); hyena (?); animal-trainer, cattle administrator (Akk. *kizû(m)*) (cf., sahar) (ki, 'place', + uš$_2$, 'to kill').

kuš$_7$...su$_{(3)}$
to level; to devastate ('devastation' + 'to immerse').

kušu[U.PIRIG̃]
(cf., kušum$_4$; kiši$_{10}$).

kušu$_2$
an aquatic animal; most likely crab, with turtle and shark as possibilities (ku$_6$, 'fish', + šu$_2$, 'to cover') [? UH$_3$ archaic frequency: 14; concatenates 2 sign variants].

kušum[BI.LUL], kušum$_2$[LUL]
to scorn, reject, despise; to abandon; to tremble; to cry (out), wail (ki, 'place', + ušum, 'solitary').

kušum/kušum$_4$(-ki)...tag
to run; to crawl (with -ki); to sneak away; to stampede (redup. tag) ('herd' (+ ground) + 'to touch').

kušum$_4$, kušu[U.PIRIG̃]
herd of cattle or sheep; livestock.

L

la
abundance, luxury, wealth; youthful freshness and beauty; bliss, happiness; wish, desire [LA archaic frequency: 20; concatenates 4 sign variants].

la-
(cf., la-ba-).

la'u$_{(2,3,4,5,6,7)}$
debt, owed amount (cf., lal'u$_6$, 'arrears').

la-ag
(cf., lag).

la-ah̬
(cf., lah̬$_{4,5,6}$).

la-ba-
the negative modal prefix (normally NU) + the conjugation prefix ba (example: la-ba-ra-sa$_{10}$, 'I did not sell it'; la-ba-ra-sa$_{10}$-an, '(my mother/ father) did not sell me') - ThSLa §360, §304.

la-bar
Emesal dialect for both lagar and lagar$_3$[MUNUS.H̬UB$_2$].

la-ga
n., vulva (cf., lu$_2$-la-ga) ('bliss' + throat phememe as in gal$_4$(-la); dug$_3$; Akkadian *gurištu*).

adj., obscene.

la-ga-ma-al
a fertility statuette (?), for which ½ to 1 ma-na of gold or silver could be assigned ('vulva' + Emesal 'to open, make available').

la-gal
(cf., lagar).

la-h̬a
(cf., lah̬$_{4,5,6}$).

^{dug}**la-h̬a-an**
bottle, flask (of pottery, stone, metal) ('happiness' + gan, 'to bring forth'; cf., a-h̬a-an; Akkadian *lah̬annu(m)*).

^{dug}**la-h̬a-an-gid$_2$-da**
slender flask ('flask' + 'long').

la-h̬a-ma
one of 50 mythical long-haired hero guardians of Enki's abzu (Akkadian *lah̬āmu(m)*, 'to be hairy').

la-h̬e
(cf., lah̬$_{4,5,6}$).

la-la
joy; appeal, charms; abundance; vigor (reduplicated 'happiness').

la-la...gi$_4$(-gi$_4$)
to bring pleasure; to become satisfied, sated ('joy' + 'to turn to, to restore').

la-la-g̃al$_2$
charming ('charms' + 'having').

$^{(MUNUS)}$la-ra-ah̬
labor of childbirth; woman suffering a difficult childbirth; hardship; anxiety ('happiness; desire' + ra-ah̬, 'to shake; to gnash'; cf., semantics of ga-ba-ra(-h̬um); gaba-ra(-ah̬); cf., gala$_2$ [MUNUS.LA], 'vagina').

la$_2$
to penetrate, pierce, force a way into (in order to see); to accuse, denounce; to show, reveal; to know; to look after; to have a beard (cf. also, lal) [LA$_2$ archaic frequency: 57].

la$_2$-e
weak; crippled; small; bound; stretched out.

la$_2$-ia$_3$
(cf., lal'u$_6$).

lag, lag̃, laka, lak[ŠID]
piece; lump, gob; clod; block, counterweight block of the shadouf; bulk size, collected mass; eczema (abundance + round).

lagab
block, slab (of stone); trunk (of tree) (cf., kilib; nig̃in$_2$) (lag, 'clod, piece', + gub, 'to stand') [LAGAB archaic frequency: 84; concatenates 2 sign variants].

$^{g̃iš/u2}$LAGAB
(cf., $^{(g̃iš)}$ellag).

$^{g̃iš}$LAGAB.RU
veneer, overlay.

LAGAB×EŠ
(cf., bul; ninna$_2$).

LAGAB.LAGAB
(cf., nig̃in).

$^{g̃iš}$LAGAB.RU
veneer, overlay.

LAGAB.U.GAG
(cf., mud$_4$).

lagab ^{na4}za-gin$_3$-na
a block of lapis lazuli ('block' + 'lapis lazuli' + genitive).

lagar
temple servant, who pronounces invocations to the god [LAGAR archaic frequency: 51; concatenates 4 sign variants].

lagar$_3$[MUNUS.H̬UB$_2$]
(divine) vizier, minister; a high ranking cultic functionary.

lag̃[ŠID]
(cf., lag, lag̃).

lah̬, ah̬$_3$[UD]; uh̬
v., to dry up; to dry out; to sparkle, shine (cf., luh̬, lah̬$_3$).

adj., dry.

lah̬$_{4,5,6}$
to bring or lead (plural); to drive off; to plunder, capture, take away; to fling (away) (suppletion class verb: plural object form, cf., de$_6$, tum$_{2,3}$) (ila$_2$, 'to bring', + h̬a$_2$, 'numerous').

lah̬$_4$-gu$_4$
ox-driver ('to bring, plural' + 'ox').

lah̬tan, lah̬ta
washbasin (luh̬/lah̬$_3$, 'to wash', + tan$_2$, 'to become clean'; Akk., *narmaktu*).

lah̬tan$_{(2)}$
beer storage vat [LAH̬TAN$_2$ archaic frequency: 7].

^{dug}lah̬tan-gid$_2$-da
beer jar, flask.

lal, la$_2$
v., to be high; to hold; to lift; to carry; to hang (from) (with -ta-); to weigh, measure; to pay; to deduct; to strap, harness, hitch (with -ši-); to dress oneself, put on; to place, set; to ensnare; to bind (a reed pillar); to stretch, extend, reach; to embrace; to load; to lessen, diminish; to become reduced, little; to be few; to fall back, retreat; to make silent (cf. also, la$_2$) (reduplicated ila$_2$, 'to carry, support', which derives from Akkadian *elû(m) III*, 'to raise/be high') (loan back into Akkadian, *alālu(m) II*, 'to hang up, suspend', preserves redup. form with vowel harmony) [LA$_2$ archaic frequency: 57].

adj., light, deficient; minus (cf. also, la$_2$).

LAL.LAGAB
(cf., usur$_4$).

LAL-NI
(cf., lal'u$_6$).

LAL$_2$.LAGAB
(cf., niĝin$_5$/nanga; usur$_4$).

$^{(u2)}$lal$_2$
n., noose, lasso (cf., lalla).

v., to hang, suspend; to bind; to silence [LAL$_2$ archaic frequency: 27; concatenates 2 sign variants].

lal$_3$
honey; date-syrup (reduplicated la, 'luxury, bliss') [LAL$_3$ archaic frequency: 14; concatenates 3 sign variants].

adj., sweet.

^{ĝiš}lal$_3$-dar(-ra)
pomegranate ('honey; date syrup' + 'sliced; crevices').

lal$_3$-ḫar; lal$_3$-ĝar
mythological lake, underground waters ('honey; date syrup' + 'ring'/'storeroom').

lal$_3$-ḫur
beeswax; shaping ('honey' + 'to sketch'; Akk., *iškūru(m)*, 'wax, for making figurines and for writing boards', prob. loan from Sum. ĝiš-ḫur, 'plan').

lalla[LAL$_2$]
shortage, deficiency (lal/la$_2$, 'to be deficient' + a, nominative suffix).

lal'u$_6$, la'u$_6$[LAL.NI]; lal'u$_{(2-7)}$, la'u$_{(2-7)}$; la$_2$-ia$_3$
remainder of debt left over, deficit, arrears; deduct! ('to pay, deduct' + imperative; cf., daḫ-ḫu).

la(l)'u$_6$-SU-ga
the restored deficit ('deficit' + 'replaced').

la(l)'u$_6$-SU-ga-im-ma
the restored deficit of the tablet ('restored deficit' + 'clay tablet' + genitive).

lam
n., abundance, luxuriance; almond tree; netherworld [LAM archaic frequency: 47; concatenates 3 sign variants].

v., to grow luxuriantly, flourish; to make grow luxuriantly (la, 'abundance' + to be).

$^{(ĝiš)}$LAM.GAL
terebinth (tree, wood, and flour-producing seed/nut, related to pistachio) (cf., $^{(ĝiš)}$eš$_{22}$, almond).

$^{(dug/gi)}$lam(-si)-sa$_2$(-re)
beer maturing vat; beer cask ('luxuriance' + 'towards being ready'; Akk. *lamsīsu*).

^{ĝiš}LAM.TUR
a nut tree (cf., $^{(ĝiš)}$eš$_{22}$, almond) (Akk. *šer'azum*).

lama$_2$, lam$_2$
an awe-inspiring quality (la, 'abundance' + me, 'function, power').

^{d}lama$_3$
(cf., ^{d}lamma, lama$_3$).

^{tug2}lamaḫuš[ZI&ZI.LAGAB]
a fine, decorative, ceremonial garment (lama$_2$, 'an awe-inspiring quality', + ḫuš, 'fiery red, terrible, awesome').

^{d}lamma, $lama_3$[KAL]
a female spirit of good fortune; guardian spirit; protective deity; tutelary genius (Akk. *lamassatu(m)*) (lam, 'to make grow luxuriantly', + a, nominative suffix).

le-el
(cf., lil_2).

le-um
plate; board; tablet (Akk. *lē'u(m)*).

li
to be happy; to rejoice; to sing [LI archaic frequency: 14].

^{ğiš}li
juniper/cedar tree (producing timber, aromatic resin, and seeds/berries); oil from the berries of *Juniperus communis* is an antiseptic and diuretic with a number of medicinal uses, including reducing skin inflammation and regulating the oiliness of skin and hair (the Latin name comes from *juvenis*, "fresh, young" and *parere*, "to produce"; cf., la, 'youthful freshness'; gub_2[LI], 'to purify, cleanse') [LI archaic frequency: 14].

^{gi}LI-bar
(cf., $^{gi}en_3$-bar).

li-bi-ir
Emesal dialect for mayor, village headman; police chief; plunderer, bandit; demon; vizier; herald (cf., $niğir_{(2)}$).

li-bi-ir(-si)
Emesal dialect for $niğir_{(2)}$-si.

li-bi_2-
the negative modal prefix (normally NU) + the conjugation prefix /bi-/ in NS and later texts - ThSLa §360, §304.

$^{(u2)}$LI-dur
(cf., en_3-dur).

$^{(im)}$li-gi_4-in
exercise tablet (loan from Akkadian *liginnu*).

li-li
celebration (reduplicated 'to rejoice').

li-li-a
offspring (Akk., *nannābu*, but cf., redup. *līpu(m)*, 'descendants, grandchildren' = Sum. $ša_3$-bal-bal, 'descendants').

^{u2}li-li-bi-zi-da
a thorny plant, probably the artichoke, used to increase bile and solve digestive disorders (cf., $^{u2}ša_3$-dib-$še_3$-ze_2-da; $ša_3$-lu-ub_2-ze_2-da) (cf., ze_2-da, 'bile'; Akk. *daddaru(m)*; Hebrew *dardar*).

^{ukuš2}li-li-$gi_{(4)}$^{sar}
colocynth (fruit) ('celebration' + 'to restore'; equated to Akk., *lalikkû*, *liligû*, 'colocynth', and *pīqu(m)*, 'narrow, tight', from its effects in relieving constipation, *napāqu(m)*; cf., $ukuš_2$-ti-gil_2-la and tam_2-šil-lum).

$^{(uruda)}$li-li-is_3[AB]$^{(zabar)}$; li-li-is_2[IŠ]
a large metal drum, with a metal head and hammered pitch spots (cf., lilis).

li-um
(cf., le-um).

li_2[NI]
n., fine oil (cf., lid_2).

v., to process or filter fine oil.

^{ğiš}li_2-id-ga
a measuring vessel set on the floor of the agrun chamber (cf., lid_2; Enmerkar and the Lord of Aratta, l. 324).

li_9
to glisten, shine.

iti ^{d}Li_9-si_4
calendar month 9 at Umma during Ur III.

lib-bar...aka
to pay attention ('sleepless' + 'outside; bright' + 'to do').

libi, lib[LUL]; lib_4[IGI]
sleepless; anxious; deathly quiet (cf., igi...$lib_{(4)}$) (li, 'to rejoice, sing', + bi, 'to lessen, diminish').

$^{(lu2)}$lib$_4$-lib$_4$[IGI.IGI]
(cf., $^{(lu2)}$lilib).

lib$_x$[I$_3$.UDU]
mutton fat; grease; tallow (abundance collected in open container; Akk. *lipium*).

libir[IGI.EŠ$_2$]
n., old age; the preceding account [LIBIR archaic frequency: 1].

v., to last long; to live long.

adj., old, ancient; traditional; used, worn (la, 'youthful freshness', + bir$_2$, 'to shrivel up' > Akk. *labīru(m)*, 'old', > *labāru(m)*, 'to become old, long-lasting').

libir-am$_3$
a plow animal group needing supplementation, supplements ('to be old').

libiš
(cf., lipiš).

lid$_2$[NI](-da-ga)
test; measuring vessel; true measure; gauge (cf., $^{\tilde{g}iš}$li$_2$-id-ga, 'a measuring vessel'; Akkadian loanword from *litiktu(m)*, 'test, esp. a measuring vessel', *latāku(m)*, 'to try out, test').

lidim
to receive (in charity) (la, 'abundance', + dim$_4$, 'to beg').

ligidba[ŠIM.^{d}NIN.URTA]; ligidba$_2$[ŠIM.^{d}MAŠ]
spurge, *Euphorbia*; the oil rich seeds of spurge produce a fine clear oil which was used as lamp oil and which possessed medicinal properties of a cathartic nature - the sign orthography confirms the use as lamp oil, referring to the faint planet Mercury, that one can only see after the sky is truly dark (Akk. *nikiptu(m) II*) (li$_2$, 'fine oil', + gid$_2$, 'to measure out' + ba, 'rations, wages').

$^{(\tilde{g}iš)}$ligima
(cf., $^{(\tilde{g}iš)}$ŠI.TUR.TUR).

lil$_{(3,5)}$
fool, moron (lallation word = unintelligible baby talk; cf., lal/la$_2$, 'deficiency').

lil$_2$
n., wind, breeze; breath; infection; haunting spirit (of a place); phantom, ghost; back or open country (reduplicated li, 'cedar scent' ?) [? KID archaic frequency: 76; concatenates 5 sign variants].

v., to infect.

adj., haunted.

lil$_2$-e...sig$_3$
smite by wind or phantoms; to be or make haunted ('wind; phantom' + 'to smite').

lil$_2$-la$_2$(-e-ne)
wind or storm demon(s) (cf., šu lil$_2$-la$_2$...dug$_4$, 'to be haunted'; u$_3$-lil$_2$-la$_2$(-en-na), 'hole, opening in the ground/lament for the dead') ('wind; to infect' + nominative (?) + plural; Akk. *lilû, lilium, lilitu(m)*).

$^{(lu2)}$lilib[IGI.IGI]
n., plunderer.

v., to steal.

lilis, liliz[AB$_2$×BALAG̃]
a large metal drum, with a metal head and hammered pitch spots - used by the gala singers to greet the evening appearance of Inanna-Venus (cf., li-li-is$_3$) (redup. li$_9$, 'to glisten, shine', + us$_2$/uz$_2$, 'side, edge, flank').

lillan[LUGAL]
stalk with ripe ear of grain.

lim$_2$
(cf., limmu$_{(2,4,5)}$, lim$_2$).

lima, limi, lim
thousand; overwhelming, awesome, fearsome (may be Akkadian loanword from *līm*, 'thousand', but a thousand is **four** hundred greater than g̃eš$_2$×u, 'six hundred'; cf., limmu$_{(2,4,5)}$, lim$_2$).

limmu$_{(2,4,5)}$, lim$_2$
four (cp., lam).

lipiš, libiš
courage; anger; core, heart; family (Akk. *libbu* 'heart').

lipiš-bala
anger, rage, fury ('heart; anger' + 'hostility; to revolt').

lipiš-ta
in anger - ThSLa §210 ('heart; anger' + 'from').

lipiš-tuku
enraged ('heart; anger' + 'having').

liru, liri
(cf., lirum).

lirum$_{(2,3)}$, liru$_{(2,3)}$, liri$_{(2,3)}$
n., physical strength; athletics.

adj., strong, powerful; combative.

liš
morsel, crumb (cf., dilim$_2$[LIŠ], 'spoon') (happiness + small + še$_3$, 'portion') [LIŠ archaic frequency: 4].

lu
n., many, much; man, men, people; sheep.

v., to be/make numerous, abundant; to multiply, increase; to mix; to graze, pasture (reduplication class [?]) (cf., lug; lu$_3$).

-lu
in the enclitic position of an imperative verb, probably represents the changed conjugation prefix /ĩ/ - ThSLa §412.

lu-ga
(cf., lug).

lu-gu$_2$
to twist; be crooked, not straight ('numerous' + 'edge'; cf., ru-gu$_2$).

lu-ḫu-um
silt, mud (luḫ, 'to wash' + im, 'clay, mud'; don't find Semitic parallels to Akk. *luḫummû*, but cf., Orel & Stolbova #1641 ***laḥaq-/*laḥiq-** 'clay'; cf., lum, 'fertilizer, manure').

lu-lim
stag, hart (male of the red deer; cf., lulim) ('to graze, pasture' + 'thousand'; Akkadian loanword from *lulīmu(m)* ?; cf., a-ia$_{10}$[A]-lum).

lu-lu-bu-na
assembly, company; offspring (?) (redup. 'numerous' + bun$_{(2)}$, 'to be swollen' + nominative; Akk., *tapḫurtu(m)*).

lu-ub$_2$^{sar}
turnip, beet ('abundant' + 'container').

^{kuš}lu-ub$_2$
leather bag for holding food; lunch bag ('abundant' + 'container'; Akk., *luppu(m)*).

^{kuš}lu-ub$_2$-šir(-ra)...aka
to prepare (gold or silver) for the precious sack (by sifting) ('leather bag' + 'scrotum' + locative case ending + 'to do').

lu$_2$
grown man; male; human being; householder; gentleman; someone, anyone; with negation, no one [LU$_2$ archaic frequency: 85].

lu$_2$-X
dependant of 'X'.

lu$_2$-1-x
person with one 'x', where 'x' can be 'ox', 'sheep', 'shekel', etc.

lu$_2$-a-tu$_5$(-a)
a priest who bathes the statues of the deities and rulers - lustration priest ('man' + 'water' + 'to wash, bathe' + nominative).

lu$_2$-a-zu
diviner; expert in lecanomancy or water-divination ('man' + 'water' + 'to know').

lu$_2$-a$_2$-tuku
strong man, influential person ('man' + 'mighty').

lu$_2$-ad(-da)
singer ('man' + 'song' + genitive).

lu_2-al-ed_2/ed_3(-de_3)
(cf., (lu2/MI2)al-ed_2/ed_3(-de_3)).

lu_2-^{ĝiš}bala
man of the spindle; spinner ('man' + 'spindle').

lu_2-bappir$_{(2/3)}$
brewer (cf., lunga) ('man' + 'beer bread').

lu_2-bar-ra
foreigner ('person' + 'outside' + genitive).

lu_2-bur_2-ru
interpreter (of omens/dreams) ('person' + 'to reveal, interpret (a dream)' + nominative with vowel harmony).

lu_2-dam-tuku
a married person ('person' + 'spouse' + 'having').

lu_2-di-da(-k)
opposing parties (in a legal case) ('person' + 'law suit' + 'with').

lu_2-du-du
vagabond ('man' + reduplicated 'walking').

lu_2-e_2-$niĝ_2$-ka
manager of the treasure-house ('man' + 'house' + 'treasure' + double genitive [a]k-a[k]).

lu_2-$erim_2$
enemy, foe ('man' + 'evil, hostile').

lu_2-$eše_2$
prisoner ('man' + 'rope'; cf., e_2-$eše_2$, 'jail' and šaĝa, 'captive').

lu_2-ga-šum
assassin ('man' + 'I will' + 'to slaughter').

lu_2-gi-di(-da)
piper ('man' + 'reed' + di-de_2, 'speaking/ doing' + genitive).

lu_2-gi-gid_2-da
flutist ('man' + 'reed' + 'long' + genitive).

lu_2-gim_4-ma, lu_2-im_2-ma
runner ('man' + 'to trot, run' + nominative).

lu_2-gu-la
despot ('man' + 'large').

lu_2-gub-ba
ecstatic ('man' + 'to stand' + nominative).

lu_2-gud_4[KUD](-da)
short person, dwarf (Akk. *kurû(m)*).

lu_2-ĝarza$_{(2)}$
an official.

lu_2-ĝeštin
vinedresser - one who cultivates, prunes, or cares for, grapevines ('man' + 'grapevine').

lu_2-ĝiš-$e_{3/11}$
doorkeeper, doorman ('man' + 'key').

(mi2)lu_2-ĝiš-gi-saĝ-$keš_2$
a cult performer ('man/woman' + 'antiphon/ chorus' + 'to pay attention').

lu_2-ĝiš-tag-ga
sacrificial priest ('man' + 'to make an offering').

lu_2-ḫu-dab_5(-bu)
a class of persons (cf., ḫe_2-dab_5(-ba), showing vowel harmony with lu_2, unless ḫu is to be read mušen).

lu_2-ḫun-$ĝa_2$
hired worker ('man' + 'to hire' + nominative).

lu_2-i-^{d}utu-ka
oppressor ('person of complaint').

lu_2-i_3-šur
oil presser ('man' + 'oil' + 'to produce a liquid, extract seed oil').

lu_2-i_3-zu
diviner; expert in lecanomancy or oil-divination ('man' + 'oil' + 'to know').

lu_2-IM
(cf., lu_2-tumu/tum_9).

lu_2-IM-zuḫ(-a)
(cf., lu_2-ni_2-zuḫ(-a)).

lu_2-im_2-ma
runner (cf., lu_2-gim_4-ma).

lu_2-inim-ma
witness ('person' + 'word/affair' + genitive).

lu_2-KA×LI-KA×LI
incantation priest (cf., tu_6, mu_7, zug_4, $uš_7$, and $uš_7$-zu).

lu_2-kal-(l)
dear one ('person' + 'precious').

lu_2-kar-ra
fugitive; runner ('person' + 'to escape' + nominative).

LU_2×KAR_2; LU_2-KAR_2
(cf., šaĝa, $še_{29}$, $ḫeš_5$).

lu_2-$kaš_4$
courier (cf., lu_2-gim_4-ma, lu_2-im_2-ma) ('man' + 'fast runner').

lu_2-ki-inim-ma
witness ('person' + 'place' + 'oath' + genitive).

lu_2-ki-na-ab-dam
(cf., [lu2]gi-na-ab-$tum_{(2)}$).

lu_2-ku_5-ku_5-ra_2
cripple (cf., lu_2-gud_4(-da), 'dwarf').

lu_2-kur_2-ra
foreigner; stranger; enemy ('man' + 'mountains, foreign country' + genitive).

lu_2-kur_6-ra
(cf., lu_2-šuku-ra-ke_4-ne).

(mi2)lu_2-$kurun_{(2)}$-na(-k)
brewer; innkeeper ('man/woman' + 'alcoholic drink' + genitive).

lu_2-la-ga
robber; rustler; plunderer; criminal (Akk., *leqû(m) II, laqû(m)*, 'to take away, carry off').

LU_2.LU_2@180; LU_2&LU_2
(cf., gigam).

lu_2-lul(-la)
unfaithful, treacherous man, liar ('man' + 'lies' + genitive).

lu_2-ma_2-gur_8
boat captain ('man' + 'large boat').

lu_2-maḫ
a linen-clad high priest, usually mentioned with the nin-diĝir, 'high priestess', who had access to the holiest shrine rooms, who performed purifications and extispicy, and who may himself have been chosen by extispicy (cf., Ur-Namma A) ('man' + 'exalted').

lu_2-mar-sa
a shipyard/arsenal person ('man' + 'shipyard').

lu_2-mar-za
(cf., (lu2)ĝarza).

lu_2-MU
(cf., (lu2)muḫaldim).

lu_2-$mu_{(2)}$-da
(cf., (lu2/MI2)al-ed_2/ed_3(-de_3), 'ecstatic; wild man', ma-$mu_{(2)}$-(d), 'dream', and su_6-mu_2, 'bearded').

lu_2-na-me
someone, anyone ('person' + indefinite pronoun).

lu_2...na-me...nu-
no man does X ('man' + 'anyone' + 'no, not'; cf., u_4-na-me...nu-tuku).

lu_2-nam-ra(-aka)
captive ('man' + 'taken as prisoner').

lu_2-nam-tag-ga
sinner ('man' + 'guilt' + genitive).

LU_2×NE; LU_2-NE
(cf., du_{14}).

lu_2-ni_2[IM]-zu(-/ak/)
thief (cf., lu_2-tumu/tum_9) ('man' + 'one's own' + 'your' + genitive).

lu_2-ni_2-zuḫ(-a); lu_2-$ni\tilde{g}_2$-zuḫ(-a)
thief ('man' + 'one's own/property' + 'to steal, rob' + nominative).

lu_2-$ni\tilde{g}_2$-dab_5
recruit; storekeeper, requisitioner ('man' + 'wages/receiver of goods').

lu_2-$ni\tilde{g}_2$-nu-tuku
poor man, debtor ('man' + 'thing' + 'not' + 'having').

lu_2-$ni\tilde{g}_2$-sam_2-aka
buyer ('man' + 'price' + 'maker').

lu_2-$ni\tilde{g}_2$-sam_2-gu_7
seller ('man' + 'price' + 'consumer').

lu_2-$ni\tilde{g}_2$-tuku
rich man, wealthy person ('man' + 'thing' + 'having').

lu_2-ru-gu_2
recalcitrant, intractable individual(s) ('man' + ru-gu_2, 'to withstand, oppose').

lu_2-ru-gu_2-da
river ordeal, to decide an insoluble legal case, which involved swimming a certain distance and returning to shore without being pulled under by the current (although a mooring pole was used to rescue a sinking person so that they could face punishment); a frequent alternative to the nam-$erim_2$ oath, but more frequent before the NS period ('man' + 'to send' + 'river bank' + 'to be near'; cf., ru-gu_2).

lu_2-sağ-lugal
royal guard ('man' + 'individual' + 'king'; cf., sağ-ur-sağ).

lu_2-sağ-$še_3$-na_2
dream interpreter ('man' + 'head' + terminative + 'bed').

lu_2-sar(-sar)
onion-growing 'men of the vegetables' ('man' + 'vegetables').

lu_2-$sila_{11}$-$\tilde{g}a_2$
baker; baker's assistant ('the man who kneads dough').

lu_2-silim
perfect man ('man' + 'good, healthy').

LU_2.SU[.A^{ki}]
(cf., šimaški).

lu_2-su-a
friend, acquaintance ('man' + su-a, 'cat').

lu_2-$šar_2$
numerous individuals, myriads ('men, people' + 'to be many').

LU_2.ŠE
(cf., $niga_2$).

lu_2 še bad-ra_2
to thresh ('man' + 'grain' + 'to open, expose, peel, release, split' + nominative).

lu_2-šim
a perfumer (?) (cf., $^{(lú)}$lunga[ŠIM], 'brewer') ('man' + 'spice, perfume').

lu_2-$šir_3$-ra
dirge singer ('man' + 'song; lament' + genitive).

lu_2-šuku-ra-ke_4-ne
persons with allotted portions, either rations or field allotments ('allotted portions' + genitive + plural).

lu_2-tir
forester; hereditary position of man working in the riverain and marsh woodlands, expected to present bundles of wood for festivals, and to assist with dike construction, harvesting, and soldiering ('man' + 'forest').

lu_2-tu-ra
a sick person ('person' + 'to be weak, sick' + nominative).

lu_2-$^{\tilde{g}iš}$tukul
armed man, soldier ('person' + 'weapon').

lu_2-$^{\tilde{g}iš}$tukul-gu-la
sergeant ('person' + 'weapon' + 'great').

lu_2-tumu/tum_9
'wind man': unreliable, dishonest person, liar (Emesal indicates that this is correct pronunciation of lu_2-IM) ('man' + 'wind').

lu_2-tur
child ('person' + 'young').

lu_2 u_2-rum
owned person; slave ('person' + 'private property').

lu_2-u_5-a
rider ('man' + 'to mount, ride' + nominative).

lu_2-u_{18}[G̃IŠGAL]-(lu), lu_2-ulu_3
mankind; human being, person; primeval man ('humans' + 'huge' [+ 'numerous']; *lā ilu*, 'not god; mortals').

lu_2-ulu_3 pap-ḫal-la(-k)
(doctor's) patient ('person' + 'confinement' + genitive; cf., pap-ḫal(-la)).

lu_2-ug_5-ga
murderer.

lu_2-ulu_3[G̃IŠGAL]-um
a foreign breed of domesticated sheep known from Drehem texts to be from Lullum or Lullubum, situated in the Zagros ranges, probably in the area of Kurdistan.

lu_2-ur-gi_7-me
kennelmen ('man' + 'dog' + 'plural').

lu_2-ur_3-ra
sculptor; supply clerk; man on the roof (Akk. *urrāku*, 'sculptor', and *marāqu(m)*, 'to rub something smooth, grind, scrape, rub away'; cf., šu-ur_3-ra, 'scraping or grinding by hand'; cf. also, e_2-ur_3-ra, 'storehouse').

lu_2-$zaḫ_3$
runaway, fugitive ('man' + 'to flee').

lu_2-zi(-d)
righteous, good man ('man' + 'faithful, true').

lu_2-zu(-a)
acquaintance; sage ('person' + 'to know; knowing' + nominative).

lu_2-zuḫ(-a)
thief ('man' + 'to steal, rob').

lu_3; lu
to disturb, agitate, trouble; to fluster, embarrass; to stir up, blend, mix; to make cloudy or muddy (reduplication class).

lu_5(-g/k)
to remain/live with, to have in safekeeping (with -da).

lu_5
(cf., lub, lul).

lu_7[G̃IŠGAL]
(cf., ulu_3 and lu_2-u_{18}[G̃IŠGAL]-(lu)).

lub[LUL](-bi)
a cut of meat.

^{uruda}lub(-bi)
an ax or rake for use in agriculture or as a weapon.

lud
a small bowl; a pestle (abundance + motion).

lug, lu
to swarm or dwell (said of birds and fish) (cf., lu-gu_2) (lu, 'to be numerous' + gu_3, 'noise, sound').

lugal
n., king; owner, master (lu_2, 'man', + gal, 'big'; glossed nu-gal at Ebla) [LUGAL archaic frequency: 80].

adj., royal (cf., $šar_3$).

lugal-$\tilde{g}u_{10}$
my lord ('king' + 'my').

lugal-ki-en-gi ki-uri(-k)
king of Sumer and Akkad ('king' + 'Sumer' + 'Akkad' + genitive).

lugal-kur-kur-ra
king of all (the foreign) lands (e.g., Enlil) ('king' + 'lands' + genitive).

lugal-kur-ra
king of the netherworld (e.g., Gilgamesh) ('king' + 'netherworld' + gen.).

lugal-mu
(cf., lugal-g̃u_{10}).

lugal-ša$_3$-la$_2$-su$_3$
merciful king ('king' + 'merciful').

lugud, lug̃ud(?) [BAD.UD; UD.BAD]
pus; serous fluid; gore (lug̃$_2$, 'fault, error' + ed$_2$, 'to issue').

lugud$_2$ [LAGAB]; lugud$_3$ [LUM.NIG̃$_2$&LUM.NIG̃$_2$]
half; short person, dwarf; misbirth, foetal anomaly (lu$_2$, 'person', + gud$_8$, 'short'; cf., lu$_2$-gud$_4$).

adj., short; weak; narrow; reduced.

lugud$_2$-da
short ('short' + phonetic complement).

lug̃a [PA.G̃A$_2$], lug̃$_2$ [PA], lu$_9$
fault, error; abusive remark; impudence.

luḫ, laḫ$_3$
to clean; to wash; to be clean, pure, fresh; to sweep (la, 'youthful freshness', + uḫ$_2$, 'spit, froth'; cf., u$_3$-luḫ).

luḫ-mar-tu$_{(2)}$ $^{(sar)}$
rue, a plant and drug, expels intestinal worms in Chinese medicine ('to clean' + mar/mur, 'worm'; Akk. *šibburratu*).

luḫummu [G̃IŠ.MI]
mud, silt (cf., lu-ḫu-um).

lukur
chaste priestess, nun; assistant and/or consort to the king (Ur III period) (lu$_2$, 'grown man', + kur$_2$, 'hostile').

lul, lu$_5$
n., liar; lie; malicious act.

v., to lie, deceive (cf., lu$_5$(-g/k)) (reduplicated lu$_3$, 'to trouble, disturb').

adj., false; treacherous; malicious.

LUL-bar...aka
(cf., lib-bar...aka).

lul...dug$_4$
to tell a lie ('lie' + 'to speak').

LUL.GU
restitution.

LUL.LUL(-na)
to be bright, shine (cf., sulug).

lul...si(-g)
to keep silent ('lie' + 'to stay silent').

lulim
stag, hart (male of the red deer; cf., maš$_2$-lulim and lu-lim) (Akk. *lulīmu(m)*).

lum
n., fertilizer, manure; cloud [LUM archaic frequency: 23].

v., to be satiated, full; to soften, soak; to grow luxuriantly, thrive; to be fertile, productive; to make productive; to bear fruit (abundance + grass, plant + to be).

LUM-...-a-ta
(in Neo-Sumerian texts, cf., murgu$_2$ [LUM]-...-a-ta).

lum-du$_8$
an adjective for small gold beads ('luxuriant' + 'to spread, adorn').

lum-ma
a fecund female ('to be fertile, productive' + nominative).

lum$_3$ [DUG]
a small drinking pot.

$^{(lu2)}$lunga/lumgi/ningi$_{(2,3)}$
brewer (lu$_2$, 'man', + nag̃, 'to drink'; Akk., *sīrāšû(m)*, 'brewer', from a type of beer; cf., šir$_3$-re-eš, 'much song').

M

-m-
a verbal prefix theorized to be a ventive element, indicating motion towards the deictic center - ThSLa §329-332, §429.

ma
v., to bind (rare meaning, but cf., al-ma-ma = *rakāsu(m)*, 'to bind') [MA archaic frequency: 250].

Emesal dialect for $\tilde{g}al_2$; $\tilde{g}a_2$.

variant for ma-a, 'where?' and for ma_4, 'to leave'.

ma-
writing of conjugation prefix /mu-/ + 1.sg. dative case element -a-, 'to me', 'for me' - ThSLa §336, §431-§432.

$^{\tilde{g}i\check{s}}$MA
(cf., $^{\tilde{g}i\check{s}}pe\check{s}_3$).

$^{\tilde{g}i\check{s}}$MA*gunû*
(cf., $^{\tilde{g}i\check{s}}$ḫašḫur).

$ma_{(3)}$; $\tilde{g}a_2$
to go (Emesal dialect) (Akk. *alāku*).

ma-a
Emesal dialect for $\tilde{g}a_2$-e and for me-a/mi_2-a, 'where ?; how ?; how many ?'.

ma-al
Emesal dialect for $\tilde{g}al_2$.

ma-al-ga
Emesal dialect for g̃alga/malga.

ma-al-ga-tum
a musical instrument or a composition for it ("from *Malgûm*").

ma-al(-$taka_4$)
Emesal dialect for $\tilde{g}al_2...taka_4$, 'to open'.

ma-al-tum
a bowl, of wood or stone (Akk., *maltu(m)*).

ma-an-ga-ga
(cf., mangaga).

$^{(uruda)}$ma-an-$gara_2$$^{(zabar)}$ (nu-ur_2-ma)
a metal basket (with precious stone pearls in the form of pomegranates) (Akk., *mangāru(m) I*).

ma-an-si-um
emblem of rulership (from Akkadian, *mesû(m) I*, 'pure, refined').

$^{(gi)}$ma-an-sim
sieve ('it sifts for me').

^{lu2}ma-an-zi-le; ma-an-zi-la_2
club-footed ? (Akk., *larsīnum*).

ma-az; ma-ra-az
n., swelling; pleasure; rejoicing; a female dancer.

v., to swell; to rejoice.

adj., exuberant, joyful; flourishing, thriving.

ma-da
district, realm, territory; foreign, conquered lands (Akkadian, *mātu(m) I*, 'land').

ma-dam
abundant yield (Akk., *mādu(m)*, 'many').

ma-gi-a
Emesal dialect for g̃agia.

$^{\tilde{g}i\check{s}}$ma-gid_2
(yoke-)shaft (of a wagon, mar) (Akk., *mašaddu*; cf., $^{\tilde{g}i\check{s}}$mar-gid_2-da) ('to bind' + 'to draw, pull, tow').

ma-ḫe
phonetic writing for maḫ.

ma-la-(g)
friend, companion (among females) ('to bind' + LA.GA, 'an obscene name for the female genitalia' per Landsberger; Akkadian *šiʾītum*, 'female neighbor; secondary wife').

$^{(uruda)}$ma-lal$^{(zabar/ku3-babbar/ku3-sig17)}$, ma-la$_2$
a type of container, usually of metal (Akk., *ma'lalum*, 'wooden mortar' ?).

ma-ma
Emesal dialect for g̃a$_2$-g̃a$_2$, 'to set, place; to present, give; to stop, detain; to tear out' (cf., g̃ar).

ma-mu$_{(2)}$-(d)
dream ('it is growing for me').

ma-na
a unit of weight measure, *mina* = ca. 500 grams (1.1 lbs.) = 60 gin$_2$ (since Akkad period, 2 ma-na = 1 sila$_3$ of water) (Akk., *manûm IV*, 'to count', > *manûm II*, *manā'um*, 'mina').

ma-na-la$_2$
weigh-master ('a weight measure' + 'to weigh').

ma-na-tur
a surface area measure, little mina = 1/3 shekel = 60 surface še = 720 square fingers; as a volume measure, = 60 še.

ma-ni-
1.sg. dative prefix ma-, 'for me, to me', + locative prefix -ni-, which with compound verbs can refer to a place or to persons and animals - ThSLa §476.

$^{g̃iš}$ma-nu
Cornelian cherry dogwood (?); dwarf ash (?); willow (?); a relatively common tree in Sumer which was used to make staffs and pegs; firewood bundle ('to bind' + nu$_{11}$, 'fire').

ma-nun
Emesal dialect for g̃a$_2$-nun.

ma-ra
Emesal dialect for g̃a$_2$-a-ra.

ma-ra-
writing of conjugation prefix /mu-/ + 2.sg. dative case element -ra-, 'to you', 'for you' - ThSLa §336, §433.

ma-ra-az
(variant of ma-az).

^{gi}ma-sa$_2$-ab
a (cult or ritual) basket; box (usually made from woven reeds, but also from bronze or silver) (imperative 'fill the bound reeds equally' - conveys a sense of social entitlement; Akk., *masabbu(m)*).

$^{(uruda)}$ma-sa$_{(2)}$-tum
lance, spear ? (Akk., *maššatum*, 'a metal weapon ?').

MA.SILA$_3$
heel; rear.

$^{(uruda)}$ma-ša-lum$^{(zabar/ku3-babbar/ku3-sig17)}$; ma-šal$_2$-lum, ma-sal$_4$-lum; mu-ša-lum
a usually bronze or silver mirror (Akkadian loanword *mušālu(m)*; cf., nig̃$_2$-šu-zabar).

$^{g̃iš}$ma$_2$
boat; raft [MA$_2$ archaic frequency: 6].

ma$_2$-a-g̃ar-ra
loaded on a ship (cf., ma$_2$(-a)... g̃ar; Akk., *maga(r)rûm*, 'travel provisions on a ship').

$^{(g̃iš)}$ma$_2$-addir
ferryboat ('boat' + 'ferry; bridge').

$^{(gi)}$ma$_2$-da-la$_2$
a thick bundle of reeds used as a life-raft or to build rafts ('boat' + 'to hold near' + 'to strap, bind'; Akk., *tillatu(m) I*, 'help, reinforcement; a piece of boat equipment').

$^{(g̃iš)}$ma$_2$-dara$_3$-abzu
the processional barge of Enki ('boat' + 'wild goat buck' + 'the deified sea').

$^{g̃iš}$ma$_2$-diri-ga
the boat sailing downstream (antonym: $^{g̃iš}$ma$_2$-ru-ru-gu$_2$); ferryboat ('boat' + 'to float (with the current)/to go over' + nominative).

${}^{\text{lu2}}$ma$_2$-DU-DU(-d)
barge captain ('boat' + ?; cf., ma$_2$-lah̲$_{4/5}$).

${}^{\text{ĝiš}}$ma$_2$-du$_3$
ship's plank ('ship' + 'to mold, shape'; cf., ${}^{\text{ĝiš}}$ĝir$_3$-ma$_2$-du$_3$).

${}^{\text{ĝiš}}$ma$_2$...du$_8$
to caulk a boat with pitch (cf., esir$_{(2)}$) ('boat' + 'to spread with pitch').

${}^{\text{(ĝiš)}}$ma$_2$-egir-ra
the stern of a boat ('boat' + 'back' + nominative).

ma$_2$-GAG
(cf., ${}^{\text{ĝiš}}$ma$_2$-du$_3$).

ma$_2$-gal-gal
a large boat or barge ('boat' + redup. 'big').

ma$_2$-gan-an-na^{ki}
Magan (a country, probably Oman, on the sea route to India) (cf., me-luh̲-h̲a^{ki} and ${}^{\text{ĝiš}}$mes-ma$_2$-gan(-an)-na) ('boats' + 'support' + 'to be high' + nominative).

${}^{\text{(ĝiš)}}$ma$_2$-gi$_{(4)}$-lum
a type of sailing boat or barge ('boat' + gilim, 'reed bundle'; Akk., *magillu(m)*).

${}^{\text{(ĝiš)}}$ma$_2$...gid$_2$
to sail (with -da-); to tow a boat or barge from the river bank (upstream) ('boat' + 'to draw, pull').

${}^{\text{(ĝiš)}}$ma$_2$-gid$_2$(-da)
hauler; tow boat; processional boat ('boat' + 'to draw, pull' + nominative).

ma$_2$-GIN$_2$
(cf., ma$_2$-tun$_3$).

ma$_2$-X-gur
(cf., ma$_2$-ĝeš$_2$-gur).

${}^{\text{(ĝiš)}}$ma$_2$-gur$_8$
a large boat, cargo boat; pot stand; silver or bronze offering boat weighing approx. ½ ma-na; a geometric figure ('boat' + 'high, deep') [MAGUR archaic frequency: 5; concatenates 2 sign variants].

${}^{\text{(ĝiš)}}$ma$_2$-gur$_8$-mah̲
a high cargo boat ('cargo boat' + 'high').

ma$_2$(-a)...ĝar
to load a boat ('boat' + 'in' + 'to place').

ma$_2$-ĝeš$_2$-gur
a boat of sixty-gur capacity ('boat' + 'sixty' + **kor** basket measure).

ma$_2$-ĝiš
a ship for transporting wood ('boat' + 'wood').

ma$_2$-i$_3$-dub
cargo ship having a capacity of 60-120 gur ('boat' + 'storage jugs').

ma$_2$-i$_7$-da
river boat ('boat' + 'river' + genitive).

MA$_2$.KASKAL.SIG$_7$
(cf., surru, sur$_9$).

${}^{\text{(ĝiš)}}$ma$_2$-la$_2$
cargo boat, freight boat, raft ('boat' + 'to extend, load').

${}^{\text{lu2}}$ma$_2$-lah̲$_{4/5}$
sailor; barge captain ('boat' + 'to drive along').

ma$_2$ ma$_2$-gan(-na)
Magan boats ('boat' + 'Magan' + genitive).

MA$_2$.MUG
(cf., ${}^{\text{(ĝiš)}}$dimgul).

ma$_2$-nisaĝ-ĝa$_2$
boat with first-fruit offerings ('boat' + 'first-fruits' + nominative).

${}^{\text{ĝiš}}$ma$_2$-ru-ru-gu$_2$
the boat sailing upstream (antonym: ${}^{\text{ĝiš}}$ma$_2$-diri-ga) ('boat' + 'to move in a direction opposite to [the current]').

^{ĝiš}ma$_2$-saĝ-ĝa$_2$
the bow of a boat; prow ('boat' + 'point, head' + nominative).

ma$_2$(-a)-si-ga
describes loading a product into a boat (for transport) ('boat' + 'in' + si-ga/ge, 'to pile up').

^{ĝiš}ma$_2$...su
(cf., ^{ĝiš}ma$_2$...du$_8$).

^{ĝiš}ma$_2$-su(-a)
sunken boat ('boat' + 'submersed' + nominative).

^{ĝiš}ma$_2$-su$_3$-a
a deep-draft boat ('boat' + 'to immerse' + nominative).

^{ĝiš}ma$_2$-še(-/ak/)
grain boat ('boat' + 'grain' + genitive).

ma$_2$-^{ĝiš}tukul
warship ('boat' + 'weapon').

ma$_2$-tun$_3$[GIN$_2$]
asphalt specialist; ship builder ('boat' + 'to bind, bandage').

$^{(ĝiš)}$ma$_2$(-a)...u$_5$
to go on board; to embark ('boat' + 'to mount').

ma$_2$-ur$_3$(-ur$_3$)
portage trail where boats or freight must be dragged overland ('boat' + 'to drag/ mountain pass').

ma$_3$
Emesal dialect for ĝa$_2$-e.

ma$_4$[SAR]
to leave, depart, go out; to grow; to ignite (cf., mud$_6$).

ma$_5$
(cf., mu$_3$).

mabi$_{(2,3)}$
(cf., amagi$_{(2,3)}$).

maḫ
n., (large) quantity, wealth, abundance (ama, 'mother of', + numerous; cf., ab$_2$-maḫ$_2$) [MAḪ archaic frequency: 6; concatenates 2 sign variants].

v., to be or make large.

adj., high; adult; exalted, supreme, great, lofty, foremost, sublime, splendid.

maḫ-bi
adv., powerfully ('great' + adverbial force suffix).

maḫ-bi-še$_3$
adv., in a magnificent way ('great, splendid' + adverbial force suffixes).

maḫ-di
exalted, prominent ('splendid' + 'doing').

maḫ$_2$[AL]
an adjective for cows that have given birth (as opposed to ĝiš for bulls).

makkaš$_{(2)}$
wailing; clamor (maḫ, 'great',? + kuš$_7$, 'devastation').

mana, mina$_3$, man, min$_3$, men$_5$[U.U]
partner; companion; equal; two (cf., mina, 'two').

mangaga
palm fiber, bast (man, 'partner', + gag, 'peg, nail', + a(k), 'genitive').

$^{(ĝiš/uruda)}$mar, ĝar$_7$
n., wagon, cart; winnowing shovel; spoon (cf., ma$_2$, 'boat', and ĝar, 'to deliver, deposit'; Akk. *marru* "shovel; spade"; Orel & Stolbova #1738 ***mar-** 'hoe') [MAR archaic frequency: 117; concatenates 2 sign variants].

v., to sow, scatter; to coat, apply; to don; to immerse.

adj., western (cf., tu$_{15}$-ĝar$_7$-du$_2$).

mar; mur
worm; earthworm.

mar
Emesal dialect for g̃ar, 'to set, place; to present, give; to tear out; storeroom; to enclose, lock up' (ma$_x$-ma$_x$ in *marû*).

$^{g̃iš}$mar-da ri-a
riding with the wagon ('wagon' + comitative + 'to be located' + nominative).

$^{g̃iš}$mar-gid$_2$-da
wagon ('wagon' + 'to draw, pull, tow' + nominative).

^{na4}mar-ḫu-ša
pyrite or marcasite (iron sulfide) (Akk., *marḫušu(m)*, 'of Marḫaši').

mar-maḫ
Emesal dialect for gudu$_4$/guda$_2$.

$^{(g̃iš)}$mar-nig̃$_2$-šur-ra
soup spoon ('spoon' + 'liquid' + genitive).

mar-ru$_{10}$ [GUR$_8$]
flood (cf., mar-uru$_5$).

mar-sa
boat transport center; shipyard and dock; arsenal ('to lock up' + 'to compensate').

$^{g̃iš}$mar-šum
litter, sedan chair, or covered wagon drawn by oxen ('wagon' + 'to hold' ?; Akk., *mayyaltu(m), maršu(m)*).

^{lu2}MAR-TU [-KI], g̃ar$_7$-du$_2$
nomad; bedouin; Amorite - Semitic nomad of the western desert ('wagon' + 'to be born').

^{tu15}MAR-TU
(cf., tu$_{15}$-g̃ar$_7$-du$_2$).

$^{(tu15)}$mar-uru$_5$ [GUR$_8$/TE*gunû*]
floodstorm, deluge, tempest (cf., e$_2$-mar-uru$_5$) ('to immerse' + 'high, deep').

mar-za
Emesal dialect and variant for g̃arza/g̃arzu.

mas
(cf., maš).

mas-su$_{(2/3)}$
leader; expert; advisor ('goat kid' + sud, su$_3$; su, 'to furnish/provide' ?; 'income' + 'to make lasting' ?; cf., maš-ki; maš-maš).

maš
one-half; twin (ma$_4$, 'to leave, depart, go out', + še$_3$, 'portion') [MAŠ archaic frequency: 133].

maš; maš$_2$
he-goat, billy goat, buck; gazelle (cf., maš-da$_3$) [MAŠ archaic frequency: 133].

maš; maš$_2$
interest (of a loan); rent; profit, income; produce, yield (of a field) (ma$_4$, 'to leave, depart, go out', + še$_3$, 'portion') [MAŠ archaic frequency: 133].

maš$_{(2)}$-a-ša$_3$-ga
a small tax on leased lands levied in advance to finance the cost of irrigation ('rent' + 'field' + genitive; cf., gana$_2$-uru$_4$-la$_2$).

maš-bi
taxes due from the recipients of a parcel of land ('goat; rent' + 'its'; cf., udu-bi).

maš-da-ri-a
(cf., maš$_2$-da-ri-a).

maš-da$_3$
gazelle (cf., mašda).

$^{(g̃iš)}$maš-dara$_3$
inscription (from Akk. *mašṭaru*, 'writing, inscription').

^{iti}maš-du$_3$-gu$_7$
calendar month 1 at Drehem through Šu-Sin 3; calendar month 2 at Drehem after Šu-Sin 3; calendar month 2 at Ur during Ur III.

MAŠ-EN-GAG; MAŠ-GAG-EN
(cf., mašda$_{2/3}$)

maš-gana$_2$
settlement (prob. Akk. loanword from *maškanum*, 'location, site; threshing floor',

cf., *šakānum* 'to place') (ZATU-356 archaic frequency: 4).

$^{ĝiš/u2}$**maš-guru$_5$(-uš)**
a medicinal plant, taken for constipation (Akkadian *šarmadu*).

^{ĝiš}**maš$_{(2)}$-gurum**
a valued tree or bush that grew in the foothills or on the high plains between the rivers ('produce' + 'heap; to be bent').

maš$_{(2)}$-ĝa$_2$-ĝa$_2$(-dam)
interest-bearing/earning ('interest' + 'to deliver' + non-finite prospective *marû*).

maš-ĝi$_6$
(cf., maš$_2$-ĝi$_6$).

^{uruda}**maš-ḫu-um**
a copper beer mug (Akk., *mašḫu(m) II*).

$^{ĝiš/u2}$**maš-ḫuš**
a thorny shrub (Akk. *giṣṣu(m)*; *kalbānu*, 'dog-plant').

maš-ka$_{15}$-en
speculative reading of mašda$_3$ [MAŠ-GAG-EN].

maš-ki
agricultural income, yield ('profit, produce, yield' + 'earth').

^{kuš}**maš-lum;** ^{kuš}**maš-li-um**
leather bucket, pail (< Akk., *mašlû(m)*).

maš-maš(-gal)
a type of priest - (great) exorcist, sorceror (cf., maš$_3$; maš, 'pure, holy').

MAŠ.PA
(cf., maš$_3$).

maš$_{(2)}$...pad$_3$
to choose by extispicy (goat + to find, declare, select).

maš-šu-gid$_2$-gid$_2$
(cf., maš$_2$-šu-gid$_2$-gid$_2$; mas-su$_{(3)}$).

maš-tab-ba
young twins ('twin' + 'to be double' + nominative).

MAŠ.U
(cf., gidim$_2$).

maš$_2$
n., extispicy (divination based on the entrails of a sacrificed animal); omen; sacrificial animal (cf., maš; maš$_2$) [MAŠ$_2$ archaic frequency: 60].

v., to scrutinize, inspect.

maš$_2$; maš
young male goat, kid [MAŠ$_2$ archaic frequency: 60].

maš$_2$-a-dara$_4$
hybrid of the domestic goat with the bezoar ('goat' + 'bezoar seed').

maš$_2$-anše
animals, domestic livestock ('goats' + 'equids').

maš$_2$-da-ri-a; maš-da-ri-a; maš-da-ra$_2$-a
a type of regular offering or tax ('goat kid' + 'driven [animal]').

maš$_2$-gaba
sucking kid ('male goat' + 'breast').

maš$_2$-gal(-niga)
full-grown male goat, billy goat, buck ('male goat' + 'large' + 'fattened').

maš$_2$-ĝi$_6$(-k); maš-ĝi$_6$(-k)
night-time vision, dream; omen ('goat/omen' + 'night' + genitive).

maš$_2$-lulim
hind (female of the red deer) (smaller goat-like animal + 'stag, hart').

maš$_2$ ma$_2$-gan$^{(ki)}$
Arabian white oryx, an antelope native to Oman (I.D. by Steinkeller) ('goat of Magan').

maš$_2$-niga
barley-fed kid (smaller goat-like animal + 'fattened').

maš$_2$-sag̃
lead goat (of a herd); leader ('goat' + 'head, leader').

maš$_2$-šu-gid$_2$(-gid$_2$)
extispicy; diviner; omen; a goat for this purpose ('goat kid' + šu... gid$_2$, 'to observe, inspect').

maš$_2$...šub
describes an animal dropping or birthing its young ('goat' + 'to drop').

maš$_2$-ud$_5$-da(-k)
breeding he-goat ('he-goat' + 'she-goat' + genitive).

maš$_2$-za-la$_2$
bearded male goat ('he-goat' + 'bleat' + 'to have a beard').

maš$_3$[MAŠ.PA]; maš
pure; holy.

mašda
gazelle (includes the goitered gazelle, the mountain gazelle, and the Dorcas gazelle) (maš$_2$, 'sacrificial animal', + du$_3$, 'to make'; cf., maš-da$_3$; $^{(\tilde{g}iš)}$maš-dara$_3$).

mašda$_{(2/3/4)}$
a class of serfs; palace dependants; poor man; destitute; commoner (this reading seems well attested, but PSD has mašga´en; cf., maš-ka$_{15}$-en; Akk. *muškēnu(m)*).

maškim
commissioner - one who investigated economic and legal matters related to a lawsuit; requisitioner, one authorized to order expenditures; inspector, monitor (maš$_2$, 'to inspect', + kig̃$_2$, 'work').

maškim...dug$_4$/du$_{11}$
to be in charge ('to be authorized to order, inspect, and monitor' + 'to effect').

me, mi$_3$; g̃e
n., essence; function, office, responsibility; ideal norm; the phenomenal area of a deity's power; divine power(s); divine decree, oracle; cult; silence [ME archaic frequency: 363; concatenates 2 sign variants].

v., to be (a particular way - not 'to exist or to be somewhere', for which see g̃ál) - ThSLa §535; the Sumerian copula; to say, tell.

Abbreviation of me-am$_3$, where is?.

Emesal dialect for g̃a$_2$-e and gin$_6$/gen$_6$.

-me-
1.pl. dative case prefix, 'to us, for us', and sometimes 1.pl. pronoun, 'us' - ThSLa §290, §428, §431, §435.

-me-
writing of conjugation prefix /mu-/ + 2.sg. pron. object -e-, 'you', if following a modal prefix, starting with OB literary texts - ThSLa §478.

-me
3.sg. form of verb 'to be'; can also be 1., 2., 3.pl. forms in OS and Gudea texts when pronominal suffix was not written - ThSLa §536, §541.

-me
1.pl. possessive suffix, 'our', - ThSLa §101.

me-a; mi$_2$-a
where ?; how ?; how many ? ('to be' + locative).

me-a
purified; refined (metal, such as silver) ('essence' + adjectival -a).

me-a-am
shepherd, in the Emesal dialect [source: Schretter, quoting C. Wilcke].

me-am$_3$
where is ? ('to be' + locative + enclitic copula).

me-da
adv., from where ?; whence?, from when; at some time.

$me-dim_2$
appearance, form, shape, handiwork; limbs ('function' + 'to build').

$^{gĩš}me-dim_2$
ship's railing (?) ('function' + 'to build').

$me-diš_2...i-i$
(cf., $me-teš_2...i-i$).

$me-du_{10}-du_{10}-ga$
the good 'me's, the beneficial functions. ('civilization's functions' + reduplicated 'sweet, good' + nominative).

-me-en; -me-e
1.sg. and 2.sg. form of verb 'to be'; I am; you are - ThSLa §95, §536, §541; I, myself - ThSLa §545; also a writing for me, 'function' ('to be' + '1st & 2nd person ending').

$me-en-de_3(-en)$
we; us; 1.pl. personal pronoun - ThSLa §90 ('to be' + '1st person plural ending').

$-me-en-de_3(-en)$
1.pl. form of verb 'to be'; we are - ThSLa §536 ('to be' + '1st person plural ending').

$me-en-ze_2(-en)$
you (plural), 2.pl. personal pronoun - ThSLa §90 ('to be' + '2nd person plural ending').

$-me-en-ze_2(-en)$
2.pl. form of verb 'to be'; you (pl.) are - ThSLa §536 ('to be' + '2nd person plural ending').

me-er
Emesal dialect for $g̃iri_2/g̃ir_2$; g̃ar - cf., mar.

me-er-ga
Emesal dialect for 'one; first'.

-me-eš
used as plural suffix, especially in late Sumerian and Akkadian context texts; 3.pl. form of verb 'to be' - ThSLa §76, §536, §541.

me-gal
great office ('function' + 'great').

me...g̃ar
to assemble; to make silent; to pay attention; to be conscious of, remember; to celebrate ('silence' + 'to set').

me-ḫuš
terrible 'me's, negative attributes ('functions' + 'terrible, angry').

me-ir
Emesal dialect for $mer_{(2)}/mir_{(2)}$.

$me-kilib_3-ba$
all the 'me's, all the functions of civilized life.

$me-lam_2/lem_4$[NE]; $me-lem_3$ [LAM]
terrifying glance; splendor, radiance; awesome nimbus, halo, aura, light (myth.); healthy glow, sheen (of a person) ('divine power' + 'awe-inspiring quality; to shine').

$me-lam_2...su_3-su_3$
to deck with splendor ('splendor' + 'to strew'; cf., $ḫi-li...su_3(-su_3)$).

me-li-e-a
interj., 'woe is me', 'alas!' - ThSLa §154.

me-a...lu(-lu)
how numerous are...? ('how ?' + 'numerous').

$me-luḫ-ḫa^{ki}$
a country - probably the Indus valley civilization in Pakistan (literally, 'cleansed rituals'; cf., $ma_2-gan-an-na^{ki}$).

me-maḫ
the high 'me's, the high functions ('function' + 'high, exalted').

$me-na(-am_3)$
when? - ThSLa §126 ('to be' + en_3, 'time; until' + enclitic copula; cf., èn-šè(-àm)).

$me-na-še_3$
how long? - ThSLa §127 ('to be' + en_3, 'time; until' + terminative; cf., èn-šè(-àm)).

me-nam-nun-na
the (god-given) 'me' of royalty ('function' + 'rulership' + genitive).

me-ni-da
along with himself ('to be' + 'self' + 'with').

me-ni_3-galam
perfected 'me's ('functions' + 'thing' + 'artistic, complicated').

me-re, me-ri
Emesal dialect for $\tilde{g}iri_3$.

me-ri
totality, all of (Emesal dialect).

me-ri; me-er
Emesal dialect for $\tilde{g}iri_2$/$\tilde{g}ir_2$.

me-ri-gub
Emesal dialect for $\tilde{g}iri_3$-gub.

me-ri-kur_2...dug_4
Emesal dialect for $\tilde{g}iri_3$-kur_2...dib_2.

me-$šar_2$-ra; me-ša-ra
all the 'me's ('functions' + 'totality; to be numerous' + nominative).

me-$še_3$
where to?, to where? - ThSLa §125 ('to be' + terminative).

me-ta
adv., from where ?; whence?, from when; at some time.

me-te
appropriate symbol, characteristic; fitting thing; suitability; unique; ornament, adornment; proper dress; dignity ('function' + 'to meet', or 'office' + 'symbol'; cf., ni_2-te).

me-te-bi-im
to suit, befit ('to be its fitting thing').

me-te...$\tilde{g}al_2$
to be fitting ('fitting thing' + 'to be').

me-te-$\tilde{g}al_2$
fitting, seemly, appropriate ('suitability' + 'having').

me-te-$\tilde{g}al_2$-sa$\tilde{g}$-$\tilde{g}i_6$-ga
adornment of the Sumerian people, such as national totems, tattoos, piercings, costumes or other symbols of the Sumerians ('proper dress' + 'having' + 'Sumerian' + genitive).

me-$teš_2$...i-i
to praise, celebrate, extol ('to be' + 'together' + 'to rise'; cf., $teš_2$...i-i).

me-a...tum_2
to prepare something for the sake of one of the civilized functions ('me' + locative + 'to be suitable; to prepare').

me(-da)...tum_3
how will X attain or succeed ('function' + comitative + 'to obtain').

me-ze_2
a type of metal drum (cf., meze; Akk. *manzû*).

(uzu)me-ze_2
jaw ('function' + 'to cut, shear').

(uzu)me-ze_2-gid_2-da; me-ze_2-gal
gums ('jaw' + 'to stretch' + nominative).

me-ze_2-er
Emesal dialect for mu-dur_7.

me_2
(cf., gig_2).

$me_{3,7,9,11}$
battle [ME_3 archaic frequency: 4].

me_3-šen(-šen-na)
battle; war ('battle' + 'combat'; cf., šen-šen).

me_6
to act, behave.

megida, megidda[TAB.TI]; $megida_2$, $megidda_2$[TAB.KUN]
sow (female pig).

mel_3
'scorching' = heartburn (?).

meli$_2$, mili$_2$, mel$_2$, ĝele$_3$, ĝili$_3$[KA×LI]; mel; mel$_3$
throat, pharynx; root of the tongue; voice (cf., mu$_7$[KA×LI]; Akk., *ma'lātu*, 'root of the tongue'; *nemlû(m)*, 'throat ?'; cf., Semitic root which manifests in Akkadian as *qâlu*, 'be silent', but which means 'voice' in Hebrew, Syriac, and Ge'ez [P.R. Bennett, *Comparative Semitic Linguistics*, p. 50).

men$_{(4)}$
n., crown, tiara (metaphor of divine en-ship) (me, 'function, office' + en, 'lord') [MEN archaic frequency: 48; concatenation of 2 sign variants].

adj., authoritative.

men-an-uraš-a
crown of heaven and earth ('crown' + 'heaven' + 'earth' + genitive).

men-dalla
beaming crown ('crown' + 'beam, ray; to be bright').

men-ri-ba; men-rib-ba
supreme crown ('crown' + 'supreme').

men-sağ
head-crown ('crown' + 'head'; cf., sağ-men).

men$_2$
both; alike (cf., mana).

men$_{2,3}$
I, myself (Emesal dialect for me-en).

mer$_{(2)}$, mir$_{(2)}$
n., storm wind; violent storm; north (wind); long side, of rectangular field inscribed on round tablet; anger; belt, girdle; an encircling snake (var. of gur$_3$, cf., gur$_{21}$) (me$_{3,7,9,11}$,'battle', + to flow) [MER archaic frequency: 48; concatenates 2 sign variants].

v., to blow fiercely; to get angry.

adj., fierce, angry, furious; northern.

mermer$_3$ [IM.EN×EN]
dust storm.

$^{(ĝiš)}$mes, meš$_3$
young man; prince; son; hackberry tree in the elm family, also known as nettle-tree, used to make furniture and carved objects including figurines (me, 'endowment', + usu, 'strength'; Akkadian loanword - *mēsu I*, 'hackberry tree'; cf., Orel & Stolbova #1766 ***mi'es-** 'tree') [MES archaic frequency: 32].

^{ĝiš}mes-gam$_3$(-ma)
a tree, grown in plantations for timber, and twig used as drug (Akk. *šaššūgu*).

^{ĝiš}mes-ma$_2$-gan(-an)-na
Magan-tree, perhaps "*Dalbergia sissoo*", used to make furniture.

meš [ME.EŠ]
the enclitic copula with plural suffix, 'they are'; [in later Sumerian texts] many, numerous; plural determinative.

meš$_3$
(cf., mes).

meze [AB$_2$×ME.EN]
a type of metal drum (function + repetitive noise; cf., me-ze$_2$).

mezem [UMBISAG$_2$]
maintenance, support (?).

mi
(cf., gig$_2$; ĝi$_6$).

mi-ir
Emesal dialect for ĝir$_2$, 'scorpion'.

mi-ni-
writing of conjugation prefix /bi-/ + 3.sg. nonpersonal locative prefix -ni- ThSLa §338, §474, §476, §480.

^{ĝiš}MI-par$_4$
(cf., ^{ĝiš}ĝi$_6$-par$_4$).

mi-ri$_2$
(cf., mer).

^{ĝiš}mi-ri$_2$-tum
a musical instrument which required tuning; harp (?) (Akk. loanword, appears as

early as Gudea Cyl. B, X, 11; cf., zag-ge$_6$[MI]-ri$_2$-tum).

^{ĝiš}mi-ri$_2$-za
small boards, planks (for a door or a boat - some sources say frame/rib).

$^{(ĝiš)}$MI(-si)-saḫar[IŠ](-ra)$^{(ku6)}$
sieve (for gold dust); moray eel (?) ('dark'(?) + 'ray-like; to fill' + 'sand, sediment' + genitive/locative).

$^{(ĝiš)}$mi-tum
a mace (cf., $^{(ĝiš)}$mitum$_{(2)}$) (Akkadian, *miṭṭu(m)*, 'a divine weapon'; Orel & Stolbova #1807, ***muṭ-** "stick", Eg *mdw*).

mi$_2$[SAL]
n., woman; female (this pronunciation of the sign found in compound words and verbs or in enclitic or proclitic position, Hallo & van Dijk, p. 85) (cf. also, mu$_{10}$, munus, min$_2$) (compounds tend to preserve older word forms) [SAL archaic frequency: 435].

adj., feminine.

adv., gently.

mi$_2$-a
(cf., me-a).

mi$_2$(-zi)...dug$_4$/du$_{11}$/e
to speak in a loving way; to (justly) praise; to approve; to treat kindly, handle gently, caress, rub; to gratify; to cherish; to take great care with, look after (often with -ni- prefix) (with loc.term. suffix -e on inanimate indirect objects); analyze ga-am$_3$-me or ga-am$_3$-e as ga-m-e-e) ('female' + 'kindly' + 'to speak, do').

MI$_2$-eden-na
she-ass of the steppe ('female' + 'steppe' + genitive).

MI$_2$-gir
heifer, young cow ('female' + 'young heifer').

MI$_2$-u$_5$-a
selected for breeding ('female' + 'to mount' + nominative).

MI$_2$-u$_8$
ewe lamb ('female' + 'ewe').

$^{(ĝiš)}$mi$_2$-us$_2$
sheath, for a sharp knife ('female' + 'to moor, join').

mi$_2$-us$_2$-sa$_2$; mi$_2$-us$_2$-sa
son-in-law; brother-in-law (sister's husband; cf., murum$_{4,5}$) (can appear as short form for niĝ$_2$-mi$_2$-us$_2$-sa$_{(2)}$) ('woman' + 'to come near to' + 'to equal in value').

mi$_2$-us$_2$-sa$_2$-tur
future son-in-law ('woman' + 'to come near to' + 'to equal in value' + 'young').

mi$_2$-zi-de$_3$-eš
appropriately ('female' + 'loyally'; cf., zi-de$_3$-eš$_{(2)}$(-še$_3$)).

$^{(ĝiš)}$middu$_{(2)}$
(cf., $^{(ĝiš)}$mitum$_{(2)}$).

mili, mil[IŠ]
(cf., milla, mili, mil).

mili$_2$
(cf., meli$_2$).

milla, mili, mil[IŠ]
a low quality flour (cf., zid$_2$-milla); saltpeter (mu$_3$, 'to mill, grind', + ila$_2$, 'to gather, deliver'; Akk., *mil'u*, 'saltpeter').

min$_{(3,5,6)}$
(cf., mina and mana).

min-a-bi
both (2 + nominative + 'their').

^{iti}min-eš$_3$
calendar month 7 at Umma during Ur III.

min(-na)-kam
an ordinal number - the second - ThSLa §141, §167 (2 + genitive + enclitic copula).

min_2[SAL], mi_2
v., care for, cherish (cf., Sjöberg, "Emar S^a Voc", #573') (cf., mi_2).

mina, $min_{(5,6)}$
two; second, another (mi_2, 'woman', + na, 'distinct things', because a woman has two breasts).

$mir_{(2)}$
(cf., $mer_{(2)}$).

$^{(muš)}$mir-$ša_4$[DU]
(sword-)belt; a fierce mythical snake ('snake' + 'belt' + 'to lament, wail').

^{ğiš}mir-tur
a type of wood/tree ('belt' + 'small').

-m-ši-
inanimate /-m-/ + terminative prefix - ThSLa §455.

$^{(ğiš)}$$mitum_{(2)}$, $middu_{(2)}$ [TUKUL.DIĞIR/KU.AN; TUKUL.BAD/KU.BAD]
mace; divine weapon; cultic object (cf., $^{(ğiš)}$mi-tum).

mu
n., name; word; year - where the words that follow could be a year-formula; line on a tablet, entry; oath; renown, reputation, fame (cf., $ğu_{10}$) [MU archaic frequency: 99].

v., to name, speak (cf., mug).

prep., because; to; toward; in.

Emesal dialect form of ğiš/ğeš. Also with additional Emesal meanings: sky; instructions; fire; house; great. Also Emesal dialect form for $ğiš_{2,3}$/$ğeš_{2,3}$/uš, man, male, penis.

mu-
conjugation prefix, suggests involvement by speaker, used especially before dative infixes, preferred for animate and agentive subjects; conjugation prefix before the 2nd person pronominal element -e- in the *ḫamṭu* transitive/two-participant conjugation - ThSLa §336, §341-§347, §280.

-MU
(cf., -$ğu_{10}$).

mu-X
year X (indicates a date according to a notable event that occurred during the year - a list of Mesopotamian Year Names is on the Internet).

mu-X
In Emesal dialect, see ğiš-X.

mu-...-a(k)-$še_3$
because (in a nominalized sentence); for somebody's sake; instead of - ThSLa §159, §201, §489 ('name' + genitive + terminative).

mu-diğir
(cf., nam-$erim_2$; mu-lugala(-bi)...pad_3/pa_3).

mu-didli, mu-dili-dili
individual entries (in a lexical series); individual accounts ('entry, line on a tablet' + 'separate, individual').

mu-dim_2
builder (personal conjugation prefix + 'to make').

mu-DU
(cf., mu-tum_2).

mu-du-lum; mu-du-li-a
n., meat meal; salted meat (cf., adkin) (Akkadian loanword, from *madālu*, "to preserve in salt").

adj., salted (Akkadian *muddulu(m)*).

mu-du-ru; mu-$duru_5$; mu-ud-ru; mu-PA
Emesal dialect form for ^{ğiš}ğidru/ğidri[PA].

mu-du_3-u_3-bi
all year long ('year' + 'to work' + 'after' + 'it').

mu...dug_4/du_{11}/e
Emesal dialect for $ğiš_3$...dug_4/du_{11}/e.

$^{(tug2)}$mu-dur$_7$[BU](-ra)
n., dirt; dirty rags.
adj., very dirty; defiled (cf., mudru$_5$).

mu-duru$_5$
Emesal dialect form for ^{giš}g̃idru/g̃idri[PA].

mu-gi$_4$-ib; mu-gi$_{17}$-ib; mu-gib$_3$[GIG]
Emesal dialect for nu-gig.

$^{(g̃iš)}$mu-gu$_2$
water lift (vowel harmony loan from Akk., *makūtu(m) II*, 'pole for a well, shaduf$^{?}$').

mu-gub
assigned lines ('word, sentence' + 'to set down').

mu ḫe$_2$-g̃al$_2$-la
a year of abundance ('year' + 'overflow; abundance' + genitive).

mu-im-ma
last year ('year' + 'last, previous').

mu-la$_2$
Emesal dialect for gal$_5$-la$_2$.

mu-lu
Emesal dialect for lu$_2$; possibly also for gala.

mu-lugala(-bi)...pad$_3$/pa$_3$
to swear by the king's name, invoking royal sanction that an agreement will be upheld ('name' + king + genitive + demonstrative suffix + 'to call, swear').

mu-mu-a
among all names = among known persons (reduplicated 'name' + locative).

mu-ni-
in compound verbs: 3.sg. animate mu- + prefix -ni-, which prefix can reference a place, persons, or animals in the locative, locative-terminative, or dative case - ThSLa §476, §479.

mu-nu-tuku
childless, without issue ('name, renown' + 'not + 'having'; Akk. *munutukû*).

mu-nu$_{10}$[KU]-(d)
Emesal dialect for unu$_3$(-d), 'chief cowherd'.

mu...pad$_3$/pa$_3$
to invoke; to choose ('name' + 'to call, swear').

mu-ri-
in compound verbs: 2.sg. mu- + prefix -ri-, which prefix can reference a place, persons, or animals in the locative, locative-terminative, or dative case; the 2.sg. prefix -ri-, which may combine the dative -ra- with locative -ni-, is not attested before the OB period - ThSLa §476, §478.

mu-ru(-b)
(cf., murub$_4$, muru$_2$; or Emesal mu-ŠUB).

mu(-še$_3$)...sa$_4$
to name; to give as name ('name' (+ terminative) + 'to name').

mu-sar
(cf., mu$_2$-sar).

mu-sar-ra
(royal) inscription; seal impression ('name, word' + 'to write' + nominative).

^{tug2}mu-sir$_2$-ra
mourning garment ('garment' + personal prefix + 'weak, feverish' + nominative).

mu-ša-lum
(cf., ma-ša-lum).

mu-X-še$_3$
because of, for, on behalf of X ('name' + terminative).

mu-ši-
1.sg. mu- + terminative prefix -ši-, 'toward me'; -šè- appears in place of later -ši- in OS texts - ThSLa §476, §478.

mu-šid(-bi-im)
numbered line of text on a tablet, count line ('line on a tablet' + 'to count' (+ 'to be its')).

itimu-šu-du7
calendar month 9 at Lagaš during Ur III.

mu-ŠUB
Emesal dialect for ĝešbu, 'bow'.

mu-X-ta
'since X'; 'X years ago'; according to the order of X - ThSLa §207.

mu-ti-in; mu-tin
Emesal dialect for ĝeštin, 'wine' (> Akk. *mu(t)tinnu*, 'choice wine').

mu-tin
Emesal dialect (?) for mušen, 'bird; (hunting) falcon'.

mu-tin; mu-ti-in
Emesal dialect for Akkadian *zikaru(m)*, 'male, virile' (cf., tin, 'life; health, vigor').

mu-tin; mu-ti-in; mu-ti-na
Emesal dialect for ki-sikil, 'young woman' (cf., tin, 'life; health, vigor').

mu-tuku
to be famous (but cf., mu-nu-tuku, 'childless') ('name; fame' + 'having').

mu-tum2
delivery (for); delivered (personal conjugation prefix + 'to bring').

mu-tun3[GIN2]
stomach (?); Emesal dialect for ĝiš-tun3, 'a small wooden container/type of ax' (?).

mu-u2-a
this year; mature young man; Emesal variant for ĝišĝidru[PA], referring to 'this year's grain measure' (Emesal mu = 'man', i.e., 'provider man'; Emesal form of ĝiš, 'stick', + 'in the plants'; cf., PA-a, 'a graphic simplification of u2-a'; cf., duru5 reading for a).

mu-ud(-da)-na
spouse; husband; wife (Emesal dialect for nitalam/nitadam).

mu-ud-ru
Emesal dialect form for ĝišĝidru/ĝidri[PA].

mu-ug
(cf., mug).

mu-un
Emesal dialect for gu2-un ?; cf., umun.

mu-un-gar3; mu-un-ga-ar
Emesal dialect for engar, 'farmer'.

mu-un-gur11[GA]; mu-un-gar3
Emesal dialect for niĝ2-gur11, 'property, possessions'.

mu-un-ku5
Emesal dialect for enku, 'fishing overseer; tax collector'.

mu-us2-sa
the following year; the year after ('year' + 'to follow' + nominative).

mu-us2-sa-bi
the second year after ('following year' + possessive suffix).

mu-us2-sa-N-bi
the Nth year after ('following year' + number + possessive suffix).

mu-uš
Emesal dialect form of ĝiš/ĝeš; also ĝešta/ĝeš2/ĝiš2, 'sixty'.

mu-uš-ki-im
Emesal dialect form of ĝiskim, 'sign'.

mu-uš-tug2
Emesal dialect for ĝeštug(2,3).

mu-uš-zal
Emesal dialect for ĝizzal, 'attention'.

mu-zal
end of the year ('year' + 'to pass'; Akk. *taqtītu(m)*).

mu2
(cf., mud6).

mu2-a
n., growth(s); vegetation (for verb, cf., mud6, mu2) ('to sprout, grow high' + nominative).

adj., sprouted, germinated.

mu_2-mu_2
always being reborn (such as the moon) (reduplicated 'to ignite; to sprout, appear').

mu_2-sar; mu-sar
(flower, vegetable) bed; garden(-plot) ('to sprout, appear' + 'vegetables').

mu_3, ma_5[KA×ŠE_3]; mu_{11}, ma_8[KA×SAR]
to mill, chop, grind, crush, pulverize; to burn (reduplication class) (cf., mur, 'to grind, mill').

mu_4
(cf., mur_{10}).

mu_5
well-formed, beautiful; plump, fattened.

mu_6[PA]-sub_3
shepherd (PA as mu_6 only occurs in this compound + 'shepherd'; Emesal mu = 'man').

mu_7[KA×LI], mun_x
to shout, scream, roar; to exorcise; exorcism.

mu_9[G̃IŠ]
Emesal dialect for 'human being'.

mu_{10}[SAL]
woman; female (cf. also, mi_2, munus) [SAL archaic frequency: 435].

mud[ḪU.ḪI]
n., progeny; blood; trembling, shivering; fear, terror, recoil [MUD archaic frequency: 88].

v., to give birth, bring forth, create, produce; to tremble, be afraid; to frighten (closed container with motion out from).

adj., dark, dim.

(g̃iš)mud
(tree) stump; handle; tube; leek; door bolt socket; metal socket for pick handle; bag; heel.

mud-g̃al_2
begetter ('to give birth' + 'being').

mud-me-mar
Emesal dialect form of mud_5-me-g̃ar.

mud_2
blood (closed container with motion out from).

$mud_{3,4}$
a large vat for beer [MUD_3 archaic frequency: 27; concatenates 4 sign variants].

mud_5
exultation, jubilation.

mud_5-me-g̃ar
to be full of joy ('exultation' + 'to celebrate'; cf., $nig̃_2$-me-g̃ar).

mud_6, mu_2[SAR]
to sing; to blow; to ignite, kindle; to make shine; to grow, make grow (tall); to sprout, appear; to be angry, aggressive, mad, rabid; to be swollen, inflamed (reduplication class) (mu, 'word', + ed_2, 'to go out').

mud_8[NUNUZ.AB_2 = LAK 449]
an amphora in the 30-60 liter range with two neck handles, = 50 ku-li, Presargonic Girsu.

mudla, madlu, mudul, madal
pole; stake (mud, 'a right-angled tool', + lal/la_2, 'to hang').

$mudru_2$
fuller; launderer (mur_{10}/mu_4, 'to clothe oneself', + $duru_5$, 'moist, fresh').

tug2$mudru_5$[SIK_2.BU]
dirty garment; mourning garment (Akk. **warāšum*, 'to be(come) dirty').

$mudru_6$, $mudra_6$[MU.BU]
(cf., mu-dur_7[BU](-ra)).

mug, muk; mu(-ug)
n., chisel; poor quality, unbleached wool; short, broken wool fibers, tow; ergot; sty, eyesore (cf., $mug_{(2)}$).

v., to hew out, hollow out; to engrave, carve; to abrade, erode (chamber + ku, 'to build').

mug...dun
to sort out the tow (from the usable, longer fibers) ('tow' + 'to heap up').

mug$_{(2)}$
n., nakedness; vulva, pudenda; shame; modesty (mu$_{10}$, 'female' + ig, 'door, entrance').

v., to be in heat.

$^{(lu2)}$muḫaldim [MU]
(chief) cook (including baking and roasting) (mu$_3$, 'to mill, chop, grind, burn', or mu$_{10}$, 'woman', + ḫal, 'to divide; portion', + dim$_2$, 'to fashion, create'; Akk. *nuḫatimmu(m)*).

mul
n., star; constellation; planet; meteor (g̃i$_6$/mi, 'night', + ul, 'star, ornament') [MUL archaic frequency: 6].

v., to (let) sparkle, shine, glow, radiate; to spread, branch out.

mul-an
celestial star; constellation(s); heavenly writing ('star' + 'heaven').

$^{(uruda)}$mul-mul (-lum)
a type of arrow (cf., Akk., *za'ānu(m)*, 'adorned').

mul-sa$_5$
the planet Mars ('star' + 'red, brown').

mul-sig$_7$, mul-sa$_7$
darkness; gloom (Akkadian *ekletu(m)*) ('stars' + sa$_7$, 'visible').

mul$_3$
a destructive insect; wood-wasp; caterpillar (mu$_3$, 'to mill, grind', + ul, 'flower, bud').

^{lu2}mumun [MU$_7$.MU$_7$]
exorcist, incantation priest (reduplicated mu$_7$, 'to shout, scream, roar; to exorcise').

munu$_{(3)}$, mun [DIM×ŠE]
salt; a tool of silver, gold, or copper [MUN archaic frequency: 24 ?; concatenates 5 ? sign variants; MUNU$_3$ archaic frequency: 15].

mun-du
emmer groats, which is emmer that has been husked and then cracked, bruised, or pounded; morning meal (time); an acceptable breakfast offering for the dead (Akk. *mundu*).

mun-gazi
spice herbs, refers to a wide range of plants and products including legumes; an industrial process of reducing the volume of goods by pulverizing until 'like salt' (?); an adjective for soil quality ('salt' + 'cassia/mustard').

mun-ur$_4$
salt-gatherer ('salt' + 'to gather in').

mun$_4$, munu$_x$ [ŠEŠ]
alkaline, brackish, salty, bitter.

munšub$_{(2)}$
hair; hairy skin; pelt, hide; horns; barber ('it falls down oneself') [? MUNŠUB archaic frequency: 3; concatenates 2 sign variants].

munšub$_{(2)}$...kud/ku5
haircut; slang for part of a sale/purchase price ('hair' + 'to cut').

munsub$_3$
(cf., musub$_3$).

munu$_2$
a caustic salt (mu$_2$, 'to make grow', + nu$_{11}$, 'fire'; saltpeter is the oxygenating ingredient in gunpowder).

munu$_4$; munu$_3$; munu
malt barley grain for brewing (cf., bappir; sun$_2$; titab$_{(2)}$; a-si$_3$-ga) (mu$_3$, 'to mill', + nud, 'to lie down, sleep').

^{iti}munu$_4$-gu$_7$
calendar month 5 at Lagaš during Ur III ('month of the malt meal feast').

$munu_4$-mu_2[SAR]
maltster ('malt' + 'to sprout, grow high').

$munu_4$-si-e_3
sprouted malt ('malt' + 'antennae' + 'to go forth').

munus[SAL]; nunus(Emesal)
female; woman (this pronunciation found in absolute inflection, cf., mi_2) (mi_2, 'woman', + nuz/nus, 'egg') (cf., mi_2/mu_{10}, nunuz, and etymology of nitaḫ).

MUNUS.GI_7/GIR_{15}
(cf., egi_2/$egir_3$).

MUNUS.$ḪUB_2$
(cf., eme_5).

munus-kar-ke_4
(cf., (MUNUS)kar-kid).

MUNUS.KU
(cf., nin_9).

munus-maḫ
princess ('woman' + 'great').

MUNUS.NITA.DAM
(cf., nitalam/nitadam).

MUNUS.TUG
(cf., nin).

MUNUS.UR
(cf., nig).

u2munzur, munzer[KI.AN.ŠEŠ.KI (KI dNANNA)]
bitter, medicinal plant; licorice plant ?; juniper shrub ? (mun_4, 'bitter', + zar, zur_4, 'to tap, flow, exude').

mur, ur_5 [ḪAR]
n., lungs; liver; fodder for fattening; lattice, grate (cf., ur_5, $muru_{12}$, and ḪAR-ḫa-da) (mu_7, 'to shout'/mud_6, mu_2, 'to sing; to blow' + ur_2, 'root, base').

v., to surround, enclose; to guard, preserve; to shout; to fatten; to grind, mill; to destroy; to spoil.

demonstrative, thus; so; in this way.

mur-gig
paralysis (?); lung cancer (?) ('lungs' + 'illness; to be sick, painful').

mur-gu_4
fodder, forage, feed for plow animals ('fodder' + 'domestic ox').

mur-ni-is-ku
fine steed; thoroughbred.

mur[ḪAR]-ra-an
a (copper) part of a wagon; a type of tree (cf., Akk. *murrānu(m)*).

mur...$ša_4$
to roar, growl, howl, bellow (said of animal or thunder) ('lungs, liver' + 'to lament, wail') (not attested as frequently as ur_5...$ša_4$ reading of ḪAR...DU).

murgu-peš; mur_7[SIG_4]-peš
(cf., peš-murgu; peš-mur_7).

$mur_{7,8}$
(cf., murgu).

mur_{10}, mu_4(-mu_4) [TUG_2]
to clothe; to dress oneself (reduplicated suggests a continuous activity) (mu_{10}, 'woman', + ur, 'to surround').

murgu
fodder; dung (from sheep) ? (cf., mur-gu_4).

$murgu_{(2)}$, $mur_{7,8}$
neck; back; shoulders; ridge (land), with very poor soil quality (mur, 'lungs', + gu_2, 'neck').

murgu-ba
turtle carapace, shell - used as a mixing bowl or trough ('back' + 'turtle').

$murgu_2$[LUM]-...(-a)-ta
after; after the death of - ThSLa §490 ('from the back of'; cf., eĝir ...-a-ta).

$murgu_3$, $urgu_2$[KA×NE]
ferocity, rage, fury, wrath (mur/ur_5 + gu_3; cf., gu_3...mur; mur...$ša_4$, ur_5...$ša_4$, 'to roar, bellow').

$muru_4$
(cf., $murum_4$).

$muru_5$ [MI_2.U_4.RU_6 = SAL.UD.EDIN]
(cf., $murum_5$).

$muru_9$ [IM.DUGUD]
fog, mist, haze; clouds; drizzle (mi, 'to be dark', + to flow; Akk. *imbaru(m)*).

$muru_{12}$ [KID; GI.KID.MAḪ; GI.KID.$ŠU_2$.MA_2]
reed mat (cf., Akkadian *mur(u)dû(m)*, 'lattice, grating').

$murub_{(2)}$
vulva; woman; sexual charm [$MURUB_2$ archaic frequency: 4].

$murub_4$, $muru_2$; $murub_6$, $muru_{13}$ [UD*gunû*]
central, median area; middle; waist, hips; skin, membrane; terrain with good, middle quality soil; interval; battle (mur_{10}, 'to dress oneself', + ib_2, 'middle; loins'; cf., $^{iti}murub_4$).

$^{iti}murub_4$
calendar month 4 at Umma during Ur III.

$murub_5$ [MUNUS.UŠ.DAM]
son-in-law (relative to wife's father) (cf., nitalam, g̃itlam; $nita_3$-dam) (Akk. *emu rabû*, 'father-in-law' ?).

$murum_{4,5}$, $muru_{3,4,5}$, $urum_2$, uru_7, ur_9
(member of) the family of the wife; relatives, kin; brother-in-law (wife's brother; cf., mi_2-us_2-sa_2; u_2-rum) (contrast $ušbar_{(3/7)}$) (mi_2, 'woman', + u_2-rum, 'own, personal').

$murum_{11}$, $muru_{11}$, urum, uru_6, ur_7
spawn, fry; father-in-law.

mussa
(read mi_2-us_2-sa_2).

$musub_3$, $munsub_3$[USAN]
shepherd (cf., mu_6[PA]-sub_3[USAN]).

muš
n., snake; reptile (eme, 'tongue'/ma_4, 'to leave, depart, go out', + $uš_2$, 'to kill'/ $uš_{11}$, 'venom, poison') [MUŠ archaic frequency: 3; BU: archaic frequency: 393; concatenation of 2 sign variants].

adj., bitter.

muš-a
water snake ('snake' + 'water').

muš-aka
combed (wool) ('snakes' + 'to do').

muš-bi-an-na; muš-bi-eden-na
an area.

muš-da-gur_4(-ra)
gecko, lizard ('reptile' + 'arms, sides' + 'plump, big').

muš-gal
great serpent (mythical beast) ('reptile' + 'great').

muš-$gu_7^{mušen}$
a bird ('snake' + 'to eat').

muš-$g̃ir_2$
a fanged snake ('snake' + 'knife').

^{na4}muš-$g̃ir_2$
a semiprecious stone, perhaps serpentine (Akk., *muššāru(m)*).

muš-ḫuš
a mythical monster; serpent-dragon; a constellation ('snake' + 'terrifying').

muš-$laḫ_5$[DU-DU]; muš-$laḫ_4$[DU&DU]
snake-charmer ('snake' + 'to drive').

muš-maḫ
a mythical serpent ('reptile' + 'foremost').

MUŠ×MUŠ.A.NA
(cf., arina/$erina_8$).

muš-SAG̃-KAL
a large snake referenced in several myths ('snake' + 'leader').

muš-ša$_3$-tur$_3$
horned viper (*Cerastes cerastes*); a mythical poisonous snake ('reptile' + 'millipede').

muš-tum$_2$
fully fermented beer (muš$_2$...de$_6$/tum$_2$, 'to stop working').

muš$_{2,3}$
n., face, appearance, aspect, glow; the irrigated, cultivated farmland which surrounded a city; precinct; surface (when followed by the genitival -k, read as the goddess Nin-anna(k) else is the sign for the storehouse goddess ^{d}INNIN; cf., šuba$_2$; suḫ/suḫ$_{10}$) (mu$_{10}$, 'female', + aš$_2$, 'to desire'; mud$_6$, 'to make grow', + eš, 'many, much') [MUŠ$_3$ archaic frequency: 284; concatenates 2 sign variants].

v., to glisten, shine.

adj., bright.

muš$_2$...de$_6$/tum$_2$; muš$_3$...de$_6$/tum$_2$
to stop working; to cease ('appearance' + 'to prepare').

muš$_2$...dub
comb or set hair ('appearance' + 'to heap up').

muš$_2$...ga; muš$_3$...ga
Emesal dialect for muš$_2$...de$_6$/tum$_2$; muš$_3$...de$_6$/tum$_2$.

MUŠ$_2$-KEŠDA
(cf., suḫ-giri$_{11}$/suḫ-kiri$_7$).

MUŠ$_3$.A
(cf., sed$_3$).

muš$_3$-am$_3$; muš$_2$-am$_3$
an exclamation used to seek or express compassion; (it is) enough!; declaration of clemency by god; petition for clemency by worshipper ('bright' + 'it is').

muš$_3$...de$_6$/tum$_2$
(cf., muš$_2$...de$_6$/tum$_2$).

MUŠ$_3$.DI
(cf., sed$_4$).

MUŠ$_3$-kar$_2$-kara$_2$-ka
(cf., suḫ$_{10}$-kar$_2$-kara$_2$-ka).

muš$_3$-me
face, features ('face, appearance' + 'to say, tell').

MUŠ$_3$.ZA
(cf., sed$_3$).

muš$_4$
a biting insect (cf., the etymology of muš, 'snake').

muš$_5$ [ŠEŠ]
bitter (eme, 'tongue', + u$_2$, 'plant', + eš, 'to anoint'; cf., šeš; še-muš$_{(5)}$).

mušen
bird (muš, 'reptile', + an, 'sky') [MUŠEN archaic frequency: 178].

Emesal dialect in some contexts apparently for nin, 'mistress' (note sign for the goddess innin, MUŠ$_3$).

mušen-du$_3$, usan$_5$-du$_3$ [ḪU-GAG]
bird-catcher, fowler; expert ('birds' + 'to fix'; Akk., *usandû(m)*, *ušandû(m)*, 'bird-catcher', *emqu(m)*, 'wise, clever', *mūdû(m)*, 'knowing, wise').

mušen-zib$_2$
owl (cf., an-zib$_2$).

muššagana, mušagana [LAGAB×MUŠ]
voracious hunger.

N

-n-
3.sg. animate (AKA personal) pronominal prefix - immediately precedes

the verbal root (or the comitative -da- and terminative -ši- prefixes that precede the root) - in transitive *ḫamṭu* forms, indicates the 3.sg. animate subject of the verb; occasionally denotes the 3.sg. animate object in *marû* forms which have no pronominal prefix as subject mark; can occur in conjugations in OB texts for reasons that are not evident - ThSLa §37, §292 (cf., -ni-).

na
n., human being; advice; incense [NA archaic frequency: 105; concatenates 3 sign variants].

adj., no.

na-
modal prefix, affirmative or emphatic in *ḫamṭu* past tense - possibly expressing an inner urge or decision, 'saw fit to'; usually prohibitive in *marû* present/ future tense, 'do not', although in some OB literary texts, that usually involve the verb e, 'to say', na- has the *marû* stem with affirmative meaning - ThSLa §371-§383.

na-
modal prefix always used in the introductory formula of Sumerian letters, /na-/ with conjugation prefix /ĩ-/ - ThSLa §378, §304.

-na-
3.sg. animate dative verbal prefix - to him/her; for him/her - denotes the being towards whom or in favor of whom an action is done - ThSLa §431, §434.

-na
combination of possessive -a.ni, "his, hers", and locative case postposition -a.

^{gi}na
(cf., ^{gi}na$_2$(-a)).

na-ab-be$_2$-a
thus does he/she speak - introductory passage of letters - ThSLa §378, §486 (affirmative + ĩ, conjugation prefix + b, inanimate pronominal prefix + e, 'to speak' in *marû* singular + e, 3rd person *marû* singular subject marker + subordinate suffix).

na-ab-da-num$_2$
meal offering (from Akk., *naptanu(m)*, 'meal').

$^{g̃iš}$na-ab-ḫa-tum
a wooden box (a variant of $^{(kuš)}$na-aḫ-ba-tum).

na-ag̃$_2$, na-am$_2$
Emesal dialect for nam.

na-ag̃$_2$-gi$_4$-in
slavery, Emesal dialect form (abstract prefix + 'slave-girl').

$^{(kuš)}$na-aḫ-ba-tum
a leather or reed carrying case or cover (e.g., for a musical instrument) (Akkadian loanword from *naḫbātu(m)*).

na-am$_2$-di-bi-dib
Emesal dialect for nig̃$_2$-dib-dib, 'adversity'.

na-am$_3$-mu-
writing of modal and conjugation prefixes /na-mu-/ in OB period - ThSLa §304.

na-an-ga-
writing for /na-ĩ-ga/, 'indeed also' - ThSLa §323, §325, §373.

-na-an-na
a postposition indicating 'without'; indicates 'except' when followed by a negative (cf., nu-me-a) ('not' + 'yes' ?).

na-aš-
Emesal dialect for nu-uš-.

na-be$_2$-a
(cf., na-ab-be2-a).

na-bi$_2$[NE]-ḫu-um
a thin gold bead, for a necklace, turban, or offering (Akk., *nabiḫum*; cf., *šurḫullu*).

na-de$_3$[IZI]
incense ('incense' + 'ashes').

na...de_5[RI](-g)
to give advice, instructions; to clarify; to cleanse, purify, consecrate; to separate; to clear away or out; to cut up trees for firewood, lumber, or simple tools; to perish (cf., na...ri(-g) and Emesal variant $ša_3$...di for $ša_3$...de_5[RI]) ('incense' + 'to purify by burning').

na-de_5(-g)(-am_3)
n., advice, instructions; clarification; ritual purification.

adj., pure, consecrated.

$^{(ĝiš)}$na$_{(4)}$-dim_2
a stonecutting tool ('stone' + 'to fashion'; Akk., *nadimmu*).

na-DU
read na...de_6 or na...ri_6, 'advice, instructions'.

na-du_3-a
(cf., na$_{(4)}$-ru_2-a).

na-ga-
OS writing for /na-ĩ-ga/, 'indeed also' - ThSLa §323, §325, §373.

na-gada
herdsman, shepherd - the lowest level in the herding hierarchy (from Akkadian *nāqidum*, 'shepherd').

na-$ĝa_2$-aḫ
fool ('human; advice' + 'to deliver' + 'spittle').

na-IZI
(cf., na-de_3).

na-kab-tum
cattle breeding house (Akk. loanword, indicating a place for cattle to be inseminated; cf., *naqābu(m)*, 'to penetrate sexually').

na-kam-tum
storehouse (Akkadian loanword, from *nakkamtu(m)*, 'treasure, treasury, storehouse'; cf., *nakāmu(m)*, 'to heap, pile up').

$^{(na4)}$na-lu-a
gravel (?) (only in Gudea inscriptions).

na-lu-ga-l(a)
(cf., nam-lugal).

na-ma
Emesal dialect for naĝa, 'alkali, soap'.

na-ma-
writing of negative modal prefix /nu-/ or affirmative modal prefix /na-/ + conjugation prefix /mu-/ + 1.sg. dative case element -a-, 'not...for me', 'indeed...to me' - ThSLa §336.

na-ma-ru-um$^{(zabar)}$
mirror (Akk. *nāmaru(m)*).

$^{(tug2)}$na-ma-ru-um
a brilliant (?) garment (Akk. *nāmaru(m)*).

na-maḫ; na-ru_2-a-maḫ
a large stele.

na-me
the indefinite pronoun: anyone; anything; somebody; whoever; with negative, "nobody; nothing" (cf., a-na me-a).

na-nam
indeed; an emphatic affirmative assertion.

-na-ne-ne
pl. possessive suffix, e.g., mìn-na-ne-ne, 'the two of them', or imin-na-ne-ne, 'the seven of them' - ThSLa §142.

na(-$še_3$)...RI(-g)
to inspect; to muster, review; to check, take stock of; to advise; to counsel in a friendly way; to gather up (cf., na...de_5) ('stone' + 'to pick; to plan').

na-RI(-ga)(-am_3)
inspector, organizer, adviser; advice, instructions (cf., na-de_5(-g) and na-DU).

na$_{(4)}$-ru_2-a
stele, dedicatory stone ('stone' + 'to erect, plant' + nominative; Akk., *narû(m)*).

na_2, nu_2
(cf., $^{ĝiš}nad_3$; nud).

$^{gi}na_2$(-a); ^{gi}na
a reed mat; resting place.

$^{\tilde{g}i\check{s}}na_2-gi_4$-rin-na
divine bed ('bed' + 'fruit, flowers' + genitive).

na_4; na
pebble, rock, ordinary stone; stone weight; token; hailstone.

na_4-ara_3/ur_5-gul-gul
manufacturer of millstones ('stone' + 'grinding' + 'to destroy utterly').

$na_4-ara_3/ur_5-\check{s}u-se_3$-ga
a millstone with handles - the upper stone of a handmill ('stone' + 'grinding' + 'hands' + 'to serve, provide').

na_4-ara_3/ur_5-šu-nu-tuku
a millstone without handles - the lower stone of a handmill ('stone' + 'grinding' + 'hands' + 'to not have').

na_4(-ki)-la_2-a
stone weight ('stone, weight' + 'area' + 'to weigh, lift' + nominative).

na_4-nunuz
egg-shaped bead.

$na_4-\check{s}ag_4-tug_2$
stone weight for cloak ('pebble, weight' + 'inside' + 'cloth garment').

$^{(\tilde{g}i\check{s})}na_5$[ŠA]
chest, box; a musical instrument.

na_8
(cf., nağ).

nab
ocean; musician; Elamite word for 'god' (ni_2, 'fear, respect', + aba, ab, 'lake, sea') [NAB archaic frequency: 10].

$^{\tilde{g}i\check{s}}nad_3$, na_2
bed, couch (na_2 = nu_2-a, 'to lie down' + nominative [from R. Englund]) [NA_2 archaic frequency: 72; concatenates 4 sign variants].

nagar
carpenter's chisel (cf., UET 3, 0752, Obv. 2, 10, nagar mu-sar zabar, 'stylus for inscribing, in bronze'); carpenter; craftsman who built furniture, doors, boats (cf., Akk. *naqāru(m)*, 'to demolish, scratch, hew out, carve, engrave', *maqqārum*, 'chisel', cf., Orel & Stolbova #1556 ***qara'-** 'cut') [NAGAR archaic frequency: 168; concatenation of 2 sign variants].

NAGAR.ZA-*tenû*
(cf., tugul).

nagga, niggi [AN.NA]
tin, pewter (Akk. *annaku(m)*).

nağ, na_8
n., drink.

v., to drink; to water, irrigate; to drink out of (with -ta-) (na_8-na_8 in *marû*) (ni_2, 'body, self', + a, 'water', + $a\tilde{g}_2$, 'to mete out to').

nağ-du_{11}-ga
flooded, leached (field) (cf., $kab_2...dug_4$) ('drink' + 'to effect' + nominative).

nağ-$ensi_2$-ka
city ruler beverage ('drink' + 'city ruler' + genitive + genitive).

nağ-$\tilde{g}a_2$
watering place ('to drink' + nominative).

NAĞ-$ku_{(5)}$
(cf., kab_2-$ku_{(5)}$).

nağ-kud[TAR], nağ-ku_5
canal regulator; settling-reservoir created by erecting embankments between the field and the side of a canal to which to divert some of the flood water within the canal - structures varied in length from 12 to 72 meters, with volumes ranging from 0.33 to 240 sar; provided irrigation water during the dry season and clean, silt-free water for drinking; device operators maintained water level and equitable distribution along length of canal ('drink' + 'to cut, divide').

nağa
soda, alkali, potash (used as soap, bleaching agent); an alkaline plant; saltwort; a food seasoning used by the poor (cf., teme; niğin$_{5,7,8,9}$/ nağa) (nağ, 'to drink', + a, 'water') [NAGA archaic frequency: 125; concatenation of 2 sign variants].

nağa...dub$_2$
to wash with soap ('soap' + 'to flop about, strike').

nağa-gaz
crushed soda (plant ?) ('soda, alkali' + 'to crush, powder').

nağa-kum
crushed soda (plant ?) ('soda, alkali' + 'to crush, bruise').

nağa-si-e$_3$
sprouted alkaline plant ('soapwort' + 'antennae' + 'to go forth').

nağa...su-ub
to rub with soap ('soap' + 'to wipe off, clean').

nağa-sub$_6$[TAG]
soap ('soap' + 'to spread on, wipe').

$^{[ğiš]}$nağa$_{3,4}$[GAZ; KUM]
n., mortar and pestle (Akk., *esittu(m) I*).

v., to crush, grind.

nam
n., (area of) responsibility; destiny, fate, lot, sign; status; function; office; governor; province; manner, way; used mainly as a prefix to form abstract or collective nouns, such as nam-lugal, 'kingship' or nam-maḫ, 'greatness' - ThSLa §56-§58 (n, 'precise essence', + am$_3$, enclitic copula, 'to be'; cf., na-me, 'indefinite pronoun: anyone, anything') [NAM archaic frequency: 30; concatenation of 4 sign variants].

prep., because of, for the sake of (with ...-ak-še$_3$); from, out of (with ...-da) ThSLa §159.

nam-
the modal prefix /na-/ is written nam- if it precedes /ĩ-m-/, /ĩ-ba-/, or /ĩ-bi-/ - ThSLa §372-§374.

NAM^{mušen}
(cf., sim^{mušen}; bir$_5$^{mušen}).

nam-10
a group of ten persons - tenship (collective prefix + number).

nam-a-a
fatherhood, parenting (abstract prefix + 'father').

nam-a-zu
medical arts (abstract prefix + 'physician').

nam-a$_2$-e$_3$
upbringing, of adopted child (abstract prefix + 'to rear, care for; foster, adopted child').

nam-a$_2$-ğal$_2$
strength, power (abstract prefix + 'arm, strength' + 'available').

nam-ab-ba
the older generation, elders; old age, seniority (abstract prefix + 'father, elder').

nam-X...aka
(cf., nam-sipa...aka).

nam-ama
motherhood (abstract prefix + 'mother').

nam-arad; nam-arad$_2$-da
slavery (Akk., *(w)ardūtu(m)*) (abstract prefix + 'slave').

nam-arad...aka
to enslave ('slavery' + 'to do').

nam-arad-še$_3$ PN-ra... gi-in/ gin[DU]
to legally award as a slave to PN ('slavery' + terminative postposition + dative postposition + 'to transfer, award').

nam-arad-še$_3$...la$_2$
to pay off a slave's status ('slavery' + terminative postposition + 'to weigh out').

nam-ba-
writing of modal and conjugation prefixes /na-ba-/ or /na-ĩ-ba-/ in NS and OB texts - ThSLa §304, n. 49.

nam-BAD
(cf., nam-uš$_2$[UŠ$_2$]; nam-suğin[TIL]).

nam-bara$_2$
monarchy; rulership (abstract prefix + 'throne dais; ruler').

nam-bi-še$_3$
therefore; for that reason - ThSLa §201 ('destiny' + 'its' + 'towards').

nam-bi$_2$-
writing of modal and conjugation prefixes /na-bi-/ or /na-ĩ-bi-/ in NS and OB texts - ThSLa §304, n. 49.

nam-buluğ$_3$-ğa$_2$
rearing of an adopted child (abstract prefix + 'to rear, make grow' + nominative).

nam-bur-šu-ma
position of elder (abstract prefix + 'elder').

nam-dam
marital status; marriage, matrimony (abstract prefix + 'spouse').

nam-dam-gar$_3$
trade (abstract prefix + 'merchant').

nam-dam-še$_3$...tuku/du$_{12}$-du$_{12}$
to get married ('marital status' + terminative + 'to get, have').

nam-diğir
divinity; divinities (abstract prefix + 'deity').

nam-DU
(cf., nam-ra$_2$).

nam-dub-sar
scribal skills (abstract prefix + 'scribe').

nam-dug$_3$/du$_{10}$
something favorable (abstract prefix + 'favorable').

nam du$_{10}$...tar
to determine an auspicious fate ('favorable' + 'to decree the fate').

nam-dugud
heaviness; importance (abstract prefix + 'heavy').

nam-dumu
childhood, youth; status of son; status of adopted son (or daughter) (cf., nam-ibila) (abstract prefix + 'child').

nam-dumu-a-ni-še$_3$...ri
to adopt (as one's heir); accept into sonship ('status of son' + 'his; her' + terminative + 'to put into').

nam-dumu-gir$_{15}$
nobles; citizenry (abstract prefix + 'citizen').

nam-egir$_{2/3}$
rulership (abstract prefix + 'princess').

nam-en(-na)
lordship; kingship; office of lord, high priest (abstract prefix + 'lord').

nam-^{d}En-lil$_2$-la$_2$
power of Enlil; divine supremacy ('function' + 'name of the most powerful god' + genitive).

nam-en-na(-k)
adj., prime quality; the best; belonging to the office of the high priest or king; describes a herd for which the shepherd is contractually bound to care.

nam-en-nu(-un/uğa$_3$)
watchfulness, guard (abstract prefix + 'to watch, safeguard'; Akk., *maṣṣartu(m)*, 'observation, guard').

nam-en-zi-da
true 'en'-ship ('lordship' + 'legitimate; true' + nominative).

nam-ensi$_2$
rulership ('office', + 'city ruler, governor').

nam-erim$_2$[NE.RU]
solemn oath invoking divine sanction, such as to decide between conflicting

court testimonies, that took place in the temple, not the court, more frequently involving witnesses than parties to the litigation, and which marked the termination of court proceedings; curse (abstract prefix + 'destruction, oath').

nam-erim$_2$(-bi-ta)...gur
to refuse to confirm by oath (takes ablative prefix, either -ra- or -ta-) ('solemn oath' (+ adverbial force and ablative suffixes) + 'to turn away from, refuse').

nam-erim$_2$(-bi)...kud/ku$_5$
to swear, confirm by oath; to perform an oath ('solemn oath' (+ adverbial force suffix) + 'to cut'; cf., nam...kud/ku$_5$).

nam-erim$_2$-e...sum/si$_3$
to turn (the decision) over to the oath process ('solemn oath' + dative case postposition for inanimate + 'to turn over to').

nam-erin$_2$
troop conscript status; field-working (abstract prefix + 'work gang').

nam-ga
perhaps.

nam-ga-
writing for /na-ĩ-ga/, 'indeed also' - ThSLa §323, §325, §373.

nam-ga-eš$_8$
trade (abstract prefix + 'traveling merchant').

nam(-ga)-me-a/am$_3$
should there not be (na, prohibitive + { ĩ, conjugation prefix + ga, conjugation prefix 'and then' + me, 'to be' } + (-a)-m, 3rd. sing. enclitic copula).

nam-gal
greatness (abstract prefix + 'great').

nam gal...tar
to decree a great fate ('great' + 'to decree the fate').

nam-gala
lamentation priesthood; post of singer (abstract prefix + 'lamentation priest; ritual singer').

nam-galam(-ma)
skilled craftsmanship; majesty, perfection (abstract prefix + 'artistic, complicated' + nominative).

nam-geme$_2$
female slavery, slave (abstract prefix + 'workwoman/slave').

nam-geme$_2$-še$_3$ PN-ra... gi-in/gin[DU]
to legally award as a slave to PN ('slavery' + terminative postposition + dative postposition + 'to transfer, award').

nam-geme$_2$-še$_3$...sum/si$_3$
to give as a female slave ('slavery' + terminative postposition + 'to give').

nam-gi$_4$-me-a-aš; nam-gi$_4$-me-eš$_3$
collegiality, fellowship (abstract prefix + 'to return, come back' + 'office, function' + locative + plural suffix) (cf., gi$_4$-me-a-aš).

nam-gilim(-ma)
destruction; epidemic, plague (abstract prefix + 'to be corrupted, destroyed' + nominative).

nam-gu-la
greatness (abstract prefix + 'great').

nam-gu$_2$
oppression (abstract prefix + 'burden').

nam-gu$_2$-ka$_{(3)}$
oppressive ('oppression' + genitive).

nam-gu$_2$-še$_3$...aka
to oppress or wrong (the weak and poor); to withdraw (in a court case) ('oppression' + terminative + 'to do').

nam-gu$_3$-ra
shouting (abstract prefix + 'to shout, roar').

nam-gudu$_4$
position/office of anointed priest (abstract prefix + 'anointed priest').

nam-gur$_4$(-ra)
greatness; great deeds; pride; feeling of importance; thickness; magnitude (abstract prefix + 'to feel big').

nam-g̃iš-šub galam
cunning spell (abstract prefix + 'spell' + 'ingenious').

nam-g̃u$_{10}$, nam-mu
why does it concern me? (a-na-am$_3$, 'why' + 'my, mine').

nam-g̃uruš
youthful vigor; manliness (abstract prefix + 'young man, worker').

^{dug}nam-ḫa-ru-um
a vessel.

nam-ḫe$_2$; nam-ḫe$_2$-g̃al$_2$
abundance (abstract prefix + 'abundant').

nam-ḫi-li
charm (abstract prefix + 'beauty/charm').

nam-ḫul
pain, discomfort; evil (abstract prefix + 'to harm').

nam-i$_3$-du$_8$
function or position of doorkeeper, gatekeeper; the doorkeeper's duty, craft, or prebend/stipend (abstract prefix + 'doorkeeper').

nam-ibila
status of heir; inheritance, estate (cf., nam-dumu) (abstract prefix + 'son; heir; inheritance').

nam-ibila-ni-ta...e$_3$
to be excluded from heir status (with ablative -ta- prefix) ('status as heir' + -a-ni, 3rd sing. animate possessive suffix, + ablative postposition + 'to go out').

nam-ibila-ni-še$_3$...g̃ar
to establish as heir ('status as heir' + -a-ni, 3rd sing. animate possessive suffix, + terminative postposition + 'to set').

nam-išib
purification; craft of the purification priest (abstract prefix + 'purification priest').

nam-kalag(-ga)
strength (abstract prefix + 'strong').

nam...kar
to take away one's destiny ('destiny' + 'to take away').

nam-kar-kid
(temple) prostitution; office or status of a temple prostitute (abstract prefix + 'prostitute'; Akk., *ḫarim(t)ūtu(m)*).

nam-ki-ag̃a$_2$
love (abstract prefix + 'to love').

nam-kiri$_4$-šu-du$_3$-a
supplication(s) (abstract prefix + 'supplication(s)').

nam-ku-li
friendship (abstract prefix + 'friend').

nam-ku$_3$-zu
wisdom, expertise, cleverness (abstract prefix + 'expert').

nam...kud/ku$_5$
to curse, insult (often with -ta-); to swear; to decide ('destiny' + 'to cut').

nam-ku$_5$-ku$_5$-ra$_2$
lameness (abstract prefix + 'lame/cripple').

^{lu2}nam-ku$_5$-ra$_2$
a man given to swearing oaths and cursing ('to swear, curse' + nominative).

nam-kur$_2$
hostility (abstract prefix + 'hostile').

PN nam-kur$_2$-re
'may PN not change it' (na, prohibitive prefix + nasal ĩ, 'impersonal conjugation prefix', + -ib-, 'it', + 'to change' in *marû* form).

nam-lilib
theft (abstract prefix + 'to steal').

nam-lu$_2$-inim-ma
the act or office of witnessing; the way that a witness testifies (abstract prefix + 'witness').

nam-lu$_2$-u$_{18}$/lu$_7$, nam-lu$_2$-ulu$_3$
people, populace, mankind, humanity; civil position, status, or origin (abstract prefix + 'human being' + 'huge').

nam-lu$_2$-ulu$_3$...aka
to treat with respect ('civil status' + 'to do').

nam-lugal
kingship (abstract prefix + 'king').

nam-luḫ
purification (abstract prefix + 'to clean').

nam-lul
treachery (cf., nam-nar[LUL]) (abstract prefix + 'to lie, deceive').

nam-ma-
writing of modal and conjugation prefixes /na-ĩ-ba-/ in OS and OB texts and /na-mu-/ + 1.sg. dative case element -a- in OB texts - ThSLa §336, §304.

nam-maḫ
greatness, majesty (abstract prefix + 'high, exalted, great').

nam-maḫ...dug$_4$/du$_{11}$/e
to exalt ('greatness' + 'to effect').

nam-me
may/shall he/she/it not be - ThSLa §379 (na, prohibitive + ĩ, conjugation prefix + 'to be').

nam(-ga)-me-a/am$_3$
should there not be (na, prohibitive + { ĩ, conjugation prefix + ga, conjugation prefix 'and then' + me, 'to be' } + (-a)-m, 3rd. sing. enclitic copula).

nam-men
authority (abstract prefix + 'crown').

nam-mi-
writing of modal and conjugation prefixes /na-ĩ-bi-/ in OS, Gudea, and OB texts - ThSLa §338, §304.

nam-mu, nam-g̃u$_{10}$
why does it concern me? (a-na-am$_3$, 'why' + 'my, mine').

nam-mu-
writing of modal and conjugation prefixes /na-mu-/ in Isin-Larsa and OB texts - ThSLa §304.

nam-mul
sparkling (abstract prefix + 'stars').

nam-munus
femininity; belonging to the world of women (abstract prefix + 'woman').

nam-nagar
carpentry (abstract prefix + 'carpenter').

nam-nar[LUL]
concert, harmony; music; musicianship; position of musician (abstract prefix + 'musician').

nam-NE.RU...kud/ku$_5$
(cf., nam-erim$_2$...kud/ku$_5$).

nam-ni$_2$
edge (abstract prefix + 'self/body').

nam-nin
rulership; position of supreme power (abstract prefix + 'queen').

nam-nir
confidence; pre-eminence; nobility (abstract prefix + 'trust').

nam-nir-g̃al$_2$
distinction, reputation; superiority (abstract prefix + 'authority; reliance').

nam-nitaḫ
(cf., ki-nam-nitaḫ).

nam-nu-tar
ill-fated ('destiny' + 'not' + 'cut').

nam-nun
nobility; dominion (abstract prefix + 'great, fine, deep').

adj., deep, profound.

nam-ra
booty; prisoner of war, used for work; captivity (abstract prefix + 'to impress with a mark').

nam-ra...aka
to take as booty, prisoner ('booty' + 'to do').

nam-ra$_2$
behavior (abstract prefix + 'to go, carry [plural]').

nam-RI-ḪU
the work of controlling birds in the fields (read dal-mušen ?; abstract prefix + 'to expel' + 'birds').

nam-sa$_6$-ga
pleasure (abstract prefix + 'to please, satisfy').

nam-sağ-ğa$_2$...aka
to treat with respect (abstract prefix + 'primary' + adjectival -a + 'to do').

nam-ses(-a)
bitterness (abstract prefix + 'to taste bitter').

nam-sikil(-la)
purity; non-slave free status (abstract prefix + 'clean, pure').

nam-silig
violence (abstract prefix + 'powerful; ax').

nam-silig...aka
to use violence ('violence' + 'to do').

nam-silig...gum/gu$_2$-ğa$_2$-am$_3$
it is disastrous (?) ('violence' + 'mortar/back of neck' + 'to place' + 'it is').

nam-sipa(-d)
shepherdship (abstract prefix + 'shepherd').

nam-sipa...aka
to practice shepherdship; to follow the trade or profession of a shepherd (abstract prefix + 'shepherd' + 'to do').

nam-suğin[TIL]
old age (abstract prefix + 'to decay').

nam-sun$_5$
humility (abstract prefix + 'modesty').

nam-sun$_7$
quarreling, bickering; arrogance (abstract prefix + 'quarrel/arrogant').

nam-ša$_3$-tam
treasurer (office of), treasurership ('function' + 'trustworthy').

nam-šeš
brotherhood (cf., nam-ses) (abstract prefix + 'brother').

nam-šilig
(cf., nam-silig).

nam-šita
prayer, supplication (abstract prefix + 'clean, bathed').

nam-šita$_4$
a type of weapon (cf., en-nam-šita$_4$) (abstract prefix + 'bound together').

nam-šu-gi$_4$
old age (abstract prefix + 'to become old').

nam-šub
incantation, spell; lot (abstract prefix + 'to cast'; cf., nam-ğiš-šub galam).

nam-šul
youth, vigor, valor (abstract prefix + 'young man, hero').

nam-tab(-ba)
companionship, partnership, assistance (abstract prefix + 'companion'; Akk., *tappûtu(m)*).

nam-tag
responsibility; guilt; sin; crime; penalty; punishment; a cry (of warning or lamentation) ('consequence' + 'to strike, afflict').

nam-tar
fate, destiny (abstract prefix + 'to determine, decide').

nam...tar
to decree the fate (most often with -ni-, or -ri-, 2. sg.; with -da- indicates that several parties are deciding the fate); to make a firm promise ('destiny' + 'to determine').

nam-še$_3$...tar
to be destined for ('destiny' + terminative postposition + 'to determine').

nam-tar-eĝir-ra(-/ak/)
the future order ('fate' + 'future' + genitive).

nam-tar-ra
decreed fate ('to decree fate' + nominalizer).

nam-tar-tar-ra
all the decreed fates; fate-deciding (reduplicated 'decreed fate').

nam-te
fear (abstract prefix + 'to be frightened').

nam-tila$_3$; nam-til-la
life (abstract prefix + 'to live').

nam-u$_{18}$-ru
large size; power (abstract prefix + 'exalted/ high').

nam-ugula[PA]
foremanship; overseer position (abstract prefix + 'foreman').

nam-ukur$_3$/uku$_2$(-r)
poverty (abstract prefix + 'to be poor').

nam-umun-na
sovereignty (abstract prefix + 'title of respect' + nominative).

nam-ur-saĝ
heroism, valor, warriorhood (abstract prefix + 'hero, warrior').

nam-ur$_5$-ra
after that, as a result ('destiny' + 'it' + genitive).

nam-uš$_2$
death; epidemic, plague (abstract prefix + 'to die'; Akk., *mūtānu(m)*).

nam-zu
wisdom (abstract prefix + 'to know').

nam$_2$[slender TUG$_2$]
planning ability; destiny; prince, noble (time; high + to be) [NAM$_2$ archaic frequency: 375].

NAM$_2$-di
swindle (?) ('planning ability' + 'doing').

namešda[ŠITA.ĜIŠ.NAM$_2$]
top warrior; king; kingship (lit., 'the lord of the mace', an early term for the ruler).

nanam
n., true measure (na$_4$, 'token, counter', + nam, 'destiny' or just reduplicated nam).

adj., reliable, true; honest, decent.

nanga$_{(2,3,4)}$
(cf., niĝin$_{5,7,8,9}$).

^{d}nanna
the moon as a god (en, 'lord', or en$_{2,3}$, 'time', + an, 'heaven', + genitive) [NANNA archaic frequency: 49; concatenation of 2 sign variants].

nar
singer; bard; musician (loan from Akkadian *nāru* II, "musician", which derives from Akk. *nāru* I, "river" in the same way that Sumerian nab means both "ocean" and "musician") [NAR archaic frequency: 69].

NAR.BALAĜ
(cf., tigi$_2$).

nar-gal
chief musician ('musician' + 'older').

NE
(cf., du$_{14}$[LU$_2$×NE or LU$_2$.NE]; du$_{17}$[NE]).

ne
this (one); that (one) (abbrev., ne-e; ne.en) [NE archaic frequency: 303; concatenation of 4 sign variants].

-ne-
3.pl. dative verbal prefix - for them - denotes the animate beings towards whom or in favor of whom an action is done - ThSLa §290, §431, §437; can also be vowel harmony writing of 3.sg. dative prefix -na- in OB and later texts - ThSLa §434.

-ne
as the final suffix after the 1. and 2. person possessive suffixes (cf., -de$_3$).

-ne
(cf., (-e)-ne).

ne-e; ne-en(-nam)
this (one); that (one); these, those; refers to objects 'here', near the speaker - ThSLa §134 (ni_3, 'thing' + e, demonstrative pronoun, this one).

ne-eš-
Emesal dialect for nu-uš-.

ne-eš$_2$
(cf., i_3-ne-eš$_2$).

NE.GI
(cf., ^{d}gira$_3$, ^{d}gir$_{18}$; ^{d}gibil$_6$).

ne-gi-bu-um
perhaps a lamp, made of bronze or silver, with gold sometimes encrusted at the base and summit (Akkadian *nēkepum*, 'a tool or container').

ne...gub
to position oneself ('precise' + 'to stand'; cf., ni_2...gub).

ne-ḫa
n., rest, repose (from Akkadian *nēḫtum*, 'peace, security').

v., to rest.

adj., safe.

^{iti}NE-izi-g̃ar
calendar month 5 at Nippur during Ur III.

NE-la$_2$-a
(cf., bil-la$_2$-a).

ne-mur
glowing coals, embers; fire; ashes.

NE-NE
(cf., bar$_7$-bar$_7$-ra, bir$_9$-bir$_9$-ra and zu$_2$...bir$_9$-bir$_9$; ^{iti}NE-izi-g̃ar).

NE-ra
(cf., bi$_2$-ra and gir$_{10}$).

NE-RU
(cf., erim$_2$, erin$_7$, rim$_3$).

ne-sag̃
(cf., nisag̃).

ne...su-ub
to kiss ('an instance' + sub, 'to suck').

ne-še$_3$
on whose behalf ?; concerning someone ('this one' + terminative postposition).

ne$_3$; ni$_2$
strength, vigor, violence; forces, host.

ne$_3$-g̃al$_2$; ne-g̃al$_2$
mighty ('strength' + 'having').

ne$_4$
(cf., ni$_2$; ne$_4$).

-neda-
(cf., -PI-).

nemur$_x$[PIRIG̃.TUR]
leopard, panther (from Akk. *nimru(m) I*).

nesag̃$_{(2)}$
(cf., nisag̃$_{(2)}$).

NI
(cf., i$_3$; zal; li$_2$; dig) [NI archaic frequency: 263; concatenation of 2 sign variants].

NI-
(cf., i$_3$-).

-ni-
locative prefix case element in the verbal chain - specifies a determinate location, but more general in meaning than the noun postpositions that it resumes, which can be locative (-a), locative-terminative (-e) and terminative (-še$_3$); the -ni- prefix, when used to denote the second object with a compound verb, can indicate a place, person or animal with either the locative, locative-terminative, or dative post-position; the -ni- prefix can indicate the 3.sg. subject Y in a three participant construction with a causative verb such as X caused Y to do Z - ThSLa §470-§482, §284, §286.

NI-du$_8$
(cf., $^{(lu2)}$i$_3$-du$_8$).

NI-dub
(cf., i_3-dub).

NI-ga
a dry measure of capacity in the Old Sumerian period (= 4 PI; cf., bariga).

ni-gi-da
unit of sixty, thing of sixty = ba-ri_2-ga (from nig̃$_2$-g̃ešta).

(šim)ni-gi_4-tum; ni-ig-tum
a resin from a plant (Akk., *nigītum*).

ni-is-ku
choice; a class of persons or animals; fine steed; thoroughbred; during the Sargonic period, appears to describe a class of people resettled by the royal Akkadian administration in southern Babylonia to be overseers and lieutenants (from Akkadian *nisqum*).

ni-iš-; ni-$iš_3$-
writing of hypothetical wish modal prefix /nu-uš-/ with conjugation prefix /ĩ-/ - ThSLa §304; Emesal dialect for nu-uš-.

ni-$iš_3$-mi-ni-
writing of modal and conjugation prefixes /nu-uš-bi-/ or /nu-uš-ĩ-bi-/ - ThSLa §304, n. 51.

NI-KUŠ-NIG̃IN_2
a vessel.

ni-me-en
Emesal dialect for nig̃in$_{(2)}$.

ni_2
self; body [NI_2 archaic frequency: 34].

ni_2; ne_4[LIL_5]
fear; respect; fearsomeness; awe.

ni_2-
reflexive pronoun; one's own (accord) - ThSLa §129-§131.

ni_2-a
by itself ('self' + locative).

ni_2-am_3
self; agitation ('self, fear' + 'to be').

ni_2-ba
by itself; by their collective self, themselves; on their own accord; spontaneously ('self' + bi, 'its' + a, locative).

ni_2-bi(-a)
(by) itself; by their collective self, themselves; on their own accord; spontaneously (cf., $teš_2$-bi) ('self' + 'its' + locative).

ni_2...bulug̃$_5$[DUB_2/BALAG̃]
to boast; to extoll ('self' + 'to elevate, extoll').

ni_2-bulug̃$_5$[DUB_2/BALAG̃]
pompous ('self' + 'to elevate, extoll').

ni_2...dar
to be fearful ('self; fear' + 'to slice, shatter').

ni_2-dig̃ir(-/ak/)
the fear of god ('fear' + 'god' + genitive).

ni_2[IM]...dirig
to sail ('self' + 'to float over'; ni_2 reading from Alster, *Sumerian Proverbs*).

ni_2...dub_2
to relax, calm, pacify ('fear' + 'to knock down').

ni_2-gal
great fear, awe, awesomeness ('fear, awe' + 'great').

ni_2...gid_2
to stretch out, to stretch oneself ('self' + 'to reach out, lengthen').

ni_2...gub
to position oneself ('self' + 'to stand'; cf., ne...gub).

ni_2-gur_3-(r); ni_2-$guru_6$
imposing, awesome ('fear, awe' + 'bearing').

ni_2...gur_4
to feel proud ('self' + 'to feel big').

ni_2-g̃a_2 [ni_2-g̃u_{10}-a]
by myself; by my own accord ('myself' + locative).

ni_2-g̃a_2 [ni_2-g̃u_{10}-ak]
my own ('myself' + genitive).

ni_2-g̃al_2
terrifying; awe-inspiring ('fear' + 'being').

ni_2-g̃u_{10}, ni_2-mu
myself ('self' + 'my').

ni_2-ḫuš
terrifying; powerful ('fear, awe' + 'furious, terrible, awesome').

ni_2...ila_2
to inspire awe; to raise oneself ('fear, awe; self' + 'to raise').

ni_2-ir_9
might, power, awesomeness ('awe' + 'strong').

ni_2...kar_2-kar_2
to circle around ('self' + 'to encircle').

ni_2(-zu)...la_2
to diminish or humiliate (your)self ('self' + 'your' + 'to diminish').

ni_2...ri
to be afraid of something; to scare; to terrify; to inspire awe or fear; to be impressive; to overwhelm (with -da-) ('fear, awe' + 'to strike').

ni_2-se_3-se_3-g/k
desire; purpose ('self' + redupl. 'to chop').

(lu2)ni_2-su-ub
coward; ecstatic, prophet ('fear' + 'to suck; to pray, prostrate oneself').

ni_2-sun_5(-na)
submissive, humble, obedient ('fear, awe' + 'humble; modesty').

ni_2 šu-a...gi_4
to submit oneself to someone's protection ('self' + 'hand, strength' + locative + 'to return to').

ni_2-te
alone; personally; (one)self; one's own ('self' + 'symbol'; cf., me-te).

ni_2-te(-a)-ne-ne
themselves ('(one)self' + 'their').

ni_2-te(-a)-ni
himself; herself ('(one)self' + 'his; her').

ni_2...te(-en)
to rest; to calm down; to relax; to cool off; to refresh oneself ('fear; body' + ten, 'to extinguish, allay, cool down').

ni_2...te/ti(-g̃e_{26})
to be scared; to panic or spread panic; to fear, to respect (with -da-) ('fear' + 'to attack').

ni_2-te-g̃a_2
filled with fear ('fear' + te-g̃e_{26}, 'to assault' + nominative).

ni_2-te-na [ni_2-te-a-ni-a]
by himself; by herself; on his own accord; on her own accord ('himself; herself' + locative).

ni_2-te-na [ni_2-te-a-ni-ak]
his own; her own ('himself; herself' + genitive).

ni_2...tuku
to experience awe or fear; to revere, have reverence for ('fear' + 'to get, have').

ni_2-tuku
careful; vigilant; zealous; fearful; reverent; awesome ('fear' + 'having').

ni_2...tur-tur
to pray; to be pious ('fear, awe' + redup. 'small').

ni_2-tur-tur(-ra)
supplication, prayer.

ni_2-ul_4
terror ('fear' + 'to hasten').

ni_2...ur_4
to fear, be scared ('fear' + 'to agitate').

ni_2-za [ni_2-zu-a]
by yourself; by your own accord ('yourself' + locative).

ni$_2$...zu
to experience fear ('fear' + 'to know').

ni$_2$-zu
yourself ('self' + 'your').

ni$_2$-zu/zuḫ
(cf., lu$_2$-ni$_2$-zu, lu$_2$-ni$_2$-zuḫ).

ni$_3$
(cf., niĝ$_2$).

ni$_5$
(cf., ne).

ni$_9$
(cf., niĝin$_3$).

ni$_9$-ĝar
storehouse (Akkadian *niggaru*) (cf., e$_2$-niĝ$_2$(-gur$_{11}$[GA]-ra)).

ni$_{10}$
(cf., niĝin$_2$).

nib
cheetah; leopard (ni$_2$, 'fear, respect' + ib$_2$, 'to be angry').

nibru^{ki}
the city of Nippur (Akkadian *nēberu*, 'crossing, ford; ferry(boat)').

nidba$_{(2)}$
(cf., nindaba).

nig[MUNUS.UR]
bitch; lioness (ni$_2$, 'strength, respect, fear' + ig, 'door, entrance'; cf., nib, 'cheetah; leopard'; mug$_{(2)}$, 'vulva').

nig$_2$
(cf., niĝ$_2$).

niga[ŠE], nigu
fattened (e.g., oxen or sheep); barley-fed (ni$_2$, 'body' or niĝ$_2$, 'thing', + gu$_7$, 'to feed, eat' + nominative a).

niga 3-kam-us$_2$
barley-fed, third grade ('fattened with barley' + 'third' + 'to follow'; cf., šeš-3-kam).

niga 4-kam-us$_2$
barley-fed, fourth grade, superior to the standard niga category ('fattened with barley' + 'fourth' + 'to follow').

niga gud-e-us$_2$-sa
the sixth and least valued category of barley-fed sheep and goats, inferior to the standard niga category, fed with barley left over from cattle feeding (?) (cf., gud-e-us$_2$-sa).

niga sag$_{10}$
barley-fed, top quality ('fattened with barley' + 'best; fine quality').

niga sag$_{10}$-us$_2$
barley-fed, top quality, next grade ('fattened with barley' + 'best; fine quality' + 'to follow').

nigida[PI]
(cf., ni-gi-da; bariga).

nigru[KA×AD+KUG]
snake charmer, magician (who probably entertained for donations) (cf., šennu).

niĝ$_2$, ni$_3$
property, goods, treasure, valuables, assets, material, stock, equipment, articles; thing; a matter; something; everything; whatever; that which; used as a prefix to form concrete nouns (self + to mete out to) [GAR archaic frequency: 409].

^{tug2}niĝ$_2$-XXX
(cf., tug$_2$-niĝ$_2$-XXX).

niĝ$_2$-a-ru
a consecrated gift ('thing' + 'to give as a votive gift').

niĝ$_2$-a$_2$-ĝar
(an act of) violence ('thing' + 'to defeat, oppress').

niĝ$_2$-a$_2$-si$_3$-ga
well-established (?) ('thing' + 'strength' + 'to set in place' + nominative).

niĝ$_2$-a$_2$-zi(-ga)
(an act of) violence ('thing' + 'violence').

nig̃$_2$-a$_2$-zi...dug$_4$
to speak unjustly ('thing' + 'violence' + 'to speak').

^{lu2}nig̃$_2$-ag̃a$_2$
a temple servant ('things' + 'to measure, check').

nig̃$_2$-ak-ak
deed; activity ('thing' + reduplicated 'to do').

nig̃$_2$-ar$_3$-ra
something that was 'ground'; milled grain; barley groats which were often soaked after grinding ('thing' + 'to grind coarsely' + nominative).

nig̃$_2$-ar$_3$-ra img̃ag̃a$_{(3)}$
emmer groats ('groats' + 'dehusked emmer').

nig̃$_2$-ba
gift, present; ration ('thing' + 'to give').

nig̃$_2$-ba...g̃ar
to make a present; to give as a present; to establish (the amount of) rations ('present' + 'to deliver, deposit').

nig̃$_2$-ba...sum
to give presents ('presents' + 'to give').

nig̃$_2$-bal-bal
trading of merchandise ('things' + 'to revolve, transfer, deliver').

nig̃$_2$-ban$_3$-da
a measuring vessel ('thing' + 'junior').

nig̃$_2$-babbar$_2$-ra
(cf., im-babbar$_2$).

$^{(g̃iš)}$nig̃$_2$-bar(-siki)-šur-ra
cloth or hide wringer ('thing' + 'fleece' (+ 'wool') + 'to expel a liquid'; Akk., *mazūru*).

^{tug2}nig̃$_2$-barag$_2$, ^{tug2}nig̃$_2$-bara$_3$(-g)
bedding ('cloth' + 'thing' + 'nest').

nig̃$_2$-bun$_2$-na$^{(ku6)}$
turtle ('thing' + 'blister; to be swollen').

nig̃$_2$-dab$_5$
something held or for which responsibility is assumed; wages; offering ('thing' + 'to hold, hire, receive').

^{lu2}nig̃$_2$-dab$_5$[-ba]-ke$_4$-ne
warehouse keepers ('thing' + 'to hold, receive').

nig̃$_2$-dag̃al
teeming; wide; vastness (cf., ninda dag̃al) ('things' + 'copious').

nig̃$_2$-dam-tak$_4$-a
divorce settlement, property division (cf., ku$_3$-dam-tak$_4$-a) ('treasure' + 'to divorce' + nominative).

nig̃$_2$-dara$_2$
(cf., arkab^{mušen}; tug$_2$-nig̃$_2$-dara$_2$).

nig̃$_2$-de$_2$-a
n., offering; marriage present; casting (of metal); something brought or poured ('thing' + 'to pour; to increase' + nominative).

adj., poured, cast (said of metal); high (water).

nig̃$_2$-dib-dib
adversity ('things' + reduplicated 'to cross').

nig̃$_2$-dim$_2$-dim$_2$-ma
created creatures ('things' + 'to fashion, create' + nominative).

$^{(g̃iš)}$nig̃$_2$-dim$_2$-ma
a utensil (cf., nig̃$_2$-ḫul-dim$_2$-ma) ('thing' + 'to fashion, create' + nominative).

nig̃$_2$-diri
excess, surplus (beyond what was contracted for; cf., nig̃$_2$-g̃ar, 'estimated yield'); additional payment for extra attributes; supplement; extra; extravagant ('thing' + 'addition').

NIG̃$_2$-DU
(cf., ninda-gin; nindan; nig̃$_2$-tum$_2$).

nig̃$_2$-du$_3$-a
a container; a measure for fruit and cheese ('thing' + 'to erect on the ground' + nominative).

nig̃$_2$-du$_7$[UL]
what is suitable, prescribed, or as it should be; what is fit for the cult (cf., nig̃$_2$-ul) ('thing' + 'suitable').

nig̃$_2$-dug$_3$, nig̃$_2$-du$_{10}$(-ga/e)
something pleasing; good things ('thing' + 'sweet, pleasing').

nig̃$_2$...dug$_4$
to say something ('thing' + 'to speak').

nig̃$_2$-dug$_4$-ga
instructions; utterances; information ('the spoken things').

nig̃$_2$-DUN
submission ('thing' + 'subordinate).

nig̃$_2$-en-na
'lord's possession' - a type of field in preSargonic texts, all of whose output went to the temple ('thing' + 'lord' + genitive).

nig̃$_2$-erim$_2$[NE.RU]
evil; wickedness; dishonesty; fraudulent claim; injustice ('thing' + 'hostile'; >Akk. *nignerûm*, 'false claim'; *raggu(m)*, 'wicked, villainous').

^{gi}nig̃$_2$-esir-ra
washbowl (made of pitch-coated reeds) ('thing' + 'bitumen' + genitive).

nig̃$_2$-ezem-ma(-k)
festival offering ('thing' + 'festival' + genitive).

nig̃$_2$-GA
(cf., nig̃$_2$-gur$_{11}$).

nig̃$_2$ ga-ti
I promise it ('thing' + 1st person cohortative modal prefix + 'to keep alive').

nig̃$_2$-gag-ti
key; lock bolt; doorkeeper ('thing' + 'peg, nail' + 'arrow').

nig̃$_2$ gal-gal
things of all sort ('thing' + reduplicated 'big').

nig̃$_2$-gi-na, nig̃$_2$-gin$_6$-na, nig̃$_2$-gen$_6$-na
justice; stability; trustworthiness; truth ('thing' + 'true, reliable' + nominative).

NIG̃$_2$-gid$_2$(-da)
(cf., ninda gid$_2$(-da); nig̃$_2$-sud-a/nig̃$_2$-su$_{13}$[BU]-a).

nig̃$_2$-gig(-ga)
n., evil; distress; illness, disease; taboo, abomination, disgust, sacrilege (>Akk. *ikkibu(m)*) ('thing' + 'illness').

adj., bitter, painful, disgusting.

nig̃$_2$-gilim-ma
sieve; ruining, spoiling; epidemic; mongoose ('thing' + 'to twist; to be corrupted' + nominative; cf., ^{d}nin-kilim; peš$_2$-nig̃$_2$-gilim-ma).

nig̃$_2$-gu$_2$-na
tools; equipment; household utensils; tax (Akk. *unūtu(m)*; *biltu(m)*; cf., gu$_2$-na).

nig̃$_2$-gu$_3$-de$_2$
commission, assignment ('thing' + 'to say').

nig̃$_2$-gu$_7$
food; glutton ('thing' + 'to eat').

nig̃$_2$-gu$_7$-a
fattened; consumption; food consumed ('thing' + 'to eat' + nominative suffix).

nig̃$_2$-gu$_7$-da
nourishment ('thing' + 'to eat' + contraction of *marû* participial and nominative suffixes).

nig̃$_2$-gu$_7$-de$_3$
something designated for consuming, for eating, such as a sheep ('thing' + 'to eat' + *marû* participial suffix).

niĝ$_2$-gug$_2$
(cf., ^{ninda}gug$_2$).

niĝ$_2$-gul
maul, a hammer-like implement used to break the clods left after harrowing ('thing' + 'to destroy').

niĝ$_2$-gur$_{11}$ [GA]
property; possession(s); goods; assets; treasure(s); property owner ('thing' + 'piled up'; Akk. *makkūru(m)*).

niĝ$_2$-ĝal$_2$ (-la)
goods on hand, stock, supply; property, livestock, riches; what is present, available, to hand; "sickle" of copper, iron, etc. used for payments ('objects' + 'to fill a storage basket' + nominative).

niĝ$_2$-ĝar (-ĝar) (-ra)
layer, such as of dates to ripen; heaped up, stored; estimated yield; cultivation agreement ('objects' + 'to set out' + nominative).

$^{(uruda)}$niĝ$_2$-ĝeštug [PI] $^{(ku3-sig17/ku3-babbar/nagga)}$
metal earrings, of gold, silver, or tin, or of copper with encrusted silver, always mentioned in an even number ('treasure' + 'ears'; cf., a-gar$_5$-ĝeštug).

niĝ$_2$-ĝir$_2$
(consonantal harmony version of nim-ĝir$_2$, lightning flash).

niĝ$_2$-ĝiri$_3$
an OAkk period term for a go-between's fee ('property' + 'intermediary').

niĝ$_2$-ĝiš-tag-ga
offering, to the king or to the gods ('object' + 'to make an offering').

niĝ$_2$-ḫa-lam-ma
destruction, annihilation; disaster ('thing' + 'to ruin, destroy, forsake, forget' + nominative).

niĝ$_2$-ḫu-ḫu-nu
helplessness ('object' + 'helpless').

niĝ$_2$-ḫul
evil ('thing' + 'evil').

niĝ$_2$-ḫul-dim$_2$-ma
(magical) procedure(s); sorceries; malevolent rites; sacrilege ('thing' + 'evil' + 'to create' + nominative).

niĝ$_2$-ḫul-e
adv., badly ('thing' + 'evil' + locative terminative -e).

niĝ$_2$-ḫul$_2$ (-ḫul$_2$) -la
joy, rejoicings ('thing' + 'very happy'; Akk. *ḫidiātum*).

niĝ$_2$-ḫuš-a
(cf., niĝ$_2$-ki-ḫuš-a).

NIĜ$_2$.IB^{mušen}
(cf., arkab^{mušen}; niĝ$_2$-dara$_2$).

niĝ$_2$-igi...nu-du$_8$-a
something never seen (by an eye) ('thing' + 'eye' + 'not' + 'to crack open' + nominative).

niĝ$_2$-il$_2$ (-l)
support ('thing' + 'to raise up').

niĝ$_2$-im-ba
loss ('thing' + 'the paid out').

niĝ$_2$-ka-bi ba-ak
account settled ('account' + 'its' + conjugation prefix + 'to make').

niĝ$_2$-ka$_9$-aka
balanced account ('account; balance' + 'made').

niĝ$_2$-kal-kal (-la)
everything valuable ('things' + reduplicated 'to value, esteem' + nominative).

niĝ$_2$-kal-la
precious ('thing' + 'to value, esteem' + nominative).

niĝ$_2$-kas$_7$/ka$_9$ [ŠID]
account; accounting; result (of a mathematical operation or calculation); balance (from Akk. *nikkassu*, 'deduction', from *nakāsu*, 'to cut off').

niĝ$_2$-kas$_7$-aka
(cf., niĝ$_2$-ka$_9$-aka).

niĝ$_2$-kas$_7$; niĝ$_2$-gaz
half-reed = 3 cubits (Akk. *nikkas*).

niĝ$_2$-keše$_2$(-d)
knot; noose; joint ('thing' + 'place of binding').

niĝ$_2$-ki
vermin; small beasts ('things' + 'ground').

NIĜ$_2$-KI-ĜAR
additional or supplementary payment (cf., iš-gana$_2$).

niĝ$_2$-ki-ḫuš-a
pitfall, trap ('small beasts' + 'to be angry, fierce' + nominative; Akk. *šuttatu(m)*).

niĝ$_2$-ki-la$_2$-bi
loss(es), such as in business, etc. ('things' + 'weight').

niĝ$_2$-ki-luḫ
broom ('thing' + 'ground, place' + 'to clean').

niĝ$_2$-ki-se$_3$
(cf., ninda-ki-si$_3$(-ga)).

niĝ$_2$-ki-za
dues, a previously determined donation ('property' + 'to make homage').

niĝ$_2$-ku$_2$
(cf., niĝ$_2$-gu$_7$).

niĝ$_2$-kud, niĝ$_2$-ku$_5$(-da)
tax, dues, customs duty; revenue, yield ('property' + 'to separate' + nominative).

niĝ$_2$-kud...aka
to tax ('tax' + 'to do').

^{ĝiš}niĝ$_2$-ku$_5$(-da)
wedge to tighten a bound join ? on a plow ('thing' + 'to separate' + nominative).

^{lu2}niĝ$_2$-ku$_5$-da
tax collector ('property' + 'to separate' + nominative).

niĝ$_2$-kur$_2$
belligerence, hostility; breaking an agreement ('thing' + 'hostile'/'to change').

$^{(tug2)}$niĝ$_2$-la$_2$
sword belt; bandage, dressing ('thing' + 'to carry; to bind'; cf., tug$_2$-niĝ$_2$-lal).

$^{(dug/uruda)}$niĝ$_2$-luḫ$^{(zabar/ku3-babbar)}$
washbowl ('thing' + 'to wash'; cf., e$_2$-šu-luḫ-ḫa).

niĝ$_2$-lul(-la)
falsehood; lie(s); dishonesty; treachery ('thing' + 'to lie, deceive' + nominative).

niĝ$_2$-maḫ
a lot; too much ('thing' + 'to be large').

niĝ$_2$-me-ĝar
assembly; silence, stillness; breath; celebration, acclaim; profit(able business) ('thing' + 'to pay attention/make silent'; cf., mud$_5$-me-ĝar).

niĝ$_2$-mi$_2$-us$_2$-sa$_{(2)}$
wedding gift, "bridewealth" brought to the house of the bride's father or guardian by the groom or his family, originally meant for the wedding feast, gradually evolved from food to various goods to money by the OB period ('treasure' + 'woman' + 'to follow' + nominative).

niĝ$_2$-mi$_2$-us$_2$-sa$_{(2)}$...aka
to bring the wedding gifts.

niĝ$_2$-na
censer; incense burner ('thing' + 'incense').

^{dug}niĝ$_2$-naĝ
drinking vessel ('vessel' + 'object' + 'to drink').

niĝ$_2$-nam(-ma); niĝ$_2$-na-me
anything, everything; property; fee ('thing' + indefinite pronoun).

$ni\tilde{g}_2$-nam-ku_3
property made of precious metal ('possessions' + abstract prefix + 'precious metal').

$ni\tilde{g}_2$-nam-nu-kal
nothing is precious ('anything' + 'not' + 'valued').

$ni\tilde{g}_2$-nam-tar-ra
nature ('thing' + 'fate').

$ni\tilde{g}_2$-NE.RU
(cf., $ni\tilde{g}_2$-$erim_2$).

$ni\tilde{g}_2$-nu-dug_3
unpleasant (things) ('things' + not + 'sweet, good').

$ni\tilde{g}_2$-nu-g̃ar-ra
foolishness; slander, lies ('goods' + 'not' + 'to store' + nominative).

$ni\tilde{g}_2$-nu-mu-da-sa_2
nothing is comparable with it ('things' + 'not' + conjugation prefix + 'with' + 'to equal in value').

$ni\tilde{g}_2$-nu-sa_6-ga
unpleasant (things) ('things' + not + 'sweet, good').

$ni\tilde{g}_2$...ra(-ra)
to throw something; to beat (up), smite ('thing' + 'to strike').

$ni\tilde{g}_2$-sa(-sa)-ḫa$_{(2)}$ (sar)
fruit(s); fruit remaining after the harvest; garden fruit; springtime fruit; minor crops ('thing' + Akk. *ṣaḫḫaru*, 'something small'; cf., also Akk. *mutḫummu*).

(uruda)$ni\tilde{g}_2$-sa-sa
roasting oven; a grill, brazier ('thing' + 'roasting').

$ni\tilde{g}_2$-sa_2[DI]
goal ('thing' + 'to compare with; to compete').

$ni\tilde{g}_2$-sa_6-ga, $ni\tilde{g}_2$-sag_9-ga
pleasure, happiness ('thing' + 'sweet, good').

$ni\tilde{g}_2$-sag̃-il_2(-la)
substitute, replacement; unit of exchange ('thing' + 'head/substitute' + 'to deliver' + nominative).

(tug2)$ni\tilde{g}_2$-sag̃-la_2-MI_2; $ni\tilde{g}_2$-sag̃-LA_2×MI_2
veil for women ('thing' + 'head' + 'to hang' + 'female').

$ni\tilde{g}_2$-saḫar-ra
(cf., uruda-$ni\tilde{g}_2$-saḫar-ra).

$ni\tilde{g}_2$-sam_2
price, value; purchase (cf., sam_2 til-la-ni) ('thing' + 'to buy, sell').

$ni\tilde{g}_2$-sam_2/sa_{10}-ma(-$\check{s}e_3$)
(for) purchase ('thing' + 'to buy, sell' + nominative [+ terminative postposition]).

$ni\tilde{g}_2$-sar
red dye for wool, in weight amounts from 1 gin_2 to 20 gin_2 (Akk., *ṣarāpu*, 'to dye (red)').

$ni\tilde{g}_2$-si
nourishment, sustenance ('thing' + 'to fill'; Akk., *ti'ûtu*).

$ni\tilde{g}_2$-si-sa_2
equity, justice, fairness ('thing' + 'straight').

$ni\tilde{g}_2$-sig-ga
weakness ('thing' + 'small, weak').

$ni\tilde{g}_2$-$sila_{11}$[ŠID]-g̃a_2
dough, of emmer ('thing' + 'to knead' + nominative).

$ni\tilde{g}_2$-su-ub
polishing, as of bronze ('treasures' + 'to wipe off, clean').

$ni\tilde{g}_2$-sud-a, $ni\tilde{g}_2$-su_3-a; $ni\tilde{g}_2$-su_{13}[BU]-a
metal plate, filigree, or powder to be added to objects ('treasures' + 'to extend; to sprinkle; to submerse' + nominative).

$ni\tilde{g}_2$-sur
(cf., $ni\tilde{g}_2$-šur).

$\text{nig̃}_2\text{-ša}_3\text{-bi}$
what is in it; contents ('things' + 'heart, interior' + 'its').

$\text{nig̃}_2\text{-ša}_3\text{-g̃ar-ra}$
famine ('thing' + 'hunger' + nominative).

$\text{nig̃}_2\text{-ša}_3\text{-te-na}$
soothing to one's heart or mood ('thing' + 'heart, mood' + 'to soothe' + nominative).

nig̃_2-ŠID
(cf., $\text{nig̃}_2\text{-kas}_7/\text{ka}_9$ and $\text{nig̃}_2\text{-sila}_{11}$[ŠID]-$\text{g̃a}_2$).

nig̃_2-šu
in the care of, the second level in the herding hierarchy ('things' + 'hands').

$^{\text{g̃iš}}\text{nig̃}_2$-šu(-gi)
chariot ('thing' + 'cross-bar').

nig̃_2-šu(-g̃a_2)
(to have) goods ('things' + 'hands' + 'in my').

$\text{nig̃}_2\text{-šu-taka}_4\text{-a}$
objects that will be given away; an official offering, gift, present, especially to another town, country, or people; consignment ('object' + 'to send, abandon' + nominative).

nig̃_2-šu-ti-a
what(ever) one receives ('object' + 'to receive' + nominative).

nig̃_2-šu-zabar
metal mirror ('object' + 'hand' + 'mirror metal').

nig̃_2...šub
to neglect something ('thing' + 'to let drop').

nig̃_2-šum-ma
meat ('thing' + 'butchered').

nig̃_2-šur
liquid (cf., $^{(\text{g̃iš})}$mar-nig̃_2-šur-ra, 'soup spoon', and gi-nig̃_2(-kaš)-šur-ra, 'drinking straw') ('thing' + šur/sur, 'to flow').

$^{\text{dug}}\text{nig̃}_2$-ta-ḫab
a (sealed) container for liquids or wet things ('vessel' + 'thing' + 'soaking').

$^{(\text{dug})}\text{nig̃}_2$-tab
oven air vent, duct; fire-box, crucible ('thing' + 'to join; to burn').

$^{(\text{dug})}\text{nig̃}_2$-tab-tur-ra
a vessel for burning incense ('ventilated fire-box' + 'small').

$\text{nig̃}_2\text{-tug}_2$
blanket (for an animal); pack-saddle; sash ('thing' + 'cloth').

nig̃_2-tuku
n., riches; possessions, property.

adj., rich, wealthy ('things' + 'having').

nig̃_2-tukum-ta(-/ak/)
something coincidental ('thing' + 'if' + 'from' + genitive).

$\text{nig̃}_2\text{-tum}_2$
delivery ('thing' + 'to bring').

nig̃_2-tur
a small amount; small piece ('thing' + 'small').

nig̃_2-U.NU-a
thread, yarn ('thing' + 'to spin' + nominative).

$\text{nig̃}_2\text{-u}_2\text{-gu-de}_2\text{-a}$
missing; damaged ('thing' + 'lost, vanished').

$\text{nig̃}_2\text{-u}_2$-rum
possession; acquisition; (hoarded) property, treasure; favorite sister or brother ('thing' + 'personal, private').

$\text{nig̃}_2\text{-u}_2\text{-zug}_4$[KA×LI]
foul food ('thing' + 'plant, food' + 'to spit out ?').

$\text{nig̃}_2\text{-u}_4\text{-da-ri}_2$(-/ak/)
everlasting, persistent ('thing' + 'days' + 'long lasting' + genitive).

niĝ$_2$-u$_4$(d)-i$_3$[ZAL]-li
something for the future ('thing' + 'tomorrow'; cf., u$_4$-i$_3$-li; u$_4$-ul-la).

niĝ$_2$-ul
distant time in the past or future; an everlasting thing; joy (cf., niĝ$_2$-du$_7$) ('thing' + 'joy; remote').

niĝ$_2$-umun$_2$-a
learned creation; scholarship ('thing' + 'knowledge' + nominative).

niĝ$_2$-ur$_2$-limmu$_{(2)}$
livestock, four-legged creature, quadruped ('thing' + 'legs' + 'four').

niĝ$_2$-ur$_5$-sa$_6$-sa$_6$
sweetness; (sexual) happiness ('thing' + ur$_5$...sa$_6$, 'to feel comfortable').

niĝ$_2$-zi
steadiness; reliability; truth ('thing' + 'faith, confidence, truth').

niĝ$_2$-zi(-ša$_3$)-ĝal$_2$
living creature(s), living thing(s) ('thing' + 'having breath; alive').

niĝ$_2$-zi-pa(-aĝ$_2$/an)
living creatures ('thing' + 'life; to breathe').

niĝ$_2$-zu
learning, education ('thing' + 'knowing').

niĝ$_2$-zu$_2$-gub
food ('thing' + 'teeth' + 'to set').

niĝ$_2$-zuḫ
something stolen ('thing' + 'to steal, rob').

^{lu2}niĝ$_2$-ZUM-DIM$_4$
a temple servant.

niĝar[NI$_9$.ĜAR]
a dark room; premature or monstrous fetus (ni$_9$,'premature birth', + ĝar,'to deliver').

niĝin$_{(2)}$
n., enclosure, circle; capacity; whole (cf., kilib and gur$_4$-gur$_4$) [NIGIN archaic frequency: 11].

v., to halt, turn away; to turn round; to start over; to surround; to enclose; to assemble; to pen up cattle; to dam a canal; to wander about; to circle; to make the rounds; to coil; to compute the square of a number (in OB math. texts) (usually niĝin$_2$[LAGAB] for *ḫamṭu* form and niĝin or ni$_{10}$-ni$_{10}$[LAGAB.LAGAB] for *marû* form) (ni$_2$;ne$_4$, 'fear', + ĝin, 'to go').

niĝin$_{(2,3)}$
vertigo (as a disease); faintness, dizziness; thirst.

NIĜIN$_2$-ba; NIĜIN-ba
(read kilib-ba and kilib$_3$-ba).

niĝin$_3$, ni$_9$[U.UD.KID]
premature or stillborn child; fetus; malformed child; monstrosity.

niĝin$_{5,7,8,9}$, nimen$_{(3,4,5)}$, nanga$_{(2,3,4)}$; naĝa
district, province (Akkadian *nagû(m) I*, 'region, district; coastal area').

niĝir$_{(2)}$, miĝir$_{(2)}$
herald, night watchman, town crier; bailiff; a bride's male attendant (conflation of separate words: Akk. *nāgiru(m)*, '(town) crier, herald' and mi$_2$,'woman' + ĝar,'to deliver') [NIMGIR archaic frequency: 62].

niĝir$_{(2)}$-si
paranymph, a man who had to take care of the bride before the young couple was married ('a bride's male attendant' + 'upright, normal').

nim, num
n., prince; flying insect; highland; east; morning; the sign for the country of Elam (high + to be) [NIM archaic frequency: 109; concatenation of 4 sign variants].

v., to be high; to lift; to multiply in arithmetic.

adj., high; early.

adv., above.

Emesal dialect for min, 'two'.

nim...ĝir$_2$
to lighten; to flash ('upper country' + 'lightning flash').

nim-ĝir$_2$
lightning (flash).

nim-mu-uš
Emesal dialect for eš$_6$, 'three'.

nim-saḫar-ra
a large fly; fly-bite ('flying insect' + 'rubbish' + genitive).

nim-še$_3$
up; probably also "to the left"; towards the upper country ('high' + 'towards').

^{ĝiš}nimbar
(cf., ^{ĝiš}ĝišimmar/^{ĝiš}ĝišnimbar).

nimgir$_{(2)}$
(cf., niĝir$_{(2)}$; dul$_4$).

nimin, nin$_5$
forty (niš, 'twenty', + min, 'two').

nimur[KI.NE]
kiln; potash; (glowing) charcoal; ashes; ash heap.

nin[MUNUS.TUG$_2$]
queen, mistress, proprietress, lady; lord (cf., ereš) (reduplicated ni$_2$, 'fear; respect; frightfulness; awe') [NIN archaic frequency: 75].

nin...aka
to exercise queenship ('lady/queen' + 'to do').

nin-diĝir
high priestess (of a particular temple and god) (cf., ereš-diĝir) ('lady' + 'god; divine'; Akk., *entu(m)*; *ugbabtu(m)*).

nin-EN
(cf., nin-uru$_{16}$).

nin-išib
lustration priestess ('lady' + 'to purify').

^{d}nin-kilim
mongoose - the Indian Mongoose lived in the Iraqi marshes, eating small rodents, reptiles, insects, young birds, eggs, and fruit ('master of moving things'; cf., niĝ$_2$-gilim).

^{d}nin-kilim-bar
otter - a sub-species of the Smooth-coated Indian Otter called Maxwell's Otter lived in the Tigris-Euphrates alluvial salt marsh - they also knew the dense reddish fur pelt of the sea otter ('mongoose' + 'fleece'; Akk., *tarpašu*; *emru I*).

^{d}nin-kilim-edin-na
a small mammal, perhaps the least weasel, which feeds on small rodents and is at home in many habitats, including steppe ('mongoose' + 'steppe' + genitive; Akk., *ayyāṣu*).

^{d}nin-kilim-tir-ra
marten, a small carnivorous mammal needing old-growth forest habitat ('mongoose' + 'forest' + genitive; Akk., *šakkadirru I*).

^{d}nin-ninna$_2$[LAGAB×EŠ]^{mušen}(-ta)
owl or hawk (cf., ^{d}nin-šara$_2$^{mušen}) ('divine proprietress' + 'owl').

NIN.PAP.SIG$_7$.NUN.ME.UBARA
(cf., ninkum).

^{mul} ^{d}nin-piriĝ$_{(3)}$(-ĝa$_2$)
a planet, called the vizier of the sun, either Venus or Mercury, see below ('mistress of the lion', cf., piriĝ).

^{d}(nin-)piriĝ-tur/banda$_3$
a planet, the same as above (?) ('mistress, lion cub', cf., piriĝ-tur; Akk., *bibbu(m)*, 'wild sheep; planet; Mercury or Saturn').

^{mul} ^{d}nin-si$_4$-an-na
the planet Venus ('lady of the evening sky'; cf., $^{(d)}$u$_2$-si$_4$-an).

^{d}nin-šara$_2$[LAGAB×SIG$_7$]^{mušen}
a bird of prey [N. Veldhuis reads imma$_x$ for LAGAB×SIG$_7$ where SIG$_7$=imma$_3$ and

considers ^{d}nin-imma$_x^{mušen}$ a variant of ^{d}nin-ninna$_2^{mušen}$, for which he proposes 'hen harrier'; cf., nu-um-ma^{mušen}, 'vulture; owl or hawk', perhaps as totem-bird of the city of Umma; LAGAB×SIG$_7$ is also read as bara$_7$, 'nest'] ('divine proprietress' + 'the patron god of Umma, son of Inanna').

nin ur$_5$ i$_3$-sag$_9$/sa$_6$
lady, sweetheart ('lady' + 'to be/make comfortable, happy').

nin-uru$_{16}$
mighty queen ('lady' + 'mighty').

nin$_5$
(cf., nimin).

nin$_9$ [MUNUS.KU]
sister; female cousin (?) (reduplicated ni$_2$, 'self; body; one's own').

nin$_9$-ab-ba (-na)
paternal aunt ('sister' + 'father' (+ ni-a(k), 'his/her' + genitive).

nin$_9$-ad-da (-na)
paternal aunt ('sister' + 'father' (+ ni-a(k), 'his/her' + genitive).

nin$_9$-ama (-na)
maternal aunt ('sister' + 'mother' (+ ni-a(k), 'his/her' + genitive).

ninda
bread loaf; bakery good; food; one day's cereal ration (cf., nindan) (niĝ$_2$, 'valuables', + dar, 'to slice') [GAR archaic frequency: 409].

ninda-ar$_3$-ra
pulpy dish (prepared) of green-malt ('bread' + 'to chew, grind' + nominative).

ninda-ar$_3$-ra-imĝaĝa [ZIZ$_2$-AN]
ninda-ar$_3$-ra made of spelt.

ninda-ar$_3$-ra-ziz$_2$
ninda-ar$_3$-ra made of emmer.

ninda-ba
bread offering ('bread' + 'to give; to divide, apportion').

ninda-bar-si
a type of bread made with bar-si emmer wheat flour.

ninda-bi
total of their bread ('bread' + 'their').

X ninda daĝal (-bi)
X rods is its width (cf., nindan).

NINDA-DU
(cf., ninda-gin; nindan).

ninda-du$_8$-a
baked bread ('bread' + 'to bake bread/bricks' + nominative).

ninda-durun$_x$ [KU.KU]-na
long-lasting bread (?); bread to eat while sitting (?) ('bread' + 'to sit, dwell; to dry out' + nominative; opposed to ninda-gub-ba, 'snack-bread').

X ninda gid$_2$ (-da)
X rods is the length (cf., nindan).

ninda-gin [DU]
regular bread ('bread' + 'ordinary').

ninda-gu
a type of bread ('bread' + 'net' ?).

ninda...gu$_7$
to eat, feast ('bread; food' + 'to eat').

ninda-gu$_7$
food ('bread; food' + 'to eat').

ninda-gug$_2$
(cf., ^{ninda}gug$_2$).

ninda-ĝiri$_2$
a type of bread ('bread' + 'expedition, trip').

ninda-ḪAR-ra
(cf., ninda-ar$_3$-ra).

ninda-i$_3$-de$_2$-a
bread with oil or fat beaten into the dough, sometimes with added honey; pastry ('bread' + 'oil/fat' + 'to pour' + nominative).

ninda-KA-gu$_7$
a type of bread ('bread' + 'mouth' + 'to eat').

ninda-ki-si$_3$(-ga)
funerary offerings (cf., ki-si$_3$-ga) ('food' + 'funerary offering').

ninda-kum$_4$[UD]-ma
a type of bread ('bread' + 'mortar-ground flour' + nominative).

ninda-pad-ra$_2$
morsels of bread ('bread' + 'bite, morsel').

ninda-sag$_{10}$
fine bread; the best bread ('bread' + 'fine quality').

ninda-sağ-gu$_7$
the best bread for eating ('bread' + 'prime' + 'to eat').

ninda-siki$_2$[UD]
a type of bread.

ninda-SILA$_3$
a type of bread ('bread' + 'liter').

ninda$_2$, inda; inda$_2$
hopper or seeding apparatus of the seeder plow; pure-bred breeding bull; funnel, tube; flower; bushel measuring vessel; fish roe; milt; ancestors (from Akk. *middatu*, *mindatu*, 'to measure') [NINDA$_2$ archaic frequency: 20].

NINDA$_2$×U$_2$+DILI^{ku6}
(cf., ugudili^{ku6}).

nindaba$_{(2)}$, nidba$_{(2)}$
food offering; sacrificial offering (ninda, 'food', + ba, 'to give').

nindan, ninda
a length measure, rod = 12 cubits (kuš$_3$) = 6 meters; one side of a sar/šar, 'garden plot' square measure (cf., ğiš-gaba-tab) (Akk. *nindanu(m)*, 'rod, pole').

^{lu2}ningi$_{(2,3)}$
(cf., $^{(lu2)}$lunga$_{(2,3)}$).

ninim[ŠA$_3$×NE]
envy (?); anger (?).

ninindu, nindu, inda$_4$
oven; stove (cf., immindu).

ninkum[NIN.PAP.SIG$_7$.NUN.ME.U BARA]
temple treasurer; guardian deity of the foundations [NINKUM archaic frequency: 11].

ninna^{mušen}, nenna^{mušen}, nenni^{mušen}; ^{mušen}ninna$_2$
nocturnal bird - owl (nin, 'fearsome lady', + a, nominative suffix or + an, 'heaven' + a(k), genitive suffix; the predatory owl with its human-like face probably gave rise to the demon Lilith myth; cf., ^{d}nin-ninna$_2$^{mušen}).

ninni$_2$
(cf., niğin).

ninni$_5$
a rush used in basketry; bulrush (reduplicated nin or nin$_9$, where reeds and rushes were seen as belonging to a young woman goddess similar to the grain goddess Nisaba).

ninnu, ninu
fifty (nimin/nin$_5$, 'forty', + ḫa$_3$/u, 'ten',).

nir
n., prince, lord; trust, authority (cf., ni$_2$-ir$_9$, 'might') [NIR archaic frequency: 45; concatenates 2 sign variants].

v., to stretch, reach, extend; to raise high; to winnow, clean grain, purify; to do someone a favor; to overcome, vanquish; to pray, beseech, appeal (to be high + to go out + to flow).

adj., victorious.

nir, ner
n., frog; omen; offspring.

adj., proper.

NIR-da
(cf., šer$_7$-da).

nir-gam(-ma)
vault ('raised high' + 'to curve').

nir...g̃al$_2$
to have authority; to be reliable; to rely, trust in (with -da-) ('authority' + 'to have').

nir-g̃al$_2$
n., noble one; authority, expert; authorities; reliance ('raised high' + 'being').

adj., noble; authoritative; tasty (said of food).

nir-g̃al$_2$-bi
confidently ('authority' + adverbial force suffix).

nir-g̃al$_2$-me$_3$-a
respected in battle ('authority' + 'battle' + locative).

nir-mu$_2$(-mu$_2$-ir)
perfumed beard with rolled up curls ('prince, lord' + 'to sprout, grow long' + 'scented').

nir-nu-g̃al$_2$
menial employee(s) ('authority' + 'not having').

nir-pad^{ku6}
a fish ? ('frog' + 'bite, small repast').

^{na4}nir$_2$[ZA.GIN$_2$]
a precious stone with black and white flecks.

^{na4}nir$_3$[ZA.NIM]
a type of stone.

^{na4}nir$_7$[ZA.MIR]
a valuable stone used for vases and ornaments (Akk. *ḫulālu(m)*).

^{na4}nir$_7$-igi
crystal (per H. Limet) ('a valuable stone used for vases' + 'to see').

^{d}niraḫ[MUŠ]
a kind of poisonous snake, such as a viper or adder (nir, 'to stretch, reach, raise high', + aḫ, 'venom').

nisag̃$_{(2)}$, nesag̃$_{(2)}$
first fruits (offering); spring time (month); dough; wine cellar ?; foremost; governor (nig̃$_2$, 'valuables', + sag̃, 'first') [NISAG$_2$ archaic frequency: 94; concatenation of 2 sign variants].

nisi
(cf., nisig).

nisig, nisi, nissa[SAR]
n., greens, vegetables (nig̃$_2$, 'valuables', + sig$_7$, 'green, yellow').

adj., beautiful; blue; green.

niskum
(cf., ni-is-ku).

nissa
(cf., nisig).

niš, neš
twenty (ni$_2$, 'self, body', + aš, 'one [finger, toe]').

nita$_{(2)}$
(cf., nitaḫ$_{(2)}$).

NITA-DUN.GI
a type of jackass ('male' + 'yoke' ?).

nita-kala-ga
strong man; manly ('male' + 'strong').

nita$_3$[MUNUS-UŠ]-dam
spouse; wife; husband (cf., nitalam/ nitadam) ('male' + 'spouse').

nitaḫ$_{(2)}$, nita$_{(2)}$
male; man; manly (ni$_2$,'self', + taḫ,'to multiply') [GIŠ$_3$ archaic frequency: 16; concatenation of 2 sign variants; UŠ archaic frequency: 101; concatenates 2 sign variants].

nitalam, nitadam [MUNUS.UŠ.DAM]
spouse; wife; husband (cf., murub$_5$, nita$_3$-dam, g̃itlam, and Emesal mu-ud(-da)-na) (nitaḫ, 'male', + dam, 'spouse').

-n-ši-
3.sg. animate /-n-/ + terminative prefix - ThSLa §455.

nu
image, likeness, picture, figurine, statue [NU archaic frequency: 101].

NU
to spin or plait (textiles or threads) (cf., sir$_5$).

nu-
no, not; without; negative indicator; modal prefix with the meaning of negation; as a negative enclitic copula, 'it is not'; a designation for non-payment - ThSLa §359-§365.

nu-
writing of negative modal prefix /nu-/ with conjugation prefix /ĩ-/ - ThSLa §304.

nu-
a pronominal prefix in a compound noun describing a person; or an archaic pronunciation of lu$_2$ - ThSLa §50-§55 (cf., u$_3$-).

nu-a
v., to lack, be without - ThSLa §365 ('not' + 'nominative).

adj., applied to domestic animals, uncertain whether to translate 'pregnant' or 'infertile, barren, sterile' ('not' + 'offspring'; cf., du$_3$-a, 'pregnant' and nud-a).

nu-banda$_{3,5}$
superintendent; supervisor of works (under the ugula; placed over the engar); lieutenant, sergeant, an officer in charge of a number of workmen; overseer of animals; high quality level of work (pronominal prefix or 'not' + 'junior; young'; > Akk., *luputtû, laputtû(m)* - cf., la-ba-).

nu-banda$_3$-gu$_4$
supervisor of plow oxen; an official who assigned manpower to cultivate domain land placed under his control for one entire year - his responsibility could range from 1 to 10 a-ša$_3$ ('supervisor' + 'oxen').

nu-bar
a cultic prostitute (pronominal prefix + 'body exterior').

nu-bi$_2$-
the negative modal prefix NU + the conjugation prefix /bi-/ in Gudea texts - ThSLa §360, §304.

nu-dug$_3$(-ga)
unpleasant ('not' + 'sweet, good' + nominative).

nu-dug$_4$-ga
not talking ('not' + 'to speak' + nominative).

nu-erim$_2$
enemy; scoundrel; oddity (pronominal prefix + 'hostile').

nu-eš$_3$(-ak)
a cultic functionary, priest - 'knife bearer' or 'sacrificer' per Kesh hymn 107 (pronominal prefix + 'sanctuary' + genitive; Akk. *nêšakku(m)*).

nu-ga-
writing of negative modal prefix /nu-/ with conjugation prefixes /ĩ-ga-/ in Gudea period - ThSLa §304.

nu-gi-in
it was not proven ('not' + gin$_6$, 'to determine').

nu-gi-na
unjust; unfit ('not' + 'just; firm' + nominative).

nu-gig(-an-na); nu-u$_8$-gig(-an-na)
a priestess devoted to the goddess; hierodule, holy woman; woman giving birth (pronominal prefix + ?; GIG = GIG$_2$.NUNUZ; cf., $\tilde{g}$i$_6$-an-na and nunuz).

nu-$\tilde{g}$ar-ra
thriftless; foolish; unreliable; disorderly ('not' + 'to store' + nominative).

$^{(lu2)}$nu-$\tilde{g}$^{iš}kiri$_6$(-k)
gardener (pronominal prefix or archaic lu$_2$; Akk. *nukaribbu(m)*, 'gardener; date-grower').

nu-ku$_3$
no money, i.e., a worthless penny ('not' + 'silver, precious metal').

nu-kur$_2$-ru-dam
which cannot ever be changed - non-finite prospective *marû* (cf., kur$_2$).

^{giš}nu-kuš$_2$(-u$_3$)
door pivot; upper and lower crosspieces of the door, by which the door was attached to the doorpost ('not' + 'to be tired').

nu-kuš$_2$-u$_3$
restlessness ('not' + 'to be tired').

nu-luḫ-ḫa$^{(sar)}$
unwashed, unrefined; a plant (asa foetida) the fetid gum resin of whose root was used as a medicine ('not' + 'to be clean' + nominative; Akk. *lā mesû(m) I*; *nuḫurtu(m)*).

nu-ma-
two possibilities: negative modal prefix nu- + conjugation prefix /mu-/ + 1.sg. dative case element -a-, 'will not for me' found in NS period; negative modal prefix nu- + conjugation prefixes /ĩ-ba-/ 'he did not' in one-participant constructions in Gudea period - ThSLa §336, §304.

nu-ma-kuš$_2$
widow ('no one cares for me'; occurs after nu-siki, 'orphan', in EDIIIB text, RIME 1.9.9.1 ex. 1 (1); cf., ša$_3$...kuš$_2$, 'to calm the heart, make love to', and kuš$_2$-a, 'hardship').

nu-ma-su
(cf., nu-mu-un-su).

nu-me-a
which is not....; without (with -da) - ThSLa §539 ('not' + 'to be' + nominative).

nu-me-en-na-ta
you don't exist ('not' + me-en, 'to be', 2nd pers. sing. + a-ta, temporal clause suffix).

nu-mi-
writing of negative modal prefix nu- + conjugation prefixes /ĩ-bi-/ in Gudea, NS periods - ThSLa §338, §304.

nu-mu-da-sa$_2$
(cf., nig̃$_2$-nu-mu-da-sa$_2$).

nu-mu(-un)-su; nu-mu-un-zu; nu-ma-su
widow (nu-ma-su is the oldest form, 'no one is replaced for me', 'no one is concerned for me'; cf., nu-ma-kuš$_2$ and kuš reading of SU).

NU.NU
spun, plaited (cf., sir$_5$).

nu-nus$_2$
Emesal dialect for munus.

nu-ra
not stamped with a seal ('not' + 'to stamp').

nu-sag$_9$, nu-sa$_6$
not good ('not' + 'sweet, good').

nu-siki/sig$_2$
orphan; in EDIII texts, can be a female or male worker in a wool workshop or state sheepfold, together with slave women and children (cf., ki-siki) (pronominal prefix + 'wool'; Akk., *ekû(m) I*, 'impoverished, orphaned, bereaved').

nu-še-ga
disobedient ('not' + 'to be obedient').

nu-tuku
to not have, to have no (cf., še-nu-tuku) ('not' + 'having').

nu-u$_8$-gig(-an-na)
(cf., nu-gig(-an-na)).

nu(-un/ub)-zu
to not know; to not recognize; to not notice ('not' (+ 'him, her'/'it') + 'to know').

nu-um-
writing of negative modal prefix /nu-/ with conjugation prefix /ĩ-/ and ventive element /-m-/ in Gudea, NS, and OB period texts - ThSLa §304.

nu-um-ma^{mušen}
vulture; owl or hawk (Akk. *zību II*; *eššebu(m)*; cf., ^{d}nin-šara$_2$^{mušen}).

nu-um-ma-
negative modal prefix nu- + conjugation prefixes /ĩ-ba-/ 'he did not' in one-participant constructions in OB period - ThSLa §336, §304.

nu-um-mi-
writing of negative modal prefix nu- + conjugation prefixes /ĩ-bi-/ in OB period - ThSLa §338, §304.

$^{(ğiš)}$nu-ur$_2$-ma
pomegranate (tree), its fruit used in leather tanning (Akk. *nurmû, lurmûm, lurīnu*; Orel & Stolbova #2122 ***riman-** 'fruit').

nu-uš-
if only; were it not for; were it but that - hypothetical wish or frustrative modal prefix - ThSLa §418-§422.

nu-uš-
writing of hypothetical wish modal prefix /nu-uš-/ with conjugation prefix /ĩ-/ - ThSLa §304.

nu-uš-in-ga-
writing for /nu-uš-ĩ-ga/, 'if only, moreover' - ThSLa §323, §304.

nu-uš-ma-
writing of hypothetical wish modal prefix /nu-uš-/ with conjugation prefix /mu-/ + 1.sg. dative - ThSLa §304.

nu-uš-mu-e-a
writing of hypothetical wish modal prefix /nu-uš-/ with conjugation prefix /mu-/ + 1.sg. dative - ThSLa §304.

nu(-un/ub)-zu
to not know; to not recognize; to not notice ('not' (+ 'him, her'/'it') + 'to know').

nu-zu
ignorant ('not' + 'knowing').

nu-zu-a
unknown ('not' + 'to know' + nominative).

nu$_2$
(cf., nud, nu$_2$).

nu$_2$-nu$_2$
to be lying down (redup. 'to lie down').

nu$_{10}$
(cf., KU).

nu$_{11}$ [ŠIR]
light; fire, lamp (cf., ğiš-nu$_{11}$ and ^{na4}ğiš-nu$_{11}$-gal) [NU$_{11}$ archaic frequency: 32].

^{na4}nu$_{11}$-gal
(cf., ^{na4}ğiš-nu$_{11}$-gal).

nud, nu$_2$
to lie down; to lie together with (with -da-); to lay down (with -ni-); to sleep; to lie in wait, to catch with a trap; to kill (cf., nu$_2$-nu$_2$; ^{ğiš}nad$_3$) (nu, 'not', + ed$_2$, 'to go out').

nud-a, nu$_2$-a
adj., applied to domestic animals, uncertain whether to translate 'pregnant' or 'infertile, barren, sterile' ('bed; to lie down; to kill' + 'offspring'/nominative; cf., du$_3$-a, 'pregnant' and nu-a).

nug
a perfume plant (Akk. *nukkatu*).

numun, nuğun$_x$, niğun$_x$
n., seed; sowing; cornfield; offspring, progeny; hereditary line (niğ$_2$, 'thing', + gun$_3$, 'dots, speckles') [NUMUN archaic frequency: 22].

v., to produce.

numun...e$_3$/i-i
to issue seed, bring forth offspring ('seed' + 'to send forth').

numun...ğar
to sow ('seed' + 'to place, deposit').

^{ğiš}numun-ğar
seeding plow ('seed' + 'to place').

^{ĝiš}numun-ĝar-GUL
a part of the seeder plow ('seed' + 'to place' + 'to break, destroy').

NUMUN-ĝisal
a tool ('seed' + 'rudder').

numun-na si_3-ga
test planting of a field after a fallow period ('seeds' + 'to demarcate a field' + nominative).

numun-sum-gaz
crushed onion seed ('seed' + 'onion' + 'crushed').

numun...til
to run out of seeds ('seeds' + 'to finish, put an end to').

numun zi...e_3/i-i
to multiply vigorously ('seed' + 'to grow tall; high' + 'to send forth').

$^{(u2)}$numun$_2$ [ZI&ZI.LAGAB]
alfalfa grass (*halfâ'*), rushes (cf., ^{u2}aški) [$NUMUN_2$ archaic frequency: 2].

$^{(u2)}$numun$_2$-bur$_{(2)}$
marsh rushes ('alfalfa grass' + 'meal/to tear out').

nun
n., prince, noble, master (ni_2, 'fear; respect', + un, 'people' ?) [NUN archaic frequency: 652; concatenation of 4 sign variants].

v., to rise up (n, 'to be high',+ u_5, 'to mount; be on top of; raised high').

adj., great, noble, fine, deep.

nun-e
adv., princely ('prince' + locative terminative -e).

$^{(d)}$nun-gal(-e-ne)
the great gods; the gods of heaven (Akkadian *Igigi*, perhaps i_2, 'five' + gi_3[DIŠ] + gi_3[DIŠ] = 'the seven, the innumerable') ('prince' + 'great' + plural).

NUN.LAGAR
(cf., tur_3).

NUN.LAGAR×BAR
(cf., immal).

NUN.LAGAR×MUNUS
(cf., šilam; $immal_2$).

NUN.ME(.PU_3)
(cf., $abgal_{(2)}$).

NUN.NUN
(cf., nir).

nundum, nundun
lip (reduplicated tun_3, 'lip').

nunuz, nunus
egg(s); offspring; female; woman (cf., na_4-nunuz) (reduplicated nuz, 'egg') [NUNUZ archaic frequency: 134; concatenation of 5 sign variants].

NUNUZ.AB_2×AŠGAB; NUNUZ.$KISIM_5$×AŠGAB
(cf., $usan_3$).

NUNUZ.AB_2×BI; NUNUZ.$KISIM_5$×BI
(cf., mud_3).

NUNUZ.AB_2×LA; NUNUZ.$KISIM_5$×LA
(cf., laḫtan).

NUNUZ.AB_2×$SILA_3$; NUNUZ.$KISIM_5$×$SILA_3$
(cf., $la\text{ḫ}tan_2$).

NUNUZ-TE
(cf., ga-nunuz-TE).

^{MUNUS}NUNUZ.ZI-^{d}.NANNA
(cf., zirru).

nuz, nus
egg (na_4,'pebble', + uz/us,'goose', cf. also, nunuz).

P

$^{(ĝiš)}$pa
leaf, bud, sprout; branch; wing; feather [PA archaic frequency: 378; concatenation of 2 sign variants].

PA-a
a graphic simplification of u_2-a.

pa-a-šu
axe, adze (loan from Akk. *pāšu(m)*).

pa-ağ₂
nostrils ('puff' + 'to mete out'; cf., za-pa-$ağ_2$; zi-pa-$ağ_2$; zi...pa-$ağ_2$).

$pa-ağ_2...ze_2$
to cut or pierce the nostrils (of a fugitive as punishment) ('nostrils' + 'to cut').

PA.AL
(cf., šabra).

PA.AMAŠ
(cf., $udul_4$).

PA.AN
(cf., billuda).

$pa_{(4)}-bil_{2/3}$-ga/gi
paternal uncle; paternal grandfather ('elder' + 'ancestor').

PA.DIĞIR
(cf., ğarza).

PA+DUG-um
an allowance, payment.

$pa...e_3$; $pa-e_3$...aka
to show; to make appear; to manifest; to let shine; to make resplendent (often with -ni- or bi_2-) ('bud, sprout' + 'to send forth' + 'to make').

PA.É
(cf., $šabra_x$).

PA.GAN
(cf., sig_{11}).

$pa_{(4)}$-ḫar
accumulation (of goods, silver) (loan from Akk. *paḫāru(m) II*).

pa-ḫal
(cf., pap-ḫal(-la)).

PA.IB
(cf., šab).

(ğiš)pa-kud
broom; trimmed branches; palm frond ('branches' + 'to cut off').

PA.LU
(cf., sipad, sibad, sipa).

PA.LUGAL
(cf., $ğarza_2$).

pa-mul(-mul)
spreading branches, foliage ('branch' + 'to spread').

pa-pa-al
bud, shoot, sprout, branch, vine stock (reduplicated 'bud, branch' + ul, 'bud, blossom').

PA.PA
(cf., kum_x-kum_x).

pa-paḫ
cella, inner sanctum of a temple (loanword from Akk. *papāḫu(m)*; cf., Orel & Stolbova #1926, ***pah-** "close, lock").

pa-ra-ga
(cf., barag, $bara_2$).

$pa-rim_4$
(cf., parim).

PA.ŠE
(cf., išin).

pa-TAR
(cf., pa-kud).

PA.TE.SI
(cf., $ensi_2$).

PA-uru
(cf., ugula-uru(-na-/ak/)).

PA+USAN
(cf., mu_6[PA]-sub_3).

pa_3
(cf., pad_3).

pa_3-da
an occupation ('to find; to declare' + nominative).

pa_3-pa_3
to intone, said of voice and strings (redup. 'to declare').

pa_4
(cf., pap).

$pa_{4,5,6}$(-r)
irrigation ditch (pa_4), small canal (pa_5), including those on top of an eg_2.

pa_4[PAP]-a-da-ga
flowing irrigation ditch ('irrigation ditch' + 'flowing with water').

pa_4...ba-al
to dig ditches ('irrigation ditch' + 'to dig').

$pa_{(4)}$-$bil_{2/3}$-ga/gi
paternal uncle; paternal grandfather ('elder' + 'ancestor').

pa_4-eg_2
(cf., eg_2-pa_5(-r)).

pa_4-šeš
(cf., pap-šeš).

itipa$_{4/5}$-u_2-e
calendar month 11 at Umma during Ur III.

$pa_{4/5}$-$ugur_2$[SIG_7]
ditch delimiting the communally controlled meadow ('irrigation ditch' + 'meadow boundary').

pa_5-sig
small branch canal ('irrigation ditch, canal' + 'small').

pab
(cf., pap, pa_4).

pad, $pa\check{r}_x$
n., bite, small repast (regularly followed by ra_2 and da; cf., bur and $buru_2$) (sprout + repetitive processing) [? PAD archaic frequency: 38; concatenation of 2 sign variants].

v., to break off or into pieces.

PAD.BI.SI+ĜIŠ[RÉC 78]
(cf., $addir_2$).

pad_3, pa_3[IGI.RU]
to show, reveal; to choose, call, appoint; to seek; to find; to remember; to declare; to swear, take an oath; to choose out of (with ablative prefix) (pa_3-de_3 in sing. *marû*; pa_3-pa_3-de_3 in plural *marû*) (sprout, branch + to go out; cp., pa...ed_2, 'to show; to make appear'; cf., er_2...pad_3) [PA_3 archaic frequency: 30].

pag, bag[ḪU]
to cage, shelter (birds); to save, spare, let go (branches + round chamber).

paḫ[LUL]
leg; a skin disease (cf., ḫal).

paḫ-zil
a disease; leprosy (?) ('legs; skin disease' + 'to divide; to peel').

$pala_{(2,3)}$
vestments, clothing (of gods and rulers); robe (cf., pa-paḫ, 'inner sanctum', and lal/la_2, 'to drape' as in tug_2-$ni\tilde{g}_2$-lal).

$palil_{(2)}$
n., advance troops, shock troops, leader (bala, 'to cross over', + lu_2, 'men').

adj., foremost.

pana, pan, ban
bow (pa, 'branch', + na_4, 'pebble, stone') [BAN archaic frequency: 27; concatenates 2 ? sign variants].

pap-
(cf., pa_4-).

pap, pab, pa_4
elder/eldest; father; brother; man; leader [PAP archaic frequency: 501; concatenation of 2 sign variants].

pap-ḫal(-la), pa_4-ḫal(-la); pa-ḫal
n., leg, thigh; confinement; poverty; share (cf., lu_2-ulu_3 pap-ḫal-la) (Akk. loan, cf., ḫal, ḫa-la).

v., to walk.

adj., walking about, movable; distraught.

PAP.NA_2
(cf., gam_3; zubu).

PAP.PAP
(cf., $munu_4$; $bulu\tilde{g}_3$).

PAP.SIG_7
(cf., pa_4-$ugur_2$).

pap-še-er
Emesal dialect for 'rope; string (of dried fruit)'.

pap-šeš, pa$_4$-šeš
older brother; leader; anointed priest ('eldest' + 'brother'; also loan from Akk. *pašīšu(m)*, 'anointed').

para$_3$, par$_3$[DAG]; para$_4$, par$_4$[KISAL]
(cf., barag$_2$).

para$_{10}$
(cf., barag).

parim
arid land; dry land (as opposed to marsh land or water) (cf., bar-rim$_4$).

pe-e
(cf., pa-e$_3$).

pe-el(-la$_2$)
to defile (cf., pel$_{(2)}$).

$^{(u2)}$pe-en-ze$_2$-er
a functionary; female genitals, pubic hair; spider web; fowler's hiding place; reed fence; a plant; a cocoon-spinning caterpillar (cf., Akk., *biṣṣūru(m)*, 'female genitals'; *būnzerru*, 'fowler's hide'; *pizzir*, 'cobweb'; cf., pi-zi-ri$_2$-um).

pel$_{(2)}$, pil$_{(2)}$
to be/make obscure; to be/make dirty, defiled, disgraced; to insult; to be weak (cf., šu pe-el-la$_2$...dug$_4$/du$_{11}$/e; pi-li-pi-li).

peš[GIR]
n., womb; soft heart/kernel; palm frond; three (cf., biš) [GIR archaic frequency: 28; concatenation of 4 sign variants] (moist container + uš$_3$, 'placental membrane'; pa, 'leaf, branch', + eš, 'many, much'; eš$_{5,6,16,21}$, 'three').

v., to expand; to be thick, wide; to fill.

adj., precious, valuable.

peš$_{(7)}$
child; son; young (1-3 years old) calf.

peš-ab-ba
(cf., gir-ab-ba).

peš-ĝal$_2$
impetuous ('young' + 'being').

peš-murgu; peš-mur$_7$[SIG$_4$]
a palm tree product - palm leaf ('palm frond' + 'ridge, spine').

peš-peš
very wide, spacious; physically handicapped (reduplicated 'womb; to expand; to be wide').

$^{(ĝiš)}$peš-tur-zi
palm tree sprout, sapling; descendant ('womb; palm frond' + 'small' + 'to rise up').

peš$_2$, piš$_2$
a type of edible mouse or rat (cf., kilim; kišib$_2$) (probably derives from peš$_3$, 'fig').

peš$_2$-$^{(ĝiš)}$gi
canebrake mouse, mole rat, bandicoot rat - an edible delicacy ('mouse' + 'reeds').

peš$_2$-ki-bal
a digging mouse, such as the desert jerboa ('mouse' + 'earth' + 'to dig').

peš$_2$-niĝ$_2$-gilim-ma
a rodent; rat (?) ('rodent' + 'spoiling, epidemic/mongoose').

peš$_2$-$^{(ĝiš)}$ur$_{(3)}$-ra
dormouse, a woodland habitat mouse with a thick, bushy tail (Akkadian *arrabu(m)*).

^{ĝiš}peš$_3$[MA], pešše
fig; fig tree or wood (moist container + še$_3$, 'portion').

^{ĝiš}peš$_3$-duru$_5$
fresh figs ('figs' + 'fresh').

^{ĝiš}peš$_3$-ḫad$_2$
dried figs ('figs' + 'dried').

$^{(na4)}$peš$_{4,11,13}$
n., sea or river shell (that resembles a vulva?); pregnancy (Akk. *išqillatu(m)*, 'a type of shell'; *arû(m) IV*, 'to be(come) pregnant, conceive'; *mērû*, 'pregnancy').

v., to be pregnant; to conceive; to swell.

peš$_{5,6}$
n., deep breathing; scent; spider; combed wool, fluff (cf., aš$_{(5)}$, 'spider').

v., to breathe deeply; to make an incision; to pluck apart; to comb and clean wool; (redup.) to anoint.

peš$_{(7)}$
child; son; young (1-3 years old) calf.

peš$_{10}$
(cf., piš$_{10}$).

pešše
(cf., ^{ğiš}peš$_{3}$).

PI
(cf., bariga).

-PI-
an OS form of the 3.pl. comitative case prefix, possibly read -neda- (for singular animate is -n.da-) ThSLa §446.

^{ğiš}PI-apin
a part of the seeder plow (barig, '36 liters in Old Sumerian period', + 'plow').

pi-il
(cf., pil$_{(2)}$).

pi-la$_{2}$
(cf., pil$_{(2)}$).

pi-li-pi-li
n., a transvestite performer in Inanna's cult (cf., pil$_{(2)}$).

v., to speak insultingly to.

pi-lu$_{5}$-da
(cf., billuda).

pi-zi-ri$_{2}$-um
gold filigree ornaments for a wreath, 9 of which weighed 1 gin$_{2}$ (cf., ki-li$_{2}$-lum) (Akk. loanword, *pizzerium* from *pazāru(m)*, 'to hide, conceal' ?, cf., pe-en-ze$_{2}$-er, 'spider web').

pil$_{(2)}$
(cf., pel$_{(2)}$).

piriğ[ĞIR$_{3}$]; piriğ$_{3}$[UG]
lion (poetic); light (bar$_{6/7}$, 'to shine', + niğ$_{2}$, 'thing'; combination of light and lion may relate to a myth in which when the horned bull of the moon gets close to the sun, the bright planet Venus, seen as a guardian lion, kills the horned moon bull - this word for lion is echoed in the name of a Hurrian planet Venus goddess Piringar) [PIRIG archaic frequency: 103; concatenation of 5 sign variants].

PIRIĞ.TUR
(cf., nemur$_{x}$).

piriğ-tur
young lion, cub.

piriğ-ugu-dili
n., rogue beast ('lion' + 'skull' + 'single'; cf., sağ-dili, 'batchelor; alone').

adj., wild, aggressive.

piriğ$_{2}$
bright.

$^{(gi)}$pisağ$_{(2/3)}$, $^{(gi)}$pisan$_{(2/3)}$, $^{(gi)}$bisağ$_{(2/3)}$
(open) basket; box, chest; container; frame - a copper pisağ weighed over 2 ma-na (bad/be, 'to open', + sağ, 'head').

pisağ[ĞA$_{2}$]-dub
container for clay tablets (cf., ğadub; ^{lu2}ša$_{14}$-dub-ba) ('vessel' + 'clay tablet').

pisağ-dub-ba, pisan-dub-ba
label, docket, etiquette, basket tag - the small and often perforated tablet describing the contents of a library archive basket begins with this term.

piš$_{10}$, peš$_{10}$[KI.A]
shore, river bank; athletic ability to jump across a stream.

$piš_{10}$...tag
to go aground (said of a boat) ('shore, river bank' + 'to touch, strike').

pu-$uḫ_2$-ru-um
assembly (Akk. *puḫru* 'assembly', cf., unkin and ub-šu-ukkin-na).

pu_2
n., well; pool; fountain; cistern, reservoir; depth; pit; breach [PU_2 archaic frequency: 37].

adj., deep.

pu_2 (-$^{ĝiš}kiri_6$)
irrigated fruit orchard ('well, cistern' + 'orchard').

pu_2-la_2
(cf., tul_2).

pu_2-$niĝ_2$-$ĝir_3$ (-/ak/)
pitfall ('well, cistern' + 'thing' + 'path' + genitive).

pu_2-$niĝ_2$-ḫuš
pitfall ('well, cistern' + 'thing' + 'terrible').

pu_2-saĝ
excavation; pit; hollow; water hole ('pit' + 'prime').

pu_2-ta (-pa_3-da)
foundling; handicapped person (can also be read tul_2-ta(-pa_3-da)) ('from a well' = 'found abandoned in a well').

pu_3
(cf., bur_{12}; bu_3).

$puniĝ_x$
(cf., $buniĝ_x$).

$puš_2$
pain; tightness; difficult circumstances (derives from $peš_4$, 'to be pregnant').

$puzur_{(2,4,5)}$, $buzur_{(2,4,5)}$
safety, security; secret, mystery; a merchandise tax (loan from Akk. *puzru(m)*, 'concealment').

$puzur_3$
hand, palm; hole, cave.

R

ra (-g/ḫ)
n., inundation [RA archaic frequency: 25].

v., to strike, stab, slay; to stir; to impress, stamp, or roll (a seal into clay); to branch out (from the side of a canal); to flood, overflow; to measure; to pack, haul, or throw away (with -ta-).

-ra-
dative verbal prefix, 2nd person singular - for you, to you - ThSLa §433.

-ra-
ablative case prefix, 'from', similar to -ta-, but without instrumental meaning - ThSLa §465-§466.

-ra
dative case postposition, for; denotes the animate being towards whom or in favor of whom an action is done; often marks the animate object of a sentence - ThSLa §175-§179.

ra-aḫ
to strike repetitively [with a hoe]; to shake; to gnash ('to strike' + ḫ, 'many, numerous').

$ra_{(2)}$-gaba
rider; courier, messenger (Akkadian *rākibu(m)*).

ra...gi_4
to thunder (like a storm) (cf., $šeg_{11}$...gi_4) ('inundation' + 'to echo').

ra-ra
to flatten; to smash; to make wide (reduplicated 'to stamp').

ra_2
(cf., re_7; a-ra_2; $šud_3$...ra_2).

ra_2-zu
(cf., a-ra-zu; a-ra_2-zu).

ra_3
(cf., ara_4).

$^{(\check{g}i\check{s})}rab_{(3)}$, rap
ring; clamp; fetter, shackle; stock; pillory; snare (to slide + open container).

$^{\check{g}i\check{s}}rad[\check{S}ITA_3]$
a tree, possibly a citrus tree [$\check{S}ITA_3$ archaic frequency: 139; concatenation of 2 sign variants].

$rag\text{-}rag^{mu\check{s}en}$, $rak\text{-}rak^{mu\check{s}en}$ [SAL-SAL]
blue heron or stork (Akkadian *laqlaqqu, raqraqqu*).

rap
(cf., $^{(\check{g}i\check{s})}rab$).

re_7; re_6, ri_6, ra_2, ir_{10}; $e\text{-}re_7$; er, ir
to accompany, lead; to bear; to go; to drive along or away; to take possession; to stir, mix (suppletion class verb: plural *ḫamṭu* $e.re_7.er$; cf., du, ğen, sub_2).

ri
v., to direct; to throw, cast; to place, pour, put into; to place upon or against (with -ši-); to be located; to touch; to moor a boat; to break open; to expel, remove, throw away, sweep away (with -ta-); to emit; to ejaculate; to inseminate, impregnate; to beget; to blow (said of a storm); to inundate; to exchange; to take; to gather up, glean, pick up (including carcasses); to plan something (ri is *ḫamṭu* form, ri-g is *marû* form, ri-ri-g is plural; cf., rig and de_5(-g)[RI]) [RI archaic frequency: 1].

adj., far, distant.

ri, re
demonstrative affix, that, those; regarding that (where the reference is to something outside the view of the speaker - over yonder, elsewhere - sometimes in the form ri-a or ri-ta) - ThSLa §135.

-ri-
In the OB period, 2.sg. locative prefix denoting the second object of a compound verb; in at least one case, 2.pl. locative prefix; the -ri- prefix can indicate the 2.sg. subject Y in a three participant construction with a causative verb such as X caused Y to do Z - ThSLa §427, §478, §481, §284.

-ri-
ablative prefix 'from' in a few cases instead of -ra- in OB literary texts - ThSLa §468.

^{iti}RI
calendar month 5 at Umma during Ur III.

ri-a
engendered ('to beget' + nominative).

ri-ba
enormous, supreme (Akkadian *rabbu*).

$^{\check{g}i\check{s}}ri\text{-}gi_4\text{-}bil\text{-}lu_2$
a tool.

ri-ḫa-mun
(cf., im-ri-ḫa-mun).

RI-ḪU
an agricultural worker in charge of controlling birds in the fields (read dal-mušen ?; 'to expel' + 'birds').

RI-RI-ga
dead, deceased (referring to deaths of two or more from natural causes, such as felled by an epidemic - not slain) (cf., $ba\text{-}u\check{s}_2$); collected; describes a tool for collecting (reduplicated de_5(-g), 'to collect from the ground').

ri_2
(cf., uru).

ri_6
(cf., re_7).

rib
to be higher in rank; surpassing; to go away (Akk. *rabbu*).

rib-ba
enormous, supreme (Akkadian *rabbu*).

rig; ri
to bring; to tend; to pull; to glean, pick, collect (reduplication class) (flowing motion such as re_7, 'to accompany, lead, drive along' + ig, 'door, entrance').

rig_3
mace, weapon (ri, 'to throw' + $ug_{5,7,8}$, 'to kill').

$rig_{5,7}$
n., list; temple ward, slave.

v., to deed, grant, bestow, present, assign (see etymology of sa_{12}...rig_7).

rig_{11} [ŠID.RU]
(cf., im-rig_{11}).

rim_4
(cf., $kaš_4$).

rin_2 [ERIM]
to be/make bright (reduplication class); to attach, join, hitch (cf., $erin_2$, rin_2) (ara_4; ar; ra_3, 'bright', + to be high).

ru
n., present, gift, offering [RU archaic frequency: 120].

v., to blow; to give; to offer; to pour out; to inflict; to send (cf., rug_2).

ru-gu_2
to withstand; to oppose; to move in a direction opposite to; to face (cf., lu_2-ru-gu_2-da; ${}^{giš}ma_2$-ru-ru-gu_2; šu...ru-gu_2; šu $teš_2$-a...ru-gu_2).

ru_2, $řu_2$
(cf., du_3).

ru_3
to be equal in size or rank.

ru_5
to send forth shoots, buds, or blossoms; to butt; to gore.

rug_2 [SU or NAM.SU]; ru
to restore, return; to replace; to pay back; to receive (reduplication class) (cf., sug_6) (ru, 'to give; to send' + entrance).

S

sa
n., sinew, tendon, muscle; vein; catgut string; cord; net; mat; bundle (tied up with a string); string of a musical instrument (the SA sign can stand for the similar E_2 sign) [SA archaic frequency: 54; concatenates 2 sign variants].

v., to roast (barley); to parch (wheat) (cf., sa-sa).

sa-2-a-ga-gul
of lyre string: eighth string ('string' + 'two' + 'rearmost').

sa-3-a-ga-gul
of lyre string: seventh string ('string' + 'three' + 'rearmost').

sa-3-sa-sig
of lyre string: third string ('string' + 'three' + 'string' + 'low, late, weak'; cf., sa-us_2).

sa-4-a-ga-gul
of lyre string: sixth string ('string' + 'four' + 'rearmost').

sa-4-tur
of lyre string: fourth string ('string' + 'four' + 'small, little').

sa-a
cat (Akk. *šurānu(m) I*, 'cat'; cf., *šarammu*[ŠE.SU_7], 'grain heap' and sur_{12}; 'catgut' is a fluke of the English language, gut strings came from lambs and sheep, so there is no etymology involving sa, 'string'; this is a vowel harmony version of su-a).

sa-a-RI(-RI); sa-a-gal
wild cat; marsh lynx; desert lynx, caracal ('the cat that creeps low to the ground', cf., de_5(-g), 'to collapse, lie down'; 'the large cat').

$^{(u2)}$sa-ad-gal
a joint disease such as arthritis (affecting sheep), or the alkaline plant that helps against it ('sinew, tendon' + 'to balk' + 'major').

sa-al-ḫab-ba
a hunting net or sack that attracts victims through odor ('net, sack' + al-ḫab-ba, 'malodorous'; Akk. *alluḫappu*; cf., al-lu$_5$-ḫab$_2$).

sa-al-ḫub$_2$(-ba)
a battle net or fishing net (ḫub$_2$, 'acrobat, athlete'; Akk. *šētu(m) I, šuškallu(m)*).

sa-al-kad$_{4/5}$
carrying net ('net, sack' + conjugation prefix + 'to bind together').

sa-am-sa-tum
a solar emblem, in gold enchased with yellow quartz (^{na4}du$_8$-ši-a) or in refined copper (uruda-luḫ-ḫa) (Akk. *šamšatu(m)*, '(sun-)disk as cult ornament').

sa-an
(cf., sag̃).

sa-bar
(cf., sa-par$_3$; sa-par$_4$; sa-bar).

$^{g̃iš}$sa-bi$_2$-tum
a musical instrument (Akk. *ṣabītu* 'gazelle').

sa-di
of lyre string: first, front; the majority opinion holds that this was the lowest note, but a minority opinion holds that this was the highest note ('string' + 'speaking/doing'; cf., diš, 'one').

sa-di-5
of lyre string: fifth string ('string' + 'speaking/doing' + 'five').

sa-še$_3$...DU
to roast ('to roast (barley)' + 'for the sake of' + 'to go' ?).

sa-du$_3$
hunting or fishing net; assistant, reinforcement ('net' + 'to erect').

$^{g̃iš}$sa-du$_8$(-a)
a tool with a blade (cf., $^{g̃iš}$eme-sa-du$_8$-a) ('roasting' + 'to loosen' + nominative).

sa-dur$_2$(-ra); ŠEŠ-dur$_2$-ra$_2$/a
moist, low-lying end of a farmer's field (cf., eg$_2$ sa-dur$_2$-ra); rump, bottom ('reed bundle, fascine' + 'seat/dam' + nominative; Akk. *aburru(m), šuburru(m)*).

$^{(g̃iš)}$sa-eš$_{(5)}$
a musical instrument ('strings' + 'many').

sa-ga
(cf., sa-gaz).

sa-gal
a muscle, tendon; hamstring injury ('muscle' + 'large'; Akk. *sagallu(m)*).

$^{(lu2)}$sa-gaz; sag̃-gaz
highway robber; murderer; criminal ('head' + 'to smash'; > Akk., *šaggāšu(m)*, 'murderer' > *šagāšu(m)*, 'to kill, slaughter').

sa-gaz...aka
to rob (someone: dative infix); to commit murder ('robber' + 'to do').

sa-gi
reed bundle(s) ('cord, bundle' + 'reeds').

sa...gi$_{(4)}$
to hoard; to prepare.

sa-gi$_{(4)}$-a
provisioned, supplied.

sa-gid$_2$-da
a musical string tuning mode = "plucked mode"; one of several rubrics or interpolated titles for part of a hymn ('string of a musical instrument' + 'to be long' + nominative).

sa-gig
illness of the tendons, joints, muscles, or veins (cf., sa-keš$_2$).

sa-giri$_{11}$[KEŠDA]
straw bale ('cord' + 'to bind neatly'; Akk., *sagrikkum*).

sa-ğar-ra
a net, for battles or fishing; a musical string tuning mode = "set mode"; one of several rubrics or interpolated titles for part of a hymn ('cord; net/string of a musical instrument' + 'to deliver; to restore' + nominative).

sa-ḫab
(metathesis of zipaḫ).

sa-ḫi-in(-du_3)
yeast ('net; to parch' + 'numerous, abundant' + 'he plants, sets up'; Akk., *sikkatu(m) III*).

sa-ḫir[KEŠDA]
carrying net; bundle (e.g., of straw) ('net' + 'produce; to tighten'; Akk., *šaḫarru(m) II*).

SA-IGI
a silver object; from context, part of a la-ga-ma-al statuette, perhaps the eyes.

sa-$keš_2$[KEŠDA] (-$keš_2$-sa)
a disease of the joints - arthritis ? ('tendon' + 'to bind'; Akk. *šaššaṭu(m), maškadu*).

sa-KU
arms, hands (? rare meaning; cf., sa-dur_2) ('sinew, tendon' + 'to build ?').

sa...lal/la_2
v., to stretch, suspend, or submerge the net; to sweep; to tie with cords ('net' + 'to stretch, suspend').

sa-la_2
adj., spared, in good condition (Akk. *padû(m), šūšuru(m)*).

sa-la_2-a
n., four-sided fishing or hunting net ('net' + 'to stretch, suspend' + nominative).

sa-li
a type of lyre ('string' + 'true measure').

sa-ma(-a)-na_2
skin disease; grain diseases such as leaf rust (Akk. *samānu* 'skin disease').

sa-par_3; sa-par_4; sa-bar
a casting net ('net' + 'to stretch out'; cf., si-par_4).

sa-sa
n., roasting, burning; stinging (reduplicated 'to roast (barley)').

v., to full newly woven woolen cloth by 'walking' or beating, turning a net of loose fibers into tight, compact cloth.

adj., reddish; fulled (cloth).

sa-sum
braid of onions ('string' + 'onion').

sa-$še_3$...DU
to roast ('to roast (barley)' + 'for the sake of' + 'to go' ?).

sa-$šu_2$-uš-gal
huge net; battle net; fish net ('cord, net' + $šuš_2$/$šu_2$, 'to cover' + 'big').

sa-tu
mountain; upper parts (Akk. *šadû(m) I*, 'mountain(s)').

sa-us_2
of lyre string: second string ('string' + 'to follow, be next to, border'; Akk. *šamūšu(m)* could be explained by transcribing sa-$ğeš_3$, where mu-uš may be the Emesal form of $ğeš_3$, but cf., am_3-mu-uš, Emesal dialect for 'three'; cf., sa-di).

sa-ZI-ZI-a; sa-ZI-ZI-$ŠE_3$
a trawling (?) net ('net' + 'to take out, extract' + locative or terminative postposition).

sa_2[DI]
n., advice, counsel.

v., to approach or equal in value; to attain, reach; to do justice; to achieve; to compare with; to yoke together; to compete (with -da-); to be zealous, competitive (reduplication class) (from sa, 'string of a musical instrument', cf., si...sa_2, 'to tune (a musical instrument)', but cf., sa_{10}, 'to be equivalent, exchange, buy').

adj., ordinary; without decoration.

$^{uruda}sa_2$-am-sa_2-am
a type of drum; a bird.

sa_2...DI
to evaluate ('value' + 'to judge').

sa_2...dug_4/du_{11}/de_3/e
to attain, reach, arrive, overwhelm, subdue, impose (often with -ni-); to succeed; to be appointed; to provide regular offerings (reduplication class) ('to equal in value, attain' + 'to effect').

sa_2-dug_4/du_{11}(-ga/ba)
a capacity measure, = 24 $sila_3$ in Presargonic Girsu and 40 $sila_3$ starting with Akkad period; regular monthly "tithe" or "offering" important to the temple economy ('to equal in value' + 'to effect'; Akk., *sattukku*).

sa_2-g̃ar
adviser, counselor ('guidance' + 'to deliver').

sa_2-nig̃in$_{(2)}$
part of a harness (?) ('guidance' + 'to halt; to turn round').

sa_2-pa
part of a harness (?) ('guidance' + 'branch; wing').

sa_2...se_3(-g/k)
to plot; to plan ('advice' + 'to apply; to compare').

sa_2 til-la-ni
(cf., sam_2 til-la-ni).

sa_4, $še_{21}$, $ša_{22}$[ḪU.NA_2]
to name; to call by name (cf., $še_{21}$).

sa_5; sa_{11}
n., red ocher.

v., to be distressed, in mourning.

adj., red, red-brown (Akk. *sāmu(m)*, 'red, brown').

sa_5-bur_2
profit(able business) ('red ocher' + 'to knap, flake').

sa_6
(cf., sag_9; in Ur III texts occasionally stands for sa_{10}).

sa_7
well-formed; flourishing; comely, beautiful; to gather, form (of clouds); visible (cf., sig_7).

sa_9[MAŠ]
n., half; midpoint; midway.

v., to halve, divide equally.

sa_{10}
to be equivalent; to exchange, buy (cf., sam_2).

sa_{11}
(cf., sa_5; sa_{11}).

sa_{12}; $ša_{24}$
(cf., sag̃).

sa_{12}-du_5
(read sa_{12}-sug_5 ?, from the Akkadian form *šassukkum*).

sa_{12}(-e-eš)...rig_7
(cf., sag̃/sa_{12}(-e-eš)...rig_7).

sa_{12}-sug_5; sa_{12}-su_5[SAG̃-KU]; sa_2-sug_5
land register manager; surveyor; registrar, recorder of deeds; librarian ('head' + 'to lay the warp of the land' ?, cf., šassuk; also read sa_{12}-du_5).

sa_{12}-ti-um^{ki}
the eastern mountains.

sa_{14}
(cf., sag_8).

sabad$_{(2,3)}$, $sad_{2,3,4}$ [G̃A_2×U, G̃A_2×BAD, G̃A_2×SIG_7]; šab, sab [PA.IB]
hips, loins; middle (su, 'body', + bad, 'to open').

$sag_{2/3}$
n., dispersal; remains (cf., $sig_{11/3}$).

v., to scatter; to flood; to push away or around (to multiply; to spread + eg_2, 'dike; to water').

adj., scattered.

sag_2...dug_4/du_{11}/e
to scatter (with -da- or -ta-) ('dispersal' + 'to effect').

sag_3
(cf., sig_3).

sag_5
(cf., zag_3).

sag_8
(cf., sig_{15}).

sag_9, $šag_5$, sig_6, sa_6, $ša_6$
n., good fortune; (divine) grace, favor.

v., to be/make good, pleasant; to please, satisfy; to improve; to be favorable; to be friendly; to kiss (with dative or -da-) (reduplicated in *ḫamṭu*; sa_6-ge in *marû*).

adj., sweet, good, pleasant; beautiful; fruitful (sa_7, 'well-formed' + $ge_{(2,6)}$, 'girl').

sag_9-ḫul
both good and bad ('good' + 'bad').

sag_{10}, sig_5[IGI.$ERIN_2$]
n., best arable land; kindness.

adj., (to be) mild, sweet, good; of fine quality.

$saga_{11}$, sag_{11}, sig_{18}[KIN]
to cut, break, harvest.

sagi [$SILA_3$.ŠU.DU_8]
cupbearer (loan from Akk. *šāqû*).

sağ, sa_{12}
head; leader (of the herd); person, individual; slave; servant (esp. of a god or king); substitute; point; front; top or beginning (of a tablet); short side (of field) in OS texts; present, gift (sa_2, 'to equal'; sa_4, 'to name', + $ğe_{26}$, $ğa_2$, myself; cf. etymology, sağ/sa_{12}(-e-eš)...rig_7) [SAG archaic frequency: 420].

adj., first, first-class, prime.

prep., in front.

sağ-a-ki-ta
lower end of a field ('head' + 'water' + 'to be lower' + nominative).

sağ...aka
to care ('head' + 'to do').

sağ-an-na
upper end of a field ('head' + 'to be high' + nominative).

sağ (an-$še_3$)...il_2
to lift the head (towards heaven); to raise up ('head' (+ 'unto heaven') + 'to lift up').

sağ-apin(-na)
plow guide; manager ('head' + 'plow' + genitive).

sağ...bala
to shake the head ('head' + 'to turn').

sağ-bi-$še_3$(...e_3)
to be superior to all; preeminent ('head; leader' + adverbial force suffix + 'towards' + 'to rise').

sağ...bul
to toss or shake the head ('head' + 'to blow', cf., sağ...bala).

sağ...DI
(cf., sağ...sa_2).

sağ-dili
batchelor; alone; unique ('head' + 'single').

sağ-du
head ('head' + 'doing').

^{ğiš}sağ-du
warp beam of weaving loom ('tool' + 'head').

sağ-du...e_3
to confront ('head' + 'to extend').

sağ-du nu-tuku
idiot, a term of derision ('head' + 'not' + 'having').

sag̃-du$_3$
triangle ('head' + 'shape'; cf., gur-sag̃-g̃al$_2$).

sag̃-dub
regular worker ('head' + 'tablet-recorded').

sag̃...dub$_2$
to smash (someone's head) (often with -da-) ('head' + 'to knock down').

SAG̃-DUN$_3$
(cf., sa$_{12}$-sug$_5$, sa$_{12}$-du$_5$, šassuk).

sag̃-en$_3$...tar
to notice ('head' + 'to investigate').

sag̃-en$_3$-tar
overseer; inspector; guardian ('head' + 'to investigate; to take care of, handle').

sag̃-gag, sag̃-kak
(cf., sag̃tag, santak$_{(2,3,4)}$).

sag̃-gaz...aka
to slay ('head' + 'smash' + 'to do'; cf., sa-gaz).

sag̃...gi$_4$
to topple; to close, block, lock ('head' + 'to send back').

sag̃...gid$_2$
(cf., sag̃-ki...gid$_2$).

sag̃-gig
headache ('head' + 'painful').

sag̃-gu$_2$-g̃al$_2$; sag̃-gu$_2$-gal; sag̃-gu$_2$-tuku
(cf., sag̃-ku$_3$-g̃al$_2$).

sag̃-gu$_2$-ne(-/ak/)
cupbearer (loan from Akk. *šāqû*).

$^{g̃iš}$sag̃-gul
(cf., sag̃-kul$_2$).

sag̃...g̃al$_2$
(same meaning as sag̃...g̃ar/g̃a$_2$-g̃a$_2$).

sag̃...g̃ar/g̃a$_2$-g̃a$_2$
to proceed, go forth, advance, lead; to shout; to confront, oppose (someone/something: -da-) ('the head' + 'to set').

sag̃-g̃ar
gift, present ('gift, present' + 'to deliver').

sag̃-G̃AR-GA-ra(-ak)
(cf., sag̃-nig̃$_2$-gur$_{11}$[GA]-ra(-ak)).

sag̃-g̃i$_6$(-ga)
black-headed people; Sumerians ('head/person' + 'black' + nominative; cf., dumu-gir$_{15}$/gi$_7$ and ki-en-gi(-r); ki-en-gir$_{15}$/gi$_7$(-r); I think that in the spoken language, this was originally 'native person', sag̃-gi$_7$, like dumu-gi$_7$, but that assimilation changed it to sag̃-g̃i and the meaning was reinterpreted).

sag̃-g̃iš...ra
to kill; to murder; to execute; to beat to death ('head' + 'wood tool' + 'to strike').

sag̃...ḫa-za
to attach securely ('head' + 'to hold, grasp, retain').

sag̃ (an-še$_3$)...il$_2$
to lift the head (towards heaven); to raise up ('head' (+ 'unto heaven') + 'to lift up').

sag̃-il$_2$(-la)
elevated; raised; tall (cf., nig̃$_2$-sag̃-il$_2$(-la)) ('head' + 'to lift up' + nominative).

sag̃-izi
torch ('head' + 'fire').

sag̃-kak
(cf., sag̃tag, santak$_{(2,3,4)}$).

sag̃...kal
to appreciate; to choose, prefer; to make foremost, prominent, excellent ('head' + 'to value').

sag̃-kal-(l)
foremost; leader ('head' + 'excellent').

sag̃...$keš_2$
to attend to; to watch, guard ('head' + 'to bind').

sag̃-$keš_2$...aka
to pay attention (with -ši-); to admonish ('head' + 'to fasten' + 'to do', cf., g̃izzal...aka).

sag̃-$keš_2$
a device (string ?) for carrying dried figs and dried apples in ED IIIb (Girsu).

^{kuš}sag̃-$keš_2$
a thong connecting the yoke to the plow ('head' + 'to bind').

^{ku6}sag̃-$keš_2$
a common edible fish ('head' + 'to bind').

sag̃-ki
forehead; brow; facial expression; front ('head, point' + 'place').

sag̃-ki...gid_2
to frown (upon); to get angry (with someone: -da-) ('brow' + 'to lengthen').

sag̃-ki-gu_4
trapezoid ('head, point' + 'location' + 'bulky like an ox').

sag̃-ki...us_2(-us_2)
to trust in ('forehead' + 'to lean against').

sag̃-ki...zalag
to smile (upon) ('facial expression' + 'to gleam; luminous'; cf., zu_2...zalag).

SAG̃-KU
(cf., sa_{12}-su_5).

sag̃-ku_3-g̃al_2
proud, splendid ('head' + 'pure, noble' + 'having').

sag̃-kul
ring; globe-lightning; an adjective for a type of metal cup ('head' + 'thick').

$^{(g̃iš/zabar)}$sag̃-kul(-la); sag̃-kul_2/gul
mace; lock bolt ('head' + 'thick'; Akk., *sankullu(m)*).

sag̃-kur-ra
a foreign slave ('slave' + 'foreign land' + genitive).

^{ku6}sag̃-kur_2[PAP]
a fish ('head' + 'strange').

sag̃-$^{g̃iš}ma_2$
bow of a boat ('head' + 'boat').

sag̃-men
head-crown (cf., men-sag̃).

sag̃-mi_2, sag̃-munus
female slave ('head; slave' + 'female').

sag̃...mu_2-mu_2
to beautify; to apply, order, and arrange the hair and makeup ('head' + 'to make shine').

sag̃-nig̃$_2$-gur_{11}[GA]-ra(-ak)
capital on hand, available goods and supplies ('in front, at first' + 'what' + 'piled up' [+ genitive]; sag̃ and 'capital' refer to the 'head' of an accounting column in different languages).

sag̃-nitaḫ
male slave; (grown) man ('head; slave' + 'male').

sag̃-NUMUN
(cf., sag̃-kul).

sag̃-rib
(cf., sag̃-kal-(l)).

sag̃/sa_{12}(-e-eš)...rig_7
to donate, bestow, grant, entrust, give as a present (with -ni- and -ri-) (with loc.term. suffix -e on inanimate indirect objects) ('present, gift' + 'to deed, grant', where these meanings derive by back-formation from this compound which derives from Akkadian *šarākum*).

sag̃-rig_7
gift; dowry, normally received by a daughter from her father.

sag̃...sa_2
to vie with (with -da-) (cf., zag...sa_2) ('head' + 'to compare').

sağ...sal-la
to be silly (?); to engage in a gesture of mourning ('head' + 'to belittle').

sağ...sar
to shave the head ('head' + 'to crop ?').

sağ...se_3/si_3-(g)
to entrust; to take care of; to pay attention; to tend ('head' + 'to apply; to surround').

sağ-sig...ğar
to bend or lower one's head (before someone/something: -ši-) ('head' + 'small, weak' + 'to place').

sağ-sig-ga
head-covering ('head' + 'small' + nominative).

sağ...sig_3
to tremble; to shake (the head) from side to side (with -da-) ('head' + 'to shake').

SAĞ-SUG_5
(cf., sa_{12}-sug_5, šassuk).

sağ...sum
to proceed; to hurry towards; to advance; to go against; to attack ('head' + 'to give').

sağ-sum-sikil
onion bulb ('head' + 'onion').

sağ X-$še_3$
instead of X ('substitute' + terminative postposition).

sağ šu...aka
to enslave ('slave' + 'to take captive').

(tug2) **sağ-$šu_4$[U]**
cap (cf., sağšu) ('head' + 'to cover').

sağ-tab
helper; cover, roof ('head' + 'to join'; cf., ka-tab).

sağ-tag
a designation of both male and female workers (cf., sağtag/santak, 'single').

sağ...tuku
to look after ('head' + 'to have, marry').

sağ-tuku
n., lookout; spy.

adj., proud; splendid ('head; first-class' + 'having'; cf., gu_2-tuku).

sağ...tum_2
to defame; to despise ('first position' + 'to carry away').

SAĞ-TUN_3
(cf., sa_{12}-sug_5, sa_{12}-du_5, šassuk).

sağ u_2-a...šub
to hide ('head' + 'in the grass' + 'to drop').

sağ-ur-sağ
eunuch; royal attendant; a powerful servant ('slave' + 'warrior').

sağ-us_2
n., supporter ('point' + 'to be moored to').

v., to be available; to support, care for something's maintenance.

adj., constant.

sağ-zi
crown, tiara ('head' + zid, 'legitimate' / zig_3, 'to raise up').

adj., exalted, high; foremost; first rate; permanent, regular; lower.

sağ zi-da
faithful.

sağ...zi(-g)
to get up, arise, set out ('head' + 'to rise up').

sağ...zi-zi(-g)
to deduct; to reduce; to breach ('head' + reduplicated 'to tear out').

$sağ_5$
(cf., zag_3).

$sağa_{2,3,4,5,6,7}$
a sprinkler, used for ritual cleaning; a purification priest (sağ, 'head', + a, 'water').

$sağdul_x$[U+SAĞ]
(read, sağšu).

sağğa, sanğa, sanğu
economic director of a temple or occupation (such as all the smiths) (function same as Akkadian loanword šabra); temple administrator; scribe of early Uruk III and Jemdet Nasr periods (cf., zag_3, sag_5, $zağ_3$, $sağ_5$[ŠID], 'to choose'; Akk., *šangû(m)*, 'priest, temple manager') [SANGA archaic frequency: 530; concatenates 3 sign variants].

(tug2) sağšu[U.SAĞ]
headdress; headcloth, turban; helmet; cap, lid; stopper, cork (sağ, 'head', + $suš_2$/$šu_2$, 'to cover'; cf., sağ-$šu_4$, 'cap') [SAGŠU archaic frequency: 14].

ğiš sağšu
socket for doorpost.

sağtag, santak$_{(2,3,4)}$
triangle; (written) wedge; single (sağ, 'head', + tag, 'to hold').

sağtuš$_x$[U.SAĞ]
hat, headdress (sağ, 'head', + tuš, 'to reside, sit').

$saḫ_4$
(cf., $suḫ_3$).

$saḫ_{6,7}$
(cf., $zaḫ_{2,3}$).

ğiš saḫab[ŠU.DIŠ]
bar, bolt (of a door); gatekeeper (?) (cf., ğiš $suḫub_{4/5}$) (sağ, 'head', + ḫub, 'hole, recess'; cf., ğiš sağ-kul; ğiš sağ-kul_2/gul, 'lock bolt').

saḫar[IŠ]
silt, dust, sand, earth, soil, mud, loam; rubbish; sediment; esquire, valet, page, body-servant, boy (loan from Akkadian *ṣuḫāru(m)*, 'boy, male child; servant') (cf., $kuš_7$; dug saḫar$_{(2)}$) (su_7, 'threshing floor', + ḫara/ara_3, 'crushed, pulverized').

saḫar-a-tuš-a
charged with excavating dirt from canals ('dirt' + locative + 'doing service').

saḫar-bi
its earth, followed by a volume amount.

SAḪAR.DU_6.TAK_4
piles of corpses.

saḫar...dub
to heap up rubbish; to raise a cloud of dust ('rubbish/dust' + 'to heap up, shake').

saḫar(-re)-eš
sand dune(s) ('sand' + phonetic complement + 'much, many').

saḫar(-da)...gi_4
to turn into dust; euphemism for 'to die' ('dust' + 'to turn, return').

(ğiš) saḫar-gi_4
dust guard, mudguard, or fender on chariot ('dust, mud' + 'to turn, return').

saḫar-ğar-ra
volume; silt ('earth' + 'to accumulate' + nominative) (cf., ki-la_2).

saḫar si-ga
to pile up earth; to fill (an eroded area) in with earth; earth piling ('earth, silt' + si-ga/ge, 'to pile up').

saḫar...su$_{(3)}$
to cover with dust or silt (redup. class) ('dust, silt' + 'to sprinkle, immerse').

saḫar šu-bala-a
to transport earth ('earth, silt' + 'hand' + 'to transfer, deliver' + nominative).

saḫar šu-ti-a
to collect earth or silt for removal ('earth' + 'to receive' + nominative).

(lu2) saḫar-šub-ba
leprosy; mange; scab; leper (cf., gan-šub-ba) ('dust' + 'to fall' + nominative).

saḫar-tun_2
dust heap ('dust' + 'heaping up').

SAḪAR.URUDA
verdigris.

saḫar zi-ga
to remove earth or silt; earth moving ('earth, silt' + 'to tear out, deduct' + nominative).

^{dug}saḫar$_2$[SAR]; ^{dug}saḫar[IŠ]
a clay pot for sprinkling (Akk., *šaḫarru I, šuḫarru*, 'porous ?').

sakar, sar
sharp (correct reading unclear, cf., u$_3$-sar...aka and u$_4$-sakar-gibil).

sal, šal
n., uterus; vulva (narrow + numerous) [SAL archaic frequency: 435].

v., to be narrow, thin, slender; to be wide, spacious; to spread out, flatten (clay); to open wide; to persist; to belittle.

adj., thin; fine, delicate; tender.

SAL.NITA.DAM
(cf., nitalam/nitadam).

SAL-SAL^{mušen}
(cf., rag-rag, rak-rak^{mušen}).

SAL.UŠ.DI
(cf., mi$_2$-us$_2$-sa$_2$; gambi$_x$^{mušen}).

sal$_4$, šal$_2$
spread out ?, dry ?, narrow ? - something done to normalize the density or specific gravity of barley and wheat before measuring their volume in gur; also an adjective for the legs of beds and chairs.

sam$_2$, šam$_2$, sa$_{10}$(-am$_3$)
n., equivalent; (barter) purchase; sale price; merchandise (Akk. loanword from *šīmu(m) I*, 'purchase (price); goods for commerce', *šâmu(m)*, 'to buy, purchase', cf., Orel & Stolbova #2281 ***su'um-** 'sell, buy'; conflated in Sumerian with sa$_2$, 'to make equal'; if sa$_{10}$ means 'to buy', then sam$_2$/sa$_{10}$-am$_3$, 'price', can be etymologized as 'it is the thing which bought') [ŠAM$_2$ archaic frequency: 51].

v., to barter, exchange; to buy (with -ši-); to sell (with -ra-, ablative) (sa$_{10}$-sa$_{10}$ in *marû*).

sam$_2$ til-la-ni, sa$_{10}$(-am$_3$) til-la-ni; sa$_2$ til-la-ni; nig̃$_2$-sam$_2$ til-la-ni
full purchase price ('price; value' + 'its fullness').

saman$_{(2,3)}$
yoke, leash, halter, or tether rope (for an ox).

sang̃a
(cf., sag̃g̃a).

sang̃a$_{2,3,4,5,6,7}$
(cf., sag̃a$_{2,3,4,5,6,7}$).

santana, šandana, šandan
herbalist, horticulturist, gardener, date orchard administrator (sag̃, 'head, human', + tin, 'to cure'; cf. also, šeg̃$_4$, 'chills' and šeg̃$_6$, 'to be hot') [ŠANDANA archaic frequency: 3; concatenates 2 sign variants].

sar, šar
a surface area measure, 'garden plot' = 1 square nindan = 60 surface shekels = 1/100 iku = 4 square reeds = 144 square cubits = 36 meters^2 - a frequent measure for the amount of reeds cut by a worker; a volume measure (for earth) of one square nindan times 1 kuš$_3$ = 144 kuš$_3$^{3} = ca. 18 cubic meters = 1,0 gur [= 60 gur] of capacity = 1,0 gin$_2$ in weight.

sar, šar
n., inscription; vegetable(s), herb(s), garden plant(s) (but cf., nisig) [SAR archaic frequency: 102; concatenates 3 sign variants].

v., to insert, enter; to begin; to write; to pay, deliver punctually; to disturb someone; to drive (with -ni-); to drive, chase away (with -ta-); to make hurry, run; to hasten (to be skilled, precise + flowing motion; for 'to drive away', cf., us$_2$, 'to follow, drive', but meaning probably derives from the act of chasing vermin from the vegetable garden, cf., kar for such a progression from the noun to the verb).

adj., driven out, pursued (sharp, cf., u_3-sar...aka and sakar).

SAR-da
n., underworld.

adj., rabid; frenzied.

sar-KA×SAR-KA×SAR
a vegetable.

SAR-SAR
(cf., mu_2-mu_2; mu_2-sar).

X-sar-ta
(each worker did) X sar.

sar_2
(cf., $šar_2$).

(u2)sas
(possible reading of KI.KAL).

(MUNUS)se_2-ek-ru-um, se_2-ek-rum
cloistered lady; a class of women (Akk. *sekretu(m)*, 'enclosed (woman)').

se_3, si_3
(cf., sig_{10}; $sig_{3,10}$).

se_{11}
(cf., si_{11}).

se_{12}, si_{12}
(cf., sig_7).

$sed_{(3,4,5,6)}$, $šed_{7,9,10,11,12}$, $še_{4,5,12,17,18,23}$
n., cold water; coldness; coolness; frost (si, 'to fill up', + ed_2, 'to go out').

v., to cool down; to repose; to be calmed, quieted; to pacify, soothe, appease, relieve; to abate, subside.

adj., cold.

ses
(cf., šeš, ses, sis).

si
n., horn(s); antenna(e); line; ray(s); radiance, light; fret or bridge of a lute, a stringed instrument; plowland (cf., sig_5) [SI archaic frequency: 417].

v., to stand upright; to be straight; to be in order; to become completely still; to shine, be bright; to light (cf., si-ga/ge).

adj., regular, normal; horned.

si; su_3; sa_5[SI.A]
v., to fill up (with loc.term. suffix -e on inanimate indirect objects); to fill with (with -da-); to occupy; to survey a field; to inundate; to be full; to be sufficient enough; to be choked up; to increase; to grow weak (probably reduplication class) (cf., sum, sig/si(-ga), sig_5).

adj., full, complete; suitable, fit.

si-2-la_2
plucked twice, attested for sheep and goats in Drehem texts ('to be straight; to be sufficient' + 'twice' + 'to lift; to diminish').

si-a
full ('to fill' + nominative).

SI.A
(cf., dirig or (gi)ušub).

SI.A
(cf., sa_5).

si am-ma-ke_4
bull's horn ('horn' + 'wild ox' + genitive).

si-dug_4
(cf., sidug).

si-ga
n., silence (cf., sig_5).

si-ga
adj., quiet; weak (cf., sig_5 and sig).

si-ga kala-ga
weak and strong points.

si-ga/ge
v., to pile or fill up (e.g., earth for a levee or temple foundation); to load; to cover or coat (as with leather) (cf., sig; si(-ga)).

si-gal
croissant ('horn-shaped' + 'large').

si gu_3...ra
to sound the horn; to signal with the horn; the horn was blown in the streets to alert the public for announcements ('horn' + 'to shout, roar'; cf., gu_3...ra(-ra)).

(uruda) si-gu_4
a copper peg or hinge (weighing one ma-na) made for a door, its pivot or post ('horn' + 'bull').

si-$\tilde{g}a_2$
cooked (cf., $še\tilde{g}_6$).

$^{\tilde{g}iš}$si-$\tilde{g}$ar
door lock, bolt; (wooden) clamp; (neck-)stock for captives ('long, narrow object' + 'storeroom').

si-i_3-tum
balance owing carried forward from an earlier account, usually from the previous year (from Akkadian *šiātum*, 'to leave behind', *šittu*, 'remainder, deficit') (cf., lal'u_6).

si-ig; si(-g); sig-ga
v., to place into the ground; to calm or put out a fire; to strike down, level; to silence.

adj., silent; weak, powerless (cf., sig_9/$šeg_5$/si(-ig)(-ga) and sig).

si-ig-dum
almond (wood and tree) - a hard wood used for weapons (Akkadian *šiqdu(m)*; cf., $^{(\tilde{g}iš)}eš_{22}$).

si-il
to split (open); to tear apart; to go away, absent oneself; to praise (cf., sila).

si-il-la_2
n., inspection (si-il, 'to split open', + nominative).

adj., reviewed, inspected, checked.

(uruda) si-im(-da)
copper branding irons; a percussion musical instrument (Akkadian *šimtu(m)*, 'mark; brand; branding iron').

si-im-da...$šu_2$/aka
to apply the branding iron (to an animal) (cf., zag...$šuš_2$/$šu_2$).

si-im-si-im...aka
to sniff (reduplicated sim, 'fragrant; to sniff' + 'to do').

si-la
controlled, acquired by; entrusted to (cf., sil).

si-li-ig
(cf., silig, šilig).

si-mu_2
to have horns; horned [can indicate a 'male' animal if only the male sex grows horns] ('horns' + 'to sprout, appear').

si-$muš_{2,3}$
splendid horns; light rays, radiance ('horns; rays' + 'to glisten, shine').

si-$par_{3,4}$
a farm tool, which yoked oxen are said to follow (cf., sa-par_4 ?) ('long, straight object' + 'to stretch out'; Akkadian *ama(n)dēnum*).

si...sa_2
to tune (an instrument); to put in order; to administer; to prepare, get ready; to do something in the right way; to make straight or just; to yoke (often with -ni- or bi_2-) (with loc.term. suffix -e on inanimate indirect objects) (redupl. class) ('fret or bridge of a stringed instrument/straightness' + 'to approach, achieve, equal').

si-sa_2
right; legal ('straightness' + 'to achieve').

si-si-ig
n., whirlwind (reduplicated sig_3, 'to demolish, flatten').

v., to silence (cf., si-ig).

si...si-sa_2
to assemble in order, to march in line; to guide.

si-šir$_3$[EZEN]
fret on a lute, a stringed instrument ('long, narrow thing' + 'song').

si-šuš-nu
a sea creature ('antennae' + 'to go down' + 'do not').

si-tum
(cf., **si-i$_3$-tum**).

si-un$_3$[BAD$_3$]-na
top of the sky, zenith ('straight up' + 'to ascend' + nominative).

^{anše}si$_2$-si$_2$
(cf., anše-zi-zi/anše-si$_2$-si$_2$).

si$_3$, se$_3$
(cf., sig$_{10}$; sig$_{3,10}$; sum).

si$_4$, su$_4$, sa$_{11}$
red; brown [SI$_4$ archaic frequency: 116; concatenates 5 sign variants].

si$_4$-lum^{sar}
a red-colored garden plant with a well-developed head, such as the beet or turnip ('reddish' + 'to grow luxuriantly').

si$_7$
(cf., simug).

si$_8$[DI]
to equal (cf., sa$_2$).

si$_{11}$, se$_{11}$[SIG]
to harvest flax and cumin by pulling (cf., sig$_7$/si$_{12}$/se$_{12}$).

si$_{12}$, se$_{12}$
(cf., sig$_7$).

si$_{12}$-si$_{12}$...g̃ar/g̃a$_2$-g̃a$_2$
to wail (cf., i-si-iš...g̃ar).

si$_{14}$
a small pot.

si$_{21}$
(cf., sig$_{15}$).

sidug
ravine; pit; pitfall; trap (sig$_3$...dug$_4$, 'to be destroyed').

sig; si(-ga)
n., evening (cf. si-ga as noun, verb, and adjective in compounds) [SIG archaic frequency: 66].

v., (cf., si-ga/ge).

adj., low; below; late; small, narrow; weak.

sig-ga
(cf., si-ig).

sig...g̃ar
to prostrate onself ('low' + 'to set').

sig-nim-ta
from everywhere ('low' + 'high' + 'from').

sig-sig
narrow (reduplicated 'small').

sig-še$_3$
down; probably also "to the right"; towards the lower country ('low' + 'towards').

sig$_2$
(cf., siki).

sig$_3$, sag$_3$; sig$_{10}$, si$_3$, se$_3$; sig$_{11}$, sag$_2$; saga$_{11}$, sig$_{18}$
n., stroke, blow (cf., sag$_{2/3}$).

v., to chop down (trees); to strike, hurt, smite, damage; to beat (rhythmically, for instance a drum); to (cause to) totter, shake, quake, tremble; to be drunk; to demolish, raze; to flatten, crush, knead, make even; to impose, subject, subdue; to remove, doff; to become still, settled (si, 'to stand upright' + ug$_{5,7,8}$, 'to kill'; cf., sug$_5$; $^{(lu2)}$su-si-ig).

sig$_3$[PA]...dug$_4$/du$_{11}$/e
to be destroyed ('stroke, blow' + 'to apply').

sig$_3$-ge-da
shadouf (AKA shadoof, shaduf, or swape), a semi-mechanical device for raising water from one level to another ('to flatten; to remove; to become settled' + 'arms; to hold').

sig_3-sig_3
whirlwind (reduplicated sig_3, 'to demolish, flatten').

sig_4
(cf., $šeg_{12}$).

SIG_4.BAD
(cf., uru_9).

SIG_4&SIG_4.$ŠU_2$
(cf., guḫšu).

sig_5
(cf., sag_{10}).

sig_7[IGI*gunû*], si_{12}(-g), se_{12}(-g), sa_7(-g)
v., to let live; to create; to live; to dwell; to complete; to be/make pleasant or beautiful; to garden; to pull out weeds; to tear out; to leave; to complain; (suppletion class verb: in the meaning 'to live (in a place)', sig_7 is the plural stem of til_3) (si, 'upright stalks' + eg_2, 'to water') [SIG_7 archaic frequency: 61].

adj., pale, sallow; green, yellow.

SIG_7[IGI*gunû*]-a
weeping; weak-sighted person (?); a common type of worker, probably a gardener.

SIG_7.ALAM
(cf., $ulutin_2$).

sig_7-g̃iš
a type of worker in the fields.

SIG_7-igi
(cf., $ugur_2$-igi).

sig_7-sig_7
to be beautiful; to be yellow (cf., igi-sig_7-sig_7) (reduplicated 'to be beautiful, pleasing; green, yellow').

SIG_7-SIG_7...g̃ar
(cf., si_{12}-si_{12}...g̃ar/$g̃a_2$-$g̃a_2$).

sig_8[GAD.KID_2.GIŠ; UMBIN]
comb (cf., siki, sig_2).

sig_9, si
to be narrow; to inlay; to place, put (cf., sig_9; $šeg_5$; si(-ig)) (narrow, fine [+neck-like]).

sig_9; $šeg_5$; si(-ig)(-ga)
n., silence.

v., to stay silent; to silence (si, 'to be still' + throat for vocalizing).

adj., calm; quiet; silenced; weary.

sig_{10}, se_3(-g), si_3(-g)
to apply, place, set, put in; to engrave; to be conscious, remember; to supply, serve, provide; to divide, demarcate a field sector; to sweep along; to do, cause; to surround; to compare; to match (cf., sum; $sig_{3,10}$; $teš_2$(-a)... sig_{10}/si_3(-ke;ga)) (combination of meanings such as: su_x, 'to spread on', sig_3, 'to knock down', and sa_2, 'to compare').

sig_{11}
(cf., sig_3).

sig_{14}
(cf., $šeg_9$).

sig_{15}[KAL]
pleasing, valuable (?) (cf., zid_2-sig_{15}; kaš-sig_{15}; esig/esi [KAL]).

sig_{17}[GI]
adj., the color of the low or setting sun = reddish yellow, gold, or tan (cf., sig).

sig_{18}
(cf., sig_3; $saga_{11}$).

sig_x[UMBIN]
comb (cf., siki, sig_2).

sigga
(cf., $šeg_9$).

siki, sik_2, sig_2
hair (of head, beard, body); wool; fur, hide (cf., tug_2-siki) (si, 'long, thin things', + ki, 'place') [SIG_2 archaic frequency: 224; concatenates 12 sign variants].

siki-ba
wool allotment, ration ('hair; wool' + 'share, rations').

siki-babbar
white wool ('hair; wool' + 'white').

siki-bar
loosely hanging hair ('hair' + 'to uncover, expose').

SIKI.BU
(cf., $zulumhi_2$; $^{tug2}mudru_5$).

siki $^{(\tilde{g}i\check{s})}$ga-rig_2-aka(-a)
carded wool.

siki-GI; siki-gin[DU]
wool of average quality, of the native sheep udu-gir_{15}.

siki-gi_6
wool of black sheep ('hair; wool' + 'dark; black').

SIKI.GID_2
(cf., $zulumhi_2$; $^{tug2}mudru_5$).

siki(-$\tilde{g}ir_2$)-gul
wool cut with knife (from dead sheep) ('wool' + 'special knife').

siki-kur-ra
low-class wool from highland sheep (cf., udu-kur-ra).

SIKI.LAM
(cf., $še\check{s}_2$; adkin).

SIKI.LAM.SUḪUR
(cf., $munšub_2$).

siki-mud_6/mu_2[SAR]
horn; hair ('hair' + 'to sprout'; may be alternate writing of munšub [SIKI.SUḪUR]).

siki-mug
mediocre (quality) wool ('hair; wool' + 'poor quality, unbleached').

siki-muš-aka
combed wool ('hair, wool' + 'snakes' + 'to do').

siki-pa
head hair; hairstyle ('hair' + 'branch').

siki...$peš_5$
to card wool ('hair, wool' + 'to comb and clean').

SIKI.SUḪUR
(cf., munšub).

$^{(tug2)}$siki-šab
combed-out hair; carded wool; cloth of carded wool.

siki-šur(-ra)
spun wool ('hair; wool' + 'to spray out, expel' + nominative).

siki-ud_5
goat's hair/wool ('hair' + 'she-goat').

siki-ur_2
pubic hair ('hair' + 'loins').

sikil
v., to be/make (cultically) clean, pure (siki, 'hair', + ul, 'to shine'; cf., $suku_5$, 'to shine brightly', sig_7, 'to create; to make beautiful') [SIKIL archaic frequency: 7].

adj., clean, fresh, pure, virginal.

sikil-du_3-a
(cf., inim-sikil-du_3-a).

sil, šil[TAR]
n., basket, quiver (?).

v., to control, acquire; to recline; to praise (cf., si-il).

sil_5
pleasure, joy.

$sil_{6,9,7}$
(cf., $asilal_{3,4,5}$).

sil_7(-la_2)
to be distant; to move away; to withdraw.

sila, sil; sil_2, zil; si-il
to cut into; to divide (si, 'long and narrow', + la_2, 'to penetrate, pierce').

sila$_{(3)}$
street; path; trail; road; market place, square (si, 'anything long and narrow', + la$_2$, 'to extend, reach').

sila-a dab$_5$-ba
(a person) seized on the street ('street' + locative + 'to seize, hire' + nominative).

sila-a g̃al$_2$-la
available on the street ('street' + locative + 'to be available' + nominative).

sila-dag̃al
broad street; city square ('street' + 'wide').

sila-kur$_2$...dab$_5$/dib$_2$
to take a different way ('street' + 'different' + 'to take'/'to traverse').

$^{(dug/g̃iš)}$sila$_3$, sil$_3$, sal$_4$, šal$_2$
n., measure of capacity, 'quart', 'liter', = 0.842 modern liters in the Neo-Sumerian period; these units expressed in vertical number signs; measuring pot (si$_{14}$, 'a small pot', + la$_2$, 'to weigh'; Akk., *qû(m) II, mīšertu(m)*) [SILA$_3$ archaic frequency: 57; concatenates 3 sign variants].

v., to drink.

$^{(dug)}$sila$_3$-ban$_3$-da
small sila$_3$-vessel ('liter' + 'junior').

$^{(dug/g̃iš)}$sila$_3$-gaz
½ sila$_3$ measure (sila$_3$, 'liter', + gaz, 'to break, divide'; Akkadian *sil(a)gazû, šarmu*, 'lopped, trimmed; term for a ½ *qû* measure', *ḫupû*).

sila$_3$-g̃ar-ra
(cf., a-sila$_3$-g̃ar-ra).

sila$_3$(-ninda)-ta
at N liters (of bread) each ('liters' + 'bread' + 'from, per').

SILA$_3$.ŠU.DU$_8$
(cf., sagi).

sila$_4$
(male) lamb; bait (cf., kir$_{11}$) (cf., silim, 'healthy, complete, perfect', for etymology) [SILA$_4$ archaic frequency: 73; concatenates 4 sign variants].

sila$_4$-ga(-sub-ba)
milk suckling lamb (-sub-ba not found in Ur III texts - occurs in earlier ED IIIb texts) ('lamb' + 'milk' + 'to suck' + nominative).

sila$_4$-gub
offspring (children or of flocks); mature young of animals ('lambs' + 'to stand').

sila$_4$-nim
early spring lamb ('lamb' + 'early').

sila$_4$-nitaḫ
lamb buck ('lamb' + 'male').

sila$_4$-nu-ur$_4$
a lamb that has not been shorn ('lamb' + 'not' + 'to shear, pluck').

silag̃, sila$_{11}$(-g̃a$_2$)
n., dough (sila/sil, 'to cut, divide', + lag/lag̃, 'lump, gob').

v., to knead (dough or clay); to slay (cf. lu$_2$-sila$_{11}$-g̃a$_2$, 'baker').

$^{(g̃iš)}$silig$_{(5)}$, šilig$_{(5)}$
n., ax (sila/sil, 'to cut, divide', + lag/lag̃, 'bulk, block').

v., to cease, stop; to lay aside one's work.

adj., extremely powerful, strong (cf., $^{g̃iš}$aga-silig and nam-silig).

silig$_2$
hand.

silig$_{3,4}$
sin.

silim[DI], sim$_3$
to be healthy, complete, perfect; to be/make in good shape; to restore (usually considered Akk. loanword, root means 'peace' in 18 of 21 Semitic languages, but Sumerians used word in greeting and root not in Orel & Stolbova's *Hamito-Semitic Etymological*

Dictionary; cf., sil_5, 'pleasure, joy', + lum, 'to grow luxuriantly').

silim...dug_4/du_{11}/di/e
to greet, say "Hello" ('health' + 'to speak').

silim-$še_3$ gu_3...de_2
to greet, say "Hello" ('health' + 'regarding' + 'to call, say').

silim-ma ḫe_2-me-en
"Welcome" ('may you be healthy').

silim...sum
to greet, say "Hello" ('greeting' + 'to give').

sim, sin_2[NAM]
to strain, sieve, filter; to sift (flour); to see through (fine, narrow + to be).

sim, $šim_2$[NAM]
v., to sniff, smell (cf., si-im-si-im...aka; ir-si-im).

adj., fragrant (cf, šim, šem, 'aromatic').

sim, $sin_2^{mušen}$
barn swallows - migratory small birds with pale underparts and blue/black upper parts, with long, deeply-forked tails, which like to feed, while flying, on insects in pasture areas and which nest in reed beds or quiet farm buildings - family Hirundinidae of order Passeriformes (Akkadian *sinuntu*).

sim_3
(cf., silim).

sim_x[GIG]-ma; sim_x[KA×GA]
suppurating wound, boil, lesion (Akk. loanword ? from *simmu*, 'wound', related to Orel & Stolbova 640, Sem ***dVm-**, 'wound; flow (of blood)' ?; cf, sim, $šim_2$, 'to sniff').

simug, si_7[$UMUN_2$]
metal-sculptor, smith (si, 'to light', + mud_6, mu_2, 'to blow; to ignite, kindle; to make shine' + aka/ag, 'to do, make'; Akk., *nappāḫu(m)*, 'smith, metalworker', from *napāḫu(m)*, 'to blow; light up; rise') [SIMUG archaic frequency: 13].

sin_2
(cf., sim).

sipa
(cf., sipad).

sipad, sibad, sipa[PA.LU]; šuba; sub_2; sub_3
n., shepherd; herder; keeper (cf. Emesal, sub_2-ba) [SIPA archaic frequency: 4].

v., to pasture, tend (si, 'to keep in order', + bad, 'to let out', or pad_3, 'to find').

sipad-ama-[ŠA.]GAN
shepherd of pregnant, mother animals ('shepherd' + 'mother' + 'to bring forth').

sipad-amar-ru-ga
shepherd of brought back (?) ('shepherd' + 'young ones' + rug_2, 'to restore' + genitive).

sipad-bibad[UZ.TUR]^{mušen}
herder of ducks ('shepherd' + 'ducks').

sipad-mušen
fowler ('shepherd' + 'birds').

sipad(-tir-ra)^{mušen}
bird with a multicolored crest; hoopoe ? ('shepherd' + 'forest' + genitive).

sipad-tur
shepherd boy, shepherd's assistant ('shepherd' + 'young').

sipad-udu-siki-ka
shepherd of wool sheep ('shepherd' + 'sheep' + 'wool' + double genitive).

sipad-ur-gi_7
dog-keeper ('shepherd' + 'dog').

^{mul}sipa-zid-an-na
the constellation Orion, the faithful shepherd of heaven ('shepherd' + 'good, faithful' + 'heaven' + genitive; Akk., *šitaddaru(m)*).

sipar
(cf., zabar).

sir_2[BU]
n., density (cf., $šer_2$).

v., to accumulate; to monitor, check; to have the harvest/event/season approach, arrive.

adj., dense; weak, feverish (si; su_3; sa_5, 'to be full; to grow weak', + $ir_{(10)}$, 'sweat').

sir_3
(cf., $šir_3$).

$^{ĝiš}sir_3$-da
carrying-pole for a litter ('to bind' + 'at the side'; cf., Akk. *sarādu(m)*, 'to tie up, pack').

sir_5; sur
(cf., $zara_5$).

sis
(cf., šeš, ses, sis).

sisi
(cf., anše-kur-ra).

$siškur_{(2)}$, $siskur_{(2)}$, $sizkur_{(2)}$
n., offering, sacrifice with entreaties, prayers, rites.

v., to pray; to sacrifice ($isiš_{2,3}$, 'to weep', + kur_9, 'to bring, deliver'; cf., i-si-iš...ĝar).

siškur...e
to say a prayer [often introduces direct, quoted speech in the texts] ('prayer' + 'to speak').

su
n., body; flesh; skin; animal hide; relatives; substitute [SU archaic frequency: 188; concatenates 2 sign variants].

v., (cf., sug_6; rug_2; $su_{(3)}$).

adj., naked.

^{lu2}SU
Subarian (cf., šubur).

^{tug2}SU.A
(cf., $^{tug2}aktum_2$).

su-a
(cf., sa_2).

su-a
cat (cf., sa-a and sur_{12}).

su-ba
(cf., sub_6).

su-bar
n., external body, exterior; adopted child; an illness (su, 'body', + bar, 'exterior/ foreign'; cf., šubur, subar).

v., to adopt.

su-bir_4^{ki}
Assyria; upper Mesopotamia (Akkadian *subartu, šubarīum*).

su-$buru_2$
quicksand, quagmire ('to immerse' + 'to dissolve, loosen'; cf., ĝiš-$buru_2$, 'trap').

su-din
butterfly; part of a wagon or plow (cf., ^{ĝiš}šudun).

su-din(-dal/$dara_2$)^{mušen}
bat ('body' + 'to cure'; Akk. *s/šu(t)tinnu*, 'bat; flying fox - a species of fruit bat'; *argabu*).

SU-ga
replaced, returned (perfect aspect) (cf., rug_2; sug_6).

su-gu_7/ku_2
famine; shortage; starvation (cf., kuš-gu_7/ku_2) ('body, flesh' + 'to eat, consume').

su-gug
mole; a skin problem, such as birthmark or scar (read kuš-gug ?) ('skin' + 'brand, birthmark, mole').

su-la_2-a
salted or cured meat ('flesh' + 'to hang' + nominative).

su-lim
terrifying appearance; awesome radiance; splendor (cf., i-lim; Akk. *rašubbatu(m)*; *šalummatu(m)*).

$su_{(11)}$-lum...mar
to disgrace, treat with contempt, mock ('body' + 'manure' + 'to coat, apply'; cf., sulummar).

su-lum-mar
insult; disgrace; slander; derision; suspicion (cf., sulummar).

su$_{(2)}$-mu-ug(-ga)
misery, trouble, distress; skin cancer (?) ('flesh' + ('my' + 'fury;storm')/('eyesore') ?).

adj., dark; darkened.

(lu2)su-si-ig
knacker, a year round collector of hides and other parts of dead/dying animals, who partly tanned the hides before bringing them into town for use in other crafts ('body' + 'to strike down; to silence'; cf., sig$_3$, 'to strike, hurt, beat, flatten, remove, divide'; Akkadian *šušikku* or *šusikkum*).

su...sig$_3$[PA]
to tremble ('body' + 'to totter, shake, quake').

su-su
to be replaced (imperfect aspect) (cf., rug$_2$; sug$_6$).

su-tab$_2$
burning sensation ('flesh' + 'to burn, be inflamed').

su-tin
(cf., su-din).

su-ub
v., to wipe off, clean (cf., sub$_6$).

adj., cleansed.

su-ul-su-ul
(cf., ĝiri$_3$ su-ul-su-ul).

su...zig$_3$/zi
to have/give gooseflesh, goose bumps; to be afraid of (with -da-) ('flesh' + zig$_3$, zi, 'to stand up, rise').

su-zi(-g)
terror; awe.

su-zig$_3$/zi...dug$_8$
to be terrified; to be terrifying ('terror; gooseflesh' + 'to amass; to adorn; to loosen').

su-zig$_3$/zi...ri
to be terrified; to be terrifying ('terror; gooseflesh' + 'to put into').

su$_2$
(cf., zu)

su$_{(3)}$
to immerse; to sink, submerge; to drown; to suffer shipwreck; to fill up; to march in procession (cf., su$_3$, sud, sug$_4$) (for semantics, cf., ab-su$_3$-na, 'irrigation furrow').

su$_3$
to sprinkle, splash, splatter; to strew (reduplication class) [SU$_3$ archaic frequency: 6].

su$_3$-a
long (?); full, plush (?) (said of cloth).

su$_3$(-ud/ra$_2$)-aĝa$_2$
n., diamond ?; electrum ?; brass ? amber ? ('to be lasting; to rejoice' + 'to measure, check').

adj., brilliant; translucent.

su$_3$-ga
deceitful(ly) (cf., sug$_4$).

su$_3$-gan
flux agent for metal smelting, such as borax ?.

su$_{(3)}$-ḫe$_2$[GAN]
a type of copper; slag, dross after smelting bronze; borax (?) powder ('to stretch' + 'to support').

su$_3$-la
a not-yet understood technical term describing plots of land (hosting grain crops).

su$_3$-ra$_2$
far-reaching; forever ('far away' + ř phoneme in sud + locative postposition).

su$_{(3)}$-ud
(cf., sud/su$_3$ and sud$_4$).

su_3-ud-g̃al_2
extended, long-lasting; patient ('distant; long in duration' + 'being').

su_4
to grow; to multiply (cf., si_4, su_4, sa_{11}).

su_5
(cf., $suḫ_5$).

su_6
(cf., sun_4).

su_6-mu_2
bearded ('beard' + 'to sprout, appear').

su_6-nam-ti-la
beard of life ('beard' + 'life' + genitive).

su_6-za-gin_3(-na)
lapis lazuli (-colored) beard; clean beard ('beard' + 'lapis lazuli; clean' + genitive; might be some wordplay with Akk. *ziqnu*, 'beard').

su_7
(cf., sur_{12}).

$^{gi}su_7$-su_7
a basket (reduplicated 'threshing floor').

su_8
(cf., sug_2, sub_2).

su_{11}
(cf., zu_2).

su_{11}...li_9-li_9
(read as zu_2...bir_9-bir_9).

su_{11}-lum
(cf., zu_2-lum(-ma)).

su_{13}
(cf., sud_4).

su_x [TAG]
(cf., sub_6).

sub; su-ub
to suck; to suckle; to clog; to bless; to pray (naked flesh + open container).

SUB-ma
(cf., sim_x[KA×GA]-ma).

$sub_{2/3}$
(cf., sipad).

sub_2-ba, su_8-ba
Emesal dialect for sipad, 'shepherd' ('to lead out, pasture, tend' + nominative).

sub_2, sug_2, su_8
to lead out, guide; to pasture, tend; to stand; to travel (suppletion class verb: plural *marû* su_8-be_2, said of two or more, such as a herd; cf., also du, g̃en, re_7).

sub_6, su_x [TAG]
to spread on, wipe, rub, caulk with, such as with pitch/bitumen.

subar
(cf., šubur).

sud, su_3(-d); su
v., to be/make remote, far away, lasting; to stretch; to extend, hold out; to sip; to wag (a tail); to furnish, provide; to help, assist (from Akk., *suddu*, 'care, maintenance') (reduplication class) (regularly followed by ra_2) (su_4, 'to grow up, multiply', + ed_2, 'to go out').

adj., distant, remote; subterranean; long (duration).

SUD-
(cf., su_3).

SUD-la
a quality of the ground ('to sprinkle, immerse' + 'freshness').

sud_2
to pound, crush; to gnash (the teeth) (su_9, 'red ochre', + motion).

sud_4, su_{13}
v., to be long; to prolong, lengthen; to last; to wear a long beard; to give, present (regularly followed by ra_2) (narrow line + repetitive process) [BU: archaic frequency: 393; concatenation of 2 sign variants].

adj., long.

^{d}suena, ^{d}suen[EN.ZU]
the moon (su$_2$, 'knowledge', + en$_{2,3}$, 'time', + -/ak/, 'of').

sug
marsh, swamp; flood basin; lake; fertile land (to fill, inundate + eg$_2$, 'levee, dike') [SUG archaic frequency: 15].

sug-zag-ge$_4$...gu$_7$
to destroy ('swamp' + 'territory' + locative/terminative + 'to swallow up, finish off').

sug$_2$, su$_8$
to stand; to be deployed, set up; to be present (suppletion class verb: plural stem; cf., gub, sub$_2$) (su, 'body' + 'long and neck-like').

sug$_4$, su$_3$(-g)
v., to strip naked, lay bare; to rejoice, feel delight; to be full of; to cut clear; to empty (su, 'body/naked' + ig, 'entrance'; cp, mug$_{(2)}$, 'nakedness').

adj., empty, vacant, destitute, desolate.

sug$_5$[GIN$_2$]
to bring low; to knock down (also read dun$_3$, du$_5$ with this meaning) (cf., tun$_3$) (si, 'to stand upright' + ug$_{5,7,8}$, 'to kill'; cf., sig$_{3,10,11,18}$) [SUG$_5$ archaic frequency: 67].

sug$_6$, su(-ga)
to compensate, repay, replace, restore, return (a loan, etc.) (reduplication class: su-su) (Akk., *riābu(m)*, 'to replace, requite') (to fill up + entrance, chamber).

sug$_7$
(cf., zug$_4$).

sug$_8$
(cf., sur$_{12}$).

sug̃in
(cf., sumun).

suḫ[MUŠ$_2$]; suḫ$_5$, su$_5$[KU]
n., encircling wall (cf., $^{g̃iš}$u$_3$-suḫ$_5$).

v., to uproot; to tear out or off; to relocate, transfer; to choose.

adj., carefully chosen; precious.

suḫ$_3$, saḫ$_4$
n., confusion, disorder, chaos (cf., zaḫ$_{2,3}$, saḫ$_{6,7}$, 'lost') [SUḪ$_3$ archaic frequency: 4].

v., to be or make troubled, confused, blurred, tangled, twisted.

suḫ$_4$, saḫ
reed matting (part of a door) (fine, narrow + plant + numerous).

suḫ$_5$-ḫa
choice (?) (applied to a high grade of onions) ('to choose' + adjectival -a).

suḫ$_{10}$[MUŠ$_3$]; suḫ[MUŠ$_2$]
hairpin, hair clasp, barrette; turban worn by farmers of the high plain, which became the headgear of the en-priestess or priest; diadem, crown; crest ('long, thin things' + 'abundance'; cf., sun$_4$, 'beard') [MUŠ$_3$ archaic freq.: 284; concat. 2 sign variants].

suḫ$_{10}$-kar$_2$-kara$_2$-ka
shining crown ('diadem' + 'to encircle; to shine').

$^{(na4)}$suḫ$_{(10)}$-giri$_{11}$, suḫ$_{(10)}$-kiri$_7$[KEŠDA]
hair ornament, equipment (cf., suḫ$_{10}$/suḫ; $^{g̃iš}$kirid, giri$_{11}$) ('hair clasp' + 'to tidy, make neat, bind up'; Akk., *tiqnu(m)*, 'equipment for putting in good order').

suḫirin[SU$_7$.SUM]
the threshing floor with the piles of grain and straw (su$_7$, 'threshing floor', + ḫirin, 'sweet smelling grass').

$^{(kuš)}$suḫub$_2$[MUL], šuḫub$_2$; šuḫub[ŠU$_2$.MUL]
n., boot(s); sandal(s) (su, 'animal hide', + ḫub$_2$, 'a type of weaver'; gub, 'to stand').

v., to step; to feed by grazing; to trample.

$^{\tilde{g}iš}$suḫub$_4$[ŠU.DI.IŠ]; $^{\tilde{g}iš}$suḫub$_5$[ŠU.GA]
bar, bolt (of a door) (cf., $^{\tilde{g}iš}$saḫab; $^{\tilde{g}iš}$šu-gi) (sag̃, 'head', + ḫub, 'hole, recess'; cf., $^{\tilde{g}iš}$sag̃-kul; $^{\tilde{g}iš}$sag̃-kul$_2$/gul, 'lock bolt').

suḫur
n., hair, scalp; tree top; crest (su$_6$, 'beard', + ḫe, 'abundant', + ur$_3$, 'roof'; cf., suḫuš) [SUḪUR archaic frequency: 239].

v., to trim or comb the hair; to scratch; to make an incision or insertion.

suḫur$^{(ku6)}$
giant carp, barbel; split, dried fish.

^{MUNUS}suḫur-la$_2$
prostitute ('hair' + 'to lift, bind; minus').

suḫur-maš$_{(2)}$^{ku6}
a type of carp - goat-fish ('carp' + 'goat').

suḫur-sun$_4$-la$_2$^{ku6}
barbel - bearded carp ('carp' + 'beard' + 'to hang').

suḫur-tun$_3$(-bar)(-gal)$^{(ku6)}$
giant carp or barbel ('carp' + 'mustache').

suḫuš, suḫ$_6$
roots; support, foundation; nest, lair, homestead; to lift; support (su$_4$, 'to grow, multiply', + ḫe, 'abundant', + uš, 'to support'; cf., suḫur).

sukkal
messenger, courier, envoy, representative; especially by Ur III period: minister, vizier, major-domo (a career step towards becoming šabra) (su, 'body', + kalag/kal, 'strong, swift') [SUKKAL archaic frequency: 130].

sukkal-maḫ
vizier, prime minister, 'minister of the interior' ('minister' + 'grand').

suku$_5$
(cf., sukud$_2$).

sukud; zugud
n., height; depth (su, 'body', + gid$_2$, 'long') [SUKUD archaic frequency: 15].

v., to be/make high.

adj., high; tall; eminent.

sukud$_2$, suku$_5$
to measure, distribute; to flash, shine brightly (cf., zu$_2$...kud/ku$_5$).

sul
(cf., šul).

sul$_2$
(cf., zal).

sul$_3$
(cf., sun$_4$).

sul$_4$
(cf., sur$_{12}$).

^{u2}sullim[BURU$_{14}$]^{sar}
a wasteland fodder crop, either chickling vetch (grass pea) or fenugreek.

sulug, zulug[LUL]
to be bright, shine (cf., zalag).

suluḫu
(cf., zulumḫi).

suluḫu$_3$
(cf., zulumḫi$_3$).

sulummar[KI.SAG̃.DU]
insult; disgrace; slander; derision; suspicion (cf., su$_{(11)}$-lum...mar).

sum, šum$_2$, sim$_2$, si$_3$(-m)
to give; to lend, entrust, turn over to (with dative) (occasionally replaces sam$_2$) (sum-mu in *marû*) (cf., sam$_2$) [SUM archaic frequency: 43; concatenates 2 sign variants].

sum, šum$_2$$^{(sar)}$
garlic; onion; bulb (Akkadian loanword from *šūmu*, 'garlic', related to *šammu*, 'plant, drug, medicine', Orel & Stolbova 2185, **sam-**, 'poison'; cf, šim).

sum-babbar
light onion ('onion' + 'white').

sum-dilmun
a type of onion during the preSargonic period ('onion' + 'honored').

sum-GAM.GAM
a rare type of onion from the Old Akkadian period ('onion' + redup. 'depth; to bend or shrivel').

sum-gar$_4$[GUD]
spring onion ('onion' + 'early').

sum-gaz
a common type of onion, probably the red onion, 'onion suitable for crushing' ('onion' + 'powder').

sum-g̃išimmar
a type of onion, earlier name for sum-sag$_9$ ('onion' + 'date palm').

sum-ḫa-din
(cf., za-ḫa-ti/din).

sum-ḫuš(-a)^{sar}
red onion; turnip (cf., sum-gaz; lu-ub$_2$^{sar}) ('onion' + 'to be fiery red'; Akk., *zimzimmu*, 'a red onion'; *laptu(m) II*, 'turnip').

$^{(u2)}$sum-kur^{sar}
a bulbous vegetable, term found only in Pre-Sargonic texts ('onion' + 'foreign'; Akk., *a'uššu(m)* etc.).

sum-sag$_9$
a type of onion ('onion' + 'good, pleasing').

sum-sikil
a common type of white onion, used for onion soup ('onion' + 'pure, bright').

sum-šir
garlic ('onion' + 'testicles').

sum-šir-dili
a single clove of garlic ('onion' + 'testicle' + 'single').

SUM-tab-ba
(cf., zar$_3$-tab-ba).

sum-TU.LU$_2$
a type of onion.

sum-us$_2$
second-class onions ('onion' + 'to follow; second-class').

sum-za-ḫa-ti/din
(cf., za-ḫa-ti/din).

sum$_4$
(cf., sun$_4$).

sum$_5$[ZIB reversed]
pauper; poor.

sumaš
a common marine fish [SUMAŠ archaic frequency: 3].

sumug$_{(3,4,5)}$, samag$_{(3,4,5)}$
mole; birthmark (su, 'flesh', + mug, 'to engrave; sty').

sumun, sug̃in, sun, šum$_4$[TIL]
n., rot, decay; something rotten; the past (su, 'body', + g̃in, 'to go'; cf., Akk., *sunginnu* > *sumkīnu*, 'rot, decay') [? ZATU-644 archaic frequency: 65; concatenation of 2 sign variants].

v., to decay; to ruin.

adj., old; used; ancient; dry, brittle.

$^{(u2)}$SUMUN.DAR
(cf., $^{(u2)}$šumunda).

^{lu2}sumun-gi$_{(4)}$
a profession that salvaged old wood from demolition ('decayed' + 'to restore').

sumun$_2$
(cf., sun$_2$).

sumur, šur$_2$, sur$_2$
n., fierceness (Akkadian loanword - *šamru*, 'fierce, enraged, wild') [ŠUR$_2$ archaic frequency: 17; concatenates 2 sign variants].

v., to be enraged (against someone: -da-).

adj., fierce; furious; impetuous; wild; stubborn.

sumur$_{(2/3)}$
roof, shelter (su,'body', + mur, 'to enclose, guard, protect').

sun
(cf., sumun).

sun_2
a shaggy-maned wild aurochs or bison; wild cow; a vessel for moistening malt grains; germinated, sprouted 'green' malt (cf., sun_4, 'bearded').

sun_2-si-mu_2
horned (or male) wild aurochs ('aurochs' + 'horned').

sun_4, sum_4, sul_3, su_6[KA×SA]
beard; chin; lower lip; fiber, thread (cf., si, 'long, thin things', and tun_3, 'lip') [SU_6 archaic frequency: 1; BU_3 archaic frequency: 21].

sun_5[BUR_2], su_{16}
n., modesty.

v., to enter (suppletion class verb ?: plural ?; cf., kur_9) (used as verb, see also dun_5).

adj., humble; with bowed head; dominated (su_9, 'to mourn, grieve' + ni_2, 'fear; respect').

sun_5-na-bi
adv., humbly ('modesty' + adverbial force suffix).

sun_7[KAL]
n., quarrel, discord.

v., to quarrel; to be arrogant; to try to control.

adj., arrogant, haughty, presumptuous.

sur
n., a garden plant; rushes; chaff, chopped straw; onion planting process [? SUR archaic frequency: 6].

v., to delimit, bound, divide, mark off, demarcate (reduplication class ?) (cf., šur) (si, 'long and narrow', + ur, 'to surround'; cf., sila, sil; sil_2, zil; si-il, 'to cut into, divide'; us_2-sa-ra_2, 'boundary').

sur_2
(cf., sumur).

sur_2-du_3[mušen], $šur_2$-du_3[mušen]
(trained) falcon - scared birds away from the crops ('fierce' + 'to work').

sur_3
ditch; deep furrow; drain (to fill, inundate + to flow; contrast sug, 'flood basin').

sur_5, $suru_5$
to hang, suspend, dangle; to hover; to wear (cf., $sur_{6,7}$; $usur_4$/$ušur_4$).

$sur_{6,7}$
height; depth; foundation pit; ditch; mound (us_2, uš, 'height; foundation; to support, lift', + $uru_{2,5,18}$, 'high, deep'; cf., $usur_4$/$ušur_4$).

sur_8
(cf., zar).

sur_9[MA_2.KASKAL.SIG_7]
(cf., surru, sur_9).

sur_{12}, sug_8, sul_4, su_7
threshing floor; grain pile; a small animal (cf., su-a/sa-a, 'cat').

surim
(cf., šurim).

surru, sur_9[MA_2.KASKAL.SIG_7]
a lamentation priest (cf., [ĝiš]al-ĝar-sur_9, 'plectrum for harp ?').

susbu[$MUŠ_2$.BU]
clean, bathed; an ablution or cleaning priest.

suš
to sit down; to reside (su, 'body, relatives', + $uš_8$, 'foundation place, base'; cf., tuš).

$suš_2$[NI]
n., fat, grease.

v., to rub, anoint (su, 'body', + eš, 'to anoint').

Š

ša
to dry up [ŠA archaic frequency: 97].

ša
a fraction of the weight measure, ma-na, *mina*.

ša-
contrapunctive modal prefix meaning 'correspondingly', 'for my part, for your part, for his part' in OB period texts - ThSLa §404-§408 ('hand; portion').

ša-
modal prefix /ša-/ with conjugation prefix /ĩ-/ in OB period - ThSLa §304.

ša-an-gu
(Akkadian spelling of sağğa).

ša-an-ša-ša
(cf., šu...ša-an-ša-ša).

ša-aš
reduplicated $\check{s}a_5$ or $\check{s}a_6$.

ša...de_5[RI]
Emesal dialect for na...de_5, 'to give advice'.

ša-dug_4-ga/ba
last night; yesterday ('to dry up' + 'utterance'; but cf., sa_2...dug_4/du_{11}/de_3/e, 'to reach, arrive; to succeed').

(ğiš/uruda)ša-ga-ru
a precious wood or copper object (Akkadian *šakarûm*).

ša-ku_8-ul-tum
divine meal (from Akkadian *šūkultu*, 'meal, banquet').

ša-ne-$\check{s}a_4$[DU]
(cf., $\check{s}a_3$-ne-$\check{s}a_4$).

ša-ra
syllabic spelling for $\check{s}ar_2$-ra, 'numerous'.

ša-ra(-g)
to dry up, wither, e.g., palm fronds ('to dry up' + 'inundation').

ša-ra-ab-du
(cf., $\check{s}ar_2$-ra-ab-du).

ša...RI
(cf., ša...de_5[RI]).

ša-ru-mi-um
a rare breed of foreign sheep found exclusively in texts from Drehem.

$\check{s}a_3$
(cf., $\check{s}ag_4$).

$\check{s}a_3$-
contrapunctive modal prefix ša- in late period texts - ThSLa §404.

$\check{s}a_3$-a-bar-ra
bastard ('womb' + locative or 'seed' + 'to be foreign' + nominative).

$\check{s}a_3$-ab
Emesal dialect for $\check{s}ag_4$, 'heart'.

$\check{S}A_3$.AB_2
creation ('womb' + 'cow').

$\check{s}a_3$ NOUN-ak-a
in the heart of, in - ThSLa §159.

$\check{s}a_3$-ba
adj., pregnant ('womb' + 'in its').

$\check{s}a_3$-ba
prep., in; among; from (them) ('midst' + 'its' + locative).

$\check{s}a_3$-ba-tuku
padded, thick; soft; one of several rubrics or interpolated titles for part of a hymn ('having in its womb').

$\check{s}a_3$-bal-bal
descendant, offspring ('womb' + reduplicated 'to revolve, deliver').

$\check{s}a_3$...bala
to breed ('womb' + 'to revolve, deliver').

$\check{s}a_3$-bala-a
'within the bala' - describes goods paid by a worker to the state as a bala contribution.

^{ku6}**ša$_3$-bar**
cleaned fish ('intestines' + 'to cut open, remove').

ša$_3$-bi SU-ga
(capital or disbursements) to be returned ('contents' + 'its' + 'replaced, returned').

ša$_3$-bi-ta
therefrom, thereof, of it; deducted from the state-bestowed capital debt (usually precedes account of credit transactions followed by zi-ga[-am$_3$]) ('contents' + 'its' + 'from').

ša$_3$-da
voluntarily ('heart' + 'with').

ša$_3$...dab$_{(5)}$
to feel hurt; to be angry; to be worried ('heart, stomach' + 'to clench, constrict').

ša$_3$-dab$_{(2/5)}$
wrath, anger; thickening, constriction.

ša$_3$...dar
to be afraid; to be heartbroken ('stomach; heart' + 'to slice', cf., ni$_2$...dar).

ša$_3$...de$_5$[RI]; ša$_3$...di
Emesal dialect for na...de$_5$, 'to give advice'.

ša$_3$-DIB
(cf., ša$_3$-dab$_{(2/5)}$ - ignore late pronunciation guide that shows ti-ib).

^{u2}**ša$_3$-dib-še$_3$-ze$_2$-da**
a thorny plant, probably the artichoke, used to increase bile and solve digestive disorders (cf., ^{u2}li-li-bi-zi-da; ša$_3$-lu-ub$_2$-ze$_2$-da) ('insides' + 'to pass' + 'towards' + 'bile'; Akk. *daddaru(m)*; Hebrew *dardar*).

ša$_3$-diğir-re-e-ne
the (secret) will of the gods ('interior; will' + 'gods').

ša$_3$...diri
to overeat ('stomach' + 'to exceed').

ša$_3$-dub-didli
recorded on an individual tablet ('contents' + 'tablet' + 'separate, individual').

ša$_3$...dug$_3$/du$_{10}$
to be satisfied ('heart' + 'to be glad').

ša$_3$-dug$_3$/du$_{10}$(-ga)
a term for young animals; health; breeding (?) ('heart, insides' + 'sweet, good').

$^{tug2/gada}$**ša$_3$-ga-du$_3$**
a woolen or linen cloth belt ('stomach' + nominative + 'to mold, shape').

ša$_3$-gada-lal/la$_2$
linen-clad (priest) ('midst' + 'linen' + 'to drape'; cf., ša$_3$-la$_2$-la$_2$).

ša$_3$-gal
fodder; food, sustenance - especially for conscript workers ('stomach' + 'enlarge').

ša$_3$-gan
physically perfect; able-bodied ('womb' + 'childbearing').

ša$_3$-gi$^{(sar)}$
radish ('heart' + 'to restore'; Akk. *puglu(m)*).

ša$_3$-gi-na
true heart; one's nature ('heart' + 'to be firm, true' + nominative).

ša$_3$-gi$_8$[IGI]-guru$_{6/7}$
a voluntary offering ('heart' + 'eyes' + 'to shine, be bright; grain heap').

ša$_3$-še$_3$...gid$_2$
to bear in mind; to take seriously; to consider carefully ('heart' + 'concerning' + 'to measure, reach out').

ša$_3$-gig-ga
an aching heart; anxiety ('heart' + 'to be sick, painful' + nominative).

ša$_3$-gu
(cf., gu ša$_3$-gu).

ša$_3$-gu$_4$
ox-driver (during plowing) ('midst' + 'oxen').

^{dug}**ša$_3$-gub**
beer-jar, used in the final stage of brewing ('vessel' + 'womb' + 'to stand'; Akk. *šagubbu*, 'a vessel').

ša$_3$...gul-gul
interpret as ša$_3$...gu-ul, 'to expand, exalt' ('heart' + reduplicated 'to enlarge').

ša$_3$-gur(-ru)
relenting, merciful ('heart' + 'to return, relent').

ša$_3$...gur$_4$
to feel wonderful ('heart' + 'to feel big').

ša$_3$(-ge)-guru$_7$
all that one wants; heart's desire; a certain sacrificial prayer ritual (siškur) ('heart, stomach' (+ 'to the') + 'to heap up').

ša$_3$-g̃al$_2$
what is in one's heart, i.e., the heart's desire ('heart' + 'to dwell').

ša$_3$-g̃ar
hunger ('stomach' + 'to deposit', cf., šag̃ar).

ša$_3$-g̃ar...tuku
to be hungry ('hunger' + 'to have').

ša$_3$-g̃ar-g̃ar
great hunger; shortage; starvation ('stomach' + reduplicated 'to deposit').

$^{(g̃iš)}$**ša$_3$-g̃išimmar**
palm-heart ('heart' + 'date-palm').

ša$_3$...ḫug̃
to pacify; to soothe the heart; to appease ('heart' + 'to rest').

ša$_3$-ḫul...dim$_2$
to grieve ('heart' + 'evil' + 'to make').

ša$_3$-ḫul-gig
hatred ('heart' + 'evil' + 'to be sick, painful').

ša$_3$...ḫul$_2$
to be happy ('heart' + 'to rejoice').

ša$_3$-ḫul$_2$-la
n., delight ('heart' + 'to rejoice' + nominative).

adv., joyously.

ša$_3$-ḫul$_2$-la...dirig
to be overflowing with joy ('delight' + 'to exceed').

ša$_3$...ḫun
(cf., ša$_3$...ḫug̃).

ša$_3$-ib$_2$-ba(-/ak/)
anger ('midst' + 'loins' + genitive).

ša$_3$ ka-tab
n., hunger ('stomach' + 'to clog, block').

v., to fast (frequently with verb nud/nu$_2$, 'to lie down').

adj., weak from hunger.

$^{g̃iš}$**ša$_3$-kal**
a type of willow tree; wood used for furniture (chairs, wheels, etc.) and household utensils ('heart' + 'excellent'; Akk. *šakkullu*).

ša$_3$(-ge)...kur$_2$/kar$_2$
to change one's mind ('heart, will, mood' + ergative agent marker + 'to change').

ša$_3$-ki-ag̃a$_2$
a loving heart ('heart' + 'to love' + nominative).

ša$_3$...kuš$_2$(-u$_3$)
v., to rest the heart; to make love to; to take counsel with (with -da-); to advise ('heart' + 'to be tired; to care, worry').

adj., thoughtful, well-informed.

ša$_3$...la$_2$
to (en)gorge, to stuff ('stomach' + 'to extend, load').

ša$_3$-la$_2$...su$_3$(-d)/su$_3$(-g)
to be merciful; to be full of pity ('heart' + 'to extend' + 'far'/'full of ?').

ša$_3$-la$_2$-la$_2$
clothed (cf., ša$_3$-gada-lal).

$\check{s}a_3$-la_2-su_3(-d)
shepherdess ('heart' + 'to extend' + 'far').

adj., merciful.

(tug2/tug2-du8-a) **$\check{s}a_3$-la_2-tum**
a rare type of cloth/textile, of wool or felt - a text describes as for 'a pair of royal chariot wheels' (Akk., *šalāṭu(m) I*, 'to rule, be in authority').

$\check{s}a_3$-lu-ub_2-ze_2-da
a thorny plant, probably the artichoke, used to increase bile and solve digestive disorders (cf., ^{u2}li-li-bi-zi-da; ^{u2}$\check{s}a_3$-dib-$\check{s}e_3$-ze_2-da) ('interior' + 'food pouch' + 'bile'; Akk. *daddaru(m)*; Hebrew *dardar*).

$\check{s}a_3$-maḫ
large intestine; paunch ('intestine' + 'great'; Akk. *šammāḫu*).

$\check{S}A_3$.MIN.TAR; $\check{S}A_3$.MIN.KASKAL; $\check{S}A_3$.MIN.DI
(cf., $tigidla_{(2/3)}$).

$\check{S}A_3\times$NE
(cf., ninim).

$\check{s}a_3$-ne-$\check{s}a_4$[DU]
supplications; compassion ('heart' + 'this' + 'to lament, wail').

$\check{s}a_3$-niĝin
intestines, entrails ('insides' + 'to coil').

$\check{s}a_3$(-ge)...pad_3
to choose ('heart, stomach' (+ 'in the') + 'to find, declare').

$\check{s}a_3$-ra(-aḫ)
lining (Akk. *šarāḫu(m) I*, 'to make splendid' ?).

$\check{s}a_3$...RI
(cf., $\check{s}a_3$...de_5[RI]).

$\check{s}a_3$...$sig_{(3)}$
to be oppressed, depressed; to feel anxious ('heart' + 'to strike, crush').

$\check{s}a_3$-$sig_{(3)}$-ga
a depressed heart; depression; a type of land - starvation land ('heart/stomach' + 'low, small, weak' + nominative).

$\check{s}a_3$-su-ga
dry river bed ('river bed' + sug_4, 'to lay bare, empty' + nominative).

$\check{s}a_3$-su_3(-ga)
hungry; starved; naked; destitute; without recompense; unproductive (fruit tree) ('stomach' + 'empty' + nominative).

$\check{s}a_3$-sud
back, torso (?) ('middle' + 'to stretch').

$\check{s}a_3$-sur
(cf., $\check{s}a_3$-šur; variant of $\check{s}a_3$-tur_3).

$\check{s}a_3$...$\check{s}ed_{7/10}$
to cool/soothe the heart ('heart' + 'to calm, cool down').

$\check{s}a_3$-šu-$ni\tilde{g}in_{(2)}$
pity, mercy ('heart, womb' + 'to quickly return, relent'; cf., $\check{s}a_3$-gur(-ru)).

$\check{s}a_3$...šur
to have diarrhea; to spawn eggs (said of a fish) ('intestines' + 'to expel a liquid').

(gi) **$\check{s}a_3$-šur**
(reed-mat) sieve ('gut-like container' + 'to press out a liquid').

$\check{s}a_3$-tam[UD]
n., administrative director, steward, treasurer, auditor, commissioner ('heart' + 'to be polished').

adj., credible, trustworthy.

$\check{S}A_3$.TAR
(cf., tigidla).

$\check{s}a_3$-$tuku_5$
mattress ('womb' + 'woven, decorated'; cf., etymology of tuku, 'to marry').

$\check{s}a_3$...$tum_{2/3}$
to decide; to plan, plot ('heart' + 'to prepare').

ša$_3$-tum$_2$
field, acre, pasture land ('womb' + 'to be suitable; to prepare; to obtain').

ša$_3$-tur$_3$
womb; millipede (cf., muš-ša$_3$-tur$_3$) ('insides' + 'birth-hut').

ša$_3$-U.NU-a
thread, that has been spun in a less common way (cf., niĝ$_2$-U.NU-a).

ša$_3$-uru(-/ak/)
town center ('interior, midst' + 'town' + genitive).

ša$_3$-zalag-ga
radiant mood; good cheer ('heart, mood' + 'to shine, smile' + nominative).

ša$_3$-zi-ga
excitement; arousal; libido; erection ('heart' + 'to rise up' + nominative).

ša$_3$-zi-ta-e$_3$-a
produced from the true womb ('womb' + 'righteous, true' + 'from' + 'to emerge' + nominative).

$^{(MUNUS/lu2)}$ša$_3$-zu
midwife; man midwife, accoucheur (if not to be read as 'your heart/your interior') ('womb' + 'knowing'; Akkadian *šabsû* and *šabsūtu(m)* must come from Emesal form, cf., ša$_3$-ab).

ša$_4$, še$_{13}$[DU]
to make noise; to lament, wail.

ša$_5$
to cut, break (reeds).

ša$_6$
(cf., sag$_9$).

^{lu2}ša$_{14}$[ĜA$_2$]-dub-ba
archivist; chief accountant (reading of ĜA$_2$ uncertain, cf., Borger MZL III 495; cf., ĝadub; pisaĝ-dub; e$_2$-ša$_3$-dub-ba).

^{dug}šab
bowl; pot; pail; vessel.

šab[PA.IB]
n., middle; stem; cut hair; plucked wool; clay sealing, sealed bulla (cf., sabad; ^{dug}šab) [ŠAB archaic frequency: 61; concatenation of 2 sign variants].

v., to subtract, deduct; to bite off; to snip out, chip out; to trim, peel off; to fall out, disappear; to apportion (lots); to gather up (portion + divide).

šabra, šapra [PA.AL]; šabra$_x$ [PA.É]
manager, administrator of a temple or royal household; prefect; commissioner (Akkadian loanword from *šāpiru(m)*, 'giver of instructions'; > *šabrû(m) I*) [ŠABRA archaic frequency: 1].

šabra-nina$_3$, šabra-nin
manager of the queen's household ('prefect' + 'queen' + genitive).

šag$_4$, ša$_3$
n., intestines; gut; heart; stomach; abdomen; entrails; content; womb; body; interior, middle, midst, inside; bed of a river; will, volition; mood; meaning, significance (grain/excrement + water/urine + chamber) [ŠA$_3$ archaic frequency: 137; concatenates 6 sign variants].

prep., in; within; at.

šag$_4$-X
(look under ša$_3$-X).

šag$_5$
(cf., sag$_9$).

šag$_5$
to slaughter (ša$_5$, 'to cut, break' + ug$_{5,7,8}$, 'to kill').

$^{(dug)}$šagan, šakan, šaman$_2$ [U.GAN]
a large pointed jar for oil; oil cruse, flask, usually with a leather seal or cover; god of wild creatures (šag$_4$/ša$_3$, 'stomach, container', + gan, 'to bring forth') [? ŠAGAN archaic frequency: 55].

šagan-la$_2$
merchant's assistant, apprentice; peddler, trader ('a large jar for oil' + 'to carry').

šaggina, šaggin, šagina, šakkan$_6$
military governor (Akk. *šakkanakku(m)* from *šaknu(m)*, 'placed, deposited; governor') [? ŠAGINA archaic frequency: 1].

šağa, še$_{29}$, ḫeš$_5$[LU$_2$×KAR$_2$; LU$_2$.KAR$_2$]
captive; wronged, oppressed person; detained person (all three readings are equally attested with same meanings) (tied up with a rope eše$_2$; cf., lu$_2$-eše$_2$).

šağan
(cf., šagan, šakan, šaman$_2$).

šağar
hunger (cf., ša$_3$-ğar).

šaḫ$_{(2)}$
domestic pig (grain + water + numerous (offspring) - pigs efficiently turn feed into meat) [ŠAḪ$_2$ archaic frequency: 39; concatenation of 3 sign variants].

šaḫ$_{(2)}$-bar-gun$_3$(-gun$_3$)-nu
porcupine (?) ('pig' + 'outside; fleece' + reduplicated 'dot, speckle'; Akk., *burmāmu(m)*).

šaḫ$_{(2)}$-ğiš-gi$_{(4)}$
"bush pig", wild boar ('pig' + 'reed thicket').

šaḫ$_{(2)}$-ğiš-gi$_{(4)}$(-i$_3$)-gu$_7$-e
porcupine (?) ('bush pig' + 'it eats'; Akk., *burmāmu(m)*).

šaḫ$_{(2)}$-niga
fattened pig ('pig' + 'fattened').

šaḫ$_{(2)}$-tur
piglet ('pig' + 'small').

šaḫ$_{(2)}$-u$_2$
pasture grazing pig ('pig' + 'plants, grass').

šaḫ$_{(2)}$-ze$_2$-da
wild boar (?) ('pig' + 'stench'; cf., the scent glands of the badger, ur-ki).

šaḫ$_{(2)}$-ze$_2$-da-bar-šur-ra
porcupine (?) ('wild boar ?' + 'outside; fleece' + 'to spray out'; Akk., *burmāmu(m)*).

šakan
(cf., šagan).

šakan-keš$_2$
basket weaver (?) ('large jar for oil', + 'to bind, wrap').

šakan$_2$, šakkan$_2$ [ĞIR$_3$]
an official in charge of checking expenditures - comptroller, auditor; may be a temporary function, not a formal title; "carried out under the supervision of", via (cf., šaggina).

šakar
milk jug (šag$_4$/ša$_3$, 'stomach, container', + kir, 'cow').

^{u2}šakira$_{(3)}$, šakir$_{(3)}$
alkaloid-rich henbane - makes beer more inebriating (loan from Akk. *šakirû(m)* from *šakāru*, 'to be(come) drunk').

^{dug}šakira$_{(3)}$, šakir$_{(3)}$
butter tub, churn; churning; pitcher (šag$_4$/ša$_3$, 'stomach, container', + kir, 'cow' + /ak/, genitive) [ŠAKIRA$_3$ archaic frequency: 56; concatenates 3 sign variants].

šakkan$_6$
(cf., šaggina).

šal
(cf., sal).

šal$_2$
(cf., sila$_3$).

šam$_2$
(cf., sam$_2$).

šaman$_2$
(cf., šagan).

šanabi
two-thirds (cf., šušana) (loan from Akkadian *šinipu*).

šandana
(cf., santana).

šapra
(cf., šabra).

šar
(cf., sar, šar).

$šar_2$, sar_2
n., totality, all; world; horizon; ball, counter, token; the number 3600 = 60^2; an area measure (many, much + ar_3, 'ring, coil').

v., to be many; to multiply or mix (with -da-); to make abundant; to slaughter; to request, implore (reduplication class).

adj., numerous; innumerable (cf., ḫi/ḫe).

$^{lu2}šar_2$
a military officer = commander of 3600.

$ŠAR_2$-da
(cf., ḫi-a; ḫi-da).

$šar_2$ du_{11}-ge $gilib_x$
to block impenetrably ('to be many' + 'to effect' + 'to cross, bar, block').

$šar_2$-gaz
a divine weapon ('many' + 'to smash, slay').

$šar_2$-$g̃al_2$
a weapon (?) ('many' + 'to be on hand; to guard, protect').

$šar_2$-ra-ab-$du_{(3/8)}$
a temple official; captain (of a boat) ('many' + 'to install, drive in'; cf., *šarrabtû*, 'an official; an underworld demon').

$šar_2$-$šar_2$
to multiply; to mix; to interchange.

$šar_2$-ur_3
a divine weapon (depicted as a bird ?) ('many' + 'to mow down').

$šar_3$[LUGAL]
royal; the best quality of cloth.

$šar_3$-ra-us_2-sa
body guard (from Akkadian *šarru*, 'king', + 'to follow' + nominative; cf., $ag̃a_2$-us_2, 'policeman, soldier').

$šar_8$[NI]
to interpret, explain.

$šar_x$[NE]
a designation of cows.

šarag[UD](-g)
(cf., ša-ra(-g)).

šaran; šarin
tick, bedbug ($šar_2$, 'to be numerous', + in, 'straw').

šardiš, šarg̃eš[$ŠAR_2$×DIŠ; ḪI×DIŠ]; $šargal_x$[$ŠAR_2$×GAL]
'216000'.

šassuk[SAG̃.GIN_2]
registrar of deeds (Akk., *šassukku(m)*, 'accountant', from *šasû(m)*, 'to read (out)' ?).

še
n., barley; generic word for any grain, like British 'corn'; a small length measure, barleycorn = 1/6 finger = 1/30 cubit = 1.67 centimeter in Presarg.-OB period; as a surface area measure = 432 square linear barleycorns = 12 square fingers; as a volume measure = 1/180 gin_2 = 1/3 gin_2-tur = 1 2/3 $sila_3$ = 360 cubic fingers = 1/10800 sar = approx. 1.667 liters; 1/180 of a gin_2 or shekel of silver = ca. 0.0463 grams (cf., še-ga/ge) [ŠE archaic frequency: 639; concatenates 3 sign variants].

v., to agree, be in agreement (cf., še-ga/ge).

adj., (cf., niga).

Emesal dialect form of izi, 'fire; incense', although normal Emesal for 'fire' is mu.

-še-; -še
demonstrative element, may indicate 'there', within the view of the speaker; 'this one here' - ThSLa §133, §136.

še-A
(cf., še-$duru_5$).

še-a-ba-aḫ-ši-in
grain harvested at an early stage of ripening (for roasting, soups, etc.) (cf.,

še-za-gin$_3$-duru$_5$) (from Akkadian *abaḫšinnu(m)*, 'stalk; an edible commodity').

še-a-ta-du$_8$-a
barley from reclaimed land ('barley' + 'reclaimed').

še ag̃
(cf., še g̃iš-e$_3$-a).

še amar-ra(-še$_3$)
barley fodder given to cultivators for young animals assigned to their care, in the amount of 120 liters/year for oxen calves and either 90 or 60 liters/year for donkey foals ('barley' + 'calf, young animal' + dative + terminative).

še-an-še
'ear' of grain ('barley, grain' + 'grain ear').

še-ba
barley/food rations distributed by the administration of the temple, palace, etc. ('barley' + 'portion, rations'; Akk., *ipru(m)*, 'ration, subsistence allowance').

še-ba
to be careless, negligent (cf., šub; šab, 'to fall, disappear').

še-bal
barley lost in processing; grain tax ('barley' + 'to demolish').

še-bala-a; ^{lu2}še-bal-la$_2$
barley winnowing - a manpower intensive activity right before hauling the barley into the granary - probably scooping and tossing the threshed barley from one pile to another to sort out small rocks, sand, and chaff; winnower; exchange ('barley' + 'to turn over' + nominative; Akk. *mušēlû*, 'that raises'; *šupêltu(m)*, 'exchange').

še-bar
grain; barley; cereals in general ('barley' + 'to divide, peel; naked').

še-bi
value-equivalence in barley (used as a standard) (cf., še kaš) ('barley' + 'its').

še-bi(-da)
n., shortfall; loss; negligence; crime (cf., še-ba, 'to be careless').

v., to act negligently, carelessly; to disdain.

adj., negligent.

še-bulug-ba-ti-la
grain whose growth is completed.

še-bur$_2$-ra
grain released for transport, storage, and further distribution ('barley' + 'to open, release').

še...de$_2$
to clean barley after winnowing ('barley, grain' + 'to pour').

še-du$_3$-a
describes grain that has arrived at the stage of the ear on the stalk ('grain' + 'to erect' + nominative).

še du$_3$-a
filling up sacks or baskets with barley ('grain' + 'to stack' + nominative).

$^{g̃iš}$še-du$_3$-a
shoot, sprout, seedling, sapling; licorice plant and root ('tree; wood' + 'flowering stalk').

$^{g̃iš}$še-dug$_3$/du$_{10}$
'sweet corn tree', probably Acacia tree, source of Arabic gum used to give body to licorice candy; the only tree used to make pana/ban, 'bows' ('corn' + 'sweet').

še-duru$_5$[A]
green barley (cf., še-za-gin$_3$-duru$_5$).

še...e$_3$
(cf., še g̃iš-e$_3$-a).

še-eb
Emesal dialect for šeg$_{12}$/sig$_4$, 'brick; brickwork'.

še-en
Emesal dialect for sim, sin_2^mušen^, 'swallow' bird; for saĝ, 'head'; for nin, 'lady'; for nin_9, 'sister'; for $niĝ_2$, 'thing'.

še-er
Emesal dialect for nir.

še-er...$ĝal_2$/$ĝa_2$-al
to have authority (Emesal dialect for nir...$ĝal_2$).

še-er; še(-er)-še-er
shine, light, glimmer (syllabic spelling of $šer_2$, 'to shine brightly').

še-er-da
Emesal dialect for $šer_7$-da.

še-er-du_8-na(-k)
part of a shaft (of a wagon or sledge) (cf., (eše2)$šer_7$).

še-er-gu/kum
a long string of dried fruit (figs or apples) (attested from Old Akkadian to Old Babylonian periods) (note Emesal pap-še-er = 'rope; string (of dried fruit)' and Emesal še-er = nir = 'to stretch').

še-er-ḫu-lum
a lightweight refined gold or silver item - necklace bead (Akk. *šurḫullu*, 'a gold or silver bead').

še-er-ka-an...dug_4/du_{11}/di/e
to cover with; to adorn, decorate, embellish (with -ni-) ($šar_2$, 'to be many' + gun_3, 'to decorate with colors' + 'to effect').

še-er-tab-ba
haystack, cornstack; a type of reed fence or enclosure ($šar_2$, 'to be many' or zar_2, 'sheaf' + 'to bind, join' + nominative).

še-er-zid
splendor; radiance; ripeness; tendrils (of a ripe cucumber plant) ('shine' + 'good, true').

še-eštub
a springtime cereal, perhaps einkorn wheat, often paired in the texts with še-muš$_{(5)}$ ('grain' + 'carp/early flood'; cf., a-eštub^(ku6)^).

še-ga/ge
n., favorite; consent.

v., to be obedient; to obey; to agree (with -ši-); to consent (cf., sig_{10}/se_3(-g)).

še-GAZ
crushed barley ('barley' + 'to crush').

še-gibil
new grain ('grains' + 'new, fresh').

še-gin_2
glue; colored dye-paste; varnish; paint, dye (measured by weight) ('grains' + 'to bind', cf., ma_2-tun_3[GIN_2]).

še-gu-nu; še-gun_3(-nu)
fine grains, good crops, late barley ('grains, barley' + $gunu_3$, 'to be good, beautiful'; Akk. *šegu(n)nû(m)*, 'grain crop').

še-gu_2
a kind of vegetable (?), measured in gur ('barley' + 'pulse/legume').

še-gub-ba
barley deposit; rent paid for a field ('barley' + 'to stand, set' + nominative).

še-GUD
(cf., še-eštub).

še gud(-ra_2) gu_7
grain spent as oxen feed ('barley' + 'bull, ox' (+ dative) + 'to feed').

še-gur_{10}-ku_5
(cf., še-sag_{11}-ku_5).

^iti^še-gur_{10}-ku_5
(cf., ^iti^še-sag_{11}-ku_5).

še $ĝa_6$-$ĝa_2$
barley carrying (in texts from Umma) ('barley' + 'to carry' + nominative).

še...ĝar
to sow barley; to buy with barley ('barley' + 'to deliver, deposit').

še-g̃ar
barley delivery ('barley' + 'to deliver, deposit').

še g̃iš-e$_3$-a
harvested grain that has just been threshed and only roughly measured with a stick; barley that is being winnowed (?) ('grain + 'stick' + 'to exit from' + nominative; cf., $^{g̃iš}$g̃idru).

še-g̃iš-i$_3$, še-i$_3$-g̃iš
sesame seeds; sesame oil; sesame was an off-season summer crop that was harvested in the fall, the red sesame seeds are high in oil but bitter, while the white sesame seeds are sweet ('grain' + 'tree' + 'oil').

še g̃iš...ra(-an/aḫ)
to thresh grain by beating with a flail ('grain' + 'stick' + 'to strike').

še-$^{g̃iš}$ḫa-lu-ub$_2$
acorn ('corn' + 'oak').

še-ḪAR-ra
(cf., še-ur$_5$-ra).

ŠE.ḪU
(cf., us, uz).

^{iti}še-il$_2$-la
calendar month 12 at Lagaš during Ur III.

še-in-nu-ḫa
a kind of cereal, said to come from the mountains ('grain + 'straw' + 'various'; Akk., *ennēnu(m)*).

^{iti}še-kar-ra-g̃al$_2$-la
calendar month 3 at Umma during Ur III.

še kaš
barley for making beer (cf., še-bi) ('barley' + 'beer').

še-KIN-ku$_5$
(cf., še-sag$_{11}$-ku$_5$; ŠE.KIN has a reading gur$_x$, 'to harvest' - cf., $^{(uruda)}$gur$_{10}$; gur$_x$).

še...ku$_5$
to reap, harvest; to cut barley; to hull barley (?) ('barley; grain' + 'to cut off').

še-kud-da
a parched grain product; pot barley or pearl barley (?) ('barley; grain' + 'to cut off, breach, separate').

še-kur-ra
a very rare cereal, perhaps 'foreign grain' (grown on an estate belonging to the head of state) ('barley; grain' + 'mountain; foreign land' + genitive).

še...la$_2$
to load or carry grain; to winnow grain ('grain' + 'to lift').

še-li
pine or juniper/cedar seeds ('grain corn' + 'juniper').

^{u2}še-li-a
rice ('plant' + 'seeds' + 'water'; Akk. *kurangu*).

še-lu$_2$$^{(sar)}$
coriander, a 1 to 3 feet high plant, the tiny round fruit of which ripens in August (often called 'seeds') ('seed' + 'many'; Akk. *kisibirrītu(m)*) [ŠELU archaic frequency: 28].

še-lum-lum
barley sprouts ('grain corn' + reduplicated 'fertilizer, manure').

še mu$_2$-a
standing crop, sprouted barley ('barley, grain' + 'growths').

še-munu$_4$
malt barley.

še-mur
Emesal dialect for nimur, 'kiln, charcoal, ashes'.

še-mur-gu$_4$
barley to be eaten by cattle ('barley' + 'fodder').

še-muš $_{(5)}$
a rare type of grain, 'bitter' barley, often paired in the texts with še-eštub ('grain' + 'bitter'; Akk., *šigūšu*).

še-na^{mušen}
Emesal dialect for sim, sin$_2$^{mušen}, 'swallow' bird.

$^{ĝiš/u2}$še-na$_2$-a; še-nu; še-na-a
the chaste tree, *Vitex agnus-castus*, a shrub resembling hemp/cannabis that grows to a height of 10-20 feet, whose flexible branches were used in the construction of plaited fences, and whose dried berries, leaves, and root were traditionally used for the treatment of menstrual and menopausal ailments as well as insufficient lactation in nursing (loanword from Akkadian, *šunā'a*, 'two each'; cf., Syriac *šunāyā*, "chaste tree" and Akkadian *šunû II*, 'chaste tree').

še-NE
Emesal dialect for KI.NE, 'brazier, oven'.

še-NE.GI-bar
a type of grain found in Pre-Sargonic texts, qualified as either 'dark' or 'light', and which M.A. Powell says "probably belongs under *Triticum*" (cf., ^{d}gira$_3$ and ^{d}gibil$_6$).

še niĝ$_2$-ĝal$_2$-la
barley on hand ('barley' + 'goods on hand').

še-nu-nir-ra
uncleaned grain ('grain' + 'not' + 'to winnow, clean grain' + nominative).

še-nu-tuku
describes a person to whom barley is not due ('barley' + 'not' + 'getting').

še-numun
barley to be used as seed ('barley' + 'seed').

še-ra
an adjective for a field - fertilized ground ('grain + 'to stir, impress, inundate').

še-ra-aḫ
threshing(s); a kind of groats ('grain + 'to strike'; cf., še ĝiš...ra(-an/aḫ)).

Emesal dialect for ^{d}niraḫ.

še-ri-ga
gleaned grain ('grain' + 'to bring').

še-sa(-a)
roasted barley ('barley' + 'to roast').

še-sag$_{11}$-ku$_5$
harvest ('grain' + 'to harvest ?' + 'to cut').

^{iti}še-sag$_{11}$-ku$_5$
calendar month 12 at Nippur during Ur III; calendar month 11 at Lagaš during Ur III; calendar month 1 at Ur during Ur III; calendar month 1 at Umma during Ur III; calendar month 12 at Drehem before Šu-Sin 3; calendar month 1 at Drehem after Šu-Sin 3.

še-SAL
(cf., še-šal).

še-SAR
(cf., še mu$_2$-a).

še-si
to fill with grain = to feed, feeders of (e.g., donkeys) ('barley' + 'to fill').

še-sig
late crop of cereals, either spring sown crops or crops sown late in the fall ('barley, grain' + 'late').

še...su-ub
to kiss, in Emesal dialect (cf., ne...su-ub).

še-sumun
grain left over from the previous year ('barley, grain' + 'old').

še...ša$_4$
Emesal dialect for še$_8$-še$_8$, 'to moan, mourn' (cf., šeš$_{2,3,4}$).

še-šal; še-ša$_2$-al
probably a collective designation for minor cereal crops, including the emmers, but excluding wheat ('barley' + 'narrow').

še-še-ga
agreement; consent (cf., še-ga/ge).

še-še-gi-ba
Emesal dialect for ša-dug$_4$-ga/ba, 'yesterday'.

še-šu-ḫu-uz
parched grain, roasted grain (cf., šu...ḫu-uz).

še...šub
to thresh grain by beating ('barley' + 'to throw').

še-šuku-ra
barley distributed back to the engar cultivator; barley for the subsistence of ... ('barley' + 'rations' + dative).

še-ta sa$_{10}$-a
purchased with barley ('barley' + instrumental case postposition, 'by means of' + 'to buy').

še-tur-ra(-me)
describes workers (or dependents ?) who get barley ('barley' + 'minor').

^{ĝiš}še-u$_3$-suḫ$_5$
pine cone ('grain corn' + 'conifer'; Akk., *terinnu*).

še-ur$_5$-ra
barley on loan, interest-barley.

še...us$_2$
'treading' by animals as a way of threshing grain ('barley' + 'to drive; to follow').

še-za-gin$_3$-duru$_5$
grain harvested at an early stage of ripening (for roasting, soups, etc.); unripe, green barley (cf., še-a-ba-aḫ-ši-in) ('grain' + 'clean, fresh' + 'moist').

še zi-ga
barley removing ('barley' + 'to remove' + nominative).

še-zi$_3$(-da)
barley for flour - flour barley ('barley' + 'flour' + -a, adjectival suffix).

še...zil-zil(-la)
to dehusk barley ('barley' + reduplicated 'to peel').

še$_3$
portion (cf., eše$_2$[ŠE$_3$]) [ŠE$_3$ archaic frequency: 152].

še$_3$-
contrapunctive modal prefix ša- in a few OS period texts - ThSLa §404.

-še$_3$-
terminative case prefix in Old Sumerian texts (cf., -ši-) - ThSLa §451.

-še$_3$
terminative case (AKA directive case or allative case) postposition /eše/ - to; unto; as far as; up to; going, but not there yet; as regards, concerning; because of, for the sake of; until - ThSLa §195.

ŠE$_3$-ba-an
a measure for fish ('portion' + 'a measure'; cf., ba-an).

še$_3$-ma-
writing of modal prefix ša- + conjugation prefixes /ĩ-ba-/ in OS period - ThSLa §304.

ŠE$_3$-mun
(cf., zid$_2$-munu4; zid$_2$-mun-du; zid$_2$-munu).

še$_4$
(cf., sed).

še$_6$
(cf., šeĝ$_6$).

še$_7$
(cf., šeĝ$_3$).

še$_8$
(cf., šeš$_2$).

še$_8$-še$_8$
(cf., šeš$_{2,3,4}$).

še$_{10}$
excrement, dung, droppings (cf., šed$_6$).

$\check{s}e_{10}$...dur_2
to fart ('excrement' + 'to break wind').

$\check{s}e_{12}$
(cf., sed_3).

$\check{s}e_{17}$
(cf., sed_4).

$\check{s}e_{21}$[ḪU.NA_2]
to lie down, repose (of animals) (cf., sa_4).

$\check{s}e_{25}$/$\check{s}e_{26}$/$\check{s}e_{27}$/$\check{s}e_{28}$...gi_4
(cf., $\check{s}eg_{10/11/12/13}$...$gi_4$(-$gi_4$)).

$\check{s}e_{26}$[KA×BALAĜ]
(cf., $\check{s}eg_{11}$).

$\check{s}e_{29}$[LU_2×KAR_2, LU_2.KAR_2]
(cf., šaĝa; $\check{s}e_{29}$-$e\check{s}_2$...dug_4/du_{11}/di/e).

$\check{s}e_{29}$-$e\check{s}_2$...dug_4/du_{11}/di/e
to enslave; to oppress.

$\check{s}ed_3$, $\check{s}id_3$[NUN-crossed-NUN]; šeššed[$\check{S}ED_3$-$\check{S}ED_3$]
copulating (birds or animals) (cf., $\check{s}ita_{(4)}$).

$\check{s}ed_6$
to defecate ($\check{s}e_{10}$, 'dung', + ed_2, 'to go out').

$\check{s}ed_{7,9,10,11,12}$
(cf., $sed_{(3,4,5,6)}$).

šedur
caterpillar cocoon ($e\check{s}e_2$, 'rope', + dur_2, 'dwelling').

$\check{s}eg_4$
frost; cold shudder, chills.

$\check{s}eg_5$
(cf., sig_9; $\check{s}eg_5$; si(-ig)).

$\check{s}eg_{8/9}$
snow; ice (cf., $\check{s}eg_9$).

$\check{s}eg_9$[$\check{S}U_2$.ŠE.KU.GAG], sigga, sig_{14}[in Labat and MZL]; $\check{s}eg_8$[$\check{S}U_2$.NAĜA]
wild mountain boar ?, wild sheep, deer, or goat ? (cf., šaḫ, $\check{s}eg_9$-bar) (cf., Orel & Stolbova #495 ***šagan-** 'goat, boar'; Akk., *sappāru(m)*, 'a wild animal, perhaps wild ram', *atūdu*, 'wild sheep; ram') [$\check{S}EG_9$ archaic frequency: 10].

$\check{S}EG_9$.BAR
(cf., $\check{s}eg_9$-bar; $ki\check{s}i_6$-$bar^{mu\check{s}en}$).

$\check{s}eg_9$-bar
a wild animal; Mesopotamian fallow deer; other suggestions include wild ram, wild boar ($\check{s}eg_9$, 'boar', + bar, 'foreign').

$\check{s}eg_{10}$; $\check{s}e_{25}$[KA×ŠID]
(cf., $\check{s}eg_{11}$...gi_4(-gi_4)).

$\check{s}eg_{11}$; $\check{s}e_{26}$[KA×BALAĜ]
(cf., $\check{s}eg_{11}$...gi_4(-gi_4)).

$\check{s}eg_{11}$; $\check{s}eg_{12}$; $\check{s}eg_x$[KA×LI]; $\check{s}eg_{10}$...gi_4(-gi_4)
to resound; to roar; to shout; to yell; to howl; to screech (reduplication class) ('walls' + 'to answer').

$\check{s}eg_{11/12}$-gi_4-a
roaring ('to resound' + nominative).

$\check{s}eg_{12}$, sig_4, $\check{s}e_{27}$
sun-dried unbaked brick; mud brick; brick of animal dung; brickwork; wall(s) (cf., $\check{s}eg_{11}$...gi_4(-gi_4)); block (such as of mun, 'salt') ($\check{s}e_{10}$, 'dung', + g, 'encircling chamber', cf., eg_2, 'levee', zig_3, 'wall, partition', zag, 'boundary, side') [? SIG_4 archaic frequency: 2].

$\check{s}eg_{12}$-ab_2
half-brick, as opposed to the older square brick ('brick' + 'cow'; Akk., *arḫu(m) III*, 'half-brick', where *arḫu(m) II*, 'cow'; cf., u_3-ku-ru-um).

$\check{s}eg_{12}$-al-ur_5-ra
kiln-burnt brick(s) (cf., izi_2-ur_5, 'coal').

$šeg_{12}$-anše...gub
to stack a brick pile ('brick' + 'donkey' + 'to set'; *imāru*, 'donkey'; *amāru*, 'brick-pile').

$šeg_{12}$-ba
turtle shell (?) ('brick; wall' + 'turtle').

$šeg_{12}$-ba$\underline{h}$ar$_2$(-ra)
baked brick (?) or potter's brick(?) ('brick' + 'potter' + genitive).

$^{iti}šeg_{12}$-ga
calendar month 3 at Nippur during Ur III.

$^{iti}šeg_{12}$-$^{\tilde{g}iš}i_3$-šub(-ba)-g̃ar
calendar month 2 at Umma during Ur III.

$šeg_{12}$ nam-tar-ra
brick of fate, fated brick - the first brick laid for a building; decreed brickwork ('brick' + 'fate' + genitive).

$šeg_{12}$ sag̃
first brick ('brick' + 'leader; first class').

šeg̃$_3$, še$_7$[A-AN]
n., rain; snow, sleet; cold; rainy season; (nocturnal) dew (šu, 'to pour' + to mete out).

v., to rain.

can be Emesal dialect for šeg̃$_6$.

šeg̃$_6$, še$_6$[NE]
to heat; to cook; to bake; to boil; to be hot; to dry a field; to fire (pottery) (redup. class) (ša, 'to dry up' + to mete out).

šeg̃$_7$[IM]
to rain.

šeg̃$_{14}$[IM.A.AN]
cloud; mist.

šeg̃$_x$[IM.A]
rain.

šem-
(cf., šim-).

šem-bi-zi-da
kohl; a paste originally made from charred frankincense resin and later from powdered antimony (stibium) or lead compounds; a darkening eye cosmetic with antibacterial properties - used as a protection against eye disease as well as giving relief from the glare of the sun ('kohl' + 'good; true' + nominative; Akk., *gu$\underline{h}$lu*, 'kohl' - cf., igi-$\underline{h}$ulu, 'evil-eye').

$^{(uruda)}$šem$_3$[AB$_2$×ŠA$_3$]$^{(zabar)}$; šem$_5$[AB$_2$×KAR$_2$]
a metal drum with a skin drumhead - kettledrum, with sound compared to thunder (*$\underline{h}$al$\underline{h}$allatu* drum in Akkadian) (cf., šen, 'copper kettle').

šembi, šimbi
kohl, i.e., a cosmetic, mascara, or eye-protection paste originally made from charred frankincense resin and later from powdered antimony (stibium) or lead compounds (cf., šem-bi-zi-da, 'kohl'; šim, 'perfumed resin'; šim-gig, 'frankincense'; im-sig$_7$-sig$_7$, 'antimony paste').

šen[SU×A]
n., a copper vessel, cauldron, kettle; combat (liquid + stone; cf., šem$_3$, 'kettledrum'; Akk. *šannu(m)*; *ruqqu(m) I*) [ŠEN archaic frequency: 66; concatenates 4 sign variants].

adj., clear, pure; polished, shiny.

šen-a$_2$-la$_2$^{zabar}
part of plow; plowshare (?) ('metal vessel' + 'arm' + 'to hang'; Akk., *nabrû*).

šen-dili$_{(2)}$; šen-da-la$_2$; šen-da-li$_2$[NI]
a small vessel with a nozzle, made of copper, bronze, or silver, usually weighing less than one ma-na, and sometimes described as a kun-řu$_2$ ('cauldron' + 'single'; Akk. *šandalum*).

šen-šen
combat, battle, fight, strife (reduplicated 'metal pots; combat'; cf., me$_3$-šen(-šen-na)).

šen-šen-bal^{mušen}
quail (?) ('combat' + phonetic complement; Akkadian *urballu*).

ŠEN-tab-ba
(cf., dur$_{10}$-tab-ba).

šen-tur
a cooking vessel ('cauldron' + 'small').

šen$_2$
verdigris.

šenbar
(cf., šeg$_9$-bar).

šennu[EN.ME.AD.KUG]
a high priest, devoted to the god Enki/Ea of Eridu or the goddess Nanshe of Eridu and Lagash, deities of mysterious arts and skills.

^{ĝiš}šennur[KIB]
plum tree (BSA, V, p. 146, where 'medlar' is rejected) (Akk. *šallūru(m)*; *uribḫu*) [ŠENNUR archaic frequency: 11; concatenates 2 sign variants].

^{ĝiš}šennur-babbar-ra
pear tree ('plum' + 'white' + nominative).

šer$_2$, šir$_2$[BU]
n., radiance; daylight (cf., sir$_2$; še-er/še(-er)-še-er) (Akkadian loan from *šēru(m) II*, 'morning').

v., to shine brightly.

šer$_3$, šir$_3$[EZEN/KEŠDA]
n., decision (cf., $^{ĝiš/uruda/kuš}$šir$_3$-šir$_3$).

v., to bind; to attribute, assign, allot; to decide (eše$_2$, 'rope', + ur, 'to surround' ?).

šer$_3$-da
a (group) contract (cf., šer$_7$-da) (šer$_3$, 'to bind; to decide', + da, 'with').

$^{(eše2)}$šer$_7$
a part in the upper $^{(ĝiš)}$targul mooring apparatus; also probably part of the pole assembly of a wagon, capable of being released (du$_8$-na) (cf., še-er-du$_8$-na(-k)) (cf., šer$_3$, 'to bind').

šer$_7$-da
sin; misdemeanor; crime; blame; criminal; debt; punishment (Akkadian *šertu* and *nerṭu*).

šer$_7$-
(cf., še-er-).

šerim$_{(2)}$, šerin, serim$_2$
a part of the loom - either the harness or the heddle [TAG archaic frequency: 48 ?; concatenates 7 ? sign variants].

šerimsur
caterpillar cocoon (šerim, 'part of a weaving loom', + zar/sur$_8$, 'to exude; to spin [a cocoon]').

šeš, šes
brother; brethren; colleague; male cousin (?) [URI$_3$=ZATU-595 archaic frequency: 77; concatenates 2 sign variants].

šeš, ses, sis
n., myrrh (reduplicated eš, 'to anoint').

v., to taste bitter.

adj., bitter, brackish.

šeš-3-kam
third brother ('brother' + '3' + /ak/, 'of' + am$_3$, 'it is').

šeš-ad-da
paternal uncle ('brother' + 'father' + genitive).

šeš-ama(-na)
maternal uncle ('brother' + 'mother' (+ ni-a(k), 'his/her' + genitive).

šeš-banda$_3$[TUR](^{da})
youngest brother ('brother' + 'young, junior').

^{iti}šeš-da-gu$_7$
calendar month 2 at Drehem through Šu-Sin 3; calendar month 3 at Drehem after Šu-Sin 3; calendar month 3 at Ur during Ur III.

ŠEŠ-dur_2-ra_2/a
(cf., sa-dur_2(-ra)).

šeš-gal
elder/oldest brother; term for a high priest; guardian, supervisor ('brother' + 'older').

šeš-tab(-ba)
brotherly companion; assistant ('brother' + 'to join' + nominative).

šeš-us_2
second brother ('brother' + 'to follow').

$šeš_{2,3,4}$
to weep, cry; to mourn; to wail (reduplication class: $še_8$-$še_8$, ši-ši) (cf., $šeš_{2,4}$) (to become moist ?).

$šeš_{4,2}$
to anoint; to rub, smear; to erase; to be dense (reduplication class: $še_{22}$-$še_{22}$) (reduplicated eš, 'to anoint') [ERIN=$ŠEŠ_4$ archaic frequency: 105].

šeššed
(cf., $šed_3$).

ši[IGI]
to be fatigued or careless (Akk., *egû(m) III*, 'to be(come) lazy; be negligent').

ši
Emesal dialect form of zi, 'life; throat'.

ši-
contrapunctive modal prefix ša- in a few OS period texts and before the prefixes ĩ- and bí- in OB period texts - ThSLa §404.

-ši-
terminative/directive/allative prefix after Old Sumerian period, typically used with verbs of motion or verbs of attention (example: in-ši-sa_{10}, 'he bought from him/it') - ThSLa §451 (cf., -$še_3$ and -$še_3$-).

-ši
suffixed quotation particle during Ur III, cf., $eše_2$[$ŠE_3$].

ši-X
Emesal dialect, cf., zi-X.

ši-bi_2-
writing of modal prefix ša- + conjugation prefix /bi-/ in Isin-Larsa and OB periods - ThSLa §304.

ši-ga-
writing of modal prefix ša- + conjugation prefixes /ĩ-ga-/ in OB period - ThSLa §323, §304.

ši-im-
writing of modal prefix ša- + conjugation prefix /ĩ-/ with ventive element /-m-/ in OB period - ThSLa §304.

ši-im-ma-
writing of modal prefix ša- + conjugation prefixes /ĩ-ba-/ in OB period - ThSLa §336, §304.

ši-im-mi-
writing of modal prefix ša- + conjugation prefixes /ĩ-bi-/ in OB period - ThSLa §304.

ši-in-
writing of modal prefix ša- + conjugation prefix /ĩ-/ + animate 3.sg. pronominal element /-n-/ in OB period - ThSLa §304.

ši-in-ga-
writing of modal prefix ša- + conjugation prefixes /ĩ-ga-/ in OB period - ThSLa §323, §304.

ši-ir
Emesal dialect for nir or zi-ir.

ši-mi-
writing of modal prefix ša- + conjugation prefixes /ĩ-bi-/ in OB period - ThSLa §304.

ši-mu-
writing of modal and conjugation prefixes /ša-mu-/ or /ša-ĩ-mu-/ - ThSLa §304, n. 50.

ši-ši
(cf., $šeš_{2,3,4}$).

$^{(\tilde{g}iš)}$ŠI.TUR.TUR
kernel; sprout (has possible reading ligima; Akk., *ligimû(m)*) ('hair-like' + reduplicated 'small').

šib, šip
exorcism (Akkadian *āšipūtu*).

$^{\tilde{g}iš}$šibir, sibir[U.BURU$_{14}$]
n., shepherd's staff ending in a curved end, i.e., a crook; also such a staff used by a god or king as a scepter; a furrow or ditch (?) Akk. *ḫeršu* (sipad; šuba, 'shepherd', + re$_7$, 'to lead; to bear').

adj., slanted, crooked.

ŠID, ŠED
(cf., šita$_5$; šid-da; lag, im-lag; zag$_3$; sag̃g̃a, umbisag̃; šudum-ma; zandara; šub$_6$).

šid-da
audit (?) ('to count' + nominative).

šid$_{3,4,5}$
(cf., šita$_{(4)}$; šed$_3$).

šidim, šitim, šidi[GIM]
mason; builder; architect (šeg$_{12}$/še$_{27}$, 'brick', + dim$_2$, 'to build, make') [ŠIDIM archaic frequency: 35].

šidim-gal
master builder; architect ('builder' + 'elder').

šika
potsherd; shell; rind (hand, portion + mouth).

šika-ri
shattered potsherds ('potsherd' + 'to break open; to throw away').

šikin$_{2,3}$
a jar for body oil, ointment, salve.

šilam[NUN.LAGAR×MUNUS]
milk-producing mother cow (cf., immal$_2$) (šu, 'to pour', + i$_3$, 'cream', + lam, 'abundance').

šilig
(cf., silig).

šim, šem
herb; aromatic wood; resin; spice; extract; drug; fragrance, perfume (see comments on sum/šum$_2$, 'garlic; onion'; *sam* is 'spice' in Hebrew; Orel & Stolbova 395, **cim-**, 'grass, plant', 488, **šiw-/šiy-**, 'grass, plant'; cf., sim, 'fragrant') [ŠIM archaic frequency: 50; concatenates 2 sign variants].

$^{(lu2)}$ŠIM
(cf., $^{(lu2)}$lunga).

šim-bi
(cf., šembi and šem-bi-zi-da).

$^{(\tilde{g}iš)}$šim-bulug/bul$_3$[BAL]/ bulug$_2$[BUR$_2$]/buk[MUG]
a tree producing an aromatic resin, possibly styrax, used as a fixative in perfumery and to treat cuts and irritated skin (>Akk. *ballukku(m)*).

šim-buluḫ[ḪAL]
a plant and its resin, probably galbanum, prescribed to relieve tension and anxiety; measured in ma-na weight units (>Akk. *baluḫḫu(m)*; buluḫ = 'to worry; to be nervous, anxious, frightened').

šim-DU
(cf., šim-gin).

$^{(\tilde{g}iš)}$šim-gam(-gam)-ma
an adhesive balsamic resin - Latin *cancamun* from the *kamkâm* tree in South Arabia, Amyris, similar to myrrh; a kind of gum bled from branches of the balsam tree, in nature caused by insect borers (šim-gam-me = Akk. *ṣumlalû(m)*; cf., *lalû II*, 'to bind'?, from Sumerian zum, 'to leak, seep, exude', + lal$_{(2)}$, 'to bind', cf., Akk., *kamû(m) II*, 'to bind' = LAL, related to Egyptian *qmy*, 'gum resin', the source of Greek kommi, 'gum'; the resin from the *kamkâm* tree and from a type of sage bush is called *d,arw* in Arabic [*d,arā* = 'it bled'] and is related to Hebrew *çori* or *çēri*, 'balsam, balm').

$^{(\tilde{g}iš)}$šim-gig
frankincense, or the more generic olibanum, a white, citrus-smelling

aromatic resin - used in making medicinal pastes and in embalming because of its antimicrobial, preservative properties; true frankincense comes from the spindly Boswellia Sacra tree of southern Arabia - the incense trade came through the recently rediscovered 5,000 year-old city of Ubar; measured in $sila_3$ volume units ('aromatic resin' + 'to be sick'; Akk. *kanaktu(m)* = $šim\text{-}mi_2\text{-}mi_2$, 'the resin of loving care', cf., Akk. *kanû(m) D*, 'treat kindly'; also, šembi and šem-bi-zi-da, 'kohl').

šim-gin
regular aromatic.

(ĝiš)šim-gu$_4$-ku-ru; šim-gug$_2$-ku-ru; šim-gug$_2$-gug$_2$; šim-ku$_7$-ku$_7$; šim-gur$_2$-gur$_2$
a tree or its aromatic product - turpentine tree, terebinth (?) (Akk. *kukuru(m)*; cf., Akkadian *kūru*, 'daze, stupor'; this product appears right after the OAkk period).

(ĝiš)šim-ĝir$_2$
myrtle (*Myrtus communis*), an evergreen shrub with scented leaves that heal wounds - its resin used to make a pleasant aromatic oil with strong anti-microbial properties ('herb' + 'knife'; Akk. *asu(m) I*; cf., ĝiš (šim)aza).

(ĝiš)šim-ḫab$_{(2)}$
the flammable gum-resin of Opopanax, resembling myrhh, of a reddish or yellowish-brown color, with a strong and disagreeable odor and an acrid, bitter taste, used for a variety of medicinal purposes (Greek opos "juice" + panax "all-healing") (Akk., *ṭūru*, 'medicinal plant, perhaps Opopanax'; *šaḫātu II*).

(ĝiš)šim-ḪAL
(cf., (ĝiš)šim-buluḫ).

šim-ḫi-a
different resins measured according to weight, or perfumes measured according to capacity (Akk. *rīqu(m) II*).

šim-i$_3$
oil extract; unguent ('aromatic substance' + 'fat').

šim-im
an aromatic substance ('aromatic substance' + 'paste; phonetic indicator').

ŠIM×KUŠU$_2$
(alternate orthography for (ĝiš)šim-bulug/bul$_3$[BAL]/bulug$_2$[BUR$_2$]/buk[MUG]).

šim-lal$_3$
sweet aromatics, used to make beer bread ('aromatics' + 'honey' - asyndetic hendiadys ?).

šim-li
juniper/cedar (resin) (cf., ĝišli).

ŠIM.dMAŠ
(cf., ligidba$_2$).

šim-mu$_2$
incantation priest; sorcerer, magician; dream interpreter ('aromatic substance' + 'to ignite').

lu2šim-naĝ
spice drinkers (?) ('spice' + 'to drink').

ŠIM.dNIN.URTA
(cf., ligidba).

šim-PI-PI
an aromatic substance from trees, possibly cypress oil (cf., u2ur-tal$_2$-tal$_2$).

šim-sag$_{10}$
finest aromatic ('aromatic substance' + 'fine quality').

šim-su-SA$_2$
cologne, perfume (?) ('aromatic substance' + 'body' + 'to equal, compete with').

(ĝiš)šim-šal
(type of) box-tree (?); pear-tree (?); source of perfumed oil ('aromatic substance' + 'to spread out'; Akk., *šimiššalû*).

$^{(ĝiš)}$šim-še-li
pine resin ('aromatic substance' + 'pine seeds'; Akk., *kikkirânu(m)*).

$^{(ĝiš)}$šim-šeš, šim-ses
myrrh, an aromatic gum which flows from a small tree or shrub resembling the acacia, Commiphora Myrrha (Akk., *murru*, 'bitterness; myrrh').

šim$_2$^{mušen}
(cf., sim, sin$_2$^{mušen}).

šimaški[LU$_2$.SU(.A^{ki})]
a Drehem text adjective for domesticated sheep and goats indigenous to Shimaski, the whole western portion of the Persian plateau.

šimbi
(cf., šembi).

^{ĝiš}šinig
tamarisk (tree), grown along edges of fields and in gardens, used to make furniture.

šip
(cf., šib, šip).

šir, sir$_4$
testicle(s); scrotum; bulb (many + to go out + to flow; cf., ḫir, nir, and ĝiš$_{2,3}$) [ŠIR archaic frequency: 24; concatenates 2 sign variants].

šir-dili
(man with a) single testicle ('testicle' + 'single').

šir$_2$
(cf., šer$_2$).

šir$_3$[EZEN]; šur
n., song; lament (Orel & Stolbova #2258 ***sir-/*sur** 'sing').

v., to sing (reduplication class).

šir$_3$
(cf., šer$_3$).

šir$_3$... ĝar/ĝa$_2$-ĝa$_2$
to perform a song ('song' + 'to deliver').

šir$_3$...aĝa$_2$
to sing; to cry (out) ('song' + 'to mete out').

šir$_3$-gid$_2$-da
a type of song composition ('song' + 'to be long' + nominative; cf., lu$_2$-gi-gid$_2$-da, 'flutist', and sa-gid$_2$-da, 'a musical string tuning mode').

šir$_3$-kug
sacred song; incantation ('song' + 'sacred, holy').

šir$_3$-nam-gala
song composed for the lamentation priesthood ('song' + 'lamentation priesthood' (+ genitive)).

šir$_3$-nam-šub(-ba-kam)
incantation song in Emesal dialect ('song' + 'incantation' (+ genitive)).

šir$_3$-nam-ur-saĝ-ĝa$_2$
song of heroism ('song' + 'heroism' + genitive).

šir$_3$-ra-nam-en-na; šir$_3$-re-nam-nir-ra
song of lordship ('song' + 'lordship' + genitive).

šir$_3$-re-eš, sir$_3$-re-eš
shout; song of praise; hymn; cry of lamentation ('song' + phonetic complement + 'much').

šir$_3$-re-eš...dug$_4$/du$_{11}$/e
to ring out in song; to cry a lament or greeting; to intone a hymn ('song' + phonetic complement + 'much').

$^{ĝiš/uruda/kuš}$šir$_3$-šir$_3$
chain; interlocked, entwined elements (probable loanword from Akkadian, *šeršerratu(m)*, 'chain, set of rings'; cf., Orel & Stolbova #2298, ***sur-** "rope").

šita, ešda$_3$[ŠITA = ŠITA$_6$ in Labat Addendum]
n., a priest; prayer, blessing; a sacred type of vessel (cf., šita$_4$) (eš, 'to anoint', + ta, da$_2$, 'by means of'/de$_2$, 'to

pour, water') [ŠITA archaic frequency: 373; concatenates 7 sign variants].

adj., clean; bathed.

ŠITA.ĜIŠ.NAM$_2$
(cf., namešda).

ŠITA-^{d}INANNA
undertaker (cf., UH̬$_3$-^{d}INANNA).

$^{(ĝiš)}$šita$_2$, ešda[ŠITA.ĜIŠ]
mace, weapon (uš$_2$, 'to kill', + ta, da$_2$, 'by means of') [EŠDA archaic frequency: 26].

šita$_3$
channel, watercourse, small canal, orchard-ditch (še$_3$, 'portion' + ida$_2$, id$_2$, i$_7$, 'main canal') [ŠITA$_3$ archaic frequency: 139; concatenation of 2 sign variants].

šita$_4$[U.KID]; šita, ešda$_3$; šid$_{3,4,5}$
n., band; bond, tie (še$_3$, 'portion', + dim, 'bond, tie'; cf., ašte, teš$_2$).

v., to bind; to be together; to join, link with; to couple.

adj., bound, intact.

šita$_5$, šiti, šit, šid, šed, šudum, šitim$_2$
n., measure; number (še$_3$/šu, 'portion', + dim, 'post'; cf., ĝiš-šudum-ma, 'herder's tally sticks', and the different readings of ŠID).

v., to count; to consider; to calculate, figure out; to memorize; to recite; to read aloud.

šita$_6$
(cf., šita).

šiten[KI.DU.GAG]
course of march; passage (šita$_3$, 'channel', + un, 'people').

šitim
(cf., šidim).

šitim$_2$
(cf., šita$_5$; šudum-ma).

šu
n., hand(s); share, portion, bundle; strength; control; authority; handle; a hired group of workers (cf., DIŠ; DIŠ$_2$[AŠ]) [ŠU archaic frequency: 360].

v., to pour; to initiate, bring about.

šu-
rare contrapunctive modal prefix ša- before the prefix mu- ThSLa §404.

šu-a...taka$_4$
to leave (something) to (someone) ('hand' + locative + 'to push').

šu-a-gi-na
regular, daily offering ('hand; portion' + locative + gin$_6$, 'to consent, act justly' + nominative [gi-na, 'regular contribution']).

šu PN-ak-ta
under the authority of PN ('from the hand of PN').

šu...aka
to take captive; to seize ('hand' + 'to do').

šu...ba
(cf., šu...bad, šu...bar).

šu-bad
length measure of 15 fingers = 25 cm. = ½ kuš$_3$; half-cubit, span (cf., šu-du$_3$-a; Akk. *ūṭu(m)*).

šu...bad
to release ('hand' + 'to open').

šu...bala
to change; to alter; to tamper; to set aside ('hand' + 'to change'; Akk., *šupêlu(m)*, 'to exchange, overturn').

šu-bala...aka
to alter; to tamper; to set aside ('hand' + 'to change' + 'to do').

šu...bar
to release, let loose (prisoner or slave) (the opposite of šu...du$_3$); to exempt (from taxes); to forget (where the forgotten entity receives an oblique case postposition such as the dative) ('hand' + 'to open, release').

šu-bar
freed, emancipated.

šu-bar(-ra)
release; (grant of) freedom; exemption.

^{gi}šu-bil-la$_2$
reed mat, portable altar ('hand' + 'to burn (incense ?)' + nominative).

šu...buru$_2$
to open the hand ('hand' + 'to open').

šu...bur$_{12}$/bu(-bu)
to pull, pluck out ('hand' + 'to tear, pull').

šu-da
hand and forearm, as a unit of measurement, ell/cubit (cf., kuš$_3$) ('hand' + 'arm').

šu...dab$_{(2,4,5)}$
to take or accept ('hand' + 'to hold, take, receive').

šu-dab$_{(5)}$(-ba)
sale ('hand' + 'to clasp, take away' + nominative).

šu...dag
to roam about; to run away; to abandon, cut off ('hand' + 'to roam').

šu-dağal...dug$_4$/du$_{11}$/e
to provide generously with (with -ni-) ('hand' + 'wide, copious' + 'to effect').

šu...dar
to slaughter (redupl. class) ('hand' + 'to slice, split, shatter').

šu-dim$_4$-ma
loyal ('hand' + 'subservient' + nominative).

šu...de$_6$
to set to work ('hand' + 'to bring').

šu-du$_2$
(variant of šu-du$_8$-a).

šu...du$_3$
to bind the hands; to apply one's hands to (the opposite of šu...bar) ('hands' + 'to fasten').

šu-du$_3$-a
length measure of 10 fingers = 16.666 cm.; handcuffs ('hands' + 'to stack').

šu...du$_7$
to embellish; to put on the finishing touches; to equip; to complete; to achieve; to assume the correct position; to bring to full force; to make perfect (with -ta-) (reduplication class) ('hand' + 'to complete').

šu...du$_8$
to hold in the hand (objects that are physically long and thin) (with -ni- or bi$_2$-); to take possession (of objects or animals) ('hand' + 'to open').

šu-du$_8$-a
guarantee; guarantor; pledge (on behalf of a person); ('to hold' + nominative).

šu-du$_8$-a...DU(de$_6$/tum$_2$)
to act as guarantor for; to guarantee surety, probably by means of a promissory oath ('guarantee' + 'to bring, carry').

šu-du$_{11}$-ga
creation ('hand' + 'to effect' + nominative).

šu...dub$_2$
to flail (at oneself); to pull out (such as hair) ('hand' + 'to flail).

šu...dug$_4$/du$_{11}$/e
to touch; to choose; to place, put; to prepare (something) ('hand' + 'to effect').

šu(-dağal)...dug$_4$/du$_{11}$/e
to supply, to provide (generously) with (with -ni-) ('hand' (+ 'wide, copious') + 'to effect').

šu-X...dug$_4$/du$_{11}$/e
to turn into X, to become X, where X is a noun phrase or descriptive adjective.

šu-dul$_5$
(cf., šudul).

šu-e-sir$_2$
shoe-mold(?).

šu...e$_3$
to honor, bless ('hand' + 'to emerge').

šu-ni...-ra-e$_3$
to escape from his/her hand ('hand' + pronominal possessive suffix + ablative infix + 'to emerge').

^{iti}šu-eš-ša
calendar month 8 at Drehem before Šu-Sin 3; calendar month 9 at Ur during Ur III.

$^{(lu2)}$šu-gal-an-zu
potter (cf., gal-zu) ('hands' + 'skillful').

šu-gana$_2$
agricultural tool ('hand' + 'field').

šu...gi
to bind ('hand' + 'to surround, lock up').

$^{\tilde{g}iš}$šu-gi
bolt, cross-bar (cf., $^{\tilde{g}iš}$suḫub$_5$) ('hand' + 'to lock up').

šu(-a)...gi$_4$(-gi$_4$)
to hand over, transfer; to return; to refund, credit; to bring back; to lead back (preceding meanings take the terminative infix -ši- in the verbal chain); to repeat (words or songs); to repay; to keep secure; to answer; to disintegrate; to surrender ('hand' (+ locative) + 'to return').

šu-gi$_{(4)}$
n., aged man; elder; senior ('hand' + 'to return' ?, 'to lock up' ?, 'reed-like' ?).

v., to become old, disintegrate.

adj., old; elderly; weak; unable to work.

šu-gibil-gibil...aka
to renew ('hand' + 'to renovate' + 'to renovate' + 'to do').

šu...gid$_2$
to accept; to observe/inspect the offering animal (cf., maš$_2$-šu-gid$_2$-gid$_2$; 'hand' + 'to reach out').

šu-gid$_2$
dues; general obligation; delivery - usually describes just one or two animals ('hand' + 'to reach out; to measure out').

šu-gid$_2$ e$_2$-muḫaldim
delivery destined for cooking ('dues' + 'kitchen pantry').

šu...gu$_4$-gu$_4$-ud
to jumpily move around ('hand' + 'to leap, dance').

šu...gur
to roll; to wrap; to wipe ('hand' + 'circular motion').

šu-guru; šu-guru$_5$[URU×GU]
ring (of gold, silver, or precious stone); vase; mat - could hold dates and most other fruit ('to roll up' + nominative).

^{tug2}šu-gur-ra; gur
turban; ghutrah, kaffiyeh ('cloth' + 'to wrap' + nominative).

$^{\tilde{g}iš}$šu-gur$_{10}$[KIN]
sickle; handle ('hand' + 'sickle/to reap'; cf., saga$_{11}$/sig$_{18}$, 'to cut, break, harvest').

šu...g̃al$_2$
to hold by the hand ('hand' + 'to place in').

šu...g̃ar/g̃a$_2$-g̃a$_2$
to perform a task; to carry out; to do someone a favor; to lift, carry; to purchase; to hold someone back; to cease doing something (with -ta-) ('hand' + 'to deliver, place').

šu(-a/še$_3$)...g̃ar
to be/place in the hand; to subdue ('hand' + locative/terminative + 'to deliver').

šu-g̃ar
effect; favor ('hand' + 'to deliver').

ŠU.G̃AR.TUR.LA$_2$-bi
(cf., tukum-bi).

šu...ḪA
(cf., šu...peš$_{11}$).

šu-ḪA; šu-GIR/$ḪA_6$
(cf., šu-ku_6/šu-ku_{17}).

šu...ḫa-za
to hold in the hand ('hand' + 'to hold, grasp').

šu-ḫal-la
open hand ('hand' + 'to divide, distribute' + nominative).

šu...ḫu-uz
to roast; to burn (cf., šu...ru-uz) (this compound may derive from Akkadian *šūḫuzu*, the **Š**-form of *aḫāzu(m)*, in the meaning "ignite, set fire to", but cf., ḫuš, "fiery red" [Akk. *ruššû*] and šu...ru-uz).

šu-ḫul...du_3
to destroy ('hands' + 'evil' + 'to make, plant').

šu ḫul...dug_4/di/du_{11}/e
to desecrate, defile, ruin ('hands' + 'evil' + 'to effect').

$^{(lu2)}$šu-i
barber ('hand' + 'sprouts' ?).

ŠU-igi-$še_3$-du
(read instead zid_2-igi-$še_3$-du).

šu...il_2
to build; to grow rich ('hand' + 'to raise').

šu-il_2-$la_{(2)}$
prayer (hand-raising); an Emesal dialect cultic song, most of which were written down after the Old Babylonian period ('hand' + 'to raise' + nominative).

šu...$kar_{(2)}$
to take away; to insult, slander, denigrate; to withdraw ('hand' + 'to take away').

^{ĝiš}šu-kar_2
tools, equipment, utensils, parts, components; fretted lute (cf., $^{(ĝiš)}a_2$-kar_2) ('hand' + 'to encircle, besiege').

šu ki-in-dar
full of cracks ('handful' + 'crevices').

šu-$kiĝ_2$
service; obeisance ('hand' + 'order, task').

šu-$kiĝ_2$...$dab_{(5)}$
to perform a service; to kneel down, prostrate oneself ('hand' + 'order, task' + 'to hold/seize').

šu-KIN
(cf., šu...sag_{11}/sig_{18}; šu(-$kiĝ_2$)...dab_5).

^{gi}šu-KIN
faggot of reeds ('hand/bundle' + ?; cf., gur_{10}, 'sickle; to gather together').

^{ĝiš}šu-KIN
(cf., ^{ĝiš}šu-gur_{10}).

šu-ku_6(-d); šu-ku6-ud-da; šu-ku_{17}
fisherman; hunter; thief; robber, bandit, plunderer; prowler, vagabond; house-breaker, burglar ('hand' + 'fish' + èd, 'to fetch, remove' + nominative; Akk., *šukuddāku*, '(temple) fisherman').

šu-ku_6 ab-ba(-k)
deep-sea fisherman ('fisherman' + 'sea').

šu-$la_2^{uruda/zabar}$
(cf., šu-ša-la_2; šu-la_2).

šu(-a)-la_2
paralyzed, folded, idle (said of hands) ('hands' + locative + 'to bind, diminish').

šu-la_2-a
entrusted ('hands' + 'to hold' + nominative).

šu...lal/la_2-la_2
to defile; to reach; to bind (the hands); to wring the hands ('hand' + 'to pierce, penetrate; to stretch; to bind; to hold').

šu-$še_3$...lal/la_2
to hold in the hand, grasp, suspend from the hands (cf., šu-ša-la_2) ('hand' + 'to bind, hold, hang').

šu lil_2-la_2...dug_4/du_{11}/e
to be haunted ('hand' + 'haunting spirit of a place' + 'to effect').

šu$_{(4)}$-luḫ
ritual cleansing, purification ritual, cleansing rite; lustration ('hand' + 'to clean').

šu/šu$_2$-luḫ...aka
to clean; to dredge (a canal) ('cleansing' + 'to do').

^{lu2}šu-luḫ-ḫa
purification ritual man, lustration priest ('ritual cleansing' + nominative).

šu lul...bala
to alter deceitfully ('hand' + 'liar' + 'to change').

šu-lum^{zabar}
a rare bronze object ('hand' + 'fertilizer' or an Akkadian loanword).

šu...ma-ma
Emesal dialect for šu...ĝar/ĝa$_2$-ĝa$_2$.

šu-maš$_2$-gid$_2$-gid$_2$
(cf., maš$_2$-šu-gid$_2$-gid$_2$).

ŠU-ME-EREN
cypress resin (cf., $^{(ĝiš)}$šu-ur$_2$-me).

$^{(na4/ĝiš)}$šu-min$_3$
a heavy object of stone, wood, or metal; with both hands; anvil; slaughtering block; metal mold, as for hatchets; hammerstone ('hands' + 'two').

šu-mu-
writing of modal and conjugation prefixes /ša-mu-/ in OB period - ThSLa §304.

$^{(u2)}$šu-mu-un
Emesal dialect for $^{(u2)}$numun$_2$, 'alfalfa grass'.

šu...mu$_2$
to enlarge; to expand (with -ni-); to pray, bless, greet (with dative) ('hand' + 'to grow').

^{na4}šu-na
pestle ('hand' + 'stone').

ŠU.NIĜ$_2$.TUR.LAL-bi
(cf., tukum-bi).

šu...niĝin$_{(2)}$/ni$_{10}$-ni$_{10}$
to proceed; to hurry; to return quickly to (plus terminative -še$_3$); to make a round trip; to circle ('hand' + 'to make the rounds').

ŠU+NIĜIN
grand total ('hand' + 'circle, whole') [? ŠUNIGIN archaic frequency: 1].

ŠU+NIĜIN$_2$
subtotal ('hand' + 'circle, whole').

šu-nim(-ma)
early (to work or to ripen) ('hand' + 'early' + nominative).

$^{(ĝiš)}$šu-nir(-ra)
standard, usually followed by for what it is a symbol; emblem or post with woolen streamers; totemic device ('hand' + 'to raise high' + nominative; Akk. *šurīnum I*, '(divine) emblem', with metathesis of consonants during borrowing).

šu-numun
sowing; seed grain ('hand' + 'seed').

^{iti}šu-numun
calendar month 4 at Lagaš during Ur III; calendar month 4 at Nippur during Ur III; calendar month 6 at Umma during Ur III.

šu pe-el-la$_2$...dug$_4$/du$_{11}$/e
to defile; to be defiled ('hand' + pel$_2$, 'to be/make dirty, defiled' + 'to effect').

šu...pel$_{(2)}$
to defile ('hand' + 'to be/make dirty, defiled').

šu...peš$_{(5/6/11)}$
to spread out, distribute; to expand, increase ('hand' + 'womb; to expand').

šu-PEŠ
(cf., šu-ku$_{17}$).

šu-peš$_5$-ri-a
the division of the harvest ('to spread out' + 'to gather up' + nominative).

šu sa_2...dug_4/du_{11}/e
to attain ('hand' + 'to reach, arrive').

šu...ra
to knead clay and form it into a tablet; to pat; to erase; to beat; to churn ('hand' + 'to beat, stir').

šu...ri
to wring the hands over (with -ši-); to clamp down ('hands' + 'to place against').

šu-ri$_{(2)}$(-a-bi)
one-half (share) ('hand/portion' + 'to take, remove' + nominative + demonstrative).

šu-rin-na
(cf., im-šu-rin-na).

šu...ru-gu_2
to withstand; to oppose (cf., šu $teš_2$-a...ru-gu_2) ('hand' + 'to oppose).

šu-ru-ub; šu-ru-ug
variant or Emesal spelling of ša-ra(-g), 'to dry up'.

šu...ru-uz
to burn; to roast; to glow (cf., šu...ḫu-uz and entry for ḫuš).

šu(-a)...sa_2(-sa_2)
to clutch; to take possession ('hand' + locative + 'to attain; to be zealous').

šu...sag_{11}/sig_{18}[KIN]
to rub ('hand' + 'to make a harvesting motion, flatten').

šu-sar
palm fiber rope; cord, string ('hand, strength' + 'garden plot measure').

šu-se_3-ga
(cf., na_4-ara_3/ur_5-šu-se_3-ga).

šu-si
finger(s); fingernail(s) ('hand' + 'horn, ray, antenna').

šu(-a)...si
to fill the hands (with); to hand over ('hand' + locative + 'to fill').

šu-$še_3$...si
to hand over; to deliver ('hand' + 'towards' + 'to fill').

šu...si-ig
to hit with the hand ('hand' + 'to strike down, silence').

šu si...sa_2
to do things to perfection; to see that all is right ('hand' + 'right; legal').

šu...sig_3(-sig_3)
to wave the hand ('hand' + 'to beat rhythmically').

šu...su-ub
to gather up; to collect; to scrape together ('hands' + 'to clean').

šu...sud/su_3
to stretch the hand out after something ('hand' + 'to make remote').

šu $suḫ_3$-a...dug_4/du_{11}/e
to confuse, disconcert; to be confused; to overturn ('hand' + 'in confusion' + 'to effect').

šu...sum/$šum_2$
to give; to entrust; to examine ('hand' + 'to give').

šu-sum-ma
gift; delivery ('to give, entrust' + nominative).

šu-šu...g̃ar
to grant a pardon ('hand' + 'hand' + 'to deliver').

šu...ša-an-ša-ša
to extend the hand; to search (parallel formation from ka...ša-an-ša-ša).

šu-ša-la_2; šu-$še_3$-la_2; šu-$la_2$$^{(zabar/ku3-babbar/uruda)}$
a hand-held metal bowl, that held from ¼ to 1 $sila_3$.

šu-ŠAKIR
(cf., šu-$guru_5$).

X šu-še
to be proclaimed as X (loan from Akk. *šasû(m)*).

šu-šu
adj., two-handed; heavy (describing an ax) (redup. 'hand').

šu...$šu_2$-$šu_2$
to clasp; to clamp down ('hand' + redup. 'to go down').

šu-$šur_2$
seizing ('hand' + 'fierce, furious').

šu-tab(-ba)
joining of hands, grasp; associate, partner ('hand' + 'to clasp, hold').

v., to double.

šu...tag
to touch; to choose by touching; to cover; to adorn, decorate (often with -ni-); to seize ('hand' + 'to weave, decorate').

šu-tag...dug_4/du_{11}/e
to adorn; to decorate (with -ni-); to sprinkle; to paint ('hand' + 'to weave, decorate, strike' + 'to effect').

šu...$taka_4$
to send, dispatch, consign (with dative) ('hand' + 'to push').

šu-a...$taka_4$
to leave (something) to (someone) ('hand' + locative + 'to push').

šu...te(-$\tilde{g}a_2$)
to confront, oppose; to take (variation of šu...ti).

šu $teš_2$-a...ru-gu_2
to applaud ('hands' + 'together' + adverbial force suffix + 'to move in a direction opposite to').

šu...ti
with conjugation prefix ba- : to accept; to receive; to take up; with conjugation prefix im-ma-(an-) : to take for a purpose; to grab; to adopt; to borrow; to gain; to be taken, accepted (with terminative and -ši-) (-$\tilde{g}e_{26}$ auslaut in *marû* aspect) ('hand' + 'to approach').

šu-ti-a
goods, staples, etc. credited as received ('to receive' + nominative).

šu-TU
(read šu-du_2; variant of šu-du_8-a).

šu...tu-bu-ur
to mix together, crush together (may derive from Akkadian *šutābulu*, 'mixed').

šu...tu-tu
to touch, face, withstand, approach (cf., šu...$tum_{2/3}$).

šu-tu-tu
escape ('hand' + reduplicated 'to interfere').

šu...$tukur_2$
to nibble or lick one's fingers ('hand' + 'to gnaw, nibble').

šu-tum; šu-tum_2; šu-tum_3; šu-tum_4
storehouse for precious goods (cf., šutum) ('hand, portion' + 'to bring, carry').

šu...$tum_{2/3}$
to carry; to apply the hand; to set to work; to touch (with magical or ritual implications) ('hand' + 'to carry; to prepare').

^{na4}šu-u
pestle (cf., ^{na4}šu-na); if a type of stone, consider 'pumice' (Akk. *šû II*, 'a stone').

šu $uḫ_3$-a...dug_4/du_{11}/e
(cf., šu $suḫ_3$-a...dug_4/du_{11}/e).

šu-um-du-um
Emesal dialect for nundum, 'lip'.

$^{(\tilde{g}iš)}$šu-ur_2-min_3[MAN]; šur-min_3; šu-ur_2-men_2[ME]
a type of cypress tree; its wood or its scented resin (cf., $^{(\tilde{g}iš)}$ḫa-šu-ur_2) (Akk. loanword ?, *šurmēnu(m)*; cf., $^{(na4/\tilde{g}iš)}$šu-min_3, 'a heavy object', and ur_2, 'trunk of a tree').

šu...ur$_3$/uru$_{12}$
to compact, flatten, spread; to erase, remove; to wipe, rub; to sharpen; to deface an inscription (with -ni- and bi$_2$-; also with -ta-) (uru$_{12}$ in the *marû* aspect) ('hand' + 'to drag over').

šu-ur$_3$-ra
scraping or grinding by hand; leveling, compacting; massage ('hand' + 'to shear' + nominative; cf., lu$_2$-ur$_3$-ra, 'sculptor'; ĝir$_2$-ur$_3$-ra, 'sharpened knife').

šu-ur$_3$(-ra)^{mušen}
a bird with clipped wings, such as the goose, kur-gi$_4$^{mušen} (Akk. *kapru III*, 'clipped').

šu...us$_2$
to send, dispatch; to push or knock on (a door); to hold out in the hand ('hand' + 'to reach out').

šu-zi
wild; aggressive; Emesal dialect for saĝ-zi, 'crown'.

šu-zi-da
right hand ('hand' + 'good, true, faithful').

šu...zi-zi(-g)
to raise one's hand (in violence); to cheat, plunder; to be angry ('hand' + reduplicated 'to rise up').

šu zi...ĝal$_2$
to bestow ('hand' + 'life; good' + 'to place'; cf., zi...ĝal$_2$).

šu zi...ĝar
to grant; to bestow generously ('hand' + 'life; good' + 'to deliver').

šu$_2$
(cf., šuš$_2$).

^{ĝiš}šu$_2$-a; ^{ĝiš}šu$_4$-a
stool ('to go down' + nominative).

ŠU$_2$.AN
(cf., en$_2$; kunga$_2$).

ŠU$_2$.AŠ$_2$
(cf., gibil$_2$).

ŠU$_2$.DUN$_4$
(cf., šudul, šudun).

ŠU$_2$.EŠ
(cf., lil$_3$).

ŠU$_2$.MUL
(cf., kunga).

ŠU$_2$.NE
(cf., lil$_5$).

šu$_2$-šu$_2$
to pour out; to pour out the voice - shout; to eat and drink; to cover (reduplicated 'to make go down').

^{sa}šu$_2$-uš-gal
(cf., sa-šu$_2$-uš-gal).

šu$_4$
(cf., šuš).

šu$_4$(-g)
to stand; to be deployed, set up; to be present (plural, reduplication class) (represents sug$_2$ in Neosumerian period legal documents).

^{ĝiš}šu$_4$-a
(cf., ^{ĝiš}šu$_2$-a).

ŠU$_4$.AN
(cf., en$_2$).

šu$_4$-luḫ
ritual cleansing, purification ritual, cleansing rite; lustration (cf., šu-luḫ).

šu$_{12}$
(cf., šude$_3$).

šub
to cast, throw; to be cast; (with -da-) to drop, let fall; to leave behind, neglect; to fall (upon); to fall into (with locative); to fell (a tree); to tear down (a wall); (with -ta-) to throw out, remove; to offer, provide (šu, 'hand' + bu$_5$, 'to rush around').

adj., abandoned, neglected (cf., šub-ba).

šub-ba
a particle expressing 'apart from'; left apart; set apart ('to fall, drop, leave behind' + nominative).

šub-lugal
subordinate of the king ('to drop; to delegate' + 'king').

(u2) $\mathbf{šub_5}$ **[ZI&ZI.LAGAB]**
rush, sedge (?) found in canals, with seven nodes (Akk. *šuppatu*).

$\mathbf{šub_6}$ **[ŠID]**
to lick (Borger MZL questions reading, but very clear instance in Inana D 60).

$\mathbf{šuba_{(2/3)}}$ **[**$\mathbf{šuba_2}$**=ZA.**$\mathbf{MUŠ_3}$**]**
n., a precious stone - agate (?); a priest (cf., sipad).

v., to be bathed, clean ('licked clean' ?).

adj., pretty; shining.

$\mathbf{šubtu_{3-7}}$ **[KASKAL.LAGAB etc.]**
seat; dwelling, quarters; animal's lair; place of ambush (Akk. *šubtu(m) I*).

šubun
(cf., g̃išbun).

šubur, subar
slave, servant, deprived person; Northerner; earth (su, 'body', + bar, 'foreign') [ŠUBUR archaic frequency: 181].

ŠUBUR
pig aged under one year - piglet, in archaic texts (cf., $šaḫ_{(2)}$-tur).

$\mathbf{šude_3}$**,** $\mathbf{šudu_3}$**,** $\mathbf{šud_3}$**,** $\mathbf{šu_{12}}$
n., prayer, blessing [$ŠU_{12}$ archaic frequency: 1].

v., to pray, bless (šu, 'hand', + de_2, 'to pour out, shape', cf., $gu_3...de_2$, 'to talk, sing').

$\mathbf{šud_3...ra_2}$
to pray ('to pray' + 'plural, to come, go').

$\mathbf{šudug_{(2)}}$**,** $\mathbf{šutug_{(2)}}$
a reed hut for purification rites; basket.

g̃iš $\mathbf{šudul_{(2,3,4,5)}}$**, g̃iš** $\mathbf{šudun_{(2,3,4,5)}}$**, g̃iš uštil**
yoke, crosspiece (šuš/$šu_4$, 'to cover', + dul_4, 'to cover, yoke', or $dun_{(4)}$, 'warp yarns connecting opposite sides of a loom frame').

šudum
(cf., $šita_5$).

šudum-ma, $\mathbf{šitim_2}$**-ma**
reckoning (cf., $šita_5$).

g̃iš šudun
(cf., g̃iššudul).

šug
(cf., šuku).

(kuš) $\mathbf{šuḫub_2}$ **[MUL];**
šuḫub [$\mathbf{ŠU_2}$**.MUL]**
(cf., (kuš)$suḫub_2$[MUL]).

šuku, $\mathbf{šukur_2}$**, šug [PAD]**
allotted food portion, (daily) ration, provision; subsistence field plot; prebend allotment; food offering (regularly followed by $ra_{(2)}$) (šu, 'portion', + kud, 'to separate'; Akk., *kurummatu(m)*, 'food allocation, ration').

lu2 $\mathbf{šuku-dab_5-ba}$
person who takes an allotted subsistence field ('allotted field plot' + 'to take' + nominative).

lu2 $\mathbf{šuku-nu-dab_5-ba}$
persons who do not take allotment plots ('allotment' + 'not' + 'to take' + nominative).

uruda/g̃iš šukur [IGI.GAG]
spear, lance (šu, 'hand', + kur_2, 'enemy'/ kur_{12}, 'fangs').

gi šukur
fence.

$\mathbf{šukur_2}$
(cf., šuku).

šukur$_2$-ud
daily ration ('food allotment' + 'day').

šul, sul
n., young man; warrior; invader; a bad disease involving skin eruptions (probably Akkadian loanword from *šalālu*, 'to plunder; to deprive').

v., to hurry, hasten, speed up (cf., ul$_4$); to rub into the skin (duplication class).

adj., strong; heroic; proud; splendid; youthful.

šul-a-lum
punishment (probably Akkadian loanword from *šalālu*, 'to plunder; to deprive').

mul dšul-pa-e$_3$-a
the planet Jupiter ('the resplendent young man'; cf., pa...e$_3$; (ĝiš)al-tar).

šul-zi
worthy young man ('young man' + 'good; true').

(uruda)šum(-me)
n., saw; knife; sickle with serrated edge - copper or bronze with a weight of 3 ma-na (ša$_5$, 'to cut, break' + eme, 'tongue, utensil' ?; cf., šag$_5$, 'to slaughter') [? TAG archaic frequency: 48 ?; concatenates 7 ? sign variants].

v., to slaughter, butcher.

šum$_2$
(cf., sum, šum$_2$).

šum$_4$
(cf., sumun).

(u2)šumunda
a long grass or weed that often caught fire (cf., (u2)SUMUN.DAR).

šun$_2$[MUL]
n., star.

v., to shine brightly.

šur, sur
to rain; to produce a liquid; to flow, drip; to extract seed oil; to process wine and juices; to press (out); to spray out; to brew (beer); to submerge; to slip through; to slither; to flash, gleam (šu, 'to pour' + to flow; cf., šeĝ$_{3,7}$).

(ĝiš)šur-min$_3$
(cf., (ĝiš)šu-ur$_2$-me).

urudašur-šur-ru-um
copper part of a knife or razor (ĝir$_2$) (Akkadian loanword).

šur$_2$
(cf., sumur).

šur$_2$-du$_3$^{mušen}
(cf., sur$_2$-du$_3$^{mušen}).

šur$_2$-ra$_2$[KUŠ$_2$.DU]
raging, furious, impetuous.

šurim, šurin, šuru, šurum, šurun
animal excrement, dung; stable (šur, 'to flow, drip', + imi/im, 'clay, mud').

šurun$_{4,5}$, šurin$_{4,5}$
cockroach; cricket.

šuš, šu$_4$; šuš$_2$, šu$_2$; šuš$_3$
n., cover, covering; surface; a musical interval sounded by lyre strings 6+3 (reduplicated šu, 'hand'; cf., šub) [ŠUŠ$_2$ archaic frequency: 243].

v., to set, become dark, be overcast (said of the sun); to cover (with -da-); to envelop, overwhelm; to overthrow; to throw down; to go down; to give way; in music, to tune down (reduplication class).

šuš$_2$-luḫ...aka
to clean (a canal) (cf., šu-luḫ...aka).

šuš$_3$[IŠ]
(cf., kuš$_7$; šuš).

šuš$_4$
to fell trees; to chop away (reduplicated šu, 'hand').

šuš$_{5,6}$, šu$_{5,6}$
bedding, litter, feed, fodder (scattered for animals) (reduplicated uš, 'to support').

šušana
one third (part) (cf., igi-3-$\tilde{g}al_2$; šanabi) (loan from Akk. *šulšan, šuššān*).

šušur$_{(2)}$
stove grill ($šuš_2$, 'to cover', + uru_3, 'hot, luminous metal').

^{gi}**šutug**$_{(2)}$
reed hut, shelter; chest; a basket for dates.

šutum[GI.NA.AB.UL]; šutum$_2$ **[GI.NA.AB.TUM]**
storehouse for precious goods (cf., šu-tum; ^{lu2}gi-na-ab-tum$_{(2)}$, 'guarantor') (šu, 'hand, portion', + tum_2, 'to bring').

^{tug2}**šutur[MAḪ]**
a ceremonial type of garment or cloth, coat (?).

T

ta, da$_2$
n., nature, character [TA archaic frequency: 34; concatenates 6 sign variants].

interrogative pronoun in Emesal dialect, the Emesal form of a-na, 'what?' - ThSLa §123.

-ta-
ablative-instrumental prefix with inanimate reference, denotes the direction from or out of the referenced something; more rarely denotes 'with, by means of' - ThSLa §460-§464.

-ta
ablative-instrumental case postposition, from, out of; under (for inanimate only); with, by means of; locative with remote deixis, to, in, over there (as in an-ta, ki-ta and saḫar-ta); suffixed to portion numbers, denotes distributive 'each'; with temporal expressions u_4/mu ...-ta, means 'since ...' or '... days/years ago', but u_4 ...-a-ta means 'from the day when ...' = 'after ...' - ThSLa §203-§213, §489-§490.

ta-a-aš
for what reason?; why? ('from' + locative + terminative ?; cf., a-na-aš(-am); a-na-še, 'why'?).

ta-am$_3$
Emesal dialect for a-na-am_3, e-ne(-am_3) and nam-mu/nam-$\tilde{g}u_{10}$, 'what is it?' - ThSLa §123.

ta-gim
Emesal dialect for a-na-gim, 'how?' - ThSLa §123.

ta-ḫab$_{(2)}$**; ta-ta-ḫab**$_{(2)}$**; ḫab**$_{(2)}$
v., to soak, saturate; to drip, libate (cf., im-ta-ḫab; ^{dug}ni$\tilde{g}_2$-ta-ḫab) (cf., Akk., *ṭubbû*, 'soaked', Orel & Stolbova #2476, ***ṭub-** "drip, be wet"; cf. also, *taḫāḫu*, 'to pour (over), drench').

adj., soaked; dripping.

-ta-ra-
ablative case prefix, 'from', ThSLa §467, §427, §465.

ta$_6$
(cf., $taka_4$).

tab
n., companion, partner, associate; brassiere; pair; both; twin; sum, whole; sting; infection; fever (cf., tab_2) (side/approach + pair, represented by the lips).

v., to hold, clasp, grasp; to bind; to shut, bolt; to cover; to block; to flatten; to join, interlock (with -da-); to be/make double (sometimes reduplicated); to reprise, repeat; paired off, arranged in pairs or parallel columns; to add up; to start, inaugurate; to appear; to burn; to heat up; to tremble, shake; to devastate; to tear down; to make haste.

adv., together (precedes the modified verb).

tab-ba
partner; doubling; describes land added to cultivation ('to join; to be double' + nominative).

TAB.KUN
(cf., $megida_2$, $megidda_2$).

TAB.TAB
(cf., ad_4).

TAB.TI
(cf., megida, megidda).

tab_2[$\tilde{G}IR_2$]; tab
to hold, squeeze; to burn, brand; to be inflamed; to suffer (written with sign for scorpion).

tabira
(cf., tibira).

taga, taka, $tuku_5$, tag, tak, ta_3
to touch, handle, hold; to weave; to decorate, adorn; to strike, hit, push; to attack; to afflict; to play an instrument; to start a fire; to fish, hunt, catch (can be reduplicated) (te, 'to approach' + aka, 'to do, place, make') [TAG archaic frequency: 48 ?; concatenates 7 ? sign variants].

^{uruda}TAG
(cf., $^{(uruda)}$šum(-me)).

TAG.ME
(cf., šum).

tag-tag(-ga)
to slaughter; slaughtered.

tag_4
(cf., $taka_4$).

taḫ
(cf., daḫ; when Sumerian words are borrowed into Akkadian, d becomes t).

taka
(cf., taga).

$taka_4$, tak_4, tag_4, ta_6, da_{13}
n., remainder.

v., to leave; to abandon; to disregard, neglect; to divorce, drive out (cf., di(-bi)-ta...tak_4); to draw up, make out (a legal document); to leave with a person, entrust; to set aside, save; to open, leave open (reduplication class - ta_6-ta_6 or da_{13}-da_{13} in *marû*) (ta, 'to, from', + ge_4, 'turn from, restore') [TAK_4 archaic frequency: 128; concatenates 2 sign variants].

TAK_4(.IM)
(cf., IM×TAK_4).

$taka_4$...lal/la_2
to open ('to open' + 'to reach').

tal
large jug (sides + abundant).

tal_2[PI]
n., breadth; understanding (sides; character + abundant).

v., to be/make wide, broad; to spread, unfold (said about wings, arms).

$tal_{3,4,5}$
(cf., $til_{4,5,6}$).

taltal
knowledge, experience, wisdom (reduplicated tal_2, 'understanding').

tam, $ta_{(5)}$, tu_2[UD]
polished; cleansed; shiny; reflective; pure; reliable; trustworthy; favorable; favorite brother ($tu_{5,17}$, 'to wash, bathe', + am_3, 'to be').

ukuš2/(g̃iš)ḫašḫur/šimtam_2-šil-lum; tam_2-ši-lum; tam_2-še-lum
colocynth, a poisonous annual plant related to the common watermelon, with fruit about the size and shape of an orange, also called bitter apple, bitter cucumber, or gourd; a drug, the extract of colocynth, a powerful laxative and cathartic, which drug was produced in weight units of 2 to 11 ma-na, where one *mina* = ca. 500 grams (Akkadian loanword from *damšillu*, 'a kind of cucumber', and *tamšilum*, 'a resin'; cf., $ukuš_2$-ti-gil_2-la).

tan_2[MEN]
to become clean, clear, light, free (ta, 'nature, character' + an, 'sky, heaven'; cf., tam).

tar
v., to cut; to separate; to distinguish; to decide; to determine; to inquire; to smoke; to cut off, break off, destroy, terminate (cf., kud, kur_5, ku_5) (ta, 'from', + ur_4, 'to shear, reap'; cf., dar, nam...tar, and en_3...tar) [TAR archaic frequency: 56; concatenates 2 sign variants].

adj., deliberate, judicious.

$^{(ĝiš)}$targul[DIMGUL], durgul
mooring pole or apparatus (dar_2, 'to bind', + gul, 'enormous').

^{ĝiš}taškarin, taskarin[TUG_2]
box shrub or small tree (or its heavy, hard wood - boxwood) (may be Akk. loan).

te, de_4
n., cheek; skin; membrane; thorn, sting; characteristic symbol, tattoo (cf., temen; me-te) [TE archaic frequency: 199].

v., to prick, pierce; to dye red; to tattoo (usually reduplicated) (cf., te, de_4, $teĝ_3$; ten/te-en).

Emesal dialect interrogative, 'when?; why?'.

te-, de_4-
Emesal dialect optative and affirmative verbal prefix, cf., $ḫe_2$- and de_3-.

-te-
(cf., -de_4-).

te, de_4, $teĝ_3$; ti, $tiĝ_4$
v., to approach, reach, meet (someone: dative; inanimate: loc.term -e); to attack, assault, hit; to harrass, trouble; to be frightened (alternating class, *ḫamṭu* stem; cf., te-$ĝe_{26}$).

TE.A
(cf., kar).

te-am_3
Emesal dialect for e-ne(-am_3) and nam-mu/nam-$ĝu_{10}$, 'what is it?'.

te-$e^{mušen}$
Emesal dialect for $tum_{12}{}^{mušen}$, $tu^{mušen}$, 'pigeon, dove'.

te-en
(cf., ten).

te-eš...dug_4/du_{11}/e
to roar, resound, thunder ($teš_2$, 'together', + 'to speak/do').

te-$ĝe_{26}$(-d)
to approach, meet (someone: dative); to attack, assault; to be frightened, worried (alternating class, *marû* stem; cf., te).

te-me-en; te-me
(cf., temen).

te-te(-ma)
(cf., te-$ĝe_{26}$).

te_3
(cf., teme).

te_8[A_2]^{mušen}
bearded vulture.

te_8-$us_{(2)}$(-gu-la)^{mušen}
a bird of prey ('bearded vulture' + us_2, 'to build (a nest)' + 'large').

tebiru
(cf., tibira).

$teĝ_3$
(cf., te, de_4; ti).

$^{ĝiš/u2}$$teḫi_3$[NIM]
(cf., $^{ĝiš/u2}$$diḫ_3$).

^{ĝiš}$teḫi_4$, $deḫi_4$[IDIM]
staff; support.

teme, $te_3$$^{(sar)}$
prickly glasswort (Salsola kali), bushy salt-loving plants growing in the saline marshes, related to the tumbleweed - sheep and cattle devoured the edible green plant for its saltish taste - glass and

lye soap were made from the soda yielded by its burnt ashes (cf., nağa) (Akk., *mangu I*, 'mung bean, sprout' ?) (te, 'to prick', + me, 'to be').

temen[TE]
perimeter; foundation(s), basis; foundation-charter; foundation platform; a figure on the ground made of ropes stretched between pegs, or the pegs themselves; excavation (often syllabically written te-me-en) (te, 'symbol'/ti, 'side, edge, stake', + men$_{(4)}$, 'crown') [TE archaic frequency: 199].

ten; te-en
n., cold, coolness (te, 'to approach, near' + en, 'time' referring to shorter days ?).

v., to trample, extinguish; to soften, allay; to cool (te-en-te in *marû*).

teš$_2$[UR]
n., sexuality, sex; vigor; shame, modesty; dignity, honor; all kinds, all sorts, all of; each of them (te, 'to approach', + aš$_2$, 'to desire'; cf., ašte).

v., to feel ashamed; to bring together.

adj., homogeneous; insulting, shameful.

adv., together (often with suffix -bi, -ba or -e).

teš$_2$[UR]-bi(-a)
altogether; in harmony; in the same manner; in equal shares; brought into accord (cf., ni$_2$-bi(-a)) - ThSLa §132, §89 ('together' + adverbial force suffix; Akk., *mithāriš*).

teš$_2$(-bi)...gu$_7$
to devour everything; to consume (cf., ur-bi-gu$_7$, 'jackal') ('together' + 'to eat').

teš$_2$...i-i
to pray ('together' + 'to rise'; cf., me-teš$_2$...i-i).

teš$_2$(-a)...sig$_{10}$/si$_3$(-ke;ga)
to make agree; to provide in equal amounts ('together' (+ locative) + 'to supply, serve, provide').

teš$_2$...(nu-)tuku
to have (no) shame; shameless ('shame, modesty' + ('not' +) 'to have').

teš$_2$-teš$_2$-a
multiplied together (in math. texts) (redup. 'bring together' + nominative).

tešlug
small young animal, fledgling.

ti
side, edge; rib; chest, torso; arrow (cf., te, ^{ğiš}ti, di$_3$, diḫ, and til$_3$) [TI archaic frequency: 105; concatenates 2 sign variants].

^{ğiš}ti
strut, brace, rib (such as for a wagon or chariot) ('rib').

ti...bala
to turn sideways, onto one's side; to signal ('rib; side' + 'to revolve, turn over').

^{ğiš}ti-bala
(wooden) sign ('wooden strut' + 'to change, revolve').

ti-gi$_4$
(cf., tigi).

ti-gid$_2$-lu$_2$$^{(mušen)}$; ti-gi$_4$-lu$^{(mušen)}$
(cf., tigidla$_{(2/3)}$$^{(mušen)}$).

^{u2}ti-gil$_2$(-la)
colocynth vine plant (cf., ukuš$_2$-ti-gil$_2$-la) ('rib' + 'to tangle' + nominative).

ti-IGI-
(cf., ti-lim-da$_{(3)}$/du$_{(3)}$).

ti-la
raw, uncooked (cf., til; til$_3$) (Akkadian *balṭu(m)*, 'living, alive').

$^{(dug)}$ti-lim-da$_{(3)}$/du$_{(3)}$ $^{(zabar/ku3-babbar/ku3-sig17)}$
a large drinking vessel, that could be made of bronze, silver, or gold (Akkadian *tilim(a)tu*, 'a drinking vessel').

ti-mar-uru$_5$
arrow quiver (cf., ^{kuš}e$_2$-mar-uru$_5$).

ti-mud...ĝal$_2$
to create life ('life' + 'to give birth' + 'to be').

ti-na
adv., strongly ('to live; healthy' + subordination suffix -a).

ti...ra
to shoot an arrow ('arrow' + 'to stab').

ti-ri$_2$-da/ga
barrier; fence; outcast; a bird that lived in the reed-banks (ĝiš-gi) (Akkadian *teriktu*, 'reed fence').

ti-ri$_2$-ĝal$_2$^{al}
(cf., al-ti-ri$_2$-gu$_7$^{mušen}).

^{gi}ti-um(-ma)
a reed mat used for covering roofs and doors ('rib' + 'rope').

^{ĝiš}ti-zu$_2$
barbed arrow ('arrow' + 'teeth; flint'; cf., e$_2$-zu$_2$).

ti$_8$^{mušen}
(cf., te$_8$).

tibir
carving knife.

tibir$_{(2,3,4,5)}$
slap, blow, strike; palm; hand (te, 'cheek', + bir, 'to wreck, break').

tibira, tebiru, tabira
metalworker, coppersmith, joiner (tab, 'to hold, clasp', + uru$_3$, 'luminous object', but cf., IE *dhabh, 'to fit together' as in L. *faber*, 'artisan who works in hard materials'; Akk., *tabīru/a*, 'coppersmith', *(w)erû(m)*, 'copper'; cf., uruda, 'copper').

tibira$_2$, ibira
merchant, tradesman (Proverb 3.108 describes how the peddler 'flays' or 'skins' the open hand, tibir, of the customer; cf., zilulu).

tibula
(read now, tigidla).

tidnum[UG.UG or UG$_2$.UG$_2$], midnum
tiger ?, leopard ? [? TIDNUM archaic frequency: 1].

tigi[BALAĜ.NAR]; tigi$_2$ [NAR.BALAĜ]; tigi$_x$ [BALAĜ.LIL$_2$]; ti-gi$_4$
drum or drummable harp; a hymn composition for which this is the lead instrument (ti, 'life', + gi$_4$, 'to restore', or gid$_2$, 'long'; cf., tigidla, 'a musical instrument').

$^{(MUNUS)}$tigi-di
wailing women ('women' + 'drum' + 'speaking/doing').

tigi-ni$_3$-du$_{10}$-ga/e
harp of beautiful sound ('harp' + 'thing' + 'sweet' + genitive).

$^{(ĝiš)}$tigidla$_{(2/3)}$$^{(mušen)}$; ti-gi$_4$-lu$^{(mušen)}$
lute; tambur; tamboura; a long-stemmed stringed instrument; a bird ('drummable harp' + 'happiness').

tiĝ$_4$
(cf., te, de$_4$; ti).

til; til$_3$[TI]
to be ripe, complete; to make complete; to perform required service; to finish paying off a contract, complete a transaction; to pluck; to put an end to, spend, exhaust, finish; to cease, perish; to be halted (became same sign as bad and idim; cf., sumun/sun) (iti, 'moon', + il$_2$, 'to be high; to shine' ?) [? ZATU-644 archaic frequency: 65; concatenation of 2 sign variants].

^{ĝiš}til-lu-ub$_2$
a tree used for roof beams in the OS period (cf., ^{ĝiš}ḫa-lu-ub$_2$).

TIL-lu-ug
elephant ('lion-killer' ? or 'battle-elephant' ?; pi_3 = BAD = TIL, Akkadian *pīru(m), pīlu, pēru*; Persian *pīr*; Hebrew *pīl*, 'elephant').

til_3, ti(-l)
n., life (te, 'to approach and meet', + li, 'to be happy').

v., to live; to keep alive; to survive (with -da-); to dwell; to be present at (with locative) (cf., til; til_3) (suppletion class verb: singular stem; cf. sig_7).

$til_{4,5,6}$, $tal_{3,4,5}$
cry, shout, scream (te; ti, 'to be frightened', + ?).

tilḫar
cloud.

tilla[URI]
a resinous bush (Akk., *urṭû*).

$tilla_2$; $tilla_3$
market place; crossroads; town square (til_3, 'to keep alive' + nominative) [$TILLA_2$ archaic frequency: 5].

$^{MUNUS}tilla_2$
'street woman', prostitute.

tilmun
(cf., $dilmun^{(ki)}$).

tim
(cf., dim).

tin
n., life; health, vigor; wine [TIN archaic frequency: 93].

v., to cure; to be healthy; to live.

$^{u2}TIN.TIR^{sar}$
(cf., $^{u2}gamun$, 'cumin spice'; with ^{ki}, the city of Babylon).

$^{(ĝiš)}tir$
forest; grove; thicket; reed-bank; bow (perhaps conflation of two compounds: ti, 'arrows' + ur_3, 'beams, rafters'; ti, 'arrow' + ru, 'to send'; cf., tir-an-na; $^{ĝiš}illuru$; ti...ra).

tir-an-na
rainbow ('bow' + 'sky' + genitive).

tirum, tiru
courtier, "son of the palace" (Akk., *tīru(m)*, 'a courtier').

$titab_{(2)}$
kiln-dried germinated malt for crushing into beer mash (cf., bappir; $munu_4$; sun_2; a-si_3-ga) (til_3/ti, 'life', + tab, 'to burn').

tu
to interfere (cf., tud and tur_5) [TU archaic frequency: 54; concatenates 3 sign variants].

$tu^{mušen}$
(cf., $tum_{12}{}^{mušen}$ and du_5-mu).

tu(-b); tu_{11}(-b)
(cf., dub; dun).

tu-da
(cf., tud).

tu-di-da; du-di-da; tu-di-tum
dress-pin (on a woman's breast) - could have a cylinder seal slipped onto the top for carrying, but the average person did not have a cylinder seal; fibula to hold a cloak closed; toggle-pin - made of bronze, copper, silver, or gold, weighing from 1 to 5 gin_2 - read KA-ba as zu_2-ba, 'its tooth, sharp point' (Akkadian *tudittu(m)*).

tu-dur
a circular blank weighing ¼ gin_2 for making a necklace bead such as ḫi-in-tum (tud, tu, 'to be born, fashioned, transformed' + 'necklace').

$TU-gur_4{}^{mušen}$
(cf., tum_{12}-$gur_4{}^{mušen}$).

tu-lu(-ub); tu-ul
to be/make loose, limp, slack, idle; to turn back; to loosen a musical string; to excuse, remit, make a gift of (Akkadian *tullû*, 'to hang up' ?).

^{ğiš}**tu-lu-bu-um;**
dulbu$_x$[GUL.BU]
plane tree or wood (Akkadian *dulbu(m)*, 'Oriental plane tree').

tu-mu
(cf., tumu).

tu-ra
(cf., tur$_5$).

TU-ru-na
(cf., duruna or $^{(im)}$duruna$_2$).

tu-ud
(cf., tud).

tu-ul
(cf., tu-lu).

tu$_2$
(cf., tam).

tu$_{3,25}$
(cf., tum$_{2,3}$).

tu$_{5,17}$
n., bath.

v., to wash, bathe; to pour; to make libation (probably reduplication class).

tu$_6$
exorcism; conjuration; magic ritual, spell; exorcistic formula.

tu$_6$-du$_{11}$-ga
spell ('spoken exorcistic formula'; Akkadian *tuduqqû*, 'spoken formula').

tu$_6$-tu$_6$
incantations, spells (reduplicated 'exorcistic formula').

tu$_7$
soup, broth; soup pitcher.

tu$_9$
(cf., tug$_2$).

tu$_9$-ba$_{13}$[TUG2-ME]
a shiny cloak or coat worn by kings and high priests/priestesses; royal robe of office (cf., tuba).

tu$_{10,11}$
(cf., dun/tun$_{(2)}$; tun$_{(2)}$/tu$_{10}$(-b)/tu$_{11}$(-b)).

tu$_{10}$-tu$_{10}$(-b); tu$_{11}$-tu$_{11}$(-b)
to smash; to overwhelm; to hit (cf., tun$_{(2)}$/tu$_{10}$(-b)/tu$_{11}$(-b)).

tu$_{15}$
(cf., tumu).

tu$_{15}$...dirig
(cf., ni$_2$...dirig).

tu$_{15}$-ğar$_7$-du$_2$
west, westwind; western ('wind' + 'western desert').

tu$_{15}$...mer
to be windy ('wind' + 'storm wind').

tu$_{15}$-mer
north, northwind ('wind' + 'anger').

tu$_{15}$-sa$_{12}$-ti-um
eastwind ('wind' + 'eastern mountains').

tu$_{15}$-si-sa$_2$
northwind ('wind' + 'straight').

tu$_{15}$-u$_{18}$-lu
southwind ('wind' + 'storm').

tu$_{17}$
(cf., tu$_5$).

tub$_x$
(cf., tun).

tuba[ME]
cloak, garment (cf., tu$_9$-ba$_{13}$).

tud, tu, dud$_2$, du$_2$
to bear, give birth to; to beget; to be born; to make, fashion, create; to be reborn, transformed, changed (cf., tur$_5$) (to approach and meet + to go out).

tud-sum
onion or garlic bulb for planting ('to beget' + 'onion').

tud$_2$[SIG$_3$.UZU]
to spank; to cane; to hit, beat, thrash (tu, 'to interfere', + motion).

tug_2, tu_9
cloth; cloth garment; robe (side + to encircle) [TUG_2 archaic frequency: 311; concatenates 3 sign variants].

$^{ĝiš}TUG_2$
(cf., ^{ĝiš}taškarin).

$^{lu2}TUG_2$
fuller (cf., $^{lu2}azlag_2$).

tug_2-ad-tab
cloth for reins ('cloth' + 'harness/reins').

tug_2-ba
clothing allotment, ration ('garment' + 'share, rations').

tug_2-bir$_7$-ra
torn clothes ('cloth' + 'to rip to pieces' + nominative).

tug_2-dim-gal(-la-k)
sail on a mast ('cloth' + 'mast' + genitive).

tug_2-du$_8$
textile fuller, felt-worker; rope-maker ('cloth' + 'residue; to bake').

tug_2-du$_8$-a
piece or bundle of felt; plaiting (of wool) ('to make felt' + nominative).

tug_2-gada-ḫi-a
wool and linen cloth ('wool cloth' + 'linen' + 'to mix').

tug_2-gu$_2$-lal
blanket (for an animal); shawl ('cloth' + 'back of neck' + 'to drape').

$^{(ĝiš)}tug_2$-gur$_8$/gur
the last plowing (before harrowing); a type of sub-soil plowshare; breaking up (of soil); a type of plow that could be used instead of or after the ^{ĝiš}apin-tug_2-sig$_{18}$/^{ĝiš}apin-šu-sig$_{18}$ (cf., ^{ĝiš}bar-dil) (originally LAK 483, 'to plow', + 'deep').

tug_2-ib$_2$-du$_3$
a woolen garment ('cloth' + 'waist, hips' + 'to mold').

TUG_2-KA
(can be misreading of zid$_2$-ka(-še$_3$)).

$^{(lu2)}tug_2$-kal-kal(-la)
tailor, stitcher, sewer, patcher ('cloth, garment' + 'to repair, mend' + nominative; Akk., *mukabbû*).

tug_2-:n:-kam-us$_2$
cloth of n-grade quality (cf., niga 3-kam-us$_2$) ('cloth' + 'nth' + 'to follow').

tug_2-KIN
(cf., tug_2-sig$_{18}$).

tug_2-ku-ru-um
mourning (?) clothes (Akkadian *kūru*, 'daze, depression, stupor').

tug_2-MAḪ
(cf., ^{tug2}šutur).

TUG2-ME
(cf., tu_9-ba$_{13}$).

tug_2-me-ze$_2$-er-ra
Emesal dialect (cf., mu-dur$_7$(-ra)).

tug_2 mu-du$_8$-um/e
felt cloth (cf., tug_2-du$_8$-a).

tug_2-mu-dur$_7$[BU]-ra
(cf., mu-dur$_7$(-ra)).

tug_2-niĝ$_2$-bara$_3$-(g)
bed spread ('cloth' + 'thing' + 'stretched out').

tug_2-niĝ$_2$-dara$_2$
loincloth ('cloth' + 'thing' + 'to bind; belt, sash, sanitary towel').

tug_2-niĝ$_2$-dara$_2$-gala$_2$-sir$_2$-ra
pubic band; sanitary towel or napkin for a woman ('cloth' + 'thing' + 'to bind; belt, sash' + 'vulva' + 'dense; feverish' + nominative).

tug$_2$-niĝ$_2$-dun$_3$-du$_3$
a woolen garment ('cloth' + 'thing' + 'to bring low' + 'to mold').

tug$_2$-niĝ$_2$-lal
a woolen garment (cf., $^{(tug2)}$niĝ$_2$-la$_2$) ('cloth' + 'thing' + 'to drape').

tug$_2$-niĝ$_2$-lam$_2$
a festive fabric or garment, dress ('cloth' + 'thing' + 'an awe-inspiring quality').

tug$_2$-niĝ$_2$-lam$_2$-tab-ba-šar$_3$
tug$_2$-niĝ$_2$-lam$_2$ cloth with double-thread ?, royal quality ('to bind, be double' + 'royal (quality)').

tug$_2$-niĝ$_2$-sal-la
a woolen garment ('cloth' + 'thing' + 'vulva' + genitive).

tug$_2$-niĝ$_2$-sig-sig
scarf, sash ('cloth' + 'thing' + redup. 'small, narrow').

tug$_2$-niĝ$_2$-ur$_5$-ra-ak-a
fine quality clothes ('cloth' + 'thing' + 'to gasp' + nominative).

tug$_2$-sig$_{18}$[KIN], tug$_2$-saga$_{11}$[KIN]
the first plowing with a deep-plow, mentioned in Umma texts from the fourth and fifth months of the year (cf., $^{(ĝiš)}$tug$_2$-gur$_8$/gur) (originally LAK 483, 'to plow', + 'to cut, break; to flatten, crush').

tug$_2$-siki
hem; fringe ('cloth' + 'hair'; Akk., *sissiktu(m), sikkum*).

TUG$_2$-ŠE.KIN
(Umma writing for tug$_2$-sig$_{18}$).

TUG$_2$-TAG
to fill or pile cloth (?) (sign may have originated as the implement LAK 483 + 'to weave; to strike').

$^{(lu2/munus)}$TUG$_2$-tag(-tag-ga)
weaver of the hem or fringe of a cloak ('cloth' ? + 'to weave, decorate, strike'; Akk., *māḫiṣu ša sissikti*, equated in lexical texts to $^{lu2\ (ĝiš)}$pana-tag-ga).

tug$_2$-TAR
short-cut robe (?) ('cloth' + 'to cut').

TUG$_2$-TUG$_2$
(cf., mu$_4$).

$^{(MUNUS/lu2)}$tug$_2$-tug$_2$-bal
a primarily female performer; ecdysiast ? ('the one who changes clothes'; Akkadian *kāpišum* and *kāpištum* from *kapāšu(m)*, 'be abundant').

tug$_2$...ur$_3$
to make a sacrifice; an act of concession by the loser in a court case ('clothing' + 'to drag').

tug$_2$-us$_2$-šar$_3$
cloth just below royal quality ('cloth' + 'to follow' + 'royal (quality)').

tug$_2$-uš-bar
woven cloth (as opposed to felt) ('cloth' + 'weaver').

tug$_2$-ZI-ZI-a
magnificent (?) robe ('cloth' + 'to spend' + nominative).

tug$_4$
(cf., tuku$_4$).

tugul
(cf., tuḫul).

tuḫ, taḫ$_2$
(cf., duḫ).

tuḫul, tugul[NAGAR.ZA-*tenû*]
hip(s), pelvis, thigh (bone) (tud/tu, 'to give birth', + ḫul$_2$, 'joy').

tuḫul-ku$_5$
crippled hip ('hip' + 'to curse'; cf., a$_2$-šu-ĝiri$_3$-ku$_5$, 'cripple').

tuku, tuk, duk$_2$, tug, du$_{12}$, tu$_{12}$
n., creditor (tuku with singing/speaking meaning, cf., du$_{12}$) [KAB/TUKU archaic frequency: 105].

v., to marry; to enter; to bring; to acquire, obtain; to receive, get; to have, own; to be respected; to have a claim, as in a debit note, against somebody (with -da-) (*marû* reduplicated form in this meaning: tuku-tuku) (te, 'to reach', + ku, 'to build; to lie down').

tuku$_4$, tuk$_4$, tug$_4$
to tremble; to be angry; to shake (probably reduplication class) (tu$_{15}$, 'wind', + ku$_4$, 'to enter').

tuku$_5$
to fill or pile cloth (?) (cf., taga).

(ĝiš)tukul[KU]
mace; weapon; arms (te, 'cheekbone', + kul, 'handle; heavy, thick', cf., Samson wielding the jawbone of an ass as a weapon in Judges 15).

ĝištukul-e...dab$_5$
engaged by force for work ('weapon' + ergative agent marker + 'to seize, bind, hire').

ĝištukul...sig$_3$
to slaughter ('mace, weapon' + 'to strike, hurt').

tukum, tukun[ŠU.NIĜ$_2$.TUR.LAL]
if, in case; perhaps; at once, soon - the Sumerian irrealis particle.

tukum-bi
if, in case (conditional clause); please; certainly (usually followed by *ḫamṭu* verb form) - ThSLa §145-§146.

tukum-bi...-nu
except - ThSLa §146 ('if' + 'not').

tukur$_2$[KA×ŠE], tukur$_3$[KA×U$_2$]
to gnaw, nibble; to grind one's teeth; to pluck; silence; silent repetitive behaviors.

tul$_2$, dul$_2$
public fountain, well, cistern; lowland; depths; reservoir (tu$_{5,17}$, 'bath', + to lift, be high, deep).

tul$_2$-ta(-pa$_3$-da)
foundling; handicapped person (can also be read pu$_2$-ta(-pa$_3$-da)) ('from a well' = 'found abandoned in a well').

tum
work, action; crossbeam; arrow quiver [TUM archaic frequency: 48; concatenates 4 sign variants].

tum$_{2,3}$, tumu$_{2,3}$, tu$_{3,25}$
to bring, deliver; to carry away; to obtain; to be suitable, fit, worthy (of somebody with dative; or something with locative/loc.-terminative infix); to prepare (suppletion class verb: *marû* singular object; cf., de$_6$, laḫ$_4$) (in *marû* plural, tum$_3$-tum$_3$[-mu] or tum$_2$-tum$_2$-mu) (ta, 'from', + u$_2$, 'food', + ma$_4$, 'to leave').

tum$_2$-ma
suitable, fit, worthy.

tum$_4$, tumu$_4$[NIM]
to carry (ta, 'from', + u$_2$, 'food', + ma$_4$, 'to leave').

tum$_9$
(cf., tumu).

tum$_{12}$^{mušen}, tu^{mušen}
dove (cf., tum$_{2,3}$, 'to bring, carry', and the term "carrier pigeon", which is actually a rock dove - name could also be onomatopoeic from the dove's monotonous cooing song).

tum$_{12}$[TU]-gur$_4$^{mušen}
a domesticated dove - this was a smaller bird that only got 4 gin$_2$ of grain, while the pigeon ir$_7$^{mušen} got 6 gin$_2$ ('dove' + 'plump').

tuma[KU]
to break wind, emit flatus (tu$_{15}$, 'wind', + ma$_4$, 'to leave, depart, go out').

tumu, tum$_9$, tu$_{15}$[IM]
wind; cardinal point, direction (ta, 'from', + mu$_2$, 'to blow').

tumu-
(cf., tu$_{15}$-).

tumu$_{2,3}$
(cf., tum$_{2,3}$).

tumu$_4$
(cf., tum$_4$).

tun$_{(2)}$, tu$_{10}$(-b), tu$_{11}$(-b)
to constrict; to defeat; to massacre; to break up, smash; to overwhelm (cf., dun).

tun$_2$
(cf., dun).

tun$_3$[DUN$_3$], dun$_3$, du$_5$
n., pocket, pouch, bag, case; bandage, wrap; leek; entire content; stomach; lip; rim (cf., gin$_2$, giĝ$_4$, 'a small ax; shekel' - DUN$_3$ lacks the *gunû* lines of GIN$_2$ in ED IIIb texts) (te, 'cheeks' + nu, 'likeness') [SUG$_5$ archaic frequency: 67].

adj., intact, bound.

TUN$_3$...bar
(cf., aga$_3$[GIN$_2$]...bar).

tun$_3$-bar
mustache ('lip' + 'outside').

^{ĝiš}tun$_3$-gal
sack lyre ('pouch, stomach' + 'large').

TUN$_3$.PAD
slice, morsel of food ('stomach; lip' + 'bite of food').

TUN$_3$.UŠ
(cf., aga$_3$-us$_2$).

tur
n., child; young (of herd animals); second in rank (tu, 'to be born', + uru$_3$, 'to watch, guard, protect') [TUR archaic frequency: 272].

v., to be/make small; to be insufficient; to reduce; to erode.

adj., small, little, young.

tur...gu$_7$
to eat modestly ('little' + 'to eat').

tur-tur(-bi)
n., little ones; young ones (cf., didi, di$_4$-di$_4$-la$_{(2)}$) (reduplicated 'little' + 'its').

adj., little.

TUR-TUR-la
(cf., di$_4$-di$_4$-la).

TUR.ZA&TUR.ZA
(cf., zizna).

tur$_3$[NUN.LAGAR] (orig. sign diff. from LAGAR); tur$_5$
animal stall; birth-hut; byre; sheepfold, cattle-pen, corral; stable; a frequent metaphor for a temple, sanctuary (cf., tur) [TUR$_3$ archaic frequency: 121; concatenates 3 sign variants].

tur$_3$-gu$_3$-nun
sanctuary with the loud voice ('birth-hut as metaphor for sanctuary' + 'voice' + 'great, noble').

tur$_5$, dur$_{11}$, tu, du$_2$
n., newborn; weakness; sickness.

v., to be or become sick; to suffer (tur$_5$-ra can be mistakenly read for kur$_9$-ra, 'to bring in', MZL 86 vs. 87).

adj., weak; sick; afflicted; incapacitated, referring to a worker.

tuš
n., home (te, 'to approach', + uš$_8$, 'foundation place, base').

verb singular, to (cause to) dwell, reside; to be at home; to settle; to encamp; to set up, establish, install; to sit, squat; to lie down; to serve (suppletion class verb: singular *ḫamṭu*, *marû* singular, tuš-u$_3$ and in *marû* participial form, tuš-u$_3$-de$_3$; cf. plural, duruna).

tuš-a
who is/are doing service, who is engaged in the service, took on for; attached/ assigned to... ('to sit' + nominative).

tuš...g̃a$_2$-g̃a$_2$
to dwell ('home' + 'to establish').

U

u
ten (cf., ḫa$_3$).

Emesal dialect for lugal and en, 'lord, master; lady; king'.

-u
(cf., /-ed/).

u$_{(2,3,4,8)}$
n., an expression of protest; cries, screams; the grunting, panting of battle; fight, dispute.

v., to bend over.

U.AD
(cf., gir$_4$; udun$_x$).

U.DIM×ŠE
(cf., gakkul).

U.GA
(cf., utu$_2$).

U.GAN
(cf., šagan, šakan).

U.GUD
(cf., ul).

U.GUN$_3$
(cf., ugun).

U.G̃AR
(cf., pad).

U.KA
(cf., ugu).

U.KID
(cf., šita$_4$).

U.MU
(cf., udun).

U.PIRIG̃
(cf., kušum$_4$; kiši$_{10}$).

U.PIRIG̃...tag
(cf., kušu/kušum$_4$(-ki)...tag).

U.SAG̃
(cf., sag̃šu; sag̃tuš$_x$).

U.U
(cf., mana, man).

U.U.U
(cf., eš).

U.UD.KID
(cf., nig̃in$_3$, ni$_9$).

u$_2$
n., plant; vegetation; herbs, weeds, thicket, grass; brushwood, firewood; vegetable; food; bread; pasture; load [U$_2$ archaic frequency: 225; concatenates 3 signs].

v., to nourish, support.

adj., strong, powerful (man); grass-fed (animal).

Emesal dialect variant for modal prefix u$_3$. Variant of Emesal dialect u$_5$, 'fat, cream, oil', in u$_2$-li ?.

^{na4}u$_2$
emery stone, the abrasive grains of which the Sumerians used to cut, polish, and pierce stone, and to pierce metal (Akk., *šammu(m)*).

u$_2$-a
caretaker, provider, provisioner ('food' + 'water, drink').

$^{(g̃iš)}$u$_2$-bil$_{(2)}$ (-la$_2$)
charcoal; charcoal-burner ('brushwood' + 'to burn' + nominative; Akk., *upellû(m)*).

u$_2$...bu-bu(-r)
to tear out plants ('plant' + reduplicated 'to tear out').

$^{(lu2)}$u$_2$-du(-l)
(cf., udul).

^{gi}u$_2$-du$_3$ (-du$_3$)
reed bundle ('plant' + 'to make'; Akk., *īlu II*).

u_2-dug_4
(cf., udug).

u_2-$durun_x$[TUŠ.TUŠ]-na
hay or dry brushwood ('grasses' + 'to dwell; to dry out' + nominative).

u_2-$ga^{mušen}$
raven (cf., $uga^{mušen}$).

u_2-gibil
fresh plant ('plant' + 'new, fresh').

u_2-gid_2-da
long grasses ('grasses' + 'long' + nominative).

u_2-$gu_{(3)}$...de_2
to shout, cry out; to lose; to disappear, vanish; to escape; to be lost ('grasses' + 'to call out').

u_2-$gu_{(3)}$-de_2-a
lost, vanished (such as an animal carcass).

u_2...gu_7
to graze; to feast ('plants, grass, food' + 'to eat').

u_2-gu_7
(plant-based) food; pasture ('plants, grass, food' + 'food, fodder').

u_2-gug
n., shortage, need; famine, starvation; burn mark, brand (cf., $^{u2}gug_4$; ^{u2}gug).

v., to lack, be in need; to burn, scorch, brand; to paralyze.

adj., deaf, mentally handicapped; paralyzed.

u_2-$\tilde{g}a_6$(-$\tilde{g}a_2$)
brushwood carrier ('plants' + 'to carry' + nominative).

u_2(-u_2)-$še_3$...$\tilde{g}$en[DU]
to go to fetch firewood (parallel, a-$še_3$...$\tilde{g}$en) ('twigs, firewood' + terminative + 'to go').

$^{\tilde{g}iš/u2}U_2$.$\tilde{G}IR_2$/U_2.$\tilde{G}IR_2$*gunû*
(cf., $^{\tilde{g}iš/u2}adda_3$; $^{\tilde{g}iš/u2}kišig$).

u_2-$\breve{h}ab_2$
a colored plant; an adjective for leather, possibly 'gallnut dyed'.

u_2-$\breve{h}$i-a
fodder crop ('grasses' + 'mixed').

u_2-$\breve{h}$i-in
(cf., u_4-$\breve{h}$i-in).

u_2...$\breve{h}ub_{(2)}$
to be deaf; to deafen (cf., u_2-$gu_{(3)}$...de_2).

u_2-$\breve{H}$UR.SA$\tilde{G}^{sar}$
(cf., $^{u2}azugna^{sar}$, $^{u2}azukna^{sar}$, $^{u2}azubir^{sar}$).

u_2-il_2(-la)
brushwood carrier ('plants' + 'to carry' + nominative).

u_2-$ki\tilde{g}_2$(-$\tilde{g}a_2$)
n., pasturage; reed bundle ('plants, grass, firewood' + 'to seek, work' + nominative).

v., to seek out (the height or depth).

u_2-ku-ug/k
(cf., u_2-gug).

u_2-kul(-la)
a grass or weed (cf., u_2-numun(-na)) ('grass' + 'heavy, thick').

u_2-kur
'mountain plant', a common medicinal spice or condiment, perhaps an earlier form of u_2-$\breve{H}$UR.SA$\tilde{G}^{sar}$ (= saffron) (cf., $kuš_2$[U_2], 'cubit'; $^{(u2)}kur$-$ra^{(sar)}$, 'a medicinal plant'; u_2-za-gin_3, 'fresh hay').

u_2...la_2
to diminish; to stem (the flow of water).

$^{gi}u_2$(-la_2)
reed bundle ('plant' + lal/la_2, 'to bind, carry'; Akk., *īlu II*).

u_2-lal$_3$
a sweet water-plant, the eating of which is a metaphor for sexual intercourse ('plant' + 'honey').

u_2-li
herb(s); Emesal for 'fine oil' ? ('plant' + 'fine smelling').

u_2-lil$_2$-la$_2$
(cf., u_3-lil$_2$-la$_2$).

u_2-lipiš-gig
nettles (?) ('plant' + 'anger/heart' + 'illness').

$u_{2/3}$-lu-lu-ma-ma
type of composition, cowherd's song (?) (cf., a-la-la).

u_2-lu$_5$-ši
(cf., ulušin).

u_2-ma-am; u_2-ma-mu
animal(s), (exotic) beast(s) (Akk., *umāmu(m)*).

U_2.NAĞA.GA^{mušen}
(cf., uga^{mušen}).

U_2-NINNI$_5$ [TIR/TIR]
a resin measured by volume.

u_2-nir-ĝal$_2$
splendid or tasty food ('plants' + 'noble, tasty').

u_2-nu-kiĝ$_2$-ĝa$_2$
untested grazing grounds (cf., u_2-kiĝ$_2$-ĝa$_2$).

u_2-numun [KUL] (-na)
wild grass; seeds; dried flower stigmas used as spice, such as saffron ('plant' + 'seed').

u_2...ri (-g)
to collect firewood ('plants' + 'to glean; to bring').

u_2-ri-in
pure (e.g., beer) (cf., gi-rin, 'pure').

u_2-rum
n., possession; property (cf., uru_3[-m], 'to watch, guard, protect').
adj., own; private, personal (property).

U_2.SA
(cf., dida; mu-us$_2$-sa).

u_2-sag$_{11}$
fascine to sustain a canal bank or levee ('plants' + 'to cut, break, harvest').

u_2-sag$_{11}$...ze$_2$
to cut fascine plants ('fascine' + 'to cut, pluck').

u_2-saĝ
first fruits; early crop (cf., nisaĝ) ('plants' + 'first').

u_2-saḫar
vegetation (and) earth used in dam work, probably dirt reinforced with grass, twigs, branches, fascines, etc. ('vegetation' + 'earth').

u_2-sal (-la)
a low-lying fertile area along a water-course - meadow; security, serenity ('grass, plants' + 'to persist').

u_2-sal-la...nu$_2$
to lie down in security ('meadow/security' + 'to lie down').

$^{(d)}u_2$-si$_4$-an
evening ('food' + 'red' + 'sky').

u_2...su$_3$-su$_3$ (-d)
to dine; to eat ('food' + 'to sip').

u_2-su$_3$-su$_3$ (-d)
meal(-time).

u_2-sug$_4$
unclean, menstruating woman (cf., uzug$_2$).

u_2 (-u_2)-še$_3$...ĝen [DU]
to go to fetch firewood (parallel, a-še$_3$...ĝen) ('twigs, firewood' + terminative + 'to go').

u_2-šim
n., grass and herbs = pasture, vegetation, greenery (a Sumerian example of asyndetic hendiadys); hunger.

adv., in hunger, hungrily.

U_2-TIR
(cf., ^{u2}gamun$_2$[TIR]).

u_2-tu-ug
phonetic writing for udug$_2$.

u_2-tul$_{(2)}$
(cf., udul).

u_2-uru$_{12}$[UR$_3$]
(cf., murum$_4$).

u_2-za-gin$_3$
fresh hay ('grass' + 'clean').

u_2-ze$_2$
to tear out thicket, brushwood ('plants' + 'to cut, pluck').

u_2-zug$_4$
foul food (?); polluted, ritually unclean (cf., uzug$_2$, 'menstruating, unclean woman').

u_2-zuḫ
cultically impure person (cf., uzug$_2$, 'menstruating, unclean woman').

u_3 [IGI.DIB]
n., sleep (cf., u$_5$, u$_{(3,4,8)}$, and dur$_x$) [according to S. Lieberman, u, u$_3$, and u$_4$ were pronounced /o/].

v., to sleep.

conj., and, and then, but, moreover - ThSLa §143 (Akkadian loanword from *u*, 'and'; cf., -bi-da(-ke$_4$)).

u_3-
prospective modal prefix, if; when; after; often used as a polite imperative - ThSLa §409-§414.

u_3-
prospective modal prefix /u-/ with conjugation prefix /ĩ-/ - ThSLa §304.

u_3-
a pronominal prefix in a compound noun, usually deriving a noun from a verb (cf., nu-).

-u_3-
represents 2.sg. pronominal prefix after mu- in Gudea period - ThSLa §291.

-u_3
in the enclitic position of an imperative verb, possibly indicates motion towards (cf. g̃e$_{26}$-nu and g̃en-na), probably represents the changed conjugation prefix /ĩ/ - ThSLa §412.

-u_3
vowel harmony version of ergative or locative/terminative postposition -e - ThSLa §172.

$u_{3/8}$(-a)
interj., woe!; alas!; also occurs as a soothing sound, but this is mainly u$_5$-a.

u_3-a
n., sleep ('to sleep' + nominative).

u_3-a-di
a type of composition, defined lexically as a complaint (*tazzimtu(m)*), however, the surviving fragmentary exemplar, *Lipit-Eštar H*, is a song in praise of Inanna.

u_3-an-bar
(cf., u$_4$-bar).

u_3-bu-bu-ul
n., pus, pustule; flame(s); part of an oven; fire arrow (pronominal prefix + reduplicated bul$_{(5)}$; bu$_{(5)}$, to ignite; to sprout; Akkadian *bubu'tu(m)*).

adj., inflamed; inflammatory.

u_3-da; u_4-da
if; introduces a conditional sentence construction (cf., u$_4$-da g̃iš-en) (prospective modal prefix + comitative suffix).

u_3-di
sleep; rest; daze, depression (cf., u$_6$-di) ('sleep' + 'doing'; cf., g̃i$_6$...di).

u_3-dub$_2$
charcoal ('sleeping' + 'to fan').

u_3-en$_3$...ša$_4$[DU]
to explain (prospective modal prefix + 'enigmatic background' + 'to make noise'; cf., en$_3$...tar, 'to investigate').

u_3-gul...g̃ar/g̃a$_2$-g̃a$_2$
to pray to; to entreat (with dative) (prospective modal prefix + 'evil' + 'to take oaths').

u_3-gul-g̃a$_2$-g̃a$_2$
pious.

u_3-ḫi-in; u_4-ḫi-in
unripe or fresh date fruit, in the autumn; a gold date-shaped jewelry piece (Akkadian loanword, from *uḫinnu(m)*, 'fresh date(s)'; cf., zu$_2$-lum(-ma)).

$^{g̃iš}u_3$-KU
(cf., $^{g̃iš}u_3$-suḫ$_5$).

u_3...ku$_{(4)}$
to sleep (reduplication class); to fall asleep; to rest ('sleep' + 'to lie down; to enter').

u_3-ku-ku^{mušen}
probably the sandgrouse, which nests on desert ground, with the female sitting tight on her nest throughout the day to protect the eggs from the sun's heat - said to be a bird of ša3-sig3-ga, 'depression' ('sleep' + 'bird'; Akk., *ṣalla(l)lu*, 'a night bird').

u_3-ku-ru-um
baked (square) brick (Akk. loanword, from *ukurrum I*; *agurrum*; cf., sig$_4$-ab$_2$).

u_3-kul[NUMUN]
an occupation (pronominal prefix + 'heavy, thick').

u_3-la
anything; nothing (pronominal prefix + 'numerous').

$^{(MUNUS)}u_3$-li-li
a soothing lament; singer, songstress (pronominal prefix + redup. 'to rejoice, sing').

u_3-lil$_2$-la$_2$(-en-na)
a hole, opening in the ground; a lament for the dead.

u_3-lu-lu-ma-ma
(cf., u$_2$-lu-lu-ma-ma).

u_3-luḫ(-gi$_4$-rin)
(a fruitful, verdant) tree seedling, scepter - a symbol of enforcing justice (pronominal prefix + 'to sweep' - a cut-off palm sapling made a handy broom ?).

u_3-luḫ...su$_3$
to send out offshoots ('tree seedling' + 'to stretch, rejoice').

u_3-lul-la...ku$_{(4)}$
to sleep badly ('sleep' + 'treacherous' + 'to lie down; to enter').

u_3-lul-la ku-ku
The One Who Feigns Sleep, lit. He Who Sleeps a False Sleep, an epithet of Enlil.

u_3-ma; u_3-na
victory, triumph (prospective modal prefix + me-a, 'when in battle').

u_3-ma-
writing of prospective modal prefix u$_3$- + conjugation prefixes /ĩ-ba-/ in Gudea period - ThSLa §304.

u_3-ma-a-du$_{11}$
would you please say? (prospective modal prefix as polite imperative).

u_3-ma/u_3-na...gub
to attain victory, triumph; to stand proudly; rearing up, rampant ('when in battle' + 'to emerge standing').

$^{(g̃iš)}u_3$-ma$_2$
(cf., $^{(g̃iš)}u_5$-ma$_2$).

u_3-mi-
writing of prospective modal prefix u$_3$- + conjugation prefixes /ĩ-bi-/ in Gudea and NS periods - ThSLa §304.

u_3-mu-un
Emesal dialect for en, nin, or lugal, 'lord, master; lady; king; queen'.

u_3-mu-un-si
Emesal dialect for $ensi_2$(-k), 'city governor'.

u_3-mun; u_3-mu-un; umun
blood (pronominal prefix + mu_2, 'to make grow', + un, 'people').

u_3-na
domineering, pugnacious, wild, impetuous (cf., $\tilde{g}i_6$-u_3-na(-k)).

u_3-na-a-dug_4
letter, missive - ThSLa §62 (from introductory formula of letters, 'when you have said it to him').

u_3-nu-g̃ar-ra
fraud (?) (pronominal prefix + 'not' + 'established' + nominative).

u_3-nu-tu
barren woman (cf., u_3-tu, 'woman able to give birth').

u_3-ri-ga
threshed ? (barley) (pronominal prefix + 'to glean; to break open' + nominative).

u_3-ri_2-in
(cf., urin).

u_3-ru-ru
crooning; soothing lament.

u_3-sa-an
whip (early spelling, from Gudea Cyl. A - cf., $usan_3$) (pronominal prefix + 'cord, sinew' + 'tall; ruling').

u_3-sa_2(-g)
sleep ('sleep' + sag_9, 'sweet' ?, Gudea Cyl. A xii, 12 has u_3-sa-ga; cf., $\tilde{g}i_6$...sa_2).

u_3-sa_2...dab_5
to be overcome by sleep (u_3-sa_2, 'sleep' + 'to seize').

u_3-sar...aka; u_3-sa-ar...aka; u_4-sar...aka
to sharpen (Akkadian *šēlu(m)* ?).

u_3-su tuku
(cf., usu-tuku).

$^{g̃iš}u_3$-suh_5
a coniferous tree, conifer, either fir or pine (if a member of the pine family, the Turkish pine (*Pinus brutia*), closely related to the Aleppo pine (*P. halepensis*), is the only species native to Iraq); from the texts, the silhouette of the tree resembled a fish skeleton, its wood was used in ship building, for punting poles (up to 6 meters long), and its seeds or fruits were edible (cf., Orel & Stolbova #115, ***'isV'-/*'isVw-** "piece of wood", Sem **'VšsV'-* 'fir-tree splinter'; Akkadian *ešše'u*, 'touchwood, tinder', *ašūḫu(m)*, 'pine-tree').

u_3-sun$_{(2)}$
wild cow, cf., sun_2.

$^{g̃iš}u_3$-šub
brick mold; a platform for molding or drying bricks (same form as udun, 'kiln for bricks'; pronominal prefix + 'to throw, drop, plop'; cf., šab, 'to chip out, apportion out').

u_3-tu
n., woman able to give birth.

u_3-tu-(d)
v., to give birth; to create; to procreate; to be born ('to lie down' + 'to create'; cf., tud).

u_3-tu(-da)
n., new birth; litter; offspring, progeny ('to give birth' + nominative).

adj., newborn.

u_3-ul-
OS writing of prospective modal prefix u_3- and the conjugation prefix al-, with meaning 'when; after' - ThSLa §354.

u_3-ur_5-re
all this (pronominal prefix + 'these').

u_4
(cf., ud, $u_{(3,4,8)}$).

u_4... [verb phrase]-a(-a)
(at the time; on the day) when... - ThSLa §489 ('time' + subordination suffix + locative).

u_4...-a-gin_7
while... ; as in ('time' + 'as; when').

u_4... [verb phrase]-a-ta
after (the time) when... - ThSLa §489, §208 ('time' + 'after').

u_4...a_2-bi/ba(-/ak/)
to be or do on time, at the right moment ('time' + 'moment' + adverbial force suffix).

u_4(-X)-am_3
for a day, within a day; for X days, within X days ('days' + number + enclitic copula).

u_4(d)-an-na
light of the heavens ('light' + 'heaven' + genitive).

u_4-aš-a
in one day ('day' + 'one' + locative).

u_4-ba
at that time; on that/this day; in those days; when; then ('time; day' + bi-a as demonstrative).

u_4-X ba-zal
on the Xth day (of the month) ('days' + 'to elapse').

u_4-bar
midday (cf., an-bar).

u_4-bi-ta
the past ('days' + 'those' + 'from').

u_4-$buru_{14}$
at the time of the harvest ('days, time' + 'harvest').

u_4-da
daily; today; in the daytime; bright light; when; if; the following verb is usually *ḫamṭu* - ThSLa §148 (cf., u_3-da; u_4-da) ('day' + 'temporal locative').

u_4-da g̃iš-en
if ('today' + irrealis suffix).

u_4-da-ta
after that ('today' + 'away from'; cf., u_4...-a-ta).

u_4-da-tuš
a clown, jester, or entertainer who performed with bears and pigs; bear-ward (= Greek *Arcturus*) ('today' + 'to set up camp').

u_4(-bar)-dag̃al
extensive daylight, long day ('day' (+ 'middle') + 'wide').

u_4-de_3
light; storm; by day; at that time, then; by storm (cf., ud, u_4).

u_4-de_3-eš(-e)
adv., like the daylight; like the sun - ThSLa §89 ('daylight; sun' + adverbial suffix).

u_4-de_3 gid_2-da
all day long ('by day' + 'to be long' + locative).

u_4-du_{10}-ga
auspicious, happy day(s) ('day' + 'sweet, good' + nominative suffix).

u_4-du_{11}-ga
an appointed time or date ('day' + 'to speak' + nominative suffix).

u_4-e_3
(cf., ^{d}utu-e_3).

u_4-gid_2-da
all day long ('day' + 'to be long' + locative).

u_4-$g̃al_2$
illuminating, glowing ('light' + 'placing').

u_4-ḫe_2-$g̃al_2$-la
days of abundance ('day' + 'overflow, abundance' + genitive).

u_4-ḫi-in
(cf., u_3-ḫi-in).

u_4-ḫuš
fierce storm ('storm' + 'furious, terrible, awesome').

u_4(d)-i_3-li; u_4(d)-ul-la
tomorrow ('day' + Akkadian *elûm*, 'to come up' and *eli*, 'above, beyond').

u_4(d)-imin
seven days ('day' + 'seven').

u_4-kur$_2$-še$_3$
in questions, 'at any time, ever'; 'forever in the future'; in the past, 'always' ('day; time' + 'to change' + terminative).

u_4 min-am$_3$
for two days - ThSLa §200 ('days' + 'two' + enclitic copula).

u_4 min-še$_3$
in two days; for two days - ThSLa §200 ('days' + 'two' + terminative).

u_4-mud
darkness; dusk ('day; light' + 'dark, dim').

u_4-na-me...nu-tuku
there was never ('time' + 'anyone' + 'not having'; cf., lu$_2$...na-me...nu-).

u_4-NE
(cf., u_4-de$_3$).

u_4-nu-du$_{10}$-ga
unhappy day(s) ('day' + 'not' + 'sweet, good' + nominative suffix).

u_4-ra$_2$-bu^{mušen}
(now read, a$_{12}$-ra$_2$-bu^{mušen}).

u_4-ri-a, u_4-re-a
in those (far remote) days ('days' + remote demonstrative affix + locative).

u_4-ri-dam
since those (far remote) days ('days' + remote demonstrative affix + ta/da$_2$ + am$_3$, 'it is from').

u_4-sa$_9$-a
half a day; midday ('day' + 'half' + nominative suffix).

u_4-sakar[SAR](-ra)
crescent moon; new moon; segment of a circle - crescent; lunar symbol; a small gold or silver jewelry piece; a plant, possibly rushes or nettles; a type of vessel ('day, light' + sal, 'to be narrow' + kara$_2$, 'to shine' + nominative suffix; Akk. *uskāru(m)*; cf., e$_2$-u_4-sakar).

u_4-sakar-gibil
reviving new moon, thin crescent moon ('crescent moon' + 'renewal'; cf., e$_2$-u_4-sakar).

u_4-su$_3$-ra$_2$(-še$_3$) [UD.SUD.DU]
for eternity ('time' + 'far-reaching' + terminative).

u_4-X-še$_3$
for X days ('day' + number + terminative case postposition).

u_4...(al-)šu$_2$-šu$_2$-ru
to become cloudy or dark ('daylight' + šuš$_2$/šu$_2$, 'to become dark' + šur, 'to rain' ? + *marû* 3rd. sing. ending with vowel harmony).

u_4-šu$_2$-uš(-e)
daily; day by day; sunset (cf., ^{d}utu-šu$_2$-a, 'sunset; west') ('day, daylight' + šuš$_2$/šu$_2$, 'to become dark' + locative-terminative postposition).

u_4-X-ta
'since X'; 'X days ago' - ThSLa §207.

u_4-te(-en)
evening ('daylight' + 'to extinguish, cool down').

u_4-te(-na)
morning ('daylight' + 'to approach').

u_4 (a-na) ti-la/til$_3$-a
lifetime ('time' + 'what' + 'to live' + nominative).

u_4-tu(-ud)-da
birthday ('day' + 'birth' + genitive).

u_4-tur(-ra)
early in the day; short in duration; youth ('time' + 'small').

u_4(d)-u
ten days ('day' + 'ten').

u_4(d)-ul(-la)
at your service ('anytime' ?).

u_4(d)-ul(-la)
ancient days; future days (cf., u_4(d)-i_3-li) ('days' + 'remote' + nominative).

u_4(d)-ul-li_2-a-aš
forever; until remote days ('days' + 'remote' + nominative + 'unto').

u_4(d)-ul-li_2-a-ta
from long ago; long since; distant time ('days' + 'remote' + nominative + 'from').

u_4-za-ḫa(-al)...aka
to disappear; to make disappear, obliterate; to waste a day ('time/light' + 'to flee, hide, be lost' + 'to cause'; cf., $zaḫ_{2,3}$; ḫal).

u_4...zal
the day dawns; to shine brightly; to gladden; to spend the day (in rest); to elapse; to bring to readiness; to continue, carry on; to waste time; to delay; to be late ('time' + 'to flow, pass').

u_4-zal-la
day, morning, dawn, daybreak; the third watch of the night, the watch of daybreak, early morning ('day' + 'to flow, elapse' + nominative).

adj., long lasting, persisting; roasted, parched (cf., gi_{16}-sa(-a)).

u_4-X zal-la
on the Xth day ('day' + 'to flow, elapse' + nominative).

u_4-zal(-le)-da
in the daytime; during the course of the day ('day' + comitative case postposition).

u_4-zal-$še_3$
tomorrow ('day' + terminative case postposition).

u_5 [ḪU.SI]
n., male bird, cock; totality; earth pile or levee; raised, unirrigable land area; cabin (on a boat); the south (sometimes written u_3) [U_5 archaic frequency: 1].

v., to mount (in intercourse); to be on top of; to mount for transport; to ride; to board (a boat); to steer, conduct.

adj., (raised) high, especially land or ground; southern (sometimes written u_3).

Emesal dialect for g̃iš/g̃eš, 'tree; wood'.

Emesal dialect for i_3, 'fat, cream, oil'.

$u_5^{mušen}$
a large white seabird described as eating 1/3 more grain than a goose - crane (?), swan (?), wild goose (?).

u_5-a
lullaby (cf., u_3-a) ('to raise high' + nominative).

$^{g̃iš}u_5$-apin
handle or attachment of a plow ('to ride' + 'plow').

u_5-$bi_2^{mušen}$; u_2-$bi_2^{mušen}$; ub-$bi_3^{mušen}$
whooping swan or crane (onomatopoeic).

$^{iti}u_5$-bi_2-gu_7
calendar month 3 at Drehem through Šu-Sin 3; calendar month 4 at Drehem after Šu-Sin 3; calendar month 4 at Ur during Ur III.

$^{g̃iš}u_5$-kun_4
step, rung (of ladder) ('to mount' + 'ladder').

$^{(g̃iš)}u_5$-ma_2; u_3-ma_2
ship's cabin, crew ('to ride' + 'boat').

$^{(g̃iš)}u_5$-šub
(cf., $^{g̃iš}u_3$-šub).

u_6
(cf., ug_6).

u_6...di/dug_4/e
to admire; to gain admiration; to observe ('admiration' + 'to speak, do').

u_6-di
admiration, amazement ('to be impressed' + 'doing').

u_6...e_3/i(-i)
to look; to appear ('to look at; to stare at' + 'to be or become visible').

u_6-e...gub
to be wonderful ('marvelous' + ergative agent marker + 'to stand').

u_6-nir
ziggurat, temple tower ('to be impressed' + 'to raise high').

u_8
mother ewe, adult female sheep (over two years of age) (pronunciation may be "ow", as in English "ouch"; cf., us_5; $u_{3/8}$(-a); $u_{(3,4,8)}$) [U_8 archaic frequency: 86].

-u_8-
allomorph of focalization marker -n- after mu- or nu- Yoshikawa, ASJ 16, 269.

u_8(-a)
interj., woe!; alas!; an expression of pain; lament.

u_8-udu-ḫa_2
sheep; (flock of) sheep and goats.

u_9
(cf., ug_5, un_3).

u_{11}
(cf., ḫu).

u_{11}-ri_2-in
(cf., ḫu-ri_2-in).

u_{18}[GIŠGAL]
huge (cf., ulu_3 and lu_2-u_{18}[ĞIŠGAL]-(lu)).

u_{18}[GIŠGAL]-lu
southwind [with classifier [tu15]]; storm; sandstorm; a demon ('huge' + 'numerous, abundant').

u_{18}-lu(-da)...dul
to cover with a storm ('storm' + 'with' + 'to cover').

u_{18}[GIŠGAL]-ru(-n)
n., a literary composition division; sighing (as of waves).

adj., exalted; high; overwhelming; mighty ('huge' + 'to send'; cf., uru_{16}(-n); uru_2).

u_{20}[ŠE]
barley.

ub
corner, angle, nook; a small room; one of the four directions [UB archaic frequency: 124].

ub-
writing of prospective modal prefix u_3- with conjugation prefix /ĩ-/ and inanimate pronominal element /-b-/ - ThSLa §409.

ub-ba...gub
to deposit in the corner ('corner' + locative + 'to set').

ub-lil_2-la_2
outdoor shrine (cf., lil_2-la_2).

ub-šu-ukkin-na
assembly (cf., pu-u$ḫ_2$-ru-um) ('corner' + 'power' + 'meeting' + genitive).

[gi]ub-zal
edible reed shoots ('bright tips' ?).

[(kuš)]$ub_{3,5}$
a rectangular frame drum.

ub_4
cavity, hole; pitfall (Akk. *ḫuppu(m) II*, 'hole, pit'; *ḫabbu*, 'a pit'; *ḫuballu(m)*, 'pit, trench').

[lu2]ub_5-ku_3-ga
keeper of the sacred drum ('drum' + 'pure, holy' + nominative).

ubara[EZEN×KASKAL]
patronage, protection.

ubi^{ku6}
a marine and fluvial fish [UBI archaic frequency: 7; concatenates 2 signs].

ubilla$_{(2)}$
charcoal; soot (u$_2$, 'plant', + bil, 'to burn', + nominative).

ubisağ
(cf., umbisağ).

ubu[AŠ]
area measure, = ½ of an iku (= 50 sar).

ubur[DAG.KISIM$_5$×GA]; ubur$_2$[DAG.KISIM$_5$×LU]; ubur$_3$[DAG.KISIM$_5$×IR]
female breast, teat, bosom; udder (ub$_4$, 'cavity', + ir$_{(2)}$, 'liquid secretion').

ud, u$_4$
n., sun; light; day; time; weather; storm (demon) [UD archaic frequency: 419].

prep., when; since.

ud-X
(cf., u$_4$).

UD.BAD
(cf., lugud).

UD.DU
(cf., e$_3$, ed$_2$; ara$_4$).

UD.KA.BAR
(cf., zabar).

^{id2}UD.KIB.NUN
(cf., ^{id2}buranun).

UD.KUŠU$_2$
(cf., uḫ$_2$).

UD.UD
(cf., babbar, dadag).

UD*gunû*
(cf., murub$_4$/murub$_6$[UD*gunû*]).

ud$_2$[AŠ$_2$]
emmer (wheat).

ud$_5$, uz$_3$, ut$_5$
she-goat, nanny goat (Akk. *enzu(m)*; cf., Orel & Stolbova #1070, ***'anaz-** or ***'azan-** 'goat, ram', Semitic **'anz-* 'she-goat') [UD$_5$ archaic frequency: 109; concatenates 3 signs].

ud$_5$-ga-nağ
milking goat ('goat' + 'milk' + 'drinking').

$^{(ğiš)}$ud$_5$-sağ
central post, pillar, bond ('lead goat').

udu
sheep; small cattle; ram, wether (reduplicated ud$_5$, 'goat', or u$_3$, 'pronominal prefix', + du, 'to walk') [UDU archaic frequency: 452; concatenates 2 signs].

udu-a-udu-ḫur-sağ
hybrid of the domestic sheep with the mouflon ('sheep' + 'mouflon seed').

udu-bar-ğal$_2$
sheep set aside from the count ('sheep' + 'outside' + 'to be').

udu-bi
taxes due from the recipients of a parcel of land ('sheep' + 'its'; cf., maš-bi).

udu-dub
tablet-recorded sheep ('sheep' + 'tablet').

udu-EME-gi(-r)
(cf., udu-uli-gi(-r)).

udu-gir$_{15}$
native or Sumerian breed of sheep (sheep + domestic).

udu-ḫur-sağ
wild sheep or Asiatic mouflon; term may have been extended to the wild urial sheep ('sheep' + 'hill-country').

udu-i$_3$
fattened sheep ('sheep' + 'dairy fat').

udu-IDIM
wild sheep; planet; Mercury ('sheep' + 'heaven').

udu-kur-ra
highland sheep, producing low-class wool; designation in Umma for udu-kungal ('sheep' + 'mountain' + genitive).

udu-maš$_2$(-ḫi-a)
sheep and goats ('sheep' + 'goat' + 'mixed').

udu-niĝ$_2$-gu$_7$-a
fattened sheep ('sheep' + 'fattened').

udu-nita$_{(2)}$
a full-grown male sheep, ram (at least two years old), wether (except for breeding males, udu-ua$_4$, all males were castrated) ('sheep' + 'male').

udu-sar
a vegetable (?) ('sheep' + 'vegetable').

udu-siki
wool sheep ('sheep' + 'wool').

udu-šag$_5$-ga
slaughtered sheep ('sheep' + 'to slaughter' + nominative).

udu-šar$_2$-a
perfect sheep ('sheep' + 'totality; to slaughter' + nominative).

udu-še-gu$_7$-a
(wool from) barley-fed sheep ('sheep' + 'barley' + 'to eat' + nominative).

udu šu-nir
sheep whose wool was used to make streamers for the group standards.

udu-u$_2$
grass-fed sheep ('sheep' + 'plant, grass').

udu-ua$_4$[AMAŠ]
rutting ram; breed ram (cf., utua/ utua$_2$) ('sheep' + u$_5$, 'to mount' + a, nominative).

udu-uli[EME]-gi(-r)
sheep which produced coarse, unclassed gi-wool.

udug, utug
pitfall; an evil demon; ghost of dead.

udug$_2$, utug$_2$
a weapon.

udul/utul$_{(3,4,5,6,10)}$
chief herdsman - the highest level in the herding hierarchy (prefer unu$_3$(-d) reading instead of udul for AB$_2$.KU) (udu, 'sheep', + lu$_2$, 'man'; Akk., *utullu(m)*) [UDUL archaic frequency: 32; concatenates 4 sign variants].

udul$_2$
(cf., utul$_2$).

udun[U.MU]; udun$_x$[GIR$_4$]
kiln (for pottery and bricks); oven.

udun-maḫ
huge baking oven ('oven' + 'huge').

udun-še-sa-a
barley roasting oven ('oven' + 'barley' + 'to roast' + nominative).

ug$_{(2)}$
n., rage, anger, fury; storm(-demon); lion; wild animal; lamentation.

adj., furious, strong.

ug-gu...de$_2$
(cf., u$_2$-gu...de$_2$).

ug$_5$
(cf., ug$_7$; ug$_5$).

ug$_6$, u$_6$[IGI.E$_2$]
n., amazement; gaze, glance (['EYE' + 'HOUSE']).

v., to look at; to stare at, gaze; to be impressed.

adj., astonishing.

ug$_7$[UŠ$_2$]; ug$_5$[BAD$_3$]
n., death; dead person.

v., to kill; to die (suppletion class verb: singular and plural *marû* stem; plural *ḫamṭu*, which is sometimes reduplicated; cf., uš$_2$; cf., lu$_2$-ug$_5$-ga, 'murderer').

uga^{mušen}; ugu$_2$^{mušen}
a corvine bird - primarily the raven, but also crows, rooks, jays, magpies and jackdaws, relentless stealers of other birds' eggs and chicks, which nest in medium-sized colonies of 20 or more birds (note that the Mesopotamian Crow, Corvus capellanus, a distinct subspecies in the hooded/carrion crow complex, has a white body and black head and wings)

(cf., u_2-ga^{mušen}, 'food + milk bird'; Akk. *erēbu(m) II*, 'rook, jackdaw; crow, raven', where *erēbu(m) I* = 'to enter' - per CDA, *āribu* in AHw).

ugnim, uĝnim
army, troops; workgang; crowd; campaign ($uĝ_3$, 'people', or ug, 'anger' + nim, 'prince, governor').

ugra
reed bundle.

ugu[U.KA/GU_3]; ugu_2[A.GU_3]
n., skull; top of the head; top side; upper part; first part; voice (cf., $ugun_3$, ugu; ugu_4) (u_3, 'after it', + gu_2, 'neck').

pron., him, her, them, this one.

prep., upon, over, on top; after; comparative enhancer of adjectives.

ugu-ba
on top of it; excessive ('top side, upper part' + bi, 'its' + a, locative).

ugu-bi-ta
from upon it ('top side' + 'its' + 'away from').

ugu-$dilim_2$(-mu)
top of the head or skull ('skull' + 'spoon').

ugu_2[A.GU_3]
debits part of account tablet (cf., uga^{mušen}/ugu_2^{mušen}).

ugu_2...ba-a-ĝar
to place in a person's debit account; to place the account at a person's disposal; to transfer (property) ('account' + impersonal conjugation prefix + locative infix + 'to deposit') (cf., gu_2-a...ĝar).

ugu_4[KU]; ugu[U.KA/GU_3]
(cf., ugu_4-bi; $ugun_3$, ugu; ugu_4).

ugu_4-bi; a-gab_2
ape, monkey ('to give birth' + inanimate demonstrative ["Inanimate are things and animals." Thomsen, p. 49]).

ugudili^{ku6}, ugudil [$NINDA_2$×U_2+DILI]^{ku6}
a fish.

ugula [PA]
overseer, inspector; captain; foreman; prefect (loan from Akkadian *(w)aklu(m)*; Orel & Stolbova #1581, ***k,ol-**, 'look, see', Sem ***mVk,ul-** 'look').

ugula-aga_3-us_2
overseer of vassals ('overseer' + 'soldier').

ugula-e_2
temple overseer ('overseer' + 'house/ temple').

ugula-ĝe$š_2$-da
officer in charge of sixty men ('overseer' + ĝešta, 'sixty' + genitival postposition -a(k)).

ugula-ila_2
foreman of the porters ('overseer' + 'to carry').

ugula-uru(-na-/ak/)
captain of the/his city; a laborer qualification ('overseer' + 'city' + 'his' + genitive).

$ugun_3$, ugu; ugu_4
n., progenitor(u_3, 'pronominal prefix', + gan, 'to bring forth, give birth').

v., to beget, bear, procreate, produce (typically in expressions: ama-$ugun_3$ or a-a-$ugun_3$, 'the mother (father) who begot me').

adj., natural, genetic.

ugunu, ugun[U.DAR/GUN_3]
adorning speckles and lines; inlaid decoration (u, 'ten, many', + gun_3, 'to decorate with colors' may be popular scribal etymology; cf., ug, 'lion, any deadly cat' + n, 'discrete point').

$ugunu_2$, $ugun_2$[GAŠAN]; ugu-nu
lady, mistress, ruler; ointment, application (for eyes); paste for decorative inlay work.

$ugur_2$[SIG_7]
lintel; arch; commons (?) boundary (ig, 'door', + ur_3, 'roof'; cf., Akk., *ugāru(m)*, 'com-munally controlled meadow'; cf., $pa_{4/5}$-$ugur_2$).

$ugur_2$-igi
eyebrow; eyebrow inlay of lapis lazuli or gold in art ('arch' + 'eye').

$u\tilde{g}a_3$, $u\tilde{g}_3$, uku_3, un(-$\tilde{g}a_2$)
people; population; crowd.

$u\tilde{g}_3$-$\tilde{g}a_6$(-me) [UN-IL_2(-me)]
porter(s); menial worker(s); emp-loyee(s); the lowest level social class, totally dependent on rations ('people' + Umma reading for ila_2 sign, 'to bear, carry' + plural; Akkadian *kinattu(m)*).

$u\tilde{g}_3$-lu-a
multitudes ('people' + 'to be numerous' + nominative).

$u\tilde{g}_3$ sa$\tilde{g}$-$\tilde{g}i_6$
black-headed people = Sumerians ('people' + 'heads' + 'black'; see note for sa$\tilde{g}$-$\tilde{g}i_6$).

$u\tilde{g}_3$ $\check{s}ar_2$(-$\check{s}ar_2$)
innumerable people, endless multitude of people ('people' + 'to be many, innumerable').

uḫ(3)
n., lice, louse; nit; flea; moth; insect, parasite, vermin; turtle eggs/young [$UḪ_3$ archaic frequency: 14; concatenates 2 sign variants].

adj., moth- or worm-eaten.

uḫ...$uš_7$
(cf., aḫ...$uš_7$).

uḫ-tag-ga
infected by lice ('lice' + 'to strike, afflict'; cf., ki...tag, 'to lay eggs').

$uḫ_2$, $aḫ_6$[UD.$KUŠU_2$]; uḫ, aḫ; $uḫ_3$[$KUŠU_2$]
spittle; phlegm; slaver; foam, froth; paste; scum; venom; malice.

$uḫ_2$-pu_2
scum or foam on standing water ('spittle' + 'pool').

$UḪ_3$-^{d}INANNA
undertaker (cf., ŠITA-^{d}INANNA).

uktin
(cf., $ulutin_2$).

uku-us_2
(cf., aga-us_2).

$uku_{2,5}$
(cf., $ukur_{3,4}$).

uku_3
(cf., $u\tilde{g}a_3$).

UKU_3.IL_2
(cf., $u\tilde{g}_3$-$\tilde{g}a_6$).

ukum
dust (devil or storm).

$ukur_2$
butcher (ug_5, 'to kill', + kir, 'cow').

$ukur_{3,4}$, $uku_{2,5}$
n., poor man, pauper; poverty.

v., to be or become poor.

$ukuš_2$$^{(sar)}$
cucumber, melon, squash; a member of the vine-growing plant family Cucurbit-aceae - a cucurbit (u_2, 'plant, food', + kuš, 'skin, hide'; Akk., *qiššû(m)*, 'cucumber').

$ukuš_2$-ti-gil_2-la; $ukuš_2$-ti-gi-la; $ukuš_2$-ti-ki-la
spongy fruit of the colocynth vine from which a cathartic drug is prepared ('cucumber' + 'colocynth'; cf., tam_2-šil-lum and ^{ukuš2}li-li-$gi_{(4)}$^{sar}).

ul[U.GUD]
n., star; flower, blossom; bud; ornament; joy, pleasure, satisfaction; a capacity measure of 36 liters in Presargonic Girsu (cf., bariga) (interaction with Akk. *ulṣu(m)*, 'pleasure, rejoicing').

v., to glitter, shine; to blossom; to remain.

adj., remote, distant (in time); ancient, enduring.

UL-ḫe$_2$
horizon ('stars' + 'numerous').

ul.KU
receiver (?).

ul-li$_2$-a-ta
(cf., u$_4$-ul-li$_2$-a-ta).

ul-lu-ul
to hasten (reduplicated ul$_4$).

ul...sig$_7$
to blossom into full strength ('bud, blossom' + 'to complete, be beautiful').

ul...šar$_2$
to gladden; to exult ('joy' + 'to multiply').

ul-šar$_2$-ra
jubilation ('joy' + 'to multiply' + nominative).

ul-še$_3$
forever ('distant' + 'towards').

ul-ta
(cf., u$_4$-ul-li$_2$-a-ta).

ul-ti(-a)
happy mood; exuberance ('joy' + 'life' + genitive).

ul$_3$
(cf., ulul).

ul$_4$
v., to be quick; to hurry, hasten, harass; to rush (against) [? KIŠIK archaic frequency: 21; concatenates 3 sign variants].

adv., promptly, without delay.

ul$_4$-la-bi
adv., very soon, swiftly, quickly ('quick' + adverbial ending).

ul$_7$
to sprout, multiply (cf., dubul).

uli(-gi)
(cf., udu-uli-gi(-r)).

ulu$_3$$^{(lu)}$
storm; south direction (towards the Gulf) (cf., tu$_{15}$-u$_{18}$-lu; u$_{18}$) (u$_{18}$, 'huge', + lil$_2$, 'wind').

ulu$_3$-di; i-lu-di
a priest devoted to ritual lamentations; frequently used as a personal name ('sad song, lament' + 'speaking/doing'; cf., i-lu...du$_{11}$/e, 'to sing a dirge').

ulul, ul$_3$[KIB]; ulul$_2$
binding; harness; leash, chain; corridor, dog-run (cf., alal$_4$) (u, 'ten, many', + lal, 'to strap, harness', or cf., ul-lu-ul, 'to hasten') [KIB archaic frequency: 7].

ulušin$_{(2/3)}$
(date-sweetened) emmer beer (ul, 'joy', + šen, 'a copper kettle or cauldron'; Akk., *ulušinnu(m), ulušennu(m)*; *dišiptuḫḫu*, 'sweet beer').

ulutin$_2$, ulutim$_2$, uktin [SIG$_7$.ALAM]
physical or facial form; image; visage; attractive, attention-getting.

$^{(gi)}$um
a rope made of reeds or rushes; vine (cf., umu).

um(-ma)^{mušen}
a plentiful diving water bird with an unpleasant voice, probably the coot.

um-
writing of prospective modal prefix u$_3$- with conjugation prefix /ĩ-/ and ventive element /-m-/ in Gudea and OB period texts - ThSLa §409, §304.

-um
(cf., -g̃u$_{10}$-um).

um-ma
elderly lady; wise woman; witch (cf., umu/um).

um-ma-
writing of prospective modal prefix u$_3$- + conjugation prefixes /ĩ-ba-/ in OB period - ThSLa §336, §304.

um-me(-da)
(cf., emeda$_{(2)}$).

um-mi-
writing of prospective modal prefix u$_3$- + conjugation prefixes /ĩ-bi-/ in Isin-Larsa period - ThSLa §304.

um-mi-a; um-me-a
schoolmaster; scholar; artisan, craftsman, specialist (umu, 'wise or skillful teacher' + 'offices, functions' + nominative or genitive; cf., umun$_2$/umum).

umaḫ
marsh, swamp (u$_2$, 'plant', + maḫ, 'high').

umbin[GAD(.KID$_2$).UR$_2$]
nail; claw; talon; hoof; nail impression (on a clay tablet); pre-cuneiform stylus; hair pin; clamp; finger, toe; a type of chisel; wheel (of a chariot, wagon); leg (of furniture) (from Akk. *ubānu(m)*, 'finger, toe' ?; cf., šu-si, 'finger') [UMBIN archaic frequency: 34; concatenates 4 sign variants].

umbin-gud
oxen hooves; oxen tracks ('hoof; footprint' + 'ox').

umbin...kiĝ$_2$
to shear ('fingernail' + 'task').

umbin...kud
to shave; to shear; to manicure ('fingernail' + 'to cut off').

umbin...lal/la$_2$
to scratch ('fingernail' + 'to place, stretch, reach').

umbin-si
fingernail; hoof ('hoof; nail' + 'long, narrow thing').

umbin-še-ba
claws - retractable, disappearing feline nails; chisel (cf., šub; šab, 'to fall, disappear' + nominative).

umbisaĝ[ŠID]
scribe; administrator (umbin, 'nail impression [on a tablet]', + saĝ, 'counted head').

ummeda$_{(2)}$
(cf., emeda$_{(2)}$).

^{kuš}ummud, ummu$_3$[EDIN.LA$_2$]
(goatskin) water bag.

umu, um
old woman; nurse; wise or skillful teacher.

umun
title of respect; Emesal dialect for en, nin, or lugal, 'lord, master; lady; king; queen' (cf., u$_3$-mun, 'blood').

umun$_2$, umum
mold; raw form or material; idea; knowledge; scholar; scholarship; school, workshop (cf., simug, 'smith') [UMUN$_2$ archaic frequency: 114].

umun$_2$...aka
to act wisely; to treat reasonably ('knowledge' + 'to do').

umun$_3$
flea; louse.

umun$_{5,6,11}$
(stagnant) pool; swamp; a swamp plant.

umuš, uš$_4$
discernment; intelligence; (good) sense; reflection, consideration; decision (umu, 'wise or skillful teacher' + uš, 'foundation').

umuš...kur$_2$
to change one's mind ('discernment; decision' + 'to change').

un
(cf., uĝa$_3$, uĝ$_3$).

un-
writing of prospective modal prefix u$_3$- with conjugation prefix /ĩ-/ and animate 3.sg. pronominal element /-n-/ in all period texts - ThSLa §409, §304.

-un
represents 1.sg. or 2.sg. pronominal suffix /-en/ after a verb ending in the vowel -u - ThSLa §296.

UN-gal
king, queen, ruler (var. of lugal, perhaps from Emesal umun).

UN-IL$_2$(-me)
(cf., uĝ$_3$-ĝa$_6$(-me)).

un$_3$, u$_9$
high; tall.

unkin, ukkin
communal assembly, folkmoot (uĝa$_3$/un, 'people', + kiĝ$_2$/kin, 'to seek, fetch'; cf., unkin-ĝar-ra) [UKKIN archaic frequency: 108; concatenates 3 sign variants].

unkin-ĝar-ra
communal assembly ('people' + 'to fetch' + 'to establish' + nominative).

unu$_2$
(cf., unug$_2$).

unu$_{(2,6)}$-gal
great dining hall ('dwelling, dining hall' + 'great').

unu$_3$(-d) [AB$_2$.KU]
chief cowherd; cattle herder; feast (cf., udul/utul$_{(3,4,5,6,10)}$).

unu$_6$
(cf., unug$_3$).

unug$_{(2)}$, unu$_{(2)}$
dwelling; dining or banquet hall; fortress; jewelry, adornment; cheek; the city of Uruk (uĝa$_3$/un, 'people', + ig, 'door') [UNUG archaic frequency: 206; concatenates 3 sign variants].

unug$_3$, unu$_6$ [TEMEN.EŠ$_3$ = TE.AB]
elevated shrine, temple; living room; sanctuary.

ur
n., dog; large carnivorous animal; servant; young man, warrior; enemy (cf., teš$_2$) [UR archaic frequency: 114; concatenation of 3 sign variants].

v., to tremble.

adj., humble.

^{iti}UR
calendar month 7 at Ur during Ur III; calendar month 10 at Umma before Šulgi 30.

ur-a
otter ('dog' + 'water'; Akk., *kalab mê*; cf., ^{d}nin-kilim-bar).

ur$_{(5)}$-da
with this (cf., ur$_5$-da) ('this' + 'with').

ur-bar-ra
wolf ('dog' + 'outside' + nominative).

UR-bi; ur$_5$-bi
together (cf., teš$_2$-bi).

ur(-bi)...gu$_7$
to devour everything; to consume ('together' + 'to eat').

ur-bi-gu$_7$
jackal(s) ('together' + 'to eat').

ur-bi-gu$_7$^{mušen}
vulture(s) ('together' + 'to eat').

ur-e-gu$_7$-a; ur-re-gu$_7$-a
eaten by dogs, usually in expression mu ur-(r)e gu$_7$-a-še$_3$, 'because eaten by dogs' ('dogs' + ergative postposition + 'to eat' + subordination suffix; cf., mu-...-a(k)-še$_3$).

ur-dib
(cf., ur-nim).

ur-gi$_7$-a
otter ('dog' + 'water'; Akk., *kalab mê*; cf., ^{d}nin-kilim-bar).

ur-gi$_7$-gal-gal
watchdogs ('dog' + redup. 'big').

ur-gi$_7$-tur-tur
young watchdogs, pups ('dog' + redup. 'young').

ur-gir$_{15}$[KU], ur-gi$_7$(-re)
domestic dog, used as livestock guardians - clay models depict thoroughbred mastiffs ('dog' + 'domestic').

$^{(\tilde{g}iš)}$ur-gu-la
lion; a musical instrument; the constellation Leo ('carnivorous beast' + 'large, great').

ur-GUG$_4$
(cf., ur-šub$_5$).

ur-idim(-ma)
wild dog; jackal; rabid dog, mad dog (cf., ur-mu$_2$-da).

ur-ki
badger ('dog' + 'earth'; Akk., *kalab urṣi*; cf., *urṣu II*).

ur-KU
(cf., ur-gir$_{15}$).

ur-maḫ
lion ('carnivorous beast' + 'mighty').

ur-mu$_2$-da
rabid dog, mad dog ('dog' + mud$_6$, 'to be mad, rabid' + nominative).

ur-nim; ur-dib; ur-zib$_2$
lion, lion cub (?); young predatory animal (?) ('carnivorous beast' + 'early'; cf., sila$_4$-nim, 'early spring lamb').

ur-re-gu$_7$-a
(cf., ur-e-gu$_7$-a).

ur-ru-ur
to roam around gathering.

ur-sa$_6$-ga
a pampered dog ('dog' + 'friendly' + nom.).

ur-sa$\tilde{g}$
hero, warrior ('young man' + 'first, in front').

ur-šub$_5$ [GUG$_4$]
a wild cat, perhaps tiger or cheetah ('beast' + 'rushes'; Akkadian *mindinu*).

ur-šub$_5$-ku$_5$-da
leopard ('beast of the cut-off rushes, i.e., who slinks below them'; Akkadian *dumāmu I*).

^{u2}ur-tal$_2$-tal$_2$
Plantago ('broad dog ears'; Akk. *āribānu*).

ur-tur
a pet dog or puppy ('dog' + 'small').

ur-ur-a...$\tilde{g}$ar
to assemble a list, schedule, or plan ('servants' + locative + 'to set').

ur-zib$_2$
(cf., ur-nim).

ur$_2$
floor; base, foundation; lap, thighs, leg(s), flanks; loins, crotch; hip; root; trunk of a tree [UR$_2$ archaic frequency: 78].

ur$_2$-da
Emesal dialect for ur$_5$-da, 'to hear, be mindful, attentive'.

ur$_2$...dun(-dun); ur$_2$...tum$_2$(-tum$_2$)
to fall to the ground, squat, grovel; to make prostate ('legs' + 'to scrape, dig; subordinate'/ tum$_2$-ma, 'suitable, fit, worthy').

ur$_2$...ze$_2$(-ze$_2$)
Emesal dialect for ur$_2$...dun(-dun).

$^{\tilde{g}iš}$ur$_2$-zi-nu
sycamore tree (?) (< Akk., *urzīnu(m)*).

$^{\tilde{g}iš}$UR$_2$×A.NA
a fruit tree, perhaps the mulberry; produced both fruit and valued timber (known from Ur and Umma texts, but Sumerian reading and Akkadian equivalents do not appear in lexical lists; Postgate in BSA III; consider reading UR$_2$×A as dul$_9$) (mulberry = Akk. *tuttu*).

ur$_3$
n., roof; entrance; mountain pass; rafter, beam; cross bar, bolt (securing a door); yoke, harness (cf., $\tilde{g}$iš-ur$_3$(-ra); ma$_2$-ur$_3$(-ur$_3$)) [UR$_3$ archaic frequency: 27; concatenation of 5 sign variants].

v., to drag (over/along the ground) (often with -ni-); to erase, smear, wipe out, destroy; to sweep over; to throw (a net) overboard; to mow (down); to clear away, strip off; to shear, pluck, reap; to bolt, shut (reduplication class).

ur_3-bad_3
rooftop(s) ('roof' + 'high').

ur_4
to collect; to gather together; to grasp; to catch; to bunch up (cf., gur_{10}; gur_{15}[UR_4]); to whirl up; to be or make disturbed, agitated [? UR_4 archaic frequency: 41; concatenation of 3 sign variants].

ur_4-ur_4
to sweep over, devastate, lay bare; to roam around, rove (reduplicated 'to harvest, shear').

ur_5[ḪAR] (-ra)
n., liver; spleen; soul; mood; bulk, main body; foundation; interest-bearing loan; obligation; interest; surplus, profit; debt; repayment; slave-woman; lamentation, dejection (cf., ḫar, mur; eš-de_2-a) [UR_5 archaic frequency: 34; concatenation of 2 sign variants].

inanimate pron., it; this, these, the referenced matter; his, hers, theirs - ThSLa §100.

v., to chew; to smell; to belch, burp; to roar; to clog, block; to imprison; to be bowed with grief; to rub something in; to rent, lease.

demonstrative, thus; so; in this way; in the same way; followed by a negation: not at all.

ur_5...aka
to gasp ('liver, soul' + 'to do').

ur_5...BAD/$UŠ_2$
(cf., ur_5...ug_7).

ur_5-bi
(cf., UR-bi).

ur_5-da
to be mindful, careful; to hear; to pay attention; to wait for (cf., $ur_{(5)}$-da) ('heart, soul' + 'with').

ur_5-di-da
famous (one) (?) (cf., lu_2-di-da).

ur_5...DU
(cf., ur_5...$ša_4$).

ur_5-e
in such manner, thus ('it; thus' + locative terminative e).

ur_5-gim, ur_5-gin_7
thus - ThSLa §100 ('like this').

ur_5...gur_2
to bow down (in grief) ('liver, soul' + 'to bow down, submit').

ur_5 $ḫe_2$-en-na-nam-ma-am_3
thus shall it be indeed; let it be so - ThSLa §540 ('thus' + 'it is indeed').

ur_5-ra...su-su
to pay off debts ('interest-bearing debt' [the famous ur_5-ra = *ḫubullu*] + sug_6, su, 'to replace, restore, return (a loan, etc.)).

ur_5-ra-ke_4-eš
thusly, by this means ('the referenced' + nominative + genitive/agent + 'towards').

ur_5-ra-$še_3$
to be like that ('in such manner' + nominative + 'towards').

ur_5-re, ur_5-e
in such manner, thus ('it; thus' + locative terminative -e).

ur_5...sag_9/sa_6
to be/make comfortable, happy ('liver, soul' + 'to satisfy'; cf., $nig̃_2$-ur_5-sa_6-sa_6).

ur_5...$ša_4$
to roar, bellow, groan ('liver, soul, mood' + 'to lament, wail') (contrast še...$ša_4$).

ur_5-$še_3$
debt with interest ('loan' + 'portion').

ur_5-$še_3$-am_3
therefore, so - ThSLa §201.

ur_5-ta
thus; from this ('this' + 'from').

ur_5...tab
to suffer ('liver, soul, mood' + 'to burn').

ur_5-tud
domestic servant ('debt' + 'to be born').

ur_5-tuku
debtor; creditor ('debt; loan' + 'having').

ur_5...ug_7
to despair; to be distressed ('liver, soul, mood' + 'to kill, die').

ur_7
(cf., $murum_{11}$).

ur_9
(cf., $murum_4$).

ur_{11}
(cf., uru_4).

ur_{11}-a
adj., planted, sowed, sowing - adjective for a field, a watch-division, or the method of planting.

uraš [IB]
earth; crooked furrow; girdle, loincloth; secret.

urbigu
n., quarrel, contest (ur-bi-gu_7, 'jackals; vultures').

adj., combative.

$urdu_2$ [ARAD×KUR]
(cf., arad).

$urgu_2$
(cf., $murgu_3$, $urgu_2$).

URI.GAL
(cf., $kindagal_2$).

$uri_{(2)}$
Akkadian (cf., $kinda_2$) [URI archaic frequency: 35; URI_2 archaic frequency: 1].

$uri_{2,5}$
(cf., $urim_{2,5}$).

uri_3 [simplified ŠEŠ]
(cf., urin).

$urim_{2,5}$, $uri_{2,5}$
doorpost; with ^{ki}, the city of Ur (cf., uru_3(-m)) [URI_5 archaic frequency: 21].

urin, uri_3 [URI_3=simplified ŠEŠ]
n., eagle; standard, emblem, banner; gate-post; blood [ŠEŠ ZATU-523 archaic frequency: 25; concatenates 2 sign variants].

adj., bloody.

urin...mul
to gleam (like a standard or banner) ('standard' + 'to gleam').

urin/uri_3-mul
sparkling, gleaming standard or emblem ('emblem' + 'to sparkle').

$ursub_{(2)}$, $urrub_{(2)}$
(cf., $zurzub_{(2)}$).

$uru^{(ki)}$, eri, iri, ri_2; uru_2; iri_{11}
city, town, village, district (Akk. *ūru IV*, 'city', from Sumerian; Orel & Stolbova derive Hebrew *'īr* from unrelated #1012, ***'ger-** "town") [URU archaic frequency: 101; concatenation of 5 sign variants; UNUG archaic frequency: 206; concatenates 3 sign variants].

uru-bala(-a)
rebel city ('city' + 'to revolt' + nominative).

uru-bar(-ra/re)
outside the city, outskirts of the city, the countryside, hinterland ('city' + 'outside').

uru-kur_2(-ra)
(in) a foreign city ('city' + 'strange' + locative).

uru-$ša_3$-ga
the interior city (contrasts to uru-bar-ra)('city' + 'inside' + nominative).

uru-ta-nu-e_3
category of unused manpower in accounting texts - the workforce never left the city ('city' + 'from' + 'not' + 'to leave').

uru-tuš
(cf., ki-tuš).

$uru_{2,5,18}$; u_{18}-ru
n., devastating flood; thunderstorm.

adj., high, deep.

uru_3(-m) [simplified ŠEŠ]
n., watch fire; light; glowing, luminous object (e.g., the moon).

v., to watch, guard, be vigilant; to protect (cf., u_2-rum).

uru_4[APIN], ur_{11}(-ru)
to till, sow, plant, cultivate.

uru_4-la_2
adjective for payment of the rent on leasehold land; tenant (cf., $gana_2$-uru_4-la_2).

uru_5
(cf., $uru_{2,5,18}$).

uru_7
(cf., $murum_4$).

uru_9
stanchion, support.

uru_{12}[UR_3]
same meaning as ur_3 with the *marû* aspect -e suffix and vowel harmony.

uru_{16}[EN] (-n)
n., a literary composition division; sighing (as of waves).

adj., valiant; strong, mighty, massive; high, lofty; clever (cf., u_{18}-ru(-n)).

uru_{18}
(cf., $uru_{2,5,18}$).

uruda, urudu, urud
copper; metal - mainly imported from northern Oman, ma_2-gan-an-na^{ki}, where the nickel content of ore samples at 0.19 percent is a close match to Sumerian copper objects ($buru_3$(-d), 'to mine', + a, nominative = 'the mined'; Akk. *(w)erû(m)*, 'copper', cf., Orel & Stolbova #55 ***'ariw**- 'metal') [URUDU archaic frequency: 61; concatenates 3 sign variants].

uruda-A-EN-da
a type of copper (a-ru_{12}-da).

uruda-gur_{10}-tur
copper clackers (musical instruments) ('copper' + 'sickle' + 'small').

uruda(-ḫu)-luḫ-ḫa
refined, pure copper ('copper' + 'to wash' + nominative; Akk., *mesû(m) I*, 'refined, purified').

uruda-$ni\tilde{g}_2$-de_2-a
object of cast copper ('copper' + 'poured, cast').

uruda-$ni\tilde{g}_2$-gid_2[BU]-da
a copper rod or wire (cf., $ni\tilde{g}_2$-sud-a/$ni\tilde{g}_2$-sud_4[BU]-a) ('copper' + 'thing' + 'to be long' + nominative; Akk., *urāku(m)*, 'a long implement, perhaps "rod"').

uruda-$ni\tilde{g}_2$-kala-ga
strong copper; a drum ('copper' + 'thing' + 'to be strong' + nominative).

uruda-$ni\tilde{g}_2$-saḫar-ra
copper pellets ('copper' + 'thing' + sand' + genitive).

urugal
the netherworld (uru, 'city', + gal, 'big').

urum, uru_6, ur_7
(cf., $murum_{11}$).

$urum_2$, uru_7, ur_9
(cf., $murum_4$).

$us^{mušen}$
(cf., $uz^{mušen}$).

us-ga
(cf., uzu_3-ga).

us_2, uz_2 [UŠ]
n., side, edge, flank; distance; path; guideline for behavior; long side (of field) in OS texts; in geometry: length; height; vertical; perpendicular.

v., to follow; to drive; to come near to, reach; to let reach; to allow (a boat) to land; to transport, bring; build (a nest); to join; to be next to, border; to moor, dock; to lean against; to reinforce (with loc.term. suffix -e on inanimate indirect objects) (cf., $\tilde{g}i\check{s}_2$).

adj., second-class (grade, e.g., of fruit).

us_2...dib$_{(2)}$
to take, follow a path ('distance; path' + 'to traverse'; cf., sila-kur_2...dab_5/dib_2).

us_2-sa
contiguous; touching; near; following; next to ('to follow; to adjoin' + adjectival -a).

us_2-sa-ra_2[DU]
boundary; border, side ('contiguous' + ra_2, 'to accompany').

adj., adjacent to.

adv., alongside.

$^{lu2}us_2$-sa-ra_2
neighbor (cf., $u\check{s}ar_{(2,3,4)}$).

us_2-sa$\tilde{g}$
rigging (of a ship) ('side; to join' + 'bow of a ship'; cf., $^{\tilde{g}i\check{s}}ma_2$-sa$\tilde{g}$-$\tilde{g}a_2$).

us_5
This reading for u_8, 'ewe', only occurs in one syllabary [S^b Voc. I].

usan$_{(2)}$
evening; nightfall (cf., u_2-si_4-an).

$usan_3$[NUNUZ.AB_2/$KISIM_5\times$AŠGAB]
whip (cf., u_3-sa-an).

$usan_3$-mar
wagon whip (?) ('whip' + 'wagon').

usar$_{(2,3,4)}$, ušar$_{(2,3,4)}$, ušur$_{(2,3,4)}$
(female) companion, neighbor (cf., us_2-sa-ra_2) [$UŠUR_3$ archaic frequency: 3; concatenates 3 sign variants].

ussu$_{(2,3)}$
eight (us_2, 'to follow', + a, nominative; cf. $su\underline{h}_3$ and imin$_{(2,3)}$).

usu[A_2.KAL]
skill; strength; force; sustenance (u_3, 'pronominal prefix', + su, 'body'; cf., u_3-su tuku).

usu-tuku
a strong, powerful person ('skill; strength' + 'having').

usug
(cf., uzug).

usu$\underline{h}$
(cf., $^{\tilde{g}i\check{s}}u_3$-$su\underline{h}_5$).

$usur_4$, $u\check{s}ur_4$
to hang, suspend (us_2, uš, 'height; foundation; to support, lift', + $uru_{2,5,18}$, 'high, deep'; cf., sur_5; $sur_{6,7}$).

uš, us_2
n., foundation (cf., us_2, $\tilde{g}i\check{s}_2$) [$GI\check{S}_3$ archaic frequency: 16; concatenation of 2 sign variants; UŠ archaic frequency: 101; concatenates 2 sign variants].

v., to support, lift; to stand upon.

UŠ
a length measure, reading unknown, = 6 ropes = 60 nindan rods. [UŠ archaic frequency: 101; concatenates 2 sign variants].

uš
variant writing for $u\check{s}_{11}$ or $u\check{s}_3$.

-uš
writing of the terminative case post-position /eše/ after the vowel -u after the NS period - ThSLa §195 (cf., -$\check{s}e_3$).

-uš
writing of the 3.pl. pronominal suffix for the intransitive verb subject after verbs with vowel [u]; can indicate the direct object of a transitive verb; can denote the 3.pl. ergative subject in two-part *ḫamṭu* forms together with the prefix -n- ThSLa §294, §281, §295.

$^{\tilde{g}iš}$uš-bar
ruler's staff; scepter ('penis' + 'to see, show'; cf., ušbar$_{(3/7)}$, 'father-in-law'; Akk. *ušparu*).

^{lu2}uš-bar
weaver (cf., $^{(\tilde{g}iš)}$bar-bar, 'part of a weaver's loom (shuttle ?)'; Akk. *išparu(m)*, *ušparu(m)* of unknown origin; cf., Orel & Stolbova #579, ***ṣafir-** 'plaiting', Hebrew *ṣfr-* 'to plait, braid'; *šfr-* 'beautiful; to embellish').

UŠ.GA
(cf., bunga).

uš-gid$_2$-da
storehouse; granary; silo (for barley, dates, oil) (cf., araḫ$_4$) ('foundation' + 'to be long' + nominative).

uš-g̃ar-ra
firm building foundation ('foundation' + 'to establish' + nominative).

UŠ.KU
(cf., gala).

uš-si$_3$-ga
unsafe building foundation ('foundation' + 'to damage' + nominative).

uš$_2$
n., blood; blood vessel; death [? ZATU-644 archaic frequency: 65; concatenation of 2 sign variants].

v., to die; to kill; to block; to dam a river (antonym: g̃al$_2$) (suppletion class verb: singular *ḫamṭu* stem; cf., ug$_5$).

adj., dead.

uš$_2$-a
piling up an earthen block or dam (cf., a uš$_2$-a) ('to block' + nominative).

uš$_2$-gi$_4$
revenge ('blood' + 'to answer').

uš$_2$-lal, uš$_2$-la$_2$
tourniquet (?) (cf., eš$_2$-lal/la$_2$) ('blood' + 'to bind').

uš$_3$
placental membrane, afterbirth.

uš$_7$; aš
spittle; mucous; spell, charm.

uš$_7$...dug$_4$
to spit ('spittle' + 'to speak, do, make').

uš$_7$-zu
sorcerer ('spittle; spell, charm' + 'knowing').

uš$_8$
foundation place, base.

uš$_{11}$
venom, poison; spittle, slaver; moistening; spell, charm.

uš$_{11}$...sig$_{10}$/si$_3$
to throw/inject venom on/in... ('venom' + 'to apply, put in').

ušar$_{(2,3,4)}$
(cf., usar$_{(2,3,4)}$).

ušbar$_{(3/7)}$, ušbur$_{(3/7)}$
n., (house of) the parents of the husband, family of the husband; father-in-law; mother-in-law; relative by marriage (contrast murum$_{4,5}$) (g̃iš$_3$/uš, 'man; penis', + bar, 'outside; foreign').

adj., belonging to the in-laws.

ušera
reed bundle (u$_2$, 'plant', + šar$_2$, 'to be many' + a, nominative).

$^{\tilde{g}iš}$uštil
(cf., $^{\tilde{g}iš}$šudul$_{(2,3,4,5)}$).

ušu
a crop-devouring insect; larva, caterpillar (u$_3$, 'pronominal prefix', + šuš$_2$/šu$_2$, 'to cover, overwhelm').

ušu$_2$[U.UD]
evening, sunset (prospective modal prefix + šuš$_2$/šu$_2$, 'to set, become dark').

ušu$_3$
thirty (eš$_5$, 'three', + ḫa$_3$/u, 'ten').

$^{(gi)}$ušub[SI.A/DIRIG]
basket; succulent reed (uš, 'to support, lift', + ub$_4$, 'cavity, hole').

ušum, ušu
n., dragon, composite creature; viper (uš$_{11}$, 'snake venom', + am, 'wild ox').

adj., solitary, alone.

ušumgal
lord of all, sovereign; solitary; monster of composite powers, dragon - thought to live in the forests (ušum, 'dragon', + gal, 'great') [UŠUMGAL archaic frequency: 21].

ušur$_{(2,3,4)}$
(cf., usar$_{(2,3,4)}$).

utaḫ, utu$_2$[U.GA]
dried, powdered milk; excess; a dish prepared with dried milk; sky, heaven(s); base of the sky (cf., ušu$_2$; zaḫan$_2$).

uttuku
(cf., nig̃$_2$-ka$_9$).

^{d}utu
the sun as a god (cf., ud).

^{d}utu-e$_3$
sunrise ('sun; day' + 'to rise, go out, become visible').

^{d}utu-šu$_2$-a
sunset; west ('sun; day' + šuš$_2$/šu$_2$, 'to set' + nominative).

utu$_2$
(cf., utaḫ, utu$_2$).

utua[DAG.KISIM$_5$×UŠ]; utua$_2$[DAG.KISIM$_5$×LU.MAŠ$_2$/AMAŠ]
breed ram; breed bull (cf., udu-ua$_4$) [UTUA archaic frequency: 74; concatenates 2 sign variants].

utug
(cf., udug).

utug$_2$
(cf., udug$_2$).

utul
(cf., udul).

$^{(dug)}$utul$_{2,7}$
large bowl, tureen, kettle, cauldron, basin (u$_2$, 'food', + tal, 'large jug').

uz, us, uzu$_3$^{mušen}[ŠE.ḪU]
domestic goose or duck (cf., bibad) (loanword *into* Akkadian, *ūsu(m) II*, 'goose') [US archaic frequency: 18; concatenation of 2 sign variants].

UZ.TUR^{mušen}
(cf., bibad^{mušen}).

uz-ga
(cf., uzu$_3$-ga).

uz$_2$
(cf., us$_2$).

uz$_3$
(cf., ud$_5$).

uzalag, uzalak[GE$_{22}$]
area measure, = 1/4 of an iku (= 25 sar).

uzu
flesh; cut of meat; omen (ud$_5$, 'goat', + ze$_2$, 'to cut').

uzu-a-bala
meat broth ('meat' + 'drawing of water').

$^{(u2)}$uzu-diri
a spongy fungus - mushroom or truffle ('flesh' + 'excess'; Akk. *kamūnu II*; cf., *kam'atum*).

uzu-ḫad$_2$
dried meat ('meat' + 'dried').

uzu-i$_3$
fatty meat ('meat' + 'fat').

uzu-lib$_x$[I$_3$.UDU]
mutton fat (Akk. *lipium*, '(animal) fat; tallow').

uzu-ur$_2$
hindquarter cut ('meat' + 'base, thigh, leg').

uzu$_3$^{mušen}
(cf., uz^{mušen}).

uzu$_3$-ga
a type of priest especially devoted to cleaning rites; a temple precinct (that received tithe offerings ?, where bird and fish offerings were fattened ?) (cf., uzug; e$_2$-uzu$_3$-ga).

uzu$_5$
(cf., ušu$_2$).

uzud
(cf., ud$_5$, uz$_3$, ut$_5$).

uzug, usug[ZAG.AN]
tithe, tenth-part set aside; pious donation; shrine, chapel, temple - associated with ^{d}lamma protective deities (cf., uzu$_3$-ga) (ḫa$_3$/u, 'ten', + zag, 'outside of'; Akkadian *sukku(m)*, 'shrine, chapel').

uzug$_{2,3,4,5}$
menstruating woman; woman isolated after birth; person under a taboo; ritually unclean (uš$_2$, 'blood', + zig$_3$, 'to expend, go out'; mi$_2$-uzug$_2$ > Akkadian *musukkum*, 'ritually unclean; impure person').

Z

za-
2.sg. pronoun; you (singular).

za$_{(2)}$
beads; hailstones; precious stone, gem-stone; pit; kernel [ZA archaic frequency: 9].

za; za$_3$
n., repetitive cry; bleat; voice; noise.

v., to make noise (occurs as the verb in compounds with repetitive, onomato-poeic syllables symbolizing a repeated monotonous noise or motion (Krebernik, *Beschwörungen*, p. 70, summarizes the different compounds that occur in ED IIIB texts) (cf., ki...za(-za); ^{MUNUS}ga-an-za-za).

-za
possessive suffix 2sg. + genitive -a(k) or locative -a, ThSLa §105 (-zu, 'yours', + -ak, genitive).

za-a-ar; za-a-ra; za-ra
2.sg. pronoun + dative; to you; for you - ThSLa §91, §96.

za-a-da; za-e-da; za-da
2.sg. pronoun + comitative; with you - ThSLa §91.

za-a-gin$_7$; za-e-gin$_7$; za-gin$_7$
2.sg. pronoun + equative; like you; as you - ThSLa §91, §96.

za-a-kam...dug$_4$/du$_{11}$
say: it is thine ('you' + /ak/, 'of' + am$_3$, 'it is' + 'to speak').

za-a-še$_3$; za-e-še$_3$; za-še$_3$
2.sg. pronoun + terminative; towards you; unto you - ThSLa §91, §96.

za-aḫ[ḪI×NUN]
a misreading of ^{za}ellağ$_2$[ḪI×ŠE].

$^{(uruda)}$za(-am)-za(-am)
a metal drum or percussion instrument; a type of song or hymn (za, 'rhythmic sound').

za-aš$_2$-da
dishonesty; crime; debt-slavery; debt-slave(s) (Akkadian *sartu(m), ṣartu(m), saštu(m)*; *kiššātum*).

$^{(ğiš)}$za-ba-lum
a variety of juniper tree, resin, or oil (Akkadian loanword from *supālu(m)*, '(a) juniper').

za-BIR
(cf., ^{za}ellağ$_2$[ḪI×ŠE]).

za-da
(cf., za-a-da).

za-dim$_2$
stone cutter (cf., zadim) ('[precious] stone' + 'to fashion').

za-e
2.sg. pronoun; you; yourself.

$za-e-en-ze_2-en$
you (plural), 2.pl. personal pronoun ('you' + '2nd person plural ending').

$za-e-me-en-ze_2-en$
you (plural), 2.pl. personal pronoun ('you' + 'to be' + '2nd person plural ending').

za-e-ne-ne
you (plural), 2.pl. personal pronoun ('you' + '3rd person plural ending').

$za-ge_6-ri_2-tum$; $za-ge_9$[NE]-ri_2-tum
(cf., $zag-ge_6$[MI]-ri_2-tum).

^{na4}za-gin_3[KUR]
lapis lazuli; precious stone (in general) ('stone' + 'colorful').

za-gin_3
clean, shining, fresh ('like a precious stone').

$^{(na4)}$za-gin_3-$duru_5$
translucent lapis lazuli (cf., še-za-gin_3-$duru_5$) ('lapis lazuli' + 'moist').

za-gin_7
(cf., za-a-gin_7).

ZA.GUL
(cf., gug).

za-ḫa; za-ḫal
(cf., $zaḫ_{2,3}$; u_4-za-ḫa(-al)... aka).

$^{(ĝiš)}$za-ḫa-da
battle-ax (stone + many + with; cf., ḫar-ḫa-da).

za-ḫa-din$^{(sar)}$, za-ḫa-tin$^{(sar)}$; za-ḫa-ti
a common type of onion, measured both by weight and by bundles (sa), suggestions include the leek, shallot, and even garlic ('kernels' + 'many' + 'to cure' where sulfur-rich garlic particularly comes to mind; Akk. *šuḫatinnû*).

za-ḫum; za-ḫu-um
a clay, bronze, or copper basin, for drinking, cooking, or brewing; a plant or drug - wormwood, vermouth, Artemisia (?) (Akkadian *šāḫu(m)*; *sīḫu(m) II*).

za-lam-ĝar
a tent, made by a weaver (zal, 'to spend the day; to tarry, wait', + enclitic copula + ĝar, 'to settle down'; cf., $ĝa_2$, 'house, stable'; Akk. *kuštāru(m)*; *šutû(m) I*).

za-na
caterpillar ('monotonous repetition' + 'distinct things or selves').

^{ĝiš}za-na
puppet.

^{ĝiš}za-na...tag
to handle a puppet ('puppet' + 'to touch, handle').

-za-na
2.pl. pronominal suffix /-enzen/ combined with the subordination suffix -a - ThSLa §298.

$^{(ĝiš)}$za-na-ru
a musical instrument (cf., Akk. *nāru II*, 'musician', and *zamāru II*, 'to sing; to repeatedly play a musical instrument').

za-pa-$aĝ_2$
sound; breath; voice quality; roar, tumult, noise (za, 'rhythmic sound' or zi, 'breathing' transformed by vowel harmony + 'puffing sound' + 'to mete out'; cf., $šir_3$...$aĝa_2$).

za-pa-aḫ
(cf., zipaḫ).

za-ra
pole, shaft of chariots, wagons, harrows, and doors (cf., ^{ĝiš}zar).

za-ra
(cf., za-a-ar).

za-ra...dug_4/du_{11}
to lecture ('to you' + 'to speak').

za-ri$_2$-in
coarsely cleaned; average quality (adj. for wool or copper) (loan from Akk. *zarinnu(m)*).

(lu2; na4)ZA-SU$_6$(-ma), sa$_3$-sum$_4$(-ma)
an occupation; a stone (? Akk. *sassumma*, 'bricklayer' ?).

za-še$_3$
(cf., za-a-še$_3$).

za-te-eb
(cf., zag...dib).

za-za
(cf., ki...za).

(uruda)za(-am)-za(-am)
a metal drum or percussion instrument (za, 'rhythmic sound').

za-za-ga
marjoram or oregano (?).

za$_3$
(cf., zag).

za$_3$[ZAG]-ḫi-li(-a)^{sar}
a garden plant yielding edible seeds that were ground in mortars; suggestions include cardamom seeds, safflower seeds, cress seeds; a condiment made from these seeds ('border, beginning' + 'charm, appeal'; Akk. *saḫlium/saḫlû*; cf., zu-ḫu-ul).

za$_3$-mi$_2$
(hymn of) praise; Hail! ('voice' + 'to cherish').

(ĝiš)za$_3$-mi$_2$
musical praise instrument - a wooden box-lyre with cow- or bull-shaped resonator; an OB geometrical figure (this term found in Nippur OB literature; cf., zag-ge$_6$[MI]-ri$_2$-tum).

za$_3$-mi$_2$...dug$_4$/du$_{11}$/e
to care for ('voice' + 'to cherish' + 'to speak, do').

(ĝiš)zabalam
juniper (cf., za-ba-lum) [? ZABALAM archaic frequency: 45; concatenates 2 sign variants].

zabar[UD.KA.BAR]
bronze; mirror metal (zil; zi; ze$_2$, 'to pare, cut', + bar$_6$, 'bright, white'; Akk. *siparrum*, 'bronze', borrowed before vowel harmony changed Sumerian word; cf., barzil, 'iron') [ZABAR archaic frequency: 1].

zabar-dab$_5$
a high functionary who dispatched armed men to get workers for the state ('bronze' + 'to seize, hire').

zabar-šu
metal hand mirror ('mirror metal' + 'hand'; cf., niĝ$_2$-šu-zabar).

zadim
jeweler; stone cutter; arrowhead, arrow, and bow maker - bow used to drill stone seals (cf., za-dim$_2$) [ZADIM archaic frequency: 2].

zadru
(cf., zandara).

zag, za$_3$
boundary, border, edge, limit, side; gums; shoulder; cusp, beginning; territory, district, place; sanctuary, shrine; percentage; a measure for fish; right (side); front; outside of; open country, plain (paired with sug) (life + to encircle) [ZAG archaic frequency: 71; concatenates 3 sign variants].

zag-10, za$_3$-u
tithe (also read as zag-šu$_4$[U], 'branding iron') ('percentage' + '10'; Akk., *ešrētu(m)*, 'one-tenth').

zag-an-na
farthest reaches of the sky, the entire sky ('boundaries' + 'sky' + genitive).

zag-bar
(metal or leather) quantity left over by cutting; shavings, scraps ('percentage; edge' + 'to pare away').

zag...dab$_5$
to surround ('border' + 'to take, seize, hold').

zag...dib
to cross over; to surpass; to make transcend ('barrier' + 'to cross').

zag-DU
(cf., zag-ša$_4$ and zag(-ga) gub).

zag-du$_8$, za$_3$-du$_8$
threshold; doorframe ('boundary' + 'to adorn').

zag-e$_3$
n., battlements; buttress(s); projection(s) (such as from a building or anything else) ('barrier' + 'to rise').

adj., outstanding.

zag e$_2$-ĝar$_8$ us$_2$
to prop against a wall ('side, shoulder, edge' + 'wall' + 'to lean against').

zag-eš$_2$-la$_2$, zag-še$_3$-la$_2$, za$_3$-eš$_2$-la$_2$$^{(zabar/ku3-babbar/ku3-sig17)}$
buckle (?) (cf., $^{(ĝiš)}$eš$_2$-lal/la$_2$).

zag-ga, za$_3$-ga
sweet; beaten.

zag(-ga) gub
to stand at the side ('side' + locative + 'to stand').

$^{(ĝiš/uruda)}$zag-ge$_6$[MI]-ri$_2$-tum$^{(zabar)}$, za$_3$-ge$_6$-ri$_2$-tum; za-ge$_6$-ri$_2$-tum; za-ge$_9$[NE]-ri$_2$-tum; za-an-ge$_9$-ri$_2$-tum
a musical instrument (I.J. Gelb speculated that this word combines za$_3$-mi$_2$ with ^{ĝiš}mi-ri$_2$-tum as 'instrument from Mari'; za-NE-ri$_2$-tum and za-an-NE-ri$_2$-tum spellings are from Ur III Umma - MVN 22 199 and MVN 09 171).

zag-gu-la; zag-gal-la
a type of chair; seat of honor ('side, shoulder' + 'great').

zag-ĝar(-ra)
n., liver; inspection; shrine.

adj., sour.

zag-ḫi-li(-a)^{sar}
(cf., za$_3$-ḫi-li(-a)^{sar}).

zag...keš$_2$
to tie up; to tie around; to don; to gird oneself with; to array oneself in; to endow with ('side' + 'to bind to').

zag-ki-a
farthest reaches of the earth, the entire earth ('boundaries' + 'earth' + genitive).

zag-KU-la$_2$$^{(zabar/ku3-babbar/ku3-sig17)}$
(cf., zag-eš$_2$-la$_2$).

zag-min$_2$
(cf., za$_3$-mi$_2$).

zag-mu(-k)
New Year (festival) ('edge, boundary' + 'name, year' + genitive).

zag-munus
(cf., za$_3$-mi$_2$).

zag...sa$_2$[DI]
to rival, parallel (cf., sağ...sa$_2$) ('limit' + 'to equal').

zag-sa$_2$[DI]; zag-ša$_4$[DU]
equal; rival ('limit' + 'to equal').

zag...sag$_2$; zag...sağ; zag...sag$_{11}$[KIN]
(cf., zag...tag).

zag-še$_{(3)}$; zag-ša$_4$
strength, endurance; bed ('limit' + 'to the').

zag-še$_3$-la$_2$$^{(zabar/ku3-babbar/ku3-sig17)}$
(cf., zag-eš$_2$-la$_2$).

$^{(uruda)}$zag-šuš$_2$/šu$_2$; zag-šuš/šu$_4$[U]
ownership mark; (copper) branding iron ('side' + 'to cover; to throw down').

zag...$šuš_2$/$šu_2$; šuš/$šu_4$
to brand; to mark (an animal) ('side' + 'to cover; to throw down'; cf., si-im-da...$šu_2$/aka).

zag...tag
to push off, launch (a boat or log); to push away; to reject; to reach one's limit; to overthrow ('edge, limit' + 'to touch, push'; Akk., *sakāpu(m) I*).

zag-u
read either as zag-10, 'tithe', or as zag-$šu_4$[U], 'branding iron'.

zag-uru
outskirts of the city ('edge, limit' + 'city').

zag...us_2
to border on; to stand by; to set aside ('edge, limit' + 'to lean against').

zag 5-us_2
a fifth (as a division) ('percentage' + 5 or other number + 'length').

zag...ze_2-$e\tilde{g}_3$
Emesal dialect for zag...tag, zag...sag_2, zag...sag̃.

zag_3, sag_5, $za\tilde{g}_3$, $sa\tilde{g}_5$[SAG_5; ŠID]
to choose; chosen (cf., igi-sag̃-$\tilde{g}a_2$).

$za\tilde{g}_3$
(cf., zag_3).

zaḫ
to be calm, tranquil; a mark or impression, esp. on the liver.

na4zaḫ
a stone used in magic and medicine (Akk., *saḫḫû*).

$zaḫ_{2,3}$, $saḫ_{6,7}$
n., secrecy (derives from zag, 'boundary, border, district', just as $ḫub_2$ relates to gub_3).

v., to flee; to hide; to escape; to abandon; to desert; to be lost; to perish (describes workers/slaves who have fled state control).

$zaḫ_2$-bi
adv., to the bitter end, until disappearance ('to perish' + adverbial force suffix).

zaḫan[U.GA.ḪI]; $zaḫan_2$[U.GA]
a garden herb, used to make a soup (cf., utaḫ, utu_2).

zal[NI]
n., supply, store (as of salted meat).

v., to be full or abundant; to flow; to continue; to pass, elapse (said about time); to dissolve, melt, break down; to spend the day or time; to be idle, waste time; to tarry, wait (often with -ni-; with -ta- in a temporal sense) (cf., zalag) (za, 'monotonous repetition' + numerous).

zalag, zalaḫ[UD]; $zalag_2$; zal
n., light, brightness; the light before dawn, early morning.

v., to shine, gleam; to illuminate; to cleanse, purify (often reduplicated) (cf., laḫ[UD]).

adj., bright, luminous, radiant; pure; cheerful.

zanbur
prowling, roaming; foraging (said of animals) (zag, 'border', + bur, 'meal').

zandara, zadru[ŠID]
one-half (share); split tally; IOU (cf., im-te_6, im-zadru) (zag, 'percentage', + dar, 'to slice, split', + nominative; cf., Akk., *mišlānū*).

zapaḫ
(cf., zipaḫ).

(g̃iš)zar
wagon shaft (cf., za-ra) (Akkadian loanword from *ṣerru(m) II*).

zar, zur_4, sur_8
to tap, pour; to spout, flow; to exude; to spin (a cocoon) (cf. the graphically similar sign, sur_{12}) (repetitive motion + to flow) [? ZAR archaic frequency: 15; concatenates 4 sign variants].

zar[LAGAB×SUM]; zar_3[SUM]
sheaf; sheaves, shock (rolled up and bound stalks and ears, cf., $zara_5$ and zar).

zar(-re-eš)...du_8
to pile up ('sheaves' + phonetic complement + 'much' + 'to open; to spread').

zar(-re-eš)...sal
to spread; to heap up ('sheaves' + phonetic complement + 'much' + 'to be wide').

zar_3-tab-ba
the work of binding sheaves; piled corn stack ('sheaf' + 'to bind' + nominative).

$zara_5$, zar_5; sir_5[NU]; sur
to spin, twine (yarn or thread); to roll up (repetitive motion + to flow).

zaraḫ[SAĜ.PA.LAGAB]
grief, wretched groaning.

ze_2, zi_2
n., stench; gall (bladder); bile; bitter anger.

v., to cut; to shear, cut hair; to pluck (cf., zil; ze_2-er).

adj., bitter.

Emesal dialect for dug_3 and for duḫ/du_8.

ze_2-ba-tum
(cf., zi-ba-tum).

ze_2-be_2-da
Emesal dialect for dugud, 'heavy, important'.

ze_2-da
stench; bile (cf., $ša\underline{h}_{(2)}$-ze_2-da; $^{u2}ša_3$-dib-$še_3$-ze_2-da).

ze_2-eb
Emesal dialect for dungu, 'cloud'.

ze_2-eb
in the Emesal dialect, 'to cry out; to make sound'.

ze_2-eb; ze_2-ba
Emesal dialect for dug_3.

ze_2-eb; ze_2-ze_2
Emesal dialect for duḫ/du_8 or for bur_{12}.

ze_2-ed
Emesal dialect for tud_2, 'to hit, beat'.

ze_2-eḫ-ru-um
a small silver or gold item - curio (Akk., *ṣeḫru(m) I*, 'small').

$^{šaḫ2}ze_2$-eḫ-tur
small pig; piglet (phonetic spelling of $ša\underline{h}_2$? + 'small'; cf., Akk., *ṣeḫru(m) I*, 'small; young').

ze_2-em_3
Emesal dialect for si_3, 'to fill up'.

ze_2-em_3
Emesal dialect for sum, 'to give; to provide'.

ze_2-em_3
Emesal dialect for tum_2, 'to bring'.

-ze_2-en
imperative 2.pl. pronominal suffix when the prefix chain ends in a consonant - ThSLa §496 (cf., -en-ze_2-en).

ze_2-er; zi-re; ze_2-ze_2
to tear up; to tear out; to remove; to pluck; to slip; to break (often with -ta-).

ze_2-ḫi-bi
(cf., ^{ĝiš}saḫab$_{(2)}$).

ze_2-me
that is yourself (za, 'you', with vowel harmony + 'to be').

ze_2-me-a
Emesal dialect for dungu, 'cloud'.

$^{ĝiš}ze_2$-na
midrib of palm frond; catapult siege weapon ('to be cut, sheared' + 'an individual case of').

ze_2-tuku
fearful (person); bitter ('bile; bitter' + 'having').

$^{(lu2)}$ze$_2$-za; $^{(lu2)}$ze$_2$-ze$_2$
oppressor, batterer; a singer who makes croaking (?) noises; 'your bile'.

ze$_2$-ze$_2$
Emesal dialect for dun$_{(4)}$-dun$_{(4)}$, 'to weave'.

ze$_2$-ze$_2$-ed
Emesal dialect for dugud, 'cloud'.

zeḫ
A reconstructed reading for ešgar, 'female goat-kid' (a more ancient word ?; cf., ^{šaḫ2}ze$_2$-eḫ-tur).

zermuššu, zermušku [SIG$_7$.KID$_2$.ALAM]
metal worker, coppersmith.

zi
n., breathing; breath; life; throat; soul (cf., zid, zig$_3$, zil, ba-zi) [ZI archaic frequency: 116; concatenates 3 sign variants].

v., (with -r Auslaut) to destroy; to annihilate; to annul, erase (cf., ze$_2$-er; zi-re).

adj., raw, uncooked.

zi-ba-tum; zi$_2$-ba-tum
lesser quality wool from the tail (Akk. *zibbatu(m)*), measured by weight (ma-na); a garden plant.

$^{(še)}$zi-bi$_2$(-tum)
a form of caraway seed (Akkadian loanword, *zibītum I*, 'a kind of spice seed', and *zībum III*, 'black cumin').

zi-de$_3$-eš$_{(2)}$(-še$_3$)
adv., loyally, faithfully, kindly ('truth' + adverbial force suffix, 'case marker').

zi-de$_3$-eš(-še$_3$)...pa$_3$-da
to faithfully choose ('faithfully' + 'to choose').

^{uruda}zi-diri
an adjective for copper from which goods are manufactured, measured in talents (gun$_2$ = 60 ma-na = 30 kg.) (zil/zi, 'to pare, cut' + 'excess').

zi-du, zid-du
a good person ('good' + 'acting').

zi...dug$_4$
to tell the truth ('truth' + 'to speak').

zi-ga
expenditure, withdrawals ('to tear out; to rise up' + nominative).

zi-ga(-am$_3$)
torn out, extracted, deducted, expended; risen up ('to tear out; to rise up' + nominative + 'it is').

zi-ga...g̃ar
to impose a levy ('to tear out, deduct' + nominative + 'to establish').

$^{g̃iš}$zi-gan
rudder, oar ('to lift, raise' + 'pestle').

zi...gi$_4$
to be on good terms; to calm down; to pacify ('faith' + 'to restore').

zi-gi$_4$-du$_3$[GAG]
a bronze ornament for an armchair.

zi-gum$_2$[LUM]
adjective for a donkey stallion that pulled chariots.

zi...g̃al$_2$
to grant life; to have life ('breath' + 'to be available; to place, put').

zi-g̃al$_2$(-la)
living creatures; alive; life-bringing ('breath' + 'having' + nominative).

zi-ḫum
(cf., zi-gum$_2$).

zi-ib-tum$^{(ku3-sig17)}$
cast gold coin, manufactured in large numbers with a uniform weight of 15 še or 1/12 gin$_2$ - witnessed only from Ur during the Ur III period (Akkadian loanword from *zi'pu*, 'mold for casting; a cast coin').

zi-ik-ru-um, zi-ik-rum
(cf., (MUNUS)se_2-ek-ru-um).

zi-in-gi
ankle; knucklebone(s) (singular: astragalus, talus; plural: astragali, tali), which are the ankle bones of cloven-hoofed animals, having four distinctly shaped sides, used as jack stones in gaming ('to stand up' + 'to turn').

zi...ir/ra
to be troubled, worried, sad; to be broken ('faith' + 'to lead away [plural]').

zi-ir
affliction; grief.

zi-ir(-ru)
polished (adj. for copper - uruda) (Akkadian *ṣīru(m) I*, 'exalted').

zi lugala
oath ('life' + 'king' + genitive).

zi-lugala(-bi)...pad_3/pa_3
to swear by the king's life, invoking royal sanction that an agreement will be upheld ('life' + king + genitive + demonstrative suffix + 'to call, swear').

zi-maḫ
legitimate (and) lofty ('legitimate' + 'lofty').

zi-pa-$ag̃_2$
throat; life (cf., za-pa-$ag̃_2$).

zi...pa-$ag̃_2$; zi...pa-an-pa(-an)
to breathe ('breath' + bun, 'to blow').

zi...pa_3(-d)
to take an oath; to conjure ('faith' + 'to swear').

zi...ra
(cf., zi...ir/ra).

zi-ra
(cf., zi(-r)).

zi-re-dam
it has to be destroyed - non-finite prospective *marû* (cf., zi; cf. also, zé-er; zi-re; zé-zé).

(g̃iš)zi-ri/ri_2-gum_2/qum
a device for moving irrigation water, involving a water bucket hanging from a swinging beam - water hoist (cf., Sumerian g̃iša_2-la_2); a reed or clay pipe or pipette (Akkadian loanword *zirīqu* from *zarāqu*).

zi-$ša_3$...$g̃al_2$
to provide (someone: -ši-) with life ('breath' + 'innards' + 'to place').

zi-$ša_3$-$g̃al_2$
n., divine encouragement; inspiration; sustenance; 'things endowed with life' = living things ('breath' + 'innards' + 'having').

adj., alive.

zi...(ši)-$tum_{2,3}$/de_6
to take refuge ('life' + ('into') + 'to bring').

zi-zi(-bi_2)-a-num_2
black cumin (Akkadian *zibibiānum, zizibiānum*).

zi-zi-i
subtracting, subtraction; to remove; to revolt, rebel; revolting; raising (reduplicated 'to tear out, raise').

zi-zi-ga
expenditure (at Sargonic Umma) (reduplicated 'to tear out').

ZI&ZI.LAGAB
(cf., (u2)$numun_2$; (u2)aški; gin_4; gug_4; $šub_5$; zukum; tug2lamaḫuš; tug2zulumḫi_3).

zi_2
(cf., ze_2, zi_2).

zi_3
(cf., zid_2).

zib; zib_2[ZIG]
haunch; stamp, brand; ownership mark; mark of debt-slavery; distinguishing mark; color; bridle, reins (of a donkey) (cf., mušen-zib_2; ḫa$š_2$[ZIG]) (izi, 'fire' + ib_2, 'thigh').

zibin$_{(2)}$
chrysalis, pupa; caterpillar (zi, 'life', + bun, 'blister').

zid, zi(-d)
n., faith, confidence; legitimacy, sanction; truth (zi, 'soul', + ed_2, 'to go forth').

v., to strengthen (e.g., the levees of a canal).

adj., right (hand); righteous, just; good; firm; well-founded; faithful; honest; true, correct; legitimate; lawful; authoritative; proper, appropriate.

adv., kindly.

zid-de_3-$eš_3$
(cf., zi-de_3-eš$_{(2)}$(-$še_3$)).

zid-du
(cf., zi-du, zid-du).

zid_2, zi_3[$ŠE_3$]
flour, meal, powder; used as glue (life + motion as in grinding).

zid_2 ba-ba
flour for porridge ('flour' + 'sweetened porridge').

zid_2-bar-si
a type of emmer wheat flour ('flour' + 'to release' + 'like a sprout').

zid_2-dub-dub
flour for the best ritual actions; flour offering ('flour' + reduplicated 'to pour, move in a circle, shake, sprinkle off, strew').

zid_2-gu
fine barley flour; used as glue ('flour' + 'net').

zid_2-gu_2-gal
chick pea flour ('flour' + 'chick pea').

zid_2-igi-$še_3$-du
first-fruit (?) flour ('flour' + 'first').

zid_2-ka(-$še_3$)
(barley sent) to the mill ('flour' + 'mouth' + 'unto').

zid_2-ku-ku
a coarse flour or groats - fed to pigs ('flour' + redup. 'to remove clothing'; cf., Debate between Silver and Copper).

zid_2-kum; zid_2-kum_4[UD](-ma)
a type of barley flour ('flour' + 'mortar-ground' + nominative).

zid_2-milla[IŠ]
a coarse, cheap type of flour - fed to pigs ('flour' + 'low quality flour'; Akk., *kukkušu(m)*).

zid_2-munu4; zid_2-mun-du; zid_2-munu
ration (of flour and malt barley); allocated provisions (zid_2-mun-du occurs only in ED IIIb texts) ('flour' + 'malt barley; groats'; Akk., *isimmānu(m)*).

zid_2-sig_{15}[KAL]
cracked barley mixed with wheat flour (?); "crushings" flour (?) ('flour' + 'pleasing; valuable'; cf., kaš-sig_{15}).

ZID_2-ŠE
(cf., dabin).

zid_2-UD
(cf., zid_2-kum_4).

zid_2-za(-tum)
a type of flour, *zātum* flour.

zig
post or wall column (> Akk., *ziqqu(m) I*).

zig_3, zi(-g)
n., wall, partition; rising; uprising, attack; troop levy, call up; sexual 'arousal' (uz_2, 'side, edge', + ig, 'door').

v., to stand up, rise; to rise up from (with -ta- or -ra-); to raise, elevate, lift; to rouse; to go out or make go out; to remove; to tear out, uproot, weed; to take out, extract; to spend or credit; to approach; to recruit; to grow tall; in music, to tune up (zi-zi in *marû*).

adj., high; raw, uncooked.

zikum[ENGUR]
heaven (cf., zid_2-kum_4-ma).

zil; zi; ze_2
to undress; to peel off; to pare, cut; to shell; to flay; to cook, boil (cf., sila; dub_3...zil) (ze_2, 'to shear, pluck', + ul, 'joy, pleasure').

zil_2[TAG]
to make beautiful, pleasing; to be loving, gentle, affectionate; to caress (usually reduplicated) (cf., zil).

zilulu[PA.ĞIŠGAL]
peddler; vagabond (zil, 'to flay, pare', + lu_2-ulu_3, 'people'; cf., $tibira_2$).

zipaḫ, zapaḫ[ŠU.BAD]
half; a length-measure, span = ½ cubit = 15 fingers = 25 cm. (ŠU.BAD: 'open hand' - approx. distance measured by span of outstretched thumb and little finger).

zirru[MUNUS.NUNUZ.ZI.^{d}.NANNA]
high priestess of the moon god.

ziz
moth (Akk. loanword from *sāsu*, 'moth' and *ašāšu*, 'moth', cf., Orel & Stolbova #1034 ***'açuç-** 'insect').

ziz_2[$AŠ_2$]
emmer (wheat) (reduplicated ze_2 or zi; Akk. *kunāšu(m)*, 'emmer').

$^{iti}ziz_2$-a
calendar month 11 at Nippur during Ur III.

ZIZ_2-AN
(cf., imğağa).

ziz_2-babbar$_{(2)}$
white/bright emmer wheat ('emmer wheat' + 'white').

ziz_2-bal
emmer wheat lost in processing ('emmer wheat' + 'to demolish').

ziz_2-da
penalty payment for theft, often a multiple of the thing stolen ('valuable grain' + 'to protect').

ziz_2...de_2-a
cleaning emmer after winnowing ('emmer wheat' + 'to pour' + nominative).

ziz_2-gu_2-nida[NUNUZ]
a gluten enriched form of emmer wheat used for breads and pastries; bread wheat (cf., $^{GIG}gu_2$-nida) ('emmer wheat' + 'chick pea' + 'bread/pastry').

ziz_3
a crop-devouring insect (see etymology for ziz).

zizna[TUR.ZA&TUR.ZA]
fish roe; abnormal growths on a fetus.

zu, su_2
n., wisdom, knowledge.

v., to know; to understand; to experience; to be familiar with; to inform, teach (in *marû* reduplicated form); to learn from someone (with -da-); to recognize someone (with -da-); to be experienced, qualified.

possessive suffix, your (singular).

pron., yours.

zu-a
acquaintance; expert; experienced person ('to know' + nominative).

ZU.AB
(cf., abzu).

zu-ḫu-ul
pierced (Akkadian *saḫlu*, 'to pass through a hole, to thread').

-zu-ne(-ne)
possessive suffix, your (plural) - ThSLa §101.

-zu-um
2.sg. possessive suffix plus enclitic copula -am_3 - ThSLa §108.

-zu-ur$_2$
2.sg possessive suffix plus dative postposition -ra - ThSLa §106 (cf., $zu_2...ur_5$, 'to chew up').

-zu-uš
2.sg. possessive suffix plus terminative postposition -$še_3$ - ThSLa §106.

zu_2, su_{11}[KA]
tooth, teeth; prong; thorn; fang; blade; ivory; flint, chert; obsidian; natural glass (as verb, cf., zuḫ).

zu_2-a-ab-ba; KA×G̃IR$_2$-a-ab-ba
coral; coral algae; coral chalk ('teeth' + 'sea').

zu_2-am-si
ivory ('teeth' + 'elephant').

$zu_2...bir_9-bir_9$[NE-NE]/ bir[UD]
to smile; to laugh ('teeth' + 'to shine').

$zu_2-bir_9-bir_9$-re
clown, jester.

$zu_2...du_3$
to bite (as by a snake) ('teeth' + 'to raise up from the ground').

zu_2...gaz
to chew; to crush with the teeth ('teeth' + 'to crush').

zu_2-gig
tooth illness - cavities (caries) or gum disease (gingivitis) ('teeth' + 'illness').

zu_2...gub
to eat ('teeth' + 'to stand').

zu_2-gub
lunch ('teeth' + 'to stand').

zu_2...gul
to break off a tooth ('teeth' + 'to destroy, break to pieces').

zu_2-g̃ar
snapping off; paralysis (cf., ḫum and ḫum-ḫum) ('teeth' + 'to set').

zu_2 g̃iš-$gana_2$-ur_3
harrow teeth ('teeth' + 'harrow').

zu_2...ḪAR
(cf., $zu_2...ur_5$).

zu_2...$keš_2$
to oblige ('teeth' + 'to bind, harness').

zu_2...kud/ku_5
to bite (as by a dog) ('teeth' + 'to cut; to curse').

$zu_2...la_2$
to bind the teeth (of a sickness demon) ('teeth' + 'to bind').

zu_2-lum(-ma)
dried date-fruit ('teeth' + 'to be satiated'; cf., u_4-ḫi-in).

zu_2-lum...mar
(cf., $su_{(11)}$-lum...mar).

zu_2-muš
snakebite ('fang' + 'snake').

zu_2...NE-NE
(cf., $zu_2...bir_9-bir_9$).

zu_2...ra(-ra)
to bite; to crush ('teeth' + usually reduplicated 'to strike, stab').

zu_2...ra-aḫ
to devour ('teeth' + 'to strike repetitively, shake').

zu_2-si(-ga)
(sheep) plucking, shearing; sheep-shearer ('teeth' + 'to fill' + nominative).

$zu_2...sud_2-sud_2$[$ŠITA_3$]
to bite; to gnash the teeth ('teeth' + 'to crush, gnash').

zu_2 uḫ
moth-eaten ('teeth' + 'parasite, moth').

$zu_2...ur_5$[ḪAR]
to bite, chew up, tear with the teeth ('teeth' + 'to chew').

zu_2...zalag
to show one's teeth ('teeth' + 'to shine, gleam'; cf., zu_2...bir_9-bir_9).

zu_5
(cf., azu).

zubu, zubi [PAP.NA_2]
sickle; bent throwing stick; watercourse; greater or lesser Zab tributaries into Tigris river; a mountain range that exported tin; water-logged ground, swamp (cf., gam_3) (zu_2, 'flint; tooth', + bu[r], 'to pull, draw, cut off'; Akkadian *zā'ibu(m)*, 'a watercourse', *zâbu(m)*, 'to dissolve, flow') [? ZUBI archaic frequency: 2; concatenates 2 sign variants].

zug_4 [KA×LI]
(cf., u_2-zug_4).

zugud, zubud
a kind of club; a fish (cf. also, sukud).

zuḫ [KA/ZU_2]
to steal, rob (zu_2, 'teeth' + numerous).

zukum [ZI&ZI.LAGAB]
to trample; to walk on; to step on (sug_2, plural 'to stand', + kum, 'to crush').

zulug
(cf., sulug).

$^{(tug2)}$zulumḫi, suluḫu [SIK_2.SUD]; $zulumḫi_2$, $suluḫu_2$ [SIK_2.BU]; $zulumḫi_3$, $suluḫu_3$ [ZI&ZI.LAGAB]
a fine ceremonial garment of long white wool or long-fleeced sheepskin; a type of long-haired sheep or its wool (cf., ^{tug2}lamaḫuš) (si, 'long, thin things', or su_6, 'beard', + 'luxuriant' + 'abundant').

zum
n., womb.

v., to leak, seep, exude, overflow; to be in labor (repetitive motion + closed container; cf., zal, 'to flow', and zar, zur_4, 'to spout, flow').

zur, zuru [AMAR]
n., offering, sacrifice; prayer (repetitive activity + to flow/protect).

v., to furnish, provide; to rock (an infant); to arrange, tend; to offer; to pray.

zur-re-eš...du_8
(cf., zar-re-eš...du_8).

zur-zur
(animal) nurse; to rock, shake (reduplicated 'to tend; to rock').

$zurzub_{(2)}$, $ursub_{(2)}$, $urrub_{(2)}$
a container provided with teat-shaped protuberances (zur_4, 'to spout, flow', + sub, 'to suckle'; Akk. *ṣurṣuppu, urṣuppu, ḫurḫuppu*).

zurzub-ga
a milk container ('a container provided with teat-shaped protuberances' + 'milk').